Germany
A New Social and Economic History

eneral Editors: Sheilagh Ogilvie and Bob Scribner

Already published

VOLUME I: 1450–1630
Edited by Bob Scribner

In preparation

VOLUME II: 1630–1800
Edited by Sheilagh Ogilvie

VOLUME III: SINCE 1800
Edited by Sheilagh Ogilvie and Richard Overy

GERMANY

A New Social and Economic History

Volume 1
1450–1630

Edited by Bob Scribner

Reader in the Social History of Early Modern Europe
University of Cambridge

A member of the Hodder Headline Group
LONDON • NEW YORK • SYDNEY • AUCKLAND

First published in Great Britain 1996 by Arnold,
a member of the Hodder Headline Group
338 Euston Road, London NW1 3BH
175 Fifth Avenue, New York, NY 10010

Second impression 1997

Distributed exclusively in the USA by
St Martin's Press Inc.
175 Fifth Avenue,
New York, NY 10010

British Library Cataloguing in Publication Data
A catalogue record for this book is available from the British Library

Library of Congress Cataloging-in-Publication Data
Germany : a new social and economic history / edited by Bob Scribner.
    p.   cm.
Includes bibliographical references and index.
Contents: Vol. 1. 1450–1630
ISBN 0–340–51332–2. — ISBN 0–340–65217–9
1. Germany—Social conditions. 2. Germany—Economic conditions.
I. Scribner, Robert W.
HN445.G472   1995
306´.0943—dc20   95-17543
                                                             CIP

ISBN 0 340 65217 9 (PB)
ISBN 0 340 51332 2 (HB)

Typeset in 10/12 Sabon by Anneset, Weston-super-Mare, Somerset
Printed and bound in Great Britain by J W Arrowsmith Ltd, Bristol

Contents

Figures and Maps

Contents of Volumes I and II

General Preface

There has long been no adequate or modern social and economic history of Germany, despite a proud tradition of Germanophone scholarship in the field since the nineteenth century, especially on the traditional themes of economic history (trade, capitalism, craft production, agriculture). In part this had been the result of the scope and complexity of the German-speaking world, whose diverse developments over the centuries have made it no less difficult to produce overviews of its political history. To complicate the problem, there have been striking new advances in several fields of history over the past generation – historical demography and family structure; the history of disease, diet, and nutrition; material culture and daily life; and climate and ecology as historical factors. There have been new approaches to the history of social structure, work, forms of production, and the relationships between town and country, while awareness of the importance of gender has radically altered our historical perspectives. There has also been a considerable interpretative reorientation. The *Annales* paradigm, with its emphasis on long-term structures and the material basis of culture and society, brought about a revolution in French historiography, but its general approach was only slowly received in German scholarship, the more so since its implicit demand for an *histoire totale* radically called into question the more compartmentalized approach of traditional economic and social history. All these developments explain why the project of a general social and economic history of Germany has become a formidable task beyond the capabilities of any one scholar.

There has been, however, a growing volume of new work in many specialist fields which makes possible a collective attempt at a synthesis suitable for use by teachers, students, and general readers. Some recent scholarship has taken the form of traditional economic history, building on and incorporating the work of the great pioneers, while a great deal of it has also been inspired by the *Annales* school. In some areas, older approaches have been cross-fertilized with the new, as in the case of agricultural history, which has profited from recent work on climatology and ecology. Newer fields of research such as demography have changed some of our commonplace generalizations, or opened up new material to historical scrutiny, as in the case of daily life. The range of expertise and coverage required to make the best of use of this scholarship demands a team of authors, each of whom is a specialist scholar, summarizing, and generalizing from, the most recent research in a number of major topics. The themes of each chapter have been chosen for attention because they either encompass structures fundamental to the development of economy and society, such as population, agriculture, consumption, trade, or industry, or else present a significant development within a given period (early capitalism, poverty and poor relief, confessionalization). It is the aim of the work as a whole to keep in view the long-term development of economy and society in Germany, while directing attention to characteristic features of a given century or phase of socioeconomic development.

Preface to Volumes 1 and 2

The period covered by the first two volumes is that of the later middle ages and early modern centuries, from *c.* 1300 to 1800. The history of these centuries can most suitably be conceived of as a *longue durée*, involving a period of contraction (1300–1450) followed by one of expansion (1450–1600), succeeded by another period of contraction (1600–1700) and incipient recovery (1700–1800). By treating this extended period as a unity, it will be possible to gain an overview of long-term structural developments in demography, agriculture, manufacture, consumption, and so on, while examining their interaction with the characteristic social formations of the medieval and early modern periods up to the eve of industrialization. However, each volume has its own distinctive focus. That of Volume I is the late medieval 'crises' – those associated with plague, population decline, economic contraction, and the 'crisis of feudalism' – and the age of the Reformation, with its characteristic themes of early capitalism, religious and social upheaval, and growing secular control of the church. Although this volume concentrates its attention more narrowly on the period 1450–*c.* 1630, it is necessary to survey some developments back to 1300 in order to gain a better appreciation of their scope and complexity. The focus of Volume II is the dislocation caused by renewed contraction and economic crisis, the impact of the Thirty Years War, the beginnings of industrialization, integration into world colonial markets, mercantilism and cameralism, and the growth of bureaucratic absolutist states. Where appropriate, German developments have been situated within a wider context of European developments.

Rather than merely repeating the same themes in both volumes for different chronological periods, each has a slightly different emphasis with complementary themes. Thus, discussion of urban networks, social and economic institutions, the nature of communities, and the socioeconomic features of gender relations are discussed in Volume I, but provide a background for Volume II. Analysis of the impact of warfare, of long-distance trade, of the growth of the middle classes and of the intervention of the state in economy and society demands special attention in Volume II. Although these themes are not absent in Volume I, the generalizations derived from the later period have applicability for the overall chronological span of the two volumes. Within each volume there has inevitably been some overlap of subject-matter, as individual authors trace the ramifications of their themes. Thus many issues are discussed from varying angles in two or three chapters, and a comprehensive grasp is made possible through the index and by comparison between chapters.

Acknowledgements

The editor wishes to thank the Ellen McArthur Fund, Cambridge University, for generous support to enable the drawing of maps and figures in this volume.

Thanks are due to R. Oldenbourg Verlag, Munich, for permission to adapt and reproduce in translation sections from Christian Pfister, *Bevölkerungsgeschichte und historische Demographie 1500–1800* (Munich, 1994), Enzyklopädie deutscher Geschichte, 28.

Abbreviations

AHR	American Historical Review
ARG	Archiv für Reformationsgeschichte
BdLG	Blätter für deutsche Landesgeschichte
CEH	Central European History
EcHR	Economic History Review
fl.	florins, gulden
GG	Geschichte und Gesellschaft
HansGbl	Hansische Geschichtsblätter
HessJbLG	Hessisches Jahrbuch für Landesgeschichte
HZ	Historische Zeitschrift
Jb	Jahrbuch
JbfränkLF	Jahrbuch für fränkische Landesforschung
JbGFeudalismus	Jahrbuch für Geschichte des Feudalismus
JbRegG	Jahrbuch für Regionalgeschichte
JbWG	Jahrbuch für Wirtschaftsgeschichte
JEEH	Journal of European Economic History
JMH	Journal of Modern History
MPIG	Max-Planck-Institut für Geschichte
P & P	Past and Present
SchweizZG	Schweizerische Zeitschrift für Geschichte
SVRG	Schriften des Vereins für Reformationsgeschichte
VSWG	Vierteljahrschrift für Sozial- und Wirtschaftsgeschichte
ZAgrarGAgrarSoz	Zeitschrift für Agrargeschichte und Agrarsoziologie
ZAGV	Zeitschrift des Aachener Geschichtsvereins
ZBLG	Zeitschrift für bayerische Landesgeschichte
ZGO	Zeitschrift für die Geschichte des Oberrheins
ZHF	Zeitchrift für historische Forschung
ZKG	Zeitschrift für Kirchengeschichte
ZRG KA	Zeitschrift für Rechtsgeschichte, Kanonische Abteilung
ZWLG	Zeitschrift für württembergische Landesgeschichte

|1|

Economic Landscapes

TOM SCOTT

From earliest times certain natural regions can be discerned in Germany, loosely defined by geology, geography, or climate. These included the main river valleys of the Rhine and Main, the East Frisian marshlands, the vast north German plain, the belt of forest stretching across central Germany from Thuringia to the Palatinate, or the Swabian Alp. Upon these were later superimposed the divisions of colonization and settlement: the frontier of the Roman *limes*, the ethnic boundary between German and Slav, and the linguistic distribution of High and Low German dialects. By the later middle ages, however, regional identities became increasingly shaped by political and economic factors. Just as local princes began to forge their scattered possessions and miscellaneous jurisdictions into coherent and consolidated territories, so too the shifting balance of land and people, resources and demand, encouraged the emergence throughout Germany of distinctive economic landscapes.

These landscapes fall broadly into three types: those which remained predominantly agrarian; those which displayed a mixture of agriculture and manufacturing based on specialized rural crops, including wool; and those which were given over to mining and industrial production dependent upon natural and mineral resources. Common to all three types, however, was the fact that their character as *economic* landscapes derived neither from endogenous conditions (soil, climate, altitude, natural resources) nor from exogenous circumstances (location and transport, organization of production, consumer demand) alone, but above all from the interplay, often highly complex, of these various factors.

To illustrate this point, let us look briefly at each type of landscape. Up to 1600 Germany remained a predominantly agrarian society, with perhaps 80 per cent of the population living and working on the land. But this bald statement conceals significant variations between regions. In many parts of Germany mixed agriculture and the traditional three-field system of the high middle ages continued unaltered, but elsewhere increasing diversity can be observed, with certain areas devoted exclusively to tillage, or to stock-rearing and dairying. Yet even in such instances, arable and pastoral husbandry cannot be entirely separated. Stock-rearing and grain-growing, as Heide Wunder has observed, were closely interlinked, since apart from supplying meat and milk pastoralism provided essential energy to the cerealist in the form of draught animals for ploughing and carting, as well as dung to manure the soil.[1] It was precisely the existence of large-scale cattle-grazing on the marshes of Frisia and Emsland, or in parts of Mecklenburg between the Elbe and the Oder, which made possible intensive forms of cereal agriculture. The annual turning of the topsoil humus admixed with stable dung (*Plaggendüngung*) permitted what became known as the 'perpetual cultivation of rye', by means of a one-field system which was able to dispense with traditional crop rotation.[2] Even in areas of virtual monoculture, moreover, the argument still applies. Beyond the grain-producing estates east of the Elbe which developed partly in response to overseas demand from Western European markets, for instance, lay a belt of pastureland in eastern Poland, Moldavia, and the Hungarian plain whose livestock likewise came to dominate Western markets in the sixteenth century.[3] Regional interdependence in such cases is merely writ much larger.

Though soil and climate clearly influenced the distribution of farming types, wider economic considerations also played a part. Since the days of von Thünen in the nineteenth century, distance from the market has above all been advanced to explain the differences in arable cultivation between, say, the multi-course rotation of the Netherlands, the regulated convertible husbandry found in Holstein, or the three-course rotation prevalent in the corn-belt of Eastern Europe. These field systems, plotted in a series of 'circles', represented the 'relatively best' agrarian system for each particular region in the light of both natural conditions and consumer demand. The merit of such a categorization is that it points away from purely structural and seemingly unchanging determinants in agricultural production towards the variable dynamics of transport costs and market-led demand.[4] Even here, though, the suggested interaction may be couched too simply. Markets, as Robert Dodgshon has reminded us, were privileged foundations rather than spontaneous creations. Their artificial character was a function of political as much as of economic interests, so that the pull of urban demand expressed through the market exerted a 'stilted' influence upon agricultural production.[5]

When we turn to the second type of economic landscape, the interconnectedness of agriculture and textile manufacturing is readily apparent. The linen industry on the northern littoral of Lake Constance provides an instructive example. The cultivation of flax and its manufacture into linen throughout Upper Swabia and into the Allgäu can be traced back to the thirteenth century. The low-lying marshy tracts along the rivers Iller and Lech, together with a high rainfall on the northern edge of the Alps, clearly created suitable conditions for flax-growing,[6] but after spinning and weaving the cloth still had to be bleached. Although various processes were employed, they all used milk at one stage or another, either for bucking (that is, steeping in an alkaline lye) or for soaking in vats of buttermilk, before the cloths were finally crofted (spread out and kept moist on bleaching-grounds for several months). The coexistence of dairying and linen manufacture in the region, therefore, was far from coincidental; the one functionally determined the other. When linen-weaving spread to other areas in the sixteenth century with dairying traditions, such as parts of Westphalia and Flanders, the rapid growth of the industry led to periodic shortages of milk for bleaching.[7]

Yet these connections by themselves are still inadequate to account for the rise of a linen industry around Lake Constance in the later middle ages. The advantages of location, while genuine enough in the Allgäu, were much less obvious at the western end of the lake, with an altogether warmer climate and less emphasis on dairying. Moreover, despite the growth of trade between Italy and southern Germany after the opening up of major Alpine passes, it is not even clear that a good location in terms of transport and trade routes was particularly decisive, for the linen industry was firmly established well before the rise of the great Swiss or Swabian merchant enterprises such as the Diesbach-Watt company of St Gallen or the Great Ravensburg trading company.[8] The development of Upper German linen (and later fustian) manufacturing seems to have depended just as much upon population growth, which created pressure within the primary sector for rural by-employment, along with a matching consumer demand from townsfolk in an area of relatively dense urbanization. The subsequent consolidation and continuing prosperity of the industry owed a great deal in their own turn both to shifts in the division of labour between town and country, notably in the emergence of the early capitalist putting-out system (*Verlagssystem*), and to the enforcement of strict quality controls (and, not least, to responsiveness to changes in fashion).[9]

In the third type of landscape, that of mining and industrial production, the links between available resources, whether natural or mineral, and the rise of certain forms of manufacturing are the most complex of all. Without the belt of forest stretching across central Germany, for instance, much of the extractive and metal-working industry of Franconia and Hesse would have been unable to flourish. But the forests were often in themselves less important than the by-products derived from timber. Even for fuel, the iron industry relied not upon raw timber but on charcoal. Many upland areas of the Sauerland were given over to charcoal-burning, with entire villages specializing in supplying the local iron foundries. Indeed, the organization of production began to display rudimentary forms of vertical integration, as miners, charcoalers, ironsmiths, and ironfounders combined in a single craft guild.[10] Other craft industries in the same region, however, required timber derivatives not for fuel, but in the treatment or manufacturing process itself. The spread of leather-working in the Siegerland presumed a particular form of deciduous arboriculture, namely coppicing

(*Haubergwirtschaft*), whereby bark from young oaks was stripped, dried, and used to make tanbark.[11] For its part, the extensive glass industry in eastern Westphalia and northern Hesse relied upon plentiful supplies of potash, made by leaching woodash which was then evaporated in pots.[12]

The most intricate equation between natural resources and the location of industry, however, occurred in the mining and refining of base and precious metals. All forms of extraction and smelting required limitless supplies of wood and water, but these were not always to be found in the vicinity of the ores themselves. The rise of the Thuringian copper-mining industry in the fifteenth century may illustrate the point. The ore was found and mined in northern Thuringia, around Mansfeld, Eisleben, and Sangerhausen, but the smelteries were, with one exception, located much further south, below Erfurt and Weimar, where the countryside was thickly forested, and watered by the rivers Gera, Ilm, and Saale.[13] But these natural features alone do not suffice to explain the location of smelteries. The new technology of liquation, upon which the fortunes of the Thuringian mining industry were built, required extensive plant, with six to eight furnaces in a row covering a considerable area. The capital cost of such investment ensured that the liquation works must be located with good access to perceived markets, as in the case of the Augsburg merchant house of Fugger's smeltery at Hohenkirchen in the Thuringian Forest, which was conveniently placed at the point of intersection of trade routes to Nuremberg, Frankfurt, and Leipzig.[14] By itself, however, the development of new technical processes of extraction, refining and manufacturing – the invention of the wet stamping mill, the switch from bloomery to blast-furnace, as well as the discovery of liquation itself – cannot fully account for the mining boom of the fifteenth and sixteenth centuries in certain parts of Germany. Some technological processes were already well known – the hydraulic pump, for instance, had been perfected in the early fifteenth century[15] – but without the finance to deploy them, these inventions lay idle. That only serves to underscore the point that the more advanced the industry the more complex was the interplay between the various factors of production.

In the genesis of economic landscapes, therefore, we may discern a hierarchy of complexity from the traditional forms of mixed agriculture up to the technically most advanced areas of specialized industrial production. Of course, the three types of economic landscape were not necessarily distinct; indeed, where they overlapped, the stimulus to economic activity was likely to be all the greater. The classic example is provided by Alsace. In the fertile valley of the Upper Rhine, agricultural diversity held the key to wider economic prosperity. On the temperate plains of the valley floor cereals throve: wheat and rye for bread; oats for bran; barley for brewing. On the slightly higher ground large flocks of sheep were pastured, which provided wool for the local textile industry. Then, on the sheltered eastern slopes of the Vosges, vineyards were strung out from Thann to Marlenheim, whose wine was the most prized in Germany. Behind them lay the moister valleys cutting into the mountains, which were largely given over to dairying and cheese-making. On the heights, alpine meadows provided pasture for fattening cattle by transhumance in the summer months. Finally, for good measure, in the higher mountain valleys such as the Val de Lièpvre and the Val du Villé, silver mines provided a lucrative source of income for urban merchants and entrepreneurs.[16] For Alsace was not only fertile: its economy was urbanized and commercialized. Wool-weaving was concentrated in Strasbourg, one of the largest cities of the Empire, with a population of around 25,000 at the turn of the fifteenth century, but there were further centres of production in Colmar, and in a cluster of Lower Alsatian cities between Wissembourg and Haguenau. In the same stretch of countryside, moreover, madder was cultivated as an industrial crop for dyeing cloth. Even in the remoter valleys textiles were woven; in Masevaux on the Doller, linen twill was manufactured to be traded at the Frankfurt fairs. Ease of transport down the rivers Ill and Rhine ensured that Alsace's produce and manufactures reached international markets; its wine, for instance, was exported as far afield as England, Scandinavia, and the Baltic.[17] What determined Alsace's economic vigour, it appears, was neither its agriculture nor its industry in isolation, but rather the interdependence of its rural and urban economies. In defining economic landscapes, therefore, the example of Alsace should caution us against ascribing a dominant role to either town or country: cities and their hinterlands should be seen as complementary dimensions of an integrated regional economy.[18] They constituted, in Hektor Ammann's words, an economic unit (*Wirtschaftseinheit*).[19]

These preliminary reflections should be borne in mind as we turn to examine the three types of economic landscape in greater detail. Within the agricultural sector patterns of inheritance, field systems and crop rotation, tenure and landlordship may all have influenced farming practices, but what was cause and what effect remains notoriously difficult to decide. Throughout most of Germany (and Scandinavia) impartible inheritance was the rule; only in south-west Germany, the Middle Rhine, much of Hesse, and pockets of Silesia can partible inheritance be found, even though it was the custom throughout most of western Europe, especially the Mediterranean lands, and much of the Slavic east (see Map 1.1). Although partible inheritance appears to have spread first along the fruitful valley and river basin landscapes in the southern, warmer latitudes, any inference that soil, topography, and climate were its chief determinants is rapidly refuted by its establishment in the less fertile upland areas to the west and east – the Hunsrück and Eifel ranges, the Westerwald, and the Bergisches Land.[20] An earlier generation of scholars, struck by the geographical peculiarity of impartibility, sought instead an explanation in ethnic or racial differences. The integrity of the Germanic kinship group, it was argued, demanded the

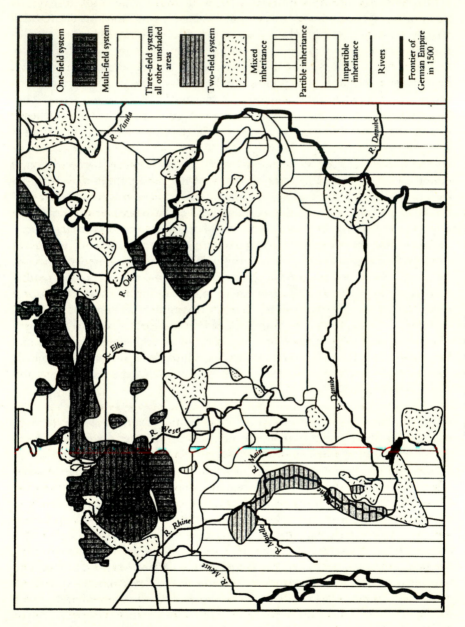

Map 1.1　Agricultural systems, c.1500

Legend:

One-field system

Multi-field system

Three-field system all other unshaded areas

Two-field system

Mixed inheritance

Partible inheritance

Impartible inheritance

Rivers

Frontier of German Empire in 1500

indivisibility of landholdings, a practice which the migrant tribes carried southwards and westwards into Roman territories. By that token, the partible inheritance of the South-West must have represented a subsequent retreat from the advance of Germanic custom.[21] When that might have occurred, however, is altogether unclear: during the era of internal colonization in the twelfth and thirteenth century impartible inheritance had become the norm in the newly settled upland areas of Swabia and Franconia.[22] Renewed pressure on land after 1500 in parts of southern Germany, moreover, impelled both landlords and tenant farmers to resist attempts to subdivide holdings and to make impartibility legally binding.[23] In general, however, what stands out is the remarkable continuity in the distribution of inheritance patterns throughout Germany from the ninth to the twentieth century; that should discourage us from seeking too close a causal connection between specific inheritance customs and certain forms of agriculture. It is true that areas of partible inheritance, especially in the Rhineland, display an abundance of viticulture and industrial crops, together with extensive rural crafts and manufacturing. Equally, such areas coincide with the greatest concentration of towns in late medieval Germany, which may have stimulated the market integration of the rural economy and therewith the commercialization of production and the creation of a land market.[24] But the rise of landscapes bearing the imprint of rural industries was by no means confined to the South-West; they arose in areas of thoroughgoing impartibility, as well, such as eastern Swabia and Westphalia. Partible inheritance should therefore not be adduced as a catch-all explanation for the economic transformation of early modern Germany towards proto-industrialization.[25]

As prevalent as, and largely coterminous with, impartible inheritance was the traditional system of open fields in Germany. On them winter cereals (wheat and rye, or in parts of the South-West, principally Württemberg, spelt) were followed by summer grains (oats and barley) and then fallow in a regulated rotation (see Map 1.1). Together with the three-field system of tillage, beasts were grazed on the common land or forest, though often the fallow year was itself used for pasturing, rather than repeatedly ploughing to aerate and improve the soil (*Schwarzbrache*).[26] In certain circumstances, however, this classic system of mixed agriculture could be sufficiently intensified in stretches of the North German plain, as we have seen, to enable a one-field system with continuous rye cultivation to develop. The origins of the two-field system in many parts of the Rhineland and its fringes are, by contrast, much harder to pin down. On the one hand, it was the ancient and primitive method of cultivation which typified Roman agriculture beyond the Mediterranean up to the ninth century.[27] This system survived in certain areas of what once had been the eastern border of Gaul, notably in the upland regions of the Palatinate. Here the prevalence of loess soils, liable to erosion, hindered the cultivation of meadow, pasture, and forest, so that the fallow had to be extended over both time and space in order to provide enough manure. In such instances, three-year rotation was practised on an infield, while on the outfield fallow succeeded oats in a system of alternate husbandry (*Feldgraswirtschaft*). Two-field systems, however, were also widespread on the lower-lying riverine lands along the Moselle and the Middle Rhine, downstream of Koblenz, where even the infield might be given over to a simple alternation between rye and fallow.[28] On the other hand, it has been argued that the spread of the two-field system in the later middle ages was attributable to the growth of specialized and commercial agriculture. Along the Rhine and Moselle, for instance, a special type of alternate husbandry developed, whereby tillage was succeeded by coppicing in order to provide tanbark and vine-props (*Lohheckenwirtschaft*).[29] By the beginning of the sixteenth century, indeed, the two-field system had apparently penetrated Alsace, in response to intensified cereal cultivation, a thriving viticulture, and the planting of industrial crops such as hemp and madder (and later tobacco).[30] Correlations of this kind clearly existed, but they must not be pressed too far. It is obvious that not all areas of loess soil had two-field systems; equally, the changes in land management contingent upon a heightened demand for grain in Alsace do not seem to have taken place in other regions of similarly dense urbanization and market demand such as Swabia.[31] To ascribe the spread of two-field cultivation in wine-growing areas to an economic conjuncture in any case presents problems. The structural requirements of viticulture in Alsace, for example, namely copious labour and plentiful manure, rather than the functional stimulus of the export market, may have promoted the two-field system by restricting the scope for traditional mixed agriculture: necessity, not opportunity, in other words, may have encouraged its spread.[32] Moreover, the two-field system in Alsace was neither new nor ubiquitous at the close of the middle ages; it can be found centuries earlier in patches on both banks of the Upper Rhine, sometimes interchangeably with a three-field system where crop rotation was not subject to regulation by course (*Verzelgung*).[33]

In certain parts of Germany mixed agriculture was beginning to give way at the end of the middle ages either to multi-course rotation, or else to an exclusive concentration on stock-rearing and dairying. In both cases, the traditional open-field system became subject to partial enclosure. In the rich pasture lands of Schleswig-Holstein and along the Frisian coast to the Dutch border a form of regulated convertible (or 'up-and-down') husbandry (*Koppelwirtschaft*) developed, whereby a series of corn years could be followed by anything from three to six years' grazing. This rotation could even dispense with a fallow year, provided that fodder crops (such as nitrogenous legumes and vetches) were planted as catch-crops in the intervening period. This pattern foreshadows the 'improved' agriculture of the eighteenth century (*Fruchtwechselbau*; in French, *assolement*).[34] Cattle-pastures (*Koppeln*) were created by intakes from both forest and waste, and from the existing common. Such pastures, however, usually involved only hurdling or folding (temporary fencing, rather than permanent enclosures, and the stint of beasts to be grazed was limited by cattle-gates. There was no widespread enclosure movement in northern Germany in the sixteenth century along the lines of England.[35] In the mountainous regions of Switzerland, by contrast, where good pasture was at a premium, much more common land in the Alps, as a study of Freiburg im Üchtland has shown, was bought up by nobles and peasants to be turned into private hay meadows for summer grazing, in order to release low-lying fields for winter fodder.[36] In general, pastoralism in northern Germany tended to serve the market for both meat and dairy produce, whereas in the Alps there was a greater concentration upon dairying. The sharply increased demand for meat from the urban centres of southern and western Germany could no longer be covered by purely regional supplies; instead, the cities came to rely upon livestock imports driven on the hoof, often over immense distances, from Burgundy, Hungary, Poland, and Scania.[37]

The pattern of landlordship had likewise undergone significant changes by 1500. The manorial system of the high middle ages had largely disappeared, or else survived in a 'petrified' form. Most secular lords had long since divested themselves of their demesne, which was parcelled out to tenants, often on short leases, and instead derived their feudal revenues purely from rents. Even monastic lords such as the Cistercians, who had pioneered direct exploitation of their estates on a commercial basis (granges; *Grangienwirtschaft*), had in most cases abandoned the practice by the sixteenth century.[38] Hereditary tenure became the rule, though there were considerable variations throughout western Germany. The strongest tenure was to be found where peasant holdings were largest – on the hereditable leaseholds of Bavaria (*Erbpacht*) or the copyhold (*Meierrecht*) prevalent in north-western Germany.[39] Revocable leases for fixed terms (*Zeitpacht*) were only common where agriculture had become commercialized, and organized on capitalist lines: on the Middle and Lower Rhine stretching into the Low Countries, and on the coastal strip of Frisia and western Holstein (Eiderstedt, Dithmarschen). Here the real (that is, tenurial) dependence of the peasantry was superseded by a purely contractual obligation.[40] Nevertheless, feudal landlordship (*Grundherrschaft*) survived as the framework for the sociolegal subjection of the peasantry, even if in some areas the economic relations between lord and tenant had been transformed.

In eastern Germany, that is, the lands east of the Elbe as far as East Prussia, *Grundherrschaft* underwent a complex and protracted transformation into a new type of large feudal seigneurie (*Gutsherrschaft*), whose peasants were progressively stripped of their land and reduced to the status of a servile labour force, in what is known as the 'second serfdom'. This concentration of seigneurial power enabled a distinctive entrepreneurial domain economy (*Gutswirtschaft*) to develop, in which the peasantry was subordinated by feudal ties ('extra-economic coercion') to a capitalist mode of production supplying overseas markets – a system reminiscent of the plantation economies of the New World. The links between domain lordship and the domain economy, however, are by no means straightforward. It used to be thought that the demand for grain from western Europe encouraged the growth of large-scale arable estates which, given the relative sparsity of population in the east Elbian territories, were obliged to resuscitate forms of feudal compulsion in order to secure an adequate work force. This argument is untenable on three counts. First, the rise of *Gutsherrschaften* preceded – by as much as three centuries in some cases - the emergence of *Gutswirtschaften*. Second, intensified feudal lordship was sometimes harnessed to forms of production quite distinct from labour-intensive cereal agriculture. Third, the development of large estates using direct labour was not confined to eastern Germany. Let us examine these points more closely.

The system of *Gutsherrschaften* was essentially in place by the beginning of the sixteenth century, but its origins lie in the fourteenth, in the aftermath of plague and epidemic. Deserted peasant holdings reverted to their seigneurs, who at that time had no incentive whatever to invest in cereal agriculture, given the slump in grain prices and the reduction in the labour force. That argument effectively disposes of any theory that *Gutsherrschaft* was predicated upon an overseas demand for corn.[41] Lords had a unique opportunity to consolidate their scattered estates by gathering rights of landlordship and feudal jurisdiction into one hand, and by attempting to stem landflight to the towns. Only with the population recovery at the end of the fifteenth century did any clear economic motive arise to develop commercial agriculture; the real demand from western Europe for grain only dates from this period, even if a trickle of exports from the Vistula estuary can be traced back to the late thirteenth century. That does not, of course, explain why lords chose direct exploitation in preference to creaming off the profits through higher peasant rents. The answer seems to be that, on terrain uniquely suitable for intensive cereal agriculture, as much as three-quarters of the crop was marketed, a proportion so high that it made direct labour not only the most efficient way to organize production, but also far more lucrative than the revenue from rents and feudal renders.[42]

The most striking exception to this pattern is to be found in Silesia and Upper Lusatia. There, as much as four-fifths of the land was held by peasants with good title and hereditary tenure, who were personally free.[43] Many of their holdings, however, were very small, 10 hectares or less, and partible inheritance was widespread. Rural by-employment and specialized crops were common, with extensive linen production, and the cultivation of madder in the district around Wroclaw. At the same time, western Silesia had become an urbanized landscape by 1500, as a string of towns was founded along the mountain ranges on the left bank of the Oder, where minerals, principally iron but also gold and silver, had been discovered in the later middle ages.[44] Against this background a domain economy was most unlikely to develop, yet by the mid-sixteenth century *Gutsherrschaft* was on the advance. Here the feudal lords used their concerted seigneurial power to promote crafts and textile production. Rather than expropriating tenants, they released demesne and common land for new settlement by cottagers, and encouraged the transfer of linen-manufacturing away from the towns to their own estates, where it was integrated into the system of feudal rents. Nevertheless, a good share of the peasantry escaped the clutches of hereditary serfdom, so that Silesia and Lusatia remained regions with a highly variegated structure of social and economic relationships.[45]

By contrast, forms of direct exploitation need not exclusively be associated with *Gutsherrschaft*. In the swathe of territories stretching from eastern Lower Saxony and Anhalt through Thuringia and Saxony itself, as well as in parts of Bavaria and Upper Austria, we encounter an interval type of landlordship, using both wage-labour from free peasants and the labour-services of serfs to manage sizeable estates, which Alfred Hoffmann has termed 'economic lordship' (*Wirtschaftsherrschaft*).[46] In one such area, the district round Magdeburg, commercial leases on the larger peasant farms co-existed with a landless servile workforce within one estate. Such domains certainly developed in response to the market, but that demand was as much local as international, and was geared towards the main crop, barley, which supplied regional brewing centres like Braunschweig, rather than the lesser crops of wheat and rye. As long as the chief means of production, namely land, remained in peasant hands, this type of domain should be regarded as a special form of *Grundherrschaft*, rather than a weakened version of *Gutswirtschaft*,[47] not least since in Bavaria serfdom in the East European sense had all but disappeared. Still, genuine *Gutswirtschaften* can also be found outside eastern Germany alongside instances of pure *Grundherrschaft*. In Schleswig-Holstein the large estates of eastern Holstein practised a domain economy which relied heavily upon serf labour, whereas central Holstein was a classic landscape of large peasant farms, hereditary and free, just as in the rest of north-west Germany.[48]

Having discussed varieties of landholding and land management, we may conclude our review of the first type of economic landscape with an examination of the non-industrial specialized crops grown in Germany, namely vines and hops. Apart from the northernmost latitudes and the Alpine slopes, there was hardly a region of Germany which had no viticulture at the end of the middle ages. Yet by 1600 the area planted with vines had begun to contract dramatically. To explain such a rapid reversal, two points need to be borne in mind. On the one hand, in the main growing regions viticulture became restricted to the most favoured sites, that is, those whose wines were in demand beyond the immediate locality, as land was taken back into cereal cultivation to feed the swelling sixteenth-century population. On the other, the high price of wine, determined above all by the labour-intensive nature of viticulture, made it vulnerable to competition from other beverages, principally beer.

Vineyards required eight times the manpower of cereal agriculture,[49] quite apart from an assured provision of manure, vine-props, barrels, and staves. It is no surprise, therefore, that they should chiefly have flourished in the areas of densest population and greatest commercial demand, in short, the urbanized regions of the South and West. By the same token, however, vineyards were planted wherever the hunger for land, the subdivision of holdings, and the prospects of a ready cash return at market were greatest – that is to say, not always in places where quality was best assured.[50] Towards the end of the sixteenth century as many as 350,000 hectares were under vines, that is, at least four times the extent of viticulture today.[51] On the fringes of the main growing areas, vines crept into the narrower, shadier valleys and up the cooler slopes: in the Rhineland, into the foothills of the Eifel around Mechernich; from Siegburg past Cologne down the Lower Rhine to Xanten; up the valleys of the Upper Ahr, the Lahn as far as Wetzlar, and the Saar to Saarbrücken; in the Palatinate, onto the higher reaches of the Haardt plateau, the Donnersberg hills, and down into Lorraine; in Württemberg, onto the foothills of the Swabian Alp and into Upper Swabia; in Franconia, over the whole of the Main plain and into Lower Bavaria and the Danube valley as far as Lower Austria and Burgenland.[52] Vines were even planted on the north German plain, in Mecklenburg, Holstein, Brandenburg, and East Prussia.[53] These marginal areas were naturally the first to contract after 1500, but there were other growing regions of considerable importance in the sixteenth century which have now also disappeared. In Lusatia there were extensive vineyards south of Frankfurt an der Oder, and in Saxony on the Elbe around Meißen. But there was also viticulture in Thuringia: in the Saale valley around Jena; on the Unstrut from Naumburg to Freyburg; and on the Gera between Arnstadt and Erfurt. These wines were not all consumed locally; rather, they supplied the needs of most of Saxony to the north and east.[54]

The main areas of good-quality wines have, by contrast, remained remarkably unchanged from the middle ages to the present day – Alsace, the Neckar valley in Württemberg, the Lower Main in Franconia, the Moselle and its tributaries, and the Rhine from Speyer down to Koblenz. It is striking that all Germany's principal viticultural regions – as in France, but unlike Italy or Spain – were situated on or close to rivers; indeed, the Rhine provided the vital artery of transport which enabled German wines to be sold outside their region of origin. Of the areas along its valley Alsace, as we have noted, enjoyed the highest reputation: its wines supplied the German South-West and Switzerland, but they were also bought up by merchants from Frankfurt and, to a lesser extent, Cologne for shipment to much of northern Europe.[55] Wine made Strasbourg's fortune in the fourteenth and fifteenth century, and severe penalties were imposed to prevent Alsatian wine being adulterated with other wines from the Breisgau on the adjoining right bank, or from further afield.[56] The reputation of Alsatian and Rhenish wines lay essentially in the white varieties, but it is well-nigh impossible to gain an accurate impression of what was grown before 1700. In Alsace the best wines were made from Muscat and Traminer grapes, with Riesling the only varietal of true quality on the Rhine and Moselle.[57] It is unlikely, however, that these wines constituted more than a fraction of production; the bulk of the harvest was made up by lesser varieties such as Sylvaner and Elbling. Surprisingly, perhaps, red-wine grapes were widely planted in Alsace and Baden (principally the burgundian Pinot Noir),[58] and much of the harvest in Württemberg, then as now, may well have been of light red wine.

Only in the sixteenth century did beer begin its triumphant march into the front rank of German beverages. Until then, the cultivation of hops and the malting of barley had been largely confined to northern Germany, where wine was less readily available and comparatively expensive. Several of the Hanseatic cities were major brewing centres – the ports of Hamburg, Lübeck, Wismar, Rostock, and Danzig along the Baltic coast, and the inland cities of Hanover, Einbeck, Goslar and Braunschweig in Lower Saxony.[59] But there was also a famous brewing tradition in eastern Franconia (Kulmbach, Bamberg, Nuremberg), and hops began to be grown in Bavaria as well, which until 1500 had been more a wine-growing region, though not until the late seventeenth century did Bavarian beer come to be highly prized.[60]

Diversification and specialization within the primary sector could reach the stage where we may identify a new type of economic landscape, in which manufacturing was based upon the cultivation of industrial crops to make cloths or dyestuffs, or on pastoralism to supply the raw material, wool. The growth of the textile industry in late medieval Germany was to have a profound influence on modes of production and the nature of town–country relations (Map 1.2). We have already referred to the rise of linen-manufacturing around Lake Constance and throughout much of Upper Swabia. Initially, production was located in the larger towns and cities, notably Constance, St Gallen, Lindau, and Kempten, which drew unprocessed flax from the surrounding countryside. But in the course of the fifteenth century production began to move out to the smaller towns and villages; rural weavers made and marketed their own (often lesser) types of cloth, upheld a separate quality control, and shunned the civic cloth-exchanges. That suggests that rural manufacturing in such circumstances – especially to the south and at the west end of Lake Constance – was not always or necessarily the outflow of a widespread putting-out system which brought country weavers into dependence upon urban capitalists.[61] Further afield in eastern Swabia, however, putting out work to country weavers occurred from the outset: in Memmingen, the urban weavers tried to counteract this threat to their livelihood by entering into collective guild

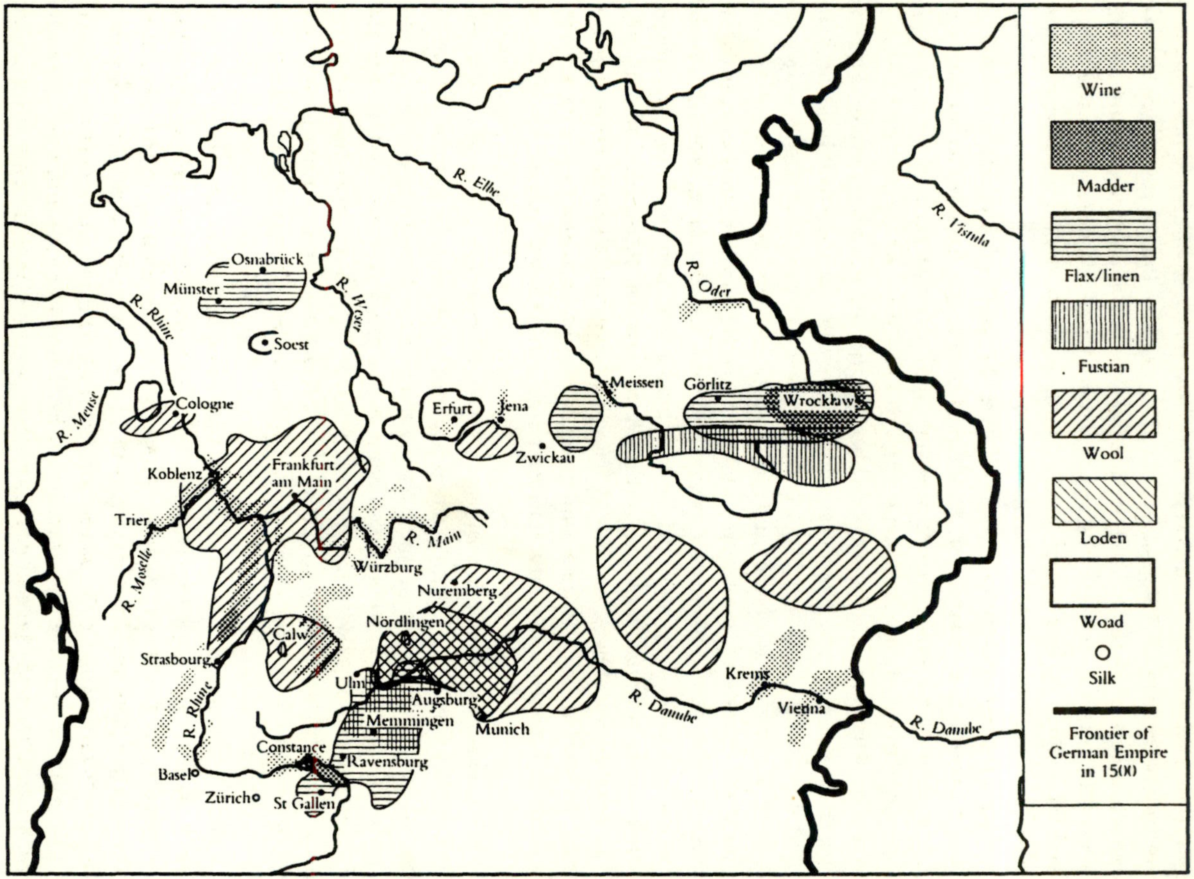
Wine
Madder
Flax/linen
Fustian
Wool
Loden
Woad
Silk
Frontier of German Empire in 1500
R. Vistula
R. Oder
R. Elbe
R. Weser
R. Rhine
R. Meuse
R. Moselle
R. Main
R. Danube
Osnabrück
Münster
Soest
Cologne
Koblenz
Trier
Frankfurt am Main
Erfurt
Jena
Zwickau
Meissen
Görlitz
Wrocław
Würzburg
Nuremberg
Nördlingen
Calw
Strasbourg
Ulm
Augsburg
Memmingen
Munich
Constance
Ravensburg
Basel
Zürich
St Gallen
Krems
Vienna

Map 1.2 Specialized crops and textiles, *c.*1500

contracts with merchants to supply cloth at an agreed price (*Zunftkäufe*).[62] To what extent put-out rural weavers should be seen as the victims of early capitalist exploitation remains an open question. In Kempten, for instance, the centre of the Allgäu linen industry, 400 urban weavers with 300 apprentices were matched by 600 'outburghers', country-dwellers in benefit of civic liberties, who were almost certainly linen-weavers.[63] Kempten may well have extended burghers' rights to this segment of the rural population in order to discourage emigration to an already populous city (on the pattern of cities such as Ghent and Bruges in fourteenth-century Flanders), but, whatever the reason, the result was an escape from serfdom and the acquisition of a certain degree of economic independence.[64]

By the sixteenth century other areas of linen production had come to the fore. In Westphalia, as woollen manufacturing declined, linen-weaving prospered, particularly in the rolling countryside between Osnabrück, Ravensberg, and Minden, and down into the plains between Diepholz and Hoya, in effect the catchment area of the rivers Ems and Weser.[65] Flax was also grown around Münster and to the south, in the Bergisches Land. Further east, flax was widely cultivated between the Erzgebirge in south-eastern Saxony and Upper Lusatia. Chemnitz was the focal point of Saxon production, whilst Lusatian cities such as Görlitz, Bautzen, Laubau, and Kamenz were not only centres of linen-weaving but also entrepôts for the trade in woollen cloth and woad.[66] Silesia's linen industry, as we have seen, was able to flourish even when integrated into feudal domain lordship. In all these northern regions *Verlag* was the standard mode of production, partly because linen production had spread in response to a growing international market, and partly because the need for rural by-employment in these areas, which, apart from Silesia, were ones of impartible inheritance, combined with a relatively weak guild tradition in the towns to leave the field open to capitalist entrepreneurs, some of whom held thousands of cottage weavers under contract.[67] From the 1560s linen exports from these areas were penetrating southern Germany, where they competed with the local cloths.[68]

The significance of linen in the definition of an economic landscape was heightened by the demand for paper after the invention of movable type in the mid-fifteenth century. Flax provided the raw material for the production of rag-paper, which was already flourishing in several south-west German and Swiss cities before the advent of printing. There were concentrations of paper mills around Ravensburg, Basel, Freiburg im Üchtland, and Épinal in the Vosges, though the technique of paper-making was quickly transferred to other centres of printing throughout Germany.[69] The natural conditions which favoured the cultivation of flax also applied to hemp, from which rough canvas and ropes were made, as well as a coarse cloth known confusingly in German as hempen linen (*Hanfleinwand*). But hemp never dominated the production of any one region so as to stamp it as an economic landscape in its own right, with the possible exception of some areas in the north, such as the Münsterland around Tecklenburg, which was heavily engaged in manufacturing canvas for the shipping industry in the Hanseatic ports.[70]

It was with the spread of fustian-manufacturing from the late fourteenth century onwards that early capitalism came to dominate the heartlands of the textile industry in Upper Swabia. Fustian, cloth woven from a linen warp and a cotton weft,[71] required the import of raw cotton from the Mediterranean, which was brought in by long-distance merchants who supplied the local spinners and weavers. While putting-out initially was confined to the larger towns, such as Nördlingen, where the merchants had their headquarters,[72] it quickly spread to the countryside, as entrepreneurs sought to circumvent guild restrictions and production limits, and to find cheaper sources of labour. In striking contrast, where fustian-manufacturing did not supplant linen-weaving – St Gallen is an obvious example – the system of *Verlag* was hardly deployed before the sixteenth century.[73] Competition between country weavers (*Gäuweber*), who supplied their capitalist employers directly, and the Swabian cities intensified during the fifteenth century. The latter tried to prohibit putting-out within a radius of 10 to 15 miles, but such edicts were mostly unsuccessful against powerful merchant companies such as the Fuggers (whose founder, Hans Fugger, had himself been a peasant and part-time weaver who emigrated to Augsburg from the Lech valley in the mid-fourteenth century), who grouped their rural weavers around rival centres of production – Weissenhorn and Pfaffenhofen, for instance, against Ulm. The latter, though, tried to hit back by enforcing more stringent quality controls and higher inspection fees, which elicited protests from its competing neighbours.[74] Similarly, Biberach saw its trade slip away to rural weavers in the pay of the Haug merchant company of Augsburg and the Zangmeisters of Memmingen.[75] Another bone of contention arose in the early 1400s as rural spinners began to warp linen-yarn ready for the loom by threading it onto cards (*Wepfen*), thereby encroaching on a more advanced state of production. The cities vacillated in their response: some, in the Allgäu, strove to confine production to the countryside; others, in Swabia, were ready to admit both urban and rural production, provided that they could prevent its organization by *Verlag*.[76] In general, however, the division of labour which marked fustian production could bring certain advantages to urban weavers, who were thereby encouraged to concentrate on the more complex finishing processes with greater added value and hence greater rewards.

By far the most extensive textile production in late medieval and early modern Germany, however, remained wool. The areas of manufacture ranged from northern Swabia, Franconia, and Bavaria, through central Württemberg, much of Lower Alsace and the Middle Rhine, to the district west of Cologne, and on eastwards through Hesse into Thuringia, Bohemia, and Moravia (see Map 1.2). Woollen manufacturing, although fully commercialized, was somewhat less exposed to the characteristic early capitalist practice of putting-out, for production was concentrated largely in towns, with only spinning as a part-time, and above all female, occupation in the countryside. But where manufacturing rapidly expanded in the sixteenth century in response to export demand – southern Thuringia is a case in point – urban weavers were obliged to accept piece-work contracts by *Verlag*.[77] Cologne, as a major metropolis both of production and distribution, also used *Verlag* to extend the manufacturing region of cloth bearing its seal of quality as far afield as Aachen.[78] These were exceptional instances, however, not the rule. Neither Strasbourg, as the mercantile capital of the Upper Rhine, nor Braunschweig, the most export-oriented of the Hanseatic cities, resorted to any degree of putting-out in order to increase their share of the market, perhaps because, in the former, workshops were geared to the production of cheaper cloths for lining rather than quality export woollens,[79] while, in the latter, the clothmakers' guild which controlled all stages of production did not display the common early capitalist division between merchant drapers and master wool-weavers.[80] Cloth production created in turn a lively market for dyestuffs and dyeing agents, notably madder, woad, and alum. The blue dye obtained from woad remained in greatest demand until it was overtaken in the sixteenth century by indigo from the Orient. Until then, Erfurt and its hinterland in Thuringia was the principal area of production, which thrived in part by supplying local manufacturers but chiefly by exporting woad to the many centres of cloth production in neighbouring Hesse.[81] A symbiosis between adjacent regions of specialized production can therefore be observed in the central German woollen industry, though elsewhere – in Alsace and on the Lower Rhine – dyestuffs were cultivated within the areas of cloth manufacture itself.

The growing demand for woollen cloth in certain instances encouraged a switch from other textiles, particularly in northern Swabia, where Nördlingen progressed from linen- through fustian-weaving to the manufacture of loden, the heavy, felted, short-pile cloth used for blankets and coats.[82] By the end of the sixteenth century, indeed, loden production had spread south-eastwards into many Bavarian towns as far as Munich. The popularity of wool over coarser, mixed cloths such as fustian was further enhanced by the development of lighter, softer woollens in the sixteenth century, known collectively as the 'new draperies'. In fact, the 'new draperies' proper were short-staple woollen cloths, pioneered in Flanders as a cheaper alternative to traditional luxury woollens, whereas the new cloths widely made in both Germany and England were either worsted (that is, long-staple) cloths, or else blends with a worsted warp and a woollen (short-staple) weft.[83] These light, unsheared cloths – sayes and serges, as they were called – had already been promoted on a territorial level in Baden and Württemberg around 1500,[84] and by the mid-sixteenth century the leading textile cities of southern Germany – Strasbourg, Ulm, Augsburg – were likewise making sayes in the form of barracans and grosgrams.[85] Apart from the 'new draperies' a few centres began to specialize in cotton and silk, notably in Switzerland, where Basel had already developed a cotton industry based on putting out work to weavers in Alsace and the Breisgau in the fifteenth century. In north Germany the only important centre of silk-weaving in the fifteenth century was Cologne, but by the mid-sixteenth refugees from Tridentine Italy had brought their expertise in silk-weaving to Zurich and other Protestant cities.[86]

The third type of economic landscape, that of mining and the metal-working industries, has sometimes been seen as the pacemaker in a decisive transformation towards a fully industrial economy based on capitalism. Yet quite apart from the restricted geographical dispersion of such areas up to the end of the sixteenth century (see Map 1.3), we should remember that the twin hallmarks of industrial production – the factory system and the replacement of manual labour by machines – only existed in rudimentary form; 'proto-factories' could survive for centuries without giving rise to any widespread industrialization.[87] In one particular branch of the extractive industry, moreover, namely salt-mining, the nature of production might in fact inhibit the development of a factory system. Where salt was extracted by evaporation from brine, as in the salt-springs of Frankenhausen in Thuringia, or Allendorf-Sooden in Hesse, the work was neither capital-intensive nor technologically complex. In Thuringia individual salt-miners were engaged in extended commodity production rather than in early capitalist entrepreneurialism.[88] No shareholding companies developed to exploit the salt works, as happened in the silver and copper mines of southern Saxony, though in Hesse the Allendorf salt-springs were run as a state monopoly on a capitalist footing.[89] Where salt had to be hewn from saliferous rock, however, as in the mines of Bavaria, Tyrol, and Salzburg, the techniques of extraction were more costly: winches and pulleys were needed to bring the salt to the surface, while the salt-pans installed in Hall, for example, were on an industrial scale. Salt-mining in the Alps was under princely control from the thirteenth century, and considerable sums were invested to improve roads over the Alps to compete in northern Italy against sea salt marketed by Venice.[90]

The other extractive industry which did not necessarily require new techniques of production was glass-making. Glassworks, as we have seen in the case of Hesse, were less dependent on the location of raw materials – silicates – than on the availability of the derivatives used in the manufacturing process itself. Both sand and clay (for the firing ovens) were plentiful in the forests of northern and southern Hesse, the Reinhard, Kaufungen, and Spessart districts. But glassworks also flourished in areas where timber (and hence potash) abounded but the soils were not especially siliceous, notably in the Black Forest, where quartz sand was

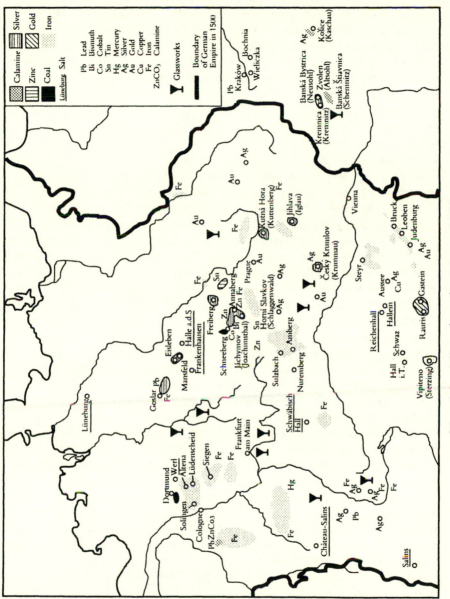

Map 1.3 Minerals and mining, c.1500

Legend:

Calamine · Silver
Zinc · Gold
Coal · Iron
Lüneburg Salt

Pb Lead
Bi Bismuth
Co Cobalt
Sn Tin
Hg Mercury
Ag Silver
Au Gold
Cu Copper
Fe Iron
ZnCO₃ Calamine

Glassworks

Boundary of German Empire in 1500

Locations (as labelled):

Lüneburg○
Goslar Pb / Fe
Eisleben
Mansfeld
Halle a.d.S
Frankenhausen
Dortmund
Werl
Altena
Lüdenscheid
Siegen
Solingen
Cologne
Pb ZnCo3
Frankfurt am Main
Schwäbisch Hall
Château-Salins
Salins
Freiberg
Schneeberg
Annaberg
Jáchymov (Joachimsthal)
Horní Slavkov (Schlaggenwald)
Sulzbach
Amberg
Nuremberg
Prague
Český Krumlov (Krummau)
Kutná Hora (Kuttenberg)
Jihlava (Iglau)
Kraków
Bochnia
Wieliczka
Banská Bystrica (Neusohl)
Kremnica (Kremnitz)
Zvolen (Altsohl)
Banská Štiavnica (Schemnitz)
Košice (Kaschau)
Vienna
Bruck
Leoben
Judenburg
Steyr
Aussee
Hallein
Reichenhall
Hall i.T.
Schwaz
Gastein
Rauris
Vipiteno (Sterzing)

hauled up from the Rhine valley. Glass foundries might be grouped into a federation of producers, as in Hesse, but it was just as common for glass-makers to remain journeymen who staked out a plot of forest which they felled until exhausted, before moving on.[91] For that reason, along with the relatively straightforward technology, glass-making remained an industry without any significant capitalist penetration of production and distribution, and, by the same token, one which rarely dominated a particular region for long enough to constitute an economic landscape. Even in Hesse, the extensive glass industry, which had already moved northwards in the course of the sixteenth century, was in decline by 1600, as woodland resources were used up.[92]

The extraction and processing of precious and base metal ores, by contrast, could only expand with sufficient capital backing and the stimulus of new technology. Where copper, silver, lead, and iron abounded – in southern Westphalia, Saxony, Bohemia, the Upper Palatinate, Tyrol, and Styria – the first genuinely industrial landscapes of late medieval and early modern Germany emerged (see Map 1.3). In many of these areas subsidiary deposits of other minerals were discovered: gold in parts of Bohemia and Lusatia; bismuth, cobalt, and tin (which, in the form of tinplate, was used to coat iron to prevent rusting) in southern Saxony. Indeed, Saxony became a region of economic diversification almost on a par with Alsace, where commercialized pastoral agriculture, the cultivation of industrial crops such as woad, and a woollen and linen industry interacted with the boom in mining and metallurgy to create a dynamic push–pull of supply and demand. Other areas, though, might acquire their distinctive economic contours from the mining of a single mineral: calamine (*Galmei*, zinc carbonate; in the USA smithsonite), which was alloyed with copper to produce brass, was discovered west of Cologne; mercury was found in the Rhineland Palatinate, while the pit-coal deposits of the Ruhr (and southern Saxony) were being mined as early as the fifteenth century.

The major technical innovation of the later middle ages in metallurgy was the invention of liquation (*Saiger-, Abdarrverfahren*), whereby silver could be extracted from argentiferous raw copper through the admixture of lead. Hitherto, the mining of silver had largely been confined to areas of argentiferous lead ores in the Carpathian and Harz Mountains, and the Austrian Alps from Tyrol through to Carinthia, with smaller reserves in the Vosges and the Black Forest. The silver was separated from the lead by cupellation, a technique known to antiquity, whereby the lead was melted in a marl-lined hearth and then oxidized, so that the silver was left as a metal 'bun' on the hearth.[93] Liquation, on the other hand, was a much more costly and time-consuming process, which required copious supplies of lead. In the copper-shale district of Thuringia, on whose southern fringes the greatest concentration of liquation works was to be found, lead, despite its weight, had to be imported from as far afield as the Eifel and Westphalia. In the liquation process itself, the lead was burnt up, which produced white lead (lead oxide); that could then be returned to lead by reduction through charcoal: nevertheless, the wastage was high.[94] The discovery of liquation transformed the mining industry of central Germany and, subsequently, the Alps, where new argentiferous copper deposits were discovered near the lead ores. By the end of the fifteenth century Schwaz in Tyrol was alone producing 80 per cent of the silver and 40 per cent of the copper of central Europe.[95] Despite the opening up of new mines, such as Kitzbühel, in the early decades of the sixteenth century, however, the silver boom quickly collapsed in the face of cheaper imports from the Americas. But the advantage of liquation was that it permitted a new phase of metallurgical enterprise to flourish through a shift in emphasis to copper production which, in its alloy of brass, supplied the growing armaments industry of the 'iron century' of warfare in early modern Europe. By the mid-sixteenth century, for instance, the bulk of Thuringian mining output was copper rather than silver, though after 1550 there appears to have been a gradual decline in the use of copper for household goods.[96]

In the mining industry the putting-out system was very widespread, not only on account of the high capital cost of extracting and refining, or the expense of transport between the mines and the smelteries, but also because its production as bullion or as metal was traded internationally. The leading merchants of Nuremberg and Augsburg were deeply involved in all the mining regions of central Europe. The Fuggers, to take the prime example, owned smelteries or maintained trading depots from Thuringia, through Hungary (at Banská Bystrica/Neusohl) to Carinthia (Fuggerau by Villach) as well as in Tyrol itself, whose economy they effectively controlled. Yet the risks were great in an industry so vulnerable to the external hazards of warfare or the loss of mining licences and monopolies, and to the internal dislocations caused by the flooding of mines, explosions, and collapse of shafts, or else incautious overproduction, let alone the perpetual threat of labour unrest. Many entrepreneurs went bankrupt, or withdrew and cut their losses, so that it comes as no surprise to find the mining industry in the area which had prospered most from the invention of liquation – Thuringia – by the 1540s no longer controlled by distant merchants but by its territorial princes, the counts of Mansfeld. A similar story can be told of the Fuggers' involvement at Banská Bystrica.[97]

These observations should make us cautious about ascribing an intrinsic dynamic to the spread of early capitalism in Germany; indeed, its most characteristic form, the putting-out system, was far from being a peculiarly late medieval development.[98] Yet in areas of iron production the entire economy might be invigorated by the manufacture of high-value metalwares – precision tools, clocks, and scientific instruments – provided that sufficient capital and technology were available. Iron-ore deposits were found in many parts of the Empire in the middle ages – the Eifel and Hunsrück, Siegerland and Sauerland, parts of the Black Forest and eastern Swabia, the Upper Palatinate, much of Bohemia into Moravia and Lusatia, and in Styria and Carinthia – but the only two areas which had made the successful transition from isolated forges employing primitive technology and supplying local needs to fully industrialized landscapes with specialized factory production by the sixteenth century were the Süderland (the county of Mark in the western Sauerland) and the Upper Palatinate. It is no accident that these two districts lay near major international trading cities – Cologne and Nuremberg – and enjoyed good communications and a strategic market position. In the Süderland, the towns of Solingen, Altena, Iserlohn, and Lüdenscheid were already famous in the fifteenth century for the manufacture of wire (by drawing, not smithying), tools, and household metal goods such as cutlery which required the use of moulds and presses as well as forges and furnaces. So advanced was production that the Süderland came to concentrate on finished articles, and was content to import pig-iron from further south in the Siegerland.[99] This latter district had undergone considerable economic development in the later Middle Ages; in its flourishing iron industry blast-furnaces had replaced bloomery by 1500, and the putting-out system was prevalent.[100] Yet, unlike the Süderland, the Siegerland never became a fully industrialized region, largely because of its remoteness and the lack of entrepreneurial initiative: iron-working remained under the control of local lords or the landgraves of Hesse, who were more concerned with domestic needs than distant export markets.

The most advanced industrial area of all was undoubtedly the district around Nuremberg, which drew on iron supplies from the Upper Palatinate with its twin metallurgical centres of Sulzbach and Amberg. By the early fourteenth century the technique of tinplating iron had been pioneered, which for long remained confined to Nuremberg and Wunsiedel in the Fichtelgebirge.[101] Likewise, the technology of wire-drawing was in use from the early fifteenth century, though not fully automated until the late sixteenth.[102] Wire mills were established all around the city on the rivers Regnitz and Pegnitz. Just as in the Süderland, Nuremberg, as the region's economic powerhouse, sought less to dominate the metallurgical processes itself than, by deploying *Verlag*, to secure supplies of semi-finished ironware which it could then manufacture into specialized finished goods. A list of crafts in the city in which the putting-out system operated records in 1535 hook-, blade-, compass-, knife-, needle- and wire-making, as well as armourers and tinsmiths, alongside certain clothing trades (fustian-weaving, glove-making) and printing. The city and its entrepreneurs used the putting-out system less to organize the surrounding countryside into an industrial zone for mass production – unlike the Upper Swabian cities with their rural linen and fustian industries – than to reserve the latter stages of production to urban craftsmen in their employ, and to export their wares to foreign markets.[103] The concept of the *Wirtschaftseinheit*, the economic unit embracing town and country, implied not so much dominance by the city of its hinterland as the fulfilment of mutual needs: the smaller surrounding

towns were as eager to grab a share of Nuremberg's industrial prosperity as the city's merchants were to control local production.[104]
The intensification of town–country relations within a given region is the most obvious hallmark of the development of economic landscapes in Germany from the later middle ages. It would be wrong to conclude this review, however, without making three qualifications. In the first place, the growth of economic regionalism was only possible where town and country made up an economic unit. Where cities earned their livelihood as entrepôts and their merchants as middlemen and carriers there, was no reason why such economic activity should impinge upon the hinterland at all. That is most noticeably the case in the coastal cities of the Hanseatic League, whose trade derived much less from importing and exporting to and from northern Germany than from long-distance cargo-carrying between Russia, the Baltic, and Western Europe. In cities such as Lübeck and Hamburg the urban economy of small commodity-producers remained largely intact; the division of labour, capital-intensive production, and the putting-out system were underdeveloped until the sixteenth century; and there was little attempt to extend commercial influence to the countryside, where the territorial lords were in any case at pains to protect their local crafts and industry from urban encroachment. Indeed, the coastal Hanseatic cities – fish out of water, rather than the natural foci of their regions – faced growing artisanal competition from their hinterlands in the course of the sixteenth century, though by then centres such as Lübeck had begun to employ put-out rural workers in the copper industry and in cooperage.[105]

Secondly, the growth of economic regions did not preclude the rise of international commerce over long distances between the Empire as a whole and its neighbours: the one, in fact, was predicated upon the other. The more the economic specialization in a particular area, the greater was the need to import goods from elsewhere. The prime example in the sixteenth century, as has already been suggested, was the development of an international trade in cattle. Population pressure and the demand for grain in the West squeezed the amount of land available for stock-rearing. Instead of the smaller, leaner cattle raised in the West, merchants began to bring in the larger grey cattle from Hungary and Poland which had been fattened, significantly enough, not on the domain estates of lords or on peasant smallholdings but on the vast tracts of semi-wild steppe.[106] A cluster of cattle markets grew up on the frontiers of the Empire around Wroław and east of Vienna, with further staging-posts in Germany itself, notably at Buttstädt in Thuringia (see Map 1.4). By the sixteenth century, however, the Eastern European cattle trade was itself in turn being challenged by imports from Denmark and Scania. Lean steers were brought via the north German cities for fattening on the lush pasturelands of the Elbe and Weser marshes, before being driven further south for sale. As pastoralism retreated before the expansion of cereal agriculture in the West, the new international system of livestock marketing became, in Ian Blanchard's words, the mainstay of met-

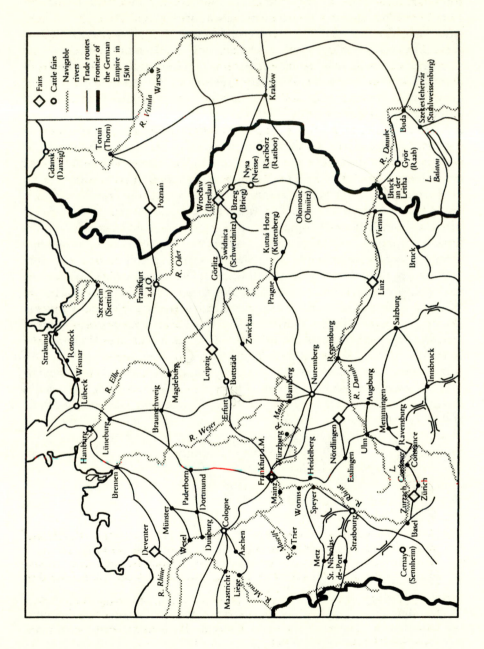

Map 1.4 Trade routes, fairs, and navigable rivers, c.1500

ropolitan meat-provisioning throughout the whole of Western Europe.[107] Yet the market exchange between areas of pastoral and cereal agriculture could also serve to intensify economic activity within a smaller compass. Alsace, as the bread-basket for much of south-west Germany and Switzerland, was dependent upon meat imports from the rich grazing lands of Burgundy and the Franche-Comté, so that the cattle-market at Cernay (Sennheim) became the hub of commercial activity between two immediately adjacent regions.[108]

The final consideration is perhaps the most important of all. Economic regions did not thrive (or decline) in a vacuum: they were vulnerable to political disruption and military depredation. The Cities' War of 1449–52, for instance, severely disrupted Nuremberg's economy and commerce and provided an opening for its rival Augsburg, of which the latter was quick to take advantage.[109] Augsburg's merchants, especially the Fuggers and Welsers, built upon that opportunity in the succeeding decades, as they forged a financial alliance with the Habsburgs in return for access to the lucrative silver and copper mines of Tyrol. Likewise, the periodic campaigns against the Turks from the 1470s brought economic dislocation to Nuremberg and many of the Swabian manufacturing cities. The *coup de grâce* for Nuremberg finally came in the mid-sixteenth century, when the Margrave's War against Albrecht Alcibiades of Brandenburg-Ansbach cost the city four-and-a-half million florins and ruined its finances.[110] In an age of transition, poised between medieval merchant-venturer capitalism and the industrial capitalism of early modern Europe, the development of economic landscapes in Germany was uneven and uncertain, constantly exposed to setbacks from without and within, that is, to political as well as economic constraints

Notes

1 Heide Wunder, 'European Agriculture', in G. R. Elton, ed., *New Cambridge Modern History* II: *The Reformation*, 2nd edn (Cambridge, 1990), p. 33.
2 Wilhelm Abel, *Geschichte der deutschen Landwirtschaft vom frühen Mittelalter bis zum 19. Jahrhundert (Deutsche Agrargeschichte* II), ed. Günther Franz, 2nd edn (Stuttgart, 1967), pp. 85–6.
3 Othmar Pickl, 'Routen, Umfang und Organisation des innereuropäischen Handels mit Schlachtvieh im 16. Jahrhundert', in Alexander Novotny and Othmar Pickl, eds, *Festschrift Hermann Wiesflecker zum sechzigsten Geburtstag* (Graz, 1973), p. 145.
4 Wilhelm Abel, *Agricultural Fluctuations in Europe. From the Thirteenth to the Twentieth Centuries* (London, 1980), pp. 113-14; Peter Kriedte, *Peasants, Landlords and Merchant Capitalists. Europe and the World Economy 1500–1800* (Leamington Spa, 1983), p. 27.
5 Robert A. Dodgshon, *The European Past. Social Evolution and Spatial Order*

(Houndmills, Hants/London, 1987), pp. 238–9.

6 Rolf Kießling, *Die Stadt und ihr Land. Umlandpolitik, Bürgerbesitz und Wirtschaftsgefüge in Ostschwaben vom 14. bis ins 16. Jahrhundert* (Städteforschung. Veröffentlichungen des Instituts für vergleichende Städtegeschichte in Münster, Reihe A XXIX) (Cologne/Vienna, 1989), p. 448.

7 Raymond van Uytven, 'Die ländliche Industrie während des Spätmittelalters in den südlichen Niederlanden', in Hermann Kellenbenz ed., *Agrarisches Nebengewerbe und Formen der Reagrarisierung im Spätmittelalter und 19./20. Jahrhundert* (Forschungen zur Sozial- und Wirtschaftsgeschichte, XXI) (Stuttgart, 1975), p. 74.

8 Wolfgang von Stromer, 'Gewerbereviere und Protoindustrien in Spätmittelalter und Frühneuzeit', in Hans Pohl, ed., *Gewerbe- und Industrielandschaften vom Spätmittelalter bis ins 20. Jahrhundert* (*VSWG* LXXVIII) (Stuttgart, 1986), pp. 47, 57.

9 Bernhard Kirchgässner, 'Der Verlag im Spannungsfeld von Stadt und Umland', in Erich Maschke and Jürgen Sydow, eds, *Stadt und Umland. Protokoll der X. Arbeitstagung des Arbeitskreises für südwestdeutsche Stadtgeschichtsforschung, Calw. 12.–14. November 1971* (Veröffentlichungen der Kommission für geschichtliche Landeskunde in Baden-Württemberg, Reihe B LXXXII) (Stuttgart, 1974), p. 86; von Stromer, 'Gewerberievere', pp. 76, 78. Cf. idem, 'Der Verlag als strategisches System einer an gutem Geld armen Wirtschaft, am Beispiel Oberdeutschlands in Mittelalter und Früher Neuzeit', *VSWG* LXXVIII (1991), pp. 153–71.

10 Hermann Kellenbenz, 'Rural Industries in the West from the End of the Middle Ages to the Eighteenth Century', in Peter Earle, ed., *Essays in European Economic History* (Oxford, 1974), p. 62.

11 Abel, *Geschichte der deutschen Landwirtschaft*, p. 83.

12 William John Wright, *Capitalism, the State and the Lutheran Reformation. Sixteenth-Century Hesse* (Athens, OH, 1988), p. 124.

13 Ekkehard Westermann, *Das Eislebener Garkupfer und seine Bedeutung für den europäischen Kupfermarkt 1460–1560* (Cologne/Vienna, 1971), p. 80; see in general Hermann Kellenbenz, *The Rise of the European Economy. An Economic History of Continental Europe 1500–1750* (London, 1976), p. 105.

14 Westermann, *Eislebener Garkupfer*, p. 78.

15 Wolfgang von Stromer, 'Verflechtungen oberdeutscher Wirtschaftszentren am Beginn der Neuzeit', in Wilhelm Rausch, ed., *Die Stadt an der Schwelle zur Neuzeit* (Beiträge zur Geschichte der Städte Mitteleuropas IV) (Linz, 1980), p. 24.

16 Hektor Ammann, 'La place de l'Alsace dans l'industrie textile du Moyen Âge', in *La Bourgeoisie alsacienne. Études d'histoire sociale* (Publications de la Société Savante d'Alsace et des Régions de l'Est, série 'grandes publications', V), 2nd edn (Strasbourg, 1967), pp. 76–7.

17 Hektor Ammann, 'Von der Wirtschaftsgeltung des Elsaß im Mittelalter', *Alemannisches Jb* (1955), p. 56.

18 John Langton and Göran Hoppe, *Town and Country in the Development of Early Modern Western Europe* (Historical Geography Research Series XI) (Norwich, 1983), p. 40 and *passim*.

19 Hektor Ammann, *Die wirtschaftliche Stellung der Reichsstadt Nürnberg im Spätmittelalter* (Nürnberger Forschungen XIII) (Nuremberg, 1970), pp. 194ff., 223.

20 Barthel Huppertz, *Räume und Schichten bäuerlicher Kulturformen in Deutschland. Ein Beitrag zur Deutschen Bauerngeschichte* (Bonn, 1939), p. 28; Abel, *Geschichte der deutschen Landwirtschaft*, pp. 71–2.

21 Huppertz, *Räume und Schichten,* pp. 53–4.
22 Kellenbenz, *Rise of the European Economy,* p. 60.
23 For Upper Swabia see David Sabean, *Landbesitz und Gesellschaft am Vorabend des Bauernkriegs. Eine Studie der sozialen Verhältnisse im südlichen Oberschwaben in den Jahren vor 1525* (Quellen und Forschungen zur Agrargeschichte XXVI) (Stuttgart, 1972), pp. 40ff.; for Hohenlohe Thomas Robisheaux, *Rural Society and the Search for Order in Early Modern Germany* (Cambridge, 1989), p. 81.
24 Huppertz, *Räume und Schichten,* p. 55.
25 Cf. Peter Kriedte, Hans Medick and Jürgen Schlumbohm, *Industrialisation before Industrialisation. Rural Industry in the Genesis of Capitalism* (Cambridge, 1981), p. 214, n. 14.
26 Friedrich-Wilhelm Henning, *Landwirtschaft und ländliche Gesellschaft in Deutschland: 800–1750,* 2nd edn (Paderborn/Munich/Vienna/Zürich, 1985), p. 78.
27 *Ibid.,* p. 79.
28 Gertrud Schröder-Lembke, 'Wesen und Verbreitung der Zweifelderwirtschaft im Rheingebiet', *ZAgrarGAgrarSoz* VII (1959), pp. 14–31.
29 Abel, *Geschichte der deutschen Landwirtschaft,* p. 83.
30 Étienne Juillard, 'L'Assolement biennal dans l'agriculture septentrionale', *Annales de géographie* (1952), pp. 34–49.
31 Hugo Ott, *Studien zur spätmittelalterlichen Agrarverfassung im Oberrheingebiet* (Quellen und Forschungen zur Agrargeschichte XXIII) (Stuttgart, 1970), pp. 94–6.
32 Abel, *Geschichte der deutschen Landwirtschaft,* p. 87.
33 Ott, *Studien zur Agrarverfassung,* p. 107.
34 Abel, *Geschichte der deutschen Landwirtschaft,* p. 176.
35 Wilhelm Abel, *Agricultural Fluctuations,* p. 140. Although this point is recognized by the author, his translator on p. 108 of the English edn erroneously translates *Koppelwirtschaft* as 'enclosure system'.
36 Hans Conrad Peyer, 'Wollgewerbe, Viehzucht, Solddienst und Bevölkerungsentwicklung in Stadt und Landschaft Freiburg i. Ue. vom 14. bis 16. Jahrhundert', in Kellenbenz, *Agrarisches Nebengewerbe,* p. 83.
37 Abel, *Geschichte der deutschen Landwirtschaft,* pp. 92–3.
38 Friedrich Lütge, *Geschichte der deutschen Agrarverfassung vom frühen Mittelalter bis zum 19. Jahrhundert (Deutsche Agrargeschichte,* ed. Günther Franz), 2nd edn (Stuttgart, 1967), pp. 89–90. He cites as a typical instance the abbey of Bebenhausen by Tübingen. For an exceptional instance of continuity in Cistercian land-management see Winfried Schenk, *Mainfränkische Kulturlandschaft unter klösterlicher Herrschaft: Die Zisterzienserabtei Ebrach als raumwirkende Institution vom 16. Jahrhundert bis 1803* (Würzburger Geographische Arbeiten LXXI) (Würzburg, 1988).
39 Kellenbenz, *Rise of the European Economy,* p. 60.
40 Henning, *Landwirtschaft,* p. 206; Lütge, *Agrarverfassung,* p.191.
41 Holm Sundhaußen, 'Zur Wechselbeziehung zwischen frühneuzeitlichem Außenhandel und ökonomischer Rückständigkeit in Osteuropa. Eine Auseinandersetzung mit der "Kolonialthese"', *GG* IX (1983), pp. 544–63.
42 Henning, *Landwirtschaft,* pp. 166–70. Those who argue that *Gutswirtschaft* preceded *Gutsherrschaft* can at least point to the fact that the structure of east Elbian society and population made increasing labour services much easier than increasing rents. Cf. Lütge, *Agrarverfassung,* p. 139.
43 *Ibid.,* pp. 126–7.
44 Ludwig Petry, 'Breslau in der schlesischen Städtelandschaft des 16. Jahrhunderts', in Rausch, *Die Stadt an der Schwelle zur Neuzeit,* pp. 259–61.

45 Abel, *Geschichte der deutschen Landwirtschaft*, p. 161; Kriedte, Medick, and Schlumbohm, *Industrialisation*, pp. 18, 20; Richard C. Hoffmann, *Land, Liberties, and Lordship in a Late Medieval Countryside. Agrarian Structures and Change in the Duchy of Wrolaw* (Philadelphia, 1989), pp. 353–5, 365–7.

46 Alfred Hoffmann, 'Die Grundherrschaft als Unternehmen', *ZAgrarGAgrarSoz* VI (1958), pp. 123–31; Lütge, *Agrarverfassung*, pp. 162–3, 170–1.

47 Hartmut Harnisch, *Bauern – Feudaladel – Städtebürgertum. Untersuchungen über die Zusammenhänge zwischen Feudalrente, bäuerlicher und gutsherrlicher Warenproduktion und den Ware-Geld-Beziehungen in der Magdeburger Börde und dem nordöstlichen Harzvorland von der frühbürgerlichen Revolution bis zum Dreißigjährigen Krieg* (Abhandlungen zur Handels- und Sozialgeschichte XX) (Weimar, 1980), pp. 190, 199–202.

48 Cf. Edgar Melton, '*Gutsherrschaft* in East Elbian Germany and Livonia, 1500–1800: A Critique of the Model', *CEH*, XXI (1988), pp. 315–49. Cf. also Michael North, 'Die frühneuzeitliche Gutswirtschaft in Schleswig-Holstein. Forschungsüberblick und Entwicklungsfaktoren', *BDLG* CXXVI (1990), pp. 223–42.

49 Roy L. Vice, 'Vineyards, Vinedressers and the Peasants' War in Franconia', *ARG* LXXIX (1988), p.139.

50 Helmut Hahn, *Die deutschen Weinbaugebiete. Ihre historisch-geographische Entwicklung und wirtschafts- und sozialgeographische Struktur* (Bonner Geographische Abhandlungen XVIII) (Bonn, 1956), p. 22.

51 Vice, 'Vineyards', p. 138.

52 Hahn, *Die deutschen Weinbaugebiete*, p. 19. For Austria see most recently Helmut Feigl and Willibald Rosner, eds, *Probleme des niederösterreichischen Weinbaus in Vergangenheit und Gegenwart. Die Vorträge des neunten Symposions des Niederösterreichischen Instituts für Landeskunde Retz. 4.–6. Juli 1988* (Studien und Forschungen aus dem Niederösterreichischen Institut für Landeskunde, XIII) (Vienna, 1990).

53 Kellenbenz, *Rise of the European Economy*, p. 94.

54 Wieland Held, *Zwischen Marktplatz und Anger. Stadt-Land-Beziehungen im 16. Jahrhundert in Thüringen* (Weimar, 1988), pp. 111–13.

55 François Joseph Fuchs, 'L'Espace économique rhénan et les relations commerciales de Strasbourg avec le sud-ouest de l'Allemagne au XVIe siècle', in Alfons Schäfer, ed., *Oberrheinische Studien III: Festschrift für Günther Haselier aus Anlaß seines 60. Geburtstages am 19. April 1974* (Karlsruhe, 1975), pp. 301–3; Wolfgang Herborn and Klaus Militzer, *Der Kölner Weinhandel. Seine sozialen und politischen Auswirkungen im ausgehenden 14. Jahrhundert* (Vorträge und Forschungen XXV) (Sigmaringen, 1980), pp. 38–40.

56 Philippe Dollinger, 'La Ville libre à la fin du Moyen Âge (1350-1482)', in Georges Livet and Francis Rapp, eds, *Histoire de Strasbourg des origines à nos jours*, II: *Strasbourg des grandes invasions au XVIe siècle* (Strasbourg, 1981), p. 153.

57 Médard Barth, *Der Rebbau des Elsaß und die Absatzgebiete seiner Weine*, I (Strasbourg/Paris, 1958), p. 88.

58 Barth, *Rebbau des Elsaß*, pp. 81–4.

59 Kellenbenz, *Rise of the European Economy*, p. 94; Abel, *Geschichte der deutschen Landwirtschaft*, p. 181.

60 Henning, *Landwirtschaft*, p. 130; Abel, *Geschichte der deutschen Landwirtschaft*, p.127.

61 Hektor Ammann, 'Die Anfänge der Leinenindustrie des Bodenseegebiets', *Alemannisches Jb* (1953), pp. 251–313, and map, p. 253; Kirchgässner, 'Verlag', p. 86.

62 Kießling, *Die Stadt und ihr Land*, p. 482.

63 Tom Scott, ed., *Die Freiburger Enquete von 1476. Quellen zur Wirtschafts- und Verwaltungsgeschichte der Stadt Freiburg im Breisgau im fünfzehnten Jahrhundert* (Veröffentlichungen aus dem Archiv der Stadt Freiburg im Breisgau XX) (Freiburg im Breisgau, 1986), pp. 15–16.
64 David Nicholas, *Town and Countryside. Social, Economic and Political Tensions in Fourteenth-Century Flanders* (Rijksuniversiteit te Gent: Werken uitgegeven door de Faculteit van de Letteren en Wijsbegeerte CLII) (Bruges, 1971), pp. 220–1, 242.
65 Kellenbenz, 'Rural Industries', p. 61.
66 Richard Dietrich, 'Das Städtewesen Sachsens an der Wende vom Mittelalter zur Neuzeit', in Rausch, *Die Stadt an der Schwelle zur Neuzeit*, p. 208.
67 Ingomar Bog, 'Wachstumsprobleme der oberdeutschen Wirtschaft 1540–1618', in Friedrich Lütge, ed., *Wirtschaftliche und soziale Probleme der gewerblichen Entwicklung im 15.–16. und 19. Jahrhundert. Berichtrüber die zweite Arbeitstagung der Gesellschaft für Sozial- und Wirtschaftsgeschichte in Würzburg 8.–10. März 1965* (Forschungen zur Sozial- und Wirtschaftsgeschichte, X) (Stuttgart, 1968), p. 53; Kellenbenz, *Rise of the European Economy*, p. 76.
68 Kießling, *Die Stadt und ihr Land*, pp. 501–2.
69 Von Stromer, 'Gewerbereviere', pp. 104–6, and map, p. 105.
70 Kellenbenz, 'Rural Industries', p. 61.
71 Not a cotton warp and a linen weft, as erroneously stated in Friedrich-Wilhelm Henning, *Wirtschafts- und Sozialgeschichte*, I: *Das vorindustrielle Deutschland 800 bis 1800*, 4th edn (Paderborn/Munich/Vienna/Zürich, 1985), p. 146.
72 Kießling, *Die Stadt und ihr Land*, p. 219.
73 Kirchgässner, 'Verlag', pp. 96–7.
74 Hermann Kellenbenz, 'The Fustian Industry of the Ulm Region in the Fifteenth and Early Sixteenth Centuries', in N. B. Harte and K. G. Ponting, eds, *Cloth and Clothing in Medieval Europe. Essays in Memory of Professor E.M. Carus-Wilson* (Pasold Studies in Textile History II) (London, 1983), p. 262.
75 Kellenbenz, *Rise of the European Economy*, pp. 81–2.
76 Rolf Kießling, 'Stadt und Land im Textilgewerbe Oberschwabens vom 14. bis zur Mitte des 16. Jahrhunderts', in Neithard Bulst, Jochen Hoock and Franz Irsigler, eds, *Bevölkerung, Wirtschaft und Gesellschaft. Stadt-Land-Beziehungen in Deutschland und Frankreich 14. bis 19. Jahrhundert* (Trier, 1983), pp. 124–6.
77 Held, *Zwischen Marktplatz und Anger*, pp. 174–5.
78 Franz Irsigler, 'Stadt und Umland im Spätmittelalter. Zur zentralitäts-fördernden Kraft von Fernhandel und Exportgewerbe', in Emil Meynen, ed., *Zentralität als Problem der mittelalterlichen Stadtgeschichtsforschung* (Städteforschung. Veröffentlichungen des Instituts für vergleichende Städtegeschichte in Münster A VIII) (Cologne/Vienna, 1979), pp. 4–5; on Cologne's cloth production in general cf. Franz Irsigler, 'Kölner Wirtschaft im Spätmittelalter', in Hermann Kellenbenz, ed., *Zwei Jahrtausende Kölner Wirtschaft* I (Cologne, 1975), pp. 218–319.
79 Ammann, 'Wirtschaftsgeltung des Elsaß', p. 81.
80 Ernst Pitz, 'Wirtschaftliche und soziale Probleme der gewerblichen Entwicklung im 15./16. Jahrhundert nach hansisch-niederdeutschen Quellen', in Lütge, *Probleme der gewerblichen Entwicklung*, pp. 39–40.
81 Hektor Ammann, 'Die Friedberger Messen', *Rheinische Vierteljahrsblätter* XV/XVI (1950/51), pp. 192–225; *Hessen und Thüringen. Von den Anfängen bis zur Reformation* (Exhibition Catalogue, Marburg and Eisenach, 1992), pp. 230–4 and map, p. 232.
82 Kießling, *Die Stadt und ihr Land*, pp. 214–15.

83 John H. Munro, 'Monetary Contraction and Industrial Change in the Late-Medieval Low Countries, 1335-1500', in N. J. Mayhew, ed., *Coinage. The Low Countries 800–1500* (British Archaeological Reports LIV) (Oxford, 1979), pp. 118–19. See also Robert S. DuPlessis, 'One Theory, Two Draperies, Three Provinces, and a Multitude of Fabrics: The New Drapery of French Flanders, Hainault, and the Tournaisis (Late Fifteenth–Late Eighteenth Centuries)', in N. B. Harte, ed., *The New Draperies* (forthcoming).

84 Kirchgässner, 'Verlag', pp. 100–2.

85 D. C. Coleman, 'An Innovation and Its Diffusion. The "New Draperies"', *EcHR* 2nd series, XXII (1969), p. 426.

86 Rudolf Holbach, 'Formen des Verlagswesens im Hanseraum vom 13. bis zum 16. Jahrhundert', *HansGbl* CIII (1985), p. 48; Kirchgässner, 'Verlag', pp. 98–9.

87 Von Stromer, 'Gewerbereviere', pp. 42ff.

88 Held, *Zwischen Marktplatz und Anger*, pp. 170–1.

89 Wright, *Capitalism, the State and the Lutheran Reformation*, p. 125.

90 Rudolf Palme, 'Alpine Salt-Mining in the Middle Ages', *JEEH* XIX (1990), pp. 117–36; Josef Riedmann, 'Mittelalter', in Josef Fontana *et al.*, eds, *Geschichte des Landes Tirol* I (Bolzano/Innsbruck/Vienna, 1985), pp. 510–11.

91 Eberhard Gothein, *Wirtschaftsgeschichte des Schwarzwaldes und der angren-zenden Landschaften* I: *Städte- und Gewerbegeschichte* (Strasbourg, 1892), p. 807.

92 Wright, *Capitalism, the State and the Lutheran Reformation*, pp. 124–5.

93 For technical information on cupellation and liquation I am deeply grateful to Dr J. W. Barnes of the University of Swansea.

94 Von Stromer, 'Gewerbereviere', p. 98. Westermann's statement in *Eislebener Garkupfer*, p. 188, that most of the lead was used up is incorrect.

95 Riedmann, 'Mittelalter', p. 515; Reinhard Hildebrandt, 'Augsburger und Nürnberger Kupferhandel 1500-1619. Produktion, Marktanteile und Finanzierung im Vergleich zweier Städte und ihrer wirtschaftlichen Führungsschicht', in Hermann Kellenbenz, ed., *Schwerpunkte der Kupferproduktion und des Kupferhandels in Europa 1500–1650* (Kölner Kolloquien zur internationalen Sozial- und Wirtschaftsgeschichte III) (Cologne/Vienna, 1977), pp. 194–5.

96 Westermann, *Eislebener Garkupfer*, pp. 25, 42–3.

97 *Ibid.*, pp. 55–6.

98 Franz Mathis, *Die deutsche Wirtschaft im 16. Jahrhundert (Enzyklopädie Deutscher Geschichte*, XI (Munich, 1992), pp. 60–5, 86–97.

99 Franz Kirns, 'Das Eisengewerbe im Süderland von 1500 bis 1650', in Hermann Kellenbenz, ed., *Schwerpunkte der Eisengewinnung und Eisenverarbeitung in Europa 1500–1650* (Kölner Kolloquien zur internationalen Sozial- und Wirtschaftsgeschichte II) (Cologne/Vienna, 1974), p. 180.

100 Fritz Geisthardt, 'Frühes Eisengewerbe an Sieg, Dill und Lahn', in Kellenbenz, *Schwerpunkte der Eisengewinnung*, p. 192.

101 Hermann Aubin, 'Formen und Verbreitung des Verlagswesens in der Altnürnberger Wirtschaft', in Stadtarchiv Nürnberg, ed., *Beiträge zur Wirtschaftsgeschichte Nürnbergs* II (Beiträge zur Geschichte und Kultur der Stadt Nürnberg XI, 2) (Nuremberg, 1967), p. 629.

102 Von Stromer, 'Gewerbereviere', pp. 87, 89.

103 Aubin, 'Formen und Verbreitung', pp. 635, 641.

104 Ammann, *Wirtschaftliche Stellung Nürnbergs*, p. 204.

105 Pitz, 'Probleme der gewerblichen Entwicklung', pp. 34, 37; Holbach, 'Formen des Verlags', pp. 53–4, 61–2.

106 Jan Baszanowski, 'Ochsenzuchtgebiete und Ochsenausfuhr aus Polen vom 16. bis 18. Jahrhundert', in Ekkehard Westermann, ed., *Internationaler*

Ochsenhandel (1350–1750). Akten des 7th International Economic History Congress Edinburgh 1978 (Beiträge zur Wirtschaftsgeschichte IX) (Stuttgart, 1979), p. 128.

107 Ian Blanchard, 'European Cattle Trades 1400–1600', *EcHR* 2nd series, XXXIX (1986), pp. 433, 441. See also Franz Lerner, 'Die Bedeutung des internationalen Ochsenhandels für die Fleischversorgung deutscher Städte im Spätmittelalter und der frühen Neuzeit', in Westermann, *Internationaler Ochsenhandel*, pp. 197–217.

108 Jean Vogt, 'Grandeur et décadence du marché de bétail de Cernay (deuxième moitié du XVIe et début du XVIIe siècle)', *Annuaire de la Société d'Histoire des Régions de Thann-Guebwiller* 1970–72, pp. 131–8.

109 Von Stromer, 'Verflechtungen', pp. 22–3.

110 Bog, 'Wachstumsprobleme der oberdeutschen Wirtschaft', pp. 71, 75.

2

The Population of Late Medieval and Early Modern Germany

CHRISTIAN PFISTER

Sources and components

The generative components of population development – fertility, nuptuality and mortality – are bound together into a system which can be called a generative structure. At one level of analysis, this structure is a component of a wider social system and as such is mutually determined by the other components in the system. The characteristic features of this interplay are subject to historical change, and it is the task of historical demography in the narrower sense to discover the characteristics of the generative structure and its modification in any given society. To do so requires a refined methodology and range of statistical tools. In the broader sense, historical demography as a social historical discipline is required to work out characteristic interconnections between population and other elements of the social system.

Population theory distinguishes between the condition of a population and population movement. The condition of a population is comprehended periodically in the form of censuses or tax enumerations, while population development – births, deaths, and marriages – is recorded continually. In order to determine changes in population numbers and to interpret them demographically, both the condition and the movement of the population have to be seen in relation to each other through a simple equation in which the population growth between any two moments of time is comprised on the one hand of the difference between births and deaths and on the other of the difference between immigration and emigration.

Population movement can be reconstituted, albeit with considerable investment of time and energy, through church registers (books recording baptisms, marriages, and burials) which extend back to the sixteenth century, despite some gaps in information. However, there are great problems in reconstituting the condition of the population for any time before the eighteenth century, the age in which primitive statistics were first systematically gathered. For earlier periods historians are forced to turn to types of sources created in the exercise of dominance over subjects, serfs, or tenants. Here the inhabitants of any place were recorded not primarily because of their residential status, but in their capacity as tax-paying subjects, rent-paying tenants, or serfs subject to feudal exactions. There was a tendency to exaggerate the number of persons recorded as if they were the entire residential population. During the early modern period there was also a variety of lords of different kinds, and it is therefore difficult to find data offering adequent coverage for any larger territory, or else to find material presenting recurrent and easily comparable figures over an extended period of time. However, it is worth discussing here the kinds of sources available for this task.

Lists or rolls recording those supplying oaths of allegiance contain the names of all those who took, or were expected to take, such oaths. This was normally performed as a formal ceremony by the subjects of a territory with each change of ruler as a swearing of binding mutual loyalty. Those liable to render such an oath of allegiance usually encompassed all male inhabitants, including servants. In the ideal case, this included the entire adult male population, as well as female heads of households. The only persons exempt from swearing allegiance were those with a special legal position (nobles, clergy, officials), and sometimes temporary residents (*Beisassen*). In the bishopric of Bamberg, where all taxable heads of households were liable to the oath, these allegiance rolls are extant in an unbroken series from the sixteenth century until well into the eighteenth.[1]

In the case of muster rolls, it is necessary to clarify whether the obligation to military service attached to the person or to the house, whether it could be commuted into a cash payment, and how far it was common to remit it on economic or other grounds. Where liability for military service was attached to the person, muster-rolls can be equated with lists of adult males. In those territories where it was attached to the house, they list the number of houses. In sixteenth-century Thuringia each rural or urban house, with only a few exceptions (buildings in the direct ownership of the nobility, or vicarages), had to present a man for military service, even where a female was head of the household. In central German territories, the muster roles based on households are well suited to provide an insight into the distribution and development of the population, even if they do not record lodgers or temporary residents.[2]

Enumerations for fiscal purposes have to be understood as the outcome of a process in which the enumerator's interest in having an accurate register was counteracted by the interest in non-registration of those liable to the exaction. We can assume that the results are more reliable according to the closeness of the enumerator to the population being recorded. In the case of some taxes, a lump sum was demanded from a territory, and this sum was then subdivided into smaller amounts to be paid by each district or province. These were further subdivided by community, and finally levied according to the wealth of each unit of liability (whether a person or a household). This raises the problem of distinguishing the tax-paying proportion of the population from those not so liable. Another kind of tax was levied as a percentage of the wealth of those liable. However, the form of taxation most useful to the historical demographer is that assessed on the individual household, enabling calculation of the total number of households, as was the case in Electoral Saxony and elsewhere. Where the hearth is used as a recording unit, we have to clarify whether the underlying concept was that of a house, a household, or an actual fireplace. A household has to to be understood as the 'whole house', which encompassed a community of production and consumption under the supervision of a patriarchal head as the bearer of political and economic rights in the community, and therefore as the basic unit of the society.

The serf registers compiled by some lordships listed the names of those regarded as liable to render tribute as serfs of a particular lord. Since free persons and the serfs of other lords were not included, these registers are only in exceptional cases useful for calculating the entire population (for example the 'population census' of 1530 in the bishopric of Speyer).[3] However, they are most useful (alongside church registers) for reconstituting the vital structure, since they frequently record women and children as well.

Lists of communicants or of those able to take communion were useful to all confessions for controlling religious practice and tracing the heterodox and Anabaptists in particular (the Jews were not included, however). Here we have to distinguish between rolls of those allowed to take communion, lists of first communicants or confirmations, and numbers of those taking communion at Easter. However, figures for communicants usually encompass that part of the population who were to be admitted to communion or the lord's supper, allowing for some variation of the age limit, both regionally and by confessional allegiance. Sometimes these rolls served as registers on the basis of which income for pastors was calculated: thus, in the bishopric of Merseburg, each potential communicant had to pay a penny to the pastor four times a year, regardless of whether he or she took communion.[4] These church registers were simultaneously instruments of religious discipline and of state control. Occasionally notes about the departure of members of a parish provide information about emigration. Besides these pastoral enumerations, there were also parish registers, the so-called *status animarum*, usually provided in the form of a list of households. In the Altenburger land (comprising some 513 km²) in 1580, the pastors had to list by name the entire membership of their parishes, household by household and including the servants, almost 30,000 persons. In the Swiss canton of Zurich, compilation of such registers was repeatedly required from 1634 onwards. During the past decade and a half, funerary sermons have been explored as a large-scale source, and around 250,000 such printed sermons have been systematically evaluated for the period 1550–1750. These provide demographical and statistical information for the Lutheran upper and middle classes, with some spillover into the lower classes, as well as illuminating the nature of familial relationships.[5]

From the fifteenth century onwards, provisioning lists were sometimes assembled at time of dearth, recording the amount of grain supplies on hand in individual households and the number of mouths to feed, largely as a countermeasure against hoarding and grain speculation. This was at first done mainly in towns, and from the later seventeenth century in rural areas as well. Because of fear of over-registration, a scrupulous watch was kept on the actual presence of all members of a family, according to which figures were calculated for the quantities of seed corn required for the following year. For example, during the great European-wide crisis of the 1690s, no fewer than four such 'grain surveys' were conducted in the territory of Basel, each time in November.[6] Citizenship registers, that is, lists of those newly granted citizen status (sometimes designated as lists, rolls, or letters) were sometimes compiled in order clearly to identify the circle of persons endowed with this particular legal status. In the case of Danzig, these citizenship registers extend back almost into the fourteenth century without any gaps.[7] However, citizenship registers most usually record the names of urban immigrants who acquired citizenship status, thus securing for themselves the right of independent economic activity, a so-called 'burgher livelihood', and who were then qualified to acquire property in the town.

Theories and key concepts

At the heart of demographic discussion and the development of demographic theory is the relationship between population, economy, and environment. The society of early modern Europe had to live with zero growth in terms of (extensive) agrarian production, and this at a low level of material existence, conditioned by marked annual fluctuations in the weather and long-term climatic changes. If more children were born in the long run than there were persons dying, the consequences were far-reaching. How was it that early modern society was able to adapt dynamic population growth to the capacity of its agriculture? This is the central problem on which the history of all traditional populations turns, and there are two contrasting explanatory models. The 'overpopulation' model, which was widespread among commentators of the sixteenth and seventeenth centuries, assumes that economy and population first develop independently of each other. However, once the population crosses a certain economic and ecological threshold, the 'carrying capacity' of the relevant region, it is then reduced by epidemics and social catastrophe (war, social disturbances). The central directing force in this model is mortality.

During the seventeenth and eighteenth century theologians discerned in both the human and animal worlds the effects of a divine plan which kept the number and resources of every species in balance. The key work, published in 1741 by the Russian army chaplain and statistician Johann Peter Süssmilch, bore the significant title 'The divine order in the changes of the human race arising from the birth, death and reproduction of the same'. In this 'equilibrium' model, which was further developed by Thomas Malthus in 1798, the central directing force was fertility. Since the 1960s, research in historical demography has demonstrated that traditional populations actually did adapt themselves to the conditions of their environment in the same way as animal populations, that is, through 'homeostatic' or 'self-regulating' systems.[8]

This model was derived from observation of the fact that the European population of the early modern period grew only slowly, yet was still able rapidly to make up for losses through epidemics. French studies have established an amazing continuity in the number of hearths and in their spatial distribution over long periods of time.[9] Mattmüller came to the conclusion that for Switzerland, over the period 1500 and 1700, the growth pattern of local and regional population remained tied to an upper limit or 'ceiling', which brought about mortality and emigration as well as affecting fertility and marital frequency.[10] Ehmer has expressed reservations about this model: in his view, it does not follow from the existence of such a limitation to growth 'that there is in any way a conclusive connection between population and the economy'.[11]

The concept of 'carrying capacity' has been much discussed within the framework of population science and population geography. It has often been used in unclear ways, and in historical discussion has mostly been confined to the problem of food supply.[12] In recent years the first elements of an ecological theory of population have been developed, a theory which attempts to lift onto a completely new plane discussion about the causal relationship of population growth and technological development.[13] Here it is necessary for the sake of conceptual clarity to distinguish between two concepts: 'ecological carrying capacity' and 'social carrying capacity'. Ecological carrying capacity is the structurally determined capacity of a given area to provide the nourishment, that is, the available per capita quantity of food, under given technological conditions and assuming equal distribution of resources, required for the basic needs of the population from both a quantitative and qualitative viewpoint and calculated purely mathematically. Social carrying capacity is understood as a situation in which an overwhelming proportion of the population is actually able to cover its food needs even within a system of social inequality. During the early modern period the social carrying capacity was in most cases dependent on harvest fluctuations, that is, it was only attained temporarily under certain favourable conjunctural circumstances, a situation that was to change only during the nineteenth century.

On the basis of this conceptual distinction, subsistence crises cannot be ascribed in any ill-considered way to a transgression of the 'limits of subsistence', since they were always rooted in the unequal distribution of available resources. While estimates of social carrying capacity can be orientated to fluctuations in grain prices, establishing the ecological carrying capacity of a given area requires the comparison of the food demands of the population (whereby one must distinguish by age and gender) with the food supply from agriculture.[14] Here we must note that the ecological carrying capacity of a given area can change both from the side of production and from that of demand: from the demand side, through a growth or contraction of population, and the consequent changes in age structure; from the production side, through reclamation or abandonment of cultivated area, through greater efficiency in buffer mechanisms (maintenance of reserves, possibilities of substitution, imports), or through changes in climate.[15] By contrast with older views (such as that of Abel), it has now been shown that good and bad years do not follow each other randomly, but that they often appear bundled together, so that there were longer runs of favourable and unfavourable periods.[16]

In order to establish a link to the varied generative pattern, we can draw on the concept of the ecotype, originally used in anthropology (Wolf). By this Ehmer and Mitterauer understand 'a regionally dominant economic form, which arose through adapting the safeguarding of existence to the spatial conditions'.[17] Alongside economic and social factors, Gehrmann includes in this concept such elements as culture and moral preconceptions, while Imhof includes the trauma of life-threatening situations.[18] It remains to be seen how far this approach, so far limited to the investigation of segmentally differentiated self-supporting societies, can also be applied to market-oriented societies with a developed division of labour (towns, proto-industrial areas).

Population development

Quite divergent estimates of the population development of Germany can be found in the literature. The inconsistencies arise in the first place because the geographical frame of reference is not stated with the desirable clarity – for example, what the borders of 'Germany' are taken to be. Moreover, the figures cited for the sixteenth century are contradictory in the sense that they take no account of the wave of population expansion so well attested in regional historiography as well as for other European states.[19] A considerable growth potential is indicated above all by certain structural data: in the population lists of the bishopric of Speyer for 1530, the proportion of couples with three or more children was amazingly high: 14 per cent with three children; 12 per cent with four children; and 20 per cent of large families with five and more children.[20] The tax register from the Abbey of Salem for the territory to the north of Lake Constance in 1578 even lists on average 3.1 unmarried children per household.[21] Population growth during the sixteenth century is indisputable; what remains controversial and unclear is exactly when we have to see the population growth as beginning and how strong it was. In upper Germany, population expansion led to conflicts within village communities as early as the end of the fifteenth century. 'Since the farms were not subdivided and there was little arable land to spare, pressure grew upon the existing means of production. The number of day-labourers rose, and they began to struggle for the common land.[22]

A basis for a solution to this problem is offered by the Jena geographer Fritz Koerner, who has produced estimates for the end of the sixteenth century which depend on using muster rolls and comparing them with other source types. Taking a selected area in the Thuringian basin of around 8800 km², he identified a broad-based number of houses and on this basis was able to establish a considerable difference in population density, determined partly by natural geographical features, partly by occupational structure, and ranging from less than two houses per km² to around 20. By using information from other broad regions of Germany, he was able to widen his base to 43,000 km², which lead him to a median density of six houses per km². In order to calculate the population density, he established from his data a number of between 5 and 5.5 persons per dwelling, and so calculated a median population density of 30 inhabitants per km². On this basis, one arrives at an estimated population for Germany within the boundaries of 1914 (540,818 km²) of 16 million, which is rather more than conventional wisdom suggests. The relevant textbooks and reference works refer to Kötzschke, who in his turn relies on Beloch.[23]

Using calculations for German-wide trends in the development of dwellings and settlements between 1520 and 1600 (see Table 2.1), we can produce a regressive analysis for an assumed population in 1500. A back-calculation of this kind, assuming a population of 16.2 million in 1600, leads to an estimate of 10 million in 1520 and 9 million in 1500. Mattmüller has also adjusted older estimates for the Swiss population downwards by a considerable amount, from 820,000 to 560,000. The lower estimate still allows for the kind of dramatic population growth in

Table 2.1 Increase in numbers of dwellings based on data from regions of south, west, north, and east-central Germany

Period	Records	Number of dwellings Beginning	End	Increase p.a. (%)	
1520–30	22	11,288	12,101	7.2	
1530–40	39	17,396	18,695	7.5	(+ 0.3)
1540–50	51	32,328	34,642	7.2	(– 0.3)
1550–60	55	31,140	33,345	7.1	(– 0.1)
1560–70	76	48,672	51,511	5.8	(– 1 3)
1570–80	70	53,902	56,409	4.6	(– 1.2)
1580–90	34	34,495	35,868	4.0	(– 0.6)
1590–1600	37	41,413	43,767	3.2	(– 0.8)

Source: Koerner, 'Bevölkerungsverteilung in Thüringen', pp. 308–9.

the first two-thirds of the sixteenth century remarked in narrative sources and confirmed by more recent research. However, it also indicates that the degree of urbanization (that is, the proportion of the population living in urban settlements of over 5,000 souls) was considerably higher on the eve of the sixteenth century (*c*.16 per cent) than Bairoch had supposed.[24] Thus, the degree of urbanization must have risen between 1400 and 1500, and then declined again during the course of the sixteenth century, a finding that appears plausible as a result of the contracting margin of subsistence and the related collapse in relative terms of prices for manufactured goods. The values for large towns with populations over 10,000 were far steadier, indicating that smaller farm-towns were more severely affected by the crisis of the later sixteenth century.[25] However, Mathis has pointed out that the population figures suggested by scholars for individual towns still display considerable variation, so that the picture sketched here will undoubtedly have to be further modified despite the extensive research conducted so far.[26] However, on the basis of the principles discussed so far, it is possible to provide an overview of general population development between 1500 and 1650.

Around 1500 there were probably 9 million persons living within the boundaries of 'Germany' (using the borders of 1914), with an average population density of 16 inhabitants per km². In the middle of the fourteenth century, epidemics of plague so severely disrupted population development that the peoples of Europe had scarcely recovered a century later. It has been estimated that there were around 170,000 settlements within Germany around 1340, that a quarter of them became deserted in the course of the agrarian depression and population contraction of the later middle ages, and that a substantial proportion were never resettled, even in the modern period.[27] The deserted areas returned to waste, and forest reclaimed many places. Around 1500 the basic lineaments of the late medieval population crisis were still evident, but there were also clear signs of a fundamental recovery.

In the following six decades, the population grew remarkably. Warm spring and summer months encouraged the planting of new vineyards and the expansion of cattle herds. The latter enabled an expansion of grain-growing through increased quantities of animal manure and thus the reclamation of abandoned landholdings. Articles of the rebellious peasants of 1525 attest that arable land was already becoming scarce as a result of population growth. In 1529 Sebastian Franck complained in his *German Chronicle* that Swabia and Bavaria were populated enough for the whole world (*aller Welt volck genuog*), and were still so continually full of people that towns and villages were flooded with them.[28] In the wake of the second wave of population growth (following that of the thirteenth century), the number of settlements grew annually between 1520 and 1560 by more than 0.7 per cent. In the bishopric of Salzburg, the population grew between 1531 and 1541 by an average of 1.2 per cent annually, of which the preceding excess of births fell in the years before the Peasants' War. In Hesse the population doubled within 100 years. An annual growth rate of 1.4 per cent has been attested for the cantons of Zurich and Berne, as well as for parts of Thuringia, a figure next reached in the nineteenth century, and there are even figures of over 3 per cent per annum attested for the principality of Hohenlohe in the years 1528–1562.[29] The 'European marriage pattern' was not yet fully developed, and in many places servants and apprentices could still marry without restriction. Detailed studies have revealed that there was a low proportion of single persons in the population, an early age of marriage, and a strong growth in the birth rate, accompanied by relatively rare mortality crises. Conjunctural upswing in the alpine mining industry, land reclamation along the Baltic sea-coast in Lower Saxony, and use of marginal lands for viticulture were all borne by the dynamic growth of the first two-thirds of the sixteenth century. The *Chronicle of the Counts of Zimmern*, written in the vicinity of Lake Constance around 1550, depicted this process as follows: 'In our time the population in Swabia, as in all other lands, has so markedly increased and multiplied that the lands have been more cultivated than at any other time in human memory, so that there is no corner, even in the most remote forest and in the highest mountains, that remains uncleared and unpopulated.'[30]

By 1560, however, the land available for new settlement had run out. The wave of population growth led to the strong growth of a class of small farmers, to manifestations of pauperism, and to ecological exhaustion, especially in the marginal lands of the Mittelgebirge. At the same time, climatic conditions deteriorated in ways extremely unfavourable to human existence. Temperatures fell in all seasons of the year, rainfall became concentrated in the high summer, and glaciers advanced down the alpine valleys. In many parts of central Europe, viticulture declined continually, right through to the turn of the sixteenth century, as a result of cold, wet summer weather. The trend towards a cold, moist climate characterized by frequent climatic anomalies and storms continued until 1630. A rise in epidemics, especially of plague, was superimposed on this deterioration of climate, peaking in the 1630s. The negative demographic effects can only be attested by certain indicators: in the principality of Hohenlohe the number of heads of households stagnated after 1562 and then rose only slowly again until the eve of the Thirty Years' War, interrupted by a fresh reversal caused by plague in the years 1596–7.[31]

The effects of such climatic deterioration on agriculture have been investigated for the area of the south-western Vogelsberg (north-east from Frankfurt) on the basis of sixteen qualitative and quantitative indicators drawn from the district accounts and stewards' accounts of the territorial ruler.[32] During the first half of the sixteenth century, grain yields were relatively high, especially for rye, corresponding to the favourable climatic conditions. Moreover, years with poorer yields could be compensated for by the better harvests of the immediately preceding or successive years. However, in the wake of climatic deterioration, the growing period became shorter. Between 1584 and 1622 the sources frequently mention snow, excessive cold, late frosts, and unseasonably heavy rainfalls. The average annual yield for rye declined remarkably, especially as the result of frost damage, there was a massive increase in mould damage to stored grain because the grain had to remain longer on the stalk and be brought in wet (which also reduced the baking quality), and the fields could often not be tilled in autumn because of the constant rainfall. In consequence of the cumulative frequency of bad rye harvests, a growing proportion of the population lived on grain that they borrowed in part from their territorial lord, so that they increasingly fell into debt and poverty. Even territorial lords found it impossible to pay their officials the quantities of rye stipulated as part of their salaries, so that they had to be content with oats, barley, or buckwheat. We can assume that there was a serious decline of dietary protein in particular, so increasing the population's susceptibility to epidemic.

The process of growth was geographically very uneven. Characteristic of the situation that had been reached in the late sixteenth century is the contrast between areas in the south-west with a relatively high density of dwellings or settlement (over 10 houses per km² in the western Black Forest, over 8 houses per km² in Württemberg) and the thinly settled regions in the north-east (2 houses per km² in Mecklemberg, 1 house per km² in Hinterpommern).[33] A population of 16 million has been calculated for 'Germany' (within the borders of 1914) in 1600. At that time, only France was more populated within Europe, with 18.5 million. Around 1634 – shortly before the battle of Nördlingen – the duchy of Württemberg had at least 50 inhabitants per km² and so belonged to the most densely settled tracts of Germany, its fertile lowlands in this respect scarcely inferior to the European zones of population concentration in the Low Countries and north Italy. Efforts to extend economic possibilities by building up an export industry in textiles and especially through expansion of viticulture could still not keep pace with population growth, so that we must assume that there was a decline of real per capita income. 'Faced with relative over-population, broad layers of the population led an existence marked by permanent underemployment and undernourishment as well as by acute need and massive mortality at time of harvest crisis.'[34]

Around 1500, 16 per cent of the German population lived in places with more than 5,000 inhabitants, 4 per cent in 'large cities' with over 10,000 inhabitants. Around 1600 the share of the urban population had declined to around 12 per cent, while the towns with more than 10,000 had been able to hold onto their share of the total population. Among the large cities – Cologne, Nuremberg, Augsburg – only Hamburg was able to record substantial population growth (from 15,000 to 40,000), because it was able to supply itself with cheap grain from the Baltic. The haemorrhage of the Thirty Years' War then reversed German population development by around a century and a half. If we assume that the population at the beginning of hostilities was around 17 million and that wartime losses ran as high as 40 per cent, then the population level around 1650 had probably fallen back to that of 1520.

Germany and the European marriage pattern

In the 'society of estates' of the early modern period, contracting marriage was a 'privilege' and as such bound by ecclesiastical, familial, and governmental regulations. The church had developed a comprehensive catalogue of incest prohibitions and prescribed a minimum age for marriage. Betrothal, meaning the granting of consent to the marriage by the bride (which usually signified commencement of sexual relations), counted as a valid conclusion of matrimony. It was only with the stipulation and implementation of a regulated, and legally binding, procedure, as well as the written registration of the marriage following the Council of Trent (1563), that premarital and marital sexual activity were separated.

The time for contracting marriage was subject to economic compulsion and custom as well as ecclesiastical prescriptions. It was characteristic of rural society that the ecclesiastically determined low point for church weddings fell during Lent, and less markedly during Advent, while the economically determined low point fell during the harvest, in August–September. In this sense, the seasonal rhythm in Catholic territories, understood as a strict observance of ecclesiastical prohibitions, was agro-liturgical, while that in Protestant territories, which took stronger account of agricultural work, was more purely agrarian. The day of the week on which a marriage took place was also regulated by custom within this 'rhythmic year'.

John Hajnal in 1965 coined one of the most successful concepts of the infant historical demography in the term 'the European marriage pattern'. He indicated that there had been since Carolingian times a specific pattern of late marriage found west of a line running from St Petersburg to Trieste, of which a constituent element was that marriage was tied to the founding of a separate household. At marriage, the new couple had to leave their parents and set up their own household. The establishment of a new socio-economic unit withdrew labour power and wealth from the parental families concerned, and usually presupposed the utilization of collective resources. Secular authorities thus demanded that the children of both sexes, regardless of their age, have the consent of the head of the parental household. Thus, the parents not only gained the right to veto the desired marriage partner but could also in effect veto marriage by their offspring completely. Further, the regulatory form of government of the early modern period subjected the contraction of marriage to arbitrary views of *raison d'état*. Thus officials, soldiers, students, widows, apprentices, and domestic servants, as well as any persons without a fixed place of abode, had to obtain permission from the secular authority to marry. One can therefore speak of marriage being made a concession by the state, in which freedom to marry remained the exception. In Bavaria the controlling authorities – the church, the family patriarch, the seigneur, the municipality, and the secular authorities – by no means pursued unified interests. The church insisted on the legitimization of the consequences of 'sinful' premarital sexual concourse by means of marriage, the secular authorities vacillated between limiting and promoting marriage, seigneurs seemed inclined to promote marriage, while many family patriarchs were interested in retaining an adequate supply of unmarried servants.

It is rare to have good data for marriages in the period before 1700, but evidence from the bishopric of Speyer indicates that very few persons there were excluded from marriage in the early sixteenth century. Around 1530 no fewer that 90 per cent of the adults in this territory were married, although we must assume that the numbers of 'children' also included unmarried adults up to the age of 30 years who were still resident in their parents' households.[35] In the Genevan upper classes, the proportion of single women over 50 years old rose between the middle of the sixteenth century and the end of the eighteenth century from 1.7 per cent to over 30 per cent, with a fourfold increase during the seventeenth century.[36]

Quasi-sovereign communities with a democratic constitution also exercised social and demographic controls. In the alpine commune of Törbel in the Vallais, which designated itself as a peasant guild, the founding of an independent household was linked not only to possession of an adequate amount of farmland and grazing but also access to communal property, the right to use communal wood and water, and the right to graze cattle on the alps. These rights were granted by the existing holders of communal usufruct only to young heads of household from their own ranks, and not to any outsider who had married a woman from the village.[37]

Such economic restrictions *de facto* excluded a considerable proportion of the population from marriage, who then had to live with their fate as best they could. However, we know virtually nothing before the late eighteenth century about that part of the population who remained permanently unmarried. Older unmarried males, and more rarely unmarried women, entered the marriage market alongside the widowed as a 'demographic reserve army', largely after epidemics of plague. The celibacy ratio, the percentage of never-married males and females under 50 years of age, varied according to different regional characteristics of the marriage system – inheritance laws, the manner and point at which farms were transferred, the age of the farm occupant.

Inheritance patterns were highly significant for access to the marriage market, since they regulated the transfer of property from one generation to the next. We must here bear in mind that it was only the majority of peasants in the territories of tenant farming west of the Elbe who enjoyed inheritance rights. The peasants on east Elbian domains had no inheritance rights, and could at best make their wishes known. Within the Germanophone areas, inheritance was regulated by the relevant territorial law, which allowed the testators certain freedom, according to local legal tradition, to dispose of their property (as in Bavaria), or else bound them more tightly to legal regulations. In Upper Bavaria the choice of marriage partner was dictated by a rule determined by seigneurial and economic constraints, which stipulated that only those persons could marry who could inherit real property and provide a suitable dowry.[38] The criterion for choosing a partner was therefore not so much a social consideration, such as belonging to a specific social class, but rather an exactly quantifiable amount of money. This strict regulation of marriage did not function as an automatic mechanism, but had to be continually reimposed in a ceaseless struggle by the secular authorities. Inheritance influenced the point at which a farm was transferred, and parents put the day off as long as possible in order to avoid the unpleasant decision. In consequence, males from the peasant classes found themselves first marrying around 30 years of age.

Besides excluding part of the population from marriage, the age of first marriage was also of importance for the West European marriage pattern. By comparison with other cultures, women married relatively late, around their mid-20s, which shortened the fertile years and so reduced the number of possible children. This pattern of late marriage was determined by the scarcity of landholdings transferred from one generation to the next. Sons and daughters from a propertied household had to wait patiently for the point at which the property, or at least the running of the farm, was transferred, while the lower classes had to save the means necessary to found a household by long-term employment as servants. The daughters of large farmers thus tended to marry younger (and so to bear more children) than those from the middling or poorer sort of farmers. Outside the area subject to the West European marriage pattern, young couples lived in the household of the groom's parents for some time, under the tutelage of the family patriarch. The size of middling households fluctuated between eight and ten persons, whereby households with several couples from time to time broke up into smaller units.

Being a domestic servant was usually a transitional life-stage. Many domestic servants met their future partners while employed away from their homeland. Even large farmers and rich artisans were content to let their children eat the bread of strangers, even if they had to be replaced by outside workers for a while. The availability of servants ensured that an equilibrium was maintained between supply of, and demand for, labour power in all branches of the economy, and was therefore an essential pre-supposition for the functioning of the economic system. In great agricul-tural enterprises the young and sturdy poor were required as workers, while the lower classes sought to be rid of superfluous mouths as quickly as possible. The households of West Europe thus limited themselves to a nuclear family, a married couple and their children as well as a number of servants, according to their material circumstances.

Thanks to the mechanism of the 'free landholding', the median age of marriage ran parallel to the scope of demographic growth, as is attested by data from funerary sermons for the pre-1750 period. Around the middle of the sixteenth century it was 22.5 years for first-married women from Protestant elites and the middling sort, in periods of epidemic it fell to 21. At the end of the sixteenth century it even fell briefly to a low point of 19.5 – probably influenced by contemporary warfare – and then it rose in the early eighteenth century to 24–6. In the Schwalm area of Hesse, in Eigeltingen (Baden), in Upper Bavaria, in the territory of Salzburg, and in the central regions of Switzerland, the rise began in the late seventeenth century following the end of the epidemics.[39] The considerable frequency of second marriages is a further characteristic of this West European marriage pattern. Widowhood within the age range of childbearing amounted to lost fertility, which could be made up by remarriage. When there was substantial adult mortality, remarriage of the widowed served as a 'first line of defence' to ensure the institutional and economic continuity of the household.[40] Widowers had considerably better chances of a second marriage than widows. Naturally, where they had under-age children to be cared for, many widowers contracted a second marriage within a few months of the demise of their wives, while the period of waiting was longer for widows because of the possibility that they might be pregnant by their deceased spouse.

Both balancing resources with demographic development and the social controls required to do so presupposes that contracting a marriage had to remain the sole legitimate way of reproduction. The long period between attainment of sexual maturity and marriage brought a danger of illegitimate births, which explains some of the rigour of European sexual norms. In order to repress premarital and extramarital sexuality in all its forms, early modern secular authorities constructed a battery of sanctions underpinned by ecclesiastical sexual morality. In many territories, premarital sexual relations were regarded as a criminal offence. In the Bavarian territorial statutes of 1553, this offence was mentioned under the rubric 'On legitimate persons, also on secret marriages and on frivolous co-habitation'. The concept of 'frivolousness' (*Leichtfertigkeit*) signifies that the pair were running the risk of pregnancy without having fulfilled the material preconditions for founding a family. Such mandates and the attitude of the church found themselves in conflict with an older village sexual morality which tolerated sexual relations within the context of a betrothal – sometimes one only informally agreed – as the basis for a full marriage. Conflicts surfaced in official records where there was a failed courtship or postponed marriage, especially in situations where a 'promise' of marriage was rather differently understood by the man and woman involved. Denunciation depended, however, on the will of the village community, and this could be manipulated flexibly, in the sense of being used as a social check against the unpopular or the disagreeable.

Illegitimate births can be traced through family reconstitution, since an interval of less than eight months between marriage and baptism serves to indicate a prenuptial conception. Family reconstitutions which extend back as far the eve of the seventeeth century reveal, in conformity with studies from other parts of Europe, a U-curve for the percentage of illegitimate to legitimate births. At the end of the sixteenth century the rate was high, in part higher than that of the early nineteenth century. It then sank to a low point in the late seventeenth and early eighteenth centuries, and began to rise again in the second half of the latter. The chances of a subsequent legitimation of such extramarital births worsened from the later seventeenth century onwards. In consequence of population growth, there were fewer holdings available, while the restrictive marriage policies which had been built into the programme of governmental social welfare were perfected with the extension of the absolutist state, so that every loophole allowing the poor to contract marriage was gradually closed.

The parents of illegitimate children were to be found predominantly in those social classes beneath the level of the peasantry. Above all, they were persons outside a household, predominantly mobile groups such as domestic servants and soldiers, who were unwilling to abstain from sexual relations for a great part of their adult lives but who could not be brought to account as easily as the sedentary population. Under these circumstances, billeting and the constant passage of troops were easily recalled nine months later by a leap in the numbers of illegitimate births. Women especially from poorer families formed sexual liaisons with soldiers, possibly in the form of prostitution, and often paid for these with pregnancies bringing social disgrace.

Various authors, invoking Norbert Elias's theory of the 'civilizing process', have ascribed the decline in illegitimacy during the sixteenth and seventeenth centuries to a 'revolution in morals' achieved by internalization of behavioural norms laid down by church and state.[41] Ussel argues that a progressive bourgeoisification of life during the fifteenth and sixteenth centuries led to a successive repression of sexuality, and Pallaver claims that this was perfected by governmental repression. Ingram adds to this picture the role of village authorities implementing the programme of ecclesiastical and state officials who had discovered a common interest in the repression of the lower classes.[42] However, on the basis of his own findings, Becker argues that village elites implemented the authorities' programme flexibly, and were able during the crisis period of the later sixteenth and early seventeenth centuries firmly to impose a 'social check'. On the other hand, Imhof believes that 'many young persons when faced with massive threats of punishment and risks of scandal learned the consequences of extramarital sexual offences and simply developed the arts of contraception and abortion into virtuoso skills'.[43]

Fertility

Three approaches have been used hitherto in interpreting fertility. The first is a canonical approach, arguing for the applicability of ecclesiastical prescriptions.[44] The Catholic church prohibited sexual relations for forty days before Christmas and for forty days before Easter, and if this had been strictly observed there should have been no children born in September and December. However, such rigid adherence to norms cannot be observed even in the strict Catholic diocese of Mainz.[45] A second, inherently demographic approach assumes that the seasonality of baptisms reflects that of marriages with a nine-month time-lag.[46] However according to Knodel's research, it was not only the first but also subsequent births which followed this seasonal pattern, albeit with weaker correlation.[47] A third approach is based on the assertion that the seasonal distribution of births, even in Catholic towns such as Mainz and Trier, was adapted to peasant work rhythms, whereby no children were conceived during the peak periods of work, during the harvest or, in areas of viticulture, during grape-picking.[48] Just how far this apparent alternation of active and passive times of love can be interpreted as a calculated and rationalized postponement of births until the quieter times of the year, or whether it was determined by the physiology of work and the weariness of the harvest period, depends on the ideological preferences of the researcher.[49] However, Schluchter's findings are worthy of note, showing that in parishes with cottage industry, which had a work rhythm spreading labour evenly throughout the year, births were also distributed quite regularly across the calendar months.[50]

As far as differences in fertility between different social strata are concerned, the little material available so far seems to indicate greater fertility among the upper classes, although the results are not entirely unambiguous. In Leezen in Schleswig-Holstein the wives of the peasant elites gave birth to one child more than those of other classes, a consequence of a lower age at first marriage and of higher marital fertility.[51] In the small town of Stockach in the Hegau, women from the lowest taxation band gave birth to 0.6 fewer children that those of the higher tax bands, a result of their later marriage.[52] On the other hand, no class-specific differences in marital fertility could be discerned in Stollhamm in Oldenburg or in Langnau in canton Berne.[53]

Discussion about the use of birth control has been conducted at two levels. There has been controversy about how far the long-running discussion of contraception in Western literature, especially by the clergy, is an indicator of its widespread use. There has been heated discussion of the thesis advanced by Heinsohn, Knieper, and Steiger, namely that the witch persecutions of the early modern period represented a targeted campaign, encapsulated in the *Hammer of Witches* (1487) and Innocent VIII's bull of 1484, primarily directed against midwives' knowledge of the arts of contraception and abortion and in favour of encouraging human reproduction. Modern studies of the witch-craze have rejected this view as monocausal, ahistorical, regionally undifferentiated, and based on false inferences from the sources. However, the grain of truth in the theory still needs to be explored on the basis of the proceedings of consistorial courts, where the contraceptive knowledge of the lower classes was a continual theme. Becker is convinced, on the basis of such material from his field of research in lower Styria, that coitus interruptus was a component of village discourse about sexuality and was transmitted to village youth. On the other hand, Breit has found no such evidence in his Upper Bavarian material.[54]

Analysis of fertility for a pre-statistical age demands refined calculations tied to family reconstitution. The more closely births can be related to the female population of childbearing age (between 15 and 45 years of age), the more reliable the figures for fertility will be. However, church registers recorded only baptisms, which can only very approximately be related to the number of births. Boundaries are drawn nowadays on medical criteria in the grey area of perinatality which cannot be replicated on the basis of the data in church registers. In Catholic territories, for example, it was not uncommon until well into the nineteenth century for stillbirths not to be recorded as such, either from negligence or out of fear for the salvation of those who had died unbaptized. Often an emergency baptism was carried out, regardless of whether the child had been born alive or whether it had been taken to a pilgrimage shrine, to be temporarily 'revived' in answer to its parents' prayers.[55]

Conceptions and births were more regularly distributed throughout the calendar months than deaths and marriages. In general, the year can be divided into three phases. Conceptions were concentrated in the months April to July, decreased markedly between August and November, and moved between December and March along a generally upwards curve until close to the median value. Thus most children were born during the quiet months of the late winter, fewest during the peak months of agricultural work in the summer. This structural distribution of birth frequency remained constant across the centuries, and made sense in terms of the survival chances of newborn infants. A new mother in a peasant society could devote more of her time to the newborn, could nurse them better, and expend more care on them during the late winter and early spring than in the hectic harvest period of the high summer and early autumn, where the labour power of women was indispensable in agricultural work.

The model of a traditional population was long predicated on the assumption that, in the absence of conscious attempts at birth control, fertility maintained a relatively uniform level and was regulated 'naturally' by nuptiality. Recent research has shown that fertility was more variable, so that any dichotomy between controlled and 'natural' fertility is no longer tenable. According to modern notions, 'natural fertility' also includes forms of behaviour designed to slow the number of births, such as prolonged breastfeeding, postnatal sexual abstinence, and temporary separation of marriage partners through migration, all of which kept the level of fertility considerably below the physiologically possible maximum.

As long as crudely effective epidemics were a relatively frequent occurrence, as was the case during the sixteenth and seventeenth centuries, the only choice was to make up population losses as quickly as possible, whether by replacing the frequent loss of newborn infants through what often looks like continuous procreation of new children, or whether through rapid remarriage following the death of a mother in childbirth. If it is true that under such circumstances a third of all conceptions ended prematurely in spontaneous abortion, that one child in three died perinatally, that 10–20 per cent of married partners were separated by early death, and that 10 per cent remained childless, then the time between marriage and menopause must have been used to the reproductive limit in order to prevent contraction of the population.

When mortality of adults and youths began to retreat after the end of the epidemics of plague, the age of marriage began to rise. Contraceptive behaviour is traceable in the urban Protestant milieu from the middle of the seventeenth century and in the rural population in the eighteenth. By contrast with Catholic teaching, Protestantism emphasized the personal responsibility of parents for their children and regarded marital sexuality more positively. The most usual method of contraception in the *ancien régime* was coitus interruptus. In order to be sure of family reproduction, contraception was first used after the initial births in the marriage, when it was certain that some children had survived the critical phase of the greatest infant mortality This strategy was reflected statistically in higher fertility at the beginning of marriage, which then declined after the first births. The birth intervals gradually grew longer, and the average age of women at the last birth declined. The practice of birth control was probably tried out first in premarital and extramarital activity, where it was necessary to avoid pregnancy.

The social and economic context of the onset of birth control has been explored for Zurich. A boom in cottage industry in the early seventeenth century multiplied the numbers of well-to-do aspirants to the limited number of places in the government, which for the elites was linked to the rising costs of placing an increasing number of male heirs, in turn a consequence of the retreat of epidemics. In order to avert status-threatening downward mobility, many couples were inclined to limit the numbers of male offspring and to concentrate their limited resources on fewer sons.[56] In the confessionally mixed small town of Oppenheim in the Rhine Palatinate, contraceptive behaviour, in the sense of limiting births to a targeted number of children, is also attested from the second half of the seventeenth century in Lutheran craftsmen families.[57]

Mortality

Sickness and death in the early modern period were largely a matter of natural causes. Most persons died in infancy or the early years of childhood, a result of diarrhoea in summer or in epidemics of plague or smallpox, while adults died from illness caused by chills and influenza in the winter and spring months. Perinatal mortality displayed clear regional differences, which were somewhat less evident in the age group of 1–2-year-olds. In the case of 3–4-year-old children, the differences between regions increasingly converge. In those parts of Germany where breastfeeding was not customary, every third infant died. In east Switzerland, where supplementary nutrition was provided through flour-based gruel and unsweetened fruit juice, it rose above 40 per cent.[58] Infant and child mortality was higher in the middling and lower classes than among the elites. The causes of this 'social inequality in death' (Perrenoud) have been discerned in poor diet and hygiene as well as in cramped living quarters. Mortality crises were an essential element of the traditional demographic system, and shaped the dynamics of population development through their frequency and intensity. It is necessary to distinguish between two basic patterns, subsistence crises and epidemic crises.

In a predominantly self-sufficient agrarian society, food shortages can be perceived through price increases and, insofar as war and natural catastrophe are excluded, can be ascribed to climatic conditions. Here we cannot assume any mechanical causation linking dearth and mortality.[59] Rigorous evidence of the effects of climatic change is first dependent on detailed reconstruction of weather conditions. The next step involves clarifying the susceptibility to weather conditions of the most important crops and of animal husbandry, within the given local agricultural conditions and legal stipulations. We then have to take account of the reality of buffer mechanisms which reduce risk or deal with crisis (such matters as substituting other foodstuffs or importing them, and what reserve foodstocks were maintained by civil authorities). Finally, the extent of social inequality comes into the overall equation.[60] Exemplary calculations reveal an alternation of periods of favourable and unfavourable climatic conditions throughout the early modern period: 1525–65, 1630–78, and 1721–66 were favourable phases; 1566–1629, 1679–1720, and 1721–66 were unfavourable.[61] These correspond in part to fluctuations in demographic development. However, in order to support this argument on a broader basis, it will be necessary to institute a systematic analysis of the rich material on weather variations available for pre-modern Germany.

Epidemic crises were caused by infectious diseases such as plague or smallpox. War often allowed both kinds of crisis to merge into one, in that it depleted the land of foodstuffs, occasioned troop movements and flight, and created a favourable hygienic and physiological soil for mass infection by concentrating troops in camps and starving masses behind city walls. This synergic effect was seen to devastating extent during the Thirty Years' War. In 1625 many peasants fled with their belongings before Tilly's troops into the fortified town of Göttingen, where the concentration of persons and animals within the confined space of the city walls, the rapid emergence of famine, and increasing confusion in the face of the siege which began in June all led to an outbreak of dysentery and plague.[62] Plague mortality varied between 10 and 30 per cent. However, the West European marriage pattern ensured that losses of this order of magnitude were made up fairly quickly, in under ten years even in smaller towns and villages. After the plague had passed on, an above-average number of marriages was concluded. These were partly a matter of second marriages, but they were partly unions delayed by the plague or brought forward by its effects. The age of marriage dropped, since the plague opened up a large number of employment possibilities which were soon filled from the reserve army of the unmarried. Premarital conceptions rose – possibly in consequence of a temporary relaxation of morality – while the birth intervals in existing marriages possibly shortened (Perrenoud). Alongside the maximal increase in fertility, any remaining losses were compensated for by in-migration from the surrounding countryside.

The character and extent of such epidemics can be seen through the example of that which raged in the years 1596–8. The outbreak began north of the Main in the years of relatively mild winters, 1596–8, and was then overlaid by a pandemic of dysentery in the hot dry summer of 1599. In Oppenheim the epidemic carried off above all older and weaker persons, and in this period all marriages were postponed. In Uelzen in Lower Saxony, very few children were begotten in the duration of the plague: plague tracts warned aganst 'deadly consorting with women'. However during the phase of recovery the birth rate rose to its highest value, of 65 per 1,000, in which the reproductive capacity, determined by the numerous youthful marriages and the desire to replace children lost to plague, almost reached its biological upper limit. Because women of childbearing age who had been spared by the plague also conceived in overwhelming numbers, there was a consequent steep rise in the birth rate, which spilled over after one or two years into the next wave of births. Together with the massive deaths among young adults, these waves must have introduced a massive skewing in the age structure of the population through an abrupt transition from a contracting to an over-large cohort, as can be seen in the example of Oppenheim. In Uelzen, population losses of over 40 per cent caused by plague and dysentery in the years 1597–9 (in Hildesheim, it was around 30 per cent) were replaced over the following six to eight years to two-thirds by births and to a third by new citizens arriving as single persons. As unmarried persons, they had incomparably good chances of taking over a business by marrying into it.[63]

In order to protect their subjects, secular authorities turned to measures for prevention, control, isolation, and hygiene. Until well into the seventeenth century these were mostly improvised and worked unsystematically; they were introduced hesitantly and were rarely coordinated with neighbouring authorities. They were also often easily evaded by allowing exceptions on economic grounds. Faced with an inability to counteract the plague once it had broken out, the provisions of secular authorities were joined by ecclesiastical measures – the ringing of bells, penitential processions – while marginal groups were often persecuted or expelled when plague broke out. The fear of a decay of morals and of contempt for social and religious norms came to the fore rather more often than concern about demographic decline. In the seventeenth century, secular authorities refined their instruments for implementing such measures by appointing sanitary inspectors and other instruments of control.

In recent years, scholarly research has directed more attention both to the spectrum of measures employed by civil authorities and to the social reactions to epidemics. Here one has sought to demonstrate that the civil statutes dealing with the plague which began to flow in great quantities from the second half of the sixteenth century were effectively implemented.[64] A more decisive framing of quarantine and control measures has emerged as a demographically significant determinant, at least in the urban sector, as well as an increasing sensitization of civil authorities to environmental hygiene.[65] The latter was reflected in efforts to improve water supply and sewage. As far as the effectiveness of these measures is concerned, there are two opposing views in recent research. Bulst represents the 'French school' in seeing the waning of epidemics as dependent on the retreat of their (medical) causal factor, and so holds that it is ultimately 'inexplicable'. On the other hand Mattmüller and Rödel ascribe a decisive role to the effectiveness of administrative measures (information, better infrastructure, quarantine, border controls), which absolutist states were increasingly able to implement in ever more efficient ways in the late seventeenth century and by means of mutual agreement. Here a continuity can be traced between the measures taken against the plague before 1750 and the prophylactic measures against epidemics in the later eighteenth and nineteenth centuries, in the sense that successful strategic measures taken to contain the plague were refurbished and redirected against other epidemics such as dysentery and smallpox.[66]

Finally, let us comment on life expectancy. By using the necrologies for princely houses, information can be obtained about long-term trends. From the turn of the thirteenth century through to the time of the Thirty Years' War, the median life expectancy declined steadily. In the sixteenth century many men were able to assume prominent positions even at 21 or 22 years of age. On the other hand, Calvin thought himself at 50 to be old and worn out, and Charles V abdicated at 55 as an exhausted greybeard. A woman of 40 was unfailingly regarded as a matron. Those over 60 represented a dwindling minority in towns and villages. One finds in funerary sermons relatively reliable information about the mortality of children and adults. Between 1550 and 1600, boys of 15 could expect on average to attain their 57th year, while girls of the same age had a life expectancy of only 38 because of higher mortality in childbirth and the physical demands of motherhood. In the first half of the seventeenth century, with its frequent epidemics of plague, the life expectancy of men decreased by a good nine years to reach a low point, while that of women, rather surprisingly, rose.[67]

The differences between town and country are striking. If a 15-year-old peasant lad in the Schwalm region of Hesse between 1600 and 1649 could expect to reach the age of 62, by contrast, members of the urban elites who appeared in funerary sermons only reached 48 years. The differences are even greater in the case of women. Schwalm women met their deaths on average at 60, but women from the elites of the nearby princely residence of Marburg departed this life on average at the age of 40.[68] Burghers were longer-lived than nobles, while the clergy were the longest-lived, probably because of their above-average standards of nutrition, relatively healthy living conditions, assured salaried incomes, and a profession involving a minimum of physical labour. Married men and women (despite the dangers of childbirth and physical exhaustion) lived considerably longer than single persons, as is also the case today. The most venerable age was attained by the widowed of both sexes, although the reasons remain wholly unclear.

The rise in life expectancy of youths and adults after 1650 went along with a reduction of gender-specific differences. Whether these differences can be extrapolated to the population at large is unknown. Apart from social inequalities, there are probably confessionally influenced differences to be considered as well. In the confessionally mixed small town of Oppenheim, Catholics died considerably earlier than Protestants of comparable social and ecological circumstances.[69]

Migration

In demographic terms, migration has effects complementary and subsidiary to the marriage pattern. However, the sources for a territorially fragmented Germany offer few useful criteria for the distinctions customarily made between emigration, immigration, and internal migration. In the case of internal migration, movement from the countryside to the towns can be traced far back into the middle ages. Maps of in-migration to towns normally reveal a picture of dense in-migration from the core area closest to the town, corresponding to its immediate marketing area with the densest network of exchange relationships, while the town's pulling power decreased with distance. However, the catchment area defined by in-migration cannot be sketched out by a line of regular circumference. Rather, there were peaks extending out in the direction of the main transport routes, between which lay areas of less dense in-migration. The distance model seems not to have applied in the case of confessional boundaries, as can be shown by the example of Koblenz. Its spatial distribution of in-migration manifests no pattern of concentric circles. The Lutheran and Calvinist territories in the neighbouring Hunsrück supplied no immigrant artisans to Catholic Koblenz, and hardly any migrated from the village of Winningen, only 7 km distant, by contrast with migration from Catholic territories much further away. Similarly, the exchange of population between the bishopric of Cologne and two neighbouring Protestant territories on the right bank of the Rhine, which split the bishopric like a wedge, was insignificant.[70]

Besides migration from countryside to town, we also have to consider inter-urban migration, from small, naturally growing towns into large towns, migration which could occur over great distances. The oversimplified rule of thumb here was that the more qualified the profession and the higher its status, the more distant and urban the place of origin was likely to be. Thus, new citizens in Nördlingen in the seventeenth century were as rich as, or richer than, existing citizens. The crafts, insofar as they required supplementary labour from outside a town, were filled up from other towns, sometimes over great distances, while the rural inflow consisted largely of the unskilled and the simpler trades from the immediate vicinity.[71] Thus, over half of the new citizens recorded by the Danzig citizenship registers originated in the coastal towns connected to Danzig by trade, or in their hinterlands. In the sixteenth and early seventeenth centuries, migrants came partly from the Netherlands, and in the eighteenth century almost exclusively from the German-colonized areas in the Baltic.[72]

The strength of immigration was determined primarily by the possibilities of finding a livelihood. Very sharp peaks in the graph of new citizens were frequently linked to outbreaks of plague. For example, in Nördlingen during a severe outbreak of plague in 1521 only half as many new citizens were accepted as the longstanding average. In the following year, however, enrolments rose to twice the average and then declined in gradual stages. The high numbers of those marrying into citizen families indicates perhaps that artisans who had been spared by the plague moved up into the positions vacated by deceased craftsmen, and the places then freed for journeymen were filled by immigrants. In a situation of plague, when a number of livelihoods were often vacated within days, the demands normally imposed on those wishing to enter a trade were temporarily relaxed, and sometimes inducements were offered to entice new members. If the livelihoods became scarce, the stream of new citizens would be throttled back by placing higher demands on applicants or by upholding existing regulations.

Only a modest proportion of the less privileged classes who constituted the larger part of immigrants came equipped with sufficient money, knowledge, or connections to rise into the ranks of merchants or craftsmen. It was not upward social mobility but an adequate livelihood that was probably the main aim of the immigrants. Half to two-thirds of them attained a position commensurate with their origins. The rest had to endure downward social mobility.

For some time now, a growing number of regional studies have led to the conclusion that the rural population, and above all those classes with fewer ties to the soil, changed their place of abode very frequently in the search for work and lodgings, of whom domestic servants were probably most inclined to migratory behaviour, adapting their migratory paths to the realities of the labour market. Migration was a matter of life-stage for servants, and this rarely transcended a space defined by the immediate vicinity of a town.

Between the waves of east Elbian colonization in the high middle ages and the streams of refugees of our own age came the migratory push precipitated by the imposition of religious uniformity in the wake of the Reformation. In the Netherlands, the recatholicization policy of the duke of Alba generated a stream of religious refugees. After the 1567 disturbances some 5,000–7,000 fled to Germany, and their numbers rose again following Farnese's conquest of Antwerp, to around 19,000 persons by the end of the century.[73] Dutch refugees were admitted into Frankfurt, Cologne, Emden, Wesel, Aachen, and Hamburg. Through their distinctive form of labour, founded on the principle of free competition, they caused great unrest in Frankfurt among those who saw themselves threatened by a superior new technology and form of enterprise, and facing downward social mobility. The religious tensions of the Reformation often strengthened older movements of migration, as was the case with wandering Scottish traders, who had already begun to settle in Pomerania in the sixteenth century (Stralsund, Greifswald). At the end of the sixteenth century, around 11,000 religious exiles entered Germany from inner Austria, Styria, Carniola, and Carinthia.[74]

The emigration of those persecuted for religious belief was usually provoked primarily by an attempt by the secular authorities to enforce a change of confession. However, the offer of asylum in territories or towns also played a role in the decision to emigrate. That the magistrates of Frankfurt, Cologne, Wesel, and Aachen, predominantly members of the merchant classes, were willing to accept Dutch refugees was influenced by hopes of technological innovation for the crisis-ridden textile industry, and of attracting new forms of trade.

The 1604 mandate of landgrave Moritz of Hesse-Kassel indicates the direction taken by mercantilist population policy in stipulating that exiles for the sake of religion were to be 'well received', housed, and allowed a two-year remission of all fees.[75] The reception of religious exiles in the seventeenth century led in some territories to the foundation of actual 'refugee towns'. An exemplary case is the town of Neuwied on the Rhine, founded in 1647 by Count Hermann III of Wied, which offered a place of freedom to seven different religious orientations (Reformed Protestants, Lutherans, Catholics, Mennonites, Inspirierten, Hutterites, and Jews).[76] Almost all newly founded absolutist residences contained a clause in their charters conceding freedom of worship.

For centuries Germany was a classic land of emigration. After migration to the east came to a halt following the plague of the fourteenth and fifteenth centuries, there was still some scattered emigration. This remained modest in scale, such as that which occurred from the Rems valley following the failed 'Poor Conrad' rebellion of 1514, or the continual long-term emigration of the Hutterites from Württemberg down the Danube to Moravia. The 1514 Treaty of Tübingen and the supplementary imperial clarification enacted in 1520 guaranteed that all who wished to emigrate from the duchy of Württemberg were permitted to do so without financial penalty, even those subjects bound by serfdom obligations.

The migrants originated for the most part from the lower rural classes, who in times of crisis were forced, or were willing, to 'strive for an improvement of their life-chances by geographical mobility.'[77] For the most part they travelled in family groups, after sending a scout on ahead to reduce uncertainty. Often they transferred their sense of neighbourhood from their old to their new homeland. In general, the emigrants were either single people or families with many children. The decision to emigrate was mostly precipitated by external events: subsistence crises, wars, confessional repression. The characteristic impulse underlying emigration movements emerged as a consequence of the interplay between the situation in the emigrants' old homeland and their expectations for the new. Great importance should be attached to the supply side of this equation, for there was always a potential for migration in the places of origin. In so far as this potential could be mobilized, it depended substantially on the actual or alleged opportunities to build a better life in another place.

Notes

1 O. Morlinghaus, *Bevölkerungs- und Wirtschaftsgeschichte des Fürstbistums Bamberg im Zeitalter des Feudalismus* (Ph.D., Erlangen, 1940).
2 F. Koerner, 'Die Bevölkerungsverteilung in Thüringen am Ausgang des 16. Jahrhunderts', *Wissenschaftliche Veröffentlichungen des Deutschen Instituts für Länderkunde*, NF 15/16 (1958), 178–315.
3 K. O. Bull, 'Die erste "Volkszählung" des deutschen Südwestens. Die Bevölkerung des Hochstifts Speyer in 1530', in K. Andermann and H. Ehmer, eds, *Bevölkerungsstatistik an der Wende vom Mittelalter zur Neuzeit* (Sigmaringen, 1990), pp. 109–35.
4 On church registers in general, P. Becker, *Leben, Lieben, Sterben. Die Analyse von Kirchenbüchern* (St Katherinen, 1989).
5 On lists for canton Zurich after 1634, W. Schnyder, *Die Bevölkerung der Stadt und Landschaft Zürich vom 14. bis 17. Jahrhundert* (Zurich, 1925); on funerary sermons, R. Lenz, *De mortuis nil nisi bene? Leichenpredigten als multidisziplinäre Quelle* (Sigmaringen, 1990).
6 M. Mattmüller, *Bevölkerungsgeschichte der Schweiz. Die frühe Neuzeit, 1500–1700* (2 vols, Basel/Frankfurt a.M., 1987) I, p. 104.
7 H. Penners-Ellwart, *Die Danziger Bürgerschaft nach Herkunft und Beruf 1537–1709* (Marburg/Lahn, 1954).
8 J. Ehmer, *Heiratsverhalten, Sozialstruktur, ökonomischer Wandel. England und Mitteleuropa in der Formationsperiode des Kapitalismus* (Göttingen, 1991), p. 63.
9 *Ibid.*, p. 64.
10 Mattmüller, *Bevölkerungsgeschichte der Schweiz* I, pp. 425–47.
11 Ehmer, *Heiratsverhalten*, p. 64.
12 F. Göttmann, 'Aspekte der Tragfähigkeit in der Ostschweiz um 1700', in J. Jahn and W. Hartung, eds, *Gewerbe und Handel vor der Industrialisierung* (Sigmaringen, 1991), pp. 152–82.
13 C. Pfister, *Das Klima der Schweiz von 1525 bis 1860 und seine Bedeutung in der Geschichte von Bevölkerung und Landwirtschaft*, 3rd edn (2 vols, Berne, 1988) II, pp. 126–9.
14 W. von Hippel, 'Bevölkerung und Wirtschaft im Zeitalter des Dreißigjährigen Krieges', *ZHF* V(1978), 413–48, esp. 420–34; C. Pfister and A. Kellerhals, 'Verwaltung und Versorgung im Landgericht Sternenberg', *Berner Zeitschrift*

für Geschichte und Heimatkunde LI (1989), pp. 151–215; Göttmann, 'Trägfähigkeit'.

15 C. Dipper, *Deutschland 1648–1789* (Frankfurt a.M., 1991), pp. 15, 45–6.

16 Cf. C. Pfister, Fluctuations climatiques et prix céréaliers en Europe du XVIe au XXe siècles', *Annales ESC* (1988), pp. 25–53.

17 J. Ehmer and M. Mitterauer, eds, *Familienstruktur und Arbeitsorganisation in ländlichen Gesellschaften* (Vienna/Cologne/Graz, 1986), p. 188. For 'ecotypes', E. R. Wolf, *Peasants* (Englewood Cliffs, NJ, 1966), p. 19.

18 R. Gehrmann, 'Einsichten und Konsequenzen aus neueren Forschungen zum generativen Verhalten im demographischen Ancien Regime und in der Transitionsphase', *Zeitschrift für Bevölkerungswissenschaft* V (1979), pp. 457–485, here p. 480; R. Lenz, *Studien zur deutschsprachigen Leichenpredigt der frühen Neuzeit* (Marburg, 1981), p. 222.

19 A. Eckhardt and H. Schmidt, eds, *Geschichte des Landes Oldenburg* (Oldenburg, 1987), p. 662; T. Robisheaux, *Rural Society and the Search for Order in Early Modern Germany* (Cambridge, 1989), pp. 26, 60–7; W. Schnyder, *Die Bevölkerung der Stadt und Landschaft Zürich vom 14. bis 17. Jahrhundert* (Zurich, 1925), p. 108; P. Blickle, *Die Revolution von 1525*, 2nd rev. edn (Munich, 1983), p. 124; M. Lasch, *Untersuchungen über Wirtschaft und Bevölkerung der Landgrafschaft Hessen-Kassel und der Stadt Kassel vom Dreißigjährigen Krieg bis zum Tode Landgraf Karls 1730* (Kassel, 1969), p. 27; G. Heckh, 'Bevölkerungsgeschichte und Bevölkerungsbewegung des Kirchspiels Böhringen auf der Uracher Alb vom 16. Jahrhundert bis zur Gegenwart', *Archiv für Rassen- und Gesellschaftsbiologie* 33 (1939), 126–69, here pp. 131–4; S. Weber, *Stadt und Amt Stuttgart zur Zeit des Dreißigjährigen Krieges* (Tübingen, 1936), p. 8; W. A. Boercke, *Wirtschaftsgeschichte Baden-Wüttembergs. Von den Römern bis heute* (Stuttgart, 1987), p. 93; H. Mauersberg, *Die Wirtschaft und Gesellschaft Fuldas in neuerer Zeit* (Stuttgart, 1969), p. 28; K. H. Ludwig, 'Neue Quellen zur Bevölkerungsentwicklung in der ersten Hälfte des 16. Jahrhunderts. Die Salzburger Mannschaftsauszüge von 1531 und 1541', *Mitteilungen der Gesellschaft für Salzburger Landeskunde* 117 (1977), 201–15; W. von Hippel, 'Bevölkerung und Wirtschaft im Zeitalter des Dreißigjährigen Krieges', *ZHF* V (1978), pp. 413–48, here p. 417.

20 Bull, 'Die erste "Volkszählung" ', p. 112.

21 Peter Bohl, 'Quellen zur Bevölkerungsgeschichte des ländlichen Raumes am Bodensee im 16. Jahrhundert', in Andermann and Ehmer, *Bevölkerungsstatistik*, pp. 47–63, here p. 55.

22 D. W Sabean, *Landbesitz und Gesellschaft am Vorabend des Bauernkriegs* (Stuttgart, 1972), p. 47; Blickle, *Revolution von 1525*, p. 123.

23 Koerner, 'Bevölkerungsverteilung in Thüringen'; R. Kötzschke, *Allgemeine Wirtschaftsgeschichte des Mittelalters* (Jena, 1924), p. 518.

24 P. Bairoch, J. Batou and P. Chèvre, *La Population des villes européennes. Banque de données et analyse sommaire des résultats 800–1850* (Geneva, 1988), p. 259.

25 J. de Vries, *European Urbanization 1500–1800* (London, 1984), p. 39.

26 *Ibid.*; Bairoch et al., *La Population*; F. Mathis, *Die deutsche Wirtschaft im 16. Jahrhundert* (Munich, 1992).

27 On general population figures, *op. cit.*, pp. 6–7, with further literature; on the number of settlements, W. Abel, *Die Wüstungen des ausgehenden Mittelalters*, 3rd edn (Stuttgart, 1976), p. 11.

28 The passage from the preface of Sebastian Franck, *Germania* (1539), cited in Sabean, *Landbesitz und Gesellschaft*, p. 37.

29 For Salzburg, K. H. Ludwig, 'Neue Quellen zur Bevölkerungsentwicklung in

der ersten Hälfte des 16. Jahrhunderts. Die Salzburger Mannschaftsauszüge von 1531 und 1541', *Mitteilungen der Gesellschaft für Salzburger Landeskunde* CXVII (1977), pp. 201–15; for Thuringia, Elizabeth Schwarze, 'Veränderungen der Sozial- und Besitzstruktur in ostthüringischen Ämtern und Städten am Vorabend des Bauernkrieges', *JbWG* III (1976), pp. 255–73, here p. 257; for Hohenlohe, Robisheaux, *Rural Society and the Search for Order*, p. 71.

30 Quoted in Sabean, *Landbesitz und Gesellschaft*, p. 37.
31 Robisheaux, *Rural Society and the Search for Order*, pp. 71–6.
32 Helmut Hildebrandt and Martin Gudd, 'Getreidebau, Missernten und Witterung im südwestlichen Unteren Vogelsberg und dem angrenzenden Vorland während des 16. und frühen 17. Jahrhunderts', *Archiv für hessische Geschichte und Altertumskunde*, NF 49 (1991), pp. 85–146.
33 On population density, von Hippel, 'Bevölkerung und Wirtschaft', p. 418; Koerner, 'Bevölkerungsverteilung in Thüringen'.
34 Von Hippel, 'Bevölkerung und Wirtschaft', p. 434.
35 Bull, 'Die erste "Volkszählung"', pp. 100–12; F. Göttmann and J. Sieglerschmidt, eds, *Vermischtes zur neueren Sozial-, Bevölkerungs- und Wirtschaftsgeschichte des Bodenseeraumes* (Constance, 1990), p. 3.
36 Mattmüller, *Bevölkerungsgeschichte* I, p. 220.
37 R. McC. Netting, *Balancing on an Alp* (Cambridge, 1981), p. 60.
38 On choices of marriage partner in Oberbayern, S. Breit *'Leichtfertigkeit' und ländliche Gesellschaft. Voreheliche Sexualität in der frühen Neuzeit* (Munich, 1991), p. 34.
39 On age of first marriage in Schwalm, A. E. Imhof, *Die verlorenen Welten. Alltagsbewältigung durch unsere Vorfahren* (Munich, 1984), p. 57; idem, 'Ländliche Familienstruktur an einem hessischen Beispiel. Heuchelheim 1690–1900', in H. Conze, ed., *Familie in der Neuzeit Europas* (Stuttgart, 1976), pp. 121–35; for Oberbayern and Switzerland, Breit, *'Leichtfertigkeit'*; for Salzburg, Ludwig, 'Neue Quellen zur Bevölkerungsentwicklung'.
40 J. Dupâquier, P. Laslett, M. Livi Bacci, H. Hélin and S. Sogner, eds, *Marriage and Remarriage in Populations in the Past* (New York, 1981), p. 3.
41 P. Becker, *Leben und Lieben in einem kalten Land. Sexualität im Spannungsfeld von Ökonomie und Demographie. Das Beispiel St. Lambrecht 1600–1850* (Frankfurt a.M., 1989), pp. 298–304.
42 W. Norden, *Eine Bevölkerung in der Krise. Historisch-demographische Untersuchungen zur Biographie einer norddeutschen Küstenregion (Butjadingen 1600–1850)* (Hildesheim, 1984), pp. 164–77; G. Pallaver, *Das Ende der schamlosen Zeit. Die Verdrängung der Sexualität in der frühen Neuzeit am Beispiel Tirols* (Vienna, 1987); J. Ussel, *Sexualunterdrückung. Die Geschichte der Sexualfeindschaft* (Giessen, 1977); M. Ingram, *Church Courts, Sex and Marriage in England 1570–1640* (Cambridge, 1987).
43 Becker, *Leben und Lieben* pp. 305–12; A. E. Imhof, *Die gewonnenen Jahre. Von der Zunahme unserer Lebensspanne seit dreihundert Jahren* (Munich, 1984), p. 57.
44 Becker, *Leben und Lieben*, p. 135.
45 W. Rödel, *Mainz und seine Bevölkerung im 17. und 18. Jahrhundert* (Wiesbaden, 1985), p. 162.
46 R. van Dülmen, 'Fest der Liebe. Heirat und Ehe in der frühen Neuzeit', in idem, ed., *Armut, Liebe, Ehe. Studien zur historischen Kulturforschung* (Frankfurt, 1988), pp. 67–102, here p. 92.
47 J. Knodel, *Demographic Behavior in the Past. A Study of Fourteen German Village Populations in the Eighteenth and Nineteenth Centuries* (Cambridge, 1988), p. 281.

48 P. Zschunke, *Konfession und Alltag in Oppenheim* (Wiesbaden, 1984), p. 152.

49 Rödel, *Mainz*, p. 162; Becker, *Leben und Lieben*, pp. 66; P. P. Viazzo, *Upland Communities. Environment, Population and Social Structure in the Alps since the Sixteenth Century* (Cambridge, 1989), p. 263; Imhof, *Die gewonnenen Jahre*, pp. 51–4.

50 A. Schluchter, *Das Gösgeramt im Ancien Regime* (Basel, 1990), pp. 182–3.

51 R. Gehrmann, *Leezen, 1720–1870. Ein historisch-demographischer Beitrag zur Sozialgeschichte des ländlichen Schleswig-Holstein* (Neumünster, 1984), pp. 253–5.

52 P. Bohl, *Die Stadt Stockach im 17. und 18. Jahrhundert* (Constance, 1987), p. 400.

53 Norden, *Bevölkerung in der Krise*, p. 159; B. Bietenhard, *Langnau im 18. Jahrhundert* (Langnau, 1988), p. 136; Zschunke, *Konfession und Alltag*, p. 199.

54 Becker, *Leben und Lieben*, p. 312; Breit, *'Leichtfertigkeit'*; the witch-craze thesis in G. Heinsohn, R. Knieper, and O. Steiger, *Menschenproduktion. Allgemeine Bevölkerungslehre der Neuzeit* (Frankfurt a.M., 1979); critique of the thesis by Wolfgang Behringer, 'Die Drohung des Schadenzaubers. Von den Regeln wissenschaftlicher Arbeit. Eine Antwort auf Heinsohn und Steiger', *Frankfurter Allgemeiner Zeitung* (7 October 1987), p. 37.

55 A. E. Imhof, *Die Verlorene Welten*, pp. 160–1; C. Pfister, 'Grauzone des Lebens', *Jb. der Schweizerische Gesellschaft für Familienforschung* XVI (1986), pp. 21–44.

56 U. Pfister, *Die Anfänge von Geburtenbeschränkung. Eine Fallstudie – ausgewählte Zürcher Familien im 17. und 18. Jahrhundert* (Berne, 1985).

57 Zschunke, *Konfession und Alltag*, pp. 198–226.

58 E. Menolfi, *Sanktgallische Untertanen im Thurgau* (St Gallen, 1980), pp. 334–42.

59 J. D. Post, 'Nutritional Status and Mortality in Eighteenth-Century Europe', in L. F. Newman, ed., *Hunger in History* (Oxford, 1990), pp. 241–80, here pp. 241–3; E. François, *Koblenz im 18. Jahrhundert* (Göttingen, 1982), p. 36.

60 Pfister, *Klima der Schweiz*, II, pp. 62–4.

61 Pfister, 'Fluctuations climatiques'.

62 E. Kier, *Epidemische Krankheiten in Göttingen bis zum Jahre 1875* (Diss. med., Göttingen, 1939).

63 E. Woehlkens, *Pest und Ruhr im 16. und 17. Jahrhundert. Grundlagen einer statistisch-topographischen Beschreibung der großen Seuchen, insbesondere in der Stadt Uelzen*, Schriften des Niedersächischen Heimatbundes, NF 26 (Hanover, 1954).

64 N. Bulst, 'Krankheit und Gesellschaft in der Vormoderne. Das Beispiel der Pest', in *Maladies et société (XII–XVIII siècles). Actes du Colloque de Bielefeld* (Paris, 1989), pp. 17–47, here pp. 30–1.

65 N. Bulst, 'Vier Jahrhunderte Pest in niedersächsischen Städten. Vom Schwarzen Tod (1349–1351) bis in die erste Hälfte des 18. Jahrhunderts', in *Katalog zur Landesausstellung Niedersachsen 1985* (Brunswick, 1985), pp. 251–70, here p. 262; Charlotte Bühl, 'Die Pestepidemien des ausgehenden Mittelalters und der Frühen Neuzeit in Nürnberg (1483/84–1533/34)', in R. Endres, ed., *Nürnberg und Bern. Zwei Reichsstädte und ihre Landgebiete* (Nuremberg, 1990), pp. 121–68, here pp. 134–6.

66 C. Pfister, 'Der Rote Tod im Kanton Bern: Demographische Auswirkungen und sozio-hygienisches Umfeld von Ruhrepidemien im 18. und 19. Jahrhundert unter dem Einfluß einer umweltorientierten Medizin', in P. Saladin, Schaufelberger, H. J. and Schläppi, P., eds, *'Medizin' für die Medizin. Arzt und Ärztin zwischen Wissenschaft und Praxis* (Basle, 1989), pp. 345–74; W.

Jungkunz, 'Die Sterblichkeit in Nürnberg 1714–1850', *Mitteilungen des Vereins für die Geschichte der Stadt Nürnberg* XLII (1951), pp. 289–352; W. Rödel, 'Pockenepidemien in Mainz im 18. Jahrhundert', *Ärzteblatt Rheinland-Pfalz* XLIII (1990), pp. 573–8.

67 Lenz, *De mortuis nil nisi bene.*

68 Imhof, *Die gewonnene Jahre*, pp. 81–3.

69 Zschunke, *Konfession und Alltag.*

70 François, *Koblenz.*

71 C R. Friedrichs, 'Immigration and Urban Society. Seventeenth Century Nördlingen', in *Immigration et société urbaine en Europe occidentale XVIe–XXe siècles. Recherche sur les civils* (Paris, 1985), pp. 65–77.

72 H. Penners-Ellwart, *Die Danziger Bürgerschaft nach Herkunft und Beruf 1537–1709* (Marburg/Lahn, 1954).

73 H. Schilling, *Niederländische Exulanten im 16. Jahrhundert* (Gütersloh, 1972).

74 I. Wechmar and R. Biederstedt, 'Die schottische Einwanderung in Vorpommern im 16. und frühen 17. Jahrhundert', *Greifswald-Stralsunder Jb.* V (1965), pp. 7–28; G. Rusam, *Österreichische Exulanten in Franken und Schwaben*, 2nd edn (Neustadt a. d. Aisch, 1989).

75 M. Lasch, *Untersuchungen über Wirtschaft und Bevölkerung der Landgrafschaft Hessen-Kassel und der Stadt Kassel vom Dreißigjährigen Krieg bis zum Tode Landgraf Karls 1730* (Kassel, 1969).

76 S. Volk, 'Peuplierung und religiose Toleranz. Neuwied von der Mitte des 17. Jh. bis zur Mitte des 18. Jh.', *Rheinische Vierteljahresblätter* LV (1991), pp. 205–31.

77 W. von Hippel, *Auswanderung aus Südwestdeutschland. Studien zur württembergischen Auswanderung und Auswanderungspolitik im 18. und 19. Jahrhundert* (Stuttgart, 1984).

Translated by Bob Scribner.

3

The Agrarian Economy,
1300–1600

WERNER RÖSENER

The agrarian depression of the later middle ages

Population decline and deserted land

The state of the agrarian economy in late medieval Germany was strongly influenced by the dramatic decline of population precipitated by successive epidemics of plague. Around a quarter of the population fell victim to the first wave of plague in the years 1347–51.[1] According to conservative estimates, the overall population of Germany declined from between 11 and 14 million around 1340 to between 7 and 10 million around 1470.[2] In considering such a global figure, one must bear in mind that the plague struck with varying intensity in different regions, and that there were consequently wide regional variations in the extent of population decline.

Population decline led to considerable losses of farms and villages, so that the settlement pattern of many regions of Germany was pockmarked by deserted landholdings. In discussing patterns of desertion, we should distinguish between deserted settlements and deserted arable land. Deserted settlements were those where residential settlement disappeared but the fields continued to be worked by neighbouring villages, whereas deserted arable meant that fields were no longer tilled at all. We can speak of partial rather than total desertion where neither the entire settlement nor the entire arable land of a village was abandoned and a remnant of the original settlement survived. The partially deserted settlements played an important role in Germany alongside those only temporarily deserted, that is, those settlements and fields which were abandoned for only a short time and then resettled and retilled. If we can assume that the number of settlements in the German Empire (using the borders of 1937) was roughly 17,000 around 1300, then they had declined to around 13,000 at the end of the fifteenth century.[3]

A map of the deserted settlements in late medieval Germany reveals that the extent of abandonment varied from region to region and that they were by no means evenly distributed across the country as a whole.[4] Their number was particularly large in the territory of Brandenburg, in the Thuringian region, and in the Hessian uplands, while the area of dispersed settlement in north-west Germany and in the Lower Rhine region was scarcely touched by the trend towards abandonment. Research on the geography of settlement patterns over the past few decades has contributed significantly to accurate mapping of the pattern of desertion.[5]

The difficulty of a quantitative assessment of the desertions results from various circumstances. Numerous deserted settlements have left no documentary record, so that they have to be recovered from archaeological evidence, from records of local place-names, and from oral evidence. Yet it is precisely in respect of those abandoned settlements that have left no documentary evidence that it is difficult to trace whether they were already deserted before the later middle ages. The partially abandoned settlements were evidently more numerous in areas where settlement survived, yet they are rarely mentioned in written records, and, moreover, were often resettled during the sixteenth century. Abandoned fields can usually only be researched by means of field archaeology and on the basis of remains of tillage (*Wölbäcker*, terraced cultivation). In regions with a favourable climate only part of the fields fell into disuse for short periods, while in those with hostile climate quite extensive areas were abandoned. For this reason there were many deserted settlements in upland regions; former arable land was reforested or used only sporadically.[6]

Besides general population decline, migration patterns accelerated the abandonment of many places. The departing peasants emigrated to a nearby town which had suffered population losses in the epidemics and which was now dependent on newcomers, or else they moved to other villages with better economic circumstances.[7] Such migration has to be reconstituted from the frequency of occurrence of abandoned settlements in particular regions or from the peculiarities of land use. Thus, it can be shown for the forested areas of the Harz, for the Thuringian uplands, and for other regions that villages which had been first settled during the high middle ages were affected by decline in unusually large numbers. In other regions, desertion can only rarely be traced among the group of the oldest settlement names, while they appear with uncommon frequency in upland regions, in areas of poor soil, and in areas more remote from major routes.

Several theories and explanatory models have been developed in the course of the search for the causes of the deserted settlements of the late middle ages.[8] The 'warfare' theory that long held pride of place assumes that abandoned places had largely been destroyed by the effects of warfare, and the numerous wars and feuds of the later middle ages were cited as evidence. Advocates of the theory of 'failed settlement' upheld the view that the deserted settlements had been largely planted on poor soil and were unable to survive because of poor yields. Adherents of the theory of 'concentration' maintained that deserted villages were the result of several places being amalgamated into a larger settlement. However, the most comprehensive theory is that of agrarian crisis, especially as formulated by Wilhelm Abel. This places population decline at the heart of its explanation, decline which was inaugurated by the famines of the years 1315–17 and then markedly intensified by the epidemics of plague of the mid-fourteenth century. This lead to a long-term fall in agrarian prices and to a shrinkage of agrarian incomes, and so to migration from the land.[9]

Trends in prices and wages during the later middle ages

The consequence of the contracting demand for grain was a long-term decline in grain prices from the second half of the fourteenth until the end of the fifteenth century. Because supply did not shrink parallel to demand, there was an over-supply which further depressed grain prices.[10] Prices for manufactured goods, however, developed in the opposite direction, leading to divergence between prices and wages.[11] Population decline brought a contraction of the labour force, so that real wages rose significantly during the later middle ages. Since manufactured products commanded relatively stable prices in contrast to agrarian produce, a substantial price difference or 'price scissors' opened up between agrarian produce and manufactured goods. The consequence was that agricultural production was confronted with higher costs as a result of higher wages, but at the same time had to adjust to lower levels of income because of falling grain prices. The low levels of grain prices affected farmers and landlords in equal measure, leading to serious decline in incomes across the agrarian sector as a whole.

Higher wages had a particular effect in the urban economy by increasing demand. The poorer social classes and urban day-labourers were now able to afford more expensive foods such as meat. Urban craftsmen profited from higher prices for manufactured goods and also increased their standard of living.[12] On the other hand, the broad mass of the rural population experienced the disadvantages of these changes in price structures. The self-sufficiency of the peasant family household was scarcely affected, but the declining returns from grain reduced the peasant's ability to acquire manufactured goods.

Since labour had become relatively expensive, wages reached a relatively high level, and although wage increases were countered by the introduction of wage tariffs, these had little success.[13] Such wage tariffs were set up in the Tyrol, in Saxony, and in other territories. In the Territorial Statutes of 1352 for the Tyrol, which specifically referred to the depopulation caused in the land by the plague, the ruler laid down maximum wages for workers, craftsmen, and servants.[14] In other statutes, employers were also blamed for causing wage rises by employing journeymen and wage-workers at too high a wage rate.

Alongside the long-term agrarian depression of the fourteenth and fifteenth centuries, which was essentially a crisis of grain distribution, we should also pay attention to short-term price rises, which continually recurred in this period as a result of poor harvests.[15] Harvest fluctuations and the resulting dearth were regular occurrences during the later middle ages, and caused hunger and immiseration among the broadest masses of the population. In 1437–8 there was a hunger crisis throughout the whole of central Europe, occasioned by massive harvest failures – severe winters and wet summers, which reduced grain yields in most regions.[16]

Changes in land use

Population decline and subsequent reduction in demand for grain led to far-reaching changes in land use. Arable was converted to grazing land or allowed to revert to woods in areas of poor soil. Other areas of good soil and with high fertility were more intensively cultivated with specialized crops.[17] Given that the population had declined by a third, according to rough estimates, we can assume that the amount of land devoted to arable was considerably reduced. None the less, there was only a gradual change in the agrarian economy during the first years following the epidemics of plague. Usually the better land was left under cultivation, so that average yields generally rose. At the same time, the increase in stocks of cattle led to better manuring, which also contributed to raising yield ratios.

The expansion of grazing land was a consequence of the reduction in the areas of arable, since all land in a village's fields that were not devoted to gardens or tillage were counted as common land available for communal grazing.[18] Even if stock-raising did not expand everywhere at the same time, none the less the increase in areas devoted to grazing produced an overall increase in the number of cattle per head of population. Thus, the expansion of stock-raising resulted in a larger number of cattle for the population of the later middle ages, and so to greater quantities of animal products than in the high middle ages. The first precise figures for consumption of meat and animal products are available for the fourteenth and fifteenth centuries. From this evidence we can see that meat consumption was relatively high; Abel even claims that the annual consumption of meat in some areas was over 100 kg per head of the population,[19] although some historians have cast doubt on this figure.[20] During the later middle ages the towns enjoyed extrordinarily favourable conditions for supplies of meat products. Low grain prices enabled the urban population to devote a great part of their expenditure to meat products. The consumption of meat at many feasts during the fifteenth century rose so much that the authorities issued statutes limiting the maximum quantity of meat and other foods permitted at such feasts.[21]

The expansion of grazing led in some areas to the establishment of sheep farms on the deserted fields, and in this way the vacant arable land of former villages became the grazing lands for great herds of sheep. This process was especially pronounced in south-west Germany, where sheep farms were set up on the deserted arable of a great number of places. The counts of Württemberg, for example, established such sheep farms on their lands and turned the arable of deserted villages over to grazing.[22]

This process of extensive farming, manifest in the expansion of grazing lands and forested areas and in the contraction of arable farming, was counterbalanced in late medieval Germany by another process leading to intensified agriculture. More fertile land was more carefully cultivated, and specialized crops spread.[23] Since these crops gave higher yields than grain-growing, they can be counted as part of a more advanced agriculture. An important impulse was provided by the expansion of urban and rural manufactures, which depended on certain industrial and market crops.[24] There was an increase in dyestuff fibres, since the textile industry required good dyeing agents. Cultivation of madder, the main red dye, on the Upper Rhine in the area around Speyer, and of the main blue dye, woad, around Erfurt in Thuringia, deserves mention. Flax was cultivated in quantities well beyond the farmers' needs, and served as a basic material for the textile industry. Cultivation of flax was extensive in south Germany, as well as in Westphalia and Lower Saxony, and provided peasants with a major source of income. Rape-seed and beets were grown in many areas, and hops increased in importance.

Viticulture and fruit-growing were also more intensively pursued during the later middle ages, since they were more profitable than grain-growing. There was a good market for fruit everywhere, as can be seen in the market statutes of various towns.[25] Wine played an especially important role, and viticulture was more extensively pursued than ever before in Germany.[26] Vines were even planted in areas completely lacking in favourable conditions. Not only were there extensive vineyards on the slopes of the Rhine, Moselle, Neckar, and Main valleys, but viticulture also expanded far into the north German lowlands.

Agrarian depression and the
crisis of manorial farming

The impact of crisis in the agrarian economy of the later middle ages had
adverse effects both on peasant producers and on landlords. Seigneurial
incomes declined in various ways, of which only the most important will
be mentioned here.[27] Many peasant farms and villages were devastated by
population losses and so provided no rents to their feudal lords.
Resettlement of abandoned farms required landlords to make various
concessions in the form of rent reductions and rebuilding subsidies for
recultivation of deserted arable. The decline in the landlords' incomes was
further accentuated by the fall in wheat prices, since a major proportion
of feudal rents had been paid in kind, and the landlords had to market
the grain tendered at low prices. Falling grain prices also affected the
products of the properties farmed by the lords themselves with wage
labour, since rising wages had a negative effect on the profitability of such
direct farming. Money rents also fell in value as the purchasing power of
money fell as a result of coinage manipulation and inflation.

All these factors contributed to worsen the situation of many landlords
during the fourteenth and fifteenth centuries. The consequences of agrarian
crisis had varying effects on a single estate such as the nobility.[28] Petty
noble families whose incomes derived from feudal rents were more heavily
hit by the crisis than those noble families who had sources of income other
than feudal rents. Thus, during the course of the fourteenth century the
masses of the petty and middle-ranking nobility fell into ever greater
difficulty through declining incomes from rents and direct farming. Studies
of the situation of the nobility in the Ortenau reveal that their incomes as
landlords fell by around a half of their previous value at the end of the
fourteenth century simply through coinage devaluation and decline in agricultural prices.[29] Added to such decline in the value of seigneurial incomes
were losses in rent through population depletion and emigration. However,
a study of families from the lower nobility in the Rhine Palatinate has
come to other conclusions by taking account of wider property interests
as well as seigneurial incomes, and although there is evidence of deep-
seated restructuring in these noble families, there was no serious economic
crisis.[30]

Alongside the large number of indebted noble families during the later
middle ages, there were clearly some nobles who pursued successful
economic activity even during periods of agricultural recession. The
economic activities of the Burggrafen of Drachenfels near Bonn can be
followed in their household accounts for the years 1458–63; it is clear from
these accounts that the properties of the lordship of Drachenfels were well
managed, and that the Burggraf's family had an adequate basis for a

lifestyle commensurate with their social standing.[31] Other less successful noble families turned partly to activity as robber-knights.[32] During the fourteenth and fifteenth centuries there were numerous instances of feuds and assaults involving knights who had fallen into economic difficulties as a result of loss of property. The threat of downwards social mobility led part of the lower nobility to secure the income they required through feuds and robbery.

Wilhelm Abel's fundamental work on the agrarian economy of the later middle ages and its interpretation as an agrarian crisis has been complemented by the research of Friedrich Lütge.[33] The epidemics of plague from 1347 to 1351 and the related population decline initiated a development which, according to Lütge, led to far-reaching changes in economy and society and precipitated a 'dynamic of contraction'.[34] In consequence of the reduction of population there developed an agrarian crisis on the one hand and a 'golden age' of the towns on the other. However, the theory of agrarian crisis has been vehemently challenged by marxist historiography. The main criticism from this viewpoint has been that demographic factors are accorded the role of a major historical influence on the one hand, while the influence of the feudal system has not been sufficiently taken into account on the other. Thus, the theory of an agrarian crisis has been confronted from the marxist side by that of a crisis of feudalism.[35] The leading economic historian of the former German Democratic Republic, Jürgen Kuczynski, firmly rejects Abel's thesis that it was population losses which ultimately caused the changes in the areas of agrarian production, prices and wages.[36] In Kuczynski's view, an agrarian crisis can only be produced during the stage of a highly developed feudalism by a crisis of the feudal mode of production, and not as a result of natural processes such as population decline caused by epidemics of plague.

The reaction of feudal lords to economic difficulties varied from region to region, and depended on the local structures of lordship and the rights of seigneurs over their subject peasants. Some sought to compensate for the decline in seigneurial incomes by heavier burdens on the peasant economy, and by demanding higher seigneurial dues.[37] Insofar as seigneurial lords were equipped with the necessary means of coercion, they also attempted to prevent peasant emigration by force. Such coercive measures took the form of extracting oaths of loyalty, imposing departure fines, and limiting peasant mobility. In the south-western regions of Germany, the agrarian crisis actually led to the strengthening of bonds of personal servitude of peasants to their lords, as many seigneurs sought to contain peasant emigration and to compensate for losses of income by increasing feudal dues.[38] For example, in the second half of the fourteenth century the monastic lordship of St Blasien in the southern Black Forest both intensified the bonds of servitude over its serfs and simultaneously increased the servile dues demanded of them.[39] Similar tendencies can be seen in other ecclesiastical and secular lordships.

In the eastern regions of Germany the results of the agrarian crisis also led to seigneurs strengthening their rights over the peasant population and extending the labour services demanded from the peasants.[40] In many areas east of the Elbe the landed nobility were able, by means of legal jurisdiction, to acquire strict rights of coercion over the peasants, and at the same time to expand the size of their estates by incorporating deserted peasant holdings. Thus, important foundations for eastern German estate farming were laid down in the period of crisis of the later middle ages, although this development only began in earnest in the sixteenth century.

The expansion of the agrarian economy in the sixteenth century

Population expansion and land reclamation

The development of the German agrarian economy in the sixteenth century was characterized by the strong population expansion which now set in after a long period of decline. The population of Germany had declined during the course of the later middle ages to somewhere between 7 and 10 million around 1470, but it now rose to around 14 million in 1560 and reached 17 million by 1618.[41] The estimates of a powerful expansion of the German population during the sixteenth century assumed by older scholarship has been confirmed by more recent research. Körner has argued that the population in Thuringia increased strongly especially during the first half of the sixteenth century; but the annual rate of increase slowed down gradually towards the end of the century.[42] Blaschke also demonstrated for Saxony that there had been substantial growth in population in the decades prior to 1550, compensating for the population losses of the late medieval decline.[43] The period around 1470–80 seems to have been a turning-point in population development, in which a phase of stagnation was followed by one of sharp increase, peaking during the first decades of the sixteenth century.

Population expansion was reflected in land reclamation and in the opening up of new arable land. This was largely a matter of land which had once been cultivated, but which had fallen into disuse during the later middle ages. It either lay on the edges of villages or else involved the land of settlements which had disappeared. At the end of the period of agrarian recession, the lands of surviving places had often been used more extensively; there was uncultivated land in the more centrally placed arable fields, the outlying fields had reverted to scrubland, and the more accessible arable land of deserted holdings were tilled only in small parcels. In recultivating former arable land, one generally proceeded as if assarting new land, so that the earlier field patterns disappeared.[44]

The recultivation of deserted arable lands was none the less insufficient to feed the growing population, especially since many former fields were already covered by forests and protected by forestry laws, so that it was necessary to open up completely new land. Research on settlement patterns has produced evidence of land being opened up in various regions.[45] In the north-east of East Prussia, a great part of the land which had become covered with dense forest during the later middle ages was resettled by the peasants.[46] Territorial officials assigned individual families patches of forest land corresponding to their needs. They paid for this with a few oxen and, and after a while, with the usual ground rents. There was extensive land reclamation along the German Baltic coast, and a substantial part of the lands that had been lost there during the later middle ages was reclaimed and repoldered.[47] In the older Germanic settlement areas, numerous waste lands were cultivated, marshes were drained, meadows turned to arable, and woods assarted. However, deforestation reached such levels that the rulers of some German territories were forced to issue forestry laws prohibiting forest clearance. There were also conflicts between peasants of various villages over the clearing of disputed lands and the resettlement of deserted land, as is attested for southern Lower Saxony.[48]

In eastern Germany there began in the sixteenth century a second wave of colonization, which has been thoroughly researched by W. Kuhn.[49] The expansion of settlement began in most east German territories in the 1530s and 1540s, and around 1550 the opening up of new lands was in full swing. Initially this involved the resettlement of deserted holdings, but the foundation of new villages quickly followed. The next stage involved the opening up of great river valleys and extensive tracts of forest. From 1547, Dutch settlers continued the drainage of the Danzig estuary and founded planned marshland villages there, while similar villages were established in the Vistula estuary near Thorn. In the second half of the sixteenth century, West Pomeranian peasants founded new villages in both eastern Pomerania and in West Prussia. Within the framework of this German eastern settlement, the settlement forms adopted were usually those which were known from the high medieval wave of colonization.

Development of prices and wages during the sixteenth century

The sixteenth century has often been described as the century of the 'price revolution'.[50] This notion is used to characterize the extraordinary rises that developed in grain prices and in those for manufactured goods. Grain prices rose during the sixteenth century by 255 per cent in Germany, by 424 per cent in England, and by 272 per cent in Austria.[51] However, the prices for manufactured goods did not keep pace with those for grain, merely doubling in this period.[52] The extent of price inflation was certainly different in various towns and territories, but the general trend was clear and the steepest price rises occurred in the second half of the sixteenth century. The difference in price trends between grain and manufactured goods is explicable in terms of the different elasticity of these goods in the face of an expanding population.[53] The demand for basic necessities was inelastic, and rising prices led to no diminution in demand; but the case was different for non-essential goods, where rising prices had a negative effect on demand. As a result of population expansion, demand for foodstuffs outstripped supply, and accordingly food prices rose more steeply than those for manufactured goods.

By contrast with grain prices, wages increased only modestly during the sixteenth century. Nominal wages certainly rose by 157 per cent in Germany and by 131 per cent in England, but they lagged well behind grain prices and those for manufactured goods.[54] This meant that real wages fell considerably during the sixteenth century, and the real wages of a building worker, to take one example, fell by more than half between 1500 and 1600. The reason for this fall in real wages resides in the fact that population increase had considerably increased the labour supply without any corresponding increase in demand. Wages could not keep pace with the rising cost of living, so that the standard of living of wage workers fell accordingly. While the production of foodstuffs stagnated or rose only marginally, the number of mouths to be fed continued to increase.

Those living on agrarian incomes – peasants and seigneurs – were the main beneficiaries of these changes in price and wage structures. Since wages and prices for manufactured goods lagged behind prices for agrarian produce, profits from the agrarian sector increased, although these accrued to the peasants only insofar as their landlords allowed them to share in the higher incomes and did not drain them off by increased feudal burdens.[55] The rents levied on individual farms certainly attest that ground rents rose: in Hainberg, near Göttingen, the rent demanded for a plot of farmland trebled during the course of the sixteenth century.[56] The alternative to renting land was independent farm management, which offered the opportunity of taking advantage of lower wages. The manager who farmed some monastic lands belonging to the Dukes of Braunschweig made a profit from the land in his charge of 40,000 gulden between 1584 and 1600 from agriculture alone.[57] Such high profits from direct farming conducted with the help of wage labour can be explained as a result of the favourable price and wage structures at the end of the sixteenth century.

Intensification of land use

The strong demand of a growing population for agrarian produce and the rise in grain prices stimulated an expansion of agricultural production. This occurred on the one hand through an extension of the area under cultivation by opening up new land, and by intensification of agriculture and the introduction of new methods of production on the other. Improved methods of cultivation were applied to land lying outside the common fields, and especially to gardens, which were the most intensively used land. Extensive garden plots were laid out in the suburbs of many towns and were carefully cultivated by the citizens. Plots designated as garden land were exempted from common access to grazing, and such designations of garden land offered the highest incentives to exploit the land for vegetables, fruit, and specialized market crops.[58] The small size of these plots encouraged making the best agricultural use of them, and they were especially well manured by their owners. Regions such as the Rhineland and Alsace were particularly notable for their flourishing gardens.[59]

Improvement on the three-field system was achieved in many areas by different crop rotation. In the Lower Rhine region, cultivation began of the fallow lying idle as a result of the three-field rotation.[60] This area was planted either with a fodder crop or with high-value plants such as peas and beans, beet, or cabbage. Animal manure or lime was used, wherever these were available, to improve soil nutrients.

We are less well informed for the sixteenth century about stock-raising than we are about arable farming. We have to assume that the area of grazing available was considerably reduced as a result of the expansion in arable use. Livestock farming could not be expanded to match the increase in population, so that meat supply must have contracted, although this was compensated for by imports of meat from neighbouring countries. Oxen were imported from Denmark into the North German regions, while large numbers of oxen were imported from Poland, reaching western and central Germany via Saxony and Thuringia. Herds of oxen originating in Hungary and the Danubian areas were brought to South Germany in substantial number. The origins of this international cattle trade can be found in the later middle ages, but the trade with oxen expanded especially in the sixteenth century.[61] The main markets for Eastern European cattle were in towns such as Vienna, Breslau, and Posen, where large numbers changed hands. In the large cities of south Germany, efficient organizations of cattledealers were established.

The intensification of agriculture is also reflected in the growth of agricultural handbooks, which thrived during the sixteenth century. Alongside translations of ancient Roman authors on agriculture such as Cato, Varro, and Columella, three authors achieved particular importance because of their agricultural handbooks: Conrad Heresbach, Martin Grosser, and Johann Coler.[62] These three works mark the beginning of the genre of the so-called 'patriarchal handbooks' (*Hausvaterliteratur*), which aimed to provide instruction for the head of a household on farm management and the running of a domestic household.[63] The mixture of advice taken from ancient Roman authors with personal observation adapted to German circumstances provided important tips for the conduct of arable farming. Conrad Heresbach's four books on agriculture are especially interesting, since he wrote them on the basis of practical experience of farming on the Lower Rhine.[64] This region had close connections to the Netherlands, where agricultural innovation was already well advanced; and Heresbach recommended increased cultivation of fruit and vegetables, market and industrial crops, as well as offering advice on fertilizing with manure from stabled animals and with lime. Heresbach's observations reflect the advances made in the agrarian economy in the neighbouring Dutch and Flemish regions. Flemish rent contracts from this period mention cultivation of cabbage, clover, and flax on the fallow fields and plentiful manuring, leading even then to very high yields for grain-growing.[65]

Changes in agrarian structure

How far the peasant population benefited from the favourable agrarian conjuncture of the sixteenth century depended, in the last resort, on the level of their feudal burdens. Large peasant farms that were not too heavily burdened, and which could produce plentiful quantities for the market, could become quite prosperous. The profits accumulated by peasant farmers during the period of favourable agrarian conjuncture are attested by magnificent peasant farmhouses and the remains of peasant domestic culture which have survived in various regions. In the German south-west, the prosperity of many large farmers grew noticeably at the end of the sixteenth century and is recognizable in the furnishing of their farmhouses as well as in their accumulated savings.[66] In the villages of the county of Hohenlohe, the trend towards the creation of an elite of prosperous peasant farmers is clearly discernible, and the social distance between a tiny upper stratum of the peasantry and the great number of small farmers increased noticeably in the sixteenth century.[67]

The majority of the middling and small peasant farmers were scarcely touched by such increases in prosperity. Their situation remained precarious, their dues high, and they generally had only the bare necessities for subsistence. In west Germany the seigneurs sought to raise rents, in money and in kind, or to supplement them through other fees. This trend is observable in the lordship of the Holy Ghost Hospital of Biberach, where the peasants farmed predominantly on lifetime leases, which reverted to the hospital on the death of the leaseholder. In order to adjust the losses of monetary income against the value of grain rents, the hospital's administrators raised the level of entry fines demanded on taking up a new lease, and these rose twelvefold in 1610–19 over the years 1500–9.[68] They thus succeeded in increasing the hospital's incomes substantially. Similar trends can be observed in the area of Ravensburg, in Upper Swabia, at the beginning of the sixteenth century. The city of Ravensburg began to buy back leases which had been conferred in hereditary tenure and to convert them to single-life leases, thus providing the city with the regular opportunity to adjust the dues from these properties and to raise them if necessary.[69]

Favourable agrarian conjuncture also had positive effects on the situation of the nobility, insofar as nobles were directly engaged in farming and could profit from higher prices. In the Weser area, the nobility erected costly Renaissance castles, while the stately residences built in Brandenburg and Pomerania attest the growing wealth of the nobility. Recent research on noble households in the Weser area has demonstrated that the favourable conjunctural circumstances of sixteenth century agriculture led to substantial increases in noble incomes, and that their profits flowed above all from the sale of grain.[70]

The agrarian structure of east Germany in the sixteenth century was decisively influenced by the improved conditions for grain exports. Grain exports from Baltic harbours were destined primarily for Western Europe, where the densely populated regions were dependent on imports of grain. The shaping of east German estate farming and the enlargement of farm enterprises were thus substantially influenced by agrarian exports.[71] Peasant freedom of movement had already been abolished in the fifteenth century in most east Elbian territories in order to hinder emigration and to ensure adequate labour for estate farming. During the sixteenth century peasant property rights deteriorated little by little; hereditary possession became an exception and unfavourable rights of occupancy the rule. This deterioration of peasant property rights served to promote estate farming more easily by tying the peasants to the soil. The area under cultivation was then enlarged by bringing waste land into cultivation. The available land had become scarce in the first half of the sixteenth century, so that farm estates could only be extended by incorporating peasant land.[72] Reducing the number of free peasants by tying the peasants to the soil also increased the servile obligations of the remaining peasants, and there gradually developed the characteristic form of east German subservience, in which the peasant counted as part of the estate's possessions and was obliged to perform heavy labour service. The children of peasants were also forced to work as servants, entering domestic service for the landlord at his request. Research on the development of manorial estates in the Mark Brandenburg reveal that such enterprises grew considerably in extent, above all in the period between 1480 and 1624.[73] In the first phase the estates were enlarged by taking over waste land and forest; in a second phase, the estates began to buy up peasant farmland and to expel the peasants. Recent research on noble-estate farming in East Prussia has revealed that noble estates there were enlarged in the second half of the sixteenth century predominantly through taking over deserted peasant farmland.[74]

East German manorial farming established itself in great measure by extension of estate farming during the sixteenth century. The economic links between peasant farms and estate farming became ever closer, and the peasant was regarded largely as the labour force of the manorial estate. The landlord exercised coercive power over the self-enclosed realm of his estate, and his manorial subjects were forced into servile dependence – a sharp contrast to western Germany, where peasants were often associated with several feudal lords.

The form of direct estate farming which developed in east German territories had essentially different characteristics from the agricultural forms in western Germany. In the south and west of Germany, the sixteenth century witnessed no formation of extensive estate farming; rather, these areas were dominated by tenant farming for landlords, on the basis of rents in money or in kind. Friedrich Lütge distinguished between five basic types of tenant farming: the north-west German, the west German, the south-west German, the central German, and the Bavarian.[75] Alongside these basic types there were a number of special types, for example in Hesse or in Franconia. In the Lower Rhine region, limited leasehold was widespread, so forming a link to the forms in the neighbouring Low Countries.[76] In Friesland, the peasants retained a relatively free position in terms of legal jurisdiction and representation in the territorial estates, despite the spread of estate farming.[77]

Within the regions assigned by Lütge to one of the five main types of farm tenure, sharp distinctions may also be found, so that any attempt at regional differentiation remains problematic. One must consider how far large regions such as the Rhineland or south-west Germany, which in the sixteenth century manifested numerous territorial divisions and economic characteristics, can provide the basis for assuming that there were unified agricultural forms. Particular types of seigneurial tenure in the west and south of Germany were dependent on structures of lordship and on the peculiarities of different kinds of lords. Thus it is necessary to distinguish between the holders of seigneuries from territorial princes, lower nobles, ecclesiastical institutions, and townsfolk.[78] The distinctiveness of individual forms of landlordship was strongly determined by whether rights of landownership were supplemented by further lordship rights, especially through legal jurisdiction.

By contrast with eastern Germany, west German territorial rulers frequently intervened in the seigneurial sphere. For example, the Welf princes of north Germany pursued a conscious agrarian policy in the sixteenth century, when the landlords attempted to raise their returns in the wake of the agrarian boom and to impair peasant rights of possession.[79] The Welf rulers hindered such exactions, and also prohibited the arbitrary expulsion of leaseholders. The landlords also were denied the right to convert peasant farms into manorial estates when leasehold contracts were properly terminated. The territorial rulers had good fiscal reasons for such policies, as well as a broad general interest in retaining a prosperous peasantry and in hindering the enlargement of noble estates at the expense of peasant holdings. At the same time, they set firm limits to peasant freedoms and prohibited the fragmentation of farmsteads. The peasants thus were assured of rights of occupancy of their holdings and of fixed levels of rent, but at the same time an eye was kept on the integrity of the holdings. In the principality of Braunschweig, peasant leasehold rights were firmly established in 1597 by the recess of the territorial diet of Salzdahlum.[80] This laid down the hereditary nature of the leaseholds, prohibited subdivision of holdings, and forbade rent increases. The expulsion of leaseholders was only possible in consequence of a penal breach of the lease contract, but the landlord had to involve the competent court and to replace the deposed leaseholder with another. Thus, the hereditary nature of landholdings in the Braunschweig area was laid down in the sixteenth century, and remained in force in the following centuries.[81]

With regard to peasant inheritance patterns, we can distinguish between those with impartible (*Anerbenrecht*) and those with partible (*Realteilung*) inheritance.[82] Regions with impartible inheritance generally retained in their villages substantial farms with large or middling peasants. Those with predominantly impartible inheritance tended towards a system of small-holdings and the formation of a lower stratum of numerous petty peasants; seigneurial rights in these areas were often sharply fragmented, since the properties were subdivided frequently and assigned as inheritance to different families. An overview of the regional distribution of farm sizes, which correlates closely with inheritance patterns, reveals that the smallest holdings in the sixteenth century were to be found in the south-west German regions.[83] They dominated on the Upper Rhine, the Neckar valley area, and the Middle Rhine, and extended into the neighbouring territories of Hesse and Franconia. Middling and large holdings, on the other hand, were concentrated in Bavaria and in north Germany (Westphalia, Lower Saxony), where impartible inheritance was dominant.

Conclusion

If we regard the period 1300–1600 as a whole from the perspective of its agrarian history, we can discern a phase of depression in the agrarian economy during the fourteenth and fifteenth century, accompanied by signs of crisis in economy, society, and lordship. This is then succeeded by a phase of expansion in the sixteenth century, characterized by rising agrarian production and high prices for agricultural produce. The impulse for the structural upheavals of the later middle ages was provided by the Black Death and subsequent epidemics of plague, as a result of which the population of Germany contracted by at least a third. This reduction in population led to a decline in demand for grain, to numerous areas of land being taken out of cultivation, and to the creation of waste arable land and deserted villages. Falling prices for grain and low agrarian incomes were the result, so that many feudal lords experienced a sharp crisis. Peasant emigration into the towns was further encouraged by rising wages. This trend turned around during the age of the price revolution (1470–1600), when a renewed population expansion radically altered the economic situation. Steeply rising agrarian prices led to sharp increases in agrarian incomes, and especially those of seigneurial lords. Agricultural production was increased by expansion of the area under cultivation; at the same time there was also an intensification of agriculture in some sectors.

In east German regions the sixteenth century witnessed a strengthening of estate farming, while the west and south German regions saw no basic change in systems of agrarian production, and the various forms of seigneurial tenure scarcely changed at all. In this sense, there emerged a bipartite division of Germany in terms of its agrarian systems, an agrarian dualism which was to persist into the nineteenth century.[84] At first there was an extension of manorial estates in the east Elbian regions through incorporation of deserted lands, and then from the second half of the sixteenth century the conversion of peasant villages into manorial lands, which was further accelerated by the expansion of direct estate farming for grain exports. At the same time, the lords strengthened their coercive rights over the peasant population and obliged them to perform heavy forced labour on their manorial estates. The reasons for this divergent development of agrarian structures in eastern and western Germany were several.[85] Western Germany was, by contrast with the east Elbian region, more heavily urbanized and had greater opportunities for the production of manufactures, so that the west German peasants had more possibilities for migration. The centuries-old dependence on feudal rights had led to sharp fragmentation of lordships, so that it was more difficult here than in the east German colonized territories to create manorial estates with self-contained manorial jurisdiction. Finally, the higher density of population also contributed to the west being more thickly populated with peasant farms and villages than the east, so that there was less land available for lords to enlarge their estates. In general, we can say that the more highly developed state of the economy in west Germany was responsible for the fact that the agrarian structure here did not develop to the disadvantage of the peasantry.

Notes

1   J. C. Russell, 'Population in Europe 500–1500', in C. M. Cipolla, ed., *The Fontana Economic History of Europe* I (London, 1972), p. 21; idem, 'Bevölkerung', in *Lexikon des Mittelalters* II (Munich, 1983), p. 14; N. Bulst, 'Der Schwarze Tod. Demographische, wirtschafts- und kulturgeschichtliche Aspekte der Pestkatastrophe von 1347–352', *Saeculum* XXX (1979), pp. 45–67.

2   E. Meuthen, *Das 15. Jahrhundert* (Munich, 1980), p. 3.

3   W. Abel, *Die Wüstungen des ausgehenden Mittelalters*, 3rd edn (Stuttgart, 1976), p. 11; K. Scharlau, 'Ergebnisse und Ausblicke der heutigen Wüstungsforschung', *BdLG* XCIII (1957), pp. 43–101; M. Born, 'Wüstungsschema und Wüstungsquotient', *Erkunde* XXVI (1972), pp. 208–18.

4   There is a map of deserted settlements in late medieval Germany in Abel, *Wüstungen*, p. 10. See also H. Pohlendt, *Die Verbreitung der mittelalterlichen Wüstungen in Deutschland* (Göttingen, 1950).

5   M. Born, *Die Entwicklung der deutschen Agrarlandschaft* (Darmstadt, 1974), pp. 22–4; H. Jäger, 'Wüstungsforschung in geographischer und historischer Sicht', in H. Jankuhn and R. Wenskus, eds, *Geschichtswissenschaft und Archäologie* (Sigmaringen, 1979), pp. 193–240; Jäger, *Entwicklungsprobleme europäischer Kulturlandschaften* (Darmstadt, 1987).

6   Born, *Agrarlandschaft*, pp. 68–71; W. Abel, ed., *Wüstungen in Deutschland* (Frankfurt a. M., 1967); W. Prange, *Siedlungsgeschichte des Landes Lauenburg im Mittelalter* (Neumünster, 1960); K. Wanner, *Siedlungen, Kontinuität und Wüstungen im nördlichen Kanton Zürich, 9.–15. Jahrhundert* (Berne/Frankfurt a. M., 1984).

7   Abel, *Wüstungen*, p. 66; Born, *Agrarlandschaft*, p. 69.

8   For the various theories on the causes of settlement desertion, Abel, *Wüstungen*, pp. 84–119.

9   W. Abel, *Agrarkrisen und Agrarkonjunktur*, 3rd edn (Hamburg/Berlin, 1978), pp. 57–103; idem, *Strukturen und Krisen der spätmittelalterlichen Wirtschaft* (Stuttgart/New York, 1980). On the crisis of the later middle ages in general, F. Graus, 'Vom Schwarzen Tod zur Reformation. Der krisenhafte Charakter des europäischen Spätmittelalters' in P. Blickle, ed., *Revolte und Revolution in Europe* (Munich, 1975), pp. 10–30; F. Seibt and W. Eberhard, eds, *Europa 1400. Die Krise des Spätmittelalters* (Stuttgart, 1984); L. Genicot, 'Crisis: From the Middle Ages to Modern Times', in M. M. Postan, ed., *The Cambridge Economic History of Europe* I, 2nd edn (Cambridge, 1966), pp. 660–741.

10 See Abel, *Agrarkrisen*, p. 57 for a graph of the movements of grain prices in central Europe 1351–1550; F.-W. Henning, *Landwirtschaft und ländliche Gesellschaft in Deutschland* I (Paderborn, 1979), p. 149; B. H. Slicher van Bath, *The Agrarian History of Western Europe* (London, 1966), pp. 170–89.

11 See Abel, *Agrarkrisen*, p. 60 for a graph of price and wage movements in Frankfurt a. M. 1351–1525.

12 *Ibid.*, pp. 61–7; F. Lütge, 'Das 14./15. Jahrhundert in der Sozial- und Wirtschaftsgeschichte', in *Studien zur Sozial- und Wirtschaftsgeschichte* (Stuttgart, 1963), p. 303; U. Dirlmeier, *Untersuchungen zu Einkommensverhältnissen und Lebenshaltungskosten in oberdeutschen Städten des Spätmittelalters* (Heidelberg, 1978).

13 Abel, *Wüstungen*, p. 107; E. Isenmann, *Die deutsche Stadt im Spätmittelalter* (Stuttgart, 1988), pp. 388–91.

14 G. Franz, ed., *Quellen zur Geschichte des deutschen Bauernstandes im Mittelalter*, 2nd edn (Darmstadt, 1974), pp. 468–71.
15 On the inflationary crisis in general, Abel, *Agrarkrisen*, pp. 22–6; idem, *Strukturen*, pp. 63–8.
16 *Ibid.*, pp. 85–95.
17 See W. Abel, *Geschichte der deutschen Landwirtschaft vom frühen Mittelalter bis zum 19. Jahrhundert*, 3rd edn (Stuttgart, 1978), pp. 118–22; F. Irsigler, 'Intensivwirtschaft, Sonderkulturen und Gartenbau als Elemente der Kulturlandschaftsgestaltung in den Rheinlanden (13.–16. Jahrhundert)', in *Atti della Undicesima Settimana di Studio: Agricoltura e trasformasione dell'ambiente secoli XIII–XVIII* (Prato, 1984), pp. 719–47.
18 L. Carlen, 'Allmende', in *Lexikon des Mittelalters* I (Munich, 1980), pp. 439–40; K. S. Bader, *Dorfgenossenschaft und Dorfgemeinde*, 2nd edn (Vienna/Cologne, 1974), pp. 119–29; A. Timm, *Die Waldnutzung in Nordwestdeutschland im Spiegel der Weistümer* (Cologne/Graz, 1960).
19 W. Abel, 'Wandlungen des Fleischverbrauchs und der Fleischversorgung in Deutschland seit dem ausgehenden Mittelalter', *Berichte über Landwirtschaft* XXII (1938), pp. 414–16; Abel, *Strukturen*, p. 41.
20 Dirlmeier, *Untersuchungen*, p. 363. However, Dirlmeier does not doubt in principle that there was an increase in meat consumption during the later middle ages.
21 *Ibid.*, pp. 357–64.
22 W. Rösener, 'Grundherrschaften des Hochadels in Südwestdeutschland im Spätmittelalter', in H. Patze, ed., *Die Grundherrschaft im späten Mittelalter* II (Sigmaringen, 1983), p. 149; H. Jänichen, *Beiträge zur Wirtschaftsgeschichte des schwäbischen Dorfes* (Stuttgart, 1970), p. 182.
23 On this, Abel, *Landwirtschaft*, pp. 128–32; Henning, *Landwirtschaft* I, p. 162.
24 H. Ammann, 'Die Anfänge der Leinenindustrie des Bodenseegebiets', *Alemannisches Jb.* (1953), pp. 251–313; W. von Stromer, *Die Gründung der deutschen Baumwollindustrie in Mitteleuropa* (Stuttgart, 1978).
25 On fruit-growing, Abel, *Landwirtschaft*, p. 129; F. J. Mone, 'Über den Obstbau vom 8. bis 16. Jahrhundert', ZGO XIII (1861), pp. 257–73.
26 See Abel, *Landwirtschaft*, p. 130 for a map of viticulture in Germany. See also F. von Bassermann-Jordan, *Geschichte des Weinbaus* I, 2nd edn (Frankfurt a. M., 1923), pp. 114–48; M. Barth, *Der Rebbau des Elsass und die Absatzgebiete seiner Weine* I (Strasburg, 1958), pp. 37–9.
27 See Lütge, *Das 14./15. Jahrhundert*, pp. 323–5; W. Rösener, *Bauern im Mittelalter*, 3rd edn (Munich, 1987), pp. 260–3; G. Bois, 'Noblesse et crise des revenus seigneuriaux en France aux XIVe et XVe siècles. Essai d'interpretation', in P. Contamine, ed., *La Noblesse au Moyen Âge, XIe–XVe siècles* (Paris, 1976), pp. 219–33; R. Sablonier, 'Zur wirtschaftlichen Situation des Adels im Spätmittelalter', in *Adelige Sachkultur des Spätmittelalters. Internationaler Kongreß Krems an der Donau 22. bis 25. September 1980* (Vienna, 1982), Veröffentlichungen der Österreichischen Akademie der Wissenschaften, Phil.- hist. Klase, Sitzungsberichte 400, pp. 9–34.
28 On the higher nobility, H. Maulhardt, *Die wirtschaftlichen Grundlagen der Grafschaft Katzenelnbogen im 14. und 15. Jahrhundert* (Darmstadt/Marburg, 1980); Rösener, 'Grundherrschaften', pp. 87–176. On the lower nobility, A. Bickel, *Die Herren von Hallwil im Mittelalter* (Aarau, 1978); W. Frese, *Die Herren von Schönau. Ein Beitrag zur Geschichte des oberrheinischen Adels* (Freiburg/Munich, 1975).
29 H.-P. Sattler, *Die Ritterschaft der Ortenau in der spätmittelalterlichen Wirtschaftskrise* (diss., Heidelberg, 1962).
30 K. Andermann, *Studien zur Geschichte des pfälzischen Niederadels im späten*

Mittelalter (Speyer, 1982).

31 F. Irsigler, 'Adelige Wirtschaftsführung im Spätmittelalter', in J. Schneider, ed., *Festschrift für Hermann Kellenbenz* I (Stuttgart, 1978), pp. 455–68.

32 W. Rösener, 'Zur Problematik des spätmittelalterlichen Raubrittertums', in H. Maurer and H. Patze, eds, *Festschrift für Berent Schwineköper* (Sigmaringen, 1982), pp. 469–88; R. Görner, *Raubritter. Untersuchungen zur Lage des spätmittelalterlichen Niederadels, besonders im südlichen Westfalen* (Münster, 1987).

33 Lütge, 'Das 14./15. Jahrhundert', pp. 281–335; idem, *Deutsche Sozial- und Wirtschaftsgeschichte*, 3rd edn (Berlin, 1966), pp. 200–11.

34 Lütge, 'Das 14./15. Jahrhundert', p. 333.

35 G. Bois, *Crise du féodalisme* (Paris, 1976); P. Kriedte, 'Spätmittelalterliche Agrarkrise oder Krise des Feudalismus?', *GG* VII (1981), pp. 42–68; R. Hilton, 'A Crisis of Feudalism', *P&P* 80 (1978), pp. 3–19.

36 J. Kuczynski, 'Einige Überlegungen über die Rolle der Natur in der Gesellschaft analäßlich der Lektüre von Abels Buch über Wüstungen', *JbWG* (1963), III, pp. 284–97.

37 Abel, *Wüstungen*, pp. 125–37; W. Rösener, 'Zur sozialökonomischen Lage der bäuerlichen Bevölkerung im Spätmittelalter', in *Bäuerliche Sachkultur des Spätmittelalters* (Vienna, 1984), Veröffentlichungen der Österreichischen Akademie der Wissenschaften, Phil.-hist. Klasse, Sitzungsberichte 439, pp. 9–47; H. Rubner, 'Die Landwirtschaft der Münchener Ebene und ihre Notlage im 14. Jahrhundert', *VSWG* LI (1964), pp. 433–53; O. Sigg, 'Spätmittelalterliche Agrarkrise', *SchweizZG* XXXI (1981), pp. 121–43.

38 P. Blickle, 'Agrarkrise und Leibeigenschaft im spätmittelalterlichen deutschen Südwesten', in H. Kellenbenz, ed., *Agrarisches Nebengewerbe und Formen der Reagrarisierung im Spätmittelalter und 19./20. Jahrhundert* (Stuttgart, 1975), pp. 39–55; H.-M. Maurer, 'Masseneide gegen Abwanderung im 14. Jahrhundert', *ZWLG* XXXIX (1980), pp. 30–99.

39 C. Ulbricht, *Leibherrschaft am Oberrhein im Spätmittelalter* (Göttingen, 1979), pp. 84–102.

40 Lütge, 'Das 14./15. Jahrhundert', pp. 327–9; Henning, *Landwirtschaft* I, pp. 165–72; W. Prange, 'Die Entwicklung der adligen Eigenwirtschaft in Schleswig-Holstein', in H. Patze, ed., *Die Grundherrschaft im späten Mittelalter* I (Sigmaringen, 1983), pp. 519–54.

41 Abel, *Landwirtschaft*, pp. 158–9; H. Lutz, *Reformation und Gegenreformation*, 2nd edn (Munich, 1982), p. 7; P. Kriedte, *Spätfeudalismus und Handelskapital* (Göttingen, 1980), pp. 28–31; R. Mols, 'Population in Europe 1500–1700', in C. M. Cipolla, ed., *The Fontana Economic History of Europe* II (London, 1976), pp. 15–82.

42 F. Körner, 'Die Bevölkerungsverteilung in Thüringen am Ausgang des 16. Jahrhunderts', *Wissenschaftliche Veröffentlichungen des Deutschen Institutes für Länderkunde* XV–XVI (Leipzig, 1958), pp. 178–315.

43 K. Blaschke, *Bevölkerungsgeschichte von Sachsen bis zur Industriellen Revolution* (Weimar, 1967), p. 85.

44 Born, *Agrarlandschaft*, p. 75.

45 Abel, *Landwirtschaft*, pp. 159–65; Born, *Agrarlandschaft*, pp. 73–84.

46 H. Mortensen and G. Mortensen, *Die Besiedlung des nordöstlichen Ostpreußen bis zum Beginn des 17. Jahrhunderts* (2 vols., Leipzig, 1937–8).

47 Abel, *Agrarkrisen*, p. 109, with a map of land reclamation on the Baltic coast.

48 See H.-J. Nitz, 'Frühneuzeitliche Wiederbesiedlung von Wüstungen im südniedersächsischen Grenzraum', in D. Brosius and M. Last, eds, *Beiträge zur niedersächsischen Landesgeschichte* (Hildesheim, 1984), pp. 1–25.

49 W. Kuhn, *Geschichte der deutschen Ostsiedlung in der Neuzeit* I

(Cologne/Graz, 1955), pp. 110–12.

50   Abel, *Agrarkrisen*, p. 122; Kriedte, *Spätfeudalismus*, pp. 63–78; H. Kellenbenz, *Deutsche Wirtschaftsgeschichte* I (Munich, 1977), pp. 213–22; F. Lütge, 'Die wirtschaftliche Lage Deutschlands vor Ausbruch des Dreißigjährigen Krieges', in *Studien zur Sozial- und Wirtschaftsgeschichte* (Stuttgart, 1963), pp. 336–95.

51   Abel, *Agrarkrisen*, p. 122.

52   *Ibid.*, pp. 124–7.

53   Kriedte, *Spätfeudalismus*, pp. 65–7.

54   Abel, *Agrarkrisen*, p. 125.

55   See Rösener, *Bauern*, pp. 272–6; idem, 'Zur sozialökonomischen Lage', pp. 9–47.

56   Abel, *Landwirtschaft*, pp. 197–201.

57   O. Fahlbusch, *Der Landkreis Göttingen in seiner geschichtlichen, rechtlichen und wirtschaftlichen Entwicklung* (Göttingen, 1960), p. 95.

58   D. Vogellehner, 'Garten', in *Lexikon des Mittelalters* IV (Munich, 1989), pp. 1122–4.

59   Irsigler, 'Intensivwirtschaft', pp. 719–47.

60   *Ibid.*, pp. 725–8.

61   On the international cattle trade in the sixteenth century, H. Wiese and J Bölts, *Rinderhandel und Rinderhaltung in norwestdeutschen Küstengebieten vom 15. bis zum 19. Jahrhundert* (Stuttgart, 1966); E. Westermann, ed., *Internationaler Ochsenhandel, 1350–1750* (Stuttgart, 1979); O. Pickl, 'Routen, Umfang und Organisation des innereuropäischen Handels mit Schlachtvieh im 16. Jahrhundert', in A. Novotny and O. Pickl, eds, *Festschrift Hermann Wiesflecker* (Graz, 1973), pp. 143–66.

62   Conrad Heresbach, *Rei Rusticae Libri Quattuor* (1570); Martin Grosser, *Kurtze und gar einfaltige anleytung der Landwirtschaft: beydes im Ackerbau und in der Viehzucht. Nach Arth und Gelegenheit dieses Land und Orth Schlesien* (1590); Johann Coler, *Oeconomia ruralis et domestica* (1593).

63   See G. Schröder-Lembke, 'Die Hausväterliteratur als agrargeschichtliche Quelle', *ZAgrarGAgrarSoz* I (1953), pp. 109–19; Abel, *Landwirtschaft*, pp. 168–72.

64   Irsigler, 'Intensivkultur', pp. 725–8.

65   See Slicher van Bath, *Agrarian History*, pp. 246–8; A. Verhulst, *Précis d'histoire rurale de la Belgique* (Brussels, 1990), pp. 140–50.

66   W. A. Boelcke, 'Bäuerlicher Wohlstand in Württemberg Ende des 16. Jahrhunderts', *Jb. für Nationalökonomie und Statistik* CLXXVI (1964), pp. 241–80.

67   T. Robisheaux, *Rural Society and the Search for Order in Early Modern Germany* (Cambridge, 1989).

68   C. Heimpel, *Die Entwicklung der Einnahmen und Ausgaben des Heiliggeistspitals zu Biberach an der Riß von 1500 bis 1630* (Stuttgart, 1966), pp. 19–21.

69   D. W. Sabean, *Landbesitz und Gesellschaft am Vorabend des Bauernkrieges* (Stuttgart, 1972), p. 24.

70   I. Richarz, *Herrschaftliche Haushalte in vorindustrieller Zeit im Weserraum* (Berlin, 1971), pp. 200–1.

71   Abel, *Agrarkrisen*, pp. 111–14; Kriedte, *Spätfeudalismus*, pp. 39–44; I. Wallerstein, *The Modern World System* I (New York, 1974); H. Rosenberg, 'Die Ausprägung der Junkerherrschaft im Brandenburg-Preußen, 1410–1618', in *Machteliten und Wirtschaftskonjunkturen* (Göttingen, 1978), pp. 24–82.

72   W. Abel, 'Verdorfung und Gutsbildung in Deutschland zu Beginn der Neuzeit', *Geografiska Annaler* XLIII (1961), pp. 1–7; H.-H. Wächter, *Ostpreußische Domänenvorwerke im 16. und 17. Jahrhundert* (Würzburg, 1958); H.

Harnisch, 'Die Gutsherrschaft in Brandenburg. Ergebnisse und Probleme', *JbWG* (1969), IV, pp. 117–47; idem, 'Die Gutsherrschaft. Forschungsgeschichte, Entwicklungszusammenhänge und Strukturelemente', *JbG-Feudalismus* IX (1985), pp. 189–240; idem, 'Probleme einer Periodisierung und regionalen Typisierung der Gutsherrschaft im mitteleuropäischen Raum', *JbGFeudalismus* 10 (1986), pp. 251–74.

73 S. Korth, *Die Entstehung und Entwicklung des ostdeutschen Großgrundbesitzes* (diss. Göttingen, 1952).

74 M. North, 'Untersuchungen zur adligen Gutswirtschaft im Herzogtum Preußen im 16. Jahrhundert', *VSWG* LXX (1983), pp. 1–20; idem, *Die Amtswirtschaften von Osterode und Soldau. Vergleichende Untersuchungen zur Wirtschaft im frühmodernen Staat am Beispiel des Herzogtums Preußen in der zweiten Hälfte des 16. und in der ersten Hälfte des 17. Jahrhunderts* (Berlin, 1982).

75 Lütge, *Sozialgeschichte*, pp. 116–27; idem, *Agrarverfassung*, pp. 188–200.

76 See F. Steinbach, 'Die rheinischen Agrarverhältnisse', in F. Petri and G. Droege, eds, *Collectanea Franz Steinbach* (Bonn, 1967), pp. 409–33; C. Reinecke, *Agrarkonjunktur und technisch-organisatorische Innovationen auf dem Agrarsektor im Spiegel niederrheinischer Pachtverträge 1200–1600* (Cologne/Vienna, 1989).

77 Lütge, *Agrarverfassung*, pp. 199–221.

78 See W. Rösener, 'Die spätmittelalterliche Grundherrschaft im südwestdeutschen Raum als Problem der Sozialgeschichte', *ZGO* CXXVII (1979), pp. 40–2; H. Patze, ed., *Die Grundherrschaft im späten Mittelalter*, (2 vols,) Sigmaringen, 1983).

79 See W. Wittich, *Die Grundherrschaft in Nordwestdeutschland* (Leipzig, 1896), pp. 379–95; D. Saalfeld, *Bauernwirtschaft und Gutsbetrieb in der vorindustriellen Zeit* (Stuttgart, 1960), pp. 16–20; M. von Boetticher, 'Nordwestdeutsche Grundherrschaft zwischen Frühkapitalismus und Refeudalisierung', *BdLG* CXXII (1986), pp. 207–28.

80 Saalfeld, *Bauernwirtschaft*, p. 18; C. Gisenius. *Das Meierrecht mit vorzüglicher Hinsicht auf den Wolfenbüttelschen Teil des Herzogtums Braunschweig-Lüneburg* I (Wolfenbüttel, 1801), pp. 465–7.

81 Wittich, *Grundherrschaft*, p. 388; Lütge, *Agrarverfassung*, pp. 190–2.

82 See Rösener, *Bauern*, p. 201 for a map of the regional variations in peasant inheritance customs in central Europe; H. Röhm, *Die Vererbung des landwirtschaftlichen Grundeigentums in Baden-Württemberg* (Remagen, 1957), pp. 66–96; J. Goody, J. Thirsk, and E. P. Thompson, eds, *Family and Inheritance. Rural Society in Western Europe, 1200–1800* (Cambridge, 1976).

83 Abel, *Landwirtschaft*, pp. 165–8.

84 See Lütge, *Agrarverfassung*, p. 188; G. Heitz, 'Zum Charakter der "zweiten Leibeigenschaft"', *Zeitschrift für Geschichtswissenschaft* XX (1972), pp. 24–39; idem, 'Die Differenzierung der Agrarstruktur am Vorabend der bürgerlichen Agrarreformen', *Zeitschrift für Geschichtswissenschaft* XV (1977), pp. 910–27; Harnisch, 'Gutsherrschaft', pp. 189–240; M. North, 'Die frühneuzeitliche Gutswirtschaft in Schleswig-Holstein. Forschungsüberblick und Entwicklungsfaktoren', *BdLG* CXXVI (1990), pp. 223–42; W. Rösener, *The Peasantry of Europe* (Oxford, 1994), pp. 104–24.

85 See Henning, *Landwirtschaft* I, p. 175; Lütge, *Sozialgeschichte*, pp. 215–17.

Translated by Bob Scribner.

4

Diet and Consumption

ULF DIRLMEIER AND GERHARD FOUQUET

The state of current research

Nutrition is undoubtedly one of the essential preconditions of human life. It is of exceptionally short duration, and is a cultural item that has to be reproduced on a daily basis. Consumption and dietary habits, the production of foodstuffs, their processing, conservation, transport, sale, and preparation are therefore a direct expression both of mundane life and of festive culture. Changes in the composition, quality, and quantity of nutrition are general manifestations of broad ecological, social, economic, and religious structures and processes within the history of any civilization.[1] Research in the Germanophone world on the history of diet and foodstuffs began in significant measure after the Second World War, and was driven forward especially by agrarian and economic history,[2] as well as by historical ethnology, medieval archaeology, and historical anthropology.[3] The theme certainly does not belong to *petite histoire*, to one of the bypaths of history, even if it does not obviously fit into any of the main fields of traditional historiography.[4]

There is no specialist history of diet and nutrition for Germany. The most recent research, by uncovering and evaluating new sources, has certainly been able to show that the stock picture of a monotonous and unvarying medieval diet does not at all correspond with reality, and that depictions of excessive consumption in the fifteenth and sixteenth centuries, 'the age of gluttony and inebriation', have been misleadingly generalized. Studies of both the qualitative and the quantitative aspects of diet have established the status-related functions of eating and drinking, and have emphasized the strongly 'differentiated consumptive habits and possibilities for consumption of the later middle ages'.[5]

From the end of the thirteenth century, information for the history of diet increases considerably in both its volume and detail. Narrative sources begin to provide pre-statistical data about the overall consumption of cities such as Florence, Nuremberg, and St Gallen. Chronicles contain observations about climate, harvest conditions, and prices, and describe the course of crises in food supply.[6] In addition, there are victualling ordinances, lists of provisions, foodstock inventories, accounts from both great ecclesiastical and secular households, and occasionally private household account books.[7] Numerous medical-dietary tracts and cookbooks also survive from the fourteenth century onwards.[8] In recent years these written sources have increasingly been supplemented by research findings in medieval archaeology, palaeobotany and palaeozoology, as well in historical anthropology (excavations of skeletons, evaluation of animal bones, vegetable remains, refuse pits, and latrines).[9]

Despite the possibilities now available for quantitative evaluation, there remain considerable areas of uncertainty. For example, lists of consumption taxes and similar documents allow calculation of the average consumption of large groups of a given population, but this remains a mere fiction unless it can be related to the social structure of the population under discussion.[10] The very detailed information which is sometimes found in accounts from private households usually concerns only small groups of consumers, and there is a problem of how far one can generalize on the basis of such information. Moreover, entries usually relate only to the purchase and cost of certain quantities of goods, but say nothing about their preparation and consumption.[11] Attempts in English, French, and German research to calculate from extant figures of the food supplied to large households the adequacy and nutritional balance (calories, vitamens, trace elements) in the medieval diet are marked by very large areas of uncertainty.[12] In general, we should note that both written sources and those drawn from material culture concentrate on princely courts, noble castles, ecclesiastical institutions, and towns. The dietary situation of the majority of the population who lived in the rural world is largely a matter of speculation and inference.[13]

Changes in dietary habits

From the thirteenth until the end of the sixteenth century, we can certainly discern changes in dietary habits, although their speed and extent lag well behind those which have occurred in recent history. The long-term persistence of systems of nutrition can be regarded as typical for traditional pre-industrial societies. Despite undeniable shifts in consumption patterns during the fourteenth, fifteenth, and sixteenth centuries, grain-based diets were still dominant in Germany, as well as in Europe as a whole, as the

most important form of calorific intake. This fact remains valid well
beyond the middle ages, indeed, until the revolution in consumption habits
that followed industrialization.[14] Despite the basic unity in the structure
of nutrition, regional differences were strengthened during the later middle
ages. Over and above this, consumption of foodstuffs became an important
status symbol in the accelerating process of social differentiation, especially
in the towns. For example, there were zones distinguished by their
dominant or exclusive consumption of wine or beer, a distinction that was
established largely by natural and local features such as the possibility of
cultivation or production (including climate and soil conditions). It was as
a result of consumer demand that there developed from the end of the thirteenth century market-oriented areas of viticulture in the climatically
favourable regions of the Rhine, the Main, the Moselle, and the Neckar.
The growth of the market for wine was only reversed around the middle
of the fifteenth century by mass consumption of quality beer in northern
Germany. Einbeck and the Baltic coastal towns developed their typical
forms of petty production into early centres of beer production. Even in
the fourteenth century, Hamburg was already known as the 'brewery of
the Hansa', and large quantities of beer were exported from there to
England, the Low Countries and the Lower Rhine. Improvements in
flavour by the use of high-quality, long-life varieties of hopped beers led
to the gradual displacement of sweeter and more easily spoiled *Grutbier*.
The comparatively low price of this mass-produced beer also led, from the
beginning of the sixteenth century, to widespread consumption of these
beers in the south of Germany. From 1613 a so-called *ainpöckisch* beer
was being brewed in the Munich Hofbräuhaus (court brewery) founded in
1589, the same as today's *Bockbier*.[15] Equally influenced by demand were
changes in grain consumption: increasingly, wheat and rye were consumed
in south Germany, but predominantly rye in north Germany, while grains
such as barley, oats, and millet, and other inferior types, became less significant in human diet, except in periods of dearth. The so-called 'Price
Revolution' occasioned by rapid monetary devaluation in the sixteenth
century led consumers from the urban lower and middle classes in south
German regions to turn increasingly to consumption of the cheaper rye,
which replaced wheat and animal products from the 1560s onwards.[16]

During the thirteenth century, continual population pressure had led to
the expansion of grain cultivation into marginal soils; but in the fourteenth
and fifteenth centuries, the growing demand of urban markets and the
increasing number of consumers with relatively strong purchasing power
furthered the development of specialized agriculture through the expansion
of market gardening in the immediate vicinity of the towns,[17] and through
increased production of animal products for consumption in zones of
intensive grassland farming (the Alps, the Mittelgebirge, coastal plains). In
Germany, as in central Europe as a whole, beef and pork were gradually
preferred to sheep meat (lamb and mutton). Game played a very minor

role as a form of meat supply, even for the nobility. In the sixteenth century the demand for beef, seen against the background of an expanding population, could only be met by a growing trade in cattle from Jutland, Denmark, Russia, Poland, and Hungary.[18] None the less the average consumption of meat at the end of the sixteenth century was considerably less than that of the fifteenth. Influenced by constant price rises and simultaneously stagnating or falling real wages (the so-called 'wage–price scissors'), the demand for meat, butter, and cheese, all relatively dependent on income levels, diminished in favour of an equally expensive cereal diet, albeit one richer in calorific content.[19] The consequences of this development for agrarian production in Germany during the sixteenth century were considerable: with the exception of the grassland regions on the North Sea and Baltic littoral, there was an expansion of arable for grain production at the expense of stock-raising. Such changes were accelerated considerably by general climatic deterioration after 1560: long, snowbound winters and wet summers led to cattle epidemics, to decimation and weakening of cattle stocks, and to collapse of milk production. At the same time, greater rainfall led to increased drainage of nutrients from the soil, which, together with the reduced availability of animal manure, produced falling yield ratios; this in turn was compensated for by expanding ploughland at the expense of pasturage, and by turning to intensive forms of agriculture such as improved crop rotation.[20]

There is absolutely no doubt that the demographic changes between the first half of the fourteenth century and the renewed population expansion of the early sixteenth century enabled consumers to switch to a more nutritious diet, a direct consequence of the changed relationship of land and population and of broad economic conditions. Bread became more refined, there was more meat and other animal products on the table, consumption of beer and wine became more common, freshwater fish and expensive imported spices were consumed in considerable quantities. This trend in consumptive habits also continued unabated throughout the sixteenth century, at least among social elites, and was further accentuated by the import of new and more luxurious items of consumption from the Americas and the West Indies and by more sophisticated culinary skills. None the less, we must be careful not to accept the idea that excessive consumption, or even an early form of an affluent consumer society, was prevalent at the end of the later middle ages and the beginning of the modern period, since the trend conceals a range of widely varying circumstances. We have already indicated that there were broad social changes in meat consumption, while the most noteworthy development of the period under discussion was the dramatic contrast between town and country, a phenomenon emerging since the high middle ages and one which was most marked in the field of nutrition. Coarse and heavy black bread, sometimes eked out with beans and other supplements, characterized the rural diet, while refined white bread in the towns was part and parcel of a self-conscious awareness on the part of townsfolk of different social status, a contrast that even found literary and visual expression in mockery of 'unrefined' peasant eating habits. It was a consequence both of the town's central function as a market and of its conscious economic policy to the detriment of rural producers that all the evidence points to the average consumption in towns being qualitatively and quantitatively better than that in the countryside.[21] Symptomatic of this relationship is the fact that rural inhabitants migrated to the towns during the hunger crises of the later middle ages because the available supplies there offered better chances of survival.[22]

Meals

Adequate daily rations during the later middle ages were made up of two meals: a morning meal (*imbs, prandium*) and an evening meal (*cena*). The earlier repast was taken, according to the season of the year, between 9 and 10.30 a.m., while one sat down for the evening meal at dusk. In addition, there were up to three intermediate mealtimes, conditioned by the seasonally determined length of the working day (sunrise to sunset): a 'morning soup' (*Morgensuppe*), an evening snack (*Abendbrot*), and a nightcap (*Schlaftrunk*). The main daily meals were relatively protracted by modern standards, and could last as long as two hours for the elite classes. The high value placed on eating in all classes of medieval society is undeniable, although the number of mealtimes should be understood as the consequence, not of greed, but of the length of the working day and the relative monotony of medieval daily working life.[23]

The five (and sometimes more) meals usually consisted of bread, gruel or mash made from grains or pulses, boiled meat, cabbage, soup, and wine or beer, more rarely mead.[24] Bread, mash or grits, and wine or beer were the basic ingredients of the main meals, except for the meals of the poor. Thus Thomas Platter of Basel in 1529 acquired a cask of wine before his household was properly set up, emphasizing thereby that it lasted for a long time and that he and his wife had never eaten without bread and wine 'no matter how poor we were'.[25] Despite the regularly recurring basic ingredients in the composition of meals, the frequently heard generalization that late medieval meals were monotonous is quite untrue. Equally incorrect is the assumption that during the fourteenth and fifteenth centuries differences in social status, festive meals excepted, were expressed largely in the quantity and regularity of consumption, but not in the quality or variety of the diet.[26]

These claims could be proven by numerous examples, but here we shall have to be content to refer only to a few.[27] Certainly, alongside more general indicators such as the predominance of references to the price of grain and wine in medieval chronicles, numerous accounts and provisioning lists speak in favour of the dominance of a few basic foodstuffs.[28] Thus, the *béguines* in Braunschweig's St Jodocus Hospice were nourished above all on bread, grits, pork or salt herring, and beer.[29] In Augsburg, during the time of danger from the Armagnacs in 1443, Burkard Zink provided himself with corn, wine, lard, and meat, and whatever else he considered necessary.[30] Even in the household accounts of the wealthy Nuremberger Paul Behaim one finds in 1548/9 under the entry 'foodstuffs' only the statement: 'that which one consumes daily, such as meat, fish, bread, beets, cabbage and other things'. However, the addendum 'and other things' found in Behaim, and similar words in Zink, indicate that such enumerations were far from complete.[31] And one certainly finds in more detailed lists and stipulations a far greater variety of foodstuffs. A rich assortment of foods has been recorded by Ulrich Richental in a list of the foodstuffs on sale in the market during the Council of Constance: white bread, pretzels and bread rings, and various pies are mentioned, followed by oats for porridge and five further kinds of porridge, alongside the sweeping statement that there was still more. Among the fresh vegetables Richental lists onions, beets, and two kinds of cabbage. In addition, six different kinds of wine of varying quality are enumerated. Most detailed is the list, provided in such specification that it is too long to recount here, of the meat on sale – all fresh and including poultry and game, as well as different kinds of fish, largely fresh.[32]

This list certainly cannot be taken to represent any normal situation, but a series of other sources indicate that the daily life of the late medieval consumer was characterized by an extraordinary variation in eating habits. In 1483 a set of accounts was produced for the tithe farm (*Zehnthof*) of the duke of Bavaria in Heilbronn, showing the foodstuffs required to feed the workers for the wine harvest. These Heilbronn fieldworkers were offered a wide range of food: white bread maslin for bread, barley, peas, oatmeal, millet, salt, pork lard, milk (butter-) lard, meat for boiling or roasting, cheese, milk, cabbage, oats, turnips, eggs, semolina, fish, stockfish, herring, onions, apples, cooking pears, and spices.[33] Daily consumptive habits were reflected in the consumption of foodstuffs for the troops of the imperial city of Rothenburg on the Tauber in the Swiss War of 1499. Naturally, bread, wine, and meat were the most common items bought and consumed. For meat the Rothenburgers preferred beef and mutton, but occasionally they also ate veal, fowl, chickens, and tripe; however, pork was completely absent from this menu. In terms of frequency of purchase, the descending order of preference was: fish, preferably freshwater fish where it could be identified, then eggs, cheese, and milk, fresh vegetables and fruit, especially cherries, flour once or twice a week, probably for porridge. Expensive imported goods such as sugar, raisins, cloves, and sweet calamus were only rarely purchased.[34]

Fast days and fasting

Daily consumptive habits were strongly influenced by ecclesiastical pre-scriptions, and offences against the obligatory fast laws could also lead to heavy fines from the secular authorities. Two or three days a week were prescribed for abstinence from meat – Friday and Saturday, and in some regions Wednesday as well – although meat could be replaced by fish and eggs. However, during the strictly observed Lenten fast and on remaining fast days, which could vary regionally, eggs and butter were also forbidden, alongside meat. Admittedly, dispensations were obtainable from the papal curia or from legates equipped with special powers of dispensation, as well as from bishops from the middle of the sixteenth century. These dispen-sations freed the holder from observing the fast from dairy foods, enabling the consumption of butter and other dairy foods, although sometimes excluding cheese. The most commonly cited ground for dispensation was the high prices of permissible foodstuffs, which included olive oil, almonds, and figs. However, the prohibition of meat and eggs was difficult to avoid. The so-called 'butter-letters' (*Butterbriefe*), dispensations from abstinence, were especially widespread from the middle of the fifteenth to the beginning of the sixteenth century, especially in south Germany.[35] At the beginning of the sixteenth century the household accounts of the Nuremberger Anton Tucher have numerous entries each year concerning the 'lard' which the family and servants had eaten on fast days.[36]

The stipulations for fasting were abolished by the Reformation, although Protestant religious practice was to retain fast days in general until the middle of the eighteenth century. For example, menus from hospices in Protestant towns attest that Fridays and Saturdays were still observed as fast days, and the same is known of princely courts in the sixteenth century.[37] On the other hand, there are sources such as the Villingen chronicle of Heinrich Hug, admittedly a traditional Catholic, who ascribed rising meat prices in 1527 to non-observance of the prescribed fast days in Strasbourg, where one ate meat on Fridays and Saturdays, showing that fast days had certainly declined in Protestant territories.[38] This conclusion is supported by the meat ordinances issued by the Rappen mint ordinance of 1555 on the Upper Rhine, also accepted by Protestant members of the association, which stated that 'because of the generally remarked shortage of meat' one should 'abstain from meat during Lent and on other days on which the abstinence has been traditionally observed, and no meat should be butchered or sold'.[39] In general, we can say that there was no decisive change in consumptive habits from the pre-Reformation period until the end of the sixteenth century.

An overall estimate of the fast days prescribed by the late medieval church whose general observance can be attested from accounts and

150
fast Days
a year

culinary ordinances comes to between 210 and 220 'meat-days' and around 150 corresponding fast days.[40] In general, meat was replaced on days of abstinence by relatively cheap preserved fish, of which dried, smoked, or salted sea fish such as salt-herring, bloaters, or stockfish were favoured even by inland consumers.[41] Alongside Lübeck, which long held the dominant role in trade with Norwegian stockfish, Cologne was an important market for sea fish, and on the basis of its staple rights and its well-functioning quality control it developed into the central market for the German South and West. Cologne merchants, who often combined trade in fish with that in wine, were often found in Frankfurt, Strasbourg, Schlettstadt, and Basel fish was shipped from Cologne to Nuremberg, Rottweil, and Augsburg, while the court of the Elector Palatine in Heidelberg at the end of the fifteenth and beginning of the sixteenth century met its annual needs for fish from the Cologne fish market.[42] Insofar as an individual household could afford it, expensive freshwater fish was also purchased for fast days, although there was a wide range of prices from the much sought-after varieties of salmon and pike down to the cheaper crayfish. The considerable purchasing power of urban and noble consumers, alongside the fast regulations, clearly boosted demand for freshwater fish at the end of the middle ages, despite its high price. As a result, there was an expanding fish-farming economy in Bohemia, Silesia, Lusatia, the Upper Palatinate, Franconia, and Württemberg, on the Upper and Middle Rhine, in Lorraine, and in Holstein, especially in the hands of ecclesiastical institutions. These fish-ponds were farmed with pike, carp, and trout, using highly developed techniques and substantial investment of capital, and although there were seasonal fluctuations in demand, there were corresponding profits. In the bishopric of Speyer around the middle of the fifteenth century, the fish stocks of the Rhine were exploited alongside all castle moats for the production of fish for the table. From the late fourteenth century, the counts of Katzenelnbogen systematically acquired and exploited salmon-breeding grounds in the Middle Rhine. In towns such as Augsburg, Basel, and Soest, town councils had ponds and moats stocked with fish. Frankfurt developed into an important market for freshwater fish for the Upper and Middle Rhine regions.[43]

The norms of prescribed fast days determined the weekly and annual menus of all classes of the late medieval population in a wholly characteristic way. The differences in the quality and preparation of foods for fast days, however, were quite considerable. A poor pensioner in the Protestant Gutenleut hospice in Speyer received, according to the statutes of 1537, two eggs for breakfast on Fridays alongside bread and the usual porridge, as well as soup, fresh or preserved fish, and cheese. For the evening meal, a milk-based soup and a further two eggs were served. The Saturday menu was the same as that for Friday, except that either eggs or fish were cooked for the midday meal.[44] The richer pensioners in Bruchsal had the right to demand fish or eggs, and 'other foods with which respectable folk made do'.[45] The servants at the court of Count Joachim of Öttingen at the beginning of the sixteenth century received on prescribed fast days soup, cabbage, baked doughnuts, porridge, and milk. On days of general abstinence they were served much the same as on fast days for the midday meal, and for the evening meal there was soup, cooked turnips or pears, and porridge.[46] In the households of the social elites, on the other hand, a greater variation and different forms of preparation of varieties of fish meals were sought. At the table of Matthias von Rammung, bishop of Speyer, three fish dishes were served for the early meal and two for the evening meal. Pike and carp were exclusively reserved for the bishop's table. Preserved seafish hardly ever appeared on the episcopal menu, with the exception of herring, and was largely purchased for consumption by the servants.[47] We have evidence of an astonishing variety of fish dishes in the household of the Cologne patrician Hermann von Goch. Between 1391 and 1394 no fewer than 28 different fish varieties were purchased, all mentioned by name.[48]

In the households of the social elites, compensation for the absence of meat was sought in better-quality cakes, in which skilled chefs sought to imitate the forbidden foods. Foods for fast days were the figs and almonds imported from southern Europe, whose remains are attested in massive quantities in the rubbish heaps of north German towns and which can be considered as typical of the better sort of cooking. Figs and especially the fat-rich almonds were also cultivated in substantial quantities on the Upper Rhine. Using figs, almonds, ginger, flour, and sugar one could, for example, create an artificial kind of 'roast deer' for fast days. Especially popular were simpler dishes such as almond purée, figs cooked in wine and flavoured with almonds, or cooked rice with almond milk.[49]

Contemporary consumers were certainly aware from their own experience that fish was less filling and nourishing than meat. Moreover, food for fast days lacked the fats from butter and pork or beef lard, most commonly used in Germany and necessary to improve the flavour and nutrition offered by a vegetable-based diet. The oil-bearing plants offering alternatives such as poppy seeds, linseed, beet seed, or hempseed were too lacking in richness and, judging from the justifications offered for 'butter dispensations', were not quite to the taste of consumers. In large households one finds even in the pre-Reformation period some menus with cheese- or milk-based soups or egg dishes. On occasion it was also stipulated that the quantity of food eaten on fast days could be increased across the board.[50]

Food as a sign of social differentiation

Socially determined differences in consumption, including qualitative differences, are a particularly striking feature of (urban) society in the later
middle ages. The spectrum within the towns extends from the highly
spiced, multi-course festive meals of the merchant patriciate upper class
through to the really irredeemably monotonous diets of the poor. The
importance of food as a sign of social differentiation and as status symbol
is clearly discernible in terminology, even if a 'sign of social differentiation' can never quite be taken as any absolute criterion. Thus, one distinguished between 'common' foods and good foods; there were 'lords' foods'
and 'servants' wine', and 'lordly bread' (*panis dominicus*). There were
certainly contemporary presuppositions about appropriate, adequate, and
sumptuous nourishment, although the spectrum covered by the terms
'appropriate' or 'adequate' was great indeed. This is clear from the statutes
of hospices, which reflected contemporary notions of social differentiation
and in which the stipulated norms are confirmed by the actual foodstuffs
purchased.[51]

The lowest level of nutrition conceivable was a simple sequence of bread
and porridge, in which the porridge, cooked with some fat, supplied the
only warm meal. Consumption of this kind is encountered in the social
field concerned with poor relief.[52] Characteristically, the poorest levels of
pension in the hospices were designated as 'porridge pensions' or 'pot-
pensions'. However, poor nutritional circumstances can also be found in
the contractual agreements regulating the food provided for craft journeymen and day-labourers. For example, the numerous contracts of
employment extant from the turn of the fourteenth century for Freiburg,
in Üchtland, usually speak only of *victus*, which signifies the usual victuals,
especially porridge made from grain or legumes.[53] Mowers on Alsatian
manors were, according to statutes of the fifteenth century, given only
plentiful amounts of bread but nothing else, or else bread, cheese, and
wine, but no meat.[54] The variety, quantity and preparation of the accompaniment (*companaticum, companagium, küchenspeise*) reveals a broad
range of possibilities for upwards differentiation compared to this exclusively cereal-based diet.

Just how fluid this transition could be can be seen in provisions for the
poor, as evidenced in the statutes of hospices. In Lindau, for example, the
difference between the best-fed elite pensioners and that supplied to the
poor consisted only in greater provision of meat.[55] In other cases, there
was a varying number of weekly meat days. Thus, the 1542 statutes for
orphaned children in Constance decreed meat only on Sundays, while
invalids in the Wimpfen hospice were given meat meals twice a week.[56]
Three meat days a week was quite frequent, as is attested in the thirteenth

century in Trier and for the poor pensioners in Markgröningen.[57] However, for the more socially eminent and pensioners from the elite, five meat days was the rule. In this latter case, moreover, it was not exclusively boiled and therefore poor-quality meat, as was uniformly the case with food for the poor, but roasts, with fruit and fresh vegetables as accompaniments.[58]

One should also mention that there are also extant statutes which can by no means be fitted into the schema of a socially differentiated pattern of nutrition. Very striking examples are two dietary statutes of 1468 and 1540 for the poor and infirm inmates of the Strasbourg hospice, which could certainly match the meat meals and courses served on feast days to the elite pensioners, and which actually exceeded them in the allocation of eggs and fruit. The statutes of 1468 are especially detailed in this regard, providing the seriously ill with night-time meals of grapes, pears, apples, sloe compote, beetroot, cherries, mulberries, and dishes baked from eggs as a supplement during the day.[59] Without going into the problem of how far these statutes were put into practice, we should note that they do not relate to any ordinary daily diet, but to that of persons especially ill. However, these statutes certainly do confirm that medieval cuisine contained great variety as well as differences between daily and exceptional consumption.

The differences between poor and good nutrition were also strongly marked in the case of feeding craftsmen and servants. By contrast with the contracts of employment mentioned above, Hamburg carpenters, for example, were fed in 1465 with rye bread, wheat grits, light beer, butter, eggs, beef, herring, cod, and cheese. Bridge-builders in Basel in 1517–18, undertaking work at a time of floods, were provided with bread, meat, fish, cheese, and butter; carpenters in Marburg in 1522 were fed with fine white bread and beer.[60] The workers in the episcopal mill in Hildesheim were fed in a special kitchen at municipal expense and, alongside basic dishes, received foodstuffs purchased in bulk, such as sides of bacon, cheese, salt, butter, fat, and even an entire ox. Some beer was brewed by the mill-hands themselves, using hops provided by the town.[61] This kind of diet based on meat and animal fats was by no means the preserve of better-placed craftsmen and servants, but is also attested for those who were, in the terminology of the day, 'poor', that is, ordinary folk. Nuremberg building workers and day-labourers around the middle of the fifteenth century received their weekly wages on Saturday mornings so that 'the workers and the poor folk ... might be able to make their purchases of meat, bread and the like' in good time.[62] In 1491 during a period of dearth, the city of Nuremberg supplied so-called 'poor' citizens and day-labourers with basic necessities, namely bread, butter, salt, salt meat, fish, vegetables, and wine.[63] In Augsburg during price rises in 1533, the town council forbade the poor to consume bread, meat, and wine.[64] The feast held annually in his own home by the Nuremberg patrician Anton Tucher for poor inmates of the hospice, and for his own farmers from the countryside, corresponds to contemporary ideas about better levels of food, with its three 'good' courses of soup-meat, mutton, and grilled sausage.[65]

The difference in dietary terms between daily life and special occasions, hinted at in the last example from the level of the rural and lower classes, seems in the case of the upper classes to have known no bounds, especially with regard to luxury consumption and the food on offer. The daily repast at the lordly table of Bishop Matthias Rammung of Speyer consisted of three meat dishes for the morning meal, but for dietary reasons was confined to two at the evening meal. However, the meals were always composed of various kinds of roast meats, which would have been regarded by the poorer classes as a feast. The rich variety of the meat dishes, on which the bishop explicitly insisted, as well as the variety and quality of the accompaniments are typical of the meals of the social elites. However, it is noteworthy that the cold leftover roast from the early meal could be served up again in the evening, as long as there were no guests in the house. The bishop also insisted that his cook should make frugal use of expensive imported spices.[66]

However, according to this same bishop, there should be no limits imposed at a feast. In 1466 Bishop Matthias laid on a banquet for the city council to honour his formal entry which certainly followed this advice and was marked by luxury, refinement, and variation. After an entrée intended to emphasize the special nature of the event, consisting of legs of venison spiced with ginger and Malvasier, an expensive imported sweet wine from Greece, there were four starter courses in which two or three different meat or fish dishes alternated with a sweet dish. The main courses ascended from sausages to chicken, wild boar, pike, capon, and veal, leading up to an aspic of fish surpassing all the others as the end of the meal. For each course there was a selection of different wines, and finally an expensive dessert of confectionery and candied fruit served with brandy, a relatively rare drink for that time.[67]

Such banquets were not confined to the noble milieu. The urban elite could keep pace with the conspicuous consumption of noble feasting, thanks to its high spending power. The social significance of public feasting as a status symbol, and its political function as a means of confirming social order within its own sphere of influence, is quite plain in many references in urban public accounts. For example, the budget of the town of Hildesheim during the first half of the fifteenth century reveals significant amounts spent on catering for the town council, especially for wine, but also for meat, fish, fruit, butter, cheese, baked cabbage, almonds, raisins, dates, ginger, and other imported spices.[68] Official dinners for the town council were always conducted with especial splendour. In 1452 the city of Constance held a dinner for 100 persons, comprised of all the elements of elite nourishment: meat, fish, poultry, eggs, cheese, dessert, and cakes were all served up.[69] In particular, 95 pounds of beef, 37 pounds of roast pork, and 18 pounds of sausage were purchased. Among the poultry, 30 broiler chickens – plump, full-grown birds – were served up, along with 31 ducks and 121 fieldfares, the last especially prized for their piquant meat. The inevitable highpoint of the feast was an aspic, which used the jelly from 300 large pieces of carp and pike. The stock for the jelly was specially prepared with 140 pieces of fish. The whole dish was spiced with 14 lot (c. 230g) of saffron, five pounds of almonds, and a half-pound of *rott traesit*, a mixture of various coarsely crushed spices and sugar. There was ginger, cinnamon, and pepper in the aspic stock.. The long pepper, almost unknown to our own day, was also used.[70] Cakes were served with the aspic: Constance cuisine used for this purpose white flour, milk, a quarter of lump sugar, and 110 eggs. For dessert, the guests were served a pound and a half of confectionery, around 25 kilos of apples, nuts, and cheese. Bread and rice were served with porridge as accompaniments. Drink was not forgotten – around 537 litres of wine was bought in, from which the cooks used a suitable amount for preparation of the aspic.

Such opulent meals are also attested for north Germany. Thus, in 1500 the patrician Confraternity of the Circle in Lübeck acquired for their Circle-feast 12 hams, a quarter of an ox, 90 chickens, and 'since they were not large', a piece of game, 900 eggs, butter, and cheese. With bread, there was a distinction made between rolls, white rolls, and cheap 'bread for the poor', intended to feed the poor, as was common on such occasions. The exclusivity of the feast is revealed by the great quantity of imported spices: ginger, pepper, expensive saffron, cloves, cinnamon, sugar, and six Lübeck pounds of raisins alone. For the dessert, several kinds of confectionery were created. Hamburg and Einbeck beer was served, alongside as much wine 'as one was able to drink'.[71]

The great urban guilds also staged prestigious feasts for special occasions. For example, the Saffron Guild in Basel, one of the four elite guilds of the city, held a dinner in August 1578 at which 155 persons were fed.[72] This feast was exceptional in its poultry and fish courses, in which 37 cocks, 8 plump chickens, 3 capons, 30 doves, 7 partridges, and 6 quail were served, as well as a special surprise and novelty, an 'Indian chicken' or turkey, which was encountered as a dish for the first time in Basel. The pike and trout supplied from Wiesental in the nearby Black Forest were distributed by the cook among five large pies. As a showpiece course there was a dish made from salmon, the most expensive and most sought-after fish. The salmon cost eight and a half Basel pounds and accounted for around 11 per cent of the total costs of the dinner.[73] The expenditure for the two calves and three lambs that were purchased, in addition to the poultry and the fish, together came to only a little more than that for the salmon. The Saffron Guild also did not overlook spices, and spent more than six and a half Basel pounds on them. Wine was also provided in considerable quantities: almost 411 litres were drunk, which amounted to over two and a half litres per person.

The enormous quantites of food purchased for such occasions, especially for the great feasts at princely courts, should not, however, be seen as equivalent to what was consumed.[74] The reason for such quantities is found not so much in 'the corpulent bodies and vehement outbreaks of passion' (Schmoller) but in the social role of generosity and hospitality, in the desire for prestige.[75] The luxury of the exceptional banquet was an important part of that form of behaviour known as 'conspicuous consumption'.[76] From the thirteenth century onwards, it was part of the table manners of the elite to serve the guests on principle with more food than they could eat. This corresponded to the expectations of the diners just as much as the fact that they had to be forced to eat. Italian travellers were continually amazed at this northern custom.[77] Moreover, the painfully exact selection of the food and drink, its careful preparation, the outstanding quality of the ingredients, and the variety on offer all determined the 'social value' of the meal. At least from the fourteenth century there developed, first at princely courts and later in the patrician milieu, a kind of informal set of rules about the foods and the courses that belonged to luxury eating that encompassed at least Italy and central and north-west Europe.

Bearing in mind the enormous spectrum which extended from the nourishment of the poorest classes to that of the most eminent, we can now offer the following generalizations. Bread was absent only in exceptional cases, and was measured along a scale of nutrition and price according to how fine and white it was. According to extant evidence of official quality-testing for bakers in Augsburg, Basel, Frankfurt am Main, Nuremberg, and Strasbourg, coarse black bread corresponded almost to the weight of the prepared grain, while bread made from the most finely ground and sifted flour, especially in the particular case of rolls and pretzels, could result in significantly less than 50 per cent. Bakery tests from the fifteenth century reveal very low yields, corresponding to the use of very refined, very white bread. This is also confirmed from estimates of bread consumption in large households in the south of France in the later middle ages. On the other hand there was a distinct tendency during the sixteenth century, especially with rye bread, for the yields to be higher, that is, to use more coarsely ground flours. There is clearly a connection here with late medieval economic conjunctures, in which the secular trend towards lower grain prices was reflected in the consumption of more refined forms of bread. The relationship between grain weight and the bread made from it also has consequences for estimates of calorific intake during the middle ages and of consumption of grain. For the modern period we can assume that, when grain is baked into an article ready for consumption, the processed weight was on average equivalent to that of the unprocessed ingredients; but for the fifteenth century at least, we have to accept that there was a substantial reduction in weight according to the kind of bread involved. Moreover, it should also be considered that consumer habits with regard to quality rather than quantity, as well as different methods of milling flour and of baking bread, could also compensate for, or even counteract, the effects of grain price movements.[78]

In the case of meat, soup-meat represented the lowest level of quality and probably originated from older work animals rather than from fattened beasts. The ascending scale of value placed roast meats, then poultry, and especially game as the food of the lordly. However, according to evaluation of remains of bones in rubbish heaps, game played only a minor role even in noble consumption as early as the thirteenth century.[79] In the wealthy household of the Cologner Hermann von Goch, no meat from red deer or roe deer or wild boar was to be found on the table; however, hares, partridges, snipe, and pheasants were consumed here.[80] The wealthy Anton Tucher of Nuremberg only purchased game for gifts, with the exception of wild ducks and fieldfares.[81] In the household of the Nuremberg patrician Michael Behaim certainly some partridges, grouse, fieldfares, and quail were consumed, indeed even squirrels, but hares or wild boar remained rare exceptions.[82]

Freshwater fish, eggs, and fresh vegetables in place of cabbage and legumes, fruit, including citrus fruit and compotes, candied fruit and confectionery were further elements of a socially elevated diet in which milk products were noticeably absent, undoubtedly as a result of problems of transport and conservation. However, butter was never absent from the better sort of household, and it represented an important item in the long-distance trade of the Hansa. The problem of preserving butter was solved in the north by salting it, but in the south the butter was turned into melted butter or dripping (in Alemannic *Anken*), which was even preferred in rich households.[83] Social distinctions were especially marked in the case of cheese consumption. In peasant households, the easily spoiled sour-milk cheese predominated, which together with bread and the byproducts of cheesemaking (cheese-soup!) formed the main nutrition in regions dominated by animal husbandry. The more readily preserved forms of rennet cheese, expensive because of their more elaborate method of production, had since the thirteenth century been consumed almost exclusively by the more eminent middle and upper social strata. Cheese was none the less a minor accompaniment to a meal, even if rennet cheese was always a component of the final course. As an item of trade, the hard cheeses from Cheshire, Flanders, Emmental, Gruyère, southern France, and northern Italy were offered for sale in Antwerp, Cologne, Strasbourg, and Basel.[84]

In the case of drinks there was, as already mentioned, a partial change in consumer habits in favour of beer and away from the previous dominance of wine, dating back to the fifteenth and even more to the sixteenth century. At the beginning of the sixteenth century in the household of Anton Tucher, alongside wine from Franconia, Alsace, and the Rhine, which was as much in favour as before, there were also copious quantities of summer and winter beer from Nuremberg breweries as well as from those in Hof in Bavaria, Einbeck, and Bohemia. In north German towns, wine consumption was restricted to the sphere of luxurious festive banquets. Nothing changed here during the sixteenth century. As a rule, foreign wine was valued more than local varieties, in terms both of price and of consumption; the most socially prestigious wines were those imported from southern Europe, as well as spiced wines.[85] Aquavit was popular in Italy, but was first taken up by the social elites in the northern Alpine regions during the second half of the fifteenth century, but it could not replace mead in the eyes of consumers before the sixteenth century.[86] A speciality of Alsace and the Middle Rhine region was 'heated wine' (*gefeuerter- Wein*), formed by a specialized fermentation procedure; however, as a sweet, heavy dessert wine, this remained confined to the feasts of the social elites.[87]

In the hierarchy of foodstuffs, expensive imported spices were found on the very top rungs, above all the luxurious saffron from the vicinity of Barcelona. The spice trade, especially that in pepper, which was retailed in Venice and, in the course of the sixteenth century, in Antwerp as well, was the most profitable item for the great trading houses of the time.[88] Consumption of expensive imported spices was not confined to the very rich. In the fifteenth century pepper became affordable for the better-placed consumer from the middle classes, at least on feast days. During the sixteenth century pepper imports increased, and so we must assume that its consumption did as well, as a result of the discovery of the sea route around the Cape of Good Hope, which lowered transport costs.[89] Some trickling-down of the social role of a foodstuff can also be seen in the case of lump sugar, which had been imported from Egypt, Sicily, Rhodes, or Cyprus since the fourteenth century and which was correspondingly expensive. From the 1450s onwards the generally insignificant demand, allied with a simultaneously intensification of sugar-cane cultivation in the Canary Islands and in Madeira, led to a substantial fall in prices, which was accentuated by imports from Brazil and the Caribbean in the sixteenth century: thus, sugar became no longer the preserve of the richest classes. However, even during the sixteenth century foods were sweetened largely with honey, as in the middle ages.[90]

Alongside quality and the exotic nature of the basic product, processing also provides distinctive characteristics, especially in the preparation of meat and egg dishes, which were expressly regarded as festive foods. This was especially true of the highly spiced – often overspiced – dishes of complicated preparation found in cookbooks and in account books, which are often regarded as 'typically medieval'. Subtle jellies of fish and meat, pies with choice fillings, heavy puddings, and spiced wine were certainly not the exclusive privilege of the upper levels of society, but with the exception of princely tables, they were far from being constant items of daily consumption.[91] On the other hand, we can certainly accept the general rule that consumption of high-value animal products was a social indicator of daily life. This is precisely attested by individual examples from the later middle ages, on the basis of large households from upper Germany and southern France in the fourteenth and fifteenth centuries, in which the calorific value of bread for the lowliest servants made up around 75 per cent of the total calorific intake, while as one went up the scale of social rank and occasion, the proportion of supplements rose to around 80 per cent and that of bread sank to 10 per cent or less.[92] Social hierarchy was expressed in the 'refinements of the table'.[93]

Average consumption and assessment of nutritional levels

There are no real grounds in the extant sources for creating average statistics of consumption in the later middle ages and early modern period in central Europe. Without running the risk of unreliable generalization, we could still none the less assume, on the basis of the population decline in the fourteenth and fifteenth centuries, that more food was available per capita, especially animal products, than there had been in the centuries of the high middle ages and was to be in the following age of mass poverty, during the early modern period.

From the available data we could calculate that, in certain cases, grain consumption reached over 600 kilos a year. Thus, considering the importance of bread as a form of nutrition, it would not be unrealistic if the average grain consumption per head of population were estimated at around 200 kilos per annum.[94] In the case of meat consumption, a clear divide is observable between northern and southern Europe. An average annual consumption of 30 kilos can be calculated for Florence in the fourteenth century, 26 kilos in Carpentras, and 40 kilos in Languedoc in the fifteenth. North of the Alps there are some instances of an annual consumption of over 100 kilos, but this figure is certainly too high to be cited as frequently as it is for an overall average.[95] That twice as much meat was consumed in Germany during the middle ages as in the highly industrialized Wilhelmine Empire at the beginning of the twentieth century seems quite incredible. It is possible that the towns north of the Alps saw an annual average consumption of around 50 kilos during the later middle ages – that is, roughly two and a half times as much as in pre-industrial Germany around 1800.[96] For wine and beer, individual reports from many regions attest daily consumption of up to two litres or up to 1,000 litres a year. That indicates an average consumption corresponding to the situation in Mediterranean towns, where between 300 and 400 litres of wine per head per annum have been attested.[97] Here we should, of course, bear in mind that the beer and wine consumed each day had a lower alcohol content than their present-day equivalents.[98]

All such calculations of average consumption, as well as all attempts to produce typical budgets, conceal the characteristic and socially determined variations of consumption discussed above. Above all, they conceal one of the most important structural features of pre-modern Europe, its fragility and propensity to crisis. The years of want at the end of thirteenth century, conditioned as they were by relative overpopulation, continued under other preconditions in subsequent periods, with their centre of gravity in the first half of the fourteenth and of the fifteenth centuries. Reports of the affluence of the 'good years' (falling prices after 1450) should be set alongside accounts of the European famines of the 1430s. Even the urban population, relatively well-off in comparison to the rural inhabitants, was hit by such years of dearth.[99] The evidence from many parts of Europe about the high proportion of inhabitants without any food reserves and of those who flocked to receive alms gives an impression of the extent of the subsistence crisis afflicting the poorest levels of society.[100] Even the available foodstuffs had their own considerable dangers, such as ergot or weed seeds mixed in with bread grains, trichinous pork, adulterated wine, foodstuffs contaminated by contact with pests, and, in the widest sense, bad drinking water. There is archaeological evidence of deficiency diseases found in skeletal remains, and of deficient hygiene in mite droppings.[101] None the less, we should beware of too casually establishing causal connections between nutrition, illness and plague, and demographic developments. The medieval periods with the lowest levels of population were also those with relatively better levels of nutrition, while the plagues with most striking demographic effects were certainly independent of nutrition.[102] Here there are basic mechanisms operating on many levels, whose interplay is not yet sufficiently explained. The state of research only allows the conclusion that the period between the thirteenth and the sixteenth century was characterized neither by perpetual hunger nor by continual excess. The uncertain availability in both quantity and quality of sufficient supplies of food was part of the multiplicity of risks to human existence in the middle ages.[103]

It is precisely this uncertainty which explains, far better than the superficial conclusion that it was an 'age of gluttony and inebriation', why late medieval society invested eating and drinking with such high symbolic value, which was then lost during an age of more assured mass consumption. Meals did not just signify an essential calorific intake; they were also a break in the grey monotony of daily life and therefore an important source, perhaps the most important source, of secular well-being. Beer and wine were quite possibly the only means of aid for chronic and acute forms of pain, occasioned by kidney stone, jawbone inflammations, and joint malformations.[104] The people of that age were endangered in their very physical existence, anxious about their 'daily bread' and concerned about the availability of both small and great pleasures over and above the minimum for existence. The background of the dream of the land of Cockayne is not an insatiable gluttony, but the wish for an existence free from hunger and want.

Notes

1 N. Elias, *Über den Prozeß der Zivilisation. Soziogenetische und psycho-genetische Untersuchungen*, 6th edn (2 vols., Frankfurt a. M., 1978), I, pp. 110–74.

2 See W. Abel, *Agrarkrisen und Agrarkonjunktur. Eine Geschichte der Land- und Ernährungswirtschaft Mitteleuropas seit dem hohen Mittelalter*, 3rd edn (Hamburg/Berlin, 1978); U. Dirlmeier, *Untersuchungen zu Einkommensver-hältnissen und Lebenshaltungskosten in oberdeutschen Städten des Spätmittelalters (Mitte 14. bis Anfang 16. Jahrhundert)* (Heidelberg, 1978); F. Irsigler, *Die wirtschaftliche Stellung der Stadt Köln im 14. und 15. Jahrhundert. Strukturanalyse einer spätmittelalterlichen Exportgewerbe- und Fernhandelsstadt* (Wiesbaden, 1979), pp. 241-318; W. Abel, *Stufen der Ernährung* (Göttingen, 1981); H. Hundsbichler, 'Nahrung', in H. Kühnel, ed., *Alltag im Spätmittelalter*, 6th edn (Graz/ Vienna/ Cologne, 1985), pp. 196–231; U. Dirlmeier and G. Fouquet, 'Ernährung und Konsumgewohnheiten im spätmittelalterlichen Deutschland', *Geschichte in Wissenschaft und Unterricht* XLIV (1993), pp. 504–26. For specific topics, still useful is M. Heyne, *Das deutsche Nahrungswesen von den ältesten geschichtlichen Zeiten bis zum 16. Jahrhundert* (Leipzig, 1901).

3 G. Wiegelmann, *Alltags- und Festspeisen. Wandel und gegenwärtige Stellung* (Marburg, 1967); *Stadtarchäologie in Deutschland und den Nachbarländern. Ergebnisse, Verluste, Konzeptionen* (Bonn, 1988); B. Herrmann, ed., *Mensch und Umwelt im Mittelalter* (Stuttgart, 1986); B. Herrmann and R. Sprandel, eds., *Determinanten der Bevölkerungsentwicklung im Mittelalter* (Weinheim, 1987); B. Herrmann, ed, *Umwelt in der Geschichte. Beiträge zur Umweltgeschichte* (Göttingen, 1989).

4 L. Stouff, *Ravitaillement et alimentation en Provence aux XIVe et XVe siècles* (Paris/La Haye, 1970), p. 15.

5 U. Dirlmeier, 'Die Ernährung als mögliche Konstante der Bevölkerungsentwicklung', in Herrmann and Sprandel, *Determinanten*, pp. 143–54, esp. p. 152.

6 On consumption statistics from city chronicles, *Cronica di Giovanni Villani*, ed. F. G. Dragomanni (4 vols., Florence, 1844–5; repr. Frankfurt a. M., 1969) III, pp. 323–6; A. Werminghoff, *Conrad Celtis und sein Buch über Nürnberg* (Freiburg im Br., 1921), pp. 200–1. Celtis's figures were taken over by Johannes Cochlaeus, *Brevis Germaniae Descriptio (1512) mit der Deutschlandkarte des Erhard Etzlaub von 1502*, ed. K. Langosch (Darmstadt, 1969), p. 77. On food supplies in St Gallen, Joachim von Watt (Vadian), *Deutsche Schriften*, ed. E. Grötzinger (3 vols., St Gallen, 1875–9) II, p. 423.

7 Numerous source references given in Dirlmeier, *Einkommensverhältnisse*, pp. 293–441. Other references can also be found in H. Hundsbichler, *Reise*,

Gastlichkeit und Nahrung im Spiegel der Reisetagebücher des Paolo Santonino (1485-1487) (Ph.D., Vienna, 1979); I. Bitsch, T. Ehlert, and X. von Ertzdorff, eds, *Essen und Trinken in Mittelalter und Neuzeit* (Sigmaringen, 1987).

8 H. Wiswe, *Kulturgeschichte der Kochkunst. Kochbücher und Rezepte aus zwei Jahrtausenden mit einem lexikalischen Anhang zur Fachsprache von E. Hepp* (Munich, 1970); T. Ehlert, *Das Kochbuch des Mittelalters. Rezepte aus alter Zeit*, 3rd edn (Zurich/Munich, 1991). On medical literature, H. Schipperges, 'Ernährung III: Diätetisch-medizinisch', *Lexikon des Mittelalters* III (Munich, 1986), pp. 2169–71; T. Ehlert, 'Wissenvermittlung in deutschsprachiger Fachliteratur des Mittelalters, oder: Wie kam die Diätetik in die Kochbücher?', *Würzburger medizinhistorische Mitteilungen* VIII (1990), pp. 137–59; T. Ehlert, 'Zum Funktionswandel der Gattung Kochbuch in Deutschland', in A. Wierlacher, G. Neuman and H. J. Teuteberg, eds, *Kulturthema Essen* (Berlin, 1993), pp. 319–41.

9 See e.g. J. Schneider, D. Gutscher, H. Etter, and J. Hanser, eds, *Der Münsterhof in Zürich* (2 vols., Olten/Freiburg im Br., 1982); S. Schutte, ed., *5 Jahre Stadtarchäologie. Das neue Bild vom alten Göttingen* (Göttingen, 1984); U. Willerding, 'Ernährung, Gartenbau und Landwirtschaft im Bereich der Stadt', in C. Meckseper, ed., *Stadt im Wandel. Kunst und Kultur des Bürgertums in Norddeutschland* (Stuttgart/Bad Cannstatt, 1985) III, pp. 569–605. *Stadtarchäologie in Braunschweig* (Hameln, 1985); B. Herrmann, 'Parasitologische Untersuchung mittelalterlicher Kloaken', in Herrmann, *Mensch und Umwelt*, pp. 160–9; *25 Jahre Archäologie in Lübeck. Erkenntnisse von Archäologie und Bauforschung zur Geschichte und Vorgeschichte der Hansestadt 1963–88*, ed. Amt für Vor- und Frühgeschichte (Bodendenkmalpflege) (Bonn, 1988); *Stadtluft, Hirsebrei und Bettelmönch. Die Stadt um 1300. Stadtarchäologie in Baden-Württemberg und in der Nordostschweiz* (Stuttgart, 1993).

10 Dirlmeier, *Einkommensverhältnisse*, pp. 491–531. For further discussion, G. Schmoller, 'Die historische Entwicklung des Fleischconsums, sowie der Vieh- und Fleischpreise in Deutschland', *Zeitschrift für die gesamte Staatswissenschaft* XXVII (1871), pp. 282–362, esp. pp. 290–1; E. Fiumi, 'Economia e vita privata dei fiorentini nelle rilevazioni statistiche di Giovanni Villani', *Archivio storico italiano* CXI (1953), pp. 207–41, esp. pp. 210–11.

11 See e.g. *Anton Tuchers Haushaltbuch (1507 bis 1517)*, ed. W. Loose (Tübingen, 1877); J. Kamann, ed., 'Aus Nürnberger Haushaltungs- und Rechnungsbüchern des 15. und 16. Jahrhunderts', *Mitteilungen des Vereins für Geschichte der Stadt Nürnberg* VII (1886), pp. 57–122; VIII (1888), pp. 39–168; F. Irsigler, 'Ein großbürgerlicher Kölner Haushalt am Ende des 14. Jahrhunderts', in E. Ennen and G. Wiegelmann, eds, *Studien zu Volkskultur, Sprache und Landesgeschichte. Festschrift Matthias Zender* (Bonn, 1972), pp. 635–68; R. Jütte, 'Household and Family Life in Late Sixteenth-Century Cologne. The Weinsberg Family', *Sixteenth Century Journal* XVII (1986), pp. 165–82.

12 See Stouff, *Ravitaillement*, pp. 219–50; U. Dirlmeier, 'Zum Problem von Versorgung und Verbrauch privater Haushalte im Spätmittelalter', in A. Haverkamp, ed., *Haus und Familie in der spätmittelalterlichen Stadt* (Cologne/Vienna, 1984), pp. 257–88; an overview in R. Roehl, 'Nachfrageverhalten und Nachfragestruktur 1000–1500: Der private Verbrauch', in C. M. Cipolla and K. Borchardt, eds, *Europäische Wirtschaftsgeschichte*, Fontana Economic History of Europe (5 vols., Stuttgart/New York, 1983) I, pp. 70–8.

13 For peasant consumption, E. Ennen and W. Janssen, *Deutsche Agrargeschichte. Vom Neolithikum bis zur Schwelle des Industriezeitalters* (Wiesbaden, 1979),

pp. 215–16; W. Rösener, *Bauern im Mittelalter* 7, 3rd edn. (Munich, 1987), pp. 106–18; D. Saalfeld, 'Wandlungen der bäuerlichen Konsumgewohnheiten vom Mittelalter zur Neuzeit', in Bitsch *et al.*, *Essen*, pp. 59–75, esp. pp. 70–2.

14 General information about the changes from the later middle ages to the early modern period in Dirlmeier, *Einkommensverhältnisse*, pp. 303–17; Abel, *Ernährung*; H. J. Teuteberg and G. Wiegelmann, *Der Wandel der Nahrungsgewohnheiten unter dem Einfluß der Industrialisierung* (Göttingen, 1972).

15 On the history of wine, still useful is F. von Bassermann-Jordan, *Geschichte des Weinbaus* 2nd edn (2 vols, Frankfurt a. M., 1923; repr. Neustadt an der Weinstrasse, 1975). Further, see G. Schreiber, *Deutsche Weingeschichte. Der Wein in Volkskunde, Kult und Wirtschaft* (Cologne, 1980); O. Volk, 'Weinbau und Weinabsatz im späten Mittelalter. Forschungsstand und Forschungsprobleme', in A. Gerlich, ed., *Weinbau, Weinhandel und Weinkultur* (Stuttgart, 1993), pp. 49–163. On beer, H. Huntemann, *Das deutsche Braugewerbe vom Ausgang des Mittelalters bis zum Beginn der Industrialisierung. Biererzeugung, Bierhandel, Bierverbrauch* (Nuremberg, 1971); G. Stefke, *Ein städtisches Exportgewerbe des Spätmittelalters in seiner Entfaltung und ersten Blüte. Untersuchungen zur Geschichte der Hamburger-Seebrauerei des 14. Jahrhunderts* (Ph.D., Hamburg, 1979); G. Fischer, H. Ganschr, B. Heizmann W. Herborn, H. G. Schulze-Berndt, *Bierbrauen im Rheinland* (Cologne, 1985); E. Plümer, 'Brauwesen und Bierhandel im spätmittelalterlichen Einbeck', in Meckseper, *Stadt im Wandel* III, pp. 303–13.

16 On grain production and the grain trade, F. Irsigler, 'Getreidepreise, Getreidehandel und städtische Versorgungspolitik in Köln, vornehmlich im 15. und 16. Jahrhundert', in W. Besch *et al.*, eds, *Die Stadt in der europäischen Geschichte. Festschrift für Edith Ennen* (Bonn, 1972), pp. 571–610; D. Ebeling and F. Irsigler, *Getreideumsatz, Getreide- und Brotpreise in Köln 1368–1797* (2 vols, Cologne/Vienna, 1976/7); W. Habermann and H. Schlotmann, 'Der Getreidehandel in Deutschland im 15. und 16. Jahrhundert. Ein Literaturbericht', *Scripta Mercaturae* XI (1977), pp. 27–55; XII (1978), pp. 107–36.

17 On market gardening, G. Franz, ed., *Geschichte des deutschen Gartenbaus* (Stuttgart, 1984), pp. 39–142; F. Irsigler, 'Intensivwirtschaft, Sonderkulturen und Gartenbau als Elemente der Kulturlandschaftsgestaltung in den Rheinlanden (13.-16. Jahrhundert)', in A. Guarducci, ed., *Agricoltura e trasformazione dell'ambiente, secoli XIII–XVIII* (Florence, 1984), pp. 719–47.

18 On agrarian developments during the agrarian crisis of the later middle ages, Abel, *Agrarkrisen*, pp. 27–103. On the cattle trade and animal husbandry, H. Wiese and J. Bölts, *Rinderhandel und Rinderhaltung im nordwesteuropäischen Küstengebiet vom 15. bis zum 19. Jahrhundert* (Stuttgart, 1966); E. Westermann, ed., *Internationaler Ochsenhandel (1350–1750). Akten des 7th International Economic History Congress, Edinburgh, 1978* (Stuttgart, 1979); J. Baszanowski, 'Zur Versorgung fürstlicher Höfe mit Ochsen aus Polen im 16. Jahrhundert', *Scripta Mercaturae* XX (1986), pp. 11–34; C. Dalhede, *Zum europäischen Ochsenhandel: Das Beispiel Augsburg 1560 und 1578* (St Katharinen, 1992).

19 On price and wage movements, M. J. Elsas, *Umriß einer Geschichte der Preise und Löhne in Deutschland vom ausgehenden Mittelalter bis zum Beginn des neunzehnten Jahrhunderts* (3 vols., Leiden, 1936–49); K. Schulz, *Handwerksgesellen und Lohnarbeiter. Untersuchungen zur oberrheinischen und oberdeutschen Stadtgeschichte des 14. bis 17. Jahrhunderts* (Sigmaringen, 1985), pp. 316–442; Abel, *Agrarkrisen*, pp. 122–51. Also see below, p. 91.

20 Abel, *Agrarkrisen*, pp. 104–21; W. Abel, *Geschichte der deutschen*

Landwirtschaft vom frühen Mittelalter bis zum 19. Jahrhundert, 2nd edn (Stuttgart, 1967), pp. 162–82; F.-W. Henning, *Landwirtschaft und ländliche Gesellschaft in Deutschland* (2 vols., Paderborn/Munich/Vienna/Zurich, 1979) I, pp. 186–202. On climatic developments in the sixteenth century and their consequences, C. Pfister, *Das Klima der Schweiz von 1525–1860 und seine Bedeutung in der Geschichte von Bevölkerung und Landwirtschaft*, 2nd edn (2 vols., Berne/Stuttgart, 1985) I, pp. 115–21; II, pp. 81–97.

21 See Dirlmeier, *Einkommensverhältnisse*, pp. 364–425. On town–country relationships, for a summary see Dirlmeier, 'Stadt und Bürgertum. Zur Steuerpolitik und zum Stadt-Land-Verhältnis', in H. Buszello, P. Blickle and R. Endres, eds, *Der deutsche Bauernkrieg* (Paderborn/Munich/Vienna/Zurich, 1984), pp. 254–80, esp. pp. 270, 275–9. See further especially R. Kießling, *Die Stadt und ihr Land. Umlandpolitik, Bürgerbesitz und Wirtschaftsgefüge in Ostschwaben vom 14. bis ins 16. Jahrhundert* (Cologne/Vienna, 1989). For the image of the peasant, H. Wunder, 'Der dumme und der schlaue Bauer', in C. Meckseper and E. Schraut, eds, *Mentalität und Alltag im Spätmittelalter* (Göttingen, 1985), pp. 34–52.

22 See Dirlmeier, *Versorgung*, p. 267 for further references.

23 See Hundsbichler, *Reise*, pp. 128–9, 293–5; Dirlmeier, *Einkommensverhältnisse*, pp. 436–7, 439.

24 On basic consumption, Dirlmeier, *Ernährung*, p. 151.

25 Thomas Platter and Felix Platter, *Zur Sittengeschichte des XVI. Jahrhunderts*, ed. H. Boos (Leipzig, 1878), p. 68.

26 G. Schiedlausky, *Essen und Trinken. Tafelsitten bis zum Ausgang des Mittelalters* (Nuremberg, 1956), p. 54; W. Wermelinger, *Lebensmittelteuerungen, ihre Bekämpfung und ihre politischen Rückwirkungen in Bern vom ausgehenden 15. Jahrhundert bis in die Zeit der Kappelerkriege* (Berne, 1971), p. 9.

27 For further references, Dirlmeier, *Einkommensverhältnisse*, pp. 303–8.

28 H. J. Schmitz, *Faktoren der Preisbildung für Getreide und Wein in der Zeit von 800 bis 1350* (Stuttgart, 1968), p. 112.

29 H. Gleitz, 'Das Hospital St Jodoci zu Braunschweig', *Niedersächsisches Jb. für Landesgeschichte* XVII (1940), pp. 37–83, esp. pp. 56–7.

30 *Die Chroniken der deutschen Städte vom 14. bis zum 16. Jahrhundert* II: *Augsburg*, ed. Historische Kommission bei der Bayerischen Akademie der Wissenschaften (Leipzig, 1866; repr. Göttingen, 1965), p. 178.

31 Kamann, Nürnberger, *Haushaltungsbücher* II, p. 54.

32 Ulrich von Richental, *Das Konzil von Konstanz*, ed. O. Feger (Starnberg/Constance, 1964), pp. 173–5.

33 E. Knupfer and M. Rauch, eds, *Urkundenbuch der Stadt Heilbronn* (4 vols., Stuttgart, 1904–22) II, pp. 312–16, no. 1370.

34 U. Dirlmeier, 'Die Kosten des Aufgebots der Reichsstadt Rothenburg ob der Tauber im Schweizerkrieg von 1499', in B. Kirchgässner and G. Scholz, eds, *Stadt und Krieg* (Sigmaringen, 1989), pp. 27–39, esp. p. 31.

35 D. Lindner, *Die allgemeinen Fastendispensen in den jeweils bayerischen Gebieten seit dem Ausgang des Mittelalters* (Munich, 1935). H. Zapp, 'Butterbriefe', in *Lexikon des Mittelalters* II (Munich/Zurich, 1983), pp. 1162–3; H. Zapp, 'Fastendispensen', *Lexikon des Mittelalters* III (Munich/Zurich, 1986), pp. 306–7.

36 Tucher, *Haushaltbuch*, pp. 71 (1509), 109 (1509–14).

37 See e.g. the *Ordnung des großen Spitals zu Straßburg, wie die armen Siechen gehalten werden* of c.1540: Friday and Saturday one abstained from meat, but eggs and cheese could be eaten; O. Winckelmann, *Das Fürsorgewesen der Stadt Straßburg vor und nach der Reformation bis zum Ausgang des sechzehnten*

Jahrhunderts (2 vols., Leipzig, 1922; repr. New York/London, 1971) II, p. 24, no. 10. Duke Julius of Braunschweig also retained the fish days in his court ordinance of 1578; Wiswe, *Kulturgeschichte*, p. 87.

38 C. Roder, ed., *Heinrich Hug's Villinger Chronik von 1495–1533* (Tübingen, 1883), p. 158.

39 After G. Adler, *Die Fleisch-Teuerungspolitik der deutschen Städte beim Ausgange des Mittelalters* (Tübingen, 1893), p. 104 (from a Freiburg source). See further E. Gothein, *Wirtschaftsgeschichte des Schwarzwaldes und der angrenzenden Landschaften* I (Strasbourg, 1892), p. 516.

40 The calculations from Dirlmeier, *Einkommensverhältnisse*, p. 360.

41 *Ibid.*, pp. 310, 312–13, 366, 369, 372, 376–8, 382, 387, 389–90, 393, 434.

42 See B. Kuske, 'Der Kölner Fischhandel vom 14.–17. Jahrhundert', *Westdeutsche Zeitschrift* XXIV (1905), pp. 227–313; M. Mayer, *Die Lebensmittelpolitik der Reichsstadt Schlettstadt bis zum Beginn der französischen Herrschaft* (Freiburg im Br., 1907), pp. 136, 150; F. Ehrensperger, *Basels Stellung im internationalen Handelsverkehr des Spätnittelalters* (Zürich, 1972), pp. 225–6; G. Fouquet, ' "Wie die kuchenspise sin solle". Essen und Trinken am Hof des Speyerer Bischofs Matthias von Rammung (1464–1478)', *Pfälzer Heimat* XXXIX (1988), pp. 12–27, esp. pp. 20–1.

43 On fish-farming and fish-ponds, R. Endres, 'Die Folgen des 30 jährigen Krieges in Franken', in H. Kellenbenz, ed., *Wirtschaftsentwicklung und Umweltbeeinflußung (14.–20. Jahrhundert)* (Wiesbaden, 1982), pp. 125–44, esp. pp. 136–8; R. Braun, *Das Benediktinerkloster Michelsberg 1015–1525. Eine Untersuchung zur Gründung, Rechtsstellung und Wirtschaftsgeschichte* (2 vols., Kulmbach, 1977–8) I, pp. 139–44; G. Schnorrenberger, *Wirtschaftsverwaltung des Klosters Eberbach im Rheingau 1423–1631* (Wiesbaden, 1977), pp. 87–8; H. Maulhardt, *Die wirtschaftlichen Grundlagen der Grafschaft Katzenelnbogen im 14. und 15. Jahrhundert* (Darmstadt/Marburg, 1980), pp. 66–71; H. Rothert, 'Die ältesten Stadtrechnungen von Soest aus den Jahren 1338, 1357 und 1363', *Westfälische Zeitschrift* CI/CII (1953), pp. 139–82, esp. pp. 159–60; Fouquet, 'Kuchenspise', p. 21. On the seasonality of the fishing (the example of the Balchen fishery in the Sempacher See since 1581), M. Körner, *Luzerner Staatsfinanzen 1415–1798. Strukturen, Wachstum, Konjunkturen* (Lucerne/Stuttgart, 1981), pp. 162–6.

44 Stadtarchiv Speyer I A 10, fo. 291ᵛ.

45 F. J. Mone, 'Armen- und Krankenpflege', *ZGO* XII (1861), pp. 142–94, esp. p. 173, no. 28.

46 W. Freiherr von Löffelholz, 'Graue Joachim salige Haußhaltung', *Anzeiger für Kunde der deutschen Vorzeit*, Neue Folge IV (1857), pp. 15–16, 44–5, 83–4, 115–16, 151–2, 186–7, 214–16, here p. 84; Wiegelmann, *Alltag*, p. 33.

47 Fouquet, 'Kuchenspise', p. 19. On the possibilities of variation required within the daily sequence of meals, see also Löffelholz, 'Graue Joachim', pp. 44–5, 84, 115.

48 Irsigler, *Kölner Haushalt*, pp. 647–50. For the exorbitant purchases of fish in great French households, see Stouff, *Ravitaillement*, pp. 201–13.

49 For examples, Hundsbichler, *Reise*, p. 238; idem, *Nahrung*, p. 229. On the growing of almonds and figs and means of preparation, Irsigler, *Intensivwirtschaft*, pp. 734–5; Willerding, *Ernährung*, pp. 578–9; Wiswe, *Kulturgeschichte*, pp. 88–92, 98, 106, 117, 135–44; H. Wiswe, 'Ein mittelniederdeutsches Kochbuch des 15. Jahrhunderts', *Braunschweiger Jb.* XXXVII (1956), pp. 19–63 (with numerous almond recipes); W. Wackernagel, ed., 'Kochbuch von Maister Hannsen des von Wirtenberg Koch', *Zeitschrift für deutsches Alterthum* IX (1853), pp. 365–73. In the household of the

Nuremberg Losunger Anton Tucher, many almonds were consumed, especially Venetian almonds; *Tucher Haushaltbuch*, pp. 18, 20, 38, 48, and *passim*.

50 Hundsbichler, *Nahrung*, p. 229; Fouquet, 'Kuchenspise', p. 19. On archaeological–paleobotanical evidence, Willerding, *Ernährung*, pp. 574–5.

51 Dirlmeier, *Einkommensverhältnisse*, pp. 308–17. Noble household statutes are also important, revealing as they do a precisely regulated hierarchy of foods, beginning with the lord's table and extending down to the servants in clearly delineated stages of decreasing quality; Löffelholz, 'Graue Joachim'.

52 See here the 1531 Enquête of Alexander Berner on South German welfare institutions, Winckelmann, *Fürsorgewesen* II, pp. 266–83, no. 204. For the example of alms in Constance, O. Feger, ed., *Die Statutensammlung des Stadtschreibers Jörg Vögeli* (Constance, 1951), pp. 29–37, no. 12 (1527).

53 H. Ammann, ed., *Mittelalterliche Wirtschaft im Alltag. Quellen zur Geschichte, Industrie und Handel des 14. und 15. Jahrhunderts aus den Notariatsregistern von Freiburg im Üchtland* (Aarau, 1942–54), p. 68, no. 693; p. 79, no. 810; p. 88, no. 901; Dirlmeier, *Einkommensverhältnisse*, p. 430.

54 J. Grimm, ed., *Weisthümer* (7 vols., Göttingen, 1840–78; repr. Darmstadt, 1957) IV, pp. 198–9, 210–11.

55 B. Zeller, *Das Heilig-Geist-Spital zu Lindau am Bodensee von seinen Anfängen bis zum Ausgang des 16. Jahrhunderts* (Lindau, 1952), p. 145.

56 Feger, *Statutensammlung*, pp. 228–37, esp. pp. 231–2, no. 361; J. von Steynitz, *Mittelalterliche Hospitäler der Orden und Städte als Einrichtungen der sozialen Sicherung* (Berlin, 1970), p. 90 (Wimpfen).

57 W. Ogris, *Der mittelalterliche Leibrentenvertrag. Ein Beitrag zur Geschichte des deutschen Privatrechts* (Vienna/Munich, 1961), p. 87 (Trier); L. F. Heyd, *Geschichte der vormaligen Oberamts-Stadt Markgröningen mit besonderer Rücksicht auf die allgemeine Geschichte Wirtembergs* (Stuttgart, 1829), p. 215.

58 Dirlmeier, *Einkommensverhältnisse*, p. 310.

59 Winckelmann, *Fürsorgewesen* II, p. 4, no. 2; pp. 20–6, no. 10.

60 Staatsarchiv Hamburg CI VII Lit. Dc. no. 7, vol. 1, fasc. 1, fo. 31ᵛ; see G. Fouquet, ' "Ad structuram civitatis". Der öffentliche Baubetrieb Hamburgs und die Errichtung von Mühlen- und Schleusenanlagen in Fuhlsbüttel während der Jahre 146–7', in U. Dirlmeier, R. S. Elkar and G. Fouquet, eds, *Öffentliches Bauen in Mittelalter und früher Neuzeit. Abrechnungen als Quellen für die Finanz-, Wirtschafts- und Sozialgeschichte des Bauwesens* (St Katharinen, 1991), pp. 206–92, esp. pp. 238–42; B. Harms, ed., *Der Stadthaushalt Basels im ausgehenden Mittelalter (Einnahmen und Ausgaben 1360-1535)* (3 vols., Tübingen, 1909–1913) III, pp. 273–4; Staatsarchiv Marburg, Bestand 330, A, II, 5 (Baurechnung 1522). For further examples of meals for building workers, K.-S. Kramer, *Bauhandwerkerbräuche in Mainfranken, insbesondere der Niederfall*, in G. Fischer, ed., *Fränkisches Handwerk* (Kulmbach, 1958), pp. 83–104.

61 U. Dirlmeier and G. Fouquet, 'Eigenbetriebe niedersächsischer Städte im Spätmittelalter', in Meckseper, *Stadt im Wandel* III, pp. 257–79, here p. 270.

62 *Endres Tuchers Baumeisterbuch der Stadt Nürnberg (1464–1475)*, ed. M. Lexer (Stuttgart, 1862; repr. Amsterdam, 1968), p. 62.

63 Werminghoff, *Celtis*, pp. 171–2.

64 *Die Chroniken der deutschen Städte vom 14. bis zum 16. Jahrhundert. Augsburg* VI (Leipzig, 1906; repr. Göttingen, 1966), p. 58.

65 *Tuchers Haushaltbuch*, pp. 26, 29, 41, 45, 49; Dirlmeier, *Einkommensverhältnisse*, p. 390.

66 Fouquet, 'Kuchenspise', pp. 17–19. On noble dietary habits, see e.g. W. Janssen, 'Ein niederrheinischer Fürstenhof um die Mitte des 14. Jahrhunderts',

Rheinische Vierteljahresblätter XXXIV (1970), pp. 219–51; H. Hundsbichler, G. Jaritz and E. Vavra, 'Tradition? Stagnation? Innovation? Die Bedeutung des Adels für die spätmittelalterliche Sachkultur', in H. Kühnel, ed., *Adelige Sachkultur des Spätmittelalters* (Vienna, 1982), pp. 35–72; W. Maleczek, 'Die Sachkultur am Hofe Herzog Sigmunds von Tirol († 1496)', in Kühnel, *Adelige Sachkultur*, pp. 133–67; W. Herborn, 'Alltagsleben auf einer Burg. Kaster im ausgehenden 14. Jahrhundert', *Dürener Geschichtsblätter* LXXV (1986), pp. 5–20.

67 F. J. Mone, ed., *Quellensammlung zur badischen Landesgeschichte* (4 vols., Karlsruhe, 1848–1867) I, p. 490 (Speyerische Chronik); for the reception of brandy in German lands, especially from the sixteenth century, H. Wiswe, 'Die Branntweinkaltschale. Studien um ein Speisebrauchtum', *Beiträge zur deutschen Volks- und Altertumskunde* VIII (1964), pp. 61–86.

68 P. Huber, *Der Haushalt der Stadt Hildesheim am Ende des 14. und in der ersten Hälfte des 15. Jahrhunderts* (Leipzig, 1901), pp. 80–2.

69 Stadtarchiv Konstanz, A VII 1, fos. 26^r–26^v; see G. Fouquet, 'Das Festmahl in den oberdeutschen Städten des Mittelalters. Zu Form, Funktion und Bedeutung öffentlichen Konsums', *Archiv für Kulturgeschichte* LXXIV (1992), pp. 83–123, esp. pp. 103–8.

70 For references see R. Jaretzky, *Lehrbuch der Pharmakognosie*, 2nd edn (Braunschweig, 1949), p. 250.

71 G. Deecke, 'Historische Nachrichten von dem lübeckischen Patriziat', *Jahrbücher des Vereins für mecklenburgische Geschichte und Alterthumskunde* X (1845), pp. 50–96, here p. 86.

72 See P. Koelner, 'Die Kuchibücher der Safranzunft', *Basler Jb.* (1929), pp. 202–69, esp. pp. 252–3, n. 136 (Edition des Festessens); for the low German region, see e.g. J. M. van Winter, 'Ernährung und Kochkunst im Hanseraum', in J. Bracker, ed., *Die Hanse. Lebenswirklichkeit und Mythos* (2 vols., Hamburg, 1989) I, pp. 406–8, esp. p. 406. For banquets in university circles, G. Erler, *LeipzigerMagisterschmäuse im 16., 17. und 18. Jahrhundert* (Leipzig, 1905).

73 In 1544 a salmon cost 3 Basel pounds, and therefore three times the price of the roast meat served with this dish for 80 persons; Koelner, *Kuchibücher*, p. 251.

74 See e.g. U. Löwenstein, ' "Ein wissen Swan mit eym gulden Snabel zu eym Schaweessen". Festessen am hanauischen Hof in 15. und 16. Jahrhundert', *Hanauer Geschichtsblätter* XXXI (1993), pp. 35–90; M. Buchner, 'Quellen zur Amberger Hochzeit von 1474', *Archiv für Kulturgeschichte* VI (1908), pp. 385–438, esp. pp. 405–10 (Bestellung der profande in die kuchen); for the no less famous Landshut marriage, A. Schultz, *Deutsches Leben im XIV. und XV. Jahrhundert* (2 vols., Prague/Vienna/Leipzig, 1892) I, p. 265. For the opulent lists of victuals for court feasts in Silesia at the close of the sixteenth century, *Merkbuch des Hans von Schweinichen*, ed. K. Wutke (Berlin, 1895), pp. 8–11, 68–70, 91–2, 149–51; *Denkwürdigkeiten des Hans von Schweinichen*, ed. H. Oesterley (Breslau, 1878), pp. 164–5.

75 Schmoller, *Fleischconsum*, p. 287.

76 T. Veblen, *Theorie der feinen Leute. Eine ökonomische Untersuchung der Institutionen* (Cologne/Berlin, 1958; repr. Munich, 1987), pp. 62–84 – originally published as *The Theory of the Leisure Class. An Economic Study of the Evolution of Institutions* (New York, 1899); G. Simmel, 'Soziologie der Mahlzeit' (1910), in G. Simmel, ed., *Brücke und Tür. Essays des Philosophen zur Geschichte, Religion, Kunst und Gesellschaft* (Stuttgart, 1957), pp. 243–50; repr. as *Das Individuum und die Freiheit* (Berlin, 1984), pp. 205–11.

77 Hundsbichler, *Reise*, p. 305.

78 Dirlmeier, *Einkommensverhältnisse*, pp. 336–57 (with source references); for the early seventeenth century, B. Roeck, *Bäcker, Brot und Getreide in Augsburg. Zur Geschichte des Bäckerhandwerks und zur Versorgungspolitik der Reichsstadt im Zeitalter des Dreißigjährigen Krieges* (Sigmaringen, 1987).

79 For a general overview, W. Meyer, 'Landwirtschaftsbetriebe auf mittelalterlichen Burgen', in Kühnel, *Adelige Sachkultur*, pp. 377–86, esp. pp. 384–6; Hundsbichler, *Nahrung*, pp. 200–1. Medieval inner Switzerland has hitherto proved an exception. As recent paleozoological research shows, a considerable part of nutritional needs in meat was met by huntable game; W. Meyer, 'Die Wüstung "Spilplätz" auf der Charretalp SZ', *Der Geschichtsfreund CXXXVI* (1983), pp. 159–60.

80 Irsigler, *Kölner Haushalt*, pp. 645–6.

81 *Tuchers Haushaltbuch*, pp. 32, 80–1, 88, 94, 103, 127, 136–7, 140, 152.

82 Kamann, Nürberger, *Haushaltungsbücher*.

83 W. Mohr and K. Koenen, *Die Butter* (Hildesheim, 1958); U. Dirlmeier, 'Butter', in *Lexikon des Mittelalters* II (Munich/Zurich, 1983), p. 1162.

84 J. A. van Houtte, 'Die Handelsbeziehungen zwischen Köln und den südlichen Niederlanden bis zum Ausgang des 15. Jahrhunderts', *Jb. des Kölnischen Geschichtsvereins* XXIII (1941), pp. 141–84, esp. pp. 146–7; F. Glauser, 'Handel mit Entlebucher Käse und Butter vom 16. bis 19. Jahrhundert', *SchweizZG* XXI (1971), pp. 1–63; Dirlmeier, *Einkommensverhältnisse*, pp. 310, 312, 376–8, 390, 395, 397, 402, 419; Pfister, *Klima* II, pp. 28–9, 32, 46, 56–7.

85 On beer and wine consumption, see pp. 87, 88, 95 above; also *Tuchers Haushaltbuch*.

86 On brandy, see p. 96 above; on dietetics, G. Keil, 'Der deutsche Branntweintraktat des Mittelalters', *Centaurus* VII (1960), pp. 53–100; on culinary uses, see e.g. Wackernagel, *Kochbuch*, pp. 367–8 (Die tugent von dem geprenten wein).

87 M. Matheus, 'Gefeuerter Wein. Zur "Weinverbesserung" in alter Zeit', *Kreis Bernkastel-Wittlich-Jb.* (1985), pp. 361–73.

88 W. Heyd, *Geschichte des Levantehandels im Mittelalter* (2 vols., Stuttgart, 1879); L. Bardenhewer, *Der Safranhandel im Mittelalter* (Bonn, 1914); H. H. Mauruschat, *Gewürze, Zucker und Salz im vorindustriellen Europa. Eine preisgeschichtliche Untersuchung* (Ph.D., Göttingen, 1975); Irsigler, *Köln*, pp. 283–303 with further literature.

89 F. Braudel, *Sozialgeschichte des 15.–18. Jahrhunderts. Der Alltag* (Munich, 1985), pp. 230–35; originally published as *Civilisation matérielle, économie et capitalisme, XVe–XVIIe siècles. Les structures du quotidien: Le possible et l'impossible* (Paris, 1979).

90 Cf. Mauruschat, *Gewürze*, pp. 30–36; Irsigler, *Köln*, pp. 291–2; Braudel, *Sozialgeschichte*, pp. 235–8. On developments in the sixteenth century, E. Schmitt, ed., *Die mittelalterlichen Ursprünge der europäischen Expansion* (Munich, 1986), pp. 140–2.

91 See the examples cited above on pp. 96, 97; also M. Zimmermann, 'Kochkunst im spätmittelalterlichen Frankreich. "Le Ménagier de Paris"', in Bitsch *et al.*, *Essen*, pp. 103–15; *Von der gesunden Lebensweise. Nach dem alten Hausbuch der Familie Cerruti* (Munich/Vienna/Zurich, 1985), originally published as *Il libro di casa Cerruti* (Milan, 1983); Hundsbichler, *Reise*.

92 Dirlmeier, *Einkommensverhältnisse*, pp. 391–425; Stouff, *Ravitaillement*, pp. 219–29.

93 G. Duby, 'La Seigneurie et l'economie paysanne dans les Alpes du Sud en 1338', *Études rurales* (1961), vol. 2, pp. 5–36, here p. 12.

94 Dirlmeier, *Ernährung*, p. 152.

95 Stouff, *Ravitaillement*, pp. 228, 230; Dirlmeier, *Einkommensverhältnisse*, pp. 295–6 with the relevant source references.

96 On the state of research, *op. cit.*, pp. 296–302, 362–3; idem, *Ernährung*, pp. 152–3. On modern conditions, Teuteberg and Wiegelmann, *Wandel*, pp. 118–24.

97 Dirlmeier, *Einkommensverhältnisse*, pp. 293–4, 317–28; Stouff, *Ravitaillement*, pp. 92, 230, 238.

98 On consumption of top-fermented small beer, R. Kleiminger, *Das Heiliggeisthospital von Wismar in sieben Jahrhunderten. Ein Beitrag zur Wirtschaftsgeschichte der Stadt, ihrer Höfe und Dörfer* (Weimar, 1962), pp. 33–4; W. Berger, *Das St-Georgs-Hospital zu Hamburg. Die Wirtschaftsführung eines mittelalterlichen Großhaushalts* (Hamburg, 1972), p. 86. Dirlmeier, *Ernährung*, p. 154.

99 Abel, *Agrarkrisen*, pp. 67–75; W. Abel, *Die Wüstungen des ausgehenden Mittelalters*, 3rd edn (Stuttgart, 1976), pp. 179–81. Dirlmeier, *Ernährung*, pp. 145–8.

100 Dirlmeier, *Versorgung*, pp. 269–70.

101 Source references in Dirlmeier, *Ernährung*, pp. 148–51; idem, 'Historische Umweltforschung aus der Sicht der mittelalterlichen Geschichte', *Siedlungforschung. Archäologie–Geschichte–Geographie* VI (1988), pp. 97–111, esp. pp. 108–10; Herrmann, *Untersuchung*, pp. 166–7; G. Freund, 'Die Reichspolizeiordnungen des 16. Jahrhunderts und das Delikt der Weinverfälschung', *Zeitschrift für neuere Rechtsgeschichte* XI (1989), pp. 1–11.

102 Abel, *Agrarkrisen*, p. 50; J. Hatcher, *Plague, Population and the English Economy 1348–1530* (London, 1977), p. 73; H.-P. Becht, 'Medizinische Implikationen der historischen Pestforschung am Beispiel des "Schwarzen Todes" von 1347/51, in B. Kirchgässner and J. Sydow, eds., *Stadt und Gesundheitspflege* (Sigmaringen, 1982), pp. 78–94, esp. pp. 81–8.

103 Dirlmeier, *Ernährung*, pp. 143–5.

104 e.g. B. Rüttimann and H. R. Gugg, 'Pathologische Befunde im Gräberfeld'; M. Steiner, 'Zahnärztliche Befunde', in Schneider *et al.*, *Münsterhof* II, respectively pp. 213–27, 228–35.

Translated by Bob Scribner

5

Urban Networks

TOM SCOTT AND BOB SCRIBNER

The German town: definition, size, and economic structure

The history of cities is most commonly written with a strong focus on their internal development, whether constitutional, legal, political, social, or economic. If a comparative mode is adopted, it is often a matter of comparing internal features or structures from one town to another. It is less common to survey the relationship of cities to one another and to the wider economic space in which they were set. Even attempts to describe city types mostly do so in atomistic ways which say little about how cities are connected into wider patterns.[1] It is the purpose of this chapter to examine the wider patterns which linked cities into what might be called urban systems or networks. The notion of some kind of patterned distribution of urban places is not a new one, and will certainly have occurred to anyone who has pondered a map showing the towns in late medieval or early modern Germany. In this period, the landscape was thickly dotted with towns, ranging from the sophisticated metropolis such as Cologne or Nuremberg to the tiny dwarf town, hardly bigger than villages, such as Mindelheim, whose walled area fitted within a trapezoid of 400 × 250 m. In the densest areas of urban settlement, the south and west of the German empire, no one had to travel for more than four or five hours to pass from one town to another and, in the more sparsely settled north and east, no more than seven or eight hours. One understanding of the nature of towns explained why this should be so: Max Weber regarded the town essentially as a market, a place of exchange where local inhabitants could sell what they produced but did not consume, and purchase what they wished to consume but did not produce. In a pre-modern agrarian economy (indeed, even in a modern economy!), no one wished to travel for more than a day to market and back (unless attending the larger fairs, stretching over several days, where overnight stays were frequent). The maximum acceptable distance to market was between two and four hours each way, perhaps between 10 km and 24 km, depending on the terrain and the state of the roads. The dispersal of urban places across the landscape could in theory be explained by such ideal-typical intervals but they quickly come up against the much more untidy nature of reality. Unravelling some of the different patterns and principles by which towns were distributed across Germany is more complex than at first appears.

Let us begin, however, with some basic notions, not least by clarifying what we understand by a town. The problem is stickier than it might seem if our concept of a town is predicated on an image of great cities such as Augsburg, Ulm, Hamburg, or Lübeck. However, these were exceptions; the majority of German towns were small places with populations of less than 2,000 souls. Neither size nor density of settlement is an adequate criterion, since a nucleated village could be more densely settled than a small farm town with large areas of unbuilt land within its walls. A town could possess as few as 200–300 inhabitants, as did Sesslach in Franconia, which consisted in 1543 of just 43 families, while a village such as Dingelstädt on the Eichsfeld, in present-day Saxony-Anhalt, living from stock-raising and agriculture, had 159 households in 1545 and a population of 800. Ilshofen in north Württemberg had a population comprising just 31 farming families, who were actually serfs of the three imperial cities (Schwäbisch Hall, Dinkelsbühl, and Rothenburg ob der Tauber) who exercised joint lordship over the town from 1398 to 1562. The existence of a city wall is also no conclusive indicator, since fortified marketplaces and villages were to be found aplenty in south Germany, while there were some towns in the Tyrol without defensive walls.[2] Weber's economic criterion, identifying the town as a market, is equally inadequate, since not all markets were towns, nor were all towns markets (one thinks of garrison or fortified towns, or the mining towns founded in abundance during the sixteenth century). Another economic-geographical criterion, similar to Weber's, regards the town as a 'central place' fulfilling social and cultural, as well as economic, functions, although monasteries and seigneurial seats had performed that role in the high middle ages, just as princely courts and even industrial villages were to do so during the early modern period. The view that towns were centres of craft rather than of primary production is equally unsatisfactory. Many villages contained large numbers of artisans, while many small towns were like Loburg in Saxony-Anhalt (lying east of Magdeburg and north of Zerbst), with a population of 900 living almost wholly from agriculture and stock-raising.[3] Just how tenuous a grasp on existence some small towns could have is illustrated by Hohenberg in Swabia, destroyed in 1449 and never rebuilt because its situation (some 900 m above sea-level) made it an uneconomic prospect. Its communal land was gratefully swallowed up by the peasant community of Deilingen.[4] Indeed, military catastrophe was often sufficient to put paid to the existence of tiny towns with few deep economic roots, as occurred to several German Swiss towns in the fourteenth century (Maschwanden, Meienberg, Richensee, Fridau, Altreu).[5]

Economic criteria are very slippery, therefore, and many historians prefer legal and political definitions of what constituted a town. Indeed, many towns were created by acts of political will, regardless of their economic viability, of which Silesia provides the classic example, where no fewer than 134 towns were founded by political fiat in the years 1210–1300.[6] The elevation of a rural settlement to urban status was also a constitutional act, with the conferment of a town charter, distinctive legal status, and a town court. But legal status itself did not make a town: villages, too, could be seats of legal jurisdictions, with their own courts and formal communal organization. Consequently, recent urban studies recognize that towns were defined by many different criteria, operating sometimes singly, sometimes in bundles. What is now seen as more important are the characteristics attached to towns within a given region, and how those towns related one to another as part of a general 'urban landscape'.

How many towns were there in late medieval and early modern Germany, and what size were they? Some historians confidently state that central Europe possessed as many as 5,000 towns around 1450, while 4,000 of these fell within the boundaries of the Holy Roman Empire.[7] These are relatively unhelpful statistics for our purposes, since 'Central Europe' is taken to extend from Bruges to Brest-Litovsk and from Falsterbo to Geneva, while the Holy Roman Empire included many non-German towns. The number of 4,000 towns has also been calculated for German (including Swiss German) towns at the end of the middle ages.[8] The calculation is complicated by the fact that historians often focus on town foundations and charters, and ignore the many towns that disappeared, either as a result of military action or because they were incapable of survival. By contrast, towns were sometimes moved by civic pride to trace their origins back to a point where local legend overtook historical fact. A plausible figure, then, might be somewhere between 2,000 and 3,000, including 88 Swiss towns and around 150 Austrian towns (according to modern territorial divisions). What is more important, however, is not some total figure but the fact that the pre-modern urban pattern of Germany was essentially complete by the end of the middle ages, with comparatively few new towns (perhaps around 200) being added between 1500 and 1800.

Agreement on the size of towns is rather easier than on the total numbers, despite the absence of any really hard statistics about urban populations. We possess relatively good information about numbers of houses, households, citizens, or tax-payers from documents such as tax-lists or muster-rolls. Using a standard multiplier (a multiplier of five for households is common, although some demographers regard it as too high or too simplistic), we can gain a rough idea of the population size of a substantial number of towns at the beginning of the early modern period. To

establish exact figures is less important than being able to apportion towns
into broad population groups which, so long as the figures are compiled
on a uniform basis, provide a useful means of comparing different kinds
of towns according to their notional size. Using a cohort of 1,865 towns
that fell within the boundaries of modern Germany, we can ascertain
plausible population figures for the sixteenth century for around two-thirds
of that number. Table 5.1 shows the distribution of towns according to
population size.

Table 5.1 Population size of German towns in the sixteenth century

Category	Population	No.	% of total
Large	20,000 and above	10	0.54
Large	10,000–20,000	18	0.97
Large–medium	5,000–10,000	57	3.05
Medium	2,000–5,000	186	9.97
Small	1,000–2,000	298	15.97
Small	500–1,000	386	20.69
Dwarf	below 500	282	15.12
	no information	628	33.67

It is apparent how few towns there were with more than 5,000 inhabitants – less than 5 per cent of the total. This figure would not change
much if we could fill in the population numbers for those towns for which
we have no information, since most of these probably belonged to the two
or three lowest-size categories. The average town, based on these figures,
had around 2,000 inhabitants, and half (undoubtedly more in reality) were
of this size or smaller, so that we can say that the German urban landscape
was dotted with small and dwarf towns. The thirty-odd large towns
dominated this landscape with their wealth and extensive economic connections, but they rested on a tiered structure of increasingly smaller urban
places, whose numbers grew as the pyramid broadened.

What was the economic character of these German towns? Here we are
better placed than with population figures, since it is possible to identify
the economic characteristics of 97 per cent of the towns in the cohort.
Working with the leading economic activity (most towns had more than
one, many had several), around 40 per cent of towns were engaged heavily
in primary production, either as farming towns (where the main activity
of the citizens was agriculture, so-called *Ackerbürger*), living mainly from
agriculture or from stock-raising, with another 4–5 per cent of towns living
from wine, fishing, or timber. Nothing underlines more the rural nature of
the bulk of German towns. Compared to the dominance of agriculture in
urban life, craft production was relatively modest. Although it was present
in significant ways in 57 per cent of all towns, it was the dominant activity
in only 15 per cent. Similarly, trade was the main activity in only 12 per

cent of all towns, although it featured significantly in around a third of all towns. This is hardly surprising when we consider that trade in significant quantities was more likely to be a feature of large–medium to large towns. Of course, not only large or largeish towns engaged in trade, as shown by Bacharach on the Rhine, with a population of 900, which was the main outlet for wine from the Rhineland Palatinate. Bearing in mind the definitions of the town as a market, it is interesting that only 12 per cent of towns could be characterized as 'markets' in their leading economic activity, while nearly a quarter (23.4 per cent) were explicitly designated as markets alongside other leading activities. Yet all towns were in some sense 'markets', and this category reveals some of the limitations of such a crude exercise in head-counting. To sum up, German urban life was most closely linked to agriculture, secondarily to petty craft production and to relatively modest degrees of trade.

This emphasizes how important it is to understand the relationship between town and country if we are fully to appreciate the parameters – social, economic, and cultural – defining urban life. Working from the notion of the town as a market, Hektor Ammann originally discerned three kinds of space around any town. There was the more narrow marketing space – what he called the smallest unit of an urban economy – constituted by those who regularly visited the town's weekly market, bringing their produce or goods for sale, and purchasing for their own needs, whether of primary produce or manufactures. A second, wider marketing space extended beyond this narrower zone, involving a broader sphere of economic influence in which the town's manufactures were sold and from which outside artisans and merchants were attracted to the town. This broader marketing space could be quite extensive, depending on the goods offered for sale, and could encompass the narrower marketing areas of many small towns. Ammann saw this as roughly equivalent to the sphere of influence of a town's annual market. The third area of economic activity was constituted by long-distance trade, which was roughly equivalent to the sphere of influence of a town's fair or larger annual market.[9] Although this threefold distinction is in principle correct, historical geographers have refined it considerably, though they still do not agree on the exact size or radius of each area; they may even overlap. The immediate market area (*Umland*), it is now suggested, can range from 10 to 30 km, depending on the pull of the urban centre. The next circle, the wider market area (*Hinterland*), may stretch up to 50 or 60 km, but rarely further. Beyond that lies a sphere of influence (*Einflußbereich*) from which visitors to the annual fair might be recruited or migrants attracted to the city's labour market.[10]

Many small and dwarf towns certainly did not rise above the narrower marketing space of a weekly market, and the sphere of economic activity for which they formed a centre was intensely local. An interesting example is Wimpfen on the Neckar, a double town formed from a riverside settlement and a hill townlet clustered around a castle, which enjoyed the status of an imperial city but whose economy depended on wine from the immediate vicinity and the trade that passed along the Neckar valley en route from the Danube to the Rhine. Its marketing area, however, was tiny, covering a 10 km deep area on its own side of the river and extending no further than 5 km radius on the other side.[11] Such towns were drawn into and formed part of the wider sphere of influence of larger or economically more significant towns; indeed, they may even have depended on a larger town for their own economic significance. A further illuminating example is Dohna in Saxony, not far from Pirna. It was described in 1445 as a *stetichen*, when it had only 100 inhabitants, growing to 160 in 1501 and 250 in 1548, and was elevated to a chartered borough only in 1569. It might be better described as a 'locality' rather than as a town, and grew up originally as a settlement by a castle. The castellans had ambitions to found a petty lordship, as a result of which the castle was destroyed in 1402, and until the middle of the fifteenth century Dohna formed the seat of a bailiff of the Elector of Saxony. At some point in the middle ages a decision was taken to plan out a rectangular market, possibly because it lay on an old road over a pass from Dresden to Prague. Somehow money was found to build a town church at the end of the fifteenth century, and to install a richly carved altar-piece in 1520, no mean achievement for a town of only 160 inhabitants. The necessary wealth undoubtedly came from its butchers' guild, which appears in 1462 with the privilege of supplying the weekly market in Dresden. The population continued to climb steadily, reaching the heady numbers of 420 in 1586, 31 of whom were butchers who, together with their households, probably accounted for around a third of the population.[12] The butchers' guild presupposes access to supplies of cattle, undoubtedly drawn from the immediate vicinity, constituting a 'narrower marketing area', but Dohna's real economic significance clearly arose from its attachment to the Dresden market. Two features of inter-urban relationships stand out in this case. First, a town may have derived its economic importance from another, larger town; second, produce did not necessarily flow directly from countryside to major urban centre, but could be routed via a subsidiary town.

   Yet marketing was much more complex in reality than a series of concentric circles of diminishing intensity might suggest. This is because of the way in which two different processes combined in the buying and selling of goods and produce. On the one hand, the market distances travelled by those selling in a given market varied for particular products. For example, cheese, butter, and poultry markets were intensely local, and no one travelled more than a few kilometres to take these to market. Grain was carried over longer distances to its first market point, perhaps 12–15 km, livestock over a wider radius (perhaps 20 km), while wool, cloth, and yarn travelled over still greater distances (32–65 km).[13] Those buying in the market travelled over different distances to acquire these products, distances which may have been determined by the quality of the items and their availability elsewhere. Moreover, merchants seeking opportunities to extend the market for their goods may have travelled far afield to visit, for example, an important annual market or fair. On the other hand, any product marketed over any considerable distance from its place of origin may actually have travelled over two or more market points before reaching its final destination, and it is most likely that those points were towns. The sources used by historians to track the movement of goods and products often conceal this complicated process, especially if they only identify at the final destination the place of origin of the goods. The temptation is to draw a line from destination to origin, thereby obscuring the intermediate marketing points. The staging-posts by means of which goods and produce flowed across Germany, from town to town, are often revealed only by tracing the routes they took and by paying heed to matters such as enforced staples and customs stations, places where goods had to be unloaded and offered for sale, often to boost the market of a particular town or even string of towns, as well as to augment customs or market fees.[14]

This provides us with two basic ways of viewing towns and their relationships both with one another and with the wider agrarian economy, on whose back they often perched in parasitic fashion. We may look at the *space* surrounding a town as a series of concentric circles, or we may look at the *routes* running out from a town and connecting it to others; indeed, we may regard the entire economic landscape as covered by a web of transport routes linking towns together, veins along which blood flowed through the economic body. Emphasizing the one leads to concentration on 'urban central places', emphasizing the other to analysing 'urban networks'. Each of these approaches can be discussed in turn to see what light they throw on our overall theme.

Towns as central places

The notion of the town as a central place has a long pedigree, and goes back to the early nineteenth century and the German economist-geographer von Thünen (d. 1851), who formulated an ideal-typical model of three zones surrounding any town: the first zone involved market-gardening and dairy products; the second and third respectively cereal production and grazing. A new dimension was added to this picture in 1933 by the German geographer Walter Christaller, who began to examine wider patterns of distribution and spacing of modern towns, fascinated by the apparent regularity in the situation, size, and numbers of towns in any given region.

Basing his observations on a market town with a service radius of 4 km, Christaller posited a regular spacing between market towns, such that their market and service functions did not overlap and so compete. Larger towns offering more developed marketing and services were also regularly spaced in the same way, at greater distances from each other, around which the smaller towns were grouped in regular patterns, and the same he held to be true of very large towns. He thus generated an ideal-typical notion of a hierarchy of towns, each related to a circle of lesser towns, within whose own circles of influence there nestled yet smaller towns.[15] When represented in diagram form, in order to tidy up the concept logically, he depicted these marketing and service areas as hexagonal in shape (Fig. 5.1). The radius of distance of one type of town from another he calculated from the distance one might have to travel from one market town to the next (4 km), from a market town to a town with a larger and more specialized range of services (12 km), thence to a large substantial medium town (21 km), and thence to a genuinely large town (36 km).

This spacing was worked out on the basis of two assumptions: first, that there was a demand threshold below which it was uneconomic to provide a certain good or service in any town, so that it was found only in a town of a certain size (small and dwarf towns would be less likely to support a goldsmith or a notary). Second, people would travel only over a given distance to obtain a good or service. As we have seen above, both assumptions have a lot of economic common sense to recommend them. Christaller, however, did not assume that the population size of a town was a reliable guide to its importance as a service centre; his mathematical model of rank–size distribution of towns, according to which towns

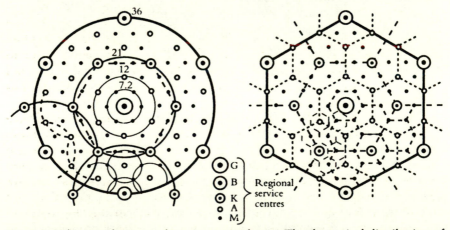

Fig. 5.1 Urban marketing and service networks: (*a*) The theoretical distribution of regional service centres; (*b*) the hexagonal pattern of regional services areas. The M centre (market town) is the basis of the whole system. The G centre is equivalent to a county town with about 30,000 to 100,000 inhabitants. The numbers in Fig. 5.1(*a*) give the radius of each circle in km. (After Christaller.)

should ideally be distributed across the terrain, was calculated on the basis of modern inter-urban communications, according to the number of telephone connections. He was, of course, aware that reality did not fit the ideal-typical model: that geography, historical accident, uneven development over time, political decisions, and administrative convenience may all have played an important part in creating more irregular patterns of cities. For example, many Swiss towns are situated in valley floors, or where the mouths of alpine valleys widen sufficiently to allow for extensive agriculture, while most of the mountainous region of Switzerland is relatively free of towns.[16]

Christaller was also aware of the wide variety of services which might be sought from a town besides those basic economic needs fulfilled by a market for food and manufactures. These included administrative, legal, religious, or financial services, as well as such concerns as health or sociability. Although he attempted to arrange these into a needs hierarchy (lower, middle, and upper grades of need), clearly such matters complicate the pattern of urban spacing, since different services may operate within wholly different spatial arrangements. Although central-place theories, much refined since Christaller's day, are used by modern urban planners, they have rarely been used to analyse how late medieval or early modern cities are related to each other. One notable attempt to do so for the middle ages by the demographer J. C. Russell, who used population size as an indicator of centrality, produced such crude and implausible results as to render the theory useless. For early modern Europe, Jan de Vries has applied sophisticated forms of statistical simulation to both population size and urban density with great success in tracing broad patterns of change over three centuries.[17] Within German urban history the notion of centrality was only slowly taken up, and it has been applied largely to establish the economic space surrounding individual towns rather than to explore patterns of inter-town relationships. Thus, it has contributed more to understanding what Hektor Ammann called the 'economic unit' of city and hinterland, which together constituted an economic region, than it has helped to define an urban network.[18]

In order to test how useful the notion might be, let us take three examples: the distribution of all our large and medium–large towns (those with population above 5,000), the distribution of towns within central Germany, and the distribution of those within the boundaries of modern Württemberg (the German south-west). The dozen largest towns are certainly widely spaced over the map (see Map 5.1): Augsburg and Nuremberg in the south, Strasbourg on the left bank of the Upper Rhine, Cologne on the Lower Rhine, with Aachen to the west, Magdeburg in central Germany, Breslau in Silesia to the east – a predominantly German town in our period. On the north coast we find Bremen with its outlet to the North Sea, Lübeck and Danzig (also predominantly German in the period) on the Baltic coast. With the exception of Cologne and Aachen,

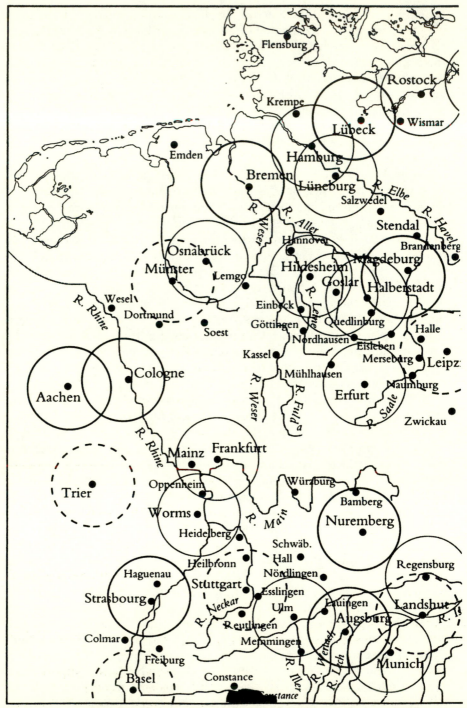

Map 5.1 Towns with population of 5,000 and above, *c.*1500

The map contains the following labels:

Flensburg

Rostock

Krempe
Wismar

Lübeck

Hamburg
Emden
Bremen
Lüneburg
R. Elbe
Salzwedel
R. Havel
Stendal
Osnabrück
Hannover
Brandenburg
Münster
Lemgo
Hildesheim
Magdeburg
Wesel
Goslar
Halberstadt
Dortmund
Einbeck
Quedlinburg
Halle
Soest
Göttingen
Nordhausen
Eisleben
Leipz
Kassel
Merseburg
R. Weser
Mühlhausen
Aachen
Cologne
Erfurt
Naumburg
R. Saale
Zwickau
R. Rhine
R. Fulda
R. Weser
R. Leine
R. Aller
R. Weser

Mainz
Frankfurt
R. Rhine
Würzburg
Oppenheim
Trier
Bamberg
Worms
Nuremberg
Heidelberg
R. Main
Schwäb.
Hall
Haguenau
Nördlingen
Regensburg
Strasbourg
Stuttgart
Esslingen
Landshut
Colmar
Ulm
Lauingen
Augsburg
R. I
Reutlingen
R. Neckar
R. Wertach
Freiburg
Memmingen
R. Lech
Munich
Basel
Constance
R. Iller
Constance

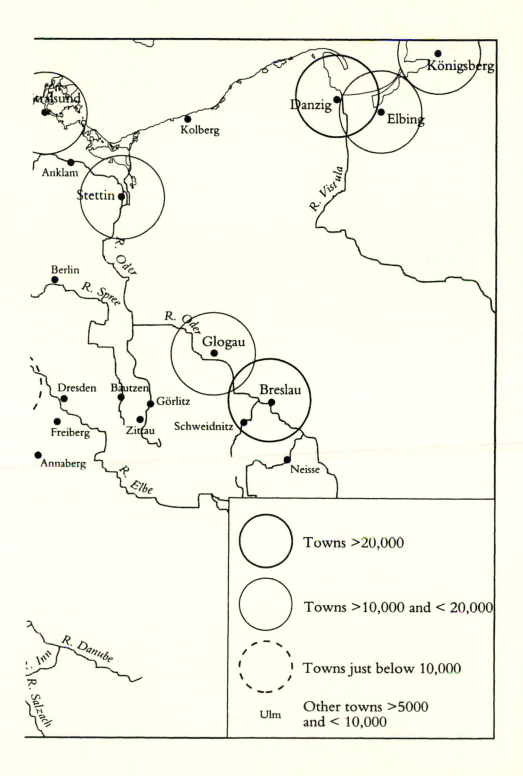

Stralsund

Kolberg

Königsberg

Danzig

Elbing

Anklam

R. Vistula

Stettin

Berlin

R. Spree

R. Oder

Glogau

Dresden

Bautzen

Görlitz

Breslau

Freiberg

Zittau

Schweidnitz

Annaberg

R. Elbe

Neisse

R. Danube

R. Inn

R. Salzach

Towns >20,000

Towns >10,000 and < 20,000

Towns just below 10,000

Ulm   Other towns >5000
        and < 10,000

which might be thought to compete for influence, we could see how each of these towns dominated a substantial swathe of territory for which they formed an economic centre. The Aachen/Cologne clash is only an apparent one, an accident of the crudity of our size categories. Aachen's size was a function of its metal trades and cloth industry, but it was clearly inferior in rank to Cologne, which was twice its size and, according to a rank–size distribution, would be graded comfortably in a category above it. Cologne contained all the services flowing from its position as seat of the ecclesiastical primate of the German church and from its extensive ecclesiastical foundations, as well as its Rhineland trade, and must count as the dominant city of the region.

If we now fill in the other large towns with populations over 10,000, we can see the intermediate spaces being occupied by further (and, according to Christaller's theory, smaller) spheres of influence. Ulm, Munich, and Regensburg in the south, Worms on the Middle Rhine, and Frankfurt on the Main; in Lower Saxony, Osnabrück, Goslar, Hildesheim, and Braunschweig; further east, Halberstadt, Erfurt in Thuringia, Glogau in Silesia; along the north coast and running to the east, Hamburg, Rostock, Stralsund, Stettin, and furthest east, in the territory of the Teutonic Knights, Elbing and Königsberg. If we draw around each of these towns, as a notional sphere of influence, a circle of 100 km radius, some anomalies immediately become apparent: Hamburg, Lübeck, and Lüneburg appear to compete for influence, as do Goslar, Hildesheim, Braunschweig, and Halberstadt, while other areas are relatively bereft of large towns. Indeed, a rectangle above the Main, and bounded to the north by a line running from Cologne through Hildesheim to Erfurt, seems not to have produced any towns over 10,000 souls, while the thinly settled tracts east of the Elbe also stand out. Some of the gaps may be filled in by providing circles of influence for those towns which just fell under the 10,000 line but were undoubtedly 'large' towns: Basel, Stuttgart and Landshut in the south, Trier to the west, Münster in Westphalia, Leipzig in Saxony.[19]

Filling in the 56 'large–medium' towns gives us a virtually complete picture of an urban network constituted by the distribution of towns with a population over 5,000. The picture shows some clusters, with some marked anomalies in which towns of the same size seem to compete for space, while some remarkably empty spaces still remain, although some of the latter are explicable. The heavily wooded, mountainous areas of the Black Forest and the Thuringia–Franconia forest account for the absence of large towns in those regions, as does the topography of north Hesse. Some of the anomalies are less marked if we compare the character of the towns involved. The 'competition' of Hamburg, Lübeck and Lüneburg is deceptive, for the relationship was rather one of complementary functions. Goods passing from the North Sea to the Baltic were unloaded in Hamburg and transferred to Lübeck and vice versa, while Lüneburg provided an outlet for goods from both directions to pass to the south, as well as supplying that essential commodity, salt, of which it was the leading producer in north Germany. The jostling of Goslar, Hildesheim, Braunschweig, and Halberstadt is also explicable by the towns' peculiarities. Goslar is most distinctive, owing its size to its mining industry – indeed, it was the wealthiest German mining town of the middle ages, while Hildesheim and Halberstadt were seats of major bishoprics as well as Hanseatic towns. However, the concentration of large and large–medium towns in such a limited area is striking, and the explanation may have less to do with any gradated structure of towns and more with the absence of certain kinds of town. Lower Saxony was under-represented with medium and small towns because urban population was more concentrated in larger settlements. The region actually had twice as many towns with population above 5,000 than the cohort of towns used here. In this case, towns were not equally distributed by size in descending order, a fact that in turn may have been the result of the more extensive agriculture of the region, which tended towards large scattered farms rather than clustered village settlements.

The exercise so far shows that there might be a rough applicability of central-place systems at the broadest and crudest levels, with the ten largest cities subordinating the score of large towns, which in their turn subordinate the fifty-odd large–medium towns into interrelated clusters. However, the distribution of towns becomes more irregular and more anomalous the further we move down the size categories. The north German coastal regions are characterized by a string of towns stretching from Bremen to Königsberg, and there are marked concentrations of towns in two broad regions, in central Germany (a band running from Lower Saxony through Thuringia-Saxony to Lower Lusatia) and in the south-west. However, there are no really regular patterns of centrality in these clusters, which in the first two cases resemble respectively a snake and a comet's-tail pattern more than that of a star-burst. Christaller based his model on towns south of the Main, rather than Germany as a whole, so that these anomalies escaped his attention. The difficulty of discerning regular patterns is even more marked if we look more closely at the central German comet-tail, assigning a circle of 50 km radius to each town of 5,000 and above (see Map 5.2). The triangle Bautzen–Görlitz–Zittau clearly forms an Upper Lusatian system, as does the diamond-shaped system Glogau–Breslau–Neisse–Schweidnitz for Silesia. There is a Saxon chain-link system running from Dresden–Freiburg–Annaberg–Zwickau, but the nearest to a coherent system is the cluster of towns running north and north-west of the line Leipzig–Naumburg–Erfurt. Those to the north of Magdeburg have clearly delimited spheres of influence; but if Magdeburg and Erfurt are taken as the dominant towns of this cluster, then there is certainly no pattern of centrality, and those two towns squeeze the others in a pincer movement. However, if we treat these two as equal in status to the other towns in the cluster, then there is a relatively even spacing of towns around the central

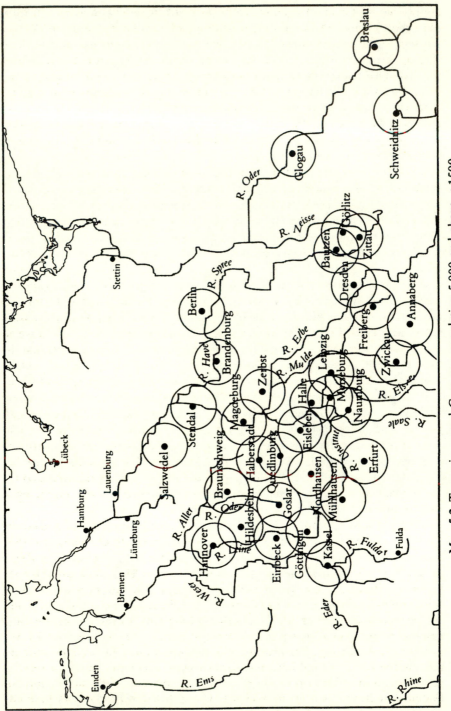

Map 5.2 Towns in central Germany, population 5,000 and above, c.1500

area of Thuringia and the Harz, with only one or two anomalies: Quedlin-burg (seat of an imperial abbey) intruding between Halberstadt and Nord-hausen, and the heavy overlaps of space Halle–Merseburg–Naumburg and Leipzig–Halle–Eisleben. If we bear in mind the trend from the middle of the sixteenth century onwards, with Leipzig rising to dominance and Erfurt declining, we could envisage these towns with smaller areas of influence, subordinate to the growing sphere of Leipzig, which appears as a stem from which the other towns hang like a bunch of grapes. Thus, centrality is not the most evident pattern, although there is undoubtedly a complex urban system at work.

Let us now turn to the south-west, in particular the region within the boundaries of modern Baden-Württemberg. The towns fall within a rectangle bounded by Switzerland to the south, the Main to the north, and the spheres of influence of Basel–Strasbourg–Worms to the west and Nuremberg–Augsburg to the East (see Map 5.1). The influence of Basel and Strasbourg is limited by the line of the Black Forest. There is only one large town directly influencing the area, Ulm on the eastern edge, although if we allow Stuttgart this status (with an eye on the future, and given that it falls only slightly below the 10,000 line), we can regard it as forming a large-town central place for the area. There are few towns with more than 5,000 inhabitants (see Map 5.3). We can leave Freiburg and Constance to one side, as centres of rather different spheres of influence, especially as that of Constance extended more towards the south. The only other large–medium towns are Heilbronn, Schwäbisch Hall, Esslingen, and Reut-lingen. Because this is an altogether smaller-scale town system, we can also add to our map all the towns in the medium category (2,000–5,000), providing them with a circle of influence of 15 km. Two features immedi-ately stand out. The five largest towns in this area (Heilbronn, Schwäbisch Hall, Stuttgart, Esslingen, and Reutlingen) compete fiercely for space (all have been given a circle of 50 km radius except – to avoid confusion – Esslingen, although its circle can easily be imagined on the map), each town contending with two other competitors.

Stuttgart is the anomaly here, growing as a capital with the ambitions of the counts and (from 1495) dukes of Württemberg to challenge the four imperial cities. Indeed, Duke Ulrich even attempted a conquest of Reut-lingen in 1519, provoking his expulsion from his lands until 1534. Gradually, Stuttgart was to overshadow its four rivals and on the basis of this future development we can construct a system around it (as Christaller did for the modern period). Stuttgart undoubtedly forms the centre of a system of medium towns with an irregular shape, constituted by Mark-gröningen, Backnang, Schorndorf, Göppingen, Tübingen, and Pforzheim, all but the last Württemberg territorial towns and seats of ducal district administration. Pforzheim was a territorial town of the margraviate of Baden, but functioned as an access link for Württemberg towns to those of the Rheinland. At this level, the notion of a central system constituted

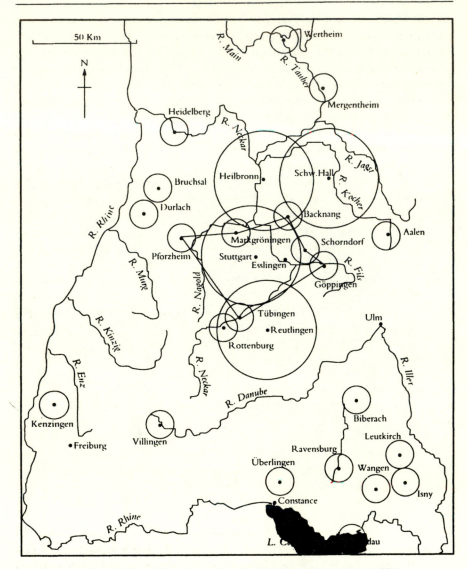

Map 5.3 The urban network of south-west Germany, *c.*1500

by service functions seems to have coherence, although it is largely the coherence of political-administrative influence. At the lower level of small towns all coherence disappears, and small towns are clustered thickly around Stuttgart in ways that seem to defy any pattern. (They also defied a pattern for Christaller, who was forced to change all his categories and to place towns rather arbitrarily into lower categories in order to make the groupings fit the theory.)[20] Meanwhile Heilbronn, Schwäbisch Hall, and Reutlingen seem to have no comparable system of satellite small towns within their sphere of influence. Moreover, the distribution of medium towns only falls into anything resembling a pattern in one other case: the cluster of towns to the north-east of the north shore of Lake Constance, Überlingen, Lindau, Ravensburg, Wangen, Isny, Leutkirch, and Biberach as an outrider, appear as a system oriented towards the only other large–medium town in their vicinity, Memmingen. There is little evidence of a central system here, even if we include Kaufbeuren in the group. However, this does correspond to a division remarked upon by Hektor Ammann, bv which Swabia falls into two distinct parts separated by the Swabian Alp: Inner Swabia in the north-west, and Upper Swabia in the south-east, both parts with distinctive economic characteristics.[21] From this perspective, it is not surprising that we find different town systems.

Let us sum up: there are undoubtedly distinctive systems of towns to be found at all levels, from the largest down to those with populations above 2,000. However, these systems are far more varied and complex than can be covered by the notion of central-place systems in the sense used by Christaller. Even allowing for the fact that the towns discussed represent only 15 per cent of the total, one might expect the sample to be sufficient to point in the right direction – and that direction is one of diversity rather than of any uniform pattern. Christaller's model was deeply indebted to the positivist notions of social science prevalent in his day, which assumed regularity and logic where often none existed. Moreover, it was based on towns shaped by the experience of industrialization and modern communications. For a better understanding of early modern urban systems, we need to turn to patterns appropriate to that period.

Urban networks

An alternative organizing concept for inter-urban links has been proposed by Hohenberg and Lees under the label of a 'network system' (see Fig. 5.2). This is predicated on the idea of towns providing trading links within a complex pattern of trade routes. The trading network relies on agriculture and basic commodity production, more appropriate than an elaborate hierarchy of services to the situation in early modern Europe, when the bulk of trade involved very basic commodities such as grain and cloth. A town may draw on the agricultural surplus of grain and raw materials to feed and sustain itself, re-exporting what it does not need, and perhaps also processing the raw materials. This demand may stimulate further production of larger surpluses, drawing on under-used reserves of land or labour; but in any case the town functions as a gateway, linking it to a wider trading network. Lesser towns may gather and ship the staple or

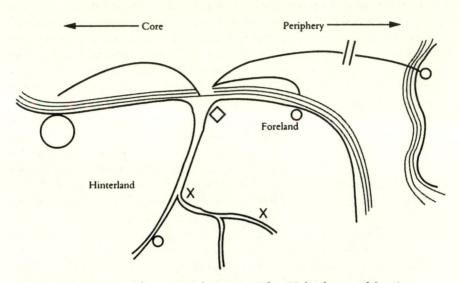

Fig. 5.2 An urban network system (After Hohenberg and Lees)

export crop, distribute a return flow of goods, and provide other central-place services. Thus an array of towns may grow up based on local trade, in which towns form centres, nodes, junctions, outposts, or relays of a trading network. The nature of the exported goods and the prosperity of the trade will affect the development and extent of the network. The concept also recognizes that political acts may influence the development of the network through the granting of new urban charters or market franchises.[22] Hohenberg and Lees rightly point to the flexibility and adaptability of the concept by contrast with the central-place system. Towns are links in a wider network, often neither the first source nor the ultimate destination of goods, so that both they and the routes are interchangeable. Shifts in marketing, political conflicts, or economic innovations can lead to the displacement of one centre by another, with a corresponding rearrangement of the network.

At the same time, a weakness in this approach may lie in its very fluidity. How do trading links and routes coalesce into a network if their pattern and development are so interchangeable? There is a real danger of super-imposing retrospectively a 'network' upon a series of bilateral contacts or random clusters of commercial activity. Does an urban network explain or merely describe the distribution of trading links? To test these assumptions, let us look at the export of wine from southern Germany in the early modern period. Immediately it is obvious that there were very different patterns of trade in wine from the Neckar region, compared to that in Alsatian or Rhine wine. Neckar wine of modest quality was traded largely within a region running south to Lake Constance, north to the Main, and east to the borders of modern Bavaria, the main artery of the trade being the line of the Danube, along which some Neckar wine even reached Vienna. The high-quality Alsatian and Rhine wines were shipped over enormously greater distances, reaching Scotland, Norway, Sweden, Finland, and Russia. The main routes of this network were down the Rhine, where they found numerous relay points in the Low Countries, whence they were reshipped to England, Scandinavia, and Eastern Europe, as well as via Frankfurt, along the land routes Magdeburg–Frankfurt an der Oder–Posen and Görlitz–Breslau, into Eastern Europe. The gateways into the trade were Colmar and especially Strasbourg for Alsatian wine, Speyer, Worms, and Bingen for Rhine wine, with Frankfurt and Cologne as key relay points, and a series of other relay and redistribution points.[23] The concept of a network system fits these inter-urban relationships far better than that of a central-place system.

The example of the wine network suggests how we might unravel some of the puzzles about systems of towns in the south-west, as well as some of the anomalies produced by a central-place perspective. A key to the distribution and interrelationships of towns is found in the elaborate river network running throughout all parts of Germany and the most striking feature of any map locating early modern towns (a point overlooked by Christaller). Much of the inland economy of early modern Europe was oriented to its great river systems. Braudel spoke of an 'isthmus' running south to north through the middle of France, constituted by the route running up the Rhône from Marseilles to Lyon and connecting with the Seine via Paris and Rouen to the Channel. For Germany, the Rhine fulfilled the same function, although the image of a pipeline might be more apposite. River systems were crucial highways of trade because they lowered transport costs. The costs of long-distance land transport were only repaid by high-value, low-bulk goods – spices, furs, silks – or else by exceptionally high prices. It has been calculated for grain that transport generated costs equal to the sale price of the grain after a distance of 375 km, so that shipping grain over long distances was only profitable when the prices were very low at the point of origin and very high at the distant point of sale. None the less, rivers had their hazards as shipment routes. They could freeze over in winter, were often strewn with rapids and rocks, and were prone to silting, marshes, and abrupt changes in course. Travel up-river also necessitated towpaths and human or animal labour to haul the boats, although the use of small, shallow-draught boats facilitated both up-river haulage and navigation of rivers with little depth: sometimes two-thirds of a metre was all that was necessary. Navigable stretches of waterway conducive to trade could also encourage customs stations which could weigh the cost differential with land transport. Moreover, on smaller rivers, the establishment of mills and sluices in the course of the middle ages hampered the river flow. Thus, water transport was often used in combination with land routes rather than as a universal solution, and the navigability of rivers, especially smaller rivers, was a cyclical matter, sometimes falling out of use, to be revived later when political will emerged to overcome the costs or hindrances. For all that, the history of river transport has been neglected and under-researched, and offers illuminating perspectives for understanding the infrastructure of many of Germany's urban networks.[24]

The logic of the distribution of the large towns along the north German coast is provided by the great river systems to which the towns formed gateways, Danzig and Elbing for the Vistula, Stettin for the Oder, Hamburg for the Elbe, Bremen for the Wesel (see Map 5.1). Goods flowed down these highways for shipment on sea routes, and other goods flowed back inland along them. The great rivers of the Oder, the Elbe, and the Danube established chain-links of towns along their routes.[25] Danzig was a harbour of the Teutonic Order until 1460, acting as the point of exit for grain collected at the Order's seat in Marienburg from the Vistula delta. The politics of the grain trade led Danzig, Elbing, and Thorn to break away from the Order in 1460 and to place themselves under Polish rule, leaving Königsberg as the Order's main outlet. Danzig concentrated grain shipments for re-export from several other towns in West Prussia, especially via Thorn, and drew on Polish grain at the point where the road from Lublin met the Vistula. In the sixteenth century, grain warehouses lined the banks of the Vistula in Danzig for 4 km, and in 1557 150 grain ships a day reached Danzig from Poland. Stettin was the outlet for grain from Pomerania, Silesia, Poland, and Bohemia flowing down the Oder and its tributaries and which was re-exported to Scotland, the Low Countries, Sweden, and Norway. The example confirms the Hohenberg and Lees model, which sees towns especially as gateways into overseas trade, so establishing an extended urban network. The Oder also provides an example of a further urban system interlinking over a distant riverine connection, in that the towns of Silesia were arrayed 'like a string of pearls' along the upper Oder or its tributaries that flowed through the whole land, and which constituted the region as one of remarkable urban concentration. This provides a more convincing logic for the system Glogau–Breslau–Neisse–Schweidnitz than central-place theory.[26]

On the Elbe, Magdeburg functioned as the collection point of a broad and corn-rich hinterland for grain flowing down the Elbe to Hamburg. Since 1309 the town had held staple rights for all grain passing along the Elbe, effectively allowing it to dominate middle Elbian trade and explaining its central position. Stendal was a further collection-point for the Mark Brandenburg to export grain to Hamburg, but the river network also extended along the branch of the Havel to Brandenburg and thence to Berlin on the Spree. The exception that proves the rule was Lübeck, which sat on no extensive riverine system and which also had no grain trade, simply meeting its own consumption needs from its modest hinterland. The town's position as a reshipment point we have mentioned above, although it also dominated a land-route trade cutting across the line of the Elbe by virtue of its central organizing role in the Hansa and so its crucial outlet to the Baltic. Its function as a gateway to a sea route outweighed its lack of riverine access. Yet Lübeck was also eventually forced to concede to the logic of water transport, and at the end of the fourteenth century invested enormous amounts in an artificial connection with the Elbe (the *Steckenitzfahrt*, opened 1397), in order to gain easier access to salt from Lüneburg.[27]

The Weser system was extremely complex, with branches from the Aller leading over Celle to the Oker and thence to Braunschweig. Further down the Aller the Leine leads south to Hanover. The Weser itself extends upriver over Minden and Hameln to Hannoversch Münden, the point of confluence of the Werra and the Fulda, with Kassel, Hersfeld, and Fulda upstream, while the Eder branches from the Fulda above Kassel to lead to Fritzlar. It has been remarked how many episcopal seats and monastic foundations are to be found along this network: the bishoprics of Bremen, Verden, and Minden on the Weser, along with monasteries on the Weser at Corvey, Hameln and Höxter, Hersfeld on the Fulda, and Elze (seat of the bishops of Hildesheim) on the Leine. Hildesheim was also reachable by small boats on the tiny Harz river, the Innerste, and the Fulda was at one stage navigable to Fulda itself (by the end of the fifteenth century, only to Kassel). From the fourteenth century the Leine, the Aller, and the Weser were made navigable, enabling grain traffic to pass from Hanover via the Weser to Bremen, and the Oker followed in the middle of the fifteenth century, allowing Braunschweig to enter the system. Indeed, stone and lime from the Harz were brought downriver to Braunschweig. Oker navigation was given a renewed boost by the dukes of Braunschweig–Wolfenbüttel during the sixteenth century in the service of their mining activities in the Harz, and Braunschweig was supplied with timber over this route.

The importance of this riverine network is shown by the political activity it generated. In the fourteenth century Bremen had to be persuaded to allow free grain transit from the Lower Saxon towns Hanover, Goslar, Hameln, and Braunschweig, while in the mid-fifteenth Lüneburg and Magdeburg protested against Braunschweig's access to the system. Lauenburg watched warily over its stretch of the Elbe, and boats from Lüneburg were only allowed as far as Lauenburg before the goods had to be transferred to Lauenburg boats. Celle and Hannoversch Münden both owed much of their prosperity to their levying of customs or enforcement of a staple respectively, hotly contested by those affected; indeed, Landgrave Karl of Hesse in 1699 even founded Karlshafen as a harbour-town for a (never completed) canal link to Kassel in order to avoid the Münden staple.[28]

The north German towns thus exemplify gateway networks, but are also connected to what we might call chain-link urban networks. The Rhine provides the most obvious example of such a network. On the right bank of the Upper Rhine, Freiburg mediated between the hills of the Black Forest and trade both up and down river, with smaller towns forming relay points in the chain – Kenzingen, Offenburg, Durlach, and Bruchsal. Offenburg was itself a link in a subsidiary chain up into the Black Forest along the Kinzig, connecting Gengenbach, Zell, Haslach, Hausach, and Wolfach, and substantial quantities of timber were rafted down this river to the Rhine (see Map 5.3). On the left bank, the network ran from Basel via Colmar, Strasbourg, and Haguenau, with alternatives of land or river routes, the latter from Basel to Speyer and Worms, a point where goods were reloaded onto deeper draught vessels for the stretch to Cologne. At Mainz, the system was joined by the Main network, although Frankfurt came to dominate this relay point rather than Mainz, undoubtedly because of the former's more favourable connection to the land routes to central Germany. Cologne formed the major node, gateway, and relay point into the Lower Rhine, via Wesel and on to the Netherlands. A string of inter-mediate towns fitted into this elongated network, all drawing their existence from the logic of the Rhine trade and the cross-routes that fed into it. How important this was for a town's economic existence is shown by the case of Duisburg, cut off from its former position on the Rhine at the beginning of the thirteenth century by a freak flood which transposed the Rhine flow a mile to its west. The citizens were forced to construct a canal at enormous cost to link the town to its former artery, but to little avail: the inconvenience of diverting from the main route deprived Duisburg of much of its relay trade and its earlier prosperity, and by the end of the middle ages it had become a sleepy farming town, reviving only in the early modern period as the mineral resources of the Ruhr became more important.

The Danube provides the spine of an even more elaborate and elongated urban network, stretching from the Black Forest to Vienna and ultimately reaching the Black Sea after almost 3,000 km. Just considering the German stretch, we see it extending up-river over key junctions linking sub-networks of rivers and their towns into an economic nerve system. At Passau, the Inn flowed down from the Alps, with the shipping stretch beginning at Hall in Tyrol; shipping salt on this route was especially important in the later sixteenth century, and the Salzach was another important route for transporting salt down from Salzburg into the Inn and Danube flows. The confluence of the Isar provided a link to Landshut and Munich, whence it was possible to travel by ship to Passau in the four-teenth century. By means of the Naab, goods from the Upper Palatinate flowed down to Regensburg, a major relay-point of medieval trade along the Danube coming up from the Black Sea before the shift of trade to the west deprived it of its enormous wealth. Regensburg had reached the peak of its wave by 1500 and was coasting steeply downhill, despite all efforts by the town goverment to rescue the situation, a good example of the impartial cruelty of the shifts affecting such trading networks. Ingolstadt and Neuburg were staging-points before the junction with the Lech, which linked southwards to Augsburg, then via Landsberg to Füssen, while the Wertach also flowed down from Kaufbeuren to join the Lech at Augsburg. The Lech was navigable by boat to Augsburg, but both the Wertach and the Lech carried freight on rafts from Kaufbeuren and Füssen respectively. At Donauwörth, the Wörnitz flowed down from Dinkelsbühl, but Ulm was the next major town, with Lauingen fulfilling the role of an intermediate relay-point. The Danube does not seem to have been navigable above Ulm, although timber was rafted down from the Black Forest, and until 1570 goods travelled down from Ulm on freight rafts rather than boats.[29] The practicality of navigation and river-borne trade on all these rivers requires exploration, although roads in any case often followed the river valleys to provide the crucial transport links in the network.

From this river-system perspective, the apparent overlap of the spheres of influence of Regensburg and Landshut, or of Munich, Augsburg, and Ulm, suggested by a central-place system makes perfect sense. Munich existed as a point of entry into the system for its surrounding countryside, Landshut as an important relay-point and further point of entry, Regensburg as a point of entry from the Upper Palatinate and a relay point. Equally Ulm, Augsburg and Munich do not really compete. Augsburg is a nodal point connecting two transalpine land routes (Reschen pass and Brenner pass) and a land route north to Nuremberg to the river system Wertach–Lech–Danube. Ulm connects similar north–south land routes with the confluence of the Iller and the Danube. We can now see the logic of the Upper Swabian system Lindau–Wangen–Isny–Leutkirch, which connects to Ulm on the Iller via Memmingen, while the Iller also links Kempten to Memmingen and Ulm, navigable by freight raft or boat down-river from Kempten, where a land route from Füssen linked into the alpine passes over the Reschen and Brenner.

By the same token, we can also unravel some of the puzzle about the distribution of towns in Württemberg (north-west Swabia), which caused Christaller so much difficulty in applying his model. At the heart of the Inner Swabian system of towns is the Neckar valley, along which are found twenty-one towns, from the river's source to its confluence with the Rhine. Most of these lie in Württemberg and, as we would expect, all but five occur before the river passes through the steeply wooded hills below Wimpfen. They include four imperial cities (Rottweil, Esslingen, Heilbronn, and Wimpfen), two princely residences (Stuttgart, Heidelberg), and two university towns (Tübingen, Heidelberg). The Württemberg towns provided a remarkable concentration of population, accounting for 24 per cent of the urban population of the duchy and around 12 per cent of its total population in the sixteenth century. Admittedly, a large part of the urban population was found in the adjoining towns Stuttgart and Esslingen; but within the range of towns smaller than 10,000 larger urban settlements are clearly over-represented, as we can see from Table 5.2, which compares

Table 5.2 Distribution of towns in the Neckar valley

		Neckar No.	%	All towns %
Large–medium	5,000–10,000	4	19.05	3.05
Medium	2,000–5,000	3	14.29	9.97
Small	1,000–2,000	10	47.61	15.97
Small	500–1,000	1	4.76	20.96
Dwarf	below 500	1	4.76	15.12
	no information	2		33.67

the size distribution of these towns with that in the total cohort.

The Neckar valley towns undoubtedly formed a coherent urban system running through the heart of the duchy of Württemberg. The economic activity of these towns was a mixture of trade (Rottweil, Esslingen, Stuttgart, Heilbronn, Heidelberg), wine (Rottenburg, Tübingen, Stuttgart, Cannstadt, Besigheim, Marbach, and Neckarsulm), timber (Nürtingen, Heilbronn, Gundelsheim, Eberbach), and a strong proportion of agricultural products (Oberndorf, Horb, Nürtingen, Marbach, Besigheim, Lauffen, Neckarsulm, and Wimpfen). The only dwarf town (Lauffen) depended largely on agriculture and stock-raising, while two other towns (Oberndorf, Marbach) also had some stock-raising. Cloth was the most important manufacture, and a string of cloth-producing towns runs the length of the valley, from Rottweil via Horb to Wimpfen. Craft production appears in significant amounts in eight towns (Rottweil, Oberndorf, Rottenburg, Tübingen, Esslingen, Stuttgart, Cannstadt, Heilbronn), while Sulz was specialized as a salt town. Clashes of spheres of influence, puzzling in terms of a central-place system, are easily explicable in terms of a network system. Rottenburg, under Habsburg lordship, competed with Tübingen, which had the additional advantage of a university founded in 1386. Esslingen clearly dominated its stretch of the Neckar until the promotion of Stuttgart as a rising capital produced a powerful competitor which was to overshadow the imperial city neighbour. Stuttgart thus emerged to become the linchpin of the system, especially since it also formed the central place for a system of satellite towns, as we have already seen. Indeed, the example shows that a network system is not incompatible with a central-place system, and Stuttgart clearly profited by both types of orientation.

The urban network of the Neckar valley, however, forms what we might call a rosary-bead system, with one or two larger beads interspersed among the smaller but roughly equal-sized beads. We can follow Ammann in envisaging the network as possessing an extended common hinterland stretching up the side valleys and so drawing in the woollen production of towns such as Weil der Stadt, Calw, and Wildberg. Moreover, the Wurm and the Nagold brought timber down from the Black Forest via Pforzheim, joining the Neckar at Besigheim to reach the major collection and reshipment point at Heilbronn, a route of such significance in the later fifteenth and early sixteenth centuries that the whole trade had to be regulated by ducal intervention in 1536. By then the rafting on the Neckar and its tributaries was so famous that it found mention in Sebastian Münster's *Cosmographia*.[30] If we regard the network as a functioning whole, we can see why its cloth industry acquired international significance well beyond German boundaries, despite the insignificant size of individual towns. As a final comment on the Neckar valley network, we might mention that it interlinks with a smaller system of towns formed by the forking of the Kocher and the Jagst from the Neckar, the former with Schwäbisch Hall as its large bead, the latter with Crailsheim.

A similar exercise could be conducted for the Main, although space does not permit the closer attention that all the riverine systems and subsystems deserve. Ammann explored the network of towns on the High Rhine (the stretch of the river from Schaffhausen to Basel) and along the Aare, and established a not dissimilar pattern.[31] However, it will be more useful to turn our attention towards central Germany again, to explore more closely an example of an urban network where rivers do not play such a dominant role but where the emphasis is provided more by the network of trade routes. The role of Erfurt as a central place for Thuringia has already been mentioned, although it has its peculiarities in that it is hardly 'central' in terms of satellite towns, since the major Thuringian towns in its local system run in a northern semicircle from Eisenach to the west, via Mühlhausen, Nordhausen, and Sangerhausen to Naumburg to the east. The occurrence of sizeable towns to the south is hampered by the Thuringian-Franconian forest. Erfurt certainly functioned as a central place for the surrounding countryside, and to ensure this role it acquired a sizeable subject territory of its own. However, its economic pre-eminence rested on more than that – in fact, on two other parameters.[32]

Erfurt was a nodal point of several major trade routes: the so-called *Hellweg*, the High Road running west–east over Cologne–Kassel–Eisenach–Erfurt–Naumburg–Leipzig–Breslau (with a road branching at Leipzig to run south to Prague). It was also a junction where several Hanseatic roads met from the north: Münster–Kassel–Eisenach–Erfurt; roads from Hanover, Hildesheim, or Braunschweig running over Nordhausen to Erfurt; and a main route from the north over Sangerhausen from Magdeburg (itself a node of routes coming from Hamburg, Lübeck, Brandenburg, and Berlin). Erfurt was a major staging-point for goods passing south through the Thuringian-Franconian forest, either via Eisenach to Frankfurt or directly south over Eisfeld and Coburg to Nuremberg. To this extent, it could fit into a central-place system, although not without some juggling. However, the third parameter shows no such element of centrality, but is constituted by the link Erfurt–Görlitz, established by the real basis of Erfurt's export prosperity, its woad trade.

Thuringia was the leading area for German production of woad, essential for the dyeing of cloth, which would otherwise be sold undyed as 'greycloth'. Woad production was a simple matter, since it grew as profusely as a weed, giving two crops a year, but the processing from the picked, chopped and balled leaves into the dried, tea-like material used for dyeing took a year and required considerable capital investment. The major 'woadtowns' in Thuringia (Erfurt, Gotha, Arnstadt, Langensalza, and Tennstedt) banded together to form a monopoly, although merchants from numerous other towns dealt in woad (Mühlhausen, Nordhausen, Naumburg, Weimar, Greussen, and Weissensee), often attempting to purchase directly from the peasant producer and so avoid the monopoly. However, Erfurt remained the central market for woad until the dyestuff was displaced by indigo in the course of the sixteenth century.

Woad and cloth production attracted each other like the opposite poles of two magnets, and the main magnetic field was Upper Lusatia and Silesia, where the towns Görlitz, Zittau, Schweidnitz, Liegnitz, and Breslau were the main poles of attraction, drawing to themselves twice as much of the Thuringian product as was shipped in other directions. Here Görlitz was the nodal point from which all woad passed into Upper Lusatia and Silesia. Görlitz itself was also a node of trade routes: two important roads ran up from Nuremberg, either via Chemnitz and Dresden or via Pilsen and Prague; while routes ran down from the north to meet the west–east High Road. In the course of the fifteenth century, Görlitz established itself as the undisputed staple for woad for the flourishing Upper Lusatian and Silesian cloth industry (the staple had existed since 1339). In 1470 the annual turnover of woad in Görlitz was 560 wagonloads, worth around 360,000 fl. – an astonishing sum for that age. Three attempts by the princes of Saxony, in 1453, 1477, and 1490, to establish a woad staple in their territory, in the last two instances at Grossenhain, were seen off by the determined city government of Görlitz. Erfurt and Görlitz thus formed two crucial centres of gravity of this essential trade, like two weights on the end of a barbell, with the connecting route over Naumburg, Leipzig, and Bautzen forming merely the bar.

Erfurt also traded woad to the south: to Nuremberg, where it was used mainly in local cloth production; to Nördlingen, where it was Erfurt's sole item of trade; and to Frankfurt, where it supplied the Middle Rhine and Upper Main cloth-producing areas; insignificant amounts travelled to the west (except for exports to the textile areas of northern Hesse), since Cologne had its own area of woad production and the Low Countries drew their woad from northern France. The Erfurt–Görlitz axis was the 'mother-trade'. Thus, Erfurt's position as a major central German town depended on a combination of its three parameters: its position as a central place for Thuringia, its nodal position on the north–south and west–east trade routes, and its barbell-like connection to Görlitz. In the course of the sixteenth century, two of these three parameters changed drastically. The loss of the woad trade to indigo occurred gradually, but the rise of Leipzig was more abrupt. Since 1459 Leipzig had run three annual markets (Easter, Michaelmas, New Year), each lasting a week, with a week either side for preparation and settling of accounts. In 1497 the duke of Saxony supplied Leipzig with a privilege for its markets, backed by imperial privileges of 1497 and 1507. The town was given staple rights within a franchise of 15 German miles (approximately 170 km), which encompassed both Erfurt and Magdeburg. In effect, this shifted the nodal point of trade to the east. Very little of what was traded at Leipzig's annual markets supplied the needs of its own local sphere of influence – it was purely a matter of transit trade, and the key link to the north and to Nuremberg shifted to the alternative roads Magdeburg–Halle–Leipzig and thence to Nuremberg over a choice of several routes: Naumburg–Jena–Coburg–Bamberg–Nuremberg, Pegau–Gera–Schleitz–Kronach–Bamberg–Nuremberg, or Zwickau–Hof–Bayreuth–Nuremberg. Being a Thuringian central place was not enough to sustain Erfurt as a major city once it had lost its position in the network.

Conclusion

There are, of course, many other links between towns, personal and cultural, as well as institutional and economic, which may constitute networks. Reacting against the notion that population size is the main determinant of urban networks, Étienne François has sought cultural indicators that reveal different patterns of inter-urban relationships, using distribution of university towns, publishing houses, and book fairs to identify broad patterns of intellectual life.[33] The distribution of publishing firms serves both as an economic and as a cultural indicator, while patterns of university matriculation have long provided insights into the drawing-power of different universities at different periods and so into variations in intellectual fashion. Such examples indicate the importance of personal networks for understanding inter-urban relations: the humanist network at the beginning of the sixteenth century undoubtedly coincided with an urban cultural network.

Two major examples of personal networks that would repay closer exploration are those formed between urban (especially mercantile) elites in different towns. Wolfgang von Stromer illustrated important patterns of intermarriage between town elites, to the extent that one can speak of explicit marriage strategies, leading to kinship links across a substantial number of towns. How deeply such networks are rooted in the urban history of medieval Germany is shown by the lasting interconnections between Westphalian elites and the new towns settled in colonized east Elbian areas, using settlers from Westphalia.[34] These socioeconomic family networks were given a further dimension in the Reformation era with the desire to preserve confessional intermarriage among Protestant elite families.[35] A second kind of network is found at a lower social level, and was recognized by Ammann on the basis of patterns of immigration into south German towns such as Constance, Esslingen, Füssen, Nördlingen, Ravensburg, Rottweil, Tübingen, and Ulm. The most striking feature was the range of journeyman immigration, from as far afield as Lusatia, Bohemia, Silesia, and East Prussia. Even if the radius of densest immigration coincided with more immediate spheres of urban influence, long-distance immigration was so consistent for such a considerable number of towns as to be more than a matter of mere accident.

To sum up, the present argument does not seek to replace a central-place system with an urban network system. In certain cases – Stuttgart has already been cited – central-place theory works well. Ammann's work on Nuremberg shows very clearly how it functioned as a central place with concentric circles of influence and satellite towns. Together, these formed what he called an 'economic region' in which metropolis and hinterland mutually stimulated economic growth. Beyond this region lay wider areas of influence (its grain measure was used up to 100 km away), while its radius of cattle supply extended into Bohemia and Hungary.[36] Significantly, Nuremberg had no water route for its trade and depended entirely on land routes, perhaps identifying the decisive factor that forced it to extend its provisioning tentacles in all directions. To take another example, many towns in Silesia uncannily exemplify Christaller's model of centrality, thanks to the strict planning with which they were founded in relationship to a supporting hinterland, with no village being more than 10 km from a town and no town more than 16.5 km from another.[37] Here political intervention rather than geography played a part, although the wider pattern of riverine networks was the dominant one, as in the Neckar valley. Thus, as inter-urban patterns are more carefully explored than is possible here, central-place models should continue to find application alongside the network systems we have identified.

Notes

1   An exception is the work represented in the volume of essays *Urbanization in History. A Process of Dynamic Interactions*, eds A. van der Woude, J. de Vries and A. Hayami (Oxford, 1990), which is characterized by a statistical-demo-

graphic approach. The discussion in Heinz Schilling, *Die Stadt in der frühen Neuzeit, Enzyklopädie Deutscher Geschichte*, XXIV (Munich, 1993), pp. 20–37 focuses on structural developments in the later part of the early modern period and mainly on large towns of population over 10,000, following Jan de Vries, *European Urbanization 1500–1800* (Cambridge, 1984). De Vries's data is flawed, however, in taking no account of towns with a population under 10,000.

2 For an overview of fortified villages, Arnold Scheuerbrandt, *Südwestdeutsche Stadttypen und Städtegruppen bis zum frühen 19. Jht.* (Heidelberger Geographische Arbeiten XXXII) (Heidelberg, 1972), map 17.

3 The town was actually created by joining two villages together; B. Schwinekoper, *Handbuch der historischen Stätten Deutschlands* XI: *Provinz Sachsen-Anhalt* (Stuttgart, 1987), pp. 282–3.

4 H. Jänichen, *Beiträge zur Wirtschaftsgeschichte des schwäbischen Dorfes* (Stuttgart, 1970), p. 204.

5 Hektor Ammann, 'Die schweizerische Kleinstadt in der mittelalterlichen Wirtschaft', in *Festschrift Walter Merz* (Aarau, 1928), pp. 158–215, here p. 168.

6 J. J. Menzel, 'Die Entstehung der mittelalterlichen Städtelandschaft Schlesiens', in F. B. Kaiser and B. Stasiewski, eds, *Stadt und Landschaft im deutschen Osten und in Ostmitteleuropa* (Cologne/Vienna, 1982), pp. 45–65, here p. 51.

7 H. Stoob, 'Stadtformen und städtisches Leben im späten Mittelalter', in H. Stoob, ed., *Die Stadt* (Cologne/Graz, 1979), pp. 157–89, here pp. 157–9.

8 Hektor Ammann, 'Wie groß war die mittelalterliche Stadt?', in C. Haase, ed., *Die Stadt des Mittelalters* I (Darmstadt, 1978), pp. 415–22.

9 Hektor Ammann, 'Vom Lebensraum der mittelalterlichen Stadt', *Berichte zur deutschen Landeskunde* XXXI (1963), pp. 284–316, here pp. 290–3.

10 Peter Schöller, 'Der Markt als Zentralisationsphänomen. Das Grundprinzip und seine Wandlungen im Zeit und Raum', *Westfälische Forschungen* XV (1962), pp. 85–92. See most recently the critique by Dorothee Rippmann, *Bauer und Städter. Stadt-Land Beziehungen im 15. Jahrhundert. Das Beispiel Basel, unter besonderer Berücksichtigung der Nahmarktbeziehungen und der sozialen Verhältnisse im Umland*, Basler Beiträge zur Geschichtswissenschaft CLIX (Basel/Frankfurt a. M., 1990), pp. 47–8.

11 Ammann, 'Vom Lebensraum', pp. 308–9; a map showing this area in Scheuerbrandt, *Südwestdeutsche Stadttypen*, fig. 14.

12 W. Schlesinger, ed., *Handbuch der historischen Stätten Deutschlands* VIII: *Sachsen* (Stuttgart, 1965), pp. 63–5; *Deutsches Städtebuch* XII, pp. 46–7; M. Winkler and H. Raußendorf, 'Die Burggrafenstadt Dohna', *Mitteilungen des Landesvereins für sächsischen Heimatschutz* XXV (1936), pp. 1–38.

13 These notional figures are most applicable to a small town; a metropolis such as Nuremberg drew its grain supplies from a radius of 100 km and its cattle supplies from as far afield as Jutland and Hungary.

14 See e.g. the illuminating map by Wolfgang Zorn, 'Schwäbische Wirtschaft im 16. Jh. (bis 1618)', in Zorn, ed., *Historischer Atlas von Bayerisch-Schwaben* (Augsburg, 1965), map 24, which identifies customs stations and salt staples.

15 Walter Christaller, *Die zentralen Orte in Süddeutschland. Eine ökonomisch-geographische Untersuchung über die Gesetzmäßigkeit der Verbreitung und Entwicklung der Siedlungen mit städtischen Funktionen* (Jena, 1933), the section referred to on pp. 63–87; trans. into English as *Central Places in Southern Germany* by Carlisle W. Bastein (Englewood Cliffs, NJ, 1966), pp. 58–83.

16 Ammann, 'Die schweizerische Kleinstadt', p. 108.

17 J. C. Russell, *Medieval Regions and their Cities* (Newton Abbot, 1972); de

Vries, *European Urbanization*. The otherwise useful discussion in Schilling, *Die Stadt in der frühen Neuzeit* largely follows de Vries, and uses an imprecise notion of urban systems or networks. More sophisticated concepts of centrality, combining administrative, judicial, ecclesiastical, cultural, and economic functions with modern urban services such as transport and health provision, have been developed on the basis of modern occupational statistics by the geographer Hans Heinrich Blotevogel, 'Methodische Probleme der Erfassung städtischer Funktionen und funktionaler Städtetypen anhand quantitativer Analysen der Berufsstatistik 1907', in Wilfried Ehbrecht, ed., *Voraussetzungen und Methoden geschichtlicher Städteforschung* (Cologne/Vienna, 1979), pp. 217–69. However, this degree of complexity cannot be achieved using sixteenth-century data.

18   For an example of this kind of application, tried out on many twentieth-century urban regions, including some in Germany, see Robert E. Dickinson, *City and Region. A Geographical Interpretation* (London, 1964). The German theoretical discussion on centrality is summed up in Peter Schöller, ed., *Zentralitätsforschung* (Wege der Forschung CCCI) (Darmstadt, 1972), and the historical approaches represented in E. Meynen, ed., *Zentralität als Problem der mittelalterlichen Stadtgeschichtsforschung* (Cologne/Vienna, 1979); the most recent discussion of the German urban network, Étienne François, 'The German Urban Network Between the Sixteenth and Eighteenth Centuries', in van der Woude and de Vries, *Urbanization in History*, pp. 84–100, works with an ill-defined notion of 'network' and is content to discern only very crude patterns of large towns.

19   Basel is not included in the cohort, which omits Swiss and Austrian towns. However, its population hovered around the 10,000 mark, being calculated as around 8,500 in 1595 and over 10,000 by 1601; Markus Mattmüller, *Bevölkerungsgeschichte der Schweiz, I: Die frühe Neuzeit 1500–1700* (Basel/Frankfurt a. M., 1987), p. 699.

20   Christaller's discussion of the modern Stuttgart system in *Die zentralen Orte*, pp. 200–16.

21   Ammann, 'Vom Lebensraum der mittelalterlichen Stadt', p. 294.

22   P. M Hohenberg and L. H. Lees, *The Making of Urban Europe 1000–1950* (Cambridge, MA., 1985), pp. 62–4. The account given here is a lightly adapted form of that by Hohenberg and Lees.

23   See Ammann, 'Vom Lebensraum der mittelalterlichen Stadt', map 1 (Neckarwein); idem, 'Hessische Wirtschaftsprobleme im Mittelalter', *HessJbLG* VIII (1958), map 29 (Alsatian and Rhine wine).

24   G. Franz, W. Abel and G. Cascorbi, *Der deutsche Landwarenhandel* (Hanover), p. 23 for costs of grain transport; the calculation was made by von Thünen, but the authors confirm it from their own work, see esp. pp. 50–1. On river transport in general, preliminary remarks by Fritz Voigt, *Verkehr II/1: Die Entwicklung des Verkehrssystems* (Berlin, 1965), pp. 225–37; and in more detail, with attention to smaller rivers, Detlev Ellmens, 'Wege und Transport. Wasser', in Cord Meckseper, ed., *Stadt im Wandel. Kunst und Kultur des Bürgertums in Norddeutschland 1150–1650* III (Stuttgart, 1985), pp. 243–55.

25   This paragraph based on Franz *et al.*, *Der deutsche Landwarenhandel*, pp. 41–6.

26   The expression 'string of pearls' is taken from Menzel, 'Mittelalterliche Städtelandschaft Schlesiens', p. 45. It was also used by Christaller, *Central Places*, p. 58, in describing towns on river networks.

27   This paragraph based on Franz *et al.*, *Der deutsche Landwarenhandel*, pp. 41–6, and Ellmers, 'Wege und Transport', pp. 245–6, 252.

28   Material on the Weser network is based essentially on *ibid* pp. 247–52, with some information from Franz *et al.*, *Der deutsche Landwarenhandel*, pp. 41–6.
29   The above information is substantially based on Ernst Neweklowsky, *Die Schiffahrt und Flößerei im Raume der oberen Donau* I (Linz, 1952), pp. 439–523 *passim*. On Ulm, Willi Zimmermann, 'Heilbronn als Floß- und Holzhandelsplatz', *Flößerei in Baden-Württemberg*, Heilbronner Museumkatalog XXVIII (Heilbronn, 1986).
30   On timber rafting, Zimmermann, 'Heilbronn als Floß- und Holzhandelsplatz'; Otto Bürk, *Die Geographie der Flößerei in nord-östlichen Schwarzwald (Enz-Nagold Gebiet)* (Tübingen, 1938), pp. 48–9 on Sebastian Münster; K. Luttenberger, *Untersuchungen über die Flößerei auf dem Neckar und seinen Nebenflüssen* (Stuttgart, 1906), p. 5 on the 1536 legislation.
31   Ammann, 'Die schweizerische Kleinstadt', pp. 173–6.
32   The following paragraphs on Erfurt are based on H. Jecht, 'Beiträge zur Geschichte des ostdeutschen Waidhandels und Tuchmachergewerbes', *Neues Lausitzisches Magazin* XCIX (1923), pp. 59–98; C (1924), pp. 57–134; W. Mädgefrau, 'Zum Waid- und Tuchhandel thüringischer Städte im späten Mittelalter', *JbWG* (1973/II), pp. 131–48; W. Held, *Zwischen Marktplatz und Anger. Stadt-Land Beziehungen im 16. Jahrhundert in Thüringen* (Weimar, 1988). Information on roads from F. Bruns and H. Weczerka, eds, *Hansische Handelsstrassen*, Quellen und Darstellungen zur hansischen Geschichte XIII–XVI (Cologne/Graz/Weimar, 1962–8).
33   François, 'The German Urban Network'.
34   Wolfgang von Stromer, 'Verflechtungen oberdeutscher Wirtschaftszentren am Beginn der Neuzeit', in Wilhelm Rausch, ed., *Die Stadt an der Schwelle zur Neuzeit* (Linz/Donau, 1980), pp. 21–40.
35   See Étienne François, *Die unsichtbare Grenze. Protestanten und Katholiken in Augsburg 1648–1806* (Sigmaringen, 1991), esp. pp. 54–64.
36   Franz *et al.*, *Deutsche Landwarenhandel*, p. 37; Hektor Ammann, *Die wirtschaftliche Stellung der Reichsstadt Nürnberg im Spätmittelalter* Nürnberger Forschungen XIII (Nuremberg, 1970), pp. 194 ff. In terms of proto-industrialization, the roles of town and country are seen as complementary, not alternative, by Hohenberg and Lees, *The Making of Urban Europe*, p. 130, who speak of the importance of a regional urban hierarchy.
37   Menzel, 'Entstehung der mittelalterlichen Städtelandschaft Schlesiens', p. 56.

6

Markets and Marketing, Town and Country

ROLF KIEßLING

It is almost a commonplace of historical research that during the later middle ages the principles of marketing – understood as the exchange of goods between producer and consumer that constituted such goods as a commodity – began to solidify and to inaugurate a development that gradually, although not without interruptions, created large-scale economic networks. The intensity and degree of differentiation of these processes remain a matter of controversy. In the nineteenth century Karl Bücher postulated a succession of economic stages extending from the 'household economy' of the early and high middle ages via the 'urban economy' of the later middle ages to the 'political economy' of the modern period.[1] This view is now outdated, since the articulation of economic circulation was too multifarious and too complex during the period under discussion (or even prior to the sixteenth century) to be described in terms of continual coexistence of two distinct systems of town and country and of simple exchange between them.

The concept of a 'market' encompasses several meanings. First, it can designate the topographical spread of a specific place subject to a particular legal form and type of periodicity which endow a regular place of exchange with a central-place function. This kind of market was usually, but not necessarily, tied to a settlement. This meaning of the term is different from that in which a market was a type of settlement founded or constituted between the thirteenth and the sixteenth century as a minor town (*Minderstadt*) with specific constitutional characteristics.[2] Certainly, such entities were usually linked to a local agrarian market, as the term implies. Finally, we have to place in a separate category the modern economic concept of a market as a mental construct, a field of exchange between supply and demand, which is certainly not present in the sources as such, but whose content certainly is.

The fundamental trends in the development of the marketing structure of central Europe appear rather disparate compared with general economic developments.[3] The demographic caesura of the fourteenth century and the subsequent 'agrarian crisis' should not be equated with a general weakening of the market.[4] Quite the contrary, it stimulated market orientation, especially when we consider that there was an attempt to counter the trend of falling grain prices by turning to intensification of agriculture in specialized crops on the one hand, or by a process of extensive agriculture on the other, leading to a regional 'division of labour'. As population losses were made good from the second half of the fifteenth century (allowing for some regional variation) and the price curve turned upwards, these changes could not simply be reversed, but were in many ways strengthened within a European framework, so that there was a rising demand to be satisfied.

From the perspective of German towns, the 'crisis' of the later middle ages looks rather different in any case. Situated within the field of activity of the two most significant European economic landscapes, northern Italy and Brabant-Flanders, long-distance trade provided decisive impulses from the later middle ages onwards, to which these towns contributed for their own part by independent commercial production. The upwards trend of the resulting exchange of goods (when allowance is made for regional variations), however, experienced various interruptions, which precipitated a stronger differentiation within the urban hierarchy. On the other hand, changes in demand during the course of the 'long sixteenth century' took effect more easily, since most people were necessarily forced to orient themselves towards cheaper mass production as a result of the opening 'price scissors' between rising prices for foodstuffs and falling real wages, which ensured that only an affluent minority were able to take advantage of the supply of more exclusive goods.[5] The newly discovered trade routes to the Indies (East and West), and the subsequent shift of the focus of economic activity from the Mediterranean–north-western European axis towards the Atlantic coast, had no immediate detrimental effects. However, the various trends in economic development generally increased the commodity character of all products and solidified the marketing structure.

Manifestations and structures of the market

The phenomenon of the 'market' was realized at different levels: within a local framework, it was implemented through exchange between town and country, while the regional market mediated goods within more broadly delineated economic landscapes. The two periodic forms of the weekly and the annual market were interlinked within this spatial differentiation, while the great fairs largely focused on interregional traffic in manufactures. The legal situation since the high middle ages had usually allowed princes and territorial lords to establish only weekly markets, while privileges for annual markets and fairs were the preserve of the king.

The growing density of market relationships from the thirteenth and fourteenth centuries onwards can already be discerned through the establishment or first mention of privileged central places, among which the new forms of the small and minor town appear alongside the other towns, but in forms quite distinct from the older, high medieval markets. In Bavaria, Duke Albrecht III stipulated in 1442 in a mandate to the territorial judge of Pfaffenhofen that 'within the territorial jurisdiction [of Pfaffenhofen], nothing in the form of cattle, cheese, eggs, lard, nor yarn and flax and other things ... is to be sold in the countryside, but we wish that all such should be brought to our regular public markets.'[6] Even making allowance for the territorial basis of the spatial density of markets,[7] they at least served to force economic penetration of territories in competition with older towns. For example, Freiburg im Breisgau found itself by 1500 confronted with sixteen market foundations within a radius of 25 km.[8] During the fourteenth century the counts of Arnsberg implemented a consistent policy of territorial enlargement between the rivers Möhne and Leine by founding towns and freedoms (*Freiheiten*) in order to make use of yields from agriculture, forestry, mining and smelting, as well as passing long-distance traffic.[9] Many of these market settlements and small towns remained no more than local markets meeting their own needs, while others were oriented towards larger centres within a commercial landscape.

Explicitly peasant trading activity still played an important role for quite some time, especially in the under-urbanized low German region.[10] The free peasant republic of Ditmarschen participated in grain trade on the Elbe and with Holland; the self-governing territory (*Landschaft*) of Eiderstedt was granted in 1572 the right of 'free commerce' and in 1607 two 'free markets' were established on the island of Nordstrand. In East Frisia, village shippers conducted trade between Westphalia and the Emsland, as well as between town and country, with a rich variety of commodities. During the sixteenth century their rural markets were furnished with scales, and even attracted buyers from great cities such as Hamburg, Braunschweig, and Cologne.

The concentration of the market phenomenon certainly encompassed quite varied forms of the process of exchange. The form most relevant to a local area was the weekly market, which took place in the respective market-places.[11] In planned settlements the market was held on a specially provided place, but in large or older towns it was usually set up in nearby streets, because of the lack of possibility for expansion. In such cases the protected area of market activity was often designated by a specific symbol (in Nuremberg, known from 1385 as the *muntat* or 'immunity'). Differentiation of the main market into specialized outlets for different commodities was juxtaposed to the development of 'particular markets', for example, fish, cattle, milk, or fruit markets, which were only partially integrated into the legally defined market area. Business was also often conducted near city gates, on bridges, in the suburbs, and in churchyards, that is, outside the 'regular' market and often took the form of a daily market, as is attested for Würzburg.[12]

Simple forms of market traffic were generally found at church sales and annual markets, whose numbers, extending right down to village settlements and hamlets, should not be underestimated.[13] The tiny settlement of Murdorf am See, lying at the junction of the roads from Rothenburg to Schwäbisch Hall and from Crailsheim to Mergentheim, celebrated its 'Murmeadow market' at Michaelmas, in which the stalls were literally erected on the meadow. Numerous markets of like kind were shifted to towns and market settlements in the fifteenth and sixteenth centuries. Their range extended even to Zurzach on the Upper Rhine, a village-like settlement with a religious foundation, in which the two great annual markets had taken on the character of fairs by 1363 at the latest.

Sales were at first conducted from simple portable stalls, tables, stools, and booths. But as early as the twelfth century there had grown up permanently erected booths for retail merchants, drapers and craftsmen, and stalls for dealers in foodstuffs, the former frequently in private hands, the latter in public ownership but rented out. In Lübeck sales pitches of this kind amounted even in 1290 to as many as 1,072.[14] Finally, we must not overlook the importance of inns or taverns: as well as being places offering food, drink, and overnight lodgings, they also served as warehouses for goods, so that many innkeepers were also active as commission agents and middlemen outside market days. Especially striking in this regard were the taverns (*Krüge*) of north-eastern Germany.[15]

Characteristic of the later middle ages, however, were the staples or warehouses in which the sale of manufactured goods was increasingly conducted.[16] These were first located in the vaults of town halls, but in some places large multi-functional warehouses also grew up, for example in Mainz, Strasbourg, and Constance. From the middle of the thirteenth century this was accompanied by a decentralization, of which the Drapers' Hall in Breslau (1241) is the best-known example, although smaller towns such as Kirchberg in the Hunsrück or Kaiserswerth could boast of their own Drapers' Halls in 1336 and 1345 respectively.[17] Characteristic of a city such as Cologne with an exceptionally large volume of trade was the number of specialized guild staples and warehouses for the display of goods, to which the town council added halls for luxury items and consumption goods, fish and meat stores, and even for beer-grits (the *Gruthaus*).[18] Fiscal control, with municipal supervision of weights and measures and an associated levying of excise, was probably decisive in this development, but could also easily have been a response to changed market conditions.

It is already clear from this example that towns attempted to prevent uncontrolled 'side-markets'. However, we should not forget that some grey areas remained, characterized by informal practices in which hawkers and occasional traders operated in hole-and-corner markets. Their share of the overall volume of trade is difficult to estimate, although the flood of prohibitions and restrictions impressively reveals their importance for daily life. Control of these was part of a general trend in guild marketing policy of 'limiting supply'. In east Swabian towns a restrictive policy of regulation was aimed not only at preventing strangers from neighbouring towns and villages offering their wares but also, as is shown by the example of Nördlingen for the years 1540–43, at excluding 'hawkers and pedlars, the so-called open-air traders known as Savoyards', who usually dealt in spices, groceries and cheap textiles; however, a general prohibition was precluded on the grounds that they 'would otherwise hawk their goods in the countryside and so draw off the trade from there, as already occurs'.[19]

The mechanisms of market regulation created a tension between free access to the market and restrictions in favour of native and local suppliers. Regulation took concrete form according to both the needs of demand as well as political forces able to assert their own interests, but these mechanisms in turn were also influenced by long-term trends and exogenous factors such as wars and epidemics. The protection offered by territorial lords in connection with the 'market-peace' could only have a limited effect in stimulating the market, and the flow of goods merely followed the law of gravity within the existing framework. The granting of market privileges as a legal-political tool involved some basic stipulations: market business was only to be conducted at specific times or dates and at specific places, using valid weights, measures and currencies, thus virtually as a centralized market which attracted the supply of goods within the economic region to itself and bundled them together. This form of enforced marketing was then reinforced with the aid of an elaborate set of requirements, which admittedly could not always be implemented.

The spatial structure was provided above all by staple and warehousing rights as well as by the right of the *Bannmeile*, the radius of a protected area from within which all goods had to be offered for sale in the central market. Staple rights, understood as 'the power of a city, rarely of a village, to halt passing trade and to reserve it to itself under exclusion of other communities'[20] in order to ensure supplies and to optimize intermediate trade, became established in Cologne before the middle of the thirteenth century for shipping on the Rhine, and in Vienna for trade on the Danube, was quickly extended, and soon included enforced use of certain routes (*Straßenzwang, die rechte landstrazz*). The interruption of transport, the unloading and reloading of goods, and the compulsory offering for sale as a form of advantage for the local resident population was often combined with the right to impose a *Bannmeile*. Similarly, some time before the middle of the thirteenth century there developed in the context of east Elbian settlement the so-called 'tavern-bann' specifically as a means of monopolizing the sale of drink, and this was soon extended to the exchange of goods and the practice of crafts in the countryside.[21] This form of restriction then developed into an increasingly differentiated and adaptable instrument of market regulation, that could be applied spatially and quite precisely in terms of particular goods or processes. It was primarily an attempt to deal with a central problem that can be traced throughout the entire period under discussion and which is subsumed under the notion of forestalling and engrossing (*Vorkauf, Fürkauf*), that is, buying up goods with the intention of price manipulation through stockpiling and monopolizing goods before they could reach the market. A manifold system of price regulation and varying support for access for foreign sellers (in the so-called 'guest-rights') completed this spatial direction of the market. Of course, the statutes only reflect intentions and not necesssarily reality, but the marketing process can actually be analysed through them in an approximate manner.

The market structure for various kinds of goods can best be described as a system of storeys, extending from local markets via regional markets up to the great fairs – admittedly each geared to the other. 'Town' and 'country' as different poles of the exchange of goods can be taken in a paradigmatic way as useful points of departure, but we must also be aware that their relationship should be understood as a matter of increasingly complex interconnections.

Local and regional exchange of foodstuffs

Even the basic supply of foodstuffs had by the later middle ages transcended any simple exchange between 'town' and 'country'. The overriding importance of grain for basic consumption made the grain market the hinge of economic activity. Although we can assume that the majority of Germany's small and miniature towns, a considerable part of whose citizens also engaged in agriculture, could fulfil their own needs for grain supply, the degree of need was disproportionately high in medium-sized and large towns. The catchment area required to supply grain for Nuremberg in the middle of the fifteenth century has been estimated as 5,000 km², and the town council reckoned on having to draw supplies from a radius of up to 100 km from Nuremberg.[22] This figure may be exaggerated, but the estimate for Lübeck of a zone of around 1,000 km² that is, a radius of around 20 km, is far too conservative.[23] However, for Augsburg a more precise analysis of the grain market produces a radius of dominant influence of 30 km.[24] The largest German town was Cologne, with around 35–40,000 inhabitants, who required over 6,000 tonnes of grain each year, corresponding to around 10,000 wagonloads or 2,400 shiploads of grain.

This was supplied largely from the bishopric of Cologne, the duchy of Jülich, and the Rheingau, but during poor harvests also from Alsace, Lorraine, and the Main region.[25] Fluctuations in harvest yields, particularly the recurrent waves of price inflation and subsistence crises of the *type ancienne* since 1437–8,[26] necessitated frequent purchases of grain well outside the actual hinterland of a town and so stimulated inter-local trade.

Larger towns intervened in the market process with regulations to ensure food supplies for their own population, intending in combination with the maintenance of their own grain stocks at least to mitigate the most severe price rises. A medium-sized town such as Memmingen in 1396 first prohibited forestalling by citizens or guests within a prohibited area of a German half-mile (*c.*3.75 km), but in 1417 this zone was extended to two German miles for grain exports and was renewed several times during periods of crisis after 1488–90[27] – a method used by other comparable towns. As a parallel measure, the town council issued prohibition of resale or else limited the quantities that could be sold by dealers in flour (*Merzler*) and bakers, normally the most important grain-dealers in the town, and by foreign exporters, all to be supervised by municipal grain measurers. At the same time, neighbouring lordships were offered positive incentives to promote supply in the market by being provided with a standardized municipal grain measure. The storehouses of external monasteries and foundations acted as a collection-point for surplus grain, and that given in payment of rent contributed to around a quarter of the regular demand. This basic system of regulatory mechanisms can be generalized to most towns.

The proportion of agricultural production which found its way into this form of marketing can only be approximately estimated. If we assume for the thirteenth and fourteenth centuries that peasant farms only offered around 10 per cent of their production for sale,[28] to which must be added a similar proportion in dues paid to feudal lords, insofar as this also found its way onto the market, then in the face of a moderately growing urban proportion of the population (rising from 10 to 13.5 per cent) there had to be an increase of around 30–35 per cent in the market share of agrarian production between 1350 and 1450. More precise research for the Magdeburger plain reveals a fairly broad range of market share in the second half of the sixteenth century.[29] On manorial farms it could vary between 9 per cent and 78 per cent in terms of independent production and rent in kind. Barley was the most important grain marketed, between 34 and 64 per cent of production, and was predominantly used by towns and lords in brewing beer. Oats and rye, the grains most in use for personal consumption, were brought to market in smaller proportions (between 9 and 60 per cent). However, on tenant farms the market share can only be estimated, and was presumably far smaller. In terms of total production, the proportion of 'circulating goods' was probably only around 25–40 per cent even for great farms. These examples, however, are taken from an eminently grain-exporting area, which extended down the Elbe from Magdeburg and in which barley for brewing in Hamburg took pride of place. In the second half of the 1570s the quantities involved reached 8,000 tonnes.

In the Upper Bavarian region of Landsberg, where soil and climatic conditions were not so favourable, a theoretical calculation for large farms in 1671 revealed an average market share of 26.8 *Doppelzentner* (= 2680 kg) or 22.5 per cent of the gross yield, of which the tenants could only market 11 per cent for their own use.[30] Admittedly, there must be added to this the various payments to rural artisans and landlords, at least some of which would have reached the market. On the other hand, small farmers were often forced to make additional purchases. In the village of Unterfinning near Landsberg on the Lech, it has been estimated for the early eighteenth century that 75–80 per cent of grain was consumed within the village itself.[31]

None the less, a dynamic did emerge from this process. Contrary to the scepticism of earlier researchers, there developed in south Germany from the fifteenth century at the latest an extensive grain trade in which various characteristic situations of exchange can be observed.[32] The boom in mining and a substantial rise in population in the first half of the fifteenth century made the land of Tyrol dependent on grain imports.[33] The favourable transport conditions from Bavaria and Austria along the Inn enabled the river docks at Hall, with their staple and enforced resale (according to a statute of 1452), to became a major entrepôt of grain and other necessities for the Tyrol. Similarly, exports from Upper Swabia were directed via Lindau and Lake Constance into eastern Switzerland. This is traceable from the beginning of the fifteenth century, and in Bregenz, according to its market and shipping statute of 1569, two ships travelled to Lindau every Saturday in order to purchase grain. From Überlingen and other markets around Lake Constance extending as far as Schaffhausen, supplies were brought to St Gallen. Zurich distributed grain from Swabia, Alsace, and the Sundgau into inner Switzerland. Basel and Strasbourg had since the fourteenth century been the most important export outlets in the south-west, for which the Rhine provided transport in large quantities, while Frankfurt, Mainz, and Cologne joined in further down-river. It seems to be a characteristic of this trade that regionally varied shortfalls caused by harvest crises of the south and south-west were covered by mutual exchange.

While the western Mittelgebirge, the territory of Berg, and the Sauerland covered most of their needs from the plains along the Hellweg, the Münsterland and Westphalia exported to Friesland and Holland. According to the Leitmeritzer customs register, Bohemian grain came along the Elbe into the Saxon-Erzgebirge mining region, which had become densely settled from the second half of the fifteenth century, carried by shippers from Schandau, Königsstein, Pirna, and Dresden.[34] Since the fourteenth century

Hamburg had advanced via the Elbe into the Altmark, the Havelland, and the Magdeburg plain, while Bremen advanced via the Weser into the entrepôt markets of Hanover, Braunschweig, and Celle.

The most significant grain trade in terms of quantity, that of the Hanseatic League, certainly developed between the exporting areas on the southern shore of the Baltic via Lübeck and the other Wendish, Prussian, or Livonian towns, bound for Flanders, Holland, Norway, and Sweden. Even if critical examination of the sources has revealed that the quantities exported during the thirteenth and early fourteenth centuries were rather less than was once thought, and that this trade also suffered considerable decline in the phase following the middle of the fourteenth century, it still increased considerably from the end of the fifteenth, including exports of flour and malt.[35] The annual quantity of grain and grain products shipped from Stralsund through the Sound alone reached an annual average of a good 1,300 tonnes in 1566. Danzig exported in the years 1490–92 almost 20,000 tonnes to Western Europe, and from the 1560s onwards the figures often reached five times that amount, while supply areas were found not just in Prussia but above all among the great landed estates of Poland, Lithuania, and the Ukraine.

The fundamental structural changes arising from the grain crisis and the high meat consumption of the fifteenth century, and then the growing long-term demand for foodstuffs in the sixteenth century, displaced the market structure towards an extensive regional traffic in commodities and in cattle for slaughtering. The widespread practice of fattening one's own pigs, not least by bakers and millers, and the inferior status of sheep as a source of meat certainly did not prevent the supply of pork and mutton extending into broader hinterlands. Augsburg was involved in extensive trade in pigs with Bavaria in the fifteenth century, while pig herds from the Münsterland and the zone along the Hellweg, or from the region of the Saarland and Lorraine, were brought to market in Cologne.[36]

However, the supra-regional structure of cattle markets was determined above all by the trade in oxen, once the European-wide process of differentiation between the densely commercialized regions of Central and Western Europe and the pasturage zones in the north and east of central Europe had taken firm shape from the end of the fifteenth century.[37] The number of cattle exported annually was probably around 150,000 head at the beginning of the sixteenth century, and grew to 350,000 around 1600, the herds travelling distances of over 1,000 km. The main routes ran in three directions. In the first the oxen were driven from Jutland, via Hamburg and Lübeck, Münster and Dortmund, into the Rhineland, to Frankfurt and Hesse (Marburg, Kassel). In the second, animals from Ruthenia, Volhynia, and Podolia reached the Silesian markets (Brieg, Breslau, Schweidnitz) via Posen and Frankfurt on the Oder, and their German destination in Silesian, Saxon, and Hessian markets. The third route from Wallachia via Hungary arrived either via Moravia at

Nuremberg, but above all via Vienna and the line of the Danube to Lower
Bavarian markets and Regensburg, then on to Augsburg and Ulm. Of lesser
importance was the supply via the Inner Austrian route Graz–Tyrol to
upper Germany. The cattle markets on the main routes were precisely determined by the droving times, but also corresponded to the dates of major
fairs in Naumburg or Leipzig, as in the case of the Saxon markets at
Buttstädt and Ohrdruf. Nuremberg's key location for south Germany
between the Danube and the Main rested on linking together imports from
the Silesian–Bohemian transit with the Austrian–Bavarian route,[38] although
this declined after the middle of the sixteenth century in favour of Poland.
The Nuremberg cattle registry in 1570 recorded 8,712 head driven to its
distribution market.

After being fattened at the place where they were to be consumed, for
which purpose the butchers used their own meadows and estates in the
hinterland of the town, the animals reached the meat markets even of
smaller towns or of individual princely courts, where they supplemented a
gradually declining local supply. The characteristic interlinkage of local,
regional, and supraregional cattle markets can be exemplified by the
household of the landgraves of Kassel and Marburg in the sixteenth
century.[39] Game and gamebirds were supplied exclusively from seigneurial
rents in kind and from the princely domains, while the fattening of pigs
in princely forests enabled around 6,000 pigs to be sent to the cattle
markets on the Ems and in Hanover in 1573. However, the oxen came
mainly from Poland and Denmark. Nördlingen shows the urban counterpart, able to supply itself adequately with sheep from its own hinterland,
while pigs were imported from Bavaria; however, imports of oxen via
Nuremberg played an increasingly greater role from the middle of the
sixteenth century.[40] That the town occupied a central position as a distribution market can be seen from the fact that the Nördlingen prices for
meat provided a norm for neighbouring towns such as Donauwörth,
Dinkelsbühl, Wemding, Aalen, and Bopfingen. When a trend towards
shortage of imports appeared as a result of the Turkish wars, the imperial
cities in the Allgäu even sought to remedy it in 1543 through common regulations.

Meat could be substituted in part by fish, and during the later middle
ages both consumption habits and ecclesiastical fast regulations influenced
an intensification of fish-farming and penetrated into both long-distance
trade and local market relationships.[41] The Hanseatic League's traditional
trade with sea-fish, especially that of Lübeck and Cologne, in the course
of which the herring trade reached west and south Germany from markets
in Scandinavia via the distribution system, was increasingly redirected
towards Holland during the fifteenth and sixteenth centuries. The supply
of fresh fish from natural resources such as lake and river fisheries was
supplemented in turn from the fifteenth century by commercialized fish-
ponds. Bohemia developed as the most important centre, although local

urban ponds also emerged as well as regional systems of supply, for example in Franconia, whence carp were sent to market, especially from Dinkelsbühl.

Increasingly, dairy products, fruit, and vegetables also became oriented towards the market. The Cologne market had been supplied as early as the thirteenth century with butter from the archbishopric of Cologne, from neighbouring territories of Berg and Jülich, and also by a wholesale trade from the Netherlands, where Antwerp played the major role for dairy-fat and milk products.[42] In Augsburg there developed during the first half of the sixteenth century a very complex set of market statutes for foodstuffs.[43] In 1523–7 prices for fresh milk supplied to households and to the market were fixed, and it was forbidden to force buyers to accept butterfat and quark. In 1521 the town council prohibited engrossing honey within six German miles (45 km) of the town, and the same radius was imposed for cabbage, onions and grapes, while in 1549 this was extended to all food-stuffs sold by pedlars.

Wholesale marketing can be seen especially in the case of the Rhineland.[44] Shiploads of fruit from the Rheingau were dispatched to Frankfurt, dried pears by the tun, chestnuts in barrels and almonds in sacks from the Breisgau, as is attested by a privilege of Frederick III for Neuenberg in the Breisgau. At the end of the fifteenth century, a farmer was able to earn 30 fl. a year by selling his cherries in Mainz.

The intensified agriculture within the vicinity of towns developed into discrete zones, determined by geographical features and by technical pos-sibilities of exploitation. Nuremberg cultivated water-meadows on the river leas in the immediate vicinity by means of numerous water-wheels;[45] in the so-called 'Garlic Land' running to the north of the city as far as Bamberg, the use of irrigation channels and manuring increased the yields for vegetable-growing, so that the city was able not only to cover its own needs but also to produce for export. In 1618 onions and beet-seed from the area could be found in Italy, France, and Spain. Although hop culti-vation remained modest and was concentrated in Spalt, for whose quality the bishop of Eichstätt conferred on the city its own hop seal in 1538, api-culture was developed in the imperial forest under urban control to the east of the city, and this honey provided the basis from the end of the four-teenth century for the growing Nuremberg industry in sweet products such as its *Lebkuchen*. Similar forms of garden cultivation are attested for the Cologne cabbage-farmers (*Kappesboore*) in the sixteenth century, although this can be traced back to the fourteenth century, as in Düsseldorf. In Erfurt, the initiatives probably began back in the thirteenth century with settlements from the Netherlands.[46]

A much more extensive marketing pattern was developed with beer and wine consumption, which experienced considerable changes in the period analysed here. Because of natural conditions, beer was a relatively cheaper mass drink in central, north, and east Germany – at the end of the fifteenth century, wine in Hamburg cost fifteen times the price of beer – while wine was widespread in the main areas of production in south and west Germany. Beer had been an item of urban trade since the thirteenth century,[47] when the use of hops increased its longevity by comparison with beer brewed from beer-grits, although local brewing traditions persisted for a long time in villages in the taverns (*Krügen*) with a monopoly on sale of drink.

Initially, the coastal towns made good use of cheap seafreight: Bremen and Hamburg (producing 70,000 hectolitres per annum in the fourteenth century) supplied beer to Friesland, Holland, and Flanders, Wismar and the neighbouring towns supplied Scandinavia, and Danzig the Baltic area. Inland towns joined the trade in greater quantities in the fourteenth century, when special brand-names such as Braunschweig's *Mumme* and Goslar's *Gose* emerged, and Einbeck's *Bockbier* won a prominent place. This particularly high-quality beer began to conquer North Germany after 1351.[48] Brewing was subject to no limitations (in 1616 there were 723 brewing rights). Occasionally Einbeck beer turned up as a speciality consumed in princely, noble, and monastic households, and was regularly offered for sale in the larger towns alongside local beers; it was exported over land routes via Hamburg to Denmark, and via Lübeck into the Baltic. When at the end of the fifteenth century competing towns tried to exclude it from their own markets – Dutch exports had some effects on the Rhineland – compensation was sought by expanding the market to south and central Germany until conflicts with territorial princes about brewing privileges damaged exports. In Bavaria, east Swabia and upper Franconia, beer-brewing also began to overtake the previously dominant consumption of wine from the first half of the sixteenth century. The Bavarian purity law (*Reinheitsgebot*) contained in statutes of 1493 and 1516, which permitted the use only of hops and malt, marked this transition, as did the construction of a local marketing system in the Swabian towns and the markets of local lordships.[49]

Thus, during the later middle ages trade in beer was geared into the wine trade from the traditional areas of production around Lake Constance, from the Upper and Middle Rhine, on the Neckar, Main, and Mosel, complemented by that from South Tyrol and Lower Austria, which had already been extensive since the high middle ages.[50] The connection between both branches of trade is especially clear in Cologne, the central exchange market for wine in north-west Europe.[51] The high-point at the close of the fourteenth century was reached with a volume of 121,000 hectolitres per annum on average (in the 1379–84, 13,830 tuns), and 269,000 hectolitres in the peak year of 1415. However, at the end of the fifteenth century the amount fell to 60,000 hectolitres, for which beer consumption was responsible. None the less, Cologne's wine merchants, who had concluded firm long-term contracts with the producers in the second half of the fifteenth century, still supplied customers throughout the Hansa region, from Bruges to Novgorod, with high-quality wine from the Rheingau, the Rhine Palatinate, and above all from Alsace. The distribution system of Alsatian wine encompassed not only south and west Germany but also Magdeburg, Breslau, and Prague.

That production was increasingly aimed at the market is shown by a classic wine-growing area such as lower Franconia, where the initial extension of viticulture into less favourable sites was reduced during the sixteenth century in favour of soft fruit, while intensification of vine-growing continued within a more limited area, but with greater concentration on quality.[52] Above all, the city estates of the Cistercians and other monastic orders maintained the wine trade in the centre of Würzburg, with an export area predominantly encompassing Bavaria, Saxony, and Thuringia, but also extending via Frankfurt and Mainz as far as England. Here, as in Württemberg, the high urban density was founded upon the marketing needs of viticulture.[53] From the beginning of the sixteenth century wine became Württemberg's main export item, and in 1599 the Württemberg Estates stated that it was 'far and away the most prominent source of income for the subjects of this duchy'. The yield from ducal properties alone amounted to almost 21,000 hectolitres in 1520–1. Stuttgart and Schorndorf were regarded as wine-towns, and Esslingen and Ulm were the most important markets among the imperial cities.

Within this basic structure, particular markets were able to develop on the basis of local cultivation, as occurred in Thuringia.[54] The yields from the area around Jena (14,493 hectolitres in 1540) were marketed at Nordhausen and Eisleben, Hof and Münchberg and into the Erzgebirge. However, as sales slackened in Zwickau in 1547 in consequence of new customs duties and excises, Jena was forced to change to other specialized market crops.

Bavaria, where viticulture was impossible with the exception of the Regensburg hinterland and a few small islands of vine-growing, was definitely an importing region, and since the high middle ages monasteries and religious foundations had drawn upon the yields of their estates in the Wachau and in South Tyrol via a chain of their own properties for transport.[55] In the east Swabian towns Bassaner, Veltliner and Friulian wines were also marketed, as well as high-quality south Italian sweet wines, although the major quantity was imported from Württemberg and Franconia, or else from Lake Constance and Alsace.[56]

The interregional character of this trade in large quantities transported over long distances stimulated the entire economy – thus the navigability of the Neckar and the shipping of wine were closely connected – and led to a system of return freight with commodities such as salt with a similar marketing pattern, as can be seen in Swabia and Bavaria from the fourteenth century.

In the south German region, the Bavarian salt-works in Reichenhall, those of the archbishop of Salzburg in Hallein, and the Austrian works in

Hallstadt, Aussee, and Hall in Tyrol built up quite stable distribution areas.[57] The route along the Salzach, Inn, and Danube had been regularly supplied with salt from Hallein since the thirteenth century, while in the first half of the fifteenth century, on the other hand, resale of Hallein salt was prohibited in Bavaria. The organization of a complex transport system from Reichenhall to the west,[58] with redistribution points at warehousing places and interconnection with return freights of wine, grain, and merchandise, enabled the salt depots, originally the sites of castles, to grow into important urban trading centres before territorial princes monopolized the trade at the beginning of the sixteenth century. The old main route was linked to specific market days: the salt sent on its way in Wasserburg on Tuesday was retailed in Munich on Wednesdays and Thursdays, resold in Augsburg from Thursdays to Saturdays, and then proceeded via Ulm to Württemberg. Parallel to this, a southern route ran to Memmingen via Landsberg, and a northern route to Donauwörth and Nördlingen. The export route to the south extended over the mule tracks to Kitzbühel, where it encountered the distribution area for Hall in Tyrol. The trade up the Danube was linked via the Passau depot to Regensburg and into the Upper Palatinate and Franconia, or via the border traffic on the so-called 'Golden Path' to Bohemia. In southern Swabia a marketing boundary with the Tyrol had already been established in the fourteenth century. The established transport route for salt from Hall to the west along the line Füssen–Kempten–Isny–Lake Constance to Schaffhausen and into Switzerland ensured distribution into southern Swabia, while Bavarian salt had its own catchment area to the north with a clear line of demarcation, similar to that in Tyrol at Kufstein. It was only in inner Swabia that production from Schwäbisch Hall attained a regional importance, often in combination with the wine trade.

Of the north German production centres, besides Halle, Lüneburg above all achieved a dominant market share.[59] Lüneburg's position was bound up with favourable transport opportunities: in the middle of the sixteenth century the main body of trade (52 per cent) moved predominantly by ship along the Ilmenau and Stecknitz canal (1396) to Lübeck, whence it flowed into Baltic trade, although overland trade (as bulk or *Weissladersalz*) extended to Holstein and Jutland, to the western coastal regions of Friesland, and to the Mark Brandenburg, while local needs for the city itself and its immediate hinterland in the nature of things accounted for only a fragment of production (*c*.0.5 per cent). The dominant role of Lüneburg salt was admittedly affected from the fourteenth century onwards by the so-called *Baiesalz*, sea-salt from the salt-pans of Western Europe, but Lüneburg succeeded in parrying this attack through a policy of acquiring privileges and compensated, during the sixteenth century, by growing inland sales, in which its own merchants did not even play the leading role in the intermediate trade.

Commercial raw materials and
their intermediate products

With flax and wool as raw materials and woad and madder as dyestuffs, the agrarian sector was tied into the commercial sector of the economy. The prevailing textile regions were thus influenced not only by the long-term trends of the industry, but also by the fundamental relationship between town and country.

The Upper Swabian linen-producing region, whose products had been exported to the Mediterranean from as early as the beginning of the thirteenth century and traded at the Champagne fairs, was initially concentrated in Constance, St Gallen, and Ravensburg.[60] From the second half of the fourteenth century, this industry experienced an enormous boom by switching over to producing fustian in its northern subregion, with centres at Augsburg, Nördlingen, Ulm, Biberach, Memmingen, and Kaufbeuren, and outlets throughout Europe as a whole. The basic raw material under local cultivation was flax, which extended from the Ries into the Allgäu, from western Upper Bavaria to the Swabian Alb and Lake Constance. Here there developed a dense network of flax and yarn markets, which were supplied partly by peasants as well as rural yarn-dealers (*Kauderer* or *Pfragner*) and partly by large merchants. The imperial cities intensified their market monopoly from the second half of the fifteenth century and thereby oriented the entire region towards themselves. In 1446 Nördlingen stipulated an exclusion zone of four German miles (30 km), while in 1513 Augsburg extended its radius of market monopoly to eight German miles, to which a lower Bavarian enclave was added during the sixteenth century; in 1512 Ulm drew its boundaries at a distance of 20–40 km. From Memmingen and Kaufbeuren to Ravensburg, the guilds agreed several times between 1476 and 1532 to maintain a protected area of raw-material supply in the Allgäu from the Lech to Lake Constance. In this way the small towns and market settlements of noble and ecclesiastical seigneurs became subordinate to the great centres.

In a parallel development, the towns reinforced their position *vis-à-vis* the countryside by means of structural changes.[61] Since around 1300, rural weavers (*Gäuweber*) and their production had been subjected to the regulation of urban supervision. This supervision developed in varying ways from town to town, in close correlation with internal constitutional conflicts, so that rural producers were forced into the position of producing half-finished fabrics, yarn, or ready-carded yarn (*Wepfen*). This development was probably provoked by fustian production, which was a mixed fabric of a linen warp and a cotton weft, so that the production techniques could be easily separated. Large-volume imports of cotton as well as exports of the finished product stimulated the Italian trade of the Swabian imperial cities, above all with Venice, and contributed to the construction of a rigidly organized caravan system (*Rott*) in alpine transit trade. At the same time, this trade favoured a putting-out organization in both town and country, which combined with a standardization of production by means of supplying goods with quality marks to increase the dependence of the countryside on the town. This had one further effect: the centres of the 'cotton industry', especially Augsburg and Ulm, set themselves apart from the multi-centred linen-region, on the basis of capital concentration achieved in the course of certain crises of the fifteenth century. The hierarchy within the urban landscape was thus intensified.

The trend towards subjecting the countryside to the conditions of production for the urban market found certain parallels in Westphalia.[62] Here too, urban trade advanced into the countryside, so that Lemgo, Bielefeld, and Herford sought from the second half of the fifteenth century to ensure a market monopoly, this time with the aid of princely privileges, against the so-called *Butenhansische*, that is, non-privileged rural traders. By contrast with Upper Swabia, where the imperial cities were able to maintain their dominance – it was only during the seventeenth and eighteenth centuries that exports to Switzerland became a problem – in Westphalia territorial rulers intervened in trade. For example, shortly after 1527 the county of Lippe organized purchase of yarn by granting licences for particular districts to individual rural families. Admittedly, the bulk of Westphalian yarn was soon drawn off from the areas in which it was produced by means of putting-out contracts with merchants from Elberfeld and other parts of the Rhineland. It was then processed in the territory of Berg and in the county of Mark, together with yarn from a broader area of production extending as far afield as Silesia, and then exported to West Europe, above all to Holland. The traditional urban markets were thus avoided by new 'black markets'. In the case of finished linen, the urban quality-control offices (*Leggen*) were able to assert themselves by means of standardization as centres for both town and country, whereby village production was possibly not integrated, for example in Bielefeld, before the late sixteenth century.

The main flax-exporting areas, however, lay in Prussia and Lithuania, where Danzig and especially Königsberg were the most important export ports.[63] Apart from destinations in England, Scotland, and the Netherlands, some of these exports also reached German textile centres. From around 1500 imports into Swabia attest the links between these areas of production, but there were even more intensive links to the Saxon–Lusatian linen region. Developments in central Germany were also largely determined locally and regionally until the end of the fifteenth century.[64] As early as 1357 linen-bleaching in Chemnitz was protected within a radius of ten German miles by means of an export prohibition on flax, yarn, and twine, and on raw narrow linen. When the area on the right bank of the Elbe around Dresden and Pirna, then Lusatia, and finally Silesia followed suit, supplies of yarn were displaced further to the east, so that professional dealers and putters-out emerged. While the earlier export areas lay in Poland and Bohemia, at the end of the fifteenth century they also extended to the west as far as Frankfurt am Main. However, from the 1530s upper German merchants, especially those from Nuremberg, took over the direction of production and sale, and channelled into the Mediterranean and overseas markets linen that was considerably coarser, and therefore cheaper, as a form of dyed bulk commodity. To this end, production was standardized according to measurements of Nuremberg and Swabian norms. In this connection, rural weavers experienced a significant boom in production, since the south German dealers were able to meet their demands for raw cloth by bypassing the urban bleaching grounds: in 1598, for example, 101 rural weavers (*Pfuscher*) were working in 21 places around Liegnitz, and considerable concentrations of production could be found (up to 16 in a village). The role of the towns as centres of linen production was thus called into question.

Although Saxon black-dyers (*Schwarzfärber*) had become more numerous since the 1530s, raw linen was increasingly sent to dyeworks in Nuremberg and in the Swabian imperial cities. This interlinkage of textile landscapes through imports to upper Germany in part also encompassed Westphalian cloth, so that Swabian producers faced difficulties in adjusting to the changed structure of demand.[65] Augsburg clearly adapted best of all, while Nuremberg linked up to blue-dying of cloth.[66] However in the course of the sixteenth century, imported goods from eastern central Germany played the dominant role, reaching their peak at the beginning of the seventeenth century.

This occasioned a considerable increase in the market for vegetable dyes. In Nuremberg, Frankfurt, and Cologne there was certainly a wide range on offer: brazilwood and sandalwood (red dyes) from India, gall-nuts (black) from Venice, safflower and madder (red), dyer's weed (yellow), and then potash as a mordant.[67] Augsburg and the Swabian textile towns used as their black dye the leaves of the bearberry from the Allgäu and the Tyrol; trade in this dye during the sixteenth century was a privilege of the subjects of the jurisdiction of Ehrenberg in the upper Lech valley, and it extended into the Vinschgau in South Tyrol.[68] Woad for blue dye was produced in many areas in response to local demand, for example on the Lower Rhine, in the duchy of Jülich, and around Cologne, but the most important area of production was Thuringia, where Erfurt rose to be the main centre from the fourteenth century onwards, until indigo displaced woad during the second half of the sixteenth century.[69] According to the oldest woad registers, from the period around 1500, 583 farmers cultivated 422.5 hectares with this plant in 35 villages within the Erfurt territory, and between 1579 and 1605 this had expanded to 1,774 farmers in around 50 villages. Alongside smaller markets such as Mühlhausen, Naumburg, and Arnstadt, 2,316,294.4 litres of balled woad entered the market under the Erfurt town council's monopoly in 1579 alone – and that at a time of contracting cultivation. The area to which it was exported encompassed the entire central European region. Since 1339–40 Görlitz had held the staple and therefore monopoly of the woad trade to Breslau in the east (*c*.1470, 560 wagonloads), until the Saxon stapel in Grossenhain emerged as a competitor. Nuremberg was the distribution centre for upper Germany and even at the close of the fourteenth century imported around 100 wagonloads annually; a hundred years later it was 300–400 and in peak years over 500 wagonloads.

The cultivation of madder for red dyes was concentrated in lower Silesia, on the Upper Rhine between Strasbourg and Speyer, and in the Netherlands. Towards the end of the sixteenth century, Silesia exported something in the order of 600–700 tonnes of madder down the Oder and via Thorn and Danzig into the cloth-producing region of the Netherlands; via Thuringia and Saxony to Nuremberg and upper Germany; and via Bohemia to Austria, Poland, and Hungary.[70]

These dyes had, of course, long been used in the production of woollen cloth. Within this second sector of cloth production, areas had developed in the same way as with linen production, with extensive market connections for raw materials, half-finished, and finished cloth.[71] Certainly, there were some basic differences in the two forms of cloth production. German woollen cloth never attained the quality of that from Flanders and Brabant, or that later from Holland and England, so that high-quality varieties of this commodity were always traded in long-distance trade within central Europe and beyond, not least as one of the main pillars supporting the Hansa trade. Despite this, there was widespread independent production in the fifteenth and sixteenth centuries, with local and regional outlets.[72] But local production of medium and cheaper bulk cloth could only compete as a supplementary source of supply. The wool used in production demanded varying degrees of processing: fine draperies were woven largely from wool imported from north-west Europe, and from the sixteenth century onwards also Spanish wool for finer cloth, while local wool was used for the cheaper and coarser greycloth and loden.

Weaving regions such as the central Rhine and Hessian cloth districts, which were fully developed during the fourteenth century, encompassed around 80 locations – with varying degrees of concentration – including above all in the sixteenth century settlements and villages in the Taunus and the Westerwald.[73] This development went hand in hand with a concentration of the marketing structure for raw-material supply, while sales took place largely at the Wetterau fairs and annual markets, which regularly supplied upper and central German regions and its border regions as a whole. However, this system fell into deep crisis during the sixteenth century as a result of competing imports.

More precise examples reveal changes in marketing structures for woollen cloth. In Cologne, the centre of Lower Rhine cloth production, the need for raw materials could not be met from the immediate vicinity of the Middle and Lower Rhine.[74] Wool from England and Flanders (and also from Scotland, from the end of the fourteenth century) reached the Cologne market as a return freight for wine. However, additional imports from Hesse, the Upper Rhine, and via Nuremberg lowered the quality. In a single year's imports of 350–500 tonnes at the close of the fourteenth century, we can see an order of magnitude which indicates a system of purchase operating on a sliding scale. Many independent master weavers could still find adequate supplies from the immediate vicinity, and in 1489 operated partly as guild engrossers within a radius of four German miles, even keeping their own sizeable sheep herds. In addition, the relatively close fairs in Brabant and Frankfurt offered good opportunities for buying and selling, so that dependence on merchants outside the guild remained small, although a putting-out system had been developed among the weavers and their assistants, a system which encompassed producers in Cologne, in neighbouring dependent small towns, and in the villages of the Eifel.

By contrast, cloth production in Nördlingen, as well as in the remaining medium-sized Franconian towns, required import over large distances of a qualitatively higher-value wool.[75] This was initially supplied via Nördlingen's own fair, but from the second half of the sixteenth century, this had become dominated by great Nuremberg and Augsburg bulk merchants. A regional market developed for the processing of local wool, once a recognizable process of substitution in the middle of the fifteenth century made loden production prominent in place of fustian. Here, however, no explicitly rural production can be discerned, and only spinning was conducted in the countryside. The urban guild first attempted to assure itself of the necessary raw materials with the well-known instrument of a market restriction, and after 1453 extended the zone for its own needs to 3–4 German miles, within which small craftsmen could make purchases. They thus clearly came into competition with the loden-weavers of the surrounding circlet of towns, which had built up their own system of supply. The rising volume of production – it is estimated that the processed wool reached *c.* 250 tonnes around 1570 – motivated some well-capitalized wool-dealers from Nördlingen after the second half of the sixteenth century to import wool from Franconia as a whole (Rothenburg, Würzburg, Bamberg, Coburg) and from Bavaria (Ingolstadt, Straubing).

In the south-west, individual territories attempted for their part to strengthen woollen production and the wool trade against traditional centres. While Strasbourg's cloth-weaving encountered difficulties around the middle of the fifteenth century, the margraves of Baden from 1486 onwards furthered rural and small town woollen weaving by means of a territorial law, and in 1527 issued regulations for wool dealing linked to an export prohibition, an example that was soon followed by Hesse in 1534 and Württemberg in 1536.[76]

Contrasted with regions of concentrated manufactures, these were rather basic structures of production, without any noticeable concentration of export business, but which instead had a broad effect, as for example with the duchy of Bavaria.[77] Both urban and rural loden-weaving, albeit without any particular areas of concentration, faced no problems of access to raw materials; quite the contrary, since the territory could supply Franconia and Swabia with wool. Sales were predominantly oriented to a strong internal market, while the level of exports, above all to the Alpine lands, remained modest. Clothmakers' guilds, especially concentrated in Munich and Ingolstadt, which worked up Bohemian and other 'foreign' wool, stagnated in the sixteenth century, not least because raw materials were more expensive, so that imports tended to increase at this level of quality.

The location of raw materials had an even more decisive influence on the market position in the metalworking sector of the economy.[78] However, there were conditions here which developed their own patterns at different levels of processing, and which were tied to the mining regions only in limited ways. Alongside inner Austria, the Upper Palatinate was the most important supplier of iron to south Germany.[79] On the basis of smelting ore from Amberg and Sulzbach, as early as 1390 at least 97 hammer forges were concentrated on the Pegnitz, Naab and Vils, whose production of iron bars rose from *c.*4,100 tonnes in 1387 to almost 8,500 tonnes in 1475, to which must be added tin of the order of 375 tonnes in 1387 and 1,075 tonnes in 1475. Of the two main export routes for this half-finished product, the water route to Regensburg was more favoured at first, since it could be traversed within a day – usually on Sundays, when the sluices were open – and from there one could travel down the Danube to Passau or else upriver to Ulm, thus reaching further distribution outlets. The second route, via Nuremberg, whose entrepreneurs had already intervened from the middle of the fourteenth century in opposition to the Amberger and Regensburger, was better placed in the long run, since Nuremberg possessed a network of privileges which opened up trade to the west via the Main, especially once imports of iron to Austria were prohibited in 1371 and Austrian iron could better assert itself in the eastern markets.

On this source of supply rested the highly differentiated Nuremberg iron-working industry, with its broad selection of specialized products, an industry which also extended its influence into the neighbouring small towns.[80] Once the Nuremberg town council had issued in 1320–30 a prohibition of putting-out within a radius of seven German miles (52.5 km), in order to secure the position of Nuremberg metalworking against uncontrolled rural craftsmen (*Staudenmeister*), even neighbouring places were producing on the Nuremberg model by the fifteenth century. According to a town council statute of 1519, all blades produced within a radius of two German miles had to be presented to Nuremberg quality control. The production from this Nuremberg district covered, via annual markets and fairs, the entirety of south Germany in a seamless network, and extended beyond it into the further regions of the Hanseatic League and West Europe.

Cologne offered an almost comparable market system, linked since the fourteenth century with the Siegerland, since the fifteenth with the territory of Berg and the Sauerland, and from the end of the fifteenth century with the northern Eifel.[81] Long-distance trade to England and Danzig with iron, steel, tin, and wire supplemented metalworking which, in much more decisive ways than Nuremberg, was founded in the fifteenth century as one of the most progressive divisions of labour between town and country. So-called ironmasters (*Eisenwirte*) mediated the raw materials while putters-out (*Verleger*) organized the import and finishing of unfinished blades from Solingen and of pan-bases from the Siegen district (on average 120,000 pieces a year, 1497–1508). In this way, the individual small towns within the area of production may also have taken on the character of subsidiary centres for the metropolis. The connection is explicable, in that the Cologne ironware market as early as 1380 followed the Siegen system of quantities and weights. The standardization of supply was later intensified, as can be seen in the contracts concluded with the steelsmiths' guild from Breckerfelde in the second half of the sixteenth century.

We can contrast another marketing structure with these two production centres, that of the forest smiths in the Hessian Bergland, of whom there were 48 at the end of the fifteenth century.[82] Their products were not passed on to independent hammersmiths, as in the larger districts, but direct to the iron trade, since in this under-urbanized area citizens were not involved in production.

In the distribution-points for ironwares, especially in the south-west, where the lines of imports from the Upper Palatinate, inner Austria, and the western Alps overlapped, there developed smaller and more specialized centres for processing.[83] The small but scattered intermediate stages of trade clearly assisted the blacksmiths, a craft which did not produce only for the local market. In the imperial cities of the Allgäu from Isny to Kaufbeuren there resided scythe-smiths, who entered in 1458 into a trans-regional production agreement with those from Munich to Schwäbisch Gmünd. Their products were exported by local merchants as far as the Upper Rhine, Burgundy, and north Italy. Many similar places of secondary production and regional distribution networks of the same kind could be identified, not only in the strongly developed existing centres such as Basel or Freiburg im Üchtland. The imitation of well-known quality control trademarks indicates that there were larger regions of distribution.[84] Thus, blades and knives with Passau's wolf symbol were forbidden in Austria as early as 1340, and in 1464 Passau was provoked to lay a complaint in Cologne against the Solingen blade industry. In the Nuremberg region the Steyr trademark found use in Wendelstein in 1465 until Frederick III granted the local masters their own symbol in 1471, in order to end such forgery. Sickles from Schwäbisch Gmünd, whose production reached

130–140,000 annually in the sixteenth century, were also famous products, exported largely to France, and led at the end of the fifteenth and beginning of the sixteenth century to tedious civil suits from putters-out because of the use of individual trademarks in nearby Giengen an der Brenz.

The kinds of fundamental structural changes that we have observed running through the textile and iron industries can at first glance appear singular, and to be a result of their overall economic importance. However, as far as we can tell from current research, other sectors of the economy also experienced them in greater or lesser measure.

This is most apparent in the case of leather-production and wood-working. Apart from Cologne, where leather-production had already taken a strong hold in the hinterland even in the fifteenth century,[85] trade with leather and leather goods advanced to regional dimensions in the course of the fifteenth and sixteenth centuries, above all in the upper German region. Naturally, there was a close connection here with the cattle trade, so that there were continual demarcation problems with the butchers. In Nördlingen the rural basis for the raw materials was laid down in the first half of the sixteenth century within a protected area with a radius of up to six German miles, while individual citizen bulk producers covered an area of 10–20 miles' radius from the town. The latter had between 4,000 and 6,000 raw hides and skins treated inside and outside the city. Just as the Nördlingen fair played a part in marketing manufacturing crafts, Frankfurt served as the most important market on the Middle Rhine for raw materials, and for the marketing of leather products.[86] In 1579 the local territorial lords and towns agreed a special ordinance for the leather-goods trade. Buying and selling took place at weekly and annual markets within an intensive network of neighbouring towns and villages. The tanners and tawers, the saddlers, furriers, and parchment-makers united in the fifteenth century into a supralocal craft association, who sought not least to resolve common marketing relationships. Just how strongly the commercially oriented trades had targeted their market can be seen from the letters of association of the boilermakers, ropemakers, and clogmakers, the potters, hat- and beret-makers. However, similar developments can also be traced outside these associations.

Finally, we should not overlook trade with timber, with its derivatives such as charcoal, pitch, and ash, and with timber-wares, commodities for which it was not so much the rurally based preparation that was decisive but the state of general demand.[87] Since the fourteenth century energy crises had become apparent in areas of population concentration, and more generally at the end of the fifteenth century, precipitating from both urban and territorial authorities the first foresty conservation measures and reafforestation plans to counteract excessive timber-felling. This led to local and supralocal market regulation, since the purchases of building timber, timber for fuel, and charcoal could frequently not be met from local forests. Even in relatively forested regions of south Germany, specific timber and

plank markets appear at the level of the medium-sized towns, with supervision, valuers, and regulations against forestalling. Both the medium-sized
and of course the large towns proceeded in the sixteenth century to buy
up whole parcels of forest from noble and monastic seigneurs, even some
distance away, to cut and market timbers.[88] Far more extensive were the
relationships established when the Mittelgebirge forests began to serve as
a long-distance timber supply, as occurred in Franconia.[89] Here Bamberg
not only became the great trans-shipment point for timber from the
Franconian forest for pitch, tanning bark, and charcoal, but also produced
vineyard poles for local viticulture, wooden barrels, wagon runners, rafts,
and oak freight-ships for traffic on the Main, as well as functioning as a
transit-point for timber-rafting via Mainz and Frankfurt and as far as the
Lower Rhine. The same was true for the Upper Rhine, especially the Black
Forest with the valley of the Murg, as it was for the Elbe, the Weser, and
the Oder, while timber exports from Prussia crossed the border into international trade via Danzig to England and Scotland.[90] As an important
small-scale structural element, we should also note that the role of the
countryside in the division of labour with the towns was not limited to
mere timber-felling, but that there was also production of half-finished
products for the urban market from the beginning of the sixteenth century
at the latest, and in Cologne even a century earlier: for example, rough
bedsteads for Nördlingen joiners, barrel staves for the coopers in Würzburg
and on the Rhine, for which specialized markets even developed, such as
that at Odernheim, and wagon-wheels for the Memmingen and Cologne
wheelwrights, who had merely to fit them with iron rims and mount them.

Annual markets and fairs

Thus, the market had, for an entire range of manufacturing trades, given
up its original function of working for local customers in favour of production for an increasingly greater range of outlets. The interlinkage of
regional commerce with distinctively long-distance trade had, therefore, to
become more intensive, and the 'upper level' of commodity exchange and
payment transactions, whose nodal points were the fairs, had to undergo
a change in character. At the same time, there was implemented between
1300 and 1600 a multiple displacement of the system of central places.[91]
The origins of Frankfurt, Leipzig, and even Nördlingen as fair cities can
be dated to the thirteenth century, but the significant commodity markets
for German long-distance trade were at this time more likely to be found
outside the boundaries of the empire: in the great trading houses of the
Hanseatic League (Bruges, London, Bergen, Novgorod), and above all, for

upper Germany, in the Champagne fairs.[92] This succession of six regular
fairs per year, each lasting several weeks, in the four towns of Provins and
Troyes (two each), Lagny and Bar-sur-Aube (one each) was fully developed
from the second half of the twelfth century and was spread virtually over
the entire year. At the heart of the business was the exchange of
Mediterranean goods for cloth from Flanders and Brabant, but furs from
northern and eastern Europe were also traded alongside upper German
linen.

During the early fourteenth century, the Champagne fairs were replaced
by the Brabant fairs in Antwerp and Bergen-op-Zoom, by that of Geneva,
and, from the 1460s, by that of Lyons as joint heirs on the one hand, while
on the other the shift of the main axis of trade to the Rhine determined
the rise of independent fairs within the closer confines of the Holy Roman
Empire, fairs which ran for shorter periods, but which none the less had
dates co-ordinated among themselves.[93] Here two parallel systems
developed at first: the Wetterau fairs with Frankfurt and Friedberg, to
which a series of supplementary regional fairs were assigned, and the
central German system, with Leipzig and Naumburg as centres.

Their structure can be described through the example of the Frankfurt
fair.[94] The older 'autumn fair' grew up from the seasonal agrarian market
on the feast of the Assumption of the Virgin (15 August) and St
Bartholomew's Day (24 August), that is, from local and regional roots.
Frankfurt was granted the privilege by Ludwig the Bavarian of holding an
additional fair at mid-Lent in 1330, and experienced its first heyday at the
end of the fourteenth century. The commodity fair at this time comprised
three different subdivisions: first, there was regional agricultural trade in
grain, wine, and horses (above all from Hungary via Nuremberg). Then
there was the craft fair, visited by all the craft guilds with their guild super-
visors and seals, occupying common living and sales quarters. This fair was
especially concerned with the purchase of raw materials and the sale of
Hessian and Middle Rhenish woollens, and extended its influence to the
Lower Rhine (Aachen) and Lorraine (Metz). As an 'extra', the fair also
attracted more explicitly long-distance trade, with a catchment area
stretching from Flanders and eastern France over Burgundy and into
Switzerland, including the entire south German region through to Tyrol and
Hungary, then east Central Europe as far as Posen and Cracow, and finally,
if not quite as densely as the others, the Hansa region (Lübeck, Danzig).
This fair served for the exchange of north-western European cloth and south
German linen, specifically Italian goods, including oriental products,
materials such as silk and spices, then furs and wax from the east, herring
from Scania, and dried cod from Norway. In the fifteenth century, more specialized textiles such as Swabian fustian came to the fore, as well as the
products of the Nuremberg iron industry, to which was added the book fair
around 1480. The prolonged boom at the end of the fourteenth century
extended the period of the fair from one to three weeks: after a preliminary

week (*Geleitswoche*) to allow for arrival, the actual week of business began, followed by a 'payments week' for settlement of accounts, payment of recurrent debts, and, in the fifteenth century, presentation of bills of exchange. In the following week, the sale of remainders was concluded with rural small dealers and departure. The safe progress of the fair was assured, alongside safe-conduct within the strict environs of the town, by the general freedom of the fair and the privilege of legal protection (held from 1360), as well as by a special 'fairs court' (in existence from 1465) for settling personal arrests and attachments of goods.

The neighbouring Friedberg fairs following Mayday (1 May) and Michaelmas (29 September) were aligned with those of Frankfurt in the first half of the fourteenth century, so that there was a continual cycle.[95] Their importance can only be indirectly appreciated, but they were significant not only for the Middle Rhine cloth-producing districts, but also for the cloth towns of the Lower Rhine and Netherlands, and were visited from upper Germany, Thuringia, and even from Cracow and Lübeck. At the end of the fourteenth century they lost their original importance and declined to the status of local annual markets, a decline to which the uncertainty of the political situation in the Wetterau as well as the attraction of the nearby Frankfurt fairs contributed.

Meanwhile, the high frequency of visitors which Frankfurt had attained at the end of the fourteenth century shrank during the fifteenth. Here competing influences were able to assert themselves, influences which were concentrated especially around 1430. Thus, Nuremberg attempted by means of a privilege of 1430 from Emperor Sigismund to establish its own imperial fair lasting 24 days, the so-called 'relics fair', occasioned by the display of the imperial regalia and other imperial treasures for four days before Easter.[96] At the same time Mainz attempted to lure Rhine traffic with two annual markets at Lent (from the sixth to the second Sunday before Easter) and at the beginning of August (1–15 August), leading to protests by Frankfurt which had no effect. Strasbourg's fairs were held on St John's Day (24 June) and at Christmas, and according to confirmations of their privileges by Emperor Sigismund were both in full swing in 1414 and 1436. These siphoned off fairs traffic from Lorraine, Burgundy, and France, while the Whitsun fair at Worms only affected the immediate catchment area of Frankfurt. By 1500 a functional differentiation had been worked out within the Middle Rhine region, whereby Worms, Speyer and Mainz marketed agrarian produce in bulk, while Frankfurt concentrated on manufactured goods.[97]

Nördlingen regarded Nuremberg's fairs ambitions as prejudicial to its own fair and resisted them firmly.[98] From the end of the thirteenth century, Nördlingen's Whitsun fair had developed into a fourteen-day rural fair, and in the fourteenth century it was significant for textiles and hides, iron and ironware, while leather-goods came more strongly to the fore in the fifteenth century. With a catchment area covering all south Germany, it

clearly filled a gap between the dates of the Frankfurt fairs and those of
Zurzach on St Verena's day (1 September) and Whitsun, which covered
the south-west and northern Switzerland.[99]

It seems to be characteristic that neither Augsburg nor Ulm could attain
any great importance within this well-established network.[100] The three
Augsburg annual markets, that at Easter, which developed as a cloth
market, and those on St Ulrich's day (4 July) and at Michaelmas (29
September), both general craft markets, corresponded within a regional
framework merely to the annual markets of neighbouring Swabian-
Bavarian towns. Ulm had also procured a fairs privilege from Emperor
Sigismund in 1429, and attempted in 1439–40 to establish a fourteen-day
fair at the beginning of July (from the beginning of the sixteenth century,
the St Veit market around 15 June), slotting in between the existing dates
in Zurzach and Nördlingen. However, until the end of the sixteenth century
Ulm's market remained merely at the level of a one- or two-day annual
market for items of consumption, and had to fit in with the other annual
markets of the region.

Linz and Bozen formed the spatial connection of this upper German distribution system, under the dominance of Frankfurt. The Linz St
Bartholomew's fair (10 August–8 September) and the so-called 'Friar's
Kirmes' (held at the monastery of the Minorites on 25 March, and which
became from the beginning of the sixteenth century a two-week Easter
market) received a decisive impetus from long-distance trade, mediated by
Salzburg and Nuremberg merchants, at the close of the fifteenth century.
These fairs served predominantly as regional mediators of 'Venetian' goods
as well as textiles – cloth from Franconia, Bavaria, and Bohemia and also
for high-value goods from Brabant via Nuremberg, for linen from Swabia,
for hides and honey, and increasingly in the sixteenth century for
metalware.[101] On the other hand, the four fairs at Bozen – mid-Lent, St
Bartholomew (24 August), St Andrew (30 November), and additionally,
around 1500, Corpus Christi – had the task of mediating non-local
exchange between Italy and upper Germany.[102] Here local interests pursued
only local and regional trade in wine, and otherwise acted as agents for
outsiders. In 1487 130 Venetians were counted as present at the mid-Lent
fair, and around 1600 there were 46 south German and 32 Italian halls.
The items of predominantly long-distance trade were oil, tropical fruits,
spices, and Italian cloth, or metals and metalware, furs, hides, leather, and
textiles.

The system of fairs in central Germany combined the dates of those
from Naumburg (St Peter and Paul, 29 June) with Leipzig (New Year and
Easter, then as a third date, the Sunday after Michaelmas). However, it
was only in the second half of the fifteenth century that the Leipzig fairs
expanded their influence into the German area as a whole and into a
European context, reflected in fairs privileges of 1497 and 1507.[103] It was
of great significance for this development that from 1507 Leipzig could

rely upon an unusually wide-ranging staple right with a radius of 15 German miles (112.5 km). This constituted merely a claim to the rights of competing towns. Leipzig was able to repel Eisleben's attempts to acquire a fair in 1522, while Naumburg, Halle, and especially Magdeburg, with its staple rights for the Elbe, were able to assert themselves more strongly. However, the growing importance of central German mining, as well as its textile production, from the close of the fifteenth century, reflected in those fairs and in the close connections with Nuremberg capital, secured Leipzig's position, so that it was able to hive off a substantial part of Frankfurt's eastern catchment area.

Just as in south Germany, other important trading towns were unable to insert themselves into this system. Emperor Charles IV's attempt to promote Hamburg through a fairs privilege of 1358, and to link it with south-eastern trade to Venice via Prague, was short-lived.[104] The privileges issued by Charles IV for Cologne's cloth and wine trade also had no conclusive effect, and Cologne's high medieval fairs declined after the thirteenth century.[105] The two fairs on St John's day (24 June) and Martinmas (11 November) – after 1387, these were transferred to the second Sunday before Easter and to St James's Day, 25 July – remained regional markets and ceased with the end of the patrician regime at the end of the fourteenth century. What remained as a focus of interest was merely an eight-day annual market in the second week after Easter (the so-called 'Lord's Garment' market). Here too the north-west European fairs system was adequately populated: Cologne's own fair could not develop between the Wetterau and the Brabant fairs – at Whitsun and on St Bavo's day (1 October) in Antwerp; at Easter and Martinmas in Bergen-op-Zoom; as well as the four Deventer fairs on St John's day (24 June), St James' day (25 July), St Aegidius' day (1 September) and Martinmas (11 November), all of which were stimulated by Cologne cloth production. Only in the east in the sixteenth century was there any possibility for towns such as Frankfurt an der Oder, Breslau, and Danzig to expand their great independent, long-distance trading markets within a regional framework.[106] On the other hand, the great ports of Emden, Bremen, and Hamburg penetrated further into the north German hinterland.

Here we must note that the system of fairs had changed in many ways in the sixteenth century by comparison with the later middle ages. First there was a recognizable trend towards regionalization of the minor fairs, as the example of Nördlingen shows.[107] That is, fairs traffic had, since the end of the fifteenth century, lost importance by comparison with market traffic during the remainder of the year. At the same time, the circle of sellers shifted more strongly towards petty dealers (pedlars and hawkers) and towards processing trades from the town itself and its immediate vicinity, while the supra-regional aspect (textiles, iron, furrier's goods) declined in importance. The attempts of the Nördlingen town council in the years 1522–42 to compensate for the decline of the Whitsun fair by setting a second date for a winter

fair (first October/November, then January) were unsuccessful. This leads
to the conclusion that the Nördlingen fair approximated to the character of
an annual market, and so was integrated into the regional marketing
structure. What was presumably decisive was the practices of early capitalist production, which frequently avoided these fairs and markets and constructed its own system of purchase and marketing with the assistance of
commission agents. The hierarchical tendency within the fairs system was
thus strengthened in favour of the great centres of Frankfurt and Leipzig,
which experienced a distinct boom during the sixteenth century. Frankfurt's
second heyday depended above all on trade in silks, jewels, and books, as
well as monetary exchange,[108] while Leipzig's lived from the eastern trade
and from its connections to north-western Europe. Second, forms of non-
cash transaction increasingly overlapped with the traditional commodity
fairs which had dominated into the sixteenth century, so that fairs of
exchange increased in importance within the international payments
system.[109] A trend that had made itself felt in Geneva and Lyons in the
fifteenth century, also for German trade, came to fruition after 1531 with
the setting up of the Borse in Antwerp, while Frankfurt linked up to the
international system of payments in 1580, and in 1585 established a specific
currency of fairs exchange, following the lead taken by Cologne in 1553
and Hamburg in 1558.

If we now attempt to sum up, we can emphasize the following aspects.
The growing market orientation encompassed the agrarian as well as the
manufacturing sectors of the economy, in which local and regional
exchange was closely geared to international trade. In the field of agricultural goods, the extensive exchange of traditional products such as wine
and salt became denser and was extended to include grain and cattle, while
specialized crops were directed to local markets.

Town and country were closely interconnected in districts with geographically extensive textile production and metalworking, in which first
the acquisition of raw materials, then production by means of a process
of division of labour, proceeded apace under limitations imposed by the
town in the course of the fourteenth and fifteenth centuries. These tendencies then began to appear in other sectors such as leather-working and
timber-working. In a second stage, these commercialized districts during
the sixteenth century entered an international network which was sustained
by the great 'early capitalist' firms. In this regard, the unity of town and
country was simultaneously weakened in places, since the urban-related
elements favouring centrality, such as market concentration and quality
control, were avoided as rural resources such as labour power made direct
contact with bulk dealers and commission agents (*Verleger*).

In general, the trend towards specialization and creation of a hierarchy
within the marketing system is striking. Within the urban landscapes, there
emerged a functional distinction between agrarian markets and those for
manufactures, local markets were tied into the field of influence emanating

from a higher-level market centre, while metropolises began to emerge. The fairs system participated in this process, as is shown by the regionalization of the minor fairs and the international linkage of the places with great fairs. Certainly, those mercantile and manufacturing towns with their own active 'foreign trade' required no fairs of their own in order to assert their central position or to acquire one. And by contrast with the newer trends of development, there were regions with a long-lived and extensive structure of outlets and strong locally-oriented market relationships for which their own internal market played a decisive role.

Notes

1 See H. Kellenbenz, 'Wirtschaftsstufen', *Handwörterbuch der Sozial wissenschaften* XII (Stuttgart/Tübingen/Göttingen, 1965), pp. 260–9.
2 See H. Stoob, 'Die Minderstädte. Formen der Stadtentstehung im Spätmittelalter', *VSWG* XLVI (1959), pp. 1–28; E. Ennen, 'Die sogenannten "Minderstädte" im mittelalterlichen Europa', in idem, *Gesammelte Abhandlungen zum europäischen Städtewesen und zur rheinischen Geschichte* II, eds D. Höroldt and F. Irsigler (Bonn, 1987), pp. 70–85; cf. also F. Fehn, 'Entstehung und Entwicklung kleinerer Städte', *Siedlungsforschung* XI (1993), pp. 9–40.
3 See in general such recent texts as H. Aubin and W. Zorn, *Handbuch der deutschen Wirtschafts- und Sozialgeschichte* I (Stuttgart, 1971); H. Kellenbenz, *Deutsche Wirtschaftsgeschichte* I (Munich, 1977); F. W. Henning, *Deutsche Wirtschafts- und Sozialgeschichte im Mittelalter und in der frühen Neuzeit* (Paderborn/Munich/Vienna/Zurich, 1991); F. Mathis, *Die deutsche Wirtschaft im 16. Jahrhundert* (Munich, 1992).
4 See E. Pitz, 'Die Wirtschaftskrise des Spätmittelalters', *VSWG* LII (1965), pp. 347–67; W. Rösener, 'Krisen und Konjunkturen der Wirtschaft im spätmittel- alterlichen Deutschland', in F. Seibt and W. Eberhard, eds, *Europa 1400* (Stuttgart, 1984), pp. 24–38; and the summary in W. Rösener, *Agrarwirtschaft, Agrarverfassung und ländliche Gesellschaft im Mittelalter* (Munich, 1992), pp. 95–102.
5 See I. Bog, 'Wachstumsprobleme der oberdeutschen Wirtschaft 1540–1615', *Jb für Nationalökonomie und Statistik* CLXXIX (1966), pp. 493–527.
6 W. Liebhart, 'Zur spätmittelalterlichen landesherrlichen Marktgründungspolitik in Ober- und Niederbayern', in P. Fried, ed., *Bayerische und schwäbische Landesgeschichte an der Universität Augsburg 1975–1977* (Sigmaringen, 1979), pp. 141–52, the quotation on p. 149.
7 See for Bavaria, M. Spindler and G. Diepolder, *Bayerischer Geschichtsatlas* (Munich, 1969), pp. 22 f.; for Württemberg, M. Schaab, 'Marktorte des Spätmittelalters und der frühen Neuzeit 1250–1828', in *Historischer Atlas von Baden-Württemberg* (Stuttgart, 1972–90), XI(2).
8 T. Scott, *Freiburg and the Breisgau* (Oxford, 1986), pp. 117 f.
9 W. Ehbrecht, 'Territorialwirtschaft und städtische Freiheit in der Grafschaft Arnsberg', in E. Meynen, ed., *Zentralität als Problem der mittelalterlichen Stadtgeschichtsforschung* (Cologne/Vienna, 1979), pp. 125–79.

10 See H. Kellenbenz, 'Bäuerliche Unternehmertätigkeit im Bereich der Nord- und Ostsee vom Hochmittelalter bis zum Ausgang der neueren Zeit', *VSWG* XLIX (1962), pp. 1–40.

11 See E. Ehmann, *Markt und Sondermarkt*, Nürnberger Werkstücke XL (Nuremberg, 1987).

12 W. Schich, *Würzburg im Mittelalter* (Cologne/Vienna, 1977), pp. 82–6.

13 The following examples from M. Schaab, 'Städtlein, Burg-, Amts- und Marktflecken Südwestdeutschlands in Spätmittelalter und früher Neuzeit', in Meynen, *Zentralität*, pp. 219–71, here pp. 245 f.

14 F. Rörig, 'Der Markt von Lübeck', in idem, *Wirtschaftskräfte im Mittelalter*, 2nd edn (Vienna/Cologne/Graz, 1971), pp. 37–132.

15 See H. C. Peyer, *Von der Gastfreundschaft zum Gasthaus* (Hanover, 1987); W. Kerntke, *Taverne und Markt*, Europäische Hochschulschriften III (326) (Frankfurt a. M., 1987).

16 See E. Isenmann, *Die deutsche Stadt im Spätmittelalter* (Stuttgart, 1988), pp. 55–7.

17 Henning, *Wirtschafts- und Sozialgeschichte*, p. 213.

18 F. Irsigler, 'Kölner Wirtschaft im Spätmittelalter', in H. Kellenbenz, ed., *Zwei Jahrhunderte Kölner Wirtschaft* (Cologne, 1975), I, pp. 217–320, here pp. 234–7.

19 R. Kießling, *Die Stadt und ihr Land. Umlandpolitik, Bürgerbesitz und Wirtschaftsgefüge in den ostschwäbischen Städten vom 14. bis ins 16. Jh.* (Cologne/Vienna, 1989), pp. 175 f.; cf. p. 479 (Memmingen).

20 Fundamental for this theme is O. Gönnenwein, *Das Stapel- und Niederlagsrecht* (Weimar, 1939), quotation on p. 357; cf. also U. Dirlmeier, 'Mittelalterliche Zoll- und Stapelrechte als Handelshemmnisse?', in H. Pohl, ed., *Die Auswirkungen von Zöllen und anderen Handelshemmnissen auf Wirtschaft und Gesellschaft vom Mittelalter bis zur Gegenwart* (Stuttgart, 1987), pp. 19–39.

21 See W. Küchler, *Das Bannmeilenrecht. Ein Beitrag der mittelalterlichen Ostsiedlung zur wirtschaftlichen und rechtlichen Verschränkung von Stadt und Land* (Würzburg, 1964).

22 G. Franz, 'Die Geschichte des deutschen Landwarenhandels', in G. Franz, W. Abel and G. Cascorbi, *Der deutsche Landwarenhandel* (Hanover, 1960), pp. 13–85, here pp. 37 f.

23 K. Fritze, *Bürger und Bauern zur Hansezeit* (Weimar, 1976,) pp. 29–45.

24 For the later middle ages R. Kießling, 'Herrschaft – Markt – Landbesitz. Aspekte der Zentralität und der Stadt-Land-Beziehungen spätmittelalterlicher Städte an ostschwäbischen Beispielen', in Meynen, *Zentralität*, pp. 180–218; for the sixteenth century, B. Roeck, *Bäcker, Brot und Getreide in Augsburg* (Sigmaringen, 1987), pp. 83–93.

25 F. Irsigler, 'Getreidepreise, Getreidehandel und städtische Versorgungspolitik in Köln im 15. und 16. Jh.', in *Festschrift E. Ennen* (Bonn, 1972), pp. 571–610.

26 See the works by W. Abel, *Agrarkrisen und Agrarkonjunktur in Mitteleuropa vom 13. bis 19. Jh.*, 3rd edn (Hamburg/Berlin, 1978); idem, *Strukturen und Krisen der spätmittelalterlichen Wirtschaft* (Stuttgart, 1980).

27 Kießling, *Die Stadt und ihr Land*, pp. 448–60.

28 Henning, *Wirtschafts- und Sozialgeschichte*, pp. 326, 407 ff.

29 H. Harnisch, *Bauern - Feudaladel - Städtebürgertum* (Weimar, 1980), pp. 127–41.

30 R. Schlögl, *Bauern, Krieg und Staat. Oberbayerische Bauernwirtschaft und frühmoderner Staat im 17. Jh.* (Göttingen, 1988), pp. 159 ff., 189.

31 R. Beck, *Naturale Ökonomie. Unterfinning. Bäuerliche Wirtschaft in einem oberbayerischen Dorf des frühen 18. Jh.* (Munich/Berlin, 1986).

32 Following H. G. v. Rundstedt, *Die Regelung des Getreidehandels in den Städten Südwestdeutschlands und der deutschen Schweiz im späteren Mittelalter und zu Beginn der Neuzeit* (Stuttgart, 1930); an evaluation of the literature for the later middle ages in W. Habermann and H. Schlottmann, 'Der Getreidehandel in Deutschland im 14. und 15. Jh.', *Scripta Mercaturae* XI (1977), pp. 27–54; XII (1978), pp. 107–36; XIII (1979), pp. 89–96.

33 O. Stolz *et al.*, 'Zur Wirtschaftsgeschichte der Stadt Hall', in *Stadtbuch Hall in Tirol* (Innsbruck, 1981), pp. 114–36; J. Fischer, *Tiroler Getreidepolitik von 1527 bis 1601* (Innsbruck, 1919).

34 See K. H. Blaschke, *Geschichte Sachsens im Mittelalter* (Munich, 1990), pp. 232–51; idem, *Sachsen im Zeitalter der Reformation* (Gütersloh, 1970), pp. 33–48.

35 K. Fritze, *Bürger und Bauern*, pp. 33–43; the following figures from P. Dollinger, *Die Hanse*, 2nd edn (Stuttgart, 1976), p. 563; W. Stark, *Lübeck und Danzig in der zweiten Hälfte des 15. Jh.* (Weimar, 1973), pp. 91–6.

36 R. Kießling, 'Augsburgs Wirtschaft im 14. und 15. Jh.', in G. Gottlieb *et al.*, eds, *Geschichte der Stadt Augsburg von der Römerzeit bis in die Gegenwart* (Stuttgart, 1984), pp. 171–81; Irsigler, 'Kölner Wirtschaft', pp. 244 f.

37 See E. Westermann, ed., *Internationaler Ochsenhandel in der frühen Neuzeit (1450–1750)* (Stuttgart, 1980); O. Pickl, 'Routen, Umfang und Organisation des innereuropäischen Handels mit Schlachtvieh im 16. Jh.', in *Festschrift für H. Wiesflecker* (Graz, 1973), pp. 143–66.

38 R. Klier, 'Der schlesische und polnische Transithandel durch Böhmen nach Nürnberg in den Jahren 1540 bis 1576', *Mitteilungen des Vereins für die Geschichte der Stadt Nürnberg* LIII (1965), pp. 195–228; Chr. Dalhede 'Zur Erforschung des Augsburger Metzgerhandwerks im 16. J. Forschungsvorschläge und Quellen', *Scripta Mercaturae* XXIV (1990), pp. 81–131; idem, *Zum europäischen Ochsenhandel. Das Beispiel Augsburg 1560 und 1578* (St Katharinen, 1992).

39 E. Westermann, 'Zum Handel mit Ochsen aus Osteuropa im 16. Jh. Materialien und Gesichtspunkte', *Zeitschrift für Ostforschung* XXII (1973), pp. 234–76.

40 Kießling, *Die Stadt und ihr Land*, pp. 196–202 (Nördlingen), 465–74 (Memmingen).

41 See Dollinger, *Die Hanse*, pp. 310–18; B. Kuske, 'Der Kölner Fischhandel vom 14. bis 17. J.', *Westdeutsche Zeitschrift* XXIV (1903), pp. 227–313; B. Hofmann, 'Die Teichwirtschaft der Reichsstadt Dinkelsbühl', *Jb des historischen Vereins für Mittelfranken* LXXVII (1958), pp. 96–151.

42 E. Ennen and F. Irsigler, in Kellenbenz, *Zwei Jahrhunderte Kölner Wirtschaft* I, pp. 131, 282, 289.

43 Kießling, 'Herrschaft – Markt – Landbesitz', pp. 195 f.

44 Kellenbenz, *Wirtschaftsgeschichte*, p. 160.

45 F. Schnelbögl, 'Die wirtschaftliche Bedeutung ihres Landgebietes für die Reichsstadt Nürnberg', in *Beiträge zur Wirtschaftsgeschichte Nürnbergs* I (Nuremberg, 1967), pp. 261–317; H. Weiß, 'Franken. Das Agrarwesen vom Spätmittelalter bis zum Ende des 18. Jh.', in M. Spindler, ed., *Handbuch der bayerischen Geschichte*, III(1) (Munich, 1971), p. 475.

46 Henning, *Wirtschafts- und Sozialgeschichte*, pp. 335 f.

47 Cf. H. Huntemann, *Das deutsche Braugewerbe vom Ausgang des Mittelalters bis zum Beginn der Industrialisierung. Biererzeugung, Bierhandel, Bierverbrauch* (Nuremberg, 1971); G. Stefke, 'Ein städtisches Exportgewerbe des Spätmittelalters in seiner Entfaltung zur ersten Blüte. Untersuchungen zur Geschichte der Hamburger Seebrauerei im 14. J.' (Ph.D., Hamburg, 1979); G. Fischer *et al.*, eds., *Bierbrauen im Rheinland* (Cologne, 1985).

48 See E. Plümer, 'Brauwesen und Bierhandel im spätmittelalterlichen Einbeck', in

C. Meckseper, ed., *Stadt im Wandel* (Stuttgart/Bad Cannstadt, 1985), III, pp. 303–13.

49 Kießling, *Die Stadt und ihr Land*, pp. 211 f., 477 f., 609 f., 676 f; K. Hackl-Stehr, *Das Brauwesen in Bayern vom 14. bis 16. Jahrhundert, insbesondere die Entstehung und Entwicklung des Reinheitsgebots (1516)* (Bonn, 1989).

50 On the wine trade in general, see G. Schreiber, *Deutsche Weingeschichte* (Cologne, 1980), pp. 133–47; A. Gerlich, ed., *Weinbau, Weinhandel und Weinkultur* (Stuttgart, 1993)

51 Irsigler, 'Kölner Wirtschaft', pp. 285–7; K. Militzer, 'Handel und Vertrieb rheinischer und elsässischer Weine über Köln im Spätmittelalter', in Gerlich, *Weinbau*, pp. 165–85; and see the map by H. Ammann in Aubin and Zorn, *Handbuch*, p. 356.

52 H. Weiß 'Agrarwesen' and E. Schremmer 'Die Entwicklung der gewerblichen Wirtschaftund des Handels bis zum Beginn des Merkantilismus', in M. Spindler, ed., *Handbuch der Bayerishchen Geschichte* III (1), (Munich, 1971), pp. 474, 498 f.; W. Störmer, 'Probleme der spätmittelalterlichen Grundherrschaft und Agrarstruktur in Franken', *ZbLG* XXX (1967), pp. 118–60; W. Schich, 'Die Stadthöfe der fränkischen Zisterzienserklöster in Würzburg', *Zisterzienserstudien* III (1977), pp. 45–95.

53 W. A. Boelcke, *Wirtschaftsgeschichte Baden-Württembergs von den Römern bis heute* (Stuttgart, 1987), pp. 60 f.; G.F. Nüske and K.H. Schröder, 'Landwirtschaftliche Sonderkulturen', in *Historischer Atlas von Baden-Württemberg*, XI(5).

54 W. Held, *Zwischen Marktplatz und Anger. Stadt-Land-Beziehungen im 16. Jh. in Thüringen* (Weimar, 1988), pp. 111–114.

55 See H. Klein, 'Die Weinsaumdienste in Nordtirol und Bayern', *Tiroler Heimat* XIII–XIV (1949–50), pp. 65–90; XVII (1953), pp. 133–9.

56 R. Kießling, 'Schwäbisch-tirolische Wirtschaftsbeziehungen 1350–1650', in W. Baer and P. Fried, eds, *Schwaben-Tirol I: Beiträge* (Rosenheim, 1989), pp. 82–201; idem, *Die Stadt und ihr Land*, pp. 208 f., 475 f.

57 See E. Schremmer, *Die Wirtschaft Bayerns* (Munich, 1970), pp. 39–63; the various contributions in W. Rausch, ed., *Stadt und Salz* (Linz, 1988); W. Dopsch, ed., *Salz-Salzburger Landesausstellung Hallein* (Salzburg, 1994).

58 H. Vietzen, *Der Münchner Salzhandel im Mittelalter* (Munich, 1936); W. Hartinger, ed., *Passau und das Salz* (Passau, 1990); Kießling, 'Wirtschaftsbeziehungen', pp. 187 f.

59 H. Witthöft, 'Die Lüneburger Saline', in Meckseper, *Stadt im Wandel* III, pp. 281–302; H. Witthöft, 'Struktur und Kapazität der Lüneburger Saline seit dem 1. Jh.', *VSWG* LXIII (1976), pp. 1–117; H. Bleeck, *Lüneburger Salzhandel im Zeitalter des Merkantilismus (16. bis 18. Jh.)* (Lüneburg, 1985).

60 Still essential is H. Ammann, 'Die Anfänge der Leinenindustrie des Bodenseegebietes', *Alemannisches Jb* (1953), pp. 251–313; on structure, Kießling, *Die Stadt und ihr Land*; W. Zorn, 'Ein neues Bild der Struktur der ostschwäbischen Gewerbelandschaft im 16. Jh.', *VSWG* LXXV (1988), pp. 153–87; R. Holbach, *Frühformen von Verlag und Großbetrieb in der gewerblichen Produktion (13.–16. Jh.)* (Stuttgart, 1994), pp. 156–66, 183–95; and see W. v. Stromer, *Die Gründung der Baumwollindustrie in Mitteleuropa* (Stuttgart, 1978).

61 R. Kießling, 'Das Umlandgefüge ostschwäbischer Städte vom 14. bis zur Mitte des 16. Jhs.', in H. K. Schulze, ed., *Städtisches Um- und Hinterland in vorindustrieller Zeit* (Cologne/Vienna, 1985), pp. 33–60; idem, 'Entwicklungstendenzen im ostschwäbischen Textilrevier während der Frühen Neuzeit', in J. Jahn *et al.*, eds, *Gewerbe und Handel vor der Industrialisierung* (Sigmaringendorf, 1991), pp. 27–48.

62 As well as B. Kuske, *Wirtschaftsgeschichte Westfalens in Leistung und Verflechtung mit den Nachbarländern bis zum 18. Jh.*, 2nd edn (Münster, 1949), pp. 82–96; E. Geiger, *Die soziale Elite der Hansestadt Lemgo und die Entstehung eines Exportgewerbes auf dem Lande in der Zeit von 1450 bis 1650* (Detmold, 1976); Holbach, *Frühformen*, pp. 166–9.

63 See Stark, *Lübeck und Danzig*, pp. 124–8.

64 See H. Aubin and A. Kunze, *Leinenerzeugung und Leinenabsatz im östlichen Mitteldeutschland zur Zeit der Zunftkämpfe* (Stuttgart, 1940); H. Aubin, 'Die Anfänge der großen schlesischen Leineweberei und -handlung', *VSWG* XXXV (1942), pp. 105–78; G. Heitz, *Ländliche Leinenproduktion in Sachsen (1470–1555)* (Berlin, 1961).

65 Kießling, *Die Stadt und ihr Land*, pp. 498–504, 733.

66 A. Kunze, 'Zur Geschichte des Nürnberger Textil- und Färbergewerbes vom Spätmittelalter bis zum Beginn der Neuzeit', in *Beiträge zur Wirtschaftsgeschichte Nürnbergs*, II (Nuremberg, 1967), pp. 669–99.

67 See F. Irsigler, *Die wirtschaftliche Stellung der Stadt Köln im 14. und 15. Jh.* (Wiesbaden, 1979), pp. 97–111.

68 Kießling, 'Wirtschaftsbeziehungen', p. 184.

69 H. Jecht, *Beiträge zur Geschichte des ostdeutschen Waidhandels und Tuchmachergewerbes* (Görlitz, 1923); Held, *Vom Marktplatz zum Anger*, pp. 107–11.

70 F. W. Henning, 'Die Produktion und der Handel mit Färberröte (Krapp) in Schlesien im 16. und im beginnenden 17. Jh.', *Scripta Mercaturae* X, (1972) pp. 25–52.

71 Essential is H. Ammann, 'Deutschland und die Tuchindustrie Nordwesteuropas im Mittelalter', *HansGbl* LXXII (1954), pp. 1–63; on the wool trade see the relevant contributions in M. Spallanzani, ed., *La lana come materia prima. I fenomeni della sua produzione e circulazione nei secoli XIII–XVII* (Florence, 1974); M. Spallanzani, ed., *Produzione, commercio e consumo dei panni di lana (nei secoli XII–XVIII)* (Florence, 1976); on structure see also Holbach, *Frühformen*, pp. 95–140.

72 R. Hohlbach, 'Zur Handelsbedeutung von Wolltuchen aus dem Hanseraum', in S. Jenks and M. North, eds, *Der hansische Sonderweg? Beiträge zur Sozial- und Wirtschaftsgeschichte der Hanse* (Cologne/Vienna/Weimar, 1993), pp. 135–90.

73 H. Ammann, 'Der hessische Raum in der mittelalterlichen Geschichte', *Hessisches Jb für Landesgeschichte* VIII (1958), pp. 37–70; A. Dietz, *Frankfurter Handelsgeschichte* (Frankfurt a. M., 1910–21) I, pp. 203–5; II, pp. 262–72; O. Dascher, 'Der mitteldeutscher Raum', in Spallanzani, *Produzione*, pp. 269–78.

74 Irsigler, *Wirtschaftliche Stellung Kölns*, pp. 37–50; idem, 'Stadt und Umland im Spätmittelalter. Die zentralitätsfordernde Kraft von Fernhandel und Exportgewerbe', in E. Meynen, ed., *Zentralität als Problem der mittelalterlichen Stadtgeschichtsforschung* (Cologne/Vienna, 1979), pp. 1–14; W. Herborn, 'Kleinstädtisches Tuchmachergewerbe im Kölner Raum bis in die frühe Neuzeit: Deutz, Münstereifel, Siegburg', *Rheinisches Jb für Volkskunde* XXVII (1987–88), pp. 59–82.

75 Kießling, *Die Stadt und ihr Land*, pp. 213–34; R. Endres, *Die Nürnberg-Nördlingischen Wirtschaftsbeziehungen im Mittelalter bis zur Schlacht bei Nördlingen* (Neustadt/Aisch, 1963), pp. 143–70.

76 E. Gothein, *Wirtschaftsgeschichte des Schwarzwaldes und der angrenzenden Landschaften* I (Strasburg 1892), pp. 545–65.

77 Schremmer, *Die Wirtschaft Bayerns*, pp. 78–99.

78 R. Sprandel, *Das Eisengewerbe im Mittelalter* (Stuttgart, 1968); the various

contributions in F. Oppl, ed., *Stadt und Eisen* (Linz, 1992); and also in general Hohlbach, *Frühformen*, pp. 209–348.

79 Especially F. R. Reß, 'Geschichte und wirtschaftliche Bedeutung der oberpfälzer Eisenindustrie von den Anfängen bis zur Zeit des 30jährigen Krieges', *Verhandlungen des historischen Vereins für die Oberpfalz und Regensburg* XCI (1950), pp. 5–186; D. Götschmann, 'Der Sulzbacher Bergbau im Mittelalter und in der frühen Neuzeit', *ZbLG* XLIX (1986), pp. 41–123; W. v. Stromer, 'Die Große Oberpfälzer Hammereinung vom 7. Januar 1387', *Technikgeschichte* LVI (1989), pp. 279–304.

80 H. Aubin, 'Formen und Verbreitung des Verlagswesens in der Altnürnberger Wirtschaft', in *Beiträge zur Wirtschaftsgeschichte Nürnbergs* II (Nuremberg, 1967), pp. 620–68; H. Ammann, *Die wirtschaftliche Stellung der Reichsstadt Nürnberg im Spätmittelalter* (Nuremberg, 1970), pp. 48–70; R. Stahlschmidt, *Geschichte des eisenverarbeitenden Gewerbes in Nürnberg von den ersten Nachrichten im 12.–13. Jahrhundert bis 1630* (Nuremberg, 1971); K. Keller, *Das messer- und schwertherstellende Gewerbe in Nürnberg von den Anfängen bis zum Ende der reichsstädtischen Zeit* (Nuremberg, 1981).

81 Irsigler, *Wirtschaftliche Stellung Kölns*, pp. 156–215.

82 Sprandel, *Eisengewerbe*, pp. 196–8.

83 G. Philipp, 'Eisengewinnung und Eisenverarbeitung im südwestdeutschen Raum von 1500 bis 1650', in H. Kellenbenz, ed., *Schwerpunkte der Eisengewinnung und Eisenverarbeitung in Europa 1500–1650* (Cologne/Vienna, 1974), pp. 204–32; R. Eirich, 'Allgäuer Kaufleute im Fernhandel mit Sensen im ausgehenden Mittelalter', *Allgäuer Geschichtsfreund* LXXXI (1981), pp. 105–22; Kießling, *Die Stadt und ihr Land*, pp. 516–19.

84 See R. Kaiser, 'Imitationen von Beschau- und Warenzeichen im späten Mittelalter. Ein Mittel im Kampf um Absatz und Märkte', *VSWG* LXXIV (1987), pp. 457–78.

85 Irsigler, *Wirtschaftliche Stellung Kölns*, pp. 217–24; cf. in general Hohlbach, *Frühformen*, pp. 488–562.

86 Kießling, *Die Stadt und ihr Land*, pp. 238–47; F. Göttmann, *Handwerk und Bündnispolitik. Die Handwerkerbünde am Mittelrhein vom 14. bis zum 17. Jh.* (Wiesbaden, 1977), pp. 417–87.

87 Cf. Hohlbach, *Frühformen*, pp. 488–562.

88 See for Augsburg, Kießling, 'Wirtschaftsbeziehungen', pp. 183 f. and in general R. Kiess, 'Bemerkungen zur Holzversorgung von Städten', in J. Sydow, ed., *Städtische Versorgung und Entsorgung im Wandel der Geschichte* (Sigmaringen, 1981), pp. 77–98.

89 E. Schremmer, 'Die Entwicklung der gewerblichen Wirtschaft und des Handels [in Franken]', in M. Spindler, ed., *Handbuch der bayerischen Geschichte*, III(1) (Munich, 1971), pp. 500–2.

90 Dollinger, *Die Hanse*, pp. 301–6; Stark, *Lübeck und Danzig*, pp. 96–113; Göttmann, *Handwerk und Bündnispolitik*, p. 18; on the Black Forest, the summary in Hohlbach, *Frühformen*, pp. 496–9; and specifically M. Scheifele, *et al.*, *Die Murgschifferschaft. Geschichte des Floßhandels, des Waldes und der Holzindustrie im Murgtal* (Gernsbach, 1988).

91 See the various contributions in R. Koch, ed., *Brücke zwischen den Völkern. Zur Geschichte der Frankfurter Messe* (3 vols., Frankfurt a. M., 1991), esp. Vol. I: H. Pohl, ed., *Frankfurt im Messenetz Europas. Erträge der Forschung.*

92 H. Ammann, 'Deutschland und die Messen der Champagne', in H. Stoob, ed., *Altständisches Bürgertum* II (Darmstadt, 1978), pp. 51–95; H. Thomas, 'Beiträge zur Geschichte der Champagne-Messen im 14. Jh.', *VSWG* LXIV (1977), pp. 433–67; idem, 'Die Champagnemessen', in Pohl, *Messenetz*, pp. 13–36.

93 In general, H. Ammann, 'Die deutschen und die Schweizer Messen des Mittelalters', in *La Foire*, Recueils de la Société Jean Bodin V (Brussels, 1953), pp. 149–73; W. Blockmans, 'Das westeuropäische Messenetz im 14. und 15. Jh.', in Pohl, *Messenetz*, pp. 37–50; W. Herborn, 'Die mittelalterlichen Messen im deutschsprachigen Raum', in Pohl, *Messenetz*, pp. 51–66.

94 A. Dietz, *Frankfurter Handelsgeschichte*, I, pp. 17–116; B. Schneidmüller, 'Die Frankfurter Messen des Mittelalters. Wirtschaftliche Entwicklung, herrschaftliche Privilegierung, regionale Konkurrenz', in Pohl, *Messenetz*, pp. 67–84.

95 H. Ammann, 'Die Friedberger Messen', *Rheinische Vierteljahresblätter* XV–XVI (1950–51), pp. 192–225.

96 R. Endres, 'Die Messestreitigkeiten zwischen Nürnberg und Nördlingen', *JbfränkLF* XXIV (1964), pp. 1–19; F. Lütge, 'Der Untergang der Nürnberger Heiltumsmesse', in idem, *Beiträge zur Sozial- und Wirtschaftsgeschichte. Gesammelte Abhandlungen*, ed. E. Schremmer (Stuttgart, 1970), pp. 193–225.

97 K. O. Bull, *Verkehrswesen und Handel an der mittleren Haardt bis zur Mitte des 19. Jh.* (Speyer, 1965), pp. 97–115.

98 H. Ammann, 'Die Nördlinger Messe im Mittelalter', in *Festschrift Theodor Mayer* (Constance, 1955), II, pp. 283–315; H. Steinmeyer, *Die Entstehung und Entwicklung der Nördlinger Pfingstmesse im Spätmittelalter mit einem Ausblick ins 19. Jh.* (Nördlingen, 1960).

99 H. Ammann, 'Die Zurzacher Messen im Mittelalter', in *Taschenbuch der historischen Gesellschaft des Kantons Aargau* (Aarau, 1923); idem, 'Neue Beiträge zur Geschichte der Zurzacher Messen', *Taschenbuch der historischen Gesellschaft des Kantons Aargau* (1929), pp. 1–208; idem, 'Nachträge zur Geschichte der Zurzacher Messen im Mittelalter; *Argovia* XXXVIII (1936), pp. 101–24.

100 H. Steinmeyer, 'Die Entwicklung der Ulmer Sommermesse (des späteren Veitsmarktes) und ihre Einordnung in das süddeutsche Handelssystem bis zum Ende der Reichsstadtzeit', *VSWG* LXXVII (1990), pp. 323–49.

101 W. Rausch, *Handel an der Donau*, I: *Die Geschichte der Linzer Märkte im Mittelalter* (Linz, 1969).

102 G. Bückling, *Die Bozener Märkte bis zum 30jährigen Kriege* (Leipzig, 1907).

103 E. Hasse, *Geschichte der Leipziger Messen* (Leipzig, 1885; rep. Leipzig, 1963); E. Müller, *Die Privilegien der Leipziger Reichsmessen* (Leipzig, 1941); M. Straube, 'Funktion und Stellung deutscher Messen im Wirtschaftsleben zu Beginn der frühen Neuzeit. Die Beispiele Frankfurt am Main und Leipzig', in Pohl, *Messenetz*, pp. 191–218.

104 See W. von Stromer, 'Der kaiserliche Kaufmann. Wirtschaftspolitik unter Karl IV.', in F. Seibt, ed., *Kaiser Karl IV. Staatsmann und Mäzen* (Munich, 1978), pp. 63–72.

105 Ennen and Irsigler in Kellenbenz, *Kölner Wirtschaft*, I pp. 113, 273 f.; F. Irsigler, 'Fernhandel, Märkte und Messen in vor- und frühhansischer Zeit', in *Die Hanse. Lebenswirklichkeit und Mythos* (Hamburg, 1989), pp. 22–7.

106 Kellenbenz, *Wirtschaftsgeschichte*, pp. 268–72; K. Heller, 'Der Handel mit dem Osten in der frühen Neuzeit', in Pohl, *Messenetz*, pp. 205–18.

107 Kießling, *Die Stadt und ihr Land*, pp. 163–72.

108 Dietz, *Frankfurter Handelsgeschichte*, I, pp. 63–76.

109 See W. von Stromer, 'Die oberdeutschen Geld- und Wechselmärkte', *Scripta Mercaturaex* (1976), pp. 23–51.

110 See also R. Holbach, 'Exportproduktion und Fernhandel als raumbestimmende Kräfte', *Jb für westdeutsche Landesgeschichte* XIII (1987), pp. 227–56.

Translated by Bob Scribner

|7|

The Nature of Early Capitalism

WILLIAM J. WRIGHT

Introduction

Capitalism emerged during the 'long sixteenth century' (1450–1610). It was, as Fernand Braudel put it, a new economic system superimposed on the economic levels of the market economy and quotidian life, levels that were already present.[1] This chapter will assess the extent of capitalistic development in the several sectors of German economic life. A large number of excellent studies of individual sectors of economic life in Germany and systematic studies of towns and regions have appeared recently, although comprehensive studies are lacking. The world-system model of Braudel, Immanuel Wallerstein, and Andre Gunder Frank seems to fit the picture of economic patterns revealed in this recent literature. Germany was involved in a system of production for sale at a maximum profit on a world market (the European world economy or the capitalist world system).[2] Germans were involved in using some labour as commodity, in commercializing some land (at least in the colonial periphery), and in promoting private over public exchange. Moreover, with the sixteenth century, Germans also participated in the first period of concentrated capital accumulation.[3]

In the fourteenth century a Malthusian crisis, with the well-known depressionary trends, prevented the development of the world market. After 1450, factors both endogenous and exogenous to Europe made possible the achievement of sustained economic growth. Those factors were the crisis of feudalism that weakened the lords; the development of European overseas empires that expanded the available land, labour resources, and markets; the new states system; and the emergence of Antwerp as the single core of the world market.

Commerce and the world market

German development began before the rise of Antwerp to capitalistic core status, and helped to make it possible. Indeed, Germany had long played a special role in the economy of the Low Countries, although it was only the cloth trade that stood out before the fourteenth century.[4] Franz Irsigler's recent study on Cologne and Upper Germany showed that the close trade network connecting Cologne and Antwerp was already in place during the early fifteenth century. Renée Doehaerd and Herman van der Wee showed that Antwerp's ascendancy, after about 1480, was due to its ability to combine the sea trade that Bruges had enjoyed with its already blossoming land trade with middle Germany. Connections with England, Spain, and Portugal came as the merchants of those countries recognized the potential of the German connection and as Bruges declined. As a Rhineland exchange place, a manufacturing town, and a member of the Hanseatic League, Cologne's connections with Antwerp grew even more extensive during the fifteenth and sixteenth centuries.[5] During the period from 1488 to 1518, 56 per cent of the foreigners residing in Antwerp were Germans, mostly from the Rhineland and Cologne.[6]

By the end of the fifteenth century, the scale of business between Antwerp and Germany was such that it engendered a transport industry with regional bases. Most freight companies and employees came from Hesse, Thuringia, or Franconia. The best-developed, or at least the biggest, freighting district was in Hesse, with its centre at Frammersbach. For this reason drivers came to be called Frammersbachers and the wagons Hessian wagons, regardless of their actual origins.[7]

The crisscross carrying of the same and very similar products charac-terized commerce in the capitalist world market. Merchants of Cologne, for example, bought raw wool, semi-finished woollen cloth, and finished woollen cloth at virtually all of the market-places where they were produced and sold; and they sold the same goods wherever there was a demand for them. They bought woollen products in England, as well as in Antwerp. They also purchased the products of the Hessian countryside and small towns. They bought finished woollen cloth made of English wool at Antwerp, but they also carried cloth finished at Cologne (out of the raw wool from various places) to Antwerp. Moreover, the merchants of Cologne were heavily involved in carrying English wool products to Frankfurt, Upper Germany, Italy, and the colonial world. Cologne and Dortrecht were the main suppliers of woollen products to the coastal Hanseatic towns.[8]

The same crisscrossing may be seen in copper exchange. Cologne, for example, not only exported raw copper, semi-finished copper, and finished copper products, but also imported copper from as far away as Spain.[9] From the late fifteenth century to the mid-sixteenth, Antwerp was the main copper market for all of Europe. From there, German copper products were marketed in England, France, Spain, and Portugal. Portugal was a major market, where copper was used for coins, weapons, naval armaments, and articles of exchange in the African and Indian trades.[10]

Other important long-distance trade items included grains, wines, fish, dairy products, fruits, vegetables, wax, honey, building wood, leather, salt, and shoes. Such an extensive exchange of goods was made profitable in the capitalistic world market by variations in the style and quality of similar products between regions, changing fashions, and regional fluctuations in supply and demand.

At the beginning of this period, it was most important for long-distance merchants to win privileges from princes or city councils, allowing them to trade in a given marketplace. At a minimum, governments had to be involved in guaranteeing the life, well-being, property (including both wares and the payment of debts), and shipping or highway protection to the foreign merchants who wished to exchange at market-places in those governments' territories. Even during the fifteenth and sixteenth centuries, after the rise of the territorial states, the escort service (*Geleit*) remained an important requirement for merchants. The merchants of the greater trading centres had acquired these basic guarantees or privileges during the twelfth century; Cologne and the duchy of Brabant, for example, made an agreement that early.[11]

Merchants sought to gain as many additional privileges as possible, depending on the political and economic influence that they had. One privilege often demanded, at least until the late fourteenth century, was the right to use their own law, or the 'law merchant'. Hanseatic merchants demanded the privilege of forming *Kontore*, that is, Hanseatic communities within the foreign towns where they did business. These communities applied the German law merchant to their members and exercized their own Hanseatic government. Moreover, their authorities enjoyed diplomatic immunity to the host country's laws.[12]

As powerful territorial governments which recognized the value of trade arose, they granted marketing rights in major market towns to merchants throughout their territories. Other privileges usually sought included freedoms from various dues, imposts, and tolls. Sometimes privileges involved a commitment that existing dues or tolls would not be raised, or that new imposts would not be imposed.[13]

Nuremberg exemplified the way merchants operated in co-operation with town, princely, and imperial government. During the fourteenth century, Nuremberg arranged 100 trading agreements. Moreover, it won 60 privileges, or freedoms, from the emperor (in 1332) for its merchants in Flanders.[14]

Family firms, partnerships, and joint-stock companies were other organizational forms used in all kinds of commerce. During the fourteenth century, Hanseatic shipping came to be dominated by partnerships. The trend was for the number of shares in the ownership of a ship to increase as ships became bigger and more expensive. Ship captains remained shareholders in, and often owners of, the cargo they carried, but they were carriers alone, and not merchants (although a merchant might become a ship captain). While most companies were small, the Teutonic Knights represented an exceptionally large ship-owning company, with four whole ships and shares in 13 others, valued at 10,000 Lübeck Marks (11,429 goldgulden) in 1404.[15]

With various kinds of partnerships, fairs, and bourses, specialized commercial agents were necessary. Companies enjoying staple privileges or visiting fairs sent factors or agents of various kinds to conduct their business and forward information on a regular basis. For example, Cologne merchants sent plenipotentiaries and factors to serve their interests at Antwerp. Plenipotentiaries were usually family members, while factors were only agents who received a percentage or a salary. Innkeepers were also employed, because guest-houses served as meeting-places, marketing centres, transfer locations, and storage facilities. Sometimes the factor and the innkeeper was the same person.[16] Wool- and linen-dealing involved greater numbers of factors than most other businesses. Moreover, these factors were fairly peripatetic, for they had to frequent many towns, or even villages, in search of raw products, yarns, and semi-finished cloth. These factors attracted much notoriety from threatened local craftsmen, who perceived veritable armies of factors buying wool and yarn from under them.

Many exchanges at fairs were undertaken by brokers. They took special oaths, making their offices public. Brokers were assigned to the exchange of specific wares, such as spices and cloth. A big town might send two or more brokers for each important ware to be exchanged at a fair. The brokers from the many towns at a fair functioned as an advisory and control organ for the host government and its employees.[17]

Attempts to win government-supported monopolies and cartels were also a feature of organization in the attempt to maximize profits. The privileges sought by the Hanseatics, for example, were often attempts to gain monopolistic control over the supply of a ware in order to make greater profits. In point of fact, cartels and attempts at monopoly, generally, were attempts to deal with competition; however, competition was usually their downfall.[18]

Capitalistic activities in finance

While considerable capital was accumulated with the fifteenth-century increase of trade, ways of intensifying or concentrating the use of that capital were necessary for continuing economic growth. While this was true in the sector of commerce itself, capitalistic financing was absolutely essential for manufacturing of textiles, metals, and various craft wares for the world market. As will be shown, the combination of commerce and manufacturing was the engine of economic growth.

The main source of all kinds of commercial credit was the urban merchant class. As is well known, much merchant capital was loaned out to the developing states of Europe. German princes and emperors were major debtors to great Augsburg and Nuremberg firms, so much so that it may have hastened the development of long-term credit and German banking.[19] Princes often based their loans on property and regal rights, although there was a tendency along the Rhine to base them on taxes. Towns also were major debtors. They based their loans on future taxes; i.e. the creditor bought some kind of *Rente* or *Zins*. It is also significant that many of these town debts were really princely debts, incurred because the town had been compelled to loan or give money to a prince.[20]

Occasionally, noblemen were involved in investment. Notably, the Holstein nobility had various investments and were also participants in the bourse at Antwerp.[21] Monasteries and various ecclesiastical endowments played a significant role as investors, especially in annuities, as the case of Saxony shows.[22]

Banking was an important aspect of capitalistic financing, although in some ways it might appear relatively primitive. According to Raymond de Roover, there was no organized exchange in Germany until the sixteenth century, when Frankfurt am Main and Hamburg became banking centres.[23] German banking firms tended to be family concerns rather than public or impersonal enterprises. There was little tendency for the formation of specialized banking systems, legally (and really) separated from other businesses.[24] Nevertheless, there were banks in Germany during the fourteenth and fifteenth centuries, which took public and private deposit, loaned money, and served as exchanges. The first of these was probably the *Wessil*, or exchange, at Frankfurt (1402).[25] Hamburg developed a similar bank by 1619.[26]

The family businesses of the Welsers, Hochstätters, and Fuggers performed the functions of modern banks. Significantly, they took deposits from non-family members, a practice which began in the early sixteenth century. In the 1520s the Hochstätters called upon the common people to save and invest in their firm. Indeed, insofar as they saw themselves more as intermediaries between capital-holders and capital-needers than their Italian models had, and less as direct investors, German capitalists advanced banking.[27] Money from deposits, with money from family resources, was invested in trade ventures, textile manufacture, and metal production.

Around 1504, state banks (i.e. banks dependent on the state) developed in the German-speaking towns of Basel and Strasbourg. These banks served as municipal exchanges. They took deposits from the town itself, other towns, and private persons. They administered transfers of capital.[28] Nuremberg sponsored a similar institution in the office of the exchangers (*Wechsler*). In 1427, four independent exchangers were replaced with one city-appointed and city-paid official. After 1472, the exchanger split the profits with the city, instead of receiving a salary, but the office remained a government office. This officer provided more than simply the services of a *Konto*, where businessmen paid debts to one another. It is clear that the exchanger administered his affairs speculatively, for the city's half of the split grew to more than 600 fl. annually.[29]

Bills or letters of exchange were widely used and dated back, at least, to the fourteenth century in Frankfurt. They were assignable, or saleable, though usually not negotiable. They involved credit and speculation, because they set payment at a future date and usually in a place other than the place of sale. They involved an exchange of moneys at different values. Appearing with them were finance bills, or promissory notes, to be drawn in currencies other than that of the original sale.[30] These bills created the need for public exchanges.

Germans were involved in a very extensive exchange of moneys within the world system. The bourses, which performed banking services, appeared in the fifteenth and sixteenth centuries and were very important for capitalistic developments in Germany. The bourse was a daily, or at least frequent and standardized, gathering of merchants in order to do business 'without exhibiting, delivering or paying for goods at the same time'.[31] Moreover, it was an impersonal securities and commodities exchange involving merchants of all nationalities. The first real bourse was the one at Antwerp (1460), which allowed merchants of all nations to trade freely with one another, without restrictions. (Bruges had established a bourse earlier, but merchant trading was restricted by privileges and regulations.)[32]

Many Germans, especially Rhinelanders and Upper Germans, were actively engaged as financiers at the Antwerp Bourse. During the 1540s, for example, the Fuggers sold shares in their business at the Antwerp Bourse. They made 12 to 13 per cent interest, while paying their depositors only 9 per cent interest. Germans were also active at Lyons, the other multinational bourse in the late fifteenth century. The rise of south German banking pre-eminence and the end of Italian dominance of banking are associated with the rise of Antwerp.[33] According to J. A. van Houtte, Cologne opened a bourse in 1553, providing an example of the movement of this institution into Germany.[34]

The great trade fairs, from which the bourses sprang, also provided some banking services, especially the extension of credit. The exchange of bills, which represented a form of commercial credit, developed out of these fairs, because the dates of fairs came to be specified as the term for large transactions and their disbursement. The fair served as a clearing-house for payments. Big merchants from Cologne, for example, arranged the payment of debts at Frankfurt's fairs, as a matter of convenience. During the fifteenth century, more than forty of them annually attended the fairs at Frankfurt.[35] The major differences between a fair and a bourse were that the former met yearly, half-yearly, or quarterly, while the latter was usually active daily; and goods were actually brought to, exhibited, and then transported from the former, but not the latter. The major fairs developed what might be called temporary bourses. By 1567, for example, Frankfurt developed a regular assembly of all the merchants on the last, official week of the fair for payment and settlement of all bills.[36]

A major form of credit during the entire period was the *Rente*, which was a form of annuity. The creditor provided capital to the debtor in return for a yearly interest payment, or *Zins*, which was paid by a secured property, for legal purposes. In the Hanseatic area these rents or bonds substituted for banks. There was considerable speculation in them. There were both non-redeemable (held mostly by charitable institutions) and redeemable rents (the main type). Even the non-redeemable rent could be sold to a third party to regain one's capital. There were organized markets for these annuities, and official records of transactions were kept.[37]

Rents were used for living expenses, short-term business crises, purchase of raw materials for production, and long-term investment in expensive equipment and plants. The bulk of the rent capital was used for profit-making.[38] An indication of the extent of rent sales, and their significance for the economy as a whole, may be seen in the market sales reports for Lübeck and Hamburg, which show their price trends fluctuating with other indicators of business trends in the Hanseatic area.[39] By 1350 rent sales were so common in Cologne that the town had to prohibit counterfeiting of the documents.

Consumer loans were available during the period, but usury concepts and laws greatly restricted their use. Lombards continued to provide personal credit to small borrowers into the sixteenth century. Charles V limited such credit to 33 per cent interest in 1540, and by 1610 it was limited to 21 per cent.[40]

There were limited means of public credit. In big towns such as Cologne, Trier, and Antwerp, the town government created boards to provide credit for craftsmen. Butchers, for example, could borrow money in order to buy animals. One could argue that where towns kept municipal registers of debt, this represented a government guarantee and, therefore, a sort of public credit. The disappearance of certain institutions of church charity with the Reformation led many towns to provide small loans to individuals at no, or very low, interest.[41]

Another device for financing, credit, and investment was provided by the *Verlagssystem*, or putting-out system. This consisted of a prepayment or advance by an entrepreneur to a worker (primary producer) for wares or services which the latter promised to deliver in a prescribed quantity, quality, and time period. Furthermore, the capitalist planned to deliver these goods to some distant market, according to the profit-maximization principle. There were many variations of this basic relationship. The advance might be in money or kind. The producer might deliver all of the goods at a set price, or deliver some, as payment, and sell the remainder of his product at a price allowing both to benefit. The entrepreneur could be an individual capitalist, a group, or a guild. The workers might or might not be skilled workers and might or might not be guildsmen. Moreover, the capitalist was as concerned with profiting from the supply of raw materials as he was with the sale of finished products on the world market.[42]

Finally, the partnership and the joint-stock company also provided investment capital for manufacturing and commerce. According to Bruno Kuske, the idea of the joint-stock company, and the German word for the shares of stock, *Actien*, were already in use by this period, and the *Aktiengesellschaft* had developed from the medieval partnerships.[43] When partnerships of worker-owners accepted capital investments from non-workers, especially in the form of deposit with a fixed interest rate, they acquired the essential features of modern corporations: transferable securities and management separated from proprietorship.

Credit in these several forms was apparently sufficient to finance the economic development of the long sixteenth century. Principalities and areas of Germany where there were no towns closely committed to long-distance trading, however, probably suffered from a lack of credit. Eckhart Schremmer has shown, in the case of Bavaria, that the absence of a class of entrepreneur putters-out, in Munich especially, in contrast to the great imperial towns of Nuremberg and Augsburg, was a major reason for the failure of economic development: manufacturing for the world market did not develop and Bavaria remained an agrarian exporter, in Schremmer's view, because under absolute monarchy merchants preferred to invest in land, court connections, and titles of nobility.[44] It appears to be a classic demonstration in reverse of Braudel's idea that the independent mercantile town was the miracle of the West.

It was not necessarily princely absolutism, however, that underlay such economic failure, because the Hanseatic coastal area also failed to develop manufacturing. Except for shipbuilding, brewing, and coopering, manufacturing industries for the world market did not develop in the coastal region. This fact was confirmed by Rudolf Holbach, who had to look at the *Binnenstädte* of the Hanseatic League, and not sea ports, in order to examine Hanseatic putting-out.[45]

It is also a curious fact that the coastal Hanseatic towns conducted a systematic campaign against the use of credit in the fifteenth century, although they had used it before, as Philippe Dollinger reported. Stuart Jenks has shown that the policy probably began as a response to a hostile Flemish policy and a shortage of gold coins.[46] However, the anti-credit policy cannot be denied; it was probably the result of an economy based solely on trade. Moreover, Hansards were lacking at the Antwerp Bourse; they depended on large numbers of short-term loans, because their concept of insurance was poorly developed.[47]

Mining and manufacturing

The rising demand for metals, metal products, and textiles on the world market led to the expansion of production, which in turn stimulated economic growth. Merchant capital from the great trading towns financed each stage of the process.[48] This made it possible for more wares to flow into the world market. Frequently, joint-stock companies were formed to do business in a certain territory, with the support and, in many cases, participation of the ruler and several of his officials. Small investors also put money into these same companies, and capital amassed in one sector might be invested in another one. Furthermore, the availability of capital allowed the widespread implementation of technological innovations, which made production more efficient.

For example, leasing companies were formed to reopen mines. Galleries were drained by using such innovative technology as a more efficient pulley system, rack-and-bundle machines, piston pumps with crankshafts, and the water-driven *Kehrrad* for raising water from mines. Tunnels were enlarged to permit the use of railed carts drawn by horses. The new technology required a considerable amount of capital. A rack machine, for example, cost 300–400 fl., a piston pump 500–700 fl., mine-rails, as at Joachimstal, 500–1,000 fl., and a *Kehrrad* 3,000 fl.[49]

The use of machines powered by hydraulic energy was extensive. Numerous mills were used in the grinding, pressing, and pumping processes for ores and metals. In 1588, for example, Augsburg had 38 mills in operation on the lower run of the Singold alone.[50] These supplied energy to various kinds of smiths, as well as to other manufacturers. Invented by 1415, the wire-drawing mill was particularly important, because it tripled the production of wire and made production for the world market possible.[51] In textiles, fulling was mechanized from the thirteenth century. The fustian industry made particular use of it, as it developed in the late fifteenth century. Yarn-spinning was also powered by mills in some places. Cologne allowed a spinning-mill from 1413 to 1498.[52]

New organizational arrangements, which resulted largely from capitalistic financing and the use of new technology, allowed the mass production of standardized products for sale on the world market. This led in turn to the development of industrial districts (i.e. districts distinguished by an economy in which the production and finishing of goods was a significant or dominating part).[53] These arrangements included various forms of putting-out, factory production, and decentralized manufacturing (i.e. a combination of putting-out and factory organization).[54]

As a principle for organizing labour, putting-out led to labour as a commodity. Putting-out was distinguished from the ideal medieval guild or *Preiswerk* system in several ways. The primary producer was neither in control of production nor knowledgeable about the several processes involved in producing and selling the ultimate product. Production tended to be divided into specialized and separate operations. The primary producer worked for, or sold to, a contractor who was not the consumer. The worker was related to the world market through his relation and dependence on the entrepreneur. In a word, the worker did not have independent economic management.[55]

Putting-out is often characterized as decentralized, in comparison to the factory system of the last century. With the factory system, all processes tended to be combined in one building complex, and under one management.[56] One should not exaggerate this distinction, however, for the production of metals and metal wares tended to be centralized in a single complex focusing on a water-mill.

Copper, silver, and alloys

As John U. Nef noted, the establishment producing copper and silver by the new *Saigernprozess*, which was a late fifteenth-century chemical advance, represented a heavier concentration of capital (two-thirds more expensive) and labour than anything previously seen.[57] The charcoal used as fuel for this multi-step smelting process meant high costs. Hydraulic energy was also required to achieve high-temperature fires, and this required expensive equipment for mills. The deepening or embossing hammers (*Tiefhämmer*) represented another costly but profitable innovation for copper producers. In a day, deepening hammers produced ten times as much as could be produced by hand. They deepened brass sheet-metal into semi-finished or finished products such as bowls and kettles.[58]

The new smelting factories employing mills on rivers were often 100 m (328 ft) in length.[59] Insofar as the complex smelting, semi-finishing, finishing, and sometimes other processes were all combined in one plant or complex of buildings, this was an example of factory organization.[60] Coppermasters, the owners of copper plants, produced bronze and semi-finished brass; whereas most finished copper, brass, and bronze wares were produced at major towns, especially Nuremberg, Augsburg, Frankfurt, Leipzig, Cologne, and Aachen.

It is well known that the partnerships of small mining and smelting operators (who invested a small amount of capital and a lot of their own labour and skills into their companies) of the thirteenth and fourteenth centuries gave way by the fifteenth century to the putting-out system and the formation of partnerships with silent partners or joint-stock companies. Entrepreneurs provided advances to the miners and smelters in return for a portion of their production. Some coppermasters became absentee owners or shareholders in factories and, in some cases, employers of many wage-workers.

Ultimately, wealthy urban capitalists became essential, because the small smelters did not have the capital to provide the charcoal and machinery, or to pay for the transport of raw materials and finished products. With their capital resources, Nuremberg and Augsburg firms tended to dominate copper and brass production.[61] After 1500, a number of partnerships including smelters and Nuremberg merchants were established in the Thuringian forest area to smelt black copper ore and produce copper and silver. Typical of these was the Arnstadt Smelting-Trade Company, founded in 1502. In 1524 another partnership, which included the count of Mansfeld and Jakob Welser, set up a plant at Leutenberg.[62] The count and Welser provided 70,000 fl. for this company. The extent of individual investment may be seen in the case of Matthäus Landauer of Nuremberg, who at his death in 1515 left an inheritance of 31,514 fl., half of which was invested in mining.[63]

The state and its agents also figured prominently in copper production. In 1535 Duke George of Saxony owned 700 mining lots with 40 works in the Annaberg district. He was, therefore, a producer himself. By 1530 two-thirds of the state income came from regalian dues on silver-mines.[64] During the sixteenth century, rulers in the whole Rhenish region, encouraged by burgher-entrepreneur bureaucracies, attempted to regulate the hammers and smelting plants and to buy shares in mines and factories. Control rendered taxation based on unquestioned regal rights easier. Princely shareholding represented an almost riskless, high-yield investment.[65] Upper Hesse provided an example of how an important bureaucrat could use his position to promote metals production and make profits for himself. In 1486 the Hofmeister Hans von Dörnberg had a concession transferred to himself for the rights on all gold, silver, copper, and lead mined within a mile of the Haina monastery.[66]

The higher costs and mechanization that dictated production on a larger scale also tended to turn labour into a commodity. In the Aachen area, and probably elsewhere, coppermasters became employers of large numbers of 'apprentices' (i.e. day wage-workers) who smelted the ore. There were 1,000 such apprentices in the 1550s. As mines became deeper, much of the mining was done by wage-workers. The need to build expensive tunnels large enough for horse-drawn carts increased the cost of mining. In Mansfeld, this resulted in greater work demands and lower wages for miners, and led to strikes in 1533 and 1536.[67]

By the late fifteenth century copper production increased and silver, as a byproduct of the refining of black copper ore, became an important product. During the sixteenth century, silver was probably the more important product, because 57 per cent of the proceeds came from silver.[68] Moreover, the demand for silver had risen because of the need for coins and because of its importance as an exchange item in Asia. The new copper-smelting process led to an increased demand for quicksilver, which was used for amalgamation. The largest European quicksilver-mining area was at Idria, not too far from the upper eastern coast of the Adriatic Sea. Idria attracted Augsburg capital with the support initially of Charles V (who subsequently attempted to produce quicksilver in Spain) and, later, Ferdinand I. It is estimated that the Idrian concession (by Ferdinand) to the brothers Hans Paul and Hans Heinrich Herwirth, between the years 1548 and 1555, was worth about 140,000 fl.[69]

Zinc-mining and smelting was the other major subsidiary industry connected with copper production. The rise of the brass industry led to large-scale investment in zinc. Mines were leased by princes or councils to mining groups such as the Altenberg Lease Company, a partnership of non-working investors. By the late fifteenth century zinc was a good invest-ment, as may be seen in the rise of the lease payments to the Burgundian heirs at Altenberg (near Aachen); the annual payment rose from 550 fl. in 1446 to 1,880 fl. in 1493. A great deal of capital from Aachen and Cologne was invested in zinc in the area. However, Nuremberg entrepreneurs also attempted to compete there; indeed, these Upper Germans introduced the deepening hammers to the area, much to the chagrin of guild craftsmen at Aachen, who tried in vain to prevent it.[70]

Tin

During the fifteenth century, tin-workers became increasingly dependent on entrepreneurs for operating capital. Some workers did not need advances, but most did; hence the putting-out system appeared. Partnerships and joint-stock companies provided the necessary capital to stimulate production and also sold the products on the world market. The following examples illustrate the organization and operation of these companies.

The Saxon example shows the way in which these kinds of firms operated in co-operation with the state. Beginning in 1491, the duke became one of the shareholders in a tin-producing company. The duke granted a privilege to the Company of the Tin Trade in 1498. This joint-stock company bought tin from mining producers and sold it to craftsmen-finishers and long-distance tin-dealers, who would sell it outside Saxony. It sold most of the tin to the tankard-makers and other pewter craftsmen in the distant town of Nuremberg; much was also sent to Breslau. The company had a number of shareholders, most of whom were close to the duke. It had a capital pool of about 30,000 fl.

There were specialized agents in such companies. In this case, the shareholders, whose names were enrolled in a company book, selected two salaried factors or officials to conduct the regular business. Factors could not have their own separate businesses, but they could invest in the company themselves. The shareholders elected from their midst commissioners, who supervised the factors, accepted quarterly account statements, and approved in advance all loans and advances to workers or buyers. A general assembly of the company met yearly in January, to approve of the account statements and pay dividends.[71]

Inasmuch as the company was created by a ducal privilege, it had the backing of public law. The factors had keys to the state-operated scales at Altenberg, where the tin was weighed and approved for sale. Thus they enjoyed the status of civil servants, much like the scalemasters. Moreover, the ducal administrative officers were instructed to provide legal council and administrative assistance (e.g. they were supposed to force debtors to pay their debts) when necessary. In 1500 the ducal government made one of several attempts to grant the company a monopoly on the wholesale tin trade, this one for three years' duration, while fixing the price on finished tin. However successful or unsuccessful such attempts at monopoly were, the companies permitted Saxons to compete with Upper Germans in producing tinplate and tinned metals.[72]

Conditions in Bohemia led the Habsburg ruler, Ferdinand, to a similar arrangement in 1548. As the ruler, Ferdinand arranged a general tin sale contract with the tin works (individually owned) in the land. Advances were provided to all needy workers in return for their promise to return their production to Ferdinand (and his entrepreneurial associates) for a twenty-year period. Nuremberg entrepreneurs provided the capital for these advances. Workers were permitted to contract with other capitalists, however. Hence, Augsburg capital also made its way into Bohemian tin production.[73]

Developments in the tin industry were similar in the Upper Palatinate. For the mid-fourteenth century, there were cartels or federations (*Einigungen*) of hammermasters producing sheet metal. In 1533 the Palatine Count-Elector Ludwig V created a joint-stock company which was given the privilege of buying all of the tinplate or tinned metal made by the hammersmiths at Amberg. The products were exported to France, the Low Countries, and Italy. The Elector was a major stockholder in this

company, with 1,000 goldgulden worth of shares, while most of his coun-
sellors invested amounts varying from 100 to 200 goldgulden. At one point
Nuremberg dealers tried to make an arrangement to monopolize the
purchase of Amberg tin products, but their degree of success is not
known.[74]

Attempts to create monopolies in tin production were basically attempts
of the entrepreneurs making loans to compete with their fellow capitalists.
The monopolies did not succeed well for at least two reasons. First, it was
not possible to buy out all the other entrepreneurs; second, princes often
prevented their operation, because they had to be certain that pewter
craftsmen had enough material with which to work.[75]

Iron

The importance of iron may be illustrated by figures from the Upper
Palatinate. In 1387 there were 150 hammer-works processing iron. The
figure rose to 200 by 1500, and declined to 180 by 1600. Moreover, nearly
12,000 people or 20 per cent of the population was employed in the entire
industry (in 1475).[76] During this period, new technology altered iron-man-
ufacturing and increased production, as was the case with copper. The
stamping-mill crushed the ore; high ovens and hydraulic bellows refined
hard iron and created poured iron. The hydraulic hammers freshened and
worked the metal; hydraulic plate-metal hammers were necessary to fashion
sheet metal. These devices appeared by the mid-fifteenth century in more
progressive places such as the Siegerland, and by the sixteenth century had
spread to the forested mountains of Hesse and Nassau.[77]

All of this machinery for increased production demanded more intensive
capital investment. Fuel was the greatest ongoing expense, costing more
than wages or transportation.[78] The higher costs led to the formation of
partnerships of miners and smelters. A clear division of these groups, and
of these from local iron-dealers, appeared earlier in the iron production
than in copper or tin production. As more capital was required, partnerships with silent partners or joint-stock companies were formed.

Partnerships of peasants were active in the Eifel, the Hessian, and
Nassauian forest districts, and the Upper Palatinate. In the latter region
the necessity of digging deep tunnels occasioned these partnerships. These
firms took some deposits from outsiders, making them something like stock
companies. The Amberg mining company, for example, with 44 members
and capital of 12,000 fl. in 1464, took deposits from non-miners.[79]

Hammer construction, on the other hand, was more capital intensive;
and for that reason, credit advances by dealers from Cologne, Nuremberg,

Amberg, and Liège to hammer-owners was the norm in the Upper Palatinate and elsewhere. The dealers were involved in carrying semi-finished metal to their towns for finishing. The earliest example of a hammer federation contracted to Nuremberg entrepreneurs was in the fourteenth century. Nuremberg entrepreneurs provided the capital for 66 hammersmiths who produced wrought iron for the dealers. The ore they processed came only from the Amberg mining company.[80]

During the sixteenth century, iron continued to attract entrepreneurial capital. Evidence from the iron-producers in the Süderland (in the duchy of Mark) shows the typical dependence on distant cities, especially Cologne. The mine at Heiligendreifältigkeit, for example, was operated with the capital of two entrepreneurs, one from Cologne, Butzbach and one from Nuremberg.[81] In the Eifel, partnerships that began with four or five shareholders who were operators permitted speculation and division of shares. By 1560, one could purchase 1/120th or 1/320th shares, indicating the participation of silent partners or, perhaps, joint-stock shareholding. Meanwhile, the directors of these firms exemplify the profit-taking involved. By 1499, Hans Wolff of Gemünd had accumulated enough capital from iron to invest 8,000 goldgulden in a copper foundry at Mariaweiler (northern Eifel).[82]

On the other hand, in the more scattered works of the Hunsrück, partnerships mainly controlled by worker-investors continued, although even they were somewhat dependent on capital from nearby towns.[83] In the Hessian forest smith district, the dealers found a demand for their capital among those affected by inheritance laws that split properties and among smiths struggling to erect hammers.[84]

As in the case of other metals, the state and wealthy merchants acted together to finance iron works. From the 1480s to 1550s, for example, the Hessian landgraves encouraged iron production. The state invested its own money and attracted investments by entrepreneurs from Frankfurt and Hessian towns. For example, Hans Dauber of Marburg and his brother-in-law, Hans Schwan, a *Schultheiss* at Gemünden (am Wohra), formed a partnership for investing profits accumulated from wool-dealing into iron production. In this manner, large capital expenditures were made possible; for example, 4,000 fl. was pooled for a foundry at Hirzenhain (1550s).[85]

Town and princely governments promoted iron production in a variety of ways. Whether town or princely, governments countered the demands of guilds in order to bring greater concentrations of wealth and production. They provided privileges, premiums, and credits. Sometimes governments even ran smelting plants during crises. Governments helped in sales of iron by establishing monopolies, as may be seen in the Saxon records.[86] The state allowed cartels to function, such as the Upper Rhenish Iron and Hammer Federation (1494), confirmed by the governor of Alsace. It limited production to stem disastrous competition and provided for shortages of ore and fuel. In 1520, the count of Mark attempted to prevent the importation of Swedish iron bars into his territory, to protect his own subjects from foreign competition.[87]

Town governments played an active role in organizing and protecting capital investment in the Upper Palatinate, always dependent, of course, on the support of the territorial government. By the fourteenth century, for example, mining families which held political power in Amberg and Sulzbach had become mostly owners of mines and hammers. With their political power, they prohibited all common wage-workers, including hammersmiths, from gaining burgher status. During the fourteenth and fifteenth centuries, they made several attempts to form effective federations of miners and hammer-owners. These were intended to function as cartels, to prevent competition from outside miners, regulate production, and control the workers. (For example, separate courts were provided for the hammersmiths, i.e. workers.) Some of the hammer-owners came from Nuremberg and Regensburg.[88] These local federations were only partially successful, because the territorial governments sometimes refused to co-operate and other entrepreneurs managed to compete.

Linen and fustian

During the fourteenth and fifteenth centuries, changes in fashion reduced the areas of linen production for the world market to a limited number of linen districts. The rise of the Portuguese and Spanish empires assured a large demand on the world market for reasonably priced linen cloth, as fashion shrank the demand in Europe. The fact that the demand was for cheap linens also made possible the extensive use of rural or village production (especially in spinning and weaving). The great towns, such as Cologne, Nuremberg, Augsburg, and Ulm, continued to produce fine linen cloth products for long-distance trade, regardless of the decline in European demand. Linen production became less important than that of other textiles after the fourteenth century.[89]

While putting-out emerged earlier in some areas than in others, by the late fifteenth century it predominated in all of them. Moreover, there was both urban and rural putting-out in all of these areas. Urban and rural spinners, weavers, and sometimes bleachers competed with one another, but were closely connected in producing for the world market. For example, Cologne linen yarn and cloth were both produced and imported for further finishing. Not only linen-dyers but dyers of other textiles dyed linen cloth in order to export it to the Low Countries and England.[90]

An intensive putting-out system emerged in the east, especially in Saxony. In Saxony, Lusatia, Silesia, and North Bohemia, entrepreneurs from the great Upper German trading centres, especially Nuremberg, developed large producing areas involving the countryside. These became industrial districts. An intensive cottage industry was established. Nuremberg entrepreneurs carried considerable amounts of cloth to Nuremberg for bleaching and dyeing. In the 1530s, for example, the Kirmayr firm of Nuremberg was active in buying up unfinished linen cloth in Saxony. During the early sixteenth century, hundreds of Saxon villages hosted spinning and weaving. Middling peasants, who held the use of very little land, tended to be most involved. Although the putting-out system limited the power of guilds, they survived because, beginning in 1522, the entrepreneurs took whole guilds and groups of masters into contract. The guilds accepted the group contracts, because they needed the advances; moreover, it was a compromise giving them some control over primary production, though their privileges were reduced.[91]

The Saxon linen arrangement was dependent on the government. By the 1470s the prince noted that rural production and putting-out were under way and irrepressible. In 1471, therefore, the state moved to recognize but limit it. Villages were allowed to host weavers as well as spinners. Urban protection from competition was only extended to a quarter of a mile around a town. Perhaps even more significantly, it appears that no noble landlord was ever punished for allowing too many village weavers.[92] It is apparent that the prince and his noble landlords gained from more certain rents.

In contrast, Westphalia showed only the individual putting-out arrangements. Whole guilds were not contracted by entrepreneurs, who preferred the more lucrative business of carrying linen cloths to the sea ports for export to colonial areas.[93]

During the fourteenth century, fustian production developed in the linen districts, especially in the south-west. It was the new style of cloth, first for the upper classes under Italian influence, which caused the decline of linen. The Lake Constance district and Silesia became the first German fustian centres because of their proximity to Venice and Milan, whence cotton was more readily available. By 1400, it was the most important industry in these areas. The prominence of fustian continued into the sixteenth century, at which time the Fuggers invested heavily in fustian production around Ulm. Like linen cloth, fustian was produced mainly for the world market. By the sixteenth century it was exported mostly westward, to England, Spain, and Portugal, while much linen had flowed south to Morocco, via Genoa.[94]

The putting-out system developed earlier in fustian than in linen production, because purchasing the imported cotton required a considerable capital investment. As in the case of linen, fustian production led to rural spinning and weaving and a limitation of guild privileges. When guildsmen in Ulm complained about rural competition in the late fourteenth century, they were told: 'Either fustian export and country weavers or no country

weavers and no fustian export.'[95] By the end of the fifteenth century, the
council had arranged a compromise similar to the Saxon linen compromise discussed above. Country weavers could have only two stools, and
they would pay a heller more than guildsmen for the inspection of their
products at Ulm. Nevertheless, the council declared that anyone could
produce fustian, because it was a foreign ware, and therefore not the
province of any single guild.[96]

The great trade centre of Cologne also had a thriving fustian industry.
Masters competed with non-guild workers. In addition to masters who
could legally have three looms, all burghers were allowed to own three in
their houses and three more for all of their direct relatives. This led to a
lively employment of wage-workers. Female labour became dominant in
yarn-making, and was also common in the south-western cities. The
notorious truck system (pay in food and materials rather than money) was
also prevalent in this industry in Cologne and the south-western cities.[97]

Occasionally, governments directly promoted the production of linen and
fustian. In 1372 the yarn-wheels for the production of linen thread were
taken over by the city government in Cologne, providing an example of
government ownership of the means of production. The city leased them
out, thereafter, to producers, who hired mostly women to operate the
machines.[98] In the late sixteenth century, Württemberg actually provided
the necessary capital for the initiation of linen and fustian production in
the town of Urach.[99]

Woollens

During the middle ages, the manufacture of woollen cloth was as widespread as that of linen cloth: there was rural production wherever there
were sheep.[100] The enduring districts for woollen cloth production for the
world market were in Upper Westphalia, Upper Germany, and the Middle
Rhineland. However, wool-weaving in the Middle Rhineland and
throughout Germany in general suffered because of competition from the
more stylish woollen products of England and the Low Countries and the
lighter, softer fabrics, such as fustian. The great trading towns continued
to produce woollen cloths, using the products of the smaller town and
country spinners and weavers. By the 1370s, Nuremberg weavers, dyers,
and finishers produced some 10,000 cloths a year, and that number doubled
by 1421. Cologne was also a great textile town with 6,000 to 8,000 people,
or between a sixth and a fifth of the population involved in the woollen
cloth industry. It is important to note that woollen cloth production was
not the main industry of either of these towns, but it was an important

export industry.[101] Even Bavaria, which was little involved in capitalistic patterns compared with the neighbouring imperial towns, produced woollen cloth for the world market.[102]

Producers of woollens in the small and middling towns also suffered from the growing demand for raw wool in the Low Countries and great towns such as Cologne. Factors bought up so much of the wool in the small and middling Rhineland towns that prices rose tremendously. From the 1510s to the 1520s in Hesse, for example, they rose by 60 per cent. Local weavers with little capital could not procure enough wool. Profit limitations and pre-emptive buying privileges for resident Hessians only modified the impact of the growing demand for wool. Attempts to make local weavers competitive with foreign producers, by introducing the new dyeing techniques, did not work either.[103]

Putting-out was important in all of these places. In Bavaria, it was mostly Bavarians who loaned advances to producers of domestic woollens. This situation only changed with the Reformation, when Dissenters moved to Augsburg, Nuremberg, and Regensburg. Apparently most of the entrepreneurs involved in putting-out tended to be Dissenters; the result was that profits from wool production began to flow out of Bavaria. Finer products made in Bavaria of imported Saxon and Bohemian raw wool also suffered decline, after the mid-sixteenth century.[104]

In Cologne, the entrepreneurs making the advances were master weavers who put their poorer colleagues' entire shops to work. Moreover, the city *Wollenamt*, recruited from the weaver putters-out, regulated the industry to their benefit. Government sponsorship allowed Cologne producers to compete on the world market, by importing English, Scottish, and even Spanish (merino) wools into Cologne. Political arrangements between towns, or between towns and princes, won trading privileges in Bruges, Antwerp, or London. Similar connections facilitated the purchase of wool throughout the Middle Rhine region.[105]

The German town of Iglau, located on the Moravian–Bohemian border, provided an example of a joint-stock company organized by a town to promote wool production and marketing. Established in 1592, and confirmed by the emperor. it took deposits from rich and humble in the town; anyone could invest with the company. The capital was used to provide advance payments to raw-wool producers and then to advance the wool to poorer cloth- and hat-makers in Iglau. The wool was sold to craftsmen who had the capital. The company sold the wares at fairs and markets as far away as Hungary.[106]

The county of Oettingen provided an example of how big firms from Upper Germany got into woollen cloth production in collusion with the governing authorities. In the 1580s the Imhof firm of Augsburg arranged an agreement with Count Gottfried, whereby it controlled the manufacturing and trade of wool and woollen cloth in the county. In the last analysis, raw-wool producers could sell only to the Imhof firm, while the

latter provided a putting-out contract to the woolweavers' guild in the
Oettingen town of Harburg. In this case the guild lost control over its
primary producers, because the putter-out determined quality and time for
production. Moreover, the putting-out was all in kind, rather than in
money.[107]

Textile subsidiary industries

Dyes and alum were the most important subsidiary products in the textiles
industries. Woad and madder, for blue and red dyes, were both produced
in Germany, although these products were also imported from other parts
of Europe. During this period, production and sale for export grew so
greatly, that the areas where these subsidiary products were produced
became industrial districts. Thuringia, Upper Jülich, and Breslau became
woad districts; and a madder district emerged on the Upper Rhine, around
Speyer and Worms.[108]

Woad production in the district of Thuringia, around Erfurt, reached
and maintained its peak between the fourteenth century and the 1620s.
The production was carried out in two parts. In the countryside, the leaves
were grown, pulverized, and pressed into balls. Hydraulic and horse-driven
mills were employed to grind the leaves. The balls were shipped to towns,
where they were moistened and hung to mould for several months in the
well-ventilated upper rooms, or attics of the woad finishers. The finishers
pulverized the moulded balls and pressed them into kegs, for shipping to
market. Before the fourteenth century, feudal landholders had been the
employers in the countryside. The urban woad-dealers slowly bought out
most of the nobility through the city government of Erfurt. Most of the
patricians were woad entrepreneurs. By 1507, Erfurt owned 83 villages,
including some small towns. The property represented no less than 610
km^2, with perhaps as many as 32,000 villagers and 18,000 burghers.
Hence, Erfurt collected the peasant rents and controlled the courts in the
countryside, so that it prevented unforeseen occurrences that nobles often
allowed to interfere with business.[109]

Ultimately, the dealer-landowner-patrician woad-producers of Erfurt controlled the entire manufacturing process. By the fifteenth century, much of
the harvesting work was done by seasonal migrant labour, while local
peasants did the remainder. Wage labour did most of the work in the town
(i.e. wetting, hanging, pulverizing, and packing). Woad production represented a variety of decentralized manufacturing with some wage labour in
a centralized location, rather than putting-out. The peasant producers in the
countryside had to sell to the dealers, and paid both rent and an acre fee to
their dealer-landlords.[110]

Other products

Space permits only a brief mention of other wares produced for the world market. Tirtey, a combination of wool and linen, and silk were important products of Cologne and the great Upper German towns.[111] Satin became a fairly large-scale industry in the south-west after 1486, replacing wool and shrinking linen production. Rural production and female labour in spinning were based on the putting-out system. It was said: 'No village is too small to make satin.'[112]

Leather and leather products were produced in Cologne, and probably other great towns, with putting-out. Advances by merchant entrepreneurs made possible the production of leather and shoes for export. In Cologne, the official *Lederwirt* served as a mediator in credit problems for his worker-clients involving people inside and outside of the city.[113] A wood industry developed on the Upper Rhine, for which Mainz provided the market centre. Peasant partnerships were organized for felling trees.[114] It has been shown elsewhere how merchant capital and government promoted salt and glass production in Hesse, and a similar example may be found in Bavaria.[115]

German investment in colonial commerce

No survey of German capitalist activity in this period would be complete without a discussion of direct German investment in colonial ventures. By the late fifteenth century at the latest, German entrepreneurs were investing their capital in Portugese colonial ventures, including the development of the sugar islands. Extant evidence shows that the great Augsburg and Nuremberg banking firms, such as the Welsers, were colonial investors from that time. Moreover, Germans became involved through their connections at Antwerp.[116]

Investment took two general forms: production and trade. In 1509, for example, the Cologne burghers Jakob Groenenberg and Johann Byse bought the Welsers' property rights on the island of Palma (Canary Islands) for 11,000 fl. It appears to have been a typical partnership in which Groenenberg, the junior investor with 3,000 fl., acted the part of the factor by taking up residence at Palma.[117] Germans also invested in American projects. In 1534, the Aachen burgher, Erasmus Schetz, who had become active in Antwerp, purchased a sugar plantation in Brazil.[118] Investment in Portuguese trade took the form of the familiar lease (*Pacht*).[119]

As sugar became a major European product of long-distance trade, German investors became involved in refining, both at the source and in Germany. Those connected to Antwerp were the first to get into the refining business; because of its connections with Antwerp, Cologne imports of sugar went up from 11,914 pounds in 1450 to 23,600 pounds in the 1490s. In the fifteenth century, a Cologne partnership set up a refinery on the island of Palma; however, most refining was done in Europe. Upper German merchants also attempted to develop profitable sugar-refining. The refining equipment was expensive: in 1547 a Nuremberg sugar-maker went into debt building one for 1,647 fl.[120]

Germans also invested in the mining and manufacture of certain metals in the Spanish colonies. Hans Tetzel, a member of a Nuremberg patrician family, provides a good example. In the 1540s he established a copper works in Cuba, near Santiago. In order to raise the necessary capital, he created the typical German family-dominated partnership, with some shares sold to other business associates.[121] American production of copper by men like Tetzel was sufficient to keep the demand for European copper in the Americas lower than that in Africa.

Notes

1 Fernand Braudel, *Capitalism and Material Life, 1400–1800*, trans. Miriam Kochan (New York, 1973), p. xiii; idem, *Afterthoughts on Material Civilization and Capitalism*, trans. Patricia M. Ranum (Baltimore, MD, 1977), pp. 47–55.
2 Immanuel Wallerstein, *The Capitalist World-Economy* (Cambridge, 1979), pp. 5–6, 14–17, 147–8.
3 Andre Gunder Frank, *World Accumulation, 1492–1789* (New York, 1978), p. 52 and Braudel, *Afterthoughts*, pp. 49–52. For the delineation of the world economy and some differences of opinion regarding the origins and timing, see Immanuel Wallerstein, *The Modern World-System: Capitalist Agriculture and the Origins of the European World-Economy in the Sixteenth Century* (New York, 1974), pp. 15–26; Janet L. Abu-Lughod, *Before European Hegemony. The World System A.D. 1250–1350* (New York, 1989), pp. 8–12; Fernand Braudel, *The Perspective of the World*, vol. III of *Civilization and Capitalism, 15th–18th Century*, trans. Siân Reynolds (New York, 1984), pp. 57, 92–6; and William J. Wright. *Capitalism, the State and the Lutheran Reformation* (Athens, OH, 1988), pp. 27–9.
4 Eckhart Schremmer, 'Antwerpen als Warenhandelsplatz im 15. und 16. Jahrhundert und seine wirtschaftlichen Beziehungen zu Mitteleuropa', *Jahrbücher für Nationalökonomie und Statistik* CLXXVIII (1965), pp. 272–3, 277; Hektor Ammann, 'Deutschland und die Tuchindustrie Nordwesteuropas im Mittelalter', *HansGbl* LXXII (1954), pp. 59–60; E. Dösseler, 'Der Niederrhein und die Brabanter Messen zu Antwerpen und Bergen op Zoom vom Ende des 14. bis zum Ende des 16. Jahrhunderts', *Düsseldorfer Jb.*

LVII–LVIII (1980), p. 52; Franz Irsigler, 'Köln, die Frankfürter Messen und die Handelsbeziehungen mit Oberdeutschland im 15. Jahrhundert', in Hugo Stehkämpfer, ed., *Historisches Archiv der Stadt Köln, Köln, das Reich und Europa*, Mitteilungen aus dem Stadtarchiv von Köln LX (Cologne, 1971), pp. 359–60.

5 For a discussion of German land routes, Jan A. van Houtte, 'Die Beziehungen zwischen Köln und den Niederlanden vom Hochmittelalter bis zum Beginn des Industriezeitalters', *Kölner Vorträge zur Sozial- und Wirtschaftsgeschichte* I (1969), pp. 51–3.

6 Schremmer, 'Antwerpen als Warenhandelsplatz,' pp. 277–80; Eberhard Quadflieg, 'Aachener als Poorter von Antwerpen im 16. Jahrhundert', *ZAGV* LXXIV (1963), p. 393; Renée Doehaerd, *Études anversoises. Documents sur le commerce international à Anvers 1488–1514*, École Pratique des Hautes Études, VIᵉ Section, ed. *Ports–Routes–Trafics* XIV (Paris, 1963), pp. 263–6.

7 Hans Pohl, 'Köln und Antwerp um 1500', in Stehkämpfer, *Köln, das Reich*, p. 503; Jakob Strieder, *Aus Antwerpener Notariatsarchiven. Quellen zur Wirtschaftsgeschichte des 16. Jahrhunderts*, Deutsche Handelsakten des Mittelalters und der Neuzeit IV (Berlin, 1930), pp. 399, xxv; Schremmer, 'Antwerpen als Warenhandelsplatz', pp. 274–5.

8 Pohl, 'Köln und Antwerp', pp. 475–81; Franz Irsigler, *Die wirtschaftlicher Stellung der Stadt Köln in 14. und 15. Jahrhundert. Strukturanalyse einer spämittelalterliche- und Fernhandelstadt*, VSWG LXIV (Wiesbaden, 1979), pp. 37–8.

9 Pohl, 'Köln und Antwerp', pp. 484–6.

10 Van Houtte, 'Beziehungen Köln und Niederlanden', p. 19.

11 Pohl, 'Köln und Antwerp', pp. 471–2; Eckhart Schremmer, *Die Wirtschaft Bayerns. Vom hohen Mittelalter bis zum Beginn der Industrialisierung. Bergbau, Gewerbe, Handel* (Munich, 1970), p. 21; Rolf Sprandel, 'Die Konkurrenzfähigkeit der Hanse im Spätmittelalter', *HansGbl* CII (1984), p. 21.

12 Philippe Dollinger, *The German Hansa*, trans. D. S. Ault and S. H. Steinberg (Stanford, CA, 1970), pp. 186–7.

13 Ulf Dirlmeier, 'Mittelalterliche Zoll- Und Stapelrechte als Handelshemmnisse', *Die Auswirkungen von Zöllen und anderen Handelshemmnissen auf Wirtschaft und Gesellschaft von Mittelalter bis zum Gegenwart* (Stuttgart, 1987), pp. 38–9.

14 Wolfgang von Stromer, *Oberdeutsche Hochfinanz 1350–1450*, VSWG LV-LVII (3 vols., Wiesbaden, 1970) I, pp. 18, 38, 138–9.

15 Dollinger, *Hansa*, pp. 151–3, 155, 167–8. For conversion information, Hans-Peter Baum, *Hochkonzentration und Wirtschaftskrise im spätmittelalterlichen Hamburg, Hamburger Rentengeschäfte 1371–1410*, Beiträge zur Geschichte Hamburgs XI (Hamburg, 1976), p. 40.

16 Pohl, 'Köln und Antwerp', p. 502.

17 Irsigler, 'Köln, Frankfurter Messen', pp. 350–1.

18 Erich Maschke, 'Deutsche Kartelle des 15. Jahrhunderts', in Wilhelm Abel *et al.*, eds, *Wirtschafts, Geschichte, Wirstschaftsgeschichte. Festschrift zum 65. Geburtstag von Friedrich Lütge* (Stuttgart, 1966), pp. 77–8; Sprandel, 'Konkurrenzfähigkeit', p. 34.

19 Jean-François Bergier, 'From the Fifteenth Century in Italy to the Sixteenth Century in Germany: A New Banking Concept', in Center for Medieval and Renaissance Studies, ed., *The Dawn of Modern Banking* (New Haven, CT, London, 1979), pp. 107–8, 119.

20 Bruno Kuske, 'Die Entstehung der Kreditwirtschaft und des Kapitalverkehrs', in *Köln, der Rhein und das Reich. Beiträge aus fünf Jahrhunderten wirtschafts-*

geschichtlicher Forschung (Cologne/Graz, 1956), pp. 99–100.

21 Hermann Kellenbenz, 'German Aristocractic Entrepreneurship. The Economic Activity of the Holstein Nobility in the Sixteenth and Seventeenth Centuries', *Explorations in Entrepreneurial History* VI (1953–4), pp. 103–6; Richard Ehrenberg, *Capital and Finance in the Age of the Renaissance. A Study of the Fuggers and Their Connections*, trans. H. M. Lucas (New York, 1896; repr. 1928), pp. 176–85, 189–90.

22 Karlheinz Blaschke, 'Die Bedeutung kirchlicher Institutionen für den Kapitalmarkt im 15. und 16. Jahrhundert', in Uwe Bestmann, Franz Irsigler and Jürgen Schneider, eds, *Hochfinanz, Wirstchaftsräume, Innovationen* I (Trier, 1987), pp. 562–3.

23 Raymond de Roover, *Money, Banking and Credit in Medieval Bruges* (Cambridge, Mass., 1948), pp. 60, 202, 210.

24 Jakob Strieder, *Studien zur Geschichte kapitalistischer Organisationsformen. Monopole, Kartelle und Aktiengesellschaften im Mittelalter und zu Beginn der Neuzeit*, 2nd edn (New York, 1971), p. 102; Friedrich Wilhelm Henning, *Das vorindustrielle Deutschland, 800 bis 1800*, 2nd edn (Paderborn, 1976), p. 203.

25 Handelskammer Frankfurt am Main, *Geschichte der Handelskammer zu Frankfurt am Main (1707–1908)* (Frankfurt, 1908), p. 4; Georg Ludwig Kriegk, *Frankfurter Bürgerzwiste und Zustände im Mittelalter* (Frankfurt, 1862), pp. 334–5; Henning, *Vorindustrielle Deutschland*, p. 204.

26 Charles P. Kindelberger, *A Financial History of Western Europe* (London, 1984), p. 116.

27 Bergier, 'From Italy to Germany', p. 126; Henning, *Vorindustrielle Deutschland*, p. 205.

28 Bergier, 'From Italy to Germany', pp. 126–7.

29 Stromer, *Oberdeutsche Hochfinanz* vol. II, pp. 347–8, 358. The same patterns have been established for south Germany by Willi A. Boelcke, *Wirtschaftgeschichte Baden-Württembergs von den Römern bis Heute* (Stuttgart, 1987), pp. 156, 158.

30 Kindelberger, *Financial History* p. 39; Kriegk, *Frankfurter Bürgerzwiste*, p. 331.

31 Ehrenberg, *Capital and Finance*, p. 54; Frederick L. Nussbaum, *A History of the Economic Institutions of Modern Europe* (New York, 1968; repr. of 1935 edn), p. 203.

32 Ehrenberg, *Capital and Finance*, pp. 238, 315–16.

33 Bergier, 'From Italy to Germany', pp. 107–8.

34 Van Houtte, 'Beziehungen Köln und Niederlanden', p. 20.

35 Irsigler, 'Köln, Frankfurter Messen', pp. 341–3, 346–7; Kuske, 'Entstehung der Kreditwirtschaft', p. 78.

36 Frankfurt, *Geschichte der Handelskammer*, pp. 5–7; Ehrenberg, *Capital and Finance*, pp. 308–10.

37 Baum, *Hochkonzentration*, pp. 9, 27–9.

38 *Ibid.*, pp. 94, 126.

39 Rolf Sprandel, 'Die Spätmittelalterliche Wirtschaftskonjunktur und ihre Regionalen Determinanten. Forschungs-Ruckblick und neue Perspektiven', *VSWG* LXXXIV (1987), pp. 168–70; Wolfgang Habermann, 'Der Getreidehandel in Deutschland im 14. und 15. Jahrhunderts', *Scripta Mercaturae* XIII (1979), pp. 89–90; Kuske, 'Entstehung der Kreditwirtschaft', pp. 124–5.

40 Jan A. van Houtte, *An Economic History of the Low Countries, 800–1800* (London, 1977), p. 218.

41 Kuske, 'Entstehung der Kreditwirtschaft', pp. 80–1; Dollinger, *Hansa*, pp. 165–6, 203–4; van Houtte, *Economic History*, pp. 218–19. Discussing

Nuremberg, Valentin Groebner argues that credit was so tight that common workers used household wares and clothing as 'economic media', *Ökonomie ohne Haus* (Göttingen, 1993), pp. 235, 243.

42 Irsigler, *Stellung*, p. 4; Kuske, 'Entstehung der Kreditwirtschaft', pp. 82–3; Strieder, *Studien*, pp. 24–5; Fridolin Furger, *Zum Verlagssystem als Organisationsform des Frühkapitalismus im Textilgewerbe*, VSWG Supplement XI (1927), p. 3; Rudolf Holbach, 'Formen des Verlags im Hanseraum vom 13. bis zum 16. Jahrhundert', *HansGbl* CIII (1985), pp. 41–2.
43 Kuske, 'Entstehung der Kreditwirtschaft', pp. 134–5.
44 Schremmer, *Wirtschaft Bayern*, pp. 86–8.
45 Holbach, 'Formen des Verlags', pp. 44–6; Ernst Pitz, 'Steigende und Fallende Tendenzen in Politik und Wirtschaftsleben der Hanse im 16. Jahrhundert', *HansGbl* CII (1984), pp. 60–2.
46 Dollinger, *Hansa*, pp. 205–6; Stuart Jenks, 'War die Hanse Kreditfeindlich?' *VSWg* LXIX (1982), pp. 305–7, 309–10; T. H. Lloyd, *England and the German Hanse, 1157–1611* (Cambridge, 1992), pp. 43–4.
47 Kindelberger, *Financial History*, pp. 44, 184, 195.
48 Philippe Braunstein, 'Innovations in Mining and Metal Production in Europe in the Late Middle Ages', *JEEH* XII (1983), p. 581; Katerina Sieh-Burens, *Oligarchie, Konfession und Politik im 16. Jahrhundert. Zur sozialen Verflechtung der Augsburger Bürgermeister und Stadtpfleger 1518–1618*, Schriften der Philosophischen Fakultät Augsburg XXIX (Munich, 1986), p. 20.
49 Hermann Kellenbenz, 'Europäisches Kupfer, Ende 15. bis Mitte 17. Jahrhundert. Ergebnisse eines Kolloquiums', in idem, *Schwerpunkte der Kupferproduktion und des Kupferhandels in Europa 1500–1650* (Cologne, 1977), pp. 294–6; Braunstein, 'Innovations', pp. 581, 586–7; John U. Nef, *The Conquest of the Material World* (Chicago, 1964), p. 135.
50 Hermann Kellenbenz, *Wirtschaftsentwicklung und Umweltbeeinflussung*, Beiträge zur Wirtschafts- und Sozialgeschichte XX (Wiesbaden, 1982), p. 264.
51 Braunstein, 'Innovations', p. 588, n. 30; Kellenbenz, 'Europäisches Kupfer', pp. 294–5; Wolfgang von Stromer, 'Innovation und Wachstum im Spätmittelalter. Die Erfindung der Drahtmühle', *Technikgeschichte* XLIV (1977), pp. 91, 98–9, 106. For an excellent case study, Herbert Mashat, *Technic, Energie und Verlagswesen. Das Beispiel der Spätmittelalterlichen Reichstadt Nürnbergs* (Munich, 1988), pp. 86, 106–7.
52 Walter Endrei and Wolfgang von Stromer, 'Textiltechnische und hydraulische Erfindung und ihre Innovatoren in Mitteleuropa im 14. –15. Jahrhundert (die Seidenzwirnmühle)', *Technikgeschichte* XLI (1974), p. 89; Elisabeth M. Carus-Wilson, 'An Industrial Revolution of the Thirteenth Century', *EcHR* XI (1941), p. 40; Wolfgang von Stromer, *Die Gründung der Baumwollindustrie in Mitteleuropa. Wirtschaftspolitik im Spätmittelalter*, Monographien zur Geschichte des Mittelalters XVII (Stuttgart, 1978), p. 18.
53 Stromer, *Gründung*, pp. 15–16; idem, 'Gewerbereviere und Protoindustrien im Spätmittelalter und Frühneuzeit', in *Gewerbe- und Industrielandschaften von Spätmittelalter bis ins 20. Jahrhundert*, VSWG Supplement LXXVIII (1986), p. 41.
54 Henning, *Vorindustrielle*, p. 141.
55 Horst Jecht, review of Fritz Furger, *Zum Verlagssystem als Organisationsform des Frühkapitalismus im Textilgewerbe*, VSWG XX (1927), pp. 514–15; Furger, *Zum Verlagssystem*, p. 3; Rudolf Endres, 'Kapitalistische Organisationsformen im Ries in der zweiten Hälfte des 16. Jahrhunderts', JbfränkLF XXII (1962), pp. 97–8.
56 Henning, *Vorindustrielle*, p. 141.

57 Nef, *Conquest*, p. 51; Kellenbenz, 'Europäisches Kupfer', pp. 294–7. For the process, Albrecht Timm, 'Die Bedeutung des Mansfelder Kupfers zwischen 1500 und 1630', in Kellenbenz, *Schwerpunkte der Kupferproduktion*, pp. 184–5.

58 Clemens Bruckner, *Zur Wirtschaftsgeschichte des Regierungsbezirks Aachen*, Schriften zur Rheinisch-Westfälischen Wirtschaftsgeschichte XVI (Cologne, 1967), p. 269; Franz Irsigler, 'Industrial Production, International Trade and Public Finances (XIVth and XVth Century)', *JEEH* VI (1977), p. 211.

59 Nef, *Conquest*, p. 51.

60 See Stromer, 'Gewerbereviere', pp. 44–6 on the idea of proto-industrialization.

61 Reinhard Hildebrandt, 'Augsburger und Nürnberger Kupferhandel 1500–1619. Produktion, Markanteile und Finanzierung im Vergleich zweier Städte und ihrer wirtschaftlichen Führungsschichte', in Kellenbenz, *Schwerpunkte der Kupferproduktion*, pp. 200–2.

62 Timm, 'Bedeutung des Mansfelder Kupfers', pp. 185–6.

63 For further examples see Hildebrandt, 'Augsburger und Nürnberger Kupferhandel', pp. 217–18.

64 Braunstein, 'Innovations', pp. 581–2.

65 Franz Irsigler, 'Rheinisches Kapital in Mitteleuropäischen Montanunternehmen des 15. und 16. Jahrhunderts', *ZHF* III (1976), p. 164.

66 Ludwig Zimmermann, *Der ökonomische Staat Landgraf Wilhelms IV, I: Der hessische Territorialstaat im Jahrhundert der Reformation*, Veröffentlichungen der Historischen Kommission für Hessen und Waldeck XVII (Marburg, 1933), pp. 318–19.

67 Timm, 'Bedeutung des Mansfelder Kupfers', p. 187.

68 Ekkehard Westermann, 'Das "Leipziger Monopolprojekt" als Symptom der mitteleuropäischen Wirtschaftskrise um 1527/28', *VSWG* LVIII (1971), pp. 3–4.

69 Hildebrandt, 'Augsburger und Nürnberger Kupferhandel', p. 210; Strieder, *Studien*, pp. 294–8; Kellenbenz, 'Europäisches Kupfer', pp. 296–7; Hermann Kellenbenz, 'Germany', in Charles Wilson and Geoffrey Parker, eds, *An Introduction to the Sources of European Economic History 1500–1800* (Ithaca, NY, 1977), p. 201.

70 Hans Pohl, 'Kupfergewinnung, Kuferverarbeitung und Kupferhandel im Aachen-Stolbgerger Raum von 1500 bis 1650', in Kellenbenz, *Schwerpunkte der Kupferproduktion*, p. 227; Bruckner, *Wirtschaftgeschichte Aachen*, pp. 57–8; Irsigler, 'Rheinisches Kapital', pp. 156–7.

71 Strieder, *Studien*, pp. 212–15, 219.

72 Hermann Kellenbenz, 'Sächsisches und Böhmisches Zinn an dem Europäischen Markt", *VSWG* LXXXIV (1982), p. 252; Strieder, *Studien*, pp. 216, 220–1.

73 Kellenbenz, 'Sächsisches und Böhmisches Zinn', pp. 246–7; Strieder, *Studien*, pp. 259–60.

74 Kellenbenz, 'Sächsisches und Böhmisches Zinn', p. 254; Strieder, *Studien*, pp. 145–6, 154–5.

75 *Ibid.*, pp. 289–92.

76 Franz Michael Ress, 'Unternehmungen, Unternehmer und Arbeiter im Eisenerzbergbau und in Eisenverhüttung der Oberpfalz von 1300 bis um 1630', *Schmollers Jb.* LXXIV (1954), pp. 49–52; Hermann Kellenbenz, 'Europäisches Eisen. Produktion – Verarbeitung – Handel (vom Ende des Mittelalters bis ins 18. Jahrhundert)', in idem, ed., *Schwerpunkte der Eisengewinnung und Eisenverarbeitung in Europa 1500–1650* (Cologne, 1974), pp. 432, 451.

77 Ress, 'Unternehmungen', p. 31; Kellenbenz, 'Europäisches Eisen', pp. 400, 423; Fritz Geisthardt, 'Frühes Eisengewerbe an Sieg, Dill und Lahn', in Kellenbenz,

Schwerpunkte der Eisengewinnung, pp. 191–9.

78 Kellenbenz, 'Europäisches Eisen', pp. 425–6.

79 *Ibid.*, pp. 409, 412.

80 Ress, 'Unternehmungen', pp. 68–9; Siegfried Sieber, 'Eisengewerbe in Schlesien, Sachsen, Thüringen, Böhmen und in der Oberpfalz', in Kellenbenz, *Schwerpunkte der Eisengewinnung*, p. 250; Kellenbenz, 'Europäisches Eisen', pp. 409, 512.

81 Franz Krins, 'Das Eisengewerbe im Süderland von 1500 bis 1650', in Kellenbenz, *Schwerpunkte der Eisengewinnung*, p. 179.

82 Hans Pohl, 'Das Eisengewerbe in der Eifel und im Hunsrück', in Kellenbenz, *Schwerpunkte der Eisengewinnung*, pp. 167–8,

83 Pohl, 'Eisengewerbe in der Eifel', pp. 164–6.

84 Geisthardt, 'Frühes Eisengewerbe', pp. 192–3.

85 Wright, *Capitalism*, pp. 122–3.

86 Kellenbenz, 'Europäisches Eisen', p. 410.

87 Krins, 'Eisengewerbe im Süderland', p. 183; Maschke, 'Deutsche Kartelle', pp. 82–3.

88 Ress, 'Unternehmungen', pp. 52, 67–72.

89 Hermann Aubin, 'Das westfälische Leinengewerbe im Rahmen der deutschen und europäischen Leinwanderzeugung bis zum Ausbruch des Industriezeitalters', *Vortragsreihe der Gesellschaft für westfälische Wirtschaftsgeschichte* XI (1964), p. 14; Hermann Kellenbenz, 'Ländliches Gewerbe und bäuerliches Unternehmertum in Westeuropa von Spätmittelalter bis ins 18. Jahrhundert', in *Deuxième conférence internationale d'histoire economique, Aix-en-Province. Congrès et colloques* VIII (Paris, 1965), pp. 402–4, 411–12.

90 Kellenbenz, 'Ländliches Gewerbe', p. 397; Irsigler, *Stellung*, pp. 28–9, 36; Karlheinz Blaschke, *Sachsen im Zeitalter der Reformation*, SVRG CLXXXV (Gütersloh, 1970), p. 37.

91 Gerhard Heitz, *Ländliche Leinenproduktion in Sachsen (1470–1555)*, Schriften des Instituts für Geschichte IV (Berlin, 1961), pp. 15–17, 28–9, 41, 52; Aubin, 'Westfälische Leinengewerbe', pp. 14–15; Blaschke, *Sachsen*, p. 37.

92 Heitz, *Ländliche Leinenproduktion*, pp. 19–21, 81.

93 Aubin, 'Westfälische Leinengewerbe', pp. 14–15.

94 Bernhard Kirchgässner, 'Der Verlag in Spannungsfeld von Stadt und Umland', in Erich Maschke and Jürgen Sydow, eds, *Stadt und Umland*, Veröffentlichungen der Kommission für geschichtliche Landeskunde in Baden-Württemberg LXXXII (Stuttgart, 1974), pp. 96–7; Stromer, *Gründung*, pp. 11–15.

95 Kirchgässner, 'Der Verlag', pp. 87–8.

96 *Ibid.*, p. 88; Stromer, *Gründung*, pp. 11–15.

97 Irsigler, *Stellung*, pp. 49–50; Kirchgässner, 'Der Verlag', p. 90.

98 Irsigler, *Stellung*, pp. 28–9.

99 Kirchgässner, 'Der Verlag', p. 107.

100 Kellenbenz, 'Ländliches Gewerbe', p. 418.

101 Hektor Ammann, *Die wirtschaftliche Stellung der Reichsstadt Nürnberg im Spätmittelalter* (Nuremberg, 1970), pp. 10–12, 47; Pohl, 'Köln und Antwerp', pp. 480–1; Stromer, 'Gewerbereviere', pp. 51, 66–7.

102 Schremmer, *Wirtschaft Bayern*, pp. 90–3.

103 Wright, *Capitalism*, pp. 149–50.

104 Schremmer, *Wirtschaft Bayern*, pp. 93–6.

105 Irsigler, *Stellung*, pp. 47–8; Pohl, 'Köln und Antwerp', pp. 480–1.

106 Strieder, *Studien*, pp. 142–5.

107 Endres, 'Kapitalistische Organisationsformen', pp. 92–8.

108 Irsigler, *Stellung*, pp. 93, 97–8; Dösseler, 'Der Niederrhein', p. 77.
109 V. E. Majer, 'Soziale und ökonomische Wandlungen im Bereich der Waidproduktion in Deutschland während des 14. bis 17. Jahrhunderts', in Werner Magdefrau, ed., *Europäische Stadtgeschichte im Mittelalter und früher Neuzeit* (Weimar, 1979), pp. 328–3.
110 *Ibid.*, pp. 231–6.
111 Irsigler, *Stellung*, pp. 11–12, 29–30, 52–3; Kirchgässner, 'Der Verlag', p. 92.
112 *Ibid.*, 'Der Verlag', pp. 100–2.
113 Irsigler, *Stellung*, pp. 321–2.
114 Hermann Kellenbenz, *The Rise of the European Economy. An Economic History of Continental Europe from the Fifteenth to the Eighteenth Century* (London, 1976), p. 100; Franz Irsigler, 'Kölner Wirtschaftsbeziehungen zum Oberrhein vom 14. bis 16. Jahrhundert', ZGO CXXII (1974), pp. 13–14, 17–21.
115 See Wright, *Capitalism*, pp. 125–6; Schremmer, *Wirtschaft Bayern*, p. 48; Nef, *Conquest*, pp. 106–7.
116 Hermann Kellenbenz, 'Wirtschaftsgeschichtliche Aspekte der überseeischen Expansion Portugals', *Scripta Mercaturae* (1970), p. 7.
117 Irsigler, 'Köln, Frankfurter Messen', p. 427; Kellenbenz, 'Aspekte Expansion', p. 7.
118 Theodor Gustav Werner, 'Die Anfänge der deutschen Zuckerindustrie und die Augsburger Zuckerraffinerie von 1573', *Scripta Mercaturae* (1972), p. 172.
119 A. Teixeira da Mota, 'Der portugiesische Seehandel in Westafrika in 15. und 16. Jahrhundert und seine Bedeutung für die Entwicklung des überregionalen Handelsverkehr', in *Kölner Vorträge zur Sozial- und Wirtschaftsgeschichte* V (Cologne, 1969), pp. 5, 8–9.
120 Werner, 'Anfänge deutschen Zuckerindustrie', pp. 167, 169, 175–6.
121 Theodor Gustav Werner, 'Die Kupferhüttenwerk des Hans Tetzel aus Nürnberg auf Kuba', *VSWG* XLVIII (1961), pp. 289, 315–19.

8

Gender and the Worlds of Work

MERRY E. WIESNER

If this chapter had been written ten or even five years ago, the title would no doubt have read 'Women's Work' and the chapter would have discussed the role of women in various sectors of the economy and the impact of economic change on their labour.[1] It would have taken the meaning of both 'women' and 'work' as self-evident: 'women' means all those born female; 'work' means production, either for subsistence or the market.

Over the last several years, however, both of those meanings have been called into question. Along with investigating the historical experience of women, historians have begun analysing the social construction of gender: how societies in the past defined what it meant to be a man or woman, and how persons born male and female were trained in their gender roles. They use methods and language often first developed by anthropologists and sociologists to explore how gender shaped human experience and how ecomonic, political, and intellectual developments affected, and in turn were affected by, changes in notions of gender.[2]

At the same time as investigations of women are broadening into investigations of gender, economic historians, both marxist and non-marxist, are becoming increasingly uncomfortable with defining work solely as production. Marxist feminist scholars stress the fact that industrial capitalism relied not only on the paid productive labour of workers in factories but also on the unpaid reproductive labour of people, largely women, in the home.[3] 'Reproductive' in this sense means not only the bearing and rearing of children, but the care and nourishment of all family members, care which allowed them to work the long hours demanded under industrial capitalism. If productive and reproductive labour are intertwined in the nineteenth century, they are even more so in the late medieval and early modern periods, when the household was often the locus of production, so that an accurate analysis of 'work' in this period must include both productive and reproductive activities.

Though working life and what we might term personal circumstances were closely related for both men and women, that relationship operated in very different ways. Male work rhythms and a man's position in the economy were to a large degree determined by age, class, and training, with boys and men often moving as a group from one level of employment to another.

Female work rhythms were also determined by age and class, but even more so by individual biological and social events. Girls rarely received formal training, so that the most dramatic change in their economic status and work responsibilities was marriage, not the completion of a training process. Their level of participation in production was influenced by their success at reproduction, for childbirth and breastfeeding took them away from production to at least some degree. After marriage, the next dramatic change in women's work status was widowhood, with possible subsequent remarriage bringing yet another change. All of these changes were experienced by women individually; they could happen at almost any time, unexpectedly.

Highlighting these gender differences somewhat obscures differences of residence and class. Rural men generally did not go through formal training programmes, and their most dramatic change in status, like that of women, was marriage, which made them independent heads of households. Unlike women, however, men's status did not change with the death of a spouse, nor was the type of work they did greatly affected by the births of children. For rural women, both marriage and widowhood brought dramatic changes in status, and the births of children shaped the waged and unwaged work they could do. Among the rural and urban poor, the work pattern of both sexes was more similar than it was for middle- and upper-class men and women, for poor boys and men often could not afford to enter into apprenticeships or start independent households, but worked as day-labourers with no job security. Their work patterns were thus more like those of women – discontinuous, largely dependent on personal events such as illness or general economic trends, and always badly paid.

For poor women, however, gender added further constraints to those of class, because the birth of children created additional hardships for those who were married, and could spell disaster for the unmarried. Class and place of residence thus created greater variation in the work experiences of men than of women. This is not simply a modern observation, but was recognised by medieval people, who classified men according to estate (*Stand*) – warriors, merchants, farmers, priests – and women according to marital or sexual status – virgin, wife, widow, nun, prostitute. This conceptual structure not only reflected their view of reality, of course, but also shaped it, encouraging men to identify with their occupation and women with their families.

In this chapter we will investigate many 'worlds' – the household, mine, fields, craft shop, marketplace – but in all of them focus on the same thing, the intersection of gender roles and economic needs. All economies need both structure and flexibility, and increasingly in the late middle ages these qualities became dichotomized and gender-identified; men provided the structure, women the flexibility. We shall start by examining how persons were socialized into their gender roles and how these roles changed throughout the life-cycle. We shall then turn to political and economic institutions which reinforced gender roles. The bulk of the chapter discusses what happened when those theoretical roles met the actual changing economies of rural and urban Germany, how women's and men's work experience was shaped by their gender.

Socialization into gender roles across the life-cycle

Socialization into gender roles began very early in childhood. Whether or to what degree medieval and early modern parents felt affection for their children has been a hotly debated topic among historians over the last thirty years, but we do know that they gave them toys, and toys that were gender-specific.[4] Girls were encouraged to play with dolls, boys with toys that involved more action; this also meant that girls played in the house, boys outside. Children were also given gender-specific household tasks and tools at a very young age, with girls getting spindles and the job of minding children while boys were sent outside to watch animals.

Gender distinctions grew larger once children reached the age of 7 or 8, particularly among urban families who were not among the very poor. At this age the sons of wealthier families began their formal schooling, starting with training in Latin. This schooling prepared them for later attendance at a university and an eventual professional career as a physician, lawyer, university professor, or government or church official. Learning Latin was in many ways a male puberty rite for upper-class urban boys, and the professionals who knew Latin were a group with high status and a strong sense of cohesion.[5] Girls were rarely taught Latin, for they were forbidden from attending a university and none of the professions which required it was open to women. A few girls did learn Latin in convents, or from their fathers or private tutors, but this was only for their private edification. Other than copying manuscripts in convents or secular scriptoria, women had no outlet for their Latin capabilities, which was particularly frustrating for them once humanist ideas about the importance of using one's education became widespread in Germany in the sixteenth century.[6]

Education in Latin for boys grew slowly more widespread during the period 1300–1600, but never involved more than a tiny portion of the population, so that class differences were more important than those of gender in determining access to Latin education. During the sixteenth century, however, Renaissance humanist ideas of the importance of education to the development of the individual and the well-being of society combined with Protestant and later Catholic ideas of the value of literacy to lead to the establishment of a large number of primary schools which taught reading and writing in German. Though many of the Protestant reformers called for the opening of girls' schools, most of the schools which were opened were for boys only, which resulted in a widening gap between male and female vernacular literacy rates in the sixteenth century.[7] Even where girls' schools did exist, girls attended for a much briefer period than their brothers, because their parents were less willing to forego their help in the household; female 'literacy' therefore often meant only the ability to read, because reading and writing were not taught simultaneously. Thus even 'literate' women could not take jobs in which writing or arithmetic was required, which did not dramatically shape their employment opportunities in 1300, when few artisans could write, but certainly did by 1600, when in many cities of Germany the majority of male artisans could both read and write.[8] Teaching women to read but not write was the result not only of an economic decision on the part of parents but also of contemporary notions about the ideal woman. Though the qualities and behaviour described as ideal for men changed dramatically over the period with the impact of the Renaissance and the Reformation, and were highly class-specific, the qualities of the ideal woman were the same across classes and centuries: she was pious, obedient, chaste and silent. The best education for girls was thus seen to be one which would encourage these qualities by providing classical and Christian models of good womanhood.[9] Learning to read would allow a girl or woman to discover more of these models on her own, and also to absorb the ideas of great (male) authors. Learning to write, on the other hand, would enable her to express her own ideas, an ability which few thinkers regarded as important and some saw as dangerous, for it broke the injunction to silence.[10]

Formal schooling in either Latin or German thus reinforced ideas about the differing roles and capabilities of males and females. The experiences of children who did not attend school also began to be more determined by gender around the age of 7. At this age, many urban boys were apprenticed in their own father's shop or to another craftsman, while girls remained at home, perhaps working in their father's shop, but without a formal apprenticeship. Boys began to identify with their occupation, knowing that in all likelihood they would remain in it their whole lives.

For a number of economic and cultural reasons, the average age at first marriage in Germany was relatively late. This meant that young adulthood (after sexual maturity, but before marriage) was a definite stage of life for most people, a stage of strong same-sex identification and orientation for both men and women. This was the period in which notions of honour became very important, notions which were highly gender-specific. Except among the nobility, for whom masculine honour still meant bravery, male honour increasingly revolved around work, around one's honesty, good craftsmanship, loyalty to craft traditions and fellow workers. Female honour centred on sexual conduct and reputation, though this was not totally unrelated to work either. Guild ordinances forbade men to marry a woman whose sexual conduct was even questionable, and demanded that members refuse to live with any wife found guilty of adultery, the reasoning being that an artisan unable to control his wife's conduct was probably also unable to control what went on in the shop.[11] Because 'honour' was one of the key qualities sought in a spouse, conformity to gender-specific notions of honour during young adulthood determined one's access to marriage partners for both sexes.

The connections between gender and work created in childhood were reinforced throughout one's life. This was a period in which occupational labels were becoming patronymics (indeed, in many instances it is difficult to tell if a name is an occupation or a patronymic), but whether occupation or patronymic, a woman's name was rarely stable through her lifetime. She was generally identified as, for example, Anna, the daughter of Hans the baker when a girl, then Anna, the wife of Martin the butcher, then the butcher's widow, then the wife of Wilhelm Smith, and so on. Trying to sort out patronymic or occupation for women in German is even more difficult than it is for men, as 'die Schmidin' could refer either to a woman whose husband was a smith or whose name was Smith, to the widow of a smith or of a man named Smith, or to a woman working as a smith herself.

It is important to recognize, however, that 'the wife of a smith' is also an occupational title in the late middle ages and did not simply indicate marital status. That title carried with it a set of responsibilities and duties which the woman herself as well as her neighbours and associates, understood; it was not an honorific in the way that calling the wife of a doctor 'die Doktorin' would be in the eigthteenth century. This conflation of occupational and marital title illustrates the fusing of work identity and family identity for women.

If names reinforced links between gender and work at a subconscious level, what historians have come to term 'popular culture' did so explicitly. Ballads and songs told about lucky young journeymen who through marrying the master's widow became wealthy and powerful. When such a marriage actually happened, a group of young men often serenaded the couple with jeering songs in an expression of their disapproval of the marriage, a disapproval which stemmed from widely held notions of the sexual voraciousness of older women, worries that she would be the dominant partner because of her status, and certainly at least a little jealousy. Woodcuts depicted timid husbands washing diapers while their wives carried swords, and court records are full of people accusing others of having harmed their reputations and honour by calling them 'she-man' (overly strong wife) or 'cuckold' in the marketplace.[12] Shops whose masters were thought to be dominated by their wives were boycotted by journeymen, who refused to work alongside anyone who upset their ideas of proper gender hierarchy.

More formal popular rituals also strengthened the links between gender identity and work identity. In city processions, men marched with their guild or occupational group while the women who worked in or even ran those same guild shops did not. Guilds themselves held celebratory meals, and created elaborate rituals to mark the acceptance of new members, events in which only the male members participated. In only a very few women's occupations, such as midwifery, were similar ceremonies developed in some cities, and in these cases the women commented specifically that they realized how important such occasions were for building up group cohesion and work identity.[13]

Institutions reinforcing gender roles

Both church and state also reinforced gender roles through sermons, published advice books, laws, and ordinances. Before the sixteenth century, few preachers or clerical writers provided much specific advice on family life or work because they viewed a life of celibacy as far superior. This began to change with the spread of Renaissance humanism, for humanists argued that the *vita activa* was the best possible life, with some going so far as to say that having a family was an important part of a man's civic duty.[14]   This championing of family life increased dramatically with the Protestant Reformation when the value of celibacy was emphatically denied. Sermons and advice manuals urged men and women to marry early, and discussed the proper comportment of husbands and wives. According to Cyriacus Spangenburg, the author of one of the best-selling of these *Ehespiegel* (mirrors of marriage), the wife was to be responsible for raising the children and keeping the house clean, and owed her husband love, patience, and obedience.[15] The husband was to be the head of the household in the same way as a ruler was the head of his territory; Andreas Musculus, another clerical author, commented that letting the wife take charge would be as bad as the Peasants' Revolt, 'when the subjects wanted to be lords'.[16] Such sermons and advice manuals, usually termed *Hausvaterliteratur*, created what was in many ways a new vocation for men in Germany, that of father and head of household, responsible for the behaviour and ideas of his wife, children, and servants. The Reformation also further exalted western Christianity's already positive assessment of labour because Protestant thinkers, at least theoretically, denied that the work of the clergy was any more important than that of the laity; all occupations became vocations.[17]

In Reformation ideology, then, men had two divinely sanctioned vocations, father and worker. Women, however, had only one: mother. Advice manuals and sermons by Protestant clergy, and later in the sixteenth century by Catholic clergy as well, all viewed whatever productive labour women did as simply part of their domestic role, of their being a helpmeet for their husband and example for their children. That idea was not just to be found in religious literature, however, but also permeates secular laws and ordinances regulating and defining work in the sixteenth century. When women performed an activity, such as sewing clothes, it was defined as *hausliche Arbeit* (domestic work), even if those clothes were not for her own family's use. When men carried out the same activity, also in their own homes, it was defined as *Erwerbsarbeit* (production), whether or not those men were members of a tailors' guild or similar organization. The gender of the worker, not the work itself or its location, marked the difference between domestic tasks and production.[18]

A similar case of other terms masking what was in fact a gender division can be seen in the notions of 'skilled' and 'unskilled' work which were supported by guild ordinances and city and state laws. Guilds often ruled that women were unfit for certain tasks, such as glass-cutting, because they were too clumsy and 'unskilled', yet those same women made lace, a job which required an even higher level of dexterity and concentration than glass-cutting. Historians of the industrial period have pointed to the deskilling of certain occupations, in which jobs which had traditionally been done by men were made more monotonous with the addition of machinery and so were redefined as unskilled and given to women, with a dramatic drop in status and pay.[19] The opposite process can be seen in the sixteenth century, in the transformation of stocking-knitting into a male-dominated occupation. When the knitting-frame was introduced into Germany, men began to argue that using it was so complicated that only men could possibly learn; the frame actually made knitting easier and much faster, but women were prohibited from using it anyway with the excuse that they were unskilled. The amount they could earn from hand-knitting was thus much less than their male counterparts using a frame, but by the end of the sixteenth century male knitters were pressuring for laws which would exclude women altogether, with the argument that all knitting was so skilled that it should be the province of men alone.[20]

Defining an occupation as skilled or unskilled according to the gender of the workers can also be seen in the largely unsuccessful attempts at silk production begun in south Germany in the sixteenth century. Though unwinding the extremely fine threads from a cocoon and twisting them into thread required great skill, patience and practice, this was an occupation largely done by girls, and often orphans at that, so it was 'unskilled'.[21]

Laws which divided skilled from unskilled labour, and productive from domestic tasks, were part of a general creation of legal systems in Germany which began in the thirteenth century. Though the political disunity of Germany meant that each territory, town, or village had a different legal system, many of them were based on the same models: in the thirteenth century the *Sachsenspiegel* and *Schwabenspiegel*, two major collections of laws collated by jurists, served as models for many territorial legal systems; in the fourteenth and the fifteenth centuries, new cities based their law codes on those of existing cities and sent difficult cases to the older cities for judgment; in the sixteenth century, university-trained lawyers introduced principles from Roman law into both territorial and urban law codes. There is thus more similarity among the law codes of Germany than one might initially expect.

A discussion of all laws which have some bearing on gender roles would be far too lengthy, so I wish to concentrate on three specific areas in which gender distinctions have an impact on the structures of work: citizenship, inheritance, and property rights. Particularly in urban areas, citizenship was often required before one could own property, join a guild or otherwise work in a town. If one was not born in a town, one could gain citizenship upon payment of a fee as long as the city council judged one to be of good character. Not surprisingly, books of new citizens record many more men gaining citizenship than women, particularly because a wife was assumed to be included in her husband's citizenship while the opposite was not the case. Women who wished to gain citizenship on their own generally had to have an occupation which a city was interested in recruiting, such as midwifery, or to have a large amount of capital so that they did not have to work.[22]

Women's access to capital was limited by inheritance laws which favoured sons (the exact formula for the division of property after a death varied widely throughout Germany, but almost all law codes favoured male children), and by the inability of married women to control even their own property without their husband's approval. Widows in Germany also had less access to capital than they did elsewhere in Europe, for only a few areas allowed a widow the absolute right to a certain part of her husband's property in the way that English common law did.[23]

Academic jurists regarded women as physically, morally and mentally weak, and so granted them the right to declare their signatures invalid on contracts and agreements if they said that they had been pressured or misled or had not understood what they were doing; this was called 'female freedom' and was said to protect women, though of course it actually gave their husbands or male relatives greater protection. This 'freedom' did not fill the needs of expanding city economies in the high middle ages, however, and most urban law codes allowed single, widowed and even married women to declare themselves 'market women' (*Marktfrauen*), able to do business without the approval of a man.[24] Many more simply carried out all sorts of financial transactions independently without any formal declaration; more harm was done to women's actual economic position by the laws which gave their husbands control over their property than by those which restricted their right to make contracts. A husband's control over his wife's property was not absolute in many cities, however. If a wife could prove her husband was in *Abfall*, wasting the family property through bad investments, gambling or drinking, the city council might step in and give her control over it; its paternalism and concern about a possible drain on city finances if the family was reduced to poverty outweighed its desire to encourage female dependence.[25] Such city laws envisioned the same ideal for adult men as the *Hausvaterliteratur* – they were to be good fathers, husbands, and providers as well as good workers.

The economic needs of medieval cities led to a gradual broadening in the legal rights of married and unmarried women, but this broadening was reversed beginning in the late fifteenth century when areas began to revise their civil codes to include procedures and principles drawn from Roman law. Unmarried women and widows were again required to have male guardians oversee all their financial decisions and husbands were given more rights to act alone or for their wives in all financial matters.

Governments recognized that women had often lost their say in family financial matters, and so required widows to pay back only half of their husband's debts. Officials trained in Roman law began to view law as a tool for shaping society, and encouraged governments to expand their codes to make them more systematic and comprehensive, and to prosecute more vigorously those who slipped through these codes. This had a particular impact on women, who had often slipped through the cracks of the older, looser codes, or whose infractions had been simply ignored.[26]

Gender roles in the actual economy: the rural world

As we might imagine, when we turn from prescriptive ideas about the roles of men and women, or laws which attempted to enforce those ideas, to the actual work experience of individuals and groups, we find much less clearly delineated gender roles and much more variation. The period from 1300 to 1600 was one of great changes in many parts of the German economy, changes which may be loosely described as the beginning of capitalism, with commercial exchange playing an increasing role in both the countryside and the cities.

The vast majority of people in Germany during this period lived in small villages, producing agricultural products for their own use and for the use of their landlords. Agricultural tasks were highly, though not completely, gender-specific, and the proper functioning of the rural household required at least one adult male and one adult female; remarriage after the death of a spouse was much faster in the countryside than in the cities. Women were largely responsible for tasks within or close to the house; they took care of poultry and small animals, prepared dairy products, beer and bread, grew flax and made linen and wool cloth. They also worked in the fields during harvest time, particularly in areas where grain-harvesting was done with a sickle; manuscript illuminations and woodcuts show women and men working side by side with sickles well into the eighteenth century. Men generally carried out all forest jobs and those involving construction and did the majority of the planting and the grain-harvesting done with a scythe, which began to be used for grain in some parts of Germany in the fifteenth century. (Earlier the scythe had been used only for hay.) Use of the scythe also created new tasks for women, gathering and binding, which were often physically more demanding than the actual cutting but did not require as much upper-body strength. Both men and women transported grain and other rural products to market, though men generally drove the teams if wagons were used.[27]

Though we often think of rural households as subsistence producers, they were actually part of a market economy in many areas of Germany as early as the fifteenth century. Rural women sold butter, eggs, cheese, soap, small animals, and fruit in market towns or cities to gain cash in order to fulfil their tax and rent obligations; unlike the sale of grain, which was restricted to harvest time, these products were sold year-round, making them a particularly important part of the household economy.

Not every family in a village had access to enough land or animals to support itself; many of them also relied on the income of family members as agricultural workers or as artisans. At the same time as craft guilds were being established in cities, men in rural areas were also specializing in certain occupations, such as smithing, weaving, carpentry work, or milling.[28] Their wives assisted them or else worked as day-labourers shearing sheep, picking hops, or at other agricultural tasks. Though in some parts of Germany women and men were paid the same for the same tasks, in most areas female agricultural labourers were paid less for the same work; traditionally female tasks, such as binding grain, earned less than tasks generally done by men, such as cutting grain with a scythe.[29]

Though almost all people who lived in rural Germany eventually married, many of them spent a period of time before their marriage as domestic servants. Their period of service was rarely determined by a written contract, but was instead sealed by a small sum of money (the *Dingpfennig* or *Mietpfennig*). Servants received room, board, and some clothing from their employers, and also an annual salary, though this was often not paid until the servant left the household. Male servants were generally paid better than female servants, though level of pay was also dependent on level of responsibility and experience. Both men and women regarded service as a time to save for the later establishment of an independent household, though young women were also occasionally forced into service to pay off their parents' feudal dues, a practice that continued into the eighteenth century in some parts of Germany.[30] By the sixteenth century, governments attempted to regulate the wages and conduct of both male and female servants, though their moves were often ineffectual, particularly because they resulted from conflicting aims: states wanted to keep wages down in order to keep landholders solvent, yet also wanted wages high enough to allow servants to save for the eventual establishment of a household; governments also wanted to keep servants living in and under the control of an employer's household, so forbade them to marry during their period of service and tried to limit unsupervised contacts between male and female servants, yet also preferred female servants to marry if they became pregnant rather than give birth out of wedlock.[31] It is not surprising that the resultant laws regarding servants were often contradictory or confused.

Servants were not the only people who worked for wages in the rural economy. In wine-growing areas, wage work began as early as the fourteenth century, with people even coming out from towns or cities to participate in the wine harvest. Unlike servants, these wage-labourers could and did marry, yet the wages of any one individual were never enough to support an entire family, so that all family members worked. They were all paid as individuals, however, and there was no clear gendered division of labour, which meant that the household was not a unit of production. Because of this, remarriage was not as common as it was for other rural residents, with widows often making up a much greater percentage of heads of household than they did in grain-growing areas. Women were generally paid less for the same job, so that widows might be forced to remarry in order to survive economically, but the structure of the economy did not require it in the way it did for peasants' widows. Female vineyard workers earned their own wages throughout their lives regardless of their marital status.[32]

In some mining areas women also worked independently for wages, though more often a male head of household was paid the wages for the work of his entire family. Though printed sources give very little information about the division of labour in mining, pictures and engravings from the fifteenth century onwards show women carrying ore, wood and salt, sorting and washing ore, and preparing charcoal briquets. Most of the work underground was carried out by adult men in the pre-industrial period, though the belief that women working underground brought bad luck was a consequence, and not a cause, of this division of labour, for it does not appear in any early modern sources. The development of large-scale capitalist mining operations which began in some parts of Germany in the late middle ages brought deeper tunnels, more use of machinery and more complex smelting techniques, all of which led to a professionalization of mining as an occupation. Though women were not always specifically prohibited from beginning an apprenticeship in mining, almost all those who learned and practised mining as a life-long career were men. This did not mean that women disappeared from mining operations, but that their labour was more clearly identified as assisting or ancillary, and consequently badly paid.[33]

Large-scale capitalist enterprise was not limited to mining areas, but began to have an impact on the rural economy in grain-growing areas as well during the fifteenth century. Urban investors began to hire rural households to produce wool, linen, and later cotton thread and cloth (or cloth that was a mixture of these), paying the household for its labour alone and retaining ownership of the raw materials and in some cases the tools and machinery used. (This is usually termed the *Verlagssystem*.) Spinning and weaving became important by-employments for peasants in many parts of Germany, providing income through the winter months. While urban cloth-production was regulated by guilds and was highly gender-stratified (women carded and spun while men wove), rural production was not, with husbands, wives, and children who were old enough all contributing. This contradicted the notions of proper gender roles for at least some observers, such as Sebastian Franck, who commented after visiting the villages around Augsburg and Ulm in the early sixteenth century: 'Not only women and maids, but also men and boys, spin. One sees contradictions; they work and gossip like women, yet are still vigorous, active, strong, and quarrelsome people, the kind any area would want to have.'[34] This is an excellent example of the point noted above, that economic need tended to outweigh gender roles; even the occupation most clearly identified as female in the pre-industrial world, spinning, could be practised by men if necessary, with at least the local popular culture adapting so that such men were not considered effeminate, though an outside observer such as Franck still had his doubts.

Gender roles in the actual economy: the urban world

In some ways, separating rural from urban economies is misleading, for the connections between cities and their surrounding villages were very close. Rural residents travelled to the cities to sell their products or, once restrictions on the travel of serfs had been lifted, to search for employment; poorer urban residents worked in the countryside during harvest and planting; wealthier city-dwellers hired rural households to produce cloth or invested in mines. Nevertheless, the cities of Germany were separate legal units, and their economic development, though linked to that of the countryside, was also distinctive. In addition, the cities have left many more sources than the countryside, so that most studies of women's work and the effects of gender roles on economic life have of necessity focused on the cities.

Though in many aspects of urban development great care must be taken to differentiate between northern and southern Germany, free imperial cities and ducal capitals, large international trading centres and regional market towns, guild-influenced governments and those controlled by patricians, when assessing the gender division of labour the similarities vastly outweigh the differences. The following discussion will thus generalize about life in all cities, with a few important regional and political differences noted.

Perhaps the most distinctive economic feature of cities in Germany were craft guilds, which were established in some parts of Germany as early as the twelfth century and in all cities by the fourteenth. The role of women in the medieval craft guilds has been a hotly debated topic since 1910, when Karl Bücher published his *Die Frauenfrage im Mittelalter*, which asserted that the sex ratio in medieval cities was highly skewed in favour of women, so that many women could not marry but had to earn their living independently.[35] This combined with the term *Lehrtochter* (female apprentice), which appeared in many early guild statutes led a number of historians to posit that, at least in the high middle ages, many guilds were open to women.[36] Bücher's demographic statistics have recently been discredited, and scholars using actual guild records rather than theoretical ordinances have pointed out that the number of women who were not masters' widows working independently as guild masters was miniscule, and that even masters' widows rarely had full guild rights.[37] They assert that, from their creation, guilds were male-dominated institutions. Not all scholars agree with this, however, citing the all-women's guilds in medieval Cologne, women's participation in the charitable and social aspects of guild life even when they were not part of the actual production process, or the fact that women *could* begin an apprenticeship in some guilds to argue that the guilds did offer opportunities for women, at least until the late fifteenth century.[38] This whole debate in many ways focuses on the wrong question, because it asks to what extent women could fit into a craft guild in exactly the same way as men. A more fruitful line of investigation, and one both less anachronistic and less male-determined, is to examine in what ways the productive and reproductive labour of women supported or undermined guild production, and how guilds in turn shaped gender roles and the actual labour of women and men.

The training process and structure of all craft guilds, even the oft-cited all-female guilds in Cologne and those that allowed female apprenticeship, followed the male life-cycle. One became an apprentice at puberty, became a journeyman four to ten years later, travelled around learning from a number of masters, then settled down, married, opened one's own shop, and worked at the same craft full-time until one died or got too old to work any longer. This process presupposed that one would be free to travel, something which was much more difficult for women than men; that on marriage one would acquire a wife as an assistant; and that pregnancy or childbirth would never interfere with one's labour.

Most guilds required that masters be married, as a sign of their stability and because they realized that the work required to keep the shop operating could not be performed by one person; they explicitly recognized that production depended on 'reproductive' tasks. The master's wife fed and clothed the resident journeymen and apprentices, often sold the products her husband had made from the shop or from a stand in the city marketplace, purchased raw materials, collected debts and kept records. There were no restrictions on what tasks she could do, and in some cases her labour was so important that she would hire wet-nurses or women to care for her children in order to work in the shop.[39] In other parts of Europe folk beliefs about menstruating or pregnant women kept masters' wives out of production at times, but I have found no evidence for this in Germany.

The master's wife was not the only woman in the shop, for the daughters of a master craftsman could learn their father's trade alongside his journeymen and apprentices. Though dowries do not appear to have gone up in German cities as they did in Italian ones in the fifteenth and sixteenth centuries, they did rise somewhat, but for masters' daughters, training and experience could substitute for or at least enhance a dowry.[40] Master craftsmen also hired female domestic servants and pieceworkers to do simple tasks like polishing, packing, and cleaning.

Thus there were girls and women working alongside the journeymen and apprentices in many capacities, but their ability to do so was not officially recognized or discussed in guild ordinances. Their work in the guilds usually did not depend on a formal apprenticeship, but on their relationship with a guild master. Guild ordinances envisioned and discussed changes of status based on levels of training (the male pattern), but a woman's status was totally dependent on personal circumstances, and, with one exception, formal guild ordinances simply chose to ignore the whole issue.

That one exception was, of course, widowhood. The death of his wife had no bearing on a man's status in the guild, but the death of her husband changed a woman's totally. The role of helpmeet, into which she had been socialized since girlhood, was no longer a possibility, leaving her at once more vulnerable and more powerful. Because a master's wife was familiar with everything involved in running the shop, she was often allowed to continue after her husband died. Masters' widows in many towns ran breweries, printing presses, brickyards and other shops, with workshops run by widows accounting for as much as 10 to 15 per cent of some crafts.[41] City governments were willing, or, better said, eager, to let widows continue in business, for this meant the family would be self-supporting and would not need public financial assistance. Widows paid all guild fees, but they could not take part in the leadership of any guild, though they could bring suits before guild courts.

Both those who see guilds as open to women's independent labour in the high middle ages and those who deny that openness agree that explicit restrictions on women's work increased in the fifteenth century, and that craft ordinances began to use more exclusively male language, simply dropping the words 'female master' or 'girl apprentice' with no explanation. Generally, restrictions on masters' widows were the first to appear: a widow was allowed to keep operating a shop for a brief period after her husband's death, or if she had a son who could inherit; she was not allowed to take on or retain journeymen or apprentices; she could only finish work that had already been begun. Tax records indicate that widows usually had the poorest households in the city, for with no apprentices or journeymen, they could not produce enough to escape poverty.[42]

The restrictions on widows were followed by limitations on the work female servants could do in a shop; even the number of his own daughters a master could employ in a shop was limited. Women were not taught new processes of production like brewing, bleaching, and dyeing, or allowed to use new tools or machinery, such as frames for knitting stockings or ribbon looms, so they could not work as fast or efficiently as men.[43]

Because women's participation in guild shops was not guaranteed by guild regulations and ordinances, and because widows had no political voice in running the guilds, women as a group were not able to protect their right to work. Individual women, especially widows, often requested that they be allowed to work despite the restrictions, appealing to the city council or other municipal authorities by stressing their poverty, old age, or number of dependent children and praising the mercy and 'Christian charity' of the authorities. These requests were often successful, for city authorities felt it was always better that one supports oneself than that one should come to the council for public charity; they never allowed women as a group to continue working, however, but limited their permission to the woman making the request.[44] Thus authorities increasingly came to view women's work as a substitute for charity or a special privilege, whereas men's work was their right.

A number of reasons have been suggested as to why women were excluded from craft guilds: the competition of commercial capitalism and rural domestic production, conflicts between guilds and city councils over who had the power to control what went on in the shop, real or fabricated concerns over the quality of products, the increasingly political nature of guilds in some cities after the guild revolutions of the fourteenth century.[45] These economic and political reasons may have played a part, but the most significant factor was an ideological one – guild honour. As

craft guilds increased the number of their celebrations and ceremonies in
the late middle ages, particularly those which welcomed in new members
or marked a young man's transition from apprentice to journeyman, they
increased the opportunity for the male members to bond with one another,
for women were generally not allowed at such ceremonies. As sociologists
and psychologists have demonstrated, male bonding can be extremely
strong, particularly if it is reinforced by economic or intellectual factors.

Economic prosperity and decline both reinforced the guilds' male
bonding by the sixteenth century: prosperity led masters to assert that their
wives and daughters did not need to work in the shop but could concentrate on domestic tasks (which were increasingly defined as not work);
decline led the whole guild, and especially the journeymen, to attempt to
exclude as many workers as possible, which was often done explicitly on
the grounds of 'honour'. Illegitimacy, servile ancestry, parents who had
worked as barbers, skinners, millers, musicians or shepherds could all make
one 'dishonourable', and by the seventeenth century having worked next
to a woman, or in a guild which still accepted women, could as well.[46]
During the sixteenth century, the ideology of the Protestant Reformation,
with its assertion that the proper role for all women was a domestic one
of wife and mother, also reinforced guild notions that the workshop was
a male preserve.

Social reality and to some degree Protestant ideology set limits as to
how far guild masters could go in their disparagement of women, however.
Though they may have hoped the labour of their wives would not be
necessary, in most cases it still was; restrictions on women's work imposed
by the guilds themselves pointedly did not include the masters' wife.
Because so much of the self-identity of a master after the Reformation was
that of husband and head of household, he could not criticize women too
sharply without implicitly criticizing himself.

These economic and ideological limits to hostility to women's work and
women in general did not apply to journeymen, who were generally
unmarried. During the late fourteenth and early fifteenth centuries, journeymen in many trades began to form separate journeymen's associations
to bargain for better wages and conditions, help journeymen who were
new in town find positions, support those who were injured or ill, and
hold religious and funeral services. There were repeated municipal and even
imperial attempts to suppress these associations, but all such attempts
failed. Their extralegal nature led to secrecy within the organizations, with
members learning secret oaths and handshakes upon initiation, and even
receiving a new, secret codename in this initiation ceremony, which was
modelled on Christian baptism.[47]

During the fifteenth century journeymen were not especially anti-female
in their aims or actions, but this began to change in the sixteenth, as craft
guilds grew more restrictive and limited membership to sons of masters or
those who married a master's widow or daughter. Journeymen could no

longer count on becoming masters themselves, but became essentially wage-labourers, working for a master all their lives. As their own work became proletarianized, they became more concerned with what Andreas Griessinger has called 'the symbolic capital of honour'.[48] Honour was important to guild masters, but even more so to journeymen, for losing one's honour meant that one lost one's right to a workplace.

Journeymen picked up on the growing sentiment among craft guilds that guild honour was something among men, but carried this idea even further. They argued not only that female servants should be excluded from a shop but that the master's female relatives and family members should as well; this not only ensured them of workplaces, but allowed the journeymen to demonstrate their power *vis-à-vis* the masters. Journeymen enforced their aims by boycotting individual masters or whole guilds which still allowed female labour, and by refusing to work next to any journeyman who had been 'tainted' by working with women.[49] All attempts to compel journeymen to relax their code of honour or allow women to work in craft shops had little effect; journeymen's associations remained staunchly male until they died out in the nineteenth century, and bequeathed their hostility to women's labour to the trade unions which followed them.

Journeymen had originally been forbidden to marry in most crafts because they were expected to live with a master's family until they could become masters themselves. As their opportunities to become masters diminished in the sixteenth century, one might have expected journeymen's guilds to push for the right to marry, which they did in a few cities, but in most they did not. Instead, they became the most vigorous enforcers of laws against married journeymen, in some cases pressuring guilds which had originally accepted married journeymen to forbid them.[50] Part of their motivation was to exclude yet another group from workplaces, but the vehemence with which they (sometimes physically) attacked married journeymen hints at something deeper. Journeymen were developing not only a hostility to women, but also to marriage and family life. Instead of demanding the right to marry, they demanded the right to live in all-male journeymen's hostels (*Herberge*), and even to have their meals sent to them in such hostels by the master's wife. They began to think of this hostel as their family, and called the couple who ran it 'father' and 'mother'.[51] Their apparent respect for their 'mother' might seem like a relaxation of their anti-family, anti-female stance, but in my opinion something else is at work here. This title is not used until after the Reformation, at a time when, especially in Protestant parts of Germany, the male-headed family was seen as the only acceptable living arrangement. Single-sex households were suspect, even all male ones. Thus by stressing that they did have 'parents', the journeymen could somewhat mitigate the authorities' distrust of their hostels. The 'mother' had no voice in the actual running of the journeymen's organization, of course, and in some ways respect for her reminds one of the cult of the Virgin among otherwise misogynist medieval monks.

The journeymen's associations thus created a very different sort of ideal for men from that envisioned by guild masters, religious leaders, and political authorities, though both were based on a linking of honour and work. For moralists and masters, masculine honour involved thrift, reliability, stability, and paternal authority. For journeymen, transience, prodigality, physical bravery, and comradeship made one a true man. This ideal not only was cut off from women, but was one which women could not share in in the least. Women could exhibit the qualities expected of an ideal head of household – permanence, honesty, control of servants and children – and were as widows quite regularly thrust into the position of household head. The qualities of the journeymen's ideal were never seen as positive in any woman, and could, in fact, land her in jail or see her banished from a town. Political and religious authorities did not see them as ideal in men, either, and tried to limit journeymen's wandering or close their hostels, but in this instance all attempts at imposing a unified moral order were unsuccessful.

The impact of gender ideology is less strong in areas of the urban economy outside of the craft guilds. All cities left the production of simple, inexpensive items such as soap, thimbles, brooms, wooden dishes, and candles open to anyone, for such things were not highly profitable so that the women or men making them were not a threat to anyone's economic well-being or social status. Municipal authorities regulated sales at the city markets, but these regulations had to do with product purity and fair trading practices and were not gender-specific; in most cities retail trade was dominated by women, while men handled long-distance trade which required capital resources and the freedom to travel. During the late middle ages, many cities set up municipal hospitals, infirmaries, and pest-houses, which were staffed by both women and men; the notion that women were too delicate to care for the sick was the product of a later period, and then really only applied to middle- and upper-class women. The growing professionalism which resulted from increased schooling did lead to the gradual exclusion of women from medical practice, and from positions as minor officials such as toll-collectors, though Germany did not see the widespread use of male midwives in the early modern period as France and England did.[52]

We can see both gender ideology and moral concerns operating in the regulation and structuring of three non-guild occupations particularly in the sixteenth century: capitalist cloth production, domestic service, and prostitution. Early modern techniques of cloth production necessitated at least twenty carders and spinners per weaver, so that cloth centres like Augsburg, Ulm, and Strasbourg could keep many urban and rural people employed. As noted above, rural spinners might be either female or male (though the vast majority were female), but in any case they usually lived in a male-headed household. Urban spinners were predominantly female, and though their low wages did not make them an economic threat, city governments viewed them somewhat suspiciously if they were not married or did not live in a male-headed household. Such women were 'masterless' in both a familial and an occupational sense, and were thus even more suspect than independent journeymen. City governments began to pass laws in the sixteenth century ordering young women to live with their parents, an older male relative, or their employer, though such laws were not effective everywhere because the numbers of young women was simply too great, and, as the Augsburg spinners commented, they were not so stupid as to work as spin-maids in the households of weavers when they could earn three times as much spinning on their own.[53] Hostility to masterless persons led to official support for the low wages already paid to spinners, with city councils reasoning that economic necessity might force women into male-headed households.

In the eyes of urban authorities, domestic service was the perfect employer for unmarried women and for men who for one reason or another could not be taken into a guild. Domestic service was a stage in life for many young people, a stage that might last twenty years because of the late average age of marriage. Servants were generally unmarried, and were considered under the authority of the head of household. As in rural areas, specific ordinances regulating the conduct, behaviour, and maximum salaries of servants grew more numerous in the cities in the sixteenth century, and prescribed an ideal for servants of both sexes that closely followed that prescribed for women of all classes; the ideal servant was to be obedient, pious, trustworthy, hard-working, chaste, and silent.[54] If widowhood gave some women the opportunity to display male virtues, service ostensibly required that men act like women. The frequency with which laws regulating servants were repeatedly issued, and the ever-stronger injunctions and admonitions they contain, indicate that the ideal was rarely achieved.

The urban occupation in which gender and work were most explicitly connected was prostitution. During the late middle ages, nearly every major city in Germany and most of the smaller ones had an official house of prostitution (*Frauenhaus*), and in the fifteenth century many cities set down strict rules for the male managers, the residents, and their customers. Such houses were purportedly set up for unmarried journeymen and apprentices (married men were, at least in theory, prohibited from entering) and for out-of-town visitors, and were justified with the comment that prostitution protected honourable girls and women from the uncontrollable lust of young men, an argument at least as old as Augustine.[55] Visiting prostitutes was associated with achieving masculinity in the eyes of young men, though for the women themselves prostitution was work. Indeed, in some cases the women had no choice, for they had been traded to the brothel manager by their parents or other people in payment for debt.

Though prostitution was legal, the position of prostitutes was always marginal, and in the late fifteenth century cities began to limit the women's freedom of movement and choice of clothing. Such restrictions increased dramatically after the Protestant Reformation, with most Protestant and then Catholic cities closing their municipal brothels, arguing that the possible benefits they provided did not outweigh their moral detriments.[56] Religious authorities suggested earlier marriage instead, in their desire to turn every man into a responsible head of household.[57] Journeymen's attitudes toward prostitutes also changed in the sixteenth century, for visiting brothels was no longer a sign of masculinity, but brought dishonour and exclusion from any journeymen's guild.[58] As we have seen, journeymen did not advocate earlier marriage, but instead a homosocial life; their hostility to women in the workplace grew into a more general aversion to all contacts with women. Journeymen's associations thus serve as a good example of a group in which the need for male bonding was 'functionally equivalent to, and probably more powerful than, the development of a sexual bond'.[59]

Conclusions

In 1300, there was no sharp split between the realms of production and reproduction for either sex; there were gender-specific tasks, and those which men usually did were more highly valued, but the tasks of women were also considered 'work'; both women and men were responsible for their family's sustenance (*Nahrung*).[60] Over the course of the next several centuries, women were excluded from some areas of production, but, more importantly, their productive tasks were increasingly defined as reproductive, as related to 'housekeeping' (*haushalten*). Women worked, but what they did was no longer thought of as 'work'.

This change in the meaning of work has often been linked to the rise of capitalism, as work became equated with participation in the market economy. This does not fully explain its gendered meaning, however, for even tasks for which women were paid (taking in sewing or boarders, for example) came to be defined as 'housekeeping' and therefore not work. Along with capitalism and the rise of market production, I see three other factors that contributed to this gradual conceptualization of male work as 'production' and female as 'reproduction'. The first was the humanist notion that education was to prepare one for a career in the world, which led to its reverse: that only those with a formal education could claim an occupational title. Women might heal people, but only men could be doctors. This professionalism trickled down to occupations which did not require university education; women might brew herbal remedies, but only men could be apothecaries. The second is the Protestant notion that a woman's proper vocation was wife and mother, whereas a man's was his occupation. This classification of men by occupation and women by marital status was not new with the Reformation, but Protestant ideology gave it a strong religious sanction by making worker or mother the ideal for all people, not simply the second-class Christians who could not remain celibate. The third factor was guild notions of honour, which increasingly defined production in a shop as what the apprentices, journeymen and masters did, and what the women did as 'assisting'. Masters and journeymen were in complete agreement that such a distinction should be made: what they disagreed about was where to draw the line, with masters claiming that certain tasks given to female servants were simply assisting while journeymen argued that these were production. Journeymen's conception of honour also led them to refuse to do tasks which they saw as 'reproductive', such as marketing or food preparation.

This gender division between production and reproduction was reinforced by city and state governments, which often allowed women to support themselves and their families with various tasks because these were not really 'work', but simply 'support'. This even included allowing women to sell items which they had made, so that governments clearly knew 'production' as we would define it was involved. Women themselves sometimes adopted the same rhetoric, for they knew arguing that they had a right to work would be much less effective than describing the children they had to support.

We often view the idea of separate spheres for men and women as a product of the nineteenth century, created by the Industrial Revolution, bourgeois notions of domesticity, and Victorian sexuality. I think we can see the roots of this idea much earlier, though the economic and physical structures which would allow actual separation developed more slowly and, as contemporary historians of the nineteenth century quickly point out, would never develop for lower-class people. What did begin in the nineteenth century, however, was the enshrinement of a gendered notion of work in statistical language, defining a man as a 'day-labourer' but a woman who took in washing, sewed curtains in other people's homes, sold eggs from her own chickens, and taught her children to read as a 'housewife', with none of these jobs contributing to the gross national product.[61] The gendered notion of work created in Renaissance Europe is to a great extent still with us.

Notes

1   See e.g. Barbara Hanawalt, ed., *Women and Work in Preindustrial Europe* (Bloomington, IN, 1986); Peter Ketsch, *Frauen im Mittelalter* (Dusseldorf, 1983) I: *Frauenarbeit im Mittelalter*; Louise Tilly and Joan Scott, *Women,*

Work and Family (New York, 1978); Merry E. Wiesner, *Working Women in Renaissance Germany* (New Brunswick, NJ, 1986).

2 See e.g. Joan W. Scott, 'Gender. A Useful Category of Historical Analysis', *AHR* XCI (1986), pp. 1053–75; Susan Staurd, 'The Dominion of Gender. Women's Fortunes in the High Middle Ages', in Renate Bridenthal, Claudia Koonz, and Susan Staurd, eds, *Becoming Visible. Women in European History*, 2nd edn (Boston, 1987), pp. 153–74.

3 Patricia Daly, 'Unpaid Family Labor', *Monthly Labor Review* (Oct. 1982), pp. 1–6; Heidi Hartmann, 'The Family as the Locus of Gender, Class and Political Struggle. The Example of Housework', *Signs* VI (1981), pp. 366–94; Joan Kelly, 'The Doubled Vision of Feminist Theory', in her *Women, History and Theory* (Chicago, 1984), pp. 51–64.

4 Philippe Ariès, *Centuries of Childhood. A Social History of Family Life* (New York, 1962); Barbara Beuys, *Familienleben in Deutschland* (Reinbek, 1980); Barbara Hanawalt, *The Ties that Bound. Peasant Families in Medieval England* (New York, 1986); Linda Pollock, *Forgotten Children. Parent–Child Relations from 1500 to 1900* (Cambridge, 1983); Lawrence Stone, *The Family, Sex, and Marriage in England, 1500–1800* (New York, 1977).

5 Walter J. Ong, SJ, 'Latin Language as a Male Puberty Rite', *Studies in Philology* LVI(2) (1959), pp. 103–24.

6 Margaret L. King, 'Book-lined Cells. Women and Humanism in the Early Italian Renaissance', in Patricia H. Labalme, ed., *Beyond Their Sex. Learned Women of the European Past* (New York, 1980), pp. 66–87.

7 Lowell Green, 'The Education of Women in the Reformation', *History of Education Quarterly* XIX (1979), pp. 93–116.

8 Michael Hackenberg, 'Books in Artisan Homes of Sixteenth-Century Germany', in Donald G. Davis, Jr, ed., *Libraries, Books, and Culture* (Austin, TX, 1986), pp. 72–90; R. A. Houston, *Literacy in Early Modern Europe. Culture and Education 1500–1800* (London, 1988), pp. 134–44.

9 Cornelia Niekus Moore, *The Maiden's Mirror. Reading Material for German Girls in the 16th and 17th Centuries* (Wiesbaden, 1988).

10 Margaret P. Hannay, *Silent but for the Word. Tudor Women as Patrons, Translators and Writers of Religious Works* (Kent, OH, 1985), pp. 7–10.

11 Rudolf Wissell, *Des alten Handwerks Recht und Gewohnheit* (Berlin, 1974) I, pp. 254–73.

12 Lyndal Roper, *The Holy Household. Women and Morals in Reformation Augsburg* (Oxford, 1989), p. 187; Munich Stadtarchiv, Stadtgericht 867 (Injurien und Rumorsachen), vols. 1–10.

13 Strasbourg, Archives Municipales, Akten der XV, 1584, fo. 12lb.

14 John K. Yost, 'Changing Attitudes toward Married Life in Civic and Christian Humanism', *Occasional Papers of the American Society for Reformation Research* I (1977), pp. 151–66.

15 Cyriacus Spangenburg, *Ehespiegel* (Strasbourg, 1570).

16 Andreas Musculus, *Wider den Eheteuffel* (Frankfurt, 1556).

17 Lynn White, 'Cultural Elements and Technological Advance in the Middle Ages', in his *Medieval Religion and Technology* (Berkeley, CA, 1978), pp. 246ff.

18 Ketsch, *Frauenarbeit im Mittelalter*, p. 118.

19 See e.g. Ava Baron, 'Questions of Gender. Deskilling and Demasculinization in the U.S. Printing Industry, 1830–1915', *Gender and History* I (1989), pp. 178–99; Sonja O. Rose, 'Gender Segregation in the Transition to the Factory. The English Hosiery Industry 1850–1910', *Feminist Studies* XIII (1987), pp. 163–84.

20 Gustav Schmoller, *Die Strassburger Tucher und Weberzünft. Urkunden und*

Darstellung (Strasbourg, 1879) II, pp. 234, 304, 307–9; Memmingen Stadtarchiv, Zünfte, 441: 1 and 3 (Strumpfstricker).

21 Stuttgart, Württembergisches Hauptstaatsarchiv, Generalreskripta A 39, Bu. 4 (1601).

22 Wiesner, *Working Women*, pp. 18–21.

23 Pearl Hogrefe, 'Legal Rights of Tudor Women and Their Circumvention', *Sixteenth Century Journal* III (1972), pp. 97–105.

24 Wilhelm Ebel, *Forschungen zur Geschichte des lübischen Rechts* (Lübeck, 1950); Luise Hess, *Die deutschen Frauenberufe des Mittelalters* (Munich, 1940), p. 52.

25 Roper, *Holy Household*, pp. 171–5; *Der verneuerte Reformation der Stadt Nürnberg* (Nuremberg, 1564), sec. 28:5.

26 Merry E. Wiesner, 'Frail, Weak and Helpless. Women's Legal Position in Theory and Reality', in Jerome Friedman, ed., *Regnum, Religio et Ratio. Essays Presented to Robert M. Kingdon* (Kirksville, MO, 1987), pp. 162–9.

27 Christina Vanja, 'Frauen im Dorf. Ihre Stellung unter besonderer Berücksichtigung landgraflich-hessischer Quellen des späten Mittelalters', *ZAgrarGAgrarSoz* XXXIV(2) (1987), pp. 147–51.

28 Anne-Marie Dübler, *Handwerk, Gewerbe und Zünft in Stadt und Landschaft Luzern* (Lucerne, 1982), pp. 381–5.

29 Wiesner, *Working Women*, pp. 92–3; Vanja, *Frauen im Dorf*, p. 152.

30 Walter Hartinger, 'Bayerisches Dienstbotenleben auf dem Land vom 16. bis 18. Jahrhundert', *ZbLG* XXXVIII(2) (1975), p. 621; Wingolf Lehnemann, 'Knechte und Mägde auf einem westfälischen Adelshof im 18. Jahrhundert', in Nils-Arvid Bringeus, ed., *Wandel der Volkskultur in Europa* (Münster, 1988) II, pp. 711–15.

31 Hartinger, 'Dienstbotenleben', p. 638.

32 Peter Feldbauer, 'Lohnarbeit im österreichichen Weinbau', *ZbLG* XXXVIII(1) (1975), pp. 227–43.

33 Christina Vanja, 'Bergarbeiterinnen. Zur Geschichte der Frauenarbeit im Bergbau, Hutten- und Salinenwesen seit dem späten Mittelalters', *Der Anschnitt* XXXIX (1987), pp. 2–11; Susan Karant-Nunn, 'The Women of the Saxon Silver Mines', in Sherrin Marshall ed., *Women in Reformation and Counter-Reformation Europe. Public and Private Worlds* (Bloomington, IN, 1989), pp. 29–46.

34 Schmoller, *Strassburger* II, p. 519.

35 Karl Bücher, *Die Frauenfrage im Mittelalter* (Tübingen, 1910).

36 Wissell, *Alten Handwerks* II, p. 439; Helmut Wachendorf, *Die wirtschaftliche Stellung der Frau in den deutschen Städten des späteren Mittelalters* (Quackenbruck, 1934), pp. 30–2.

37 Ketsch, *Frauen*, pp. 113–14; Kurt Wesoly, 'Der weibliche Bevölkerungsanteil in spätmittelalterlichen und frühneuzeitlichen Städten und die Betätigung von Frauen im zünftigen Handwerk (insbesondere am Mittel- und Oberrhein)', *ZGO* LXXXIX (1980), pp. 69–117; Yoriko Ichikawa, 'Die Stellung der Frauen in den Handwerksämtern im spätmittelalterlichen und frühneuzeitlichen Lübeck', *Zeitschrift des Vereins für lübeckische Geschichte und Altertumskunde* LXVI (1986), pp. 91–118.

38 Edith Ennen, 'Die Frau in der Mittelalterlichen Stadtgesellschaft Mitteleuropas', *HansGbl* XCVIII (1980), pp. 12–14; Barbara Handler-Lachmann, 'Die Berufstätigkeit der Frau in den deutschen Städten des Spätmittelalters und der beginnenden Neuzeit', *HessJbLG* XXX (1980); Margaret Wensky, *Die Stellung der Frau in der stadtkölnische Wirtschaft im Spätmittelalter* (Cologne, 1981); see also the debate in Hans Pohl and Wilhelm Treue, eds., *Die Frau in der deutschen Wirtschaft* (Wiesbaden, 1985), pp.

45–50.
39 Wiesner, *Working Women*, pp. 152–5; Mary Lindemann, 'Love for Hire. The Regulation of the Wet-Nursing Business in Eighteenth-Century Hamburg', *Journal of Family History* (1981), p. 385.
40 David Herlihy and Christiane Klapisch-Zuber, *Les Toscans et leurs familles. Une étude du catasto florentin de 1427* (Paris, 1978), pp. 414–18; Marian A. Kaplan, *The Marriage Bargain. Women and Dowries in European History* (Binghamton, NY, 1985).
41 Rainer Stahlschmidt, *Die Geschichte des eisenverarbeitende Gewerbes in Nürnberg von den ersten Nachrichten im 12.–13. Jahrhundert bis 1630* (Nuremberg, 1971), pp. 186–7.
42 Munich, Stadtarchiv, Steuerbücher; Klaus-Joachim Lorenzen-Schmidt, 'Zur Stellung der Frauen in der frühneuzeitlichen Stadtegesellschaft Schleswigs und Holsteins', *Archiv für Kulturgeschichte* LXI (1979), pp. 328–35.
43 Wiesner, *Working Women*, pp. 158, 181.
44 Strasbourg, *Archives municipales*, Akten der XV: 1617, fo. 247.
45 Wiesner, *Working Women*, pp. 161, 168; Martha Howell, *Women, Production and Patriarchy in Late Medieval Cities* (Chicago, 1986), pp. 174–83, and her 'Citizenship and Gender. Women's Political Status in Northern Medieval Cities', in Mary Erler and Maryanne Kowaleski, eds, *Women and Power in the Middle Ages* (Athens, GA, 1988), pp. 37–60.
46 Mack Walker, *German Home Towns. Community, State, and General Estate 1648–1871* (Ithaca, NY, 1971), pp. 104–5.
47 Wilfried Reininghaus, *Die Entstehung der Gesellengilden im Spätmittelalter* (Wiesbaden, 1981), pp. 84–6; Knut Schulz, *Handwerksgesellen und Lohnarbeiter. Untersuchungen zur oberrheinischen und oberdeutschen Stadtgeschichte des 14. bis 17. Jahrhunderts* (Sigmaringen, 1985), pp. 136–7.
48 Andreas Griessinger, *Das symbolische Kapital der Ehre. Streikbewegungen und kollektives Bewusstsein deutscher Handwerksgesellen im 18. Jahrhundert* (Frankfurt, 1981).
49 Frank Göttman, *Handwerk und Bundnispolitik. Die Handwerkerbände am Mittelrhein vom 14. bis 17. Jahrhundert* (Wiesbaden, 1977), pp. 153, 280; Wissell, *Alten Handwerks* I, pp. 222–45.
50 *Ibid.*, pp. 446–50.
51 Schulz, *Handwerksgesellen*, p. 182.
52 Wiesner, *Working Women*, pp. 37–109.
53 Claus-Peter Clasen, *Die Augsburger Weber. Leistungen und Krisen des Textilgewerbes um 1600* (Augsburg, 1981), pp. 132–3.
54 Merry E. Wiesner, 'Paternalism in Practice. The Control of Servants and Prostitutes in Early Modern German Cities', in Phillip N. Bebb and Sherrin Marshall, eds., *The Process of Change in Early Modern Europe* (Athens, OH, 1988), pp. 180–6.
55 James Brundage, 'Prostitution in the Medieval Canon Law', *Signs* I(4) (1976), pp. 825–45.
56 Roper, *Holy Household*, pp. 96–7; Wiesner, *Working Women*, p. 99.
57 Roper, *Holy Household*, p. 108.
58 Wissell, *Alten Handwerks*, I, p. 271; Göttman, *Handwerk*, 153.
59 Quoted by Lionel Tiger, *Men in Groups* (New York, 1969), p. 172.
60 Lyndal Roper, 'Housework and Livelihood. Towards the *Alltagsgeschichte* of Women', *German History* II (1985), pp. 3–9.
61 Nancy Folbre and Marjorie Abel, 'Women's Work and Women's Households. Gender Bias in the pre-1940 U.S. Censuses', *Social Research* LVI(3) (1989), pp. 545–69; Marilyn Waring, *If Women Counted. A New Feminist Economics* (New York, 1988).

|9|

German Social Structure 1300–1600

CHRISTOPHER R. FRIEDRICHS

Inequality is a feature of every human society. The uneven distribution of wealth, power, prestige or opportunity is such a basic characteristic of the human condition that some aspects are almost taken for granted. In all societies children are socially and economically weaker than adults. In most societies, females are unthinkingly regarded as inferior to males. Other forms of inequality, by contrast, are widely acknowledged. The members of almost every society recognize the existence of a hierarchy of social ranks and positions, and hopes of moving up the social ladder or fears of moving down can powerfully influence human behaviour. Yet the exact shape of the ladder is often hard to describe. Sociologists have trouble enough agreeing on the structure of modern societies; the analysis of past societies can be even more difficult.[1] Even the most articulate observers frequently differ in describing their own societies. And modern theories of social structure are not always readily applicable to the past.[2] Contemporary sociology, for example, tends to emphasize occupational roles as the chief determinants of social rank. In past societies, by contrast, social rank more often determined occupation.

Historians and social scientists do tend to agree, however, that most human societies fall into one of three basic categories: a society may be stratified by caste, by class, or by 'orders'.[3] In a caste society, inequality is fixed for life: rank and occupation are determined by birth, and change is impossible. In a class society, by contrast, everyone is legally equal and opportunity is theoretically open to all, though in reality individuals are sharply differentiated along economic lines. A society of 'orders' stands midway between the other two categories: each person is born into a particular rank, estate, or order, which in most cases determines his or her occupation and economic prospects. But movement from one estate or order to another is possible, especially when formally sanctioned by the ruler.

There is little dispute that late medieval and early modern Germany conformed broadly to the category of a 'society of orders'.[4] Almost everyone accepted the existence of a hierarchy of ranks. Birth normally determined status, but upward mobility was possible and, within limits, encouraged.

Yet the exact construction of the social hierarchy was by no means obvious. We can see this, for example, in what is surely the most famous attempt to describe and depict German society in early modern times: the *Ständebuch* of 1568. In woodcuts and verse, the Nuremberg engraver Jost Amman and poet Hans Sachs attempted to provide 'a true description of all the ranks on earth, high and low, religious and secular, and of all arts, crafts and trades, from the greatest to the humblest'.[5] A total of 114 social and occupational categories were presented, awkwardly mingled together. Amman and Sachs followed social convention by beginning with members of the church, traditionally regarded as the first estate; though they were Protestants working in a Protestant town, they nevertheless started with the Pope, followed by cardinals, bishops, priests, monks, and wandering pilgrims. Next came the nobility: Holy Roman Emperor, king, princes, and ordinary noblemen – the latter ever hopeful of promotion to dukes. Then came the learned professions and 14 skilled crafts. Suddenly the merchant appeared, followed, surprisingly, by the moneylending Jew – here an apparent similarity in economic function overrode the social attitudes which would normally have placed the Jew much further down. Countless urban craftsmen came next, interrupted from time to time by such rural types as the peasant, the hunter, the fisherman and the vine-grower. Towards the end appeared the wandering musicians – and finally the fools.

Though promising to present every *Stand* 'from the greatest to the humblest', the authors of the *Ständebuch* could never have established a formal social ranking whose validity all would accept. Indeed, even the concept of *Stand* was ambiguous, as it could refer to social or political rank in one context and to occupation in another.[6] But the basic notion that society consisted of the sum of individual *Stände* was common to all.

In fact, much of the *Ständebuch* could have been published – had printing existed – 200 years earlier. For the basic contours of German social structure remained intact between 1300 and 1600. To say this is not to belittle changes whose importance historians have rightly emphasized. The spread of capitalism, the growing influence of the legal profession, and of course the Protestant Reformation significantly transformed some aspects of German social structure in the fifteenth and sixteenth centuries. But even so, the overall framework remained stable. Most Germans in 1600 would have understood the structure of their society in much the same way as their ancestors had three centuries before.

Bauer, Bürger, Edelmann – everybody in late medieval or early modern Germany was familiar with these three fundamental social categories of peasant, citizen, and nobleman.[7] At the pinnacle of German social structure stood the *Adel*, or nobility. Moralists and clergymen might place members of the church first in their descriptions of the social order, but this hardly corresponded to social reality. In fact, high ecclesiastics and members of cathedral chapters normally had to be of noble birth even to qualify for such positions. It was noble status, not ecclesiastical rank, that commanded the greatest amount of respect.

A nobleman normally possessed one or more landed estates, over which he exercised seigneurial rights and, in most cases, some degree of juridical authority as well. But the German nobility was by no means an exclusively rural order. Some nobles lived in cities, and there was a substantial degree of intermarriage and social contact between the lower nobility and the higher ranks of urban society.

The German nobility, like that of every European society in the late middle ages, encompassed members who differed greatly in their degree of wealth, prestige, and local power. Broadly speaking, however, the nobility was divided into two major groups, each of course with its own subcategories. The higher nobility (*Hochadel*) consisted essentially of rulers of territories, though the size of these territories could differ enormously. Indeed, the higher nobility itself was made up of two main subgroups: one included electors, margraves, dukes, and other princes of the Empire while the other consisted chiefly of counts (*Grafen*) and barons (*Herren*) whose lands, though also held directly from the Emperor, were much more modest in scale. Vastly greater in number than any sector of the higher nobility, however, were the members of the lower nobility (*niederer Adel*). These nobles normally held their land as fiefs from the territorial ruler. Most of them were known as knights, or *Ritter*, though in some areas they were also known as *Junker*. This was the basic picture. But there were countless anomalies. Many nobles had more than one estate, and it was possible for a nobleman to hold most of his land as the vassal of a territorial prince, yet to qualify as a member of the higher nobility because of one independent estate he possessed outside the prince's territory. By contrast, the *Reichsritter*, or imperial knights, in Franconia, Swabia, and the Rhineland held much of their land as fiefs from territorial rulers but were still recognized as having no personal overlord other than the Emperor. This gave them a status higher than that of ordinary knights, but they were not regarded as members of the higher nobility.

Even within a single territory there might be tremendous differences in wealth among the members of the lower nobility. A recent study of the Mark Brandenburg makes the point clear. Of the roughly 300 knightly families in Brandenburg in in the mid-sixteenth century, a mere 14 families appear to have possessed almost one-third of the group's total landholdings.[8] But wealth was not the only source of differences among knightly families, and to many nobles it was not even the most significant one. For in Germany, as elsewhere in Europe, nobles were deeply concerned with the antiquity and authenticity of their titles. By the late middle ages in most parts of Germany, the once significant distinction between true vassals and mere *ministeriales* – nobles descended from servants of a ruling house – had largely been forgotten. For all nobles whose titles dated back to the high middle ages by now shared a common interest in showing that their status was higher than that of nobles whose titles originated more recently.

In fact, new noble families were constantly emerging. At times the Emperor granted noble status in return for services rendered – or even for cash. A famous decree issued by the Habsburg court in 1545 specified a charge of 400 gulden for ennoblement as a count, with correspondingly lower charges for lesser ranks.[9] But it was also possible for sufficiently rich non-nobles to slide into noble status by acquiring a landed estate, holding a 'noble' office, or making a suitable marriage. Some contemporary nobles accepted that this process of constant renewal was inevitable. Here, for example, is what Wiguleus Hundt von Lauterbach, a Bavarian official and historian of the mid-sixteenth century, had to say about the subject:

> I would not want to criticize the ordinary new nobles who have arrived at this status by service to their rulers, by warfare or by other honorable means, and who behave in accordance with their new rank, since the families that die out obviously must be replaced by others and the noble estate can thus be maintained – for what is now 'new' will eventually become 'old', and what is now 'old' was 'new' years ago; but just as I cannot praise the old nobles who lack noble virtues, even less can I have any regard for new nobles who participate in burgher   trades   or   marriages,   as   is   the   case   in   many places...[10]

Hundt's position, however, was to some extent self-interested: his father was of noble stock, but his mother was not.[11] Other nobles fought more vigorously against the admission of newcomers to their ranks – but almost always in vain.

If older noble families could not prevent the emergence of new ones, they could at least try to block them from being accepted as social equals. In Bavaria, for example, ordinances of the late fifteenth century specified which noble families could participate in chivalric tournaments as *Turnieradel*. Though the higher nobility hoped to bar members of the lower nobility from participating in these events, this proved impossible; some lower nobles had to be accepted. But this in turn meant that those who got into the *Turnieradel* became an exclusive group within the lower nobility.[12] A century later, in 1557, the older Bavarian nobles secured an even more advantageous ruling, which granted special judicial powers only to those families which had possessed a noble estate 50 years earlier. The main effect of this ruling was to establish which families qualified as members of the true Bavarian nobility. But, like all such attempts to stem the tide of newcomers, this was a hollow victory – for actual political powers in the Bavarian state increasingly fell to nobles of foreign extraction, or to the new nobles whose rank derived from their service to the ruler.[13]

Another strategy by which noble families attempted to maintain their exclusiveness was by strictly enforcing the rule of *Ebenbürtigkeit*, or equality of birth, according to which marriages were to be made only between persons of equal rank. Children born to 'unequal' marriages might suffer in their inheritance rights. But this rule was not always rigidly enforced. If the spouse of lower background was sufficiently wealthy, the difference in status was more likely to be overlooked.[14] In 1485 the *Turnieradel* of Franconia reluctantly agreed not to exclude any member who had married the daughter of an urban patrician – as long as the bride's dowry exceeded 4,000 gulden. Even the children of such marriages would be accepted at future tournaments.[15]

In the long run, then, sufficient wealth could always secure noble status. But wealth was needed to sustain it as well. Noble families often died out: typically this happened when declining wealth made it difficult to find suitable marriage partners, but sometimes a noble family was unable to sustain the required lifestyle, and slipped quietly back into the ranks of commoners.[16] In fact the rate of attrition among noble families was always high: most such families lasted no more than a few generations.[17] But there was never any shortage of ambitious newcomers eager to take their places.

There were different patterns by which new nobles emerged. By and large, it was individuals or their families who achieved noble status. In some cases, however, entire categories of people asserted their noble status on a collective basis. With the introduction of Roman law in Germany, lawyers as a group became more socially assertive, and doctors of jurisprudence claimed noble status by virtue of their degrees.[18] And in some cities the leading social group, the *Geschlechter* or patricians, asserted a collective claim to noble rank. Many such claims were eventually accepted; the wealth and influence of some urban elites made this inevitable. But to understand this more fully, we must turn to the structure of urban society in late medieval and early modern Germany.

Town-dwellers made up a distinct minority of the population of Germany in the late middle ages and the sixteenth century – certainly no more than a quarter of the total, if as much.[19] But the structure of urban society in Germany has attracted particular attention from historians. One reason for this is the sheer richness and variety of urban life. Another is the importance of the city for long-term social change. An earlier generation of historians placed the city at the heart of what was once the dominant model for understanding European history of late medieval and early modern times: the transition from feudalism to capitalism, a process in which the urban bourgeoisie was held to play the central role. The basic notion of a transition from feudalism to capitalism remains attractive to many historians. More emphasis is given today than was the case earlier to the transformation of agrarian relations and the role of rural elites in introducing the capitalist economy.[20] Yet the city is still seen to have played a central part in the overall spread of the market economy. No less important was the city's role – especially in Germany – in such crucial developments as the emergence of literacy and the Protestant Reformation.

The study of German urban society in the late medieval and early modern era has been enhanced by the existence of a rich body of source materials. By the fourteenth century, German cities had developed methods for keeping records which continued to grow in volume and precision in the centuries that followed. Detailed information about property transactions, loans, taxes, muncipal finances and the administration of justice can be found in the archives of almost every German city. Since taxes were levied on all citizens according to carefully documented scales – and harsh punishments might be inflicted on those who cheated – tax records can give historians remarkably precise information about relative wealth levels among a large group of urban inhabitants. But other factors – legal, political, and economic – were of scarcely less importance in making up the social structure of the late medieval or early modern German city.

In fact, urban social structure is best examined in two stages. First we should consider the social organization of cities in terms of legal or occupational categories generally familiar to the town dwellers themselves. Then we may examine the somewhat different perspective made possible by modern historians through the quantitative analysis of data from German town records.

Certainly, any discussion of German urban society in the late medieval or early modern period must begin with the most fundamental aspect of every city's social structure: the division of its inhabitants into citizens and non-citizens.[21] The citizens, or *Bürger*, were the permanent members of the community, who enjoyed an unquestioned right to live and work there. Non-citizens were merely tolerated outsiders who participated in the social and economic life of the community only by permission of the magistrates. Membership in the *Bürgerschaft* was normally inherited, but outsiders might be admitted if they met the criteria and paid the fees laid down by the city's rulers.

The *Bürgerschaft* encompassed men, women, and children, but their status was not equal. The full rights of citizenship were exercised only by adult male heads of households. Sons and daughters of citizens had a diminished status, though their right to live in the community could not be abrogated. When the son of a citizen was prepared to get married and begin to practise a trade, he took the oath of citizenship and was recognized as a full member of the *Bürgerschaft*, thereby assuming some political rights and many obligations – notably to pay civic taxes and serve in the civic militia. When a male citizen died, his widow assumed some of his rights; for example, she could continue to carry out her husband's trade, though the actual work might be done by male underlings. She paid taxes, but would not be expected to fulfil the political and military obligations of citizenship

Whether or not one belonged to the citizenry was the most important single aspect of a town-dweller's identity. But there were other groupings as well. Larger cities were divided into numerous parishes. Many cities also grouped people for administrative purposes into neighbourhoods, quarters, or even streets, sometimes with their own 'captains' to maintain order or represent the inhabitants. But by far the most important organizations in every city were the guilds. Depending on regional tradition, guilds were known as *Zünfte, Gilden, Innungen, Ämter,* or even just as *Handwerke* (crafts). In some cities, each craft had its own distinct guild; elsewhere, various crafts were grouped for administrative or political purposes into larger guilds.

Everywhere the guilds functioned above all as organizations to regulate the training of apprentices, the hiring of journeymen, the admission of new masters, and the administration of rules regarding the production and sale of goods. Whether the guild's functions were limited to these, however, varied from city to city. In some cities – Nuremberg is the most celebrated example – the authorities consistently strove to control the crafts and prevent them from acting independently. In many other cities, by the late middle ages guilds had acquired extensive powers of self-administration and their leaders occupied specific positions in the city government. These powers were precarious, however: often the authorities struggled to reduce the guilds' role. In the mid-sixteenth century, for example, the Emperor Charles V revoked the constitutions of dozens of imperial cities in southern Germany, eliminating guild representatives from their seats on the town councils and reducing the guilds themselves to carefully supervised craft associations. Yet even in cities like these, the guilds retained some influence as interest groups whose wishes the city council could never entirely ignore.[22]

Membership in the guilds tended to become more exclusionary between the fourteenth and sixteenth century. In the earlier period in most cities admission to a guild – and to citizenship as well – was relatively easy for anyone who could demonstrate adequate credentials to function effectively as a master of his trade. Gradually, however, as urban economies lost their expansionary dynamic, the guilds in many parts of Germany pressured city authorities to tighten the standards of admission and thus limit the number of newcomers admitted to the trades.[23] In much the same way, women were pushed out of active participation in the guilds. In the fourteenth century, many women appear to have been accepted as masters; by the sixteenth century this was increasingly rare.[24]

The guild members were not equal in status. Many cities had a recognized hierarchy of guilds, with greater prestige or political power granted to the older or larger guilds or to those whose members carried out more refined crafts. And even within a single guild, the masters were generally far from equal in status. Positions of leadership within the guilds – and as guild representatives on the city council – almost always tended to go to the wealthiest members.[25]

All guild masters were citizens, but not all citizens were members of guilds. In many cities, members of the social and political elite considered it beneath their dignity to belong to an ordinary guild. There were special organizations which members of the elite could join – and by joining these organizations, they could prove that they were indeed members of the elite. Yet the very existence of such organizations suggests how difficult it sometimes was for contemporaries to know precisely who belonged to the urban elite. Obviously every city had an elite – or, to use the terminology favoured by modern historians, an *Oberschicht* or *Führungsschicht*.[26] But the exact composition of this group and its relationship both to the other citizens and to elites outside the community was often problematic to contemporaries – and remains so for modern historians.

Many cities had elite groups which aspired to noble status, yet only a handful of cities had a true nobility. Until the early sixteenth century, Schwäbisch Hall had a clearly defined *Stadtadel*, made up of families descended from ministerial knights of the high middle ages.[27] But cases like this were rare. The haughty *Erbmänner* of Münster remained highly exclusive in their choice of marriage partners, chiefly to reinforce their claims to noble descent, but in actual fact the origins of this group were much less exalted.[28] For in Münster, as in most German cities, the origins of the social elite lay among members of the *Bürgerschaft*.

Part of the elite group in virtually every city was made up of *Kaufleute* or merchants. Some were descended from families long active in trade, others were craftsmen who had been able to make the transition from workshop to counting room. Larger towns, however, generally also had a group of prominent families – the *Geschlechter* – who claimed a status superior to that of the merchants. Many were themselves descended from merchant families, but the fact that they had turned away from commerce to live primarily off rents and investments was taken as an indication of superior social standing. By the late sixteenth century the Roman term 'patrician' was adopted in some cities to describe the members of this group, and historians have come to use the term broadly to cover all those families who ranked higher than ordinary merchants in German cities of the late middle age or early modern times.[29] To refer to prominent merchants or members of other leading families whom the patricians did not accept as their equals, historians generally use the term *Honoratioren*.[30]

In the course of the sixteenth century, a third group increasingly came to be included in the urban elites as well. These were the members of the learned professions – especially lawyers but also medical doctors and, where applicable, university professors. The growing secularization and prestige of the professions made it inevitable that men with academic credentials – especially those serving as city officials – should be regarded not just as public servants but as leading members of their community. They were themselves generally sons of patricians or merchants, but their claims to elite status came as much from their professional identity as from their ancestry.[31]

The urban elite, broadly defined, was not an encapsulated group. Like the nobility, the urban elites needed constant replenishment from below to take the places of families that had lost their fortunes or died out. Yet many members of the urban elites, especially the patricians, struggled against the pressure from below. In many cities, especially the largest ones, members of the *Geschlechter* sought to close off their ranks and prevent newcomers from joining them. The reason for this, in most cases, was simple: the patricians wanted to achieve recognition as being nobles or equal in rank to nobles. The more exclusive they were, the more convincingly they might argue that membership in their ranks amounted *ipso facto* to noble status. Arranging for the grant of a coat of arms and purchase of a country estate would help – but the refusal to admit newcomers or to marry beneath their rank was even more important.

Hermann von Kerssenbrock, a school rector and chronicler of late sixteenth-century Münster, penned an evocative description of that city's patriciate. Much of what he said would apply to many other cities as well:

> The noble patricians are citizens and descendants of the old families, who are commonly known as *Erbmänner*, which is to say by birth and inheritance successors to the rights of their ancestors, who transmit their families' hereditary coats of arms without stain to their descendants and do not accept among themselves anyone from the ranks of citizens, no matter how rich he is, unless he has patrician parents. Thus it has come about that this group, which is clearly distinguished from the citizens, has maintained its existence for a long time. These patricians live off their rents and from the proceeds of agriculture, and they imitate the knights.[32]

In many cities, patrician status was linked to *Ratsfähigkeit* – eligibility for membership on the city council or for those council seats which were not explicitly reserved for merchants or craftsmen. But in many cities the patricians developed other means, often focusing on social activities, to reinforce their exclusive status. The patricians of Nuremberg, who struggled for centuries to achieve recogition as nobles, attempted to limit their membership for all time in the famous *Tanzstatut* of 1521. This edict specified which families could participate in dances at the city hall – and by extension defined which families were eligible for the patrician seats on the city council.[33] But patrician ranks were never completely closed: even in Nuremberg itself an additional family was admitted in 1536, and in most cities the patriciate was much more permeable. Nor was the patriciate always a uniform group: in Augsburg the true patriciate clearly consisted of the *Geschlechter*, but an additional number of families were recognized as *Mehrer der Gesellschaft*, with some but not all of the social privileges of patricians.[34]

Many cities had patrician drinking-clubs or other social organizations whose main purpose was not so much to promote companionship as to clarify social status. Frankfurt am Main had four patrician clubs in the middle ages, which were eventually consolidated into two: the more exclusive Alt-Limpurg society and the smaller but less restrictive Frauensteiner. In the course of the sixteenth century, the Alt-Limpurg society admitted fewer and fewer new families – and after 1584 newcomers were only accepted if they could show that their families had abstained from retail commerce for two generations.[35] In Braunschweig the uncertain boundaries of the patriciate were clarified by the establishment of a *Geschlechtergesellschaft* in 1569. Prominent families who did not qualify as patricians were relegated to a secondary group known as the *weisse Ringe* due to the fact that the women of these families could wear only silver jewel-clasps on their bosoms as opposed to the gold ones sported by patricians' wives.[36]

How did the merchants respond to the patrician insistence on excluding them from their ranks? In some cases they might retreat from commercial activity and seek admission to the patrician ranks; in other cases they might establish their own associations. Many cities had merchants' guilds, of course, but a merchants' drinking-club had rather different connotations, for it implied an attempt by the merchants to assert their own social status while aping the patrician style.[37] Tension between merchants and patricians was a persistent feature of political and social life in some German cities, but it was only compounded by the fact that many merchants were themselves unsure whether they wanted to work their way individually into the patriciate or assert their rights collectively as a group.

Nor were the patricians themselves always completely divorced from commerce. In some cities a *rentier* lifestyle was regarded, at least in theory, as a formal requirement of patrician status, but in many places patricians openly engaged in trade.[38] The Leipzig jurist Christoph Cuppener, in fact, argued in 1508 that while commerce was unsuitable for members of the higher nobility, it was an acceptable pursuit both for lower nobles and for urban patricians – for 'an honourable rich citizen or merchant who is in a position to support himself substantially can be equated with a poor nobleman of the lowest level of nobility'.[39]

Probably no individual family better illustrates the complex problem of defining membership in the urban elite than the famous Fuggers of Augsburg. Certainly the Fuggers present a remarkable example of social mobility. Hans Fugger immigrated to Augsburg in 1367 as a weaver. Within a hundred years his descendants had become major merchants, and by the early sixteenth century the Fuggers were financiers of international importance on whom the house of Habsburg was heavily dependent. Eventually the Fuggers became members of the higher nobility, ruling their own small territories in southern Germany. Yet their progression to noble status was an unusual one. The Emperor granted the Fuggers the rank of *Reichsgrafen* in 1526 and 1530 – but only in 1538 were they admitted to the patriciate of their own city. Nor did their status as territorial nobles lead to a rapid alienation either from commercial life or from identification with their home city; indeed, it has been noted that the Fuggers were more involved with political affairs in Augsburg in the second half of the sixteenth century than they had been earlier.[40] More predictable, perhaps, was their lukewarm reception by the established dynasties, who could recall how recently the Fuggers had been mere merchants. At the grand wedding of Count Anton II Fugger to the countess of Helfenstein, the groom complained that his wife had been seated in a position too modest for her rank. None less than a duchess of Bavaria informed Anton haughtily that by marrying him, his bride had lost her rank: 'She is no longer a countess, but just a Fugger ... and now tell me this: just what are you yourself, other than a mere Fugger?'[41]

A duchess's scorn could hardly counter the fact that the Fuggers had in fact risen into the high aristocracy. At the same time, however, they remained members of the *Bürgerschaft* of Augsburg – a rank they shared in common with thousands of ordinary craftsmen. In fact, in virtually every German city the citizens and their families made up a substantial majority of the total population. But there was always also a significant minority of non-citizens.

Not all non-citizens were of low social status. Some were prosperous individuals who had been granted the right to live in one city while retaining their citizenship in another. Priests, monks, and other clerics of the old church were exempt from citizenship in the towns where they lived. For many citizens, in fact, this was a sore point which contributed to anti-clerical sentiment before and during the Reformation.[42] But most non-citizens were members of the city's disadvantaged lower orders – the urban *Unterschicht*.[43] Some were householders who practised unskilled or menial occupations and lacked the cash or credentials to be admitted to citizenship. Some were wage-labourers. Many were male or female servants living in the homes of their masters. Some had no fixed residence at all.

Many of the householders without full rights of citizenship at least enjoyed a relatively secure status as 'associate citizens', *Beisassen* or *Pfahlbürger* who had been granted permission to live in the city or its suburbs. Too poor or too unskilled to join the system of guilds, many of them were occupied with agricultural or semi-agricultural pursuits.[44] Others worked as wage-labourers.

A special category within the group of non-citizens was formed by the *Gesellen*, or journeymen. Aspiring to eventual admission to the guilds as craft masters, and thus also to membership in the citizenry, the journeymen had much in common with the masters for whom they worked. This did not prevent the journeymen from eventually developing a strong sense of solidarity with each other. But the special status of journeymen and their recognition of shared interests evolved only slowly. Originally, masters simply hired qualified men to work for them as *Knechte* or *Knappen*. In the course of the fourteenth century, however, some of these hired workers – especially younger, unmarried ones – began to form regional organizations to protect their right to move from city to city and seek employment on the

most advantageous terms wherever they could.[45] Borrowing the very term
which the masters used to describe themselves, these organized workers
called themselves 'companions,' or *Gesellen*. By the early fifteenth century,
at least in southern Germany, their organizations had become so powerful
in setting the terms of employment that many cities joined in trying to limit
their powers; in the sixteenth century imperial legislation was passed to the
same end. But all this was to little avail. In many trades, especially less
populous ones in which the supply of labour was weak, the
Gesellenorganisationen used boycotts or other forms of pressure to protect
the interests of their members with great effectiveness. Certainly these organizations challenged the authority of the guild masters and even, at times,
the city governments. But they always operated within the framework of a
guild-based organization of production, and in this broader sense they may
have contributed to the ultimate stability of the guild system.

The journeymen, however, represented a unique element among the non-
citizens. Much of their power came from the fact that their specialized
skills made them indispensable to their masters. Less skilled or less specialized wage-workers and house servants – male and female – had no
organizations to give voice to their interests. For this reason, most members
of this stratum appear in civic records not as members of any recognized
group but as isolated individuals whose circumstances only occasionally
interested the governing circles. What does seem clear is that most members
of this group immigrated to the cities from the surrounding countryside in
hopes of employment and economic advance. A few fortunate servants
succeeded in marrying into the *Bürgerschaft*. Most did not, and eventually
drifted back home or died unmarried in the city itself.

Even servants, however, occupied a higher position on the social ladder
than the floating population of beggars, prostitutes, criminals and vagrants.
Every community had its local poor – citizens or other established residents
who had fallen into distress and were recognized by the community as having
some claim to charity. But in addition, almost every town – certainly every
larger one – had a significant floating population of people regarded as social
undesirables.[46] Historians are uncertain whether these marginal groups
should be regarded as an authentic social stratum.[47] But they remained a
persistent element in the urban environment even when, especially in the
sixteenth century, city authorities made strenuous efforts to banish them.

Two other social groups occupied an anomalous situation at the lower
end of the urban social order. Their rights of residence in the town were
more secure than those of the floating population, but their social status
was in some respects even lower. One of these groups consisted of persons
who carried out 'dishonourable' occupations – above all the municipal executioners and the *Abdecker*, who were charged with removing carrion and
other offensive material. Concern with *Ehre*, or honour, was a persistent
theme in German urban self-consciousness; increasingly, for example, ille-
gitimates were barred from the guilds on the basis of their dishonoured

birth. But practitioners of the dishonoured trades occupied a unique social niche in most German cities: executioners, for example, were well paid for their indispensable services, yet they were strictly barred from social contact or intermarriage with ordinary citizens.[48] The case of the executioner of Schwäbisch Hall who in 1614 married the daughter of a prominent clergyman stands out as a remarkable exception to a social taboo which persisted in most German towns until the end of the *ancien régime*.[49]

An even more anomalous niche was occupied by the Jews. Though socially entirely isolated from the Christian population and often the object of bitter hostility, the Jews had a recognized right, protected by the Emperor, to live in numerous German cities. Many imperial cities strove to eliminate their Jewish populations in the late fourteenth and throughout the fifteenth century – and, with the Emperor's permission, many succeeded.[50] But the Jews continued to live in major towns like Frankfurt and Worms, and found new havens in numerous territorial cities.

The social structure of German cities thus encompassed a remarkably broad range of groups, from patricians with aristocratic aspirations down to marginal groups subject to ceaseless harassment. Contemporary observers struggled with the problem of classifying these diverse elements into a coherent pattern. Finer differentiations, however, were often reserved to the upper ranges of the urban social order. The late fifteenth-century humanist Conrad Celtis divided the inhabitants of Nuremberg into five groups in a scheme that attempted to reconcile elements of social prestige, political power, and economic importance. The first category consisted, of course, of the *Geschlechter*, who were entitled to most seats on the city council. The next three categories consisted chiefly of those who belonged to the city's powerless but prestigious large council – divided into major merchants who engaged in long-distance commerce with their own resources, merchants who worked as agents for richer investors, and retailers or craftsmen of sufficient standing to sit on the larger council. The fifth and largest category included everyone else.[51] Many city governments drew up ordinances or codes – sometimes with a view to regulating modes of dress – which classified the inhabitants into specific ranks. An ordinance issued by the government of Frankfurt in the early seventeenth century grouped the city's inhabitants into five social orders: the patricians; other council members and distinguished merchants; distinguished retailers and members of the legal establishment; craftsmen and ordinary retailers; and unskilled workers.[52] Yet try as the authorities might to take into account all the relevant criteria of prestige, power and wealth, a satisfactory ranking of all citizens into a clear vertical hierarchy was often difficult to establish.

Modern historians have found it no less difficult to reduce the social structure of German cities to a clear-cut hierarchical order. Classical marxist historiography interpreted tensions in the late medieval German city by positing a three-way division between patricians, their bourgeois opponents, and more democratic 'plebeian' opponents.[53] Non-marxist historians have generally rejected this model as overly schematic. Yet theories of social structure derived from modern sociological thought rarely seem to correspond any more effectively to the social realities of a late medieval German city. Many historians have chosen instead to adopt an empirical approach, attempting to construct a model of urban social structure drawn from the sources themselves. The vast amounts of data pertaining to individual inhabitants of the German city – much of it capable of quantitative analysis – have certainly encouraged this approach.

The most important sources of this sort are registers of the property taxes which were levied in many cities on the head of each citizen household. Of course, these records omit many inhabitants: women generally appeared only when they headed a household as widows, and non-citizens were normally excluded altogether. Though most tax-payers were assessed at a fixed percentage of their total wealth, in some cities special rules applied to citizens at the top or the bottom of the scale. The analysis of tax records can lead to a distorted picture of social reality, especially if historians treat property-holding as the only significant indicator of social position and reify tax brackets into actual social categories. Even so, these records have provided historians with a rich fund of data about the distribution of wealth in many German cities.[54]

Consider, for example, the meticulously studied city of Schwäbisch Hall in southern Germany. In 1396, a total of 1,202 citizens were taxed. Their total wealth was reckoned at about 262,000 gulden. But the distribution of wealth was highly uneven: 250 tax-payers paid a nominal fee or nothing at all, while at the top of the scale 21 citizens – about 2 per cent of the total – paid taxes corresponding to 39 per cent of the city's total wealth.[55] In exactly the same year the city of Augsburg recorded a total of 3,617 taxpayers. Half of them were listed as *Habnits* – citizens whose savings and property were too negligible to be assessed – while at the same time a mere 74 tax-payers had fortunes of 1,200 gulden or more.[56] These patterns remained constant over the following centuries. In 1618 in Schwäbisch Hall 18 per cent of the citizens were assessed as having minimal property, while a mere 4 per cent controlled almost 40 per cent of the community's wealth.[57] In Augsburg in the same year, over 40 per cent of the citizens were still listed as *Habnits*, while less than 2 per cent of the taxpayers controlled over half of the city's wealth.[58]

Distributions like these can be duplicated for city after city. They can be also duplicated when the urban population is broken down into specific occupational groups. To be sure, if one looks at average wealth, certain trades tended to come out ahead of others. The victualling trades, for example, frequently appear relatively high on the scale. But within each craft – or, to put it another way, among the members of a single guild – one could invariably find a vast range of wealth levels.[59] Certainly the significance of differences in wealth can be overstated. To be listed as 'having nothing' did not imply abject poverty; many citizens who had no savings or not enough wealth to be taxed still had a relatively secure source of income from the practice of their craft. But it is clear that the citizenry in any German city was a far from homogeneous group.

Given that the distribution of wealth was highly skewed in all cities, historians have nevertheless attempted to determine whether the degree of inequality varied significantly from city to city. A pioneering analysis published in 1926 posited that cities in which there was extensive production for export tended to have a more uneven and more unstable distribution of wealth than cities which produced chiefly for a local market.[60] It is certainly true that export-oriented production created more opportunities for rich merchants to reduce poor masters to economic dependency on the putting-out system. It has been suggested that the late medieval Hanseatic cities, which depended more heavily on commerce and local production than on production for export, tended to have less extreme differences of wealth than the export-oriented centres of southern Germany.[61] But uniform correlations between economic structure and the distribution of wealth are hard to demonstrate.

Given the abundance of available data, it is inevitable that historians will group the citizens of a German town into strata according to wealth: treatments of this topic abound with categories like *obere Mittelschicht, untere Mittleschicht*, and so on. This approach is sound enough when used as a measure of inequality, but a division of citizens into categories based on arbitrarily selected wealth brackets can be misleading if this is taken as an actual indication of any particular individual's social position. For, in fact, people frequently moved from one wealth level to another in the course of a lifetime.[62] A man who appeared poor in early adulthood could marry, inherit, or work his way up into far greater prosperity. Only a few citizens experienced dramatic changes in the course of a lifetime, but some degree of upward mobility was a constant aspiration and a frequent occurrence. Downward mobility, of course, took place as well – sometimes in the course of one lifetime, sometimes over a period of generations. In the late fifteenth century, for example, Peter Welser – a member of the enormously wealthy Welser family of Augsburg – moved to the town of Zwickau in Saxony, where he engaged in commercial enterprises that soon placed him at the pinnacle of the local wealth hierarchy. But his descendents steadily lost their inherited wealth, and Peter Welser's great-grandson was reduced to working as a gravedigger.[63] The social ladder in German cities was always crowded with traffic, going either way.

The vast majority of Germany's inhabitants in the late middle ages belonged to the peasantry. But one would hardly know it from consulting the *Ständebuch* of 1568. Amman and Sachs described nearly 100 different urban occupations, but the entire peasantry of Germany was subsumed under a single entry:

> By nature I am but a *Bauwr*,
> Work for me is hard and sour...[64]

In actual fact, of course, rural society was highly complex, and peasants – who made up most though not all of the population of the countryside – were far from uniform in their social and economic standing.

The social position of individual peasants was affected by numerous factors. Each peasant, as a member of the church, belonged to a rural parish. Each peasant also stood under the authority of a territorial ruler, although before the sixteenth century the direct impact of the state on peasants' lives was often small. In most cases, two other factors were much more decisive in shaping the individual's place in rural society: the peasant's relationship to the seigneur, and the peasant's social and economic standing within the community itself. These factors were often related – but the connection between them was not simple or obvious. It is best to consider them one at a time.

Not every peasant had a seigneur. A small number of peasants cultivated allodial land on their own, owing nothing to a lord. But the overwhelming majority of peasants in Germany did have seigneurs to whom they had to render various dues and services. The seigneurs were generally nobles, but they might also be institutions like monasteries, or even wealthy town-dwellers. Sometimes the seigneur and the political ruler were the same; more often they were not.

The exact nature of the obligations which peasants owed to their seigneurs could vary enormously over time and place. Some peasants were serfs. In fact the history of agrarian relations in Germany – like that of Europe as a whole – is often described in terms of a great paradox: the gradual decline of serfdom in the west and the simultaneous rise of serfdom in the east.[65] When German colonists began to settle the lands east of the Elbe river in the high middle ages, they attracted new peasants by offering generous terms which made the peasants essentially free. But from the late middle ages onward, seigneurs in the east increasingly found that they could profit from the growing demand for grain all over Europe if only they could make more efficient use of their labour supply. So they steadily imposed tighter controls on their tenants, leading to what is sometimes called the 'second serfdom'. That this happened is widely agreed. But to speak of a simultaneous 'decline' of serfdom in the western part of Germany raises many more questions.

To start with, the exact definition of serfdom and the precise boundary between serfs and non-serfs was not always clear. Certainly before the fourteenth century most peasants in western Germany were in bondage to their seigneurs. They were required to provide labour services on the manorial estate and forbidden to marry or emigrate from the village without permission – though many tried, and some succeeded. By the fourteenth century, however, many seigneurs had found it more convenient to transfer much or all of the manorial lands to the peasants themselves, in return for having the peasants render various dues or fulfil other obligations. Under the new system, a peasant could normally bequeath the land he cultivated – the *Hofstätte* or *Hufe* – to his heirs. Concerned chiefly with getting a steady flow of revenues, the seigneurs permitted much of the work of administering the village to devolve on the peasants themselves, so that the village became a self-governing community, or *Gemeinde*.[66]

That was the general pattern. But the peasants' continuing obligations to their seigneurs differed enormously from place to place. In many villages the lords still imposed personal bondage, restricting the peasants' freedom to move or marry outside the community. Sometimes an heir could inherit the father's property only after paying a substantial death-duty to the lord. There was little uniformity. But where the obligations were most onerous and restrictions on freedom most severe, the peasants could still be considered serfs – or, to use the term that became increasingly common in the sixteenth century, *Leibeigene*.

Even within a single village there could be differences in status among the peasants. One peasant might be a serf while his neighbour was not. In many parts of Germany, especially in the east, the village was likely to have one seigneur and all villagers might be equal in status. But elsewhere, especially in some parts of southern Germany, different peasants within a single village might have different seigneurs. It was even possible for an individual peasant to have more than one seigneur. In some places a peasant's land was inherited from the father but personal status as a serf was inherited from the mother. Thus, a single person might hold his land from one seigneur but be in personal bondage to another.[67]

Certainly serfdom declined in western Germany between the fourteenth and the eighteenth century. But there was no steady, step-by-step progression to ever less onerous obligations. Indeed, in some parts of southwestern Germany, seigneurs in the fifteenth and early sixteenth century tried to tighten their control over their peasants. New forms of dependency, not necessarily similar to those of earlier times, were sometimes imposed.[68] This revival or 'intensification' of serfdom was, of course, bitterly resented by the peasants themselves; their anger contributed to the fury of the Peasants' War of 1524–5, in which the complete abolition of serfdom was often a major objective.[69] Though that uprising was firmly suppressed, in the long run seigneurs in western Germany were generally less able to impose and sustain the rigours of serfdom as effectively as seigneurs east of the Elbe. Even so, the idea of a simple and steady decline of serfdom in western Germany must obviously be modified.

Yet serfdom was only one factor in determining a peasant's social position. For each peasant also had a social standing within the community based essentially on the extent and security of his holding. The social differences among peasants within a single village were often acute – and this could apply whether the village had a single seigneur or multiple lords.

In every village, the leading peasants were those who possessed one or more full-sized holdings. To possess a *Hufe* or *Hofstätte* meant that one had a fixed share of the main fields of the village, along with access to the common pastures and a full voice in the deliberations of the *Gemeinde*. But most villages, especially from the late middle ages onward, also had inhabitants of lesser standing. Some peasants had only part of a full-sized holding. But there were also villagers who held small parcels of land entirely outside the main fields. The terminology to describe this group varied from region to region: they were *Gärtner* in Saxony, *Kossäten* in Brandenburg, *Kötter* in Westphalia, *Seldner* in Swabia. No matter what they were called, they almost always stood substantially beneath the other peasants in the extent of their holdings and prestige within the community. Yet they were by no means at the bottom of the rural social order. For many villages also had an even lower stratum of cottagers, or *Häusler*, who possessed no land at all and supported themselves by working for the peasants who did have land. Finally there were mere servants, or *Gesinde*, who lived in their masters' homes.[70]

Records of peasant wealth are less abundant than comparable urban sources, but when they are examined they tend to reveal a highly unequal distribution of wealth among the inhabitants of the German village.[71] A recent study of sixteenth-century Hohenlohe shows that there the distribution of rural wealth corresponded closely to differences in property-holding, with full tenants clustered at the top of the scale, smallholders concentrated in the middle ranges, and propertyless cotters all grouped at the bottom.[72]

How had these differences arisen? Sometimes they reflected the way in which the village had originally been settled or the way in which land had originally been allocated. But differences among villagers could also arise over relatively short periods of time owing to accidents of marriage or customs of inheritance. Some parts of Germany had partible inheritance, in which each heir would get part of the father's holdings; this, of course, could result in endless subdivisions which eventually made the holdings scarcely viable. In most regions this was avoided by impartible inheritance, which required that each holding be passed on intact to a single heir. In these areas it was typical for one son – often the youngest one – to inherit the parents' holding; any other heirs were supposed to receive compensation for their share of the inheritance and were expected to settle elsewhere, perhaps by marrying someone who had inherited a holding. This worked well enough when the population was relatively stable. But if the population were rising, the non-inheriting siblings might be unable to take over any vacant holdings and would slip down into the ranks of village wage-workers, far removed in social status from the one brother who had inherited the land. In some villages the disproportionate wealth and status among different members of the community could lead to serious tension – all the more so if they were in fact closely related to each other.[73]

Rural society was never composed only of peasants. A large village might include a resident member of the clergy, a miller, an innkeeper, and a small group of craftsmen, perhaps also a seigneurial official. The differences between urban and rural society were sharp, but the barrier was permeable. Many villagers moved to the cities. By the late middle ages it would have been difficult for an unskilled villager to qualify for admission to a guild, but towns constantly absorbed surplus members of rural society as servants or unskilled labourers. Peasants also moved to neighbouring villages, especially when they married. No rural community was socially encapsulated.

The basic social structure of most German villages remained constant from the fourteenth to the sixteenth centuries. But few villages were immune from the long-term impact of political or economic change. The steady expansion of the market economy during these centuries could not fail to affect rural society, although different regions responded in highly different ways. In the sparsely populated regions of eastern Germany it was the seigneurs who took advantage of the opportunity to produce grain for export to distant markets. Here the villagers were often the victims, as seigneurs worked to tighten controls over their peasant. In the densely populated regions of western Germany, by contrast, where urban markets were often more accessible, wealthier peasants whose holdings generated a surplus became increasingly involved in production for the market. This in turn, however, might only widen the gulf between the dominant peasants with full holdings and the less propertied members of the community.[74]

Rural social structure was also affected by the changing role of the state. In the late middle ages, few villagers were directly affected by the territorial state; the seigneur was of greater importance to most peasants, and even many of the seigneur's functions were carried out by the *Gemeinde* itself. Gradually, however, the institutions of the territorial state began to intrude themselves into rural society – especially in connection with the collection of taxes and administration of justice, but also through attempts to codify and regulate economic and social norms. In fact many of these trends became fully apparent only in the seventeenth century, but already in the sixteenth century some communities had begun to experience the transition from what has been called a system of power exercised 'with' peasants to one exercised 'over' them.[75] This transition had a significant impact on the seigneurs (except, of course, in those places where the ruler himself was the seigneur). In some regions the state extended its powers most effectively by co-opting the seigneurs into becoming agents of the state itself; in other areas the seigneurs were bypassed as professional bureaucrats assumed more and more administrative functions. But either way, the extension of state power was also bound to have an impact on social relations within the village. Officials of the emerging state preferred to deal directly with individual tax-paying households rather than filtering their demands through communal institutions. As a result, the *Gemeinde* tended to lose its autonomy. But this did not necessarily diminish the dominant role of the richer peasants: where, as often happened, the peasants with large holdings were willing to co-operate with state officials, their power in the community was, if anything, likely to be enhanced. The emerging absolutist state may well have tried to reduce all those under its sway to a uniform status as subjects, or *Untertanen*.[76] But the social structure of the German village remained highly stratified as rural society moved from the middle ages toward the *ancien régime*.

We need look no further than the *Communist Manifesto* for a brief description of German social structure in the late middle ages with which almost every historian would agree: 'In the earlier epochs of history,' wrote Marx and Engels, 'we find almost everywhere a complicated arrangement of society into various orders, a manifold gradation of social ranks... in the middle ages, feudal lords, vassals, guild-masters, journeymen, apprentices, serfs; in almost all of these classes, again, subordinate gradations.'[77] In short: a society of orders.

Far more problematic, of course, is the broader framework of feudal society into which Marx and Engels fitted this description. For they assumed that 'lord and serf, guild-master and journeyman, in a word, oppressor and oppressed, stood in constant opposition to one another', and that this contributed to the eventual collapse of feudalism and the emergence of a capitalist system in which the complex social groupings of earlier times would give way to the simple antagonism of bourgeoisie and proletariat.

Despite the criticisms which have battered it for over 100 years, the marxist view of history, with its powerful capacity to place all historical developments into a meaningful pattern of long-term change, has never lost its attraction to large numbers of historians. Even when the marxist perspective is not adopted as a whole, specific categories of analysis remain inviting. Only orthodox marxist historiography pictured the social and political upheavals of the Reformation era as an 'early bourgeois revolution'.[78] But many other historians would accept that the reassertion of control by the social and political elites after 1525 can be seen as a process of 'refeudalization'.[79]

Yet whether or not the social structure of late medieval Germany is thought to conform to the marxist model depends, ultimately, on one's understanding of what happened next. If later epochs really experienced the triumph of the capitalist bourgeosie, followed in turn by the formation of an increasingly cohesive proletariat, then it is easy enough to see in the history of earlier times some intimations of the coming collapse of feudalism and the origins of what would eventually become new classes. It is not clear, however, that class formation was really a significant factor in German society before the eighteenth or nineteenth century. If classes are assumed to be social groups defined by antagonistic economic interests of which their members become increasingly conscious, it would be difficult to find them in German society of the fourteenth to sixteenth centuries.

Of course there were social conflicts, but they did not necessarily follow clear lines of economic interest. The thrust to expropriate was constantly modified by concerns about status, prestige, and precedent. Indeed, it could scarcely be otherwise when the boundaries between 'oppressed' and 'oppressors' were so often blurred by 'a complicated arrangement of society into various orders, a manifold gradation of social rank'.

Some historians have attempted to rescue the notion of class for late medieval or early modern society by positing the concept of a 'one-class society': only members of the nobility, broadly defined, were 'banded together in the exercise of collective power, political and economic' and thus qualified as a class in the modern sense.[80] But it is difficult to apply this notion to the German nobility of the fourteenth to sixteenth centuries. For there was so much uncertainty and conflict among the nobles themselves about who exactly qualified as members of the nobility that their capacity to think and act in a collective manner was crippled. There are many indications that members of older noble families attempted to close their ranks or prevent the admission of newcomers with particular vigour in the late fifteenth and early sixteenth century. But on closer inspection it almost always appears that these efforts represented anxious and fearful responses to the steady intrusion of newcomers, often as a result of their service to the territorial princes. The *Beamtenadel* of early modern times were simply a new version of the *ministeriales* whose social advance had forced a redefinition of nobility hundreds of years earlier.

In fact, the Germany of the fourteenth to sixteenth centuries is best thought of not as a class society but as a society of orders. This does not mean, of course, that the social structure remained static, nor that it was unaffected by economic factors. Quite the contrary. The spread of the market economy generated opportunities which many people grasped in order to make possible some social advance for themselves or their families. But they were not all members of a single social group. Depending on local conditions, it might be the seigneur or the burgher or even the rich peasant who most avidly exploited the opportunities of the expanding market.

Religious and cultural changes were also significant, not only in offering individual opportunities but in reshaping the social structure as a whole. The Protestant Reformation eliminated the power of the old church in many imperial cities and territorial states, but it also created a new social group: the Protestant pastorate. As Roman law steadily supplanted customary legal norms as the basis for conflict resolution, university-trained lawyers rose steadily in social status – not only as individuals but as a group. Other educated professionals followed in their wake.

The social ladder was complex, but people always knew which way was up. Wealth played a crucial part in taking them there: in case after case, money bought status. But there were limits to this process. Precisely because status was so precious a commodity, old elites could use non-economic weapons to defend their own standing or delay the full acceptance of newcomers. Jacob Herbrot, a wealthy merchant who served as a mayor of Augsburg and was granted the title of royal councillor by the Habsburgs in 1551, still had to beg the abbot of Weingarten to stop addressing him with the familiar 'du' normally used for social inferiors.[81] The Fuggers could be snubbed at their own wedding celebrations by a duchess of Bavaria. Yet to others, a polite gesture from the Fuggers carried immense social value. When the distinguished medical doctor and author Achilles Pirmin Gasser invited Hans Jacob Fugger to his wedding in 1546, he explained the invitation with remarkable candour: 'Since I am a "new man" of modest birth, not only will your presence make me appear more estimable to my fellow-citizens, but social contact with such an important man will also make me more respected and appreciated by my in-laws.'[82] A society of orders is always sensitive to economic pressures. But ultimately what counted most, especially in the higher ranks of the social order, were prestige, honour, and status.

Notes

1 Michael Mitterauer, 'Probleme der Stratifikation in mittelalterlichen Gesellschaftssystemen', in Jürgen Kocka, ed., *Theorien in der Praxis des Historikers*, Geschichte und Gesellschaft 3 (Göttingen, 1977), pp. 13–43; Ingrid Bátori, 'Soziale Schichtung und soziale Mobilität in der Gesellschaft Alteuropas. Methodische und theoretische Probleme', in Ilja Mieck, ed., *Soziale Schichtung und soziale Mobilität in der Gesellschaft Alteuropas* (Berlin, 1984), pp. 8–28.
2 Erdmann Weyrauch, 'Über soziale Schichtung', in Ingrid Bátori, ed., *Städtische Gesellschaft und Reformation. Kleine Schriften* II (Stuttgart, 1980), pp. 5–57; Mitterauer, 'Probleme', pp. 14–37.
3 Roland Mousnier, *Social Hierarchies, 1450 to the Present*, trans. Peter Evans (New York, 1973), esp. pp. 21–40; on how Mousnier was influenced by modern sociological thought, Armand Arriaza, 'Mousnier and Barber. The Theoretical Underpinnings of the "Society of Orders" in Early Modern Europe', *P & P* LXXXIX (Nov. 1980), 38–57.
4 Even an influential work which argues against the 'society of orders' in favour of a model based on (non-economic) classes still concedes that 'the 'historian must work with estate and class categories simultaneously': Thomas A. Brady, Jr, *Ruling Class, Regime and Reformation at Strasbourg, 1520–1555* (Leiden, 1978), p. 33.
5 [Jost Amman and Hans Sachs], *Eygentliche Beschreibung Aller Stände auff Erden/Hoher und Nidriger/Geistlicher und Weltlicher/Aller Künsten/ Handwercken und Händeln/u. vom grösten biß zum kleinesten/* ... (Frankfurt am Main, 1568). A reproduction of the book has been published as *The Book of Trades (Ständebuch)* (New York, 1973).
6 Mitterauer, 'Probleme', pp. 17–20.
7 Gerd Wunder, 'Bauer, Bürger, Edelmann', in Wunder, *Bauer, Bürger, Edelmann* (Sigmaringen, 1984), pp. 49–57.

8   Peter-Michael Hahn, *Struktur und Funktion des brandenburgischen Adels im 16. Jahrhundert* (Berlin, 1979), pp. 24–9, 239.

9   Gerhard Benecke, 'Ennoblement and Privilege in Early Modern Germany', *History* LVI (1971), pp. 360–70, here p. 365.

10 Friedrich W. Euler, 'Wandlungen des Konnubiums im Adel des 15. und 16. Jahrhunderts', in Hellmuth Rössler, ed., *Deutscher Adel 1430–1555* (Darmstadt, 1965), pp. 58–94, here p. 63.

11 *Ibid.*, pp. 87–8.

12 Heinz Lieberich, *Landherren und Landleute. Zur politischen Führungsschicht Bayerns im Spätmittelalter* (Munich, 1964), pp. 16–32; Euler, 'Wandlungen', pp. 62–5.

13 Klaus von Andrian-Werburg, 'Der Altbaierische Adel im standesfürstlichen Staat der Wittelsbacher bis zum Abschluss der ritterschaftlichen Verfassung', in Rössler, *Adel 1430–1555*, pp. 48–57, here pp. 55–6.

14 For two striking cases, see Euler, 'Wandlungen', pp. 66–7. But the normal pattern is suggested by a recent study of 15 dynasties of *Grafen* and *Herren* between the thirteenth and the early sixteenth centuries: in 551 of 630 marriages (87.5 per cent) both partners came from families of *Grafen* or *Herren*; in 40 cases one partner came from a family of higher-ranked *Fürsten* and in 39 cases one partner came from a family of lower-ranked *Ritter*: Karl-Heinz Spiess, *Familie und Verwandtschaft im deutschen Hochadel des Spätmittelalters. 13. bis Anfang des 16. Jahrhunderts* (Stuttgart, 1993), pp. 398–400.

15 Lieberich, *Landherren*, pp. 30–1.

16 Heinrich Kramm, *Studien über die Oberschichten der mitteldeutschen Städte im 16. Jahrhundert. Sachsen, Thüringen, Anhalt* (2 vols., Cologne/Vienna, 1981) I, pp. 532–7.

17 This is well illustrated for Hessen by Hellmuth Gensicke, 'Der Adel im Mittelrheingebiet', in Rössler, *Adel 1430–1555*, pp. 127–52, here pp. 128–30.

18 Gerald Strauss, *Law, Resistance and the State. TheOpposition to Roman Law in Reformation Germany* (Princeton, NJ, 1986), pp. 166–8; Kramm, *Oberschichten* I, pp. 562–3.

19 Germany had roughly 3,000 to 4,000 cities and towns at the end of the middle ages; Klaus Gerteis, *Die deutschen Städte in der frühen Neuzeit. Zur Vorgeschichte der 'bürgerlichen Welt'* (Darmstadt, 1986), pp. 59–60, estimates that these cities may have accounted for almost 25 per cent of Germany's total population in the sixteenth century. Jan de Vries, *European Urbanization, 1500–1800* (Cambridge, Mass., 1984), pp. 38–9, records the urban share of Germany's total population in 1500 as only 3.2 per cent, but this calculation is limited to cities of more than 10,000; for one region, Saxony, de Vries estimates the total urban share in 1550 at over 30 per cent (pp. 60–2).

20 E.g. Robert Brenner, 'Agrarian Class Structure and Economic Development in Pre-Industrial Europe', *P & P* LXX (Feb. 1976), pp. 30–75; see also T. H. Aston and C. H. E. Philpin, eds, *The Brenner Debate* (Cambridge, 1985).

21 For a general introduction to this topic, Hans Mauersberg, *Wirtschafts- und Sozialgeschichte zentraleuropäischer Städte in neuerer Zeit* (Göttingen, 1960), pp. 80–92.

22 For examples from Augsburg, Claus-Peter Clasen, *Die Augsburger Weber. Leistungen und Krisen des Textilgewerbes um 1600* (Augsburg, 1981), pp. 70–89; Bernd Roeck, *Bäcker, Brot und Getreide in Augsburg. Zur Geschichte des Bäckerhandwerks und zur Versorgungspolitik der Reichsstadt im Zeitalter des Dreissigjährigen Krieges* (Sigmaringen, 1987), pp. 160–2.

23 Knut Schulz, *Handwerksgesellen und Lohnarbeiter. Untersuchungen zur oberrheinischen und oberdeutschen Stadtgeschichte des 14. bis 17. Jahrhunderts* (Sigmaringen, 1985), pp. 209–48, 312–15, shows that in southern Germany

this trend, which is normally attributed to the late middle ages, only began in the sixteenth century.

24   Merry E. Wiesner, *Working Women in Renaissance Germany* (New Brunswick, NJ, 1986), pp. 150–2.
25   Erich Maschke, 'Verfassung und soziale Kräfte in der deutschen Stadt des späten Mittelalters, vornehmlich in Oberdeutschland', *VSWG* XLVI (1959), pp. 289–349, 433–76.
26   Volker Press, 'Führungsgruppen in der deutschen Gesellschaft im Übergang zur Neuzeit um 1500', in Hanns Hubert Hofmann and Günther Franz, eds., *Deutsche Führungsschichten in der Neuzeit. Eine Zwischenbilanz* (Boppard a. R., 1980), pp. 29–77, esp. pp. 52–65; Heinz Schilling, 'Wandlungs- und Differenzierungsprozesse innerhalb der bürgerlichen Oberschichten West- und Norddeutschlands im 16. und 17. Jahrhunderts', in Marian Biskup and Klaus Zernack, eds, *Schichtung und Entwicklung der Gesellschaft in Polen und Deutschland im 16. und 17. Jahrhundert* (Wiesbaden, 1983), pp. 121–73.
27   Gerd Wunder, *Die Bürger von Hall. Sozialgeschichte einer Reichsstadt, 1216–1802* (Sigmaringen, 1980), pp. 57–69.
28   Helmut Lahrkamp, 'Das Patriziat in Münster', in Hellmuth Rössler, ed., *Deutsches Patriziat 1430–1740* (Limburg/Lahn, 1968), pp. 195–207.
29   The best overview is by Ingrid Bátori, 'Das Patriziat der deutschen Städte. Zu den Forschungsergebnissen über das Patriziat besonders der süddeutschen Städte', *Zeitschrift für Stadtgeschichte, Stadtsoziologie und Denmalpflege* II (1975), pp. 1–30. For specific cities or regions, see Rössler, *Patriziat*.
30   Schilling, 'Differenzierungsprozesse', pp. 127–41.
31   *Ibid.*, pp. 141–8.
32   Lahrkamp, 'Patriziat', pp. 198–9.
33   Gerhard Hirschmann, 'Das Nürnberger Patriziat', in Rössler, *Patriziat*, pp. 257–76, here p. 265.
34   Katarina Sieh-Burens, *Oligarchie, Konfession und Politik im 16. Jahrhundert. Zur sozialen Verflechtung der Augsburger Bürgermeister und Stadtpfleger, 1518–1618* (Munich, 1986), pp. 24–6.
35   Gerald L. Soliday, *A Community in Conflict. Frankfurt Society in the Seventeenth and Early Eighteenth Centuries* (Hanover, NH, 1974), pp. 71–84.
36   Werner Spiess, *Geschichte der Stadt Braunschweig im Nachmittelalter, vom Ausgang des Mittelalters bis zum Ende der Stadtfreiheit (1491–1671)* (2 vols., Braunschweig, 1966) II, pp. 466–7, 475–6.
37   Peter Eitel, 'Die politische, soziale und wirtschaftliche Stellung des Zunftbürgertums in den oberschwäbischen Reichsstädten am Ausgang des Mittelalters', in Erich Maschke and Jürgen Sydow, eds, *Städtische Mittelschichten* (Stuttgart, 1972), pp. 80–93, here pp. 85–6; Sieh-Burens, *Oligarchie*, pp. 26–8.
38   Cf. Bátori, 'Patriziat', p. 22.
39   Kramm, *Oberschichten* I, pp. 530–1.
40   Olaf Mörke, 'Die Fugger im 16. Jahrhundert. Städtische Elite oder Sonderstruktur?', *ARG* LXXIV (1983), pp. 141–61.
41   Sieh-Burens, *Oligarchie*, p. 128.
42   Peter Blickle, *Gemeindereformation. Die Menschen des 16. Jahrhunderts auf dem Weg zum Heil* (Munich, 1985), pp. 98–100.
43   A useful overview is provided by Erich Maschke, 'Die Unterschichten der mittelalterlichen Städte Deutschlands', in Erich Maschke and Jürgen Sydow, eds, *Gesellschaftliche Unterschichten in den südwestdeutschen Städten* (Stuttgart, 1967), pp. 1–74.
44   The importance of agricultural activity by urban inhabitants is emphasized by Gerteis, *Städte*, pp. 125–36.

45 For this entire topic, see Schulz, *Handwerksgesellen*, esp. pp. 443–56.
46 Franz Irsigler and Arnold Lassotta, *Bettler und Gaukler, Dirnen und Henker. Randgruppen und Aussenseiter in Köln, 1300–1600* (Cologne, 1984) covers the topic thoroughly for one city with numerous references to other communities.
47 Robert Jütte, *Abbild und soziale Wirklichkeit des Bettler- und Gaunertums zu Beginn der Neuzeit. Sozial-, mentalitäts- und sprachgeschichtliche Studien zum Liber Vagatorum (1510)* (Cologne/Vienna, 1988), pp. 26–43, esp. p. 35.
48 Richard van Dülmen, *Theater des Schreckens. Gerichtspraxis und Strafrituale in der frühen Neuzeit* (Munich, 1985), pp. 91–7.
49 Wunder, *Bürger von Hall*, pp. 150–1.
50 Markus J. Wenninger, *Man bedarf keiner Juden mehr. Ursachen und Hintergründe ihrer Vertreibung aus den deutschen Reichsstädten im 15. Jahrhundert* (Vienna, 1981).
51 Hanns Hubert Hofmann, 'Nobiles Norimbergenses. Beobachtungen zur Struktur der reichsstädtischen Oberschicht', in Theodor Mayer, ed., *Untersuchungen zur gesellschaftlichen Struktur der mittelalterlichen Städte in Europa* (Constance/Stuttgart, 1966), pp. 53–92, here p. 79.
52 Soliday, *Community in Conflict*, pp. 61–4.
53 Johannes Schildhauer, *Soziale, politische und religiöse Auseinandersetzungen in den Hansestädten Stralsund, Rostock und Wismar im ersten Drittel des 16. Jahrhunderts* (Weimar, 1959).
54 For a classic exposition of the interpretive issues, see Bernhard Kirchgässner, 'Probleme quantitativer Erfassung städtischer Unterschichten im Spätmittelalter, besonders in den Reichsstädten Konstanz und Esslingen', in Maschke and Sydow, *Unterschichten*, pp. 75–89. For practical guidance on how to use a major tax-register series, see Claus-Peter Clasen, *Die Augsburger Steuerbücher um 1600* (Augsburg, 1976).
55 Wunder, *Bürger von Hall*, p. 266.
56 Friedrich Blendinger, 'Versuch einer Bestimmung der Mittelschicht in der Reichsstadt Augsburg vom Ende des 14. bis zum Anfang des 18. Jahrhunderts', in Maschke and Sydow, *Mittelschichten*, pp. 32–78, here pp. 44–5.
57 Wunder, *Bürger von Hall*, p. 269.
58 Blendinger, 'Versuch', pp. 50, 71. For a comprehensive examination of Augsburg's social structure in 1618, see Bernd Roeck, *Eine Stadt in Krieg und Frieden. Studien zur Geschichte der Reichsstadt Augsburg zwischen Kalendenstreit und Parität* (2 vols., Göttingen, 1989) I, pp. 301–15.
59 Adolf Laube, 'Wirtschaftliche und soziale Differenzierung innerhalb der Zünfte des 14. Jahrhunderts, dargestellt am Beispiel mecklenburgischer Städte', *Zeitschrift für Geschichtswissenschaft* V (1957), pp. 1181–97; for similar evidence from a much later period, see Clasen, *Weber*, pp. 33–4.
60 Horst Jecht, 'Studien zur gesellschaftlichen Struktur der mittelalterlichen Stadt', *VSWG* XIX (1926), pp. 48–85.
61 Ahasver von Brandt, 'Die gesellschaftliche Struktur des spätmittelalterlichen Lübeck', in Mayer, *Untersuchungen*, pp. 215–39, here pp. 229, 236–7; Ernst Pitz, 'Wirtschaftliche und soziale Probleme der gewerblichen Entwicklung im 15./16. Jahrhundert nach hansisch-niederdeutschen Quellen', in Friedrich Lütge, ed., *Wirtschaftliche und soziale Probleme der gewerblichen Entwicklung im 15.–16. Jahrhundert* (Stuttgart, 1968), pp. 16–43, here pp. 40–2.
62 For some quantitative evidence from the late sixteenth century, Christopher R. Friedrichs, *Urban Society in an Age of War. Nördlingen, 1580–1720* (Princeton, NJ, 1979), pp. 95–7, 125–7.
63 Kramm, *Oberschichten* I, p. 196.

64 *Ständebuch*, p. Mii. The only other essentially rural occupation listed is that of vine-grower; some other occupations, though depicted in the *Ständebuch* as being practised in the countryside, were not generally part of the rural social order, e.g. huntsmen, fishermen, and miners.

65 Jerome Blum, 'The Rise of Serfdom in Eastern Europe', *AHR* LXII (1957), pp. 807–36.

66 Peter Blickle, *Deutsche Untertanen. Ein Widerspruch?* (Munich, 1981), pp. 23–51.

67 David Sabean, 'Family and Land Tenure. A Case Study of Conflict in the German Peasants' War (1525)', *Peasant Studies Newsletter* III (Jan. 1974), pp. 1–15, here p. 7–8; the article also appeared as 'Famille et tenure paysanne. Aux origines de la guerre des paysans en Allemagne (1525)', *Annales ESC* XXVII (1972), pp. 903–22. The confusions that could arise from such situations are well illustrated by Tom Scott, *Freiburg and the Breisgau. Town–Country Relations in the Age of Reformation and Peasants War* (Oxford, 1986), pp. 77–113.

68 Friedrich Lütge, *Geschichte der deutschen Agrarverfassung vom frühen Mittelalter bis zum 19. Jahrhundert*, 2nd edn (Stuttgart, 1967), pp. 106–8.

69 Peter Blickle, *The Revolution of 1525*, trans. Thomas A. Brady, Jr and H. C. Erik Midelfort (Baltimore, MD, 1981), pp. 25–35.

70 Günther Franz, *Geschichte des deutschen Bauernstandes vom frühen Mittelalter bis zum 19. Jahrhundert* (Stuttgart, 1970), pp. 210–17; Willi A. Boelcke, 'Wandlungen der dörflichen Struktur während Mittelalter und Neuzeit', in Heinz Haushofer und Willi A. Boelcke, eds, *Wege und Forschungen der Agrargeschichte* (Frankfurt a.M., 1967), pp. 80–103.

71 Franz, *Geschichte*, pp. 210–12, 223–4.

72 Thomas Robisheaux, *Rural Society and the Search for Order in Early Modern Germany* (Cambridge, 1989), pp. 86–7.

73 David Sabean, 'German Agrarian Institutions at the Beginning of the Sixteenth Century. Upper Swabia as an Example', in Janos Bak, ed., *The German Peasant War of 1525* (London, 1976), pp. 76–88.

74 See Robisheaux, *Rural Society*, pp. 147–62.

75 Heide Wunder, *Die bäuerliche Gemeinde in Deutschland* (Göttingen, 1986) formulates this as the transition from 'Herrschaft mit Bauern' to 'Herrschaft über Bauern'.

76 Peter Blickle, 'Untertanen in der Frühneuzeit. Zur Rekonstruktion der politischen Kultur und der sozialen Wirklichkeit Deutschlands im 17. Jahrhundert,' *VSWG* LXX (1983), pp. 483–522, esp. p. 497.

77 Karl Marx and Friedrich Engels, *Manifesto of the Communist Party* (Moscow, 1971), pp. 35–6.

78 Max Steinmetz, 'Die frühbürgerliche Revolution in Deutschland (1476–1535)', in Rainer Wohlfeil, ed., *Reformation oder frühbürgerliche Revolution?* (Munich, 1972), pp. 42–55.

79 Blickle, 'Untertanen', p. 479.

80 Peter Laslett, *The World We Have Lost. England Before the Industrial Age*, 2nd edn (New York, 1971), pp. 23–4. A more nuanced version of this argument, for late medieval Europe as a whole, is presented by Rhiman A. Rotz, 'Class Structure, Western (1300–1500)', in Joseph R. Strayer, ed., *Dictionary of the Middle Ages* (13 vols., New York, 1982–9) III, pp. 419–29.

81 Sieh-Burens, *Oligarchie*, pp. 129–30.

82 Karl Heinz Burmeister, *Achilles Pirmin Gasser (1505–1577). Artz und Naturforscher, Historiker und Humanist* (3 vols., Wiesbaden, 1970–5) III, pp. 87–91.

|10|

Economic and Social Institutions

THOMAS A. BRADY, JR.

One morning in the year 1338, as the Emperor Charles IV lay sleeping, a young knight woke him with the cry, 'Sire, get up, the Last Day has arrived, for the whole world is covered with locusts!' Charles arose, dressed, and went out to see how large the swarm was; he rode nearly 30 miles without coming to the end of it.[1] Ten years later, a tremendous earthquake rocked the Carinthian town of Villach and threw down its castle, monastery, churches, and walls, while the earth opened up in the middle of the city and poured out water and sulphur, killing at least 5,000 persons. The plague – it was the dreadful new Black Death – that followed closely on this catastrophe raged so fiercely in Vienna, 'that in a single day 1,200 bodies were buried in St. Colman's cemetery. . . . The great mortality was blamed on the Jews, and . . . the common people rose up in the towns of Stein and Krems, . . . seized the Jews, and killed them all.'[2] Famine, earthquake, plague, pogrom – signs of the fourteenth century, signs of the waning middle ages, signs of crisis so many and massive that historians call it an 'age of crisis'.[3]

The economic crisis began in the 1310s – at least three decades before the Black Death raged across Latin Christendom in 1347–50 – and it lasted more or less until the 1470s and 1480s, when all the principal economic indicators – population, settlement, prices – began to indicate recovery.[4] This secular rhythm, a 150-year trough between the economic boom of the high middle ages and the more laboured expansion of Fernand Braudel's 'long sixteenth century', frames the late medieval era in the Holy Roman Empire from the Swiss Jura to Pomerania and from Flanders to the Hungarian border. In this space lived perhaps 14 million persons on the eve of the Black Death, a figure which dropped to c.10 million by 1450 and did not recover pre-plague levels until the mid-sixteenth century.[5] Human densities, which were always highest in the Empire's western and southern sectors, reached a peak of 45 persons/km² in Brabant (1435) and the Lower Rhenish region, dropping to perhaps 23 persons/km² (c.1300) in Saxony and half that in Silesia. Most of the people lived in one of the approximately 170,000 settlements, including 4,000 towns and cities, within the boundaries of the

Empire (in 1300 almost exactly the size of Germany in 1937). In the fourteenth century only Cologne – and perhaps Prague – reached 40,000, the
size of Roman Trier in the fourth century, and no city in the Empire rivalled
contemporary Venice, Milan, Florence, or Paris, though at least four others
– Brussels, Metz, Lubeck, and Danzig – surpassed 20,000. Seven other cities
had around 20,000, and over a dozen more exceeded 10,000, but, outside
of the Empire's densely settled north-west, its towns typically housed fewer
than 2,000 souls.

From the end of the medieval boom through the long depression and
into the age of recovery, the Empire's peoples adapted inherited customs
and practices in response to the great new forces, and created or developed
the characteristic social and economic institutions of pre-industrial Central
Europe. The new forces produced the long agrarian depression: the fall or
stagnation of populations and grain prices, the recession of cultivation and
settlement, the expansion of market relations, and the appreciation of the
value of human labour relative to land. The general economic movement
favoured the town over the land and the peasants over their lords, so that
the depression's global effect was to devolve, in the absence of effect cen-
tralised government, more and more self-management and even self-gov-
ernance into the hands of the common people. The late medieval era thus
advantaged the Central European common people relative to their social
betters in both town and countryside, though to call this harsh era their
'golden age' is perhaps going too far. Yet the peoples of this harsh, freer
era proved extremely creative. If the medieval expansion had created the
Empire's basic social topography – the patterns of forest and clearing, the
roads, and the villages and towns – the later middle ages fixed the economic
and social institutions that would structure social life until the Empire's
demise: the household, the guild, the commune, and the firm.[6] Only one
institutional system – the church – retained a much older structure, for its
shapes reached back to the post-Carolingian centuries and beyond.

Household

Theoretical and taxonomic considerations aside, the predominant small
community in which late medieval German-speakers lived was the household
(*Haus*), the basic unit of co-residence, production, and reproduction in the
towns as on the land.[7] Nearly all we know about the structure and size of
late medieval households comes from the cities, and there from the middle
and upper classes; but we may accept in general that the late medieval
German household conformed to the northern European type based on a
nuclear couple who had first married rather late – perhaps the mid-20s –

and at roughly the same age, and who, together with their children and servants – perhaps seven to nine persons in all – formed the most important unit of co-residence and production.[8] The urban regimes recognized this fact by requiring that all citizens 'keep fire and smoke', that is, maintain a household in the city.[9] In principle, in the city as on the land, only those who owned their own houses were allowed to have families – the nobility, the burghers, the peasants, but not the servants, the journeymen, or the farmhands. Yet, our scanty evidence suggests the towns' resident poor (*Hausarmen*) also formed and lived in households, which were typically composed, like those of solid burghers, of a man, his wife (*uxor, husfrauw, wieff*), their children and possibly grandparents, the remnants of a 'deracinated and fluid' multi-generational family.[10]

Many households were headed by women, whose discriminatory exclusion from many trades made them disproportionately poor. Among 2,400 taxpayers surveyed at Trier in 1364, for example, a quarter – but two-thirds of the female heads of households – belonged to the poorest class. Women could and did head urban households, however, despite the customary law which still placed each woman in the custody (*mundium, Munt*) of a man, usually a father or a husband, a norm which in practice often bent to the economic reality of the household.[11]

Kinship, an older and in some respects alternative principle of social organization, continued to flourish without threatening the household's predominance. The kin community, based on real or fictive descent from a common ancestor, bore in German the name *Geschlecht* (pl. *Geschlechter*) but in Latin a variety of names – *familia, gens, progenies, genus, stirps*, and *genealogia* – which suggests its fluidity as contrasted to the solid monotony of the term *Haus*.[12] The feeling for kin or family in this sense remained as strong among the German-speakers as among the other peoples of Christendom, for whom it formed the primary metaphor for their religious sense of community as the great body of the kinsmen and kinswomen of Jesus Christ.[13] This powerful religious metaphor kept kinship on people's minds, and so did the confusingly contradictory rules that delimited potential marriage partners on the basis of consanguinity, even though the church did not really succeed in imposing its authority over 'the forms and patterns of marriage at all levels' until the sixteenth and seventeenth centuries.[14]

In practice the shape of family had become very fluid and its size as large, Erich Maschke wrote resignedly, 'as family sense made it'.[15] The point can be illustrated from wills at Lübeck: the widow Alheyd Wessel named in her second will of June 1354 thirteen relatives from three generations as her heirs; Elisabeth, the childless widow of Conrad Cruse, named in 1351 as heirs her sister's four children, four grand-nieces, and her brother-in-law's three children; and Gerhard Warendorp, a substantial merchant, named in two wills of 1356 and 1359 twenty persons, including eight maternal uncles and a paternal uncle and aunt.[16] The Lübeck wills show a family sense which extended over great distances but embraced, at most, the four generations of living memory. Different limits can be seen in the household books kept by wealthy southern merchants. When, for example, Lucas Rem (1481–1541) of Augsburg brought his great-grandfather's list (*verzeichnus*) up to date, he included only his own line of descent and excluded collaterals, which means that his sense of family was long but narrow.[17]

The Rems belonged to the very top of the smaller, more favoured of the two classes recognized by late medieval urban social discourse, rich (*dives, reich*) and poor *(pauper, arm)*. The civic tax registers give us a more nuanced insight into the shapes of wealth and poverty among urban households, and allow us to see them *ensemble* as a social structure. Around 1500 the possession of property worth 25–30 fl. or an income of 15 fl. per annum – the absolute minimum for a single person – meant true poverty. The possession of property worth 100 fl. meant modest prosperity, those who possessed 500 fl. were rich, and more than 5,000 fl. made one the late medieval equivalent of a millionaire. A nest-egg of 200 fl. was considered 'quite a lot of money'.[18]

The relationship between urban social stratification and economic structure may be illustrated by comparing tax-payers at Lübeck in 1460 with those of Augsburg in 1475: the rich and upper middle classes made up 18 per cent and 4.9 per cent, the middling ones 68 per cent and 27 per cent, and the poor 14 per cent and 66 per cent respectively.[19] Deficiencies of data aside, these figures reveal dramatically different social structures: Lübeck, a classic late medieval shape of an onion or turban – small point, large middling bulge, and modest base; and Augsburg, a pyramid shaped by the rapid development of large-scale production for export – tiny super-rich point, modest middling sector, and very large base. The key to social and political stability, of course, lay in the social and political behaviour of the bulge of middling folk.[20]

Most late medieval households, of course, formed and lived not in the cities but in the thousands of villages, hamlets (*Weiler*), and dispersed rural settlements, where the interplay of household and kinship responded to customary laws of inheritance of status and property, the presence of economic opportunity, and 'the gradual, long-drawn-out process' of 'the transfer of authority from parents to children'.[21] This process was regulated by inheritance regimes, and modern research teaches us great caution about assuming fixed correspondences between family structures and inheritance customs, the more so because rural families cannot be traced until the coming of parish registers in the middle years of the sixteenth century. No one, however, doubts that customary law powerfully influenced the inheritance of status and property during the later middle ages. In this era the line between servility and freedom, for example, was still quite visible, and its enforcement devolved, along with other legal functions, on the rural communes. At Ettenheimmünster in Baden, a manorial court (*Dinghof*) composed of leading male householders (*von mengem erberen Manne*) dealt with the offspring of a servile father and a free mother. If both parents were servile, they judged, the child would follow its mother, but if the father is servile and the mother free, the child should be servile and not follow its mother.[22]

The agrarian depression none the less eroded servility, along with the old patterns of management and governance of the manor, and created opportunities by loosening the rules of inheritance. Although the German-speaking lands are famous for their division into zones of partible and impartible inheritance, we cannot establish a clear correlation between impartible inheritance, size of holding, and the formation of a stem or multi-generation family, which was in any case predominant only in the eastern Alpine lands.[23] We may suppose that rules of impartibility encouraged larger, more complex households, and that partibility made the formation of stem families unlikely, but the evidence all comes from a later era.[24] Indeed, the typically fixed and regular patterns of rural inheritance in the German-speaking lands is a product less of the medieval than of the early modern era, when rising population pressure and the state's fiscal interest encouraged strict and uniform regulation of the generational transfer of real property. Even then, the state's preference for impartibility on fiscal grounds did not extinguish the great zones of partibility in the Rhineland, Württemberg, Baden, Lower Franconia, Hesse, south-western Westphalia, and parts of central Germany (Thuringia, south-west Saxony, southern Hanover).[25] This is so because different forces acted for different rules of inheritance – the state for impartibility and population pressure for partibility – so that the two systems might come to predominate in neighbouring regions, as, for example, Upper Swabia (impartibility) and Württemberg (partibility).[26]

It is difficult now, so powerful is the image of a static middle ages, to imagine the opportunities that opened up for young people to form new households during the late medieval agrarian crisis. Many fields were abandoned and whole settlements disappeared – perhaps 23 per cent of the total – ranging from low levels (10 per cent) in the Netherlands, to higher ones (17 per cent) in Alsace, and highest levels (40 per cent) in Brandenburg, Mecklenburg, and Hesse's uplands. A survey of the Mark Brandenburg in 1375 found 'an empty, deserted land' (*öde, wust land*), of which only a third to a half was occupied.[27] The shift of the land–labour ratio favoured the farmers by giving opportunities to find land and found households. How peasants seized such opportunities is suggested by an undated late medieval customary (*Weistum*) from western Germany, which says that if a stranger should ask for land, the village mayor (*Schultheiß*) should take the stranger up behind him on his horse and ride out into the land. When the stranger saw land which pleased him, he should dismount and mark the place, whereupon the mayor should mark off 15 Morgen (5.4 ha) for him to farm.[28]

Such evidence conveys the impression of an age, from about 1350 to about 1450, when very favourable conditions reigned for the formation and preservation of farming households and constitution of villages as groups of households. Villages averaged perhaps 12 households and 70 persons, who were related to one another in complex ways: consanguinity, affinity, godparenthood, co-ownership, employment, indebtedness, and faction. Although the village was a bastion of equality, compared with the society as a whole, every village formed a hierarchy of households. At the top were the rich, influential families, who in regions such as Westphalia (where they were called *Schulten*) and Franconia might pay as much tax as a well-to-do burgher in a nearby town. Such households formed the backbone of many small territories, such as the abbey of Göß in Styria, the boundaries of whose 25 large farms (*Meierhöfe*) survive to this day.[29]

The middling farmers, called *Vollbauern* or *Huber*, possessed one or more *Hufen* of ploughland and formed the stable element in every village. Below them stood the cotters (*Häusler*), who rented house and garden but, having little or no right to ploughland, worked in others' fields or as artisans or loggers. Below all these farmers stood those who lacked full rights in the village, called by different names in the different regions, who were often younger, non-inheriting brothers of full and middling peasants. A 1486 tax register from the county of Mark, a smallish territory on the Lower Rhine, offers a glimpse into rural stratification: a ninth of the 3,766 households had property worth less than 12.5 fl., of whom 38 per cent were too poor to pay any tax (*nil habet*); of the fifth worth more than 125 fl. each, only 2 per cent could pay nothing; and two-thirds of the tax-paying farmers were middling men with holdings worth between 20 and 125 fl.[30]

Most noble households also formed and lived in the countryside, where they shared the peasants' vulnerability to the price scissors created by falling revenues and rising costs of labour and manufactured goods. As the Bavarian Estates complained in 1510, 'all the grain and other things, which the peasant must sell to pay his taxes, are in little demand now; but the things he must buy in the town do not fall in price and are not regulated by law, but they cost ever more.'[31] Such conditions indeed favoured the burghers, who began in the later middle ages to invade the countryside as moneylenders and even as landlords, providing the nobles with competition they could rarely withstand.[32] The depression threatened the noble household more than it did the peasants, who at least benefited from cheaper and more accessible land; and it did so earliest and most strongly where agriculture was already market-oriented and demesne farming had declined, as in the Upper Rhine Valley. A study of sixteen families of lesser (*ritteradlige*) nobles in the fourteenth-century Ortenau, a district of Middle Baden, reveals that a community of noble households – they endowed masses and even built a chapel together to serve their dead – suffered grievously from the fall of grain prices and the debasement of coinage, which depressed their incomes faster than those of their tenants.[33] The plunge in their fortunes stabilized around 1400, but other evidence indicates that south-western rural nobles' incomes remained depressed right to the end of the later middle ages.[34]

This picture of the noble household standing helpless before the agrarian depression can none the less be misleading. One of the defining characteristics of nobles, lineage or descent, helped them to defend themselves against the ravages of the economic depression. They used it, for example, to guard their monopoly of many clerical corporations, such as the cathedral chapters, by enforcing requirements for noble ancestry – the 'four-ancestor rule' was used at Freising and Regensburg, the 'sixteen-ancestor rule' at Bamberg, Würzburg, and Mainz – for admission. Strasbourg, most aristocratic of all, admitted only men whose families held seats in the Imperial Diet, which meant that, as Desiderius Erasmus once quipped, Jesus Christ lacked sufficient noble ancestors to become a canon of Strasbourg.[35]

Then, too, in complicated noble lineages fortunate households could make up the losses suffered by less fortunate ones. This process can be seen in the history of the lords (since 1467, barons) of Fleckenstein, the most successful noble lineage of Lower Alsace during the later middle ages.[36] They recouped some of their late fourteenth-century losses by entering Palatine service in the next century, but the failure of one line, the Dagstuhls, to produce sufficient and timely heirs depressed its fortunes in comparison with its kinsmen. The family as a whole, however, survived the depression in good shape, thanks as much to political environment as to improved economic conditions.[37] This story reminds us that bonds between lines and between households provided types of support – for example, in the mortgage, sale, and purchase of lands and rents, and providing surety for loans – lacked by the burghers generally and the peasants almost universally.

While evidence from the south-west reveals hard times for the lesser nobles, the picture further east, in Saxony, shows more light and shadow, perhaps because the greater degree of economic autarchy in the more sparsely populated east helped noble households better to withstand the depression's effects. Hans von Honsperg of Klöden, for example, reported to the electoral Saxon treasury in 1474 that his incomes barely met household expenses. For cloth alone he allotted annually the equivalent of 41,700 kg of rye, half for himself, a third for his wife, and the rest for his daughters. This was less than half the limit (100,000 kg of rye) that Regensburg's sumptuary law placed on the price of a single dress for a burgher's wife or daughter. Burghers often lived far better than country gentlemen did, and not only in the east. In 1519 Lucas Rem of Augsburg, for example, spent half again as much (991 fl.) on a single wedding as the Swabian knight Werner von Zimmern had paid (650 fl.) in 1453 for an entire village.[38]

There are none the less signs of modest if rough prosperity in the (self-assessed) tax returns of the Saxon nobles in 1474. Seiffard von Lüttichau, lord of Kmehlen on the Bohemian–Lusatian border, for example, described his considerable household: wife, daughter, four sons, two squires, secretary, bailiff, watchman, carpenter, lady's maid, cook, children's nanny, and others – a total of twenty-four persons.[39] This junker was also lord of five villages, perhaps 1,000 souls, from whose rents he and his folk lived roughly but well – his inventory includes spices, figs, almonds, and raisins – though he complained that his barns and fish-ponds lay in ruins.

Guild

Just as the lineage cushioned the noble household, the guild shielded the burgher household against the shocks of the late medieval age of crisis. Trade and manufacturing, the late medieval German city's most important economic functions, were managed, trade partly and manufacturing almost entirely, through corporations called 'guilds'.[40] It is customary to distinguish between two types of guild, the older merchants' guild (*Gilde*), which went back to eleventh-century antecedents and was chiefly a north German form, and the newer artisans' and shopkeepers' guild (*Zunft*), which emerged in south Germany around 1200 and slowly spread northward. The many names – *Gilde* and *Amt* in north Germany, *Innung* in central Germany, *Zeche* in Austria, Bavaria, Bohemia, Moravia, and Silesia, and *Zunft* in south Germany – all refer to an institution which, in Otto von Gierke's words, 'combined religious, social, moral, private, and political goals'.[41] A community of fortune of persons having common economic and social interests, the guild regulated their work, represented and defended their liberties, managed their spiritual lives and social welfare, and, in many cities, shared in the governance of the city.[42] The guild consisted of three overlapping communities. First, it was an economic association which possessed an exclusive right to conduct a trade or trades and jurisdiction over all aspects of the trades, which was exercised by a guildmaster (*Zunftmeister*) and guild court (*Schöffen, Sechser, Zwölfer*). Secondly, the guild was a religious confraternity (*Seelzunft*), which assumed religious obligations, managed burials, and marked the anniversaries of deaths (*Jahrzeiten*), and to which a good many outsiders, including clergy, might belong. Thirdly, the guild maintained a social club (*Stube, Gesellschaft*), often separate from its headquarters as a trade association (*Laube*). Guilds also varied greatly in size, from a dozen or so masters in the small towns of south-western Germany to 300 weavers at Frankfurt in 1387 and 700 gardeners at Strasbourg around 1500.

Like the household, the guild was thus both an economic and a social institution. Just as the household was a unit of co-residence and production supplemented by literal kinship relations, the guild was an association of producers and sellers supplemented by religious and social relations of fictive or spiritual kinship. The economic core of the guild was monopoly (*Zunftzwang*), which bound to guild membership the right to exercise a trade and access to the civic market, the control of production processes and the quality of products, and limitation of production to specific places – notably not the countryside.

Only master artisans, traders, merchants, and shopkeepers could be full members of an urban guild, though journeymen and apprentices enjoyed a kind of passive membership and shared the guild's protection. Admission to a guild depended on ability to demonstrate free, legitimate, and honourable birth, performance of an apprenticeship and journeymanship (2–8 years, though 2–4 years was normal), a probation period (1–3 years), and, since the early fourteenth century, execution of a masterwork. New guildsmen had normally to become citizens (*Bürgerrecht*), to pay a fee (*Zunftkauf*), and either to furnish arms for militia service or to pay a fee (*Harnischgeld*). Such was the model guild in its classic, south German form between the fourteenth and the sixteenth centuries. While in the south the guilds tended to become subsidiary corporations of the urban communes, giving the masters political voice and weight, over most of northern Germany and in a few southern towns, notably Nuremberg, the older mercantile elites maintained their political monopolies.

The number of a city's guilds was determined not by the number of its trades but through political negotiation: 15 at Basel, 13 at Zurich, 28 (later 20) at Strasbourg, 7 at Überlingen, 17 at Ulm, 12 at Magdeburg, 16 at Danzig, and 50 at Lübeck. The number of crafts, on the other hand, underwent an explosive increase during the later middle ages. There were 148 trades in 1378 and 191 in 1440 at Frankfurt am Main, and 206 at Erfurt around 1500. Frankfurt had 32 metalworking trades alone, while Nuremberg had more than 40 trades, and by 1420 more than 500 masters worked in the iron branch there. Hamburg had 457 brewers in 1376; Cologne 200 weavers around 1400.[43] Specialization and strict control of quality brought some German products to high reputation by the fifteenth century, such as Constance's linens, Nuremberg's metalwares, Augsburg's and Ulm's fustians, and Solingen's knives. This soaring reputation of German craftsmen tends to hide the parallel growth of the humbler service and victualling trades, whose numbers reached astonishing levels for such small populations: 71 butchers at Nuremberg (1363), 116 at Lübeck (c.1370), 109 at Basel (1451), and 75 at Frankfurt am Main (1481); 187 brewers at Lübeck (1407), 182 at Wismar (1464), 378 at Danzig (1416), and 457 at Hamburg (1378).[44]

These figures suggest the degree to which the urban common good (*gemeiner Nutz*) depended on the prosperity and discipline of its artisanate which bore the main brunt of civic taxation. The inculcation and enforcement of this discipline fell to the guilds, for

> with the objective norms of craft and status (*Stand*) went a strict moral code, which demanded exemplary moral conduct from the entire households – master, wife, journeymen, and apprentices – both at work and in social intercourse. The code forbade them to associate

at home or in public with persons of evil reputation and provided the norms for their way of life in all matters, including how they dressed and ate. The guild encased (*überformte*) family and household.[45]

The guild, from this point of view, was the middle instance in the hierarchy of household, guilds, and commune.

From another point of view the guild looked like a federation of households formed to serve common economic, social and religious needs. It did so, in part, by closing off access to work and markets to non-members. This is clearest in its economic functions the cartel-like character of which has been subject to a very long debate.[46] Guilds restricted the sizes of shops (one or two journeymen was usual), the rights to practise a craft or sell manufactured goods, and access to raw materials, and they engaged in many kinds of price-fixing. During the fifteenth century, too, guilds and regulated crafts began to restrict the numbers of masters: Nuremberg set a limit of 12 master bronzesmiths, while Hamburg reduced the master coopers from 200 in 1437 to 150 in 1458 and 120 in 1501. These acts were exclusions, but even more exclusionary were the restrictions on males who had no households and on women, whether heads of households or not.

Domestic servants, apprentices, and journeymen made up the bulk of the urban working poor, who lacked the independence to form households and economically belonged to the have-nots (*habenitse*).[47] These servants (*Knechte*), who worked for wages and keep, made up about a quarter (22–28 per cent) of the populations of fifteenth century cities. Many of them were domestic servants, who served in every urban household of substance and belonged to its inner core. They might well be persons of respect – in 1441 and again in 1459, 'our maid, Grete', stood godmother to sons of Augsburg's Jakob Fugger[48] – but their disability lay in that, while in service, they could not form households of their own.

One type of servant, the journeyman, had no household of his own, though he could hope to form one as a master. Journeymen – apprenticeship became a distinct status only in the fourteenth century – worked under masters for a fixed term, most commonly six months, of service (*Dienst*), and despite their English name (the German *Geselle* has no such connotation), the requirement to travel began to appear only in the mid-fifteenth century and did not become general until around 1600. During the fifteenth century, the guilds began to regulate wages (*Lidlon*), work hours – 8–16 hours for an average of 11–12 hours per day, about 256 days per year minus free ('blue') Mondays – and other conditions. The journeyman's nominal wage – a third to a half in cash – often remained fixed for very long periods, even in the face of great price fluctuations, as at Frankfurt am Main, for example, where construction workers were paid at the same weekly rate from about 1350 until 1553.

The guilds supervised journeymen in part to reduce competition for their labour and in part to counter their own corporate activity, for the journeymen called themselves 'comrades' (*Geselle*, from *Saalgenosse*) and organized in imitation of the masters with whom they worked very closely – rarely more than two journeymen per shop in the Rhenish cities. Such journeymen's guilds (*Knechtzünfte*) began to appear in the Upper Rhenish cities, especially among the weavers, and flourished from about 1350 until about 1410 – the period of rising real wages. The journeymen also formed regional and sometimes transregional brotherhoods with rules, treasuries, assemblies, courts, and religious activities. The journeyman bakers of Strasbourg and Freiburg even built and maintained their own chapels in the civic hospitals. They also staged strikes, the first by journeyman belt-makers at Breslau in 1329 and the most spectacular in 1470 by Strasbourg's journeyman furriers, who decamped to Haguenau and called out their comrades all through the region. Gradually, however, the masters, allied to the communes, harnessed the journeymen to the allied structures of commune, guild, and household and undermined their ability to organize and bargain, and by the mid-fifteenth century they worked under a single set of regulations from northern Switzerland to Cologne.

The journeyman was at least potentially a full-fledged master; the working woman was usually not. The role of gender in the interplay of household and guild was complicated. The city depended on women's work and working women, both within the household and outside it.[49] Women worked in retail trades in all cities. At Nuremberg, for example, women worked as tailors, shopkeepers, money-changers, and innkeepers; Speyer recognized 'women merchants' (*koufmennine, koufvrouwe, institutrices*); Lübeck allowed a female shopkeeper (*cremersche*) to continue her work after marrying a guildsman; women belonged to the confraternity of the iron-mongers at Trier in 1285; and women made up more than half (27 of 52) of the retail grocers (*Gremper*) in a Strasbourg list of the fifteenth century.[50]

Women also worked in shops as artisans, sometimes as masters. At Lübeck female masters (*sulvesvrouwen*) were active in many crafts; at Strasbourg around 1430, 25 women were members of the cloth guild (*Tucherzunft*), and in 1484 the guild ordered that the guild's women (*frowenspersone*) should perform all duties of a guild member with the exception of the city watch; and at Basel in the late thirteenth century, women were active in several trades, including the plasterers and the coopers.[51] Many guilds recognized the 'widow's right' to continue her husband's shop, though sometimes only to complete current work. The role of women in a given branch varied enormously, even in neighbouring regions. It was very important in the draperies of Douai in Flanders, far less so in those of Lier in Brabant.[52]

A special case is presented by late medieval Cologne, where the role of women in guilds assumed an unprecedented and unmatched proportion. A few of Cologne's guilds – tailors, harness-makers, cloth-cutters – discriminated against women, but many others did not, including the needle-makers, purse-makers, furriers, sash-makers, and weavers of linen, fustians, and woollens, as well as the butchers. And in Cologne, alone in the German-speaking world, women artisans formed their own guilds of yarn-makers, gold-spinners, and silk-weavers. The last-named counted between 1437 and 1504 a total of 116 masters and 765 apprentices.[53]

The entire development of women's participation in retail sales, crafts, and the corresponding guilds reflected the economic realities of rising wages, and rising prices for manufactured goods.[54] Against it stood the feelings represented by the ideal of the burgher's household, a closed and secure unit represented to the outside world of guild and commune by its male head. In effect, in the burgher's world all social roles were, in the last analysis, gendered roles, and when the economic trends changed after 1450 with the recovery of populations and prices, such views began to make themselves felt in a new way.[55] Gradually, as work became scarcer and cheaper, and access to the guilds' privileges correspondingly more valuable, women were pushed out of many trades and lost their rights in many guilds. The beginnings of this process, most of which belongs to the succeeding, early modern era, can be detected in the fifteenth century.[56] At Frankfurt, for example, where nine of the twenty guilds and brotherhoods had had provisions for women in the fourteenth century, only three of them did so after 1500. Women continued to perform 'women's work', such as the needle trades, midwifery, and certain kinds of baking, but their day as active participants in the corporate economic and social institutions of the German-speaking cities was past.[57] The location of the limits to which late medieval economic reality stretched attitudes about work and gender is illustrated by the near-total absence of women from the institutions that drove large-scale and long-distance economic operations, firms, and mining syndicates.

Firm

Many kinds of economic operations in the late medieval Empire – long-distance trade and banking, mining operations, and certain other branches, such as printing – were conducted not by corporate associations of producers or sellers but by entrepreneurs operating by means of what is here called a 'firm'.[58] Varieties of firms in the late medieval Empire did all long-distance trade and most banking. Along the roads – the great constrictor of trade – and rivers and across the northern seas, the German merchants transported goods produced and consumed by the Empire's peoples. Their two most important networks connected the Hanseatic merchants to the trade of the North and Baltic seas and the southern cities' merchants to the trade of the Mediterranean basin.[59]

The two chief zones of German trade evolved quite different institutions. Hanseatic firms were small – two to four partners – and formed for a short term – usually a single venture. The Lübecker Hermann Mornewech, for example, formed or renewed eighteen different firms between 1323 and 1335. This practice, plus the assembly of capital from wide circles, including rural nobles, clergymen, and even harbour workers, spread the northern trade's high risks. So did the Hanseatic merchants' custom of avoiding specialization in trade. Their operations were protected by a vast economic and military federation of cities, the Hansa itself, which from its centre at Lübeck stretched out its two wings in the Baltic and North Seas to protect its merchants' trade along the axis Novgorod–Reval–Visby–Lübeck–Hamburg–Bruges–London. Westward flowed the wax, timber, rye, fish, copper, and furs; eastward went salt, cloth, and other manufactures; and along both wings flowed German beer. Although by the fifteenth century the Germans began to feel the challenge to which they would later succumb, from the Hollanders, until the end of the later middle ages the Hanseatic League remained cock of the north, so powerful that it made war on Denmark (1426–35), the Netherlands (1438–41), and England (1470–74).

The contrast between Hanseatic and southern merchants' practices has been characterized thus: 'the Hanseatic merchant had businesses, the South German merchant had a business.'[60] The southerners founded powerful, long-lasting firms, often around a single family, in which the principal partners supplied both capital and management skills, for an average of four to six years, often renewed. The evolution of the southern firms is illustrated by the Great Ravensburg Company, established by three Swabian merchant families in 1380, which from its headquarters around Lake Constance strove to monopolize the linen trade through thirteen offices scattered from Ravensburg to Barcelona. At its height the company had partners from 121 families, all burghers of free cities, and 117,000 fl. in working capital. Whereas the Ravensburg company was run by a troika of partners and avoided banking, Jakob Fugger (1459–1525) ran his family-based firm, pursued both trade and finance, and over the years 1484 to 1524 made 15–20 per cent per year to the Ravensburgers' 7.5 per cent. By 1510, when his firm was worth about 245,000 fl., he had surpassed the Ravensburgers for good.

Although the south German merchants never dominated the trade of any land outside the Empire, they operated all through the area bounded by the line Rome–Seville–Lisbon–Toulouse–Paris–Antwerp–London–Lübeck–Cracow–Lvov/Lemberg–Constantinople. The Nuremberg firms, which since 1350 operated in all sectors, formed true economic conglomerates, combining long-distance trade in goods, large manufacturing enterprises, and mining operations with banking and the trade in offices and regalian rights. Nurembergers pioneered in all areas and all branches from the early fourteenth century, only to be overhauled after 1470 in certain sectors by

Augsburg firms. Like the Nurembergers under the Luxemburg dynasty in the fourteenth century, the Fuggers and lesser Augsburg firms bound their destinies to the Habsburg dynasty at the end of the fifteenth. A deposit of 300,000 fl. – two-and-a-half times the Ravensburg Company's entire capitalization – by Bishop Melchior von Meckau of Brixen (Bressanone) suggests the scale on which they operated. The firms spread the techniques they learned from others, chiefly the Italians, such as double-entry book-keeping (introduced by Praun and Tucher of Nuremberg in 1476–84) and the bill of exchange. From the early 1400s onwards the Nurembergers, and later the Fuggers, codified their knowledge in books modelled on Francesco Balducci Pegolotti's *La Practica della mercatura* (1337–40).

Despite the spread of guilds, there were always some branches in which production could be and was organized by merchant-investors. The handiest instrument for such situations was the *Verlag*, a term which comes from the verb *vorlegen* in the sense of 'to extend credit'.[61] The investor, usually a large merchant or a firm, extended credit in cash (*Geldverlag*) or materials and tools (*Gezeugverlag*) to the producers in return for an exclusive right to buy the products at a fixed price. This system was suited to branches, such as mining, in which the producers themselves could no longer raise the amounts of capital they required. It was also a powerful instrument for the extension of urban economic power over the hinterland and for co-ordinating whole regions' economies with those of large cities.[62] Versions of it achieved great prominence in the new, or newly reorganized, industries of the later fifteenth century, notably mining and printing.

During the later fifteenth century, mining in the Empire expanded from a subsidiary branch conducted by small, part-time producers, such as the *Eisenbauern* of Styria and Carinthia, into what became by 1500 the greatest industrial branch in Europe.[63] The major watershed came in the second half of the fifteenth century when Central Europe witnessed an explosion of mineral production, largely because of technological improvements in drilling, drainage, and ventilation, which permitted the exploitation of previously untappable gold, silver, and copper deposits in the Saxon-Bohemian Erzgebirge, in the alpine regions of the Tyrol, Styria, and Carinthia, and in Upper Hungary. The scale of this upsurge may be suggested by what happened in Salzburg's Gastein valley, a silver region, the population of which rose from c.1,800 in 1456 to c.3,000 in 1497 to 5,000 (of whom 1,200 were miners) in the following century. In the Tyrol, the greatest mining region in Europe, by the early sixteenth century the industry employed perhaps a quarter of the entire population.

Three aspects of the mining boom provided special opportunities to urban firms. First, the mines and smelters required capital far in excess of what could be raised by the syndicates of miners or supplied by any other local source. Secondly, the regalian right to mine, in the Empire a prerogative of princes, suggested a partnership between mining princes and urban firms to exploit mines, smelters, and metal markets to mutual advantage. And thirdly, the mines, the chief form of rural industry, lay far beyond the reach of the urban guilds, which strove with might and main to crush every shoot of rural industry.[64] These factors, plus the tremendous demand for metals, made mining an ideal sector for the operations of firms.[65]

The Nurembergers again led the way, having gained control of the Carpathian metals trade as early as 1396–1412. Around 1450 they began to invest in the first modern smelters (*Saigerhütten*) in Thuringia, and in 1478 investors from Nuremberg, Bautzen, and Cracow (Jan Thurzo) nego- tiated a half-interest in the Goslar mining district called *Trostenfahrt* in return for the erection of a modern smelter. They were also heavily involved in exploiting the Saxon silver bonanzas of the Erzgebirge at Annaberg and Schneeberg. Once the capitalists gained access to the mines through agree- ments with the princes, they got control by buying up shares (*Kuxen*) in the highly fragmented mining syndicates (*Gewerke*). The operation was then tied together by contracts (*Käufe*), paid in advance, for deliveries of metals to the princes. In effect, the developments since 1470 enabled princes and investors to exploit the ore deposits, and the miners, on a scale unknown to the old, co-operative mining syndicates.

The system worked much the same way in the great mines of the Tyrol, where silver production tripled and copper more than doubled between 1470 and 1520.[66] Starting at Villach in Carinthia in 1495, the Fuggers of Augsburg gained a dominant position in Europe's greatest mining region. They organized the production and sale of metals and held a monopoly of the import of foodstuffs, in return for which they lent huge sums to Emperor Maximilian I (r.1493–1519), who owed them and other Augsburgers about 6,000,000 fl. at his death in 1519.[67]

New methods or machinery sometimes favoured exploitation by firms rather than by guilds. The rising cost of wages in the later middle ages made labour-saving devices, such as the silk-spinning mill, which Walter Kesinger brought from Lucca to Cologne in 1412/13, all the more desirable.[68] One such new process that well suited the institution of the firm was printing with movable type, which emerged during the 1450s in the firm which Johann Gutenberg (Gensfleisch) of Mainz had organised in 1448. The branch's profit depended on using relatively cheap raw materials – paper cost a third of parchment – and the relatively high literacy of the German burghers, and soon printed books cost about a fifth as much as manuscripts. Under these conditions, printing firms spread through the Empire during the second half of the fifteenth century, until by 1500 about 300 presses were operating in about 65 cities. Of the 450 known printers of this era, very few came from the older crafts, but more than 100 were university men, many of them clergymen. Almost all the printers were investors, organizers, and managers of their firms, though few became rich from the trade. The greatest of them, Anton Koberger of Nuremberg, is said to have employed 100 employees working 25 presses.

Around 1500, on the eve of the early modern era, it might have seemed as if the firms were taking over the world. This was certainly the impression conveyed by the anti-monopoly movement of the 1520s, and it was certainly fostered by theologians such as Johann Geiler von Kaysersberg (1445–1510), who defended the corporatist ethic from his pulpit in Strasbourg's cathedral:

> The Holy Sacrament should be refused those who buy as cheaply as possible and those who sell as dearly as possible . . . for this is against brotherly love. You should add a modest profit, also your trouble and effort, but to buy as cheaply and sell as dearly as you can, that is false![69]

In fact, around 1500 the corporate way of life was enjoying the last phase of its golden age. It was partly protected by the fact that it had evolved from its economic base a socio-political institution well suited to the management of small social orders through the coordination of households and, in the cities, guilds. This institution was the commune.

Commune

The commune (*Gemeinde*), a sworn association of heads of household for the purposes of governance – the defence of homes and rights, the management of everyday life, the provision of justice, and representation to the outside world – arose from origins in the thirteenth century to become the most characteristic social institution of the common people in the late medieval Empire. The comparability of rural and urban communes is now widely accepted.[70] There were important differences, but their basis, the contrast between agriculture and trade and manufacturing, was not great. More than two-thirds (67.1 per cent) of the Empire's cities were either small agricultural towns (*Ackerbürgerstädte*) or contained at least some farmers, and in some rich regions, notably Alsace, large numbers of urban guildsmen were actually engaged in some form of agriculture.[71] Whether in the town or in the village, the commune was an oath-bound association, admission to which depended on the possession of a farm or a house; its assembly possessed the power to form statutes (*Satzungen, Weistümer*) for the purposes of securing justice and regulating the use of common property. The commune's decisive norm was the common good, service to which was binding on all members. Neither in the village nor in the town did the commune include, even by inference (as it did women and children), all residents, nor was it ever a purely associative institution.

Even where, as in the imperial free cities, the lord's authority disappeared, the commune evolved a city council as a governing institution, which soon began to consider itself a 'ruler' (*Obrigkeit*) and the citizens its 'subjects' (*Untertanen*).[72] From its origins in the thirteenth century, the German urban communal regime developed into a fully-fledged city-state with council (Rat), town clerk (*Stadtschreiber, Ratschreiber*), and attorney (*Consulent, Syndicus*), judicial functions, taxation, military organization, and welfare institutions.[73] It may be argued that these communes and their regimes were primarily political rather than social or economic, but, in truth, in these milieux such distinctions are not very helpful. The commune and its regime were both social and economic institutions, because there were no boundaries between private and public life in the towns, and the civic regime, like the guild regime, reached its fingers into every aspect of the burghers' economic and social lives. The burgher's government dealt with war and peace, assaults and insults, fashion and finance, goods and services, bread and wine, taverns and brothels, beggars and bishops, clothing and trash, and marriage, birth, and death.[74]

In some sectors, the late medieval communal regimes did not just manage, they pioneered, and in none more notably than in finance. Urban regimes managed by merchants and other burghers practically invented the entire foundations of finance and banking in the Empire. They adapted to this purpose their favourite instrument, annuities (*Renten*), for which the purchaser deposited a fixed sum in return for a guaranteed annual income. Originally 'perpetual' (*ewig*), that is, non-redeemable, in the fourteenth century annuities generally became negotiable and redeemable, and perpetual ones were commonly forbidden (1240 in Lübeck, 1360 in Vienna, 1439 in Frankfurt). For small folk the annuity was the most popular form of social insurance, especially after the introduction of life annuities (*census vitalitius, Leibgedinge*), i.e. annuities paid only for the life of the purchaser, on which the interest gradually fell from 12–15 per cent to a standard 5 per cent at the end of the fifteenth century. The sale of annuities drew very large sums from private hands toward public purposes. Lübeck's Castorp brothers, for example, around 1490 held civic debt to the sum of 30,000 Lübeck pounds. The inability to redeem such debts led to the continuing need to service them. At Basel, for example, service on the public debt rose from around 2 per cent of total civic outlay in the 1360s to over 50 per cent by the 1430s, and remained above 30 per cent for most of the rest of the century.[75] The communal regime was indeed an organ of justice and governance, but it was also the foremost urban economic institution.

The late medieval German urban communes exhibit many variations in their histories and shapes. There were many intermediate phases between the first consular regimes around 1200 (Utrecht, 1196; Lübeck, 1201; Cologne, 1216) and the full-blown southern guild regimes of the fourteenth and fifteenth centuries, just as there were many urban communes which never gained full autonomy, for example, the many towns of the German east which were endowed by the princes with some rights of self-govern-ment.[76] The late medieval phase of urban development none the less possessed its own characteristic signatures. The first was the conjuncture, collision, and collaboration of the communal development, on the one side, and the rise of the guilds, on the other. This process, which drew strength from the appreciation of the value of human labour during the depression, gave the economic and social weight of the middle – the bulge in the onion – political weight and voice.[77]

Civic struggles – another name for guild revolts[78] – produced typical guild-based constitutions at Strasbourg in 1334, Zurich in 1336, Augsburg in 1352/68, Braunschweig in 1374, Lübeck in 1380/84, Cologne in 1396, Hamburg in 1484.[79] Often the guilds won and held a substantial share of civic offices – one-half at Ulm, two-thirds at Strasbourg, and, briefly, all at Basel – but elsewhere their bid for sharing power was beaten back by the older elites. At Lübeck, for example, a city ruled by the merchants, the guilds (*Ämter*) lost their independent jurisdiction in 1384 and functioned only as reporting bodies (*Ruginstanz*) for the civic regime, while from around 1400 the guilds of Danzig, Stendal, and Hamburg were allowed to meet only in the presence of two councillors. Over much of north Germany, indeed, though not at Cologne, the guilds remained regulated crafts, closely supervised by a non-guild ruling group. The most notorious example of this outcome in south Germany was at Nuremberg, where the mercantile elite crushed the guilds with the emperor's aid in 1348; thereafter the city knew only various types of regulated crafts (*Handwerke*).

Where the guilds did gain direct access to communal government, it did not mean that artisans as such ruled the towns. Plain artisans did sit in the council chambers of many (especially southern) German towns during the later middle ages, but the ominous gap between their economic needs and the onerous but poorly remunerated civic offices tended to keep the main weight of civic business in the hands of the well-to-do, who in the Upper Swabian towns were called 'men of leisure' (*Müßiggänger*).[80] This tendency, plus the growing complication and tempo of civic business, stimulated a pronounced trend toward oligarchy – more offices in the hands of fewer, richer families – and sometime around 1450 came the watershed between an age of devolution of political voice to the guildsmen and an age of its re-concentration in the hands of the noble and mercantile elites.[81] Gradually, the great age of popular activism in the towns came to a close – Maschke counted 170 disturbances between 1301 and 1520 – as the economic recovery and falling real wages reinforced the oligarchical trend and made the guild towns more and more like Nuremberg, where, as Dr Christoph Scheurl noted in 1516, 'the common folk [*das gemain völklein*] have no authority, as they properly should have none, for all authority comes from God, and gover-nance is granted to only those few who are specially gifted by the special wisdom of Him who created nature and all things.'[82]

The history of rural communes in the late medieval Empire displays great variations.[83] In general, it is recognized that the commune (*Gemeinde*), as a sworn association of the principal male householders of a village, took shape in the space left by the disintegration of the primary economic and social unit of the preceding era, the manor. Like its urban counterpart, the rural commune was older than the economic crisis that set in after 1300, though it acquired its classic form only gradually, in the depression's wake, as rights of local governance associated with the manor disintegrated into separable and often separate components – landlordship (*Grundherrschaft*), mastery of serfs (*Leibherrschaft*), and judicial authority (*Gerichtsherrschaft*).[84] The process, which occurred earlier in the other settled areas of Germany than east of the Elbe, created a new space for the rural commune.

The typical rural commune was a sworn corporate association of households, each represented by its adult male householder – communal government was almost exclusively a male affair – and presided over by a mayor (*Schultheiß*) and a village court (*scabini, jurati, Schöffen, échevins*) of six, eight, or twelve men. This body co-operated with, rivalled, and sometimes superseded the nobles' local governance, especially where property rights and territorial government were greatly fragmented. At Ebersmünster in Lower Alsace, for example, the abbot as both seignieur and landlord nominated the village mayor, while at Hüningen, which belonged to the abbot of St Alban in Basel, the village elected its administrator (*Meier*), who assessed taxes with the aid of four or six full farmers (*Huber*).[85] Here, as elsewhere in southern Germany, the general tendency during the later middle ages was for local rule to pass from seignieurial into communal hands.

No general notion of liberty, but only 'specific and precise rights', underlay this intensely local development.[86] There did arise a notion, however, that somehow things were out of joint on the land, or, as the Strasbourg merchant and mystic Rudolf Merswin (1307–82) put it, 'the peasants in these villages live like animals, lacking all fear of God, and they have become wicked and quite proud, and are of quite perverse mien'.[87] Where feudal governance was weak, they became truly obstreperous, as rural federations combined into permanent, sworn associations to pacify and defend the countryside. In the Swiss forest cantons, the Graubünden, and the Valais, mature political federations developed on a communal basis, and unsuccessful attempts to 'turn Swiss' in this sense erupted in Vorarlberg, the Tyrol, the Swabian Allgäu, and the belt of lands from Lake Constance west to Alsace during the fifteenth century.[88] If they did not succeed in imitating their Swiss neighbours, at least they were able to push their ways into established territorial diets (*Landschaften*).[89] This occurred chiefly in the Empire's southern belt, which was also the main theatre of the sixty or so rural revolts between 1336 and 1525.[90]

One important cause of rural revolts, which often were organized by communes, arose from their lords' efforts to recover what the agrarian crisis had taken. One way to do this was to retain labour on the land by offering very favourable terms, as the prince-bishop of Augsburg did at Pfronten in the Allgäu in 1403, or heritability of tenures, as the provost of Berchtesgaden did in 1377.[91] Another was to reinforce servile customs: some south German abbots demanded that their serfs swear, on pain of a heavy fine, never to leave the land.[92] Harsher yet, since around 1400 some south German lords began to restore full servility by revoking the rights to free mobility and to free choice of guardian or marriage partner.[93] It was partly this temporary reversion to serfdom that lay behind the Upper Swabian rebels' complaint in 1525 that serfdom 'is pitiable, given that Christ has purchased and redeemed us with his precious blood, the shepherd the same as the Emperor'.[94]

In the southern lands, this relapse into servility did not succeed in either quashing the rural communes or keeping them out of the territorial parliaments.[95] East of the Elbe, however, a very different story unfolded. The rural communes of the eastern lands harked back to the Netherlands and the Weser and Elbe marshes, whence their founders had migrated.[96] As in Old Germany, the communes formed, often under very favourable circumstances, during the age of German-speaking colonization, which the Black Death brought to an end. Yet, in some parts of the east, notably in East Prussia, the rural communes continued to expand their competencies until well into the fifteenth century.[97] For a number of reasons, however, such as ethnic diversity in the villages, expansion of urban power, and the late and deep effects of the depression, the rural communes of the east never gained political representation in the territorial parliaments, leaving the rural folk open to a solution to the labour problem from above. Although the agrarian depression may not have caused the east Elbian 'second serfdom' of the early modern era, its deep and late inroads on rural economies surely weakened the peasants' abilities to defend their liberties.[98] Nothing shows more clearly the importance of circumstances than the dramatically different fates of the farming folk in the two zones of the German-speaking world.

Others

The explosive development of corporate forms among the Empire's common people – household–guild–commune in the towns, household–commune on the land – is one of the most remarkable aspects of late medieval German history. It led, as Italian observers of the German towns noted, to levels of popular politics known nowhere else in Europe.[99] So intense was the corporate process in the towns, indeed, that the 'commonalty' (*Gemeinheit*) of all householders 'sometimes emerges as a legitimate political category, distinct from the traditional patriciate on the one hand, and the "brotherhood" of the guilds on the other'.

The cities contained, however, groups of persons whose way of life drew them away from this corporate order, either because they were drawn toward different social spheres, where different values reigned, or because the corporate order itself excluded them. The first possibility applies to the urban patricians.[100] Whether their origins were purely mercantile, as at Lübeck and Hamburg, largely noble and ministerial, as at Metz, or mixed noble and mercantile, as at Strasbourg, Ulm, Augsburg, and Nuremberg, their common ethos was the desire for 'honour', that is, for the respect and prestige claimed by who lived nobly. The Strasbourgeois Hans Armbruster spoke for them all about 1477: 'Whom God has granted riches, also wants honour.'[101] 'Honour' in the noble sense meant living nobly, that is, without work; it meant the expansion of a sense of family from the household to the lineage; it meant dress, manners, and recreation – such as jousting – which the common folk might enjoy but could not emulate. This honourable style of life attracted both the offspring of rural nobles, such as Nuremberg's Paumgartners, and those of merchants, such as Strasbourg's Wurmsers. At Hamburg and Freiburg im Breisgau, at Rostock and Frankfurt am Main, they bought land, rents, and castles, became seigniers, jousted with rural nobles, and sometimes married their daughters. Such men sat beside merchants and craftsmen in the town halls, but in their clubs – Lübeck's *Zirkelgesellschaft*, Lindau's *Sünfzen*, and Strasbourg's *Hohensteg* – they decided who was socially acceptable and who was not. The Nurembergers could speak freely in 1489 what the other patricians all thought, namely, that only he was an 'honourable and worthy man' (*ehrbar und bescheiden Mann*), 'who lives nobly and honestly, deals in nothing dishonourable, and pursues no craft' (*wer sich ehrbar und reddish hält, nichts Unehrbars handelt oder Handwerk treibt*).[102]

Those repelled by the corporate order included the unemployed, under-employed, and seasonally unemployed; fatherless families, poor widows and spinsters, orphans, and beggars, plus the itinerants (*fahrende Leute*) – lepers, gamblers, prostitutes, quack physicians, poor students, and unemployed soldiers – and the practitioners of 'dishonourable trade', such as cesspool cleaners, renderers, gravediggers, travelling players, and, universally, executioners, who plied 'the most dishonourable of the dishonourable professions'.[103] Their numbers are hard to grasp, though when Basel counted mouths in preparation for a siege in 1444, they reckoned the propertyless at 20–30 per cent of the city's population.[104] These truly poor were disproportionately female. At Strasbourg, when civic poor relief was established in 1523, a survey found that 69 per cent of the persons needing assistance were women, and that 79 per cent of the needy women (versus 21 per cent of the men) lived alone.[105] These poor, native (*Hausarmen*) and itinerant, lodged where they could in cellars, alleyways, and back courts, where 24.6 per cent of tax-paying Lübeckers lived in 1460.[106] They had special claim on the surplus that the church dispensed through hospitals (*Spitäler*) and poor-houses (*Almosen*), the most important of which was Cologne's great Hospital of the Holy Spirit, where 700 poor folk ate each day.[107]

Repelled, too, were the Jews. Once eligible for citizenship on the same basis as Christians, savage persecutions at the time of the Black Death pushed them into countryside and the shadows, from which they did not re-emerge for nearly four centuries. The late medieval diaspora brought Jews into about 500 places where no previous settlement is known, leaving larger communities of 150 or more in only two dozen towns – all south of a line from Dortmund to Goslar to the Baltic sea coast.[108] With the destruction in 1519 of Regensburg's Jewry, in 1500 nearly 15 per cent of the city's residents, the disaster and the diaspora became complete.

One other group stood largely outside the new social and economic institutions associated with the corporate structure of household, guild, and commune. It was, oddly enough, the clergy. Oddly, because the regular clergy supplied the oldest public models for social organization on the basis of fraternity rather than kinship. Oddly, too, because the clergy, especially the mendicants, supplied the religious language for that order's justification, linking the idea of the common good – the foundation value of guilds and communes – to the Christian virtue of *caritas* (altruistic love).[109] As the new guild regime at Augsburg announced in 1368, it intended 'with God's help to ordain and establish all things in the best, safest and most Christian way'.[110]

The parish, the most common form of community in the Empire, represented medieval Christianity's most important adaptation to European conditions.[111] The parish's congregation formed a community and was so regarded throughout the middle ages, and pastor (*rector ecclesiae*) or his vicar (*vicarius*), who was responsible for its spiritual welfare and sacramental life, could be regarded either as his flock's leader or as its lord.[112] Thus dualism of associative and hierarchical features replicated the character of all other 'communal' institutions and was, therefore, in itself nothing provocative. Yet, as communal institutions grew denser in the later middle ages, external patronage, which meant the right to nominate priests and sometimes to collect the tithe, tended to grow more irksome. In the cities, where the number of parishes bore little relationship to the population's size – 28 at Erfurt, at least 20 at Cologne, 9 each at Strasbourg and Regensburg, 6 at Augsburg, 2 at Nuremberg, and only one at Frankfurt am Main, Bamberg, Freiburg im Breisgau, and Ulm – something could be done about patronage. The Ulmers, for example, in 1446 took pride in paying the immense sum of 25,000 fl. to the abbot of Reichenau for their church's patronage, thereby acquiring 'a higher stage of control over the church' than any other power in medieval Europe.[113] In the towns, too, the parishes competed with other churches, both in the urban skyline and for the citizens' hearts, and the major ecclesiastical towns, those 'German Romes', sprouted spires like barley fields: by 1350 Cologne had 11 collegiate chapters, 20 religious houses, 19 parishes, 24 autonomous and 20 other chapels, and 62 houses of *béguines* and *béghards*; and Erfurt, the most churched town in Central Europe, possessed 2 chapters, 22 monasteries, 23 other churches, 36 chapels, and 6 hospitals, plus 28 parishes.[114]

In the countryside things were quite different: the parish church was the only church, if the village were lucky enough to possess one, and the patronage rights of distant lords grew the more intrusive the firmer the local communal structure became. The range of patrons was immense. In Alsace they included nobles and commoners, monasteries and convents, and clerical corporations of every conceivable description.[115] The village communes tried to gain control over the patronage and the tithe of existing churches and, where none existed, to found and endow them with repatriated tithes.[116]

One aim of this 'communal reformation', the roots of which lay well back in the later middle ages, was to use the tithe to support the village poor.[117] This corresponded to the immense expansion of charitable institutions in the towns, often under clerical leadership or control – hospitals, poor-houses, orphanages, and schools.[118] Their rise was nourished by the ethos of spiritual kinship and fraternal love that formed the heart of popular Christianity, for 'the state of charity, meaning social integration, was the principal end of the Christian life, and any people that claimed to be Christian must embody it somehow, at some time, in this world'.[119] Charity, which involved both the living and the dead and aimed both at peace in this world and at eternal salvation in the next, lay behind the donations that jammed the churches with altars, retables, windows, tombs, tablets, and chapels, as the living endowed masses for the souls of their kin, natural and spiritual. The urban rich endowed by family, the middling folk by confraternity, a kind of 'consensual parish' that boomed in such cities as Lübeck (over 70) and Cologne (80) around 1350 and Hamburg (99) around 1520 – and sometimes grew to enormous size – 4,000 in Ulm's Rosary Confraternity (est. 1483).[120] Their charitable activities swelled the flow of prayers and wealth to the hospitals and poor-houses. Most of them drew their resources from donations of the burghers, such as Cologne's Dr Peter Rynck, who in 1500 left 4,300 marks to clothe and feed 'the poor foundlings, who are cared for as abandoned and unwanted children'.[121]

In this story of expansion, one point seems clear. The expanding institutions – confraternities, hospitals, and poor-houses – were all lay religious institutions, even when clerically led. The numbers of dioceses and deaneries (subdivisions of dioceses) remained fixed in their earlier sizes and configurations; collegiate churches did not grow in numbers or importance; and the patterns of monastic life changed very little, if at all.[122] Only one type of purely ecclesiastical institution did continue to grow during this age, rural parishes, but only in villages which for some reason – poverty, custom, or oversight – had hitherto lacked parishes of their own. Otherwise, while the later middle ages was very rich in new or newly prominent lay economic and social institutions, it was very poor in new clerical ones.[123]

Reflection on the fit between the older, clerical, or clerically led institutions and the newer or newly prominent lay corporate institutions sheds some light on this contrast. The archetypal form of clerical community, the monastery, was based on the separation of genders and communal property. The lay communities of the late medieval Empire, by contrast, were based on the co-ordination of genders and more exclusive forms of property peculiar to the household.[124] Here we seem to encounter a genuine divide, a difference not of religious belief but of moral sensibility, for the burghers and, perhaps, the peasants were coming to see the fulfilment of God's command in terms of a way of life based on labour structured both by age and by gender. The imperial church might in time have adjusted to this sensibility, and probably did so in many ways, but not enough and not swiftly enough. Its immobility stemmed partly from its incorporation, long ago, into the Empire's very structure, partly from its economic basis in an increasingly archaic institution, the benefice, and partly from its vulnerability to the imperial nobility's rapacious use of the church to soften the depression's worst effects.[125] Most of the upper nobles probably shared Emperor Frederick III's belief that 'what the priests own, belongs to our treasury' (*Pfaffengut ist unser Kammergut*).[126] When the clerical corporations responded successfully to the agrarian crisis, as they did in the diocese of Strasbourg, their very success fomented conflict with the laity provoked by clerical usury and clerical involvement in the trade in foodstuffs. Their wealth, in turn, drew many foreigners – Swabians, Bavarians, and Lorrainers – into the region, which also tended to estrange the laity from their clergy.[127]

The new anti-clericalism of the pre-Reformation decades arose partly from this growing unconformity between clerical social institutions and those of the laity, to which they had to some degree provided models and values. The burghers, and perhaps also the peasants, increasingly saw the world less as a family bound by ties of kinship and more as a household structured by the conservation of and transmission of property and by division of labour according to gender and age.[128] This new world valued service over mediation, instruction over ritual, and thrift over display.

One side of this nonconformity impressed Johann Geiler of Kaysersberg at Strasbourg. He sensed that the laity felt that 'we should take half of what the priests own. Why should they have so much property? They have too much.'[129] His answer was to try to teach the Strasbourgeois that the clergy returned spiritual goods for material ones, forming with the laity one vast division of spiritual and material labour. Geiler believed that the anti-clerical sentiments he commonly witnessed – 'You laymen, you hate us priests!' – flowed from the laity's incomprehension of this truth. He was half right. For another moral sentiment had emerged from the long evolution of lay society and its institutions over the later middle ages, from the first shadows on the medieval boom around 1300 through the Black Death in the late 1340s, the agrarian depression of the following century, and the quickening recovery after 1450. This strong, new sentiment, like most others, had long been taught by the clergy. It held that God intended men and women to live and work together.

Notes

1 *Vita Caroli quarti. Die Autobiographie Karls IV.*, ed. E. Hillenbrand, ch. 10, quoted by Hartmut Boockmann, *Stauferzeit und spätes Mittelalter. Deutschland 1125–1517* (Berlin, 1987), p. 228.

2 Quoted by Karl Brunner and Gerhard Jaritz, *Landherr, Bauer, Ackerknecht. Der Bauer im Mittelalter. Klischee und Wirklichkeit* (Vienna/Cologne/Graz, 1985), p. 121.

3 Frantisek Graus, *Pest–Geissler–Judenmorde. Das 14. Jahrhundert als Krisenzeit*, Veröffentlichungen der MPIG LXXXVI (Göttingen, 1987), p. 555.

4 On the agrarian cycle, the current state of knowledge is described by Thomas W. Robisheaux, 'The World of the Village', Thomas A. Brady, Jr, Heiko A. Oberman, and James D. Tracey, eds, *Handbook of European History, 1400–1600. Late Middle Ages, Renaissance, and Reformation* I (Leiden, 1994), pp. 79–112.

5 These figures are taken from Wilhelm Abel. Substantially lower ones (10 million and 7.5 million respectively) are given by Peter Moraw.

6 And, of course, the territorial state, which falls outside this chapter's scope.

7 Michael Mitterauer and Reinhard Sieder, *The European Family. Patriarchy to Partnership from the Middle Ages to the Present*, trans. Karla Oosterveen and Manfred Hörzinger (Chicago, 1982), p. 8; Erich Maschke, *Die Familie in der deutschen Stadt des späten Mittelalters*, Sitzungsberichte der Heidelberger Akademie der Wissenschaften, Phil.-hist. Klasse, Jahrgang 1980, no. 4 (Heidelberg, 1980), pp. 11–15. I agree with the reservations expressed by Mitterauer and Sieder (p. 9) about using the term 'the whole house' (*das ganze Haus*), for which see Otto Brunner, 'Das "ganze Haus" und die alteuropäische "Ökonomik"', in Brunner, *Neue Wege der Verfassungs- und Sozialgeschichte*, 2nd end (Göttingen, 1968), pp. 103–27 (originally published in 1958). A survey of the entire subject of household and family in a European context is Merry E. Wiesner, 'Family, Household, and Community', in Brady *et al.*, *Handbook of European History, 1400–1600* I, pp. 51–78.

8 Jan de Vries, 'Population', in Brady *et al.*, *Handbook of European History, 1400–1600* I, pp. 1–50.

9 I give the form used at Strasbourg, 'feuer und rauch halten', but there are many others.

10 Maschke, *Die deutsche Familie*, p. 11, based on the members of the 'Elenden-Bruderschaft', in Trier, 1437–65.

11 *Ibid.*, p. 33; Martha C. Howell, *Women, Production, and Patriarchy in Late Medieval Cities* (Chicago, 1986), pp. 9–46. For evidence of practice, see Erika Uitz, 'Zur gesellschaftlichen Stellung der Frau in der mittelalterlichen Stadt', *Magdeburger Beiträge zur Stadtgeschichte* I (1977), pp. 20–34, esp. the table after p. 34.

12 Maschke, *Die deutsche Familie*, p. 13; Brunner, 'Das "ganze Hause" und die alteuropäische "Ökonomik", pp. 42–3.

13 For the religious importance of spiritual kinship in late medieval religion, see John Bossy, *Christianity in the West, 1400–1700* (Oxford, 1985); and on the

family as a social metaphor in general, see Mitterauer and Sieder, *The European Family*, pp. 2–3.

14 Jack Goody, *The Development of the Family and Marriage in Europe* (Cambridge, 1983), p. 148. I do not mean to slight the importance of these restrictions, and Goody (p. 145) cites the example of the Imperial Recess of Mainz in 1439, which asked the church to reduce the prohibitions to the second degree.

15 Maschke, *Die deutsche Familie*, p. 15.

16 Ahasver von Brant, ed., *Regesten der Lübecker Bürgertestamente des Mittelalters*,Veröffentlichungen zur Geschichte der Hansestadt Lübeck, 18, 24 (2 vols Lübeck, 1964–73) II, p. 76, no. 535; pp. 26–7, no. 444; pp. 102–3, no. 587, here cited from Maschke, *Die deutsche Familie*, p. 18.

17 This document is evaluated in *Ibid.*, pp. 19–22. Maschke's treatment of this genre (pp. 19–30) suggests that the strong familial sense it documents does not yield much to the famous Florentine *ricordi*.

18 Walter Jacob, *Politische Führungsschicht und Reformation. Untersuchungen zur Reformation in Zürich 1519–1528*, Zürcher Beiträge zur Reformationsgeschichte I (Zurich, 1970), pp. 102–3.

19 Isenmann, *Die deutsche Stadt*, pp. 266–7.

20 Erich Maschke, 'Mittelschichten in deutschen Städten des Mittelalters', in Maschke, *Städte und Menschen. Beiträge zur Geschichte der Stadt, der Wirtschaft und Gesellschaft 1959–1977* (Wiesbaden, 1980), pp. 275–305.

21 David Warren Sabean, *Property, Production, and Family in Neckarhausen, 1700–1870* (Cambridge, 1990), p. 16.

22 Günther Franz, ed., *Quellen zur Geschichte des deutschen Bauernstandes im Mittelalter* (Darmstadt, 1974), p. 418, no. 186 (24 Feb. 1363).

23 John W. Cole and Eric R. Wolf, *The Hidden Frontier. Ecology and Ethnicity in an Alpine Valley* (New York, 1974), pp. 181–2, show that adjacent regions with similar ecologies but different inheritance systems could in fact emerge with farms of similar size, though they do not study typical farming landscapes.

24 The literature on the stem family in the eastern alpine lands centres on the early modern era, not the late medieval period. See Michael Mitterauer, 'Familiengroße – Familientypen – Familienzuklus', *GG* I (1975), pp. 235–55; Lutz Berkner, 'The Stem Family and the Developmental Cycle of the Peasant Household. An Eighteenth Century Example', *AHR* LXXVII (1972), pp. 398–418; idem, 'Inheritance, Land Tenure and Peasant Family Structure. A German Regional Comparison', in Jack Goody, Joan Thirsk, and E. P. Thompson, eds, *Family and Inheritance. Rural Society in Western Europe, 1200–1800* (Cambridge, 1976), pp. 71–95.

25 On the geography of inheritance, see Barthel Huppertz, *Räume und Schichten bäuerlicher Kulturformen in Deutschland. Ein Beitrag zur deutschen Bauerngeschichte* (Bonn, 1939), pp. 25–7, and map 1, who also describes (pp. 27–9) the debate about why some regions (especially the south-west) practised partibility and others impartibility and concludes that there are no environmental reasons for it.

26 Sabean, *Property, Production, and Family*, p. 15, who also suggests the impossibility of correlating family patterns with inheritance customs before the introduction of parish registers in the sixteenth century.

27 Wilhelm Abel, 'Landwirtschaft 1350–1500', in Hermann Aubin and Wolfgang Zorn, eds, *Handbuch der deutschen Wirtshafts- und Sozialgeschichte* I (Stuttgart, 1971), p. 303.

28 Wilhelm Abel, *Agrarian Fluctuations in Europe. From the Thirteenth to the Twentieth Centuries*, trans. Olive Ordish (New York, 1980), p. 79.

29 Peter Moraw, *Von offener Verfassung zu gestalteter Verdichtung. Das Reich*

im späten Mittelalter 1250 bis 1490 (Berlin, 1985), p. 89.

30 Wilhelm Abel, *Geschichte der deutschen Landwirtschaft vom frühen Mittelalter bis zum 19. Jahrhundert,* Deutsche Agrargeschichte II (Stuttgart, 1962), p. 132.

31 Quoted in *Ibid.,* p. 131, n. 1.

32 Rolf Kießling, *Die Stadt und ihr Land. Umlandpolitik, Bürgerbesitz und Wirtschaftsgefüge in Ostschwaben vom 14. bis ins 16. Jahrhundert,* Städteforschungen, series A, XXIX (Cologne/Vienna, 1989); Tom Scott, *Freiburg and the Breisgau. Town–Country Relations in the Age of Reformation and Peasants' War* (Oxford, 1986).

33 Hans-Peter Sattler, 'Die Ritterschaft der Ortenau in der spätmittelalterlichen Wirtschaftskrise', *Die Ortenau* XLII (1962), pp. 220–58; XLIV (1964), pp. 22–39; XLV (1965), pp. 32–57; XLVI (1966), pp. 32–58. The chapel, built at Neuweier in 1329, is noted in pt. II, vol. 44, p. 31.

34 K. O. Müller, 'Zur wirtschaftlichen Lage des schwäbischen Adels am Ausgang des Mittelalters', *ZWLG* III (1939), pp. 285–328, who found that two-thirds of the Swabian lesser nobility had annual incomes less than 200 fl., while only 2 per cent enjoyed incomes over 800 fl.

35 *Die Chronik der Grafen von Zimmern,* ed. Hansmartin Decker-Hauff and Rudolf Seigel (3 vols., Darmstadt, 1964–72) III. p. 72, II. 37–38: 'Christus het [in] das collegium, da sie nit dispensirt, nit angenomen werden megen.'

36 Peter Müller, *Die Herren von Fleckenstein im späten Mittelalter. Untersuchungen zur Geschichte eines Adelsgeschlechts im pfälzisch-elsässischen Grenzgebiet,* Geschichtliche Landeskunde XXXIV (Stuttgart, 1990). The Fleckensteins were the only Alsatian family that was able to found a miniature territorial state.

37 *Ibid.,* pp. 292–5.

38 Abel, *Agricultural Fluctuations,* p. 76; idem, *Geschichte der deutschen Landwirtschaft,* p. 129.

39 Franz, *Quellen,* pp. 570–5, no. 228, used by F. R. H. Du Boulay, *Germany in the Later Middle Ages* (London, 1983), pp. 73–4, 87, 174–6. This household, it may be noted, was larger than that of a dowager duchess in Hannoversch-Münden in 1397–8, which contained 20–30 persons; Wilhelm Abel, 'Neue Wege der handwerksgeschichtlichen Forschung', in Abel, ed., *Handwerksgeschichte in neuer Sicht,* Göttinger Beiträge zur Wirtschafts- und Sozialgeschichte I (Göttingen, 1978), pp. 1–25, here p. 11.

40 Fundamental is Eberhard Isenmann, *Die deutsche Stadt im Spätmittelalter 1250–1500. Stadtgestalt, Recht, Stadtregiment, Kirche, Gesellschaft, Wirtschaft* (Stuttgart, 1988), here pp. 299–319. See also Erich Maschke, 'Deutsche Städte am Ausgang des Mittelalters', in Maschke, *Städte und Menschen,* pp. 56–99.

41 Otto von Gierke, *Das deutsche Genossenschaftsrecht* (4 vols, Berlin; 1868–1913; repr. Graz, 1954) I, p. 228.

42 Isenmann, *Die deutsche Stadt,* pp. 315–19.

43 Rolf Sprandel, 'Gewerbe und Handel 1350–1500', in Aubin and Zorn, *Handbuch der deutschen Wirtschafts- und Sozialgeschichte,* I, pp. 335–6.

44 Isenmann, *Die deutsche Stadt,* pp. 342–3.

45 *Ibid.,* p. 312.

46 See Reinhard Ennen, *Zünfte und Wettbewerb. Möglichkeiten und Grenzen zünftlicherischer Wettbewerbsbeschränkungen im städtischen Handel und Gewerbe des Spätmittelalters,* Neue Wirtschaftgeschichte III (Cologne/Vienna, 1971).

47 Erich Maschke, 'Die Unterschichten in der mittelalterlichen Städte Deutschlands', in Maschke, *Städte und Menschen,* pp. 306–79.

48 Maschke, *Die deutsche Familie*, p. 48. This was Jakob the Elder (d. 1468), not his far more famous son, Jakob the Rich (1459–1525).

49 The following paragraphs are based on *Ibid.*, pp. 35–45; Isenmann, *Die deutsche Stadt*, pp. 314–15; Margarete Wensky, *Die Stellung der Frau in der stadtkölnischen Wirtschaft im Spätmittlalter* (Cologne, 1981); Martha C. Howell, *Women, Production, and Patriarchy in Late Medieval Cities* (Chicago, 1986); Merry E. Wiesner, *Working Women in Renaissance Germany* (New Brunswick, NJ, 1986). For the European context, see idem, *Women and Gender in Early Modern Europe* (Cambridge, 1993), pp. 102–6.

50 Maschke, *Die deutsche Familie*, pp. 36–7.

51 *Ibid.*, p. 37.

52 Howell, *Women, Production, and Patriarchy*, pp. 161–73.

53 Wensky, *Die Stellung der Frau*.

54 But probably not a permanent surplus of women in the cities. This widespread notion goes back to Karl Bücher; it is demolished by Kurt Wessoly, 'Die weibliche Bevölkerungsanteil in spätmittelalterlichen und frühneuzeitlichen Städten und die Betätigung von Frauen im zünftigen Handwerk (insbesondere am Mittel- und Oberrhein)', ZGO LXXXIX (1980), pp. 69–117.

55 See esp. Lyndal Roper, *The Holy Household. Women and Morals in Reformation Augsburg* (Oxford, 1989).

56 On this trend, see Heide Wunder, *'Er ist die Sonn, sie ist der Mond'. Frauen in der frühen Neuzeit* (Munich, 1992), pp. 120–5.

57 Wiesner, *Working Women in Renaissance Germany*.

58 John H. Munro, 'Patterns of Trade, Money, and Credit', in Brady *et al.*, *Handbook of European History, 1400–1600* I, pp. 147–96.

59 Based on Sprandel, 'Gewerbe und Handel 1350–1500', pp. 347–52; Isenmann, *Die deutsche Stadt*, pp. 358–80.

60 Jacob Strieder, *Studien zur Geschichte kapitalistischer Organisationsformen. Monopole, Kartelle und Aktiengesellschaften im Mittelalter und zu Beginn der Neuzeit*, 2nd edn (Munich/Leipzig, 1935), p. 97.

61 Isenmann, *Die deutsche Stadt*, pp. 353–6; Bernhard Kirchgäßner, 'Der Verlag im Spanngsfeld von Stadt und Umland', in Erich Maschke and Jürgen Sydow, eds., *Stadt und Umland* (Stuttgart, 1974), pp. 72–128.

62 Hektor Ammann, *Die wirtschaftliche Stellung der Reichsstadt Nürnberg im Spätmittelalter*, Nürnberger Forschungen XIII (Nuremberg, 1970), pp. 194–224; Kießling, *Die Stadt und ihr Land*.

63 Michael Mitterauer, 'Produktionsweise, Siedlungsstruktur und Sozialformen im österreichischen Montanwesen des Mittelalters und der Frühen Neuzeit', in Mitterauer, ed., *Österreichisches Montanwesen. Produktion, Verteilung, Sozialformen* (Vienna, 1974), pp. 234–315; K. Klein, 'Die Bevölkerung Österreichs vom Beginn des 16. bis zur Mitte des 18. Jahrhundert', in Heimold Helczmanovszki, ed., *Beiträge zur Bevölkerungs- und Sozialgeschichte Österreichs* (Vienna, 1973), pp. 47–112.

64 Sprandel, 'Gewerbe und Handel 1350–1500', p. 339.

65 Isenmann, *Die deutsche Stadt*, pp. 351–2; Adolf Laube, *Studien über den erzgebirgischen Silberbergbau von 1470 bis 1546*, 2nd edn (Berlin, 1976); Strieder, *Studien zur Geschichte kapitalistischer Organisationsformen*; Mitterauer, *Österreichisches Montanwesen*.

66 Sprandel, 'Gewerbe und Handel 1350–1500', pp. 340–2.

67 Hermann Wiesflecker, *Kaiser Maximilian I. Das Reich, Österreich und Europa an der Wende zur Neuzeit* (5 vols., Munich, 1971–86) V, pp. 576–80.

68 Isenmann, *Die deutsche Stadt*, pp. 347–8.

69 Quoted by Strieder, *Studien zur Geschichte kapitalistischer Organisationsformen*, p. 62. See Thomas A. Brady, Jr, *Turning Swiss. Cities and Empire*,

1450–1550 (Cambridge, 1985), pp. 120–30.

70 To the credit, above all, of Peter Blickle. See his *Deutsche Untertanen. Ein Widerspruch* (Stuttgart, 1981); idem, *The Communal Reformation. The Quest for Salvation in Sixteenth-Century Germany*, trans. Thomas Dunlap (Atlantic Highlands, NJ, 1992), pt. 3. The following is based on Günter Vogler, Dorfgemeinde und Stadtgemeinde zwischen Feudalismus und Kapitalismus', in Peter Blickle, ed., *Landgemeinde und Stadtgemeinde in Mitteleuropa*, *HZ* Supplement XIII (Munich, 1991), pp. 39–64, here pp. 39–51.

71 Anne-Marie Imbs, 'Tableaux des corporations alsaciennes, XIVe–XVIIIe siècles', and Jean Rott, 'Artisanat et mouvements sociaux à Strasbourg autour de 1525', in *Artisans et ouvriers d'Alsace*, Publications de la Société Savante d'Alsace et des Régions de l'Est IX (Strasbourg, 1965), pp. 35–45, 158. The percentage of *Ackerbürgerstädte* is based on a survey of 1911 towns by Renate Schilling, cited by Vogler, 'Dorfgemeinde und Stadtgemeinde', p. 46.

72 There is a classic statement of this dualistic principle by Otto Brunner, 'Souveränitätsproblem und Sozialstruktur in den deutschen Reichsstädten der frühen Neuzeit', in his *Neue Wege der Verfassungs- und Sozialgeschichte*, 2nd edn, pp. 294–321, here p. 303. For the European context, see Steven Rowan, 'The Urban Community. Rulers and Ruled', in Brady *et al.*, *Handbook of European History, 1400–1600*I, pp. 197–230.

73 See the superb systematic description by Isenmann, *Die deutsche Stadt*, pp. 131–98.

74 See the splendid overview in *Ibid.*, pp. 146–60.

75 Josef Rosen, 'Zins und Zinsaufwand', in Rosen, *Finanzgeschichte Basels im späten Mittelalter. Gesammelte Beiträge 1971–1987* (Stuttgart, 1989), pp. 170–3.

76 Isenmann, *Die deutsche Stadt*, pp. 109–13, is clear and nuanced on these gradations.

77 Erich Maschke, 'Mittelschichten in deutschen Städten des Mittelalters', in Maschke, *Städte und Menschen*, pp. 275–305.

78 Karl Czok, 'Die Bürgerkämpfe in Süd- und Westdeutschland im 14. Jahrhundert', *Jb für Geschichte der oberdeutschen Reichsstädte* XII–XIII (1966–7), pp. 40–72.

79 Sprandel, 'Sozialgeschichte 1350–1500', p. 378.

80 Isenmann, *Die deutsche Stadt*, p. 139; and see Erich Maschke, 'Verfassung und soziale Kräfte in der deutschen Stadt des späten Mittelalters, vornehmlich in Oberdeutschland', in Maschke, *Städte und Menschen*, pp. 170–274.

81 Isenmann, *Die deutsche Stadt*, pp. 132–3; Vogler, 'Dorfgemeinde und Stadtgemeinde', pp. 49–50. See Thomas A. Brady, Jr, *Ruling Class, Regime, and Reformation at Strasbourg, 1520–1555*, Studies in Late Medieval and Reformation Thought XXII (Leiden, 1978), pp. 163–96, where the trend is documented from the mid-fifteenth century.

82 Christoph Scheurl's famous 'Epistel über die Verfassung der Reichsstadt Nürnberg', in *Die Chroniken der fränkischen Städte. Nürnberg V* vol. 5 = Chroniken der deutschen Städte, XI (Leipzig, 1874); repr. Göttingen, 1961), pp. 781–804, here p. 791. On the number of urban revolts, see Maschke, 'Deutsche Städte am Ausgang des Mittelalters', p. 95, n. 206. The effect of falling real wages on popular political activity is argued by Jean-Pierre Kintz, *La Société Strasbourgeoise du milieu du XVIe siècle à la fin de la Guerre de Trente Ans 1560–1650. Essai d'histoire démographique, économique et sociale* (Paris, 1984).

83 Robisheaux, 'The World of the Village', pp. 99–102.

84 See Heide Wunder, *Die bäuerliche Gemeinde in Deutschland* (Göttingen, 1986); idem, 'Die ländliche Gemeinde als Strukturprinzip der spätmittelalter-

lich-neuzeitlichen Geschichte Mitteleuropas', in *Landgemeinde und Stadt-gemeinde in Mitteleuropa*, pp. 385–402. It is now recognized that rural communes were typical of central Europe as a whole, not just their classic landscape in the Empire's southern and western lands. Wunder, *Die bäuerliche Gemeinde*, pp. 63–7; and see the contributions of Karlheinz Blaschke, Hartmut Harnisch, Evamaria Engel, and Carl-Heinz Hauptmeyer to *Landgemeinde und Stadtgemeinde in Mitteleuropa*, pp. 119–44, 289–384.

85 Henri Dubled, 'Grundherrschaft und Dorfgerichtsbarkeit in Elsaß vom 13. bis zum 15. Jahrhundert und ihr Verhältnis zueinander', *Deutsches Archiv für Erforschung des Mittelalters* LXVII (1961), pp. 518–19.

86 Du Boulay, *Germany in the Later Middle Ages*, p. 172. For the very wide regional variations in rural communes, see Wunder, *Die bäuerliche Gemeinde*, pp. 67–77.

87 Franz, *Quellen*, p. 479, no. 187 (*c.*1370).

88 Brady, *Turning Swiss*, pp. 34–42.

89 Peter Blickle, *Landschaften im Alten Reich. Die staatliche Funktion des gemeinen Mannes in Oberdeutschland* (Munich, 1973).

90 Peter Bierbrauer, 'Bäuerliche Revolten im Alten Reich. Ein Forschungsbericht', in Peter Blickle, ed., *Aufruhr oder Empörung? Studien zum bäuerlichen Widerstand im alten Reich* (Munich, 1980), pp. 62–5.

91 Franz, *Quellen*, pp. 497–501, no. 196; 479–83, no. 188. The first document is summarized (somewhat inaccurately) by Du Boulay, *Germany in the Later Middle Ages*, p. 174.

92 Abel, *Geschichte der deutschen Landwirtschaft*, p. 127.

93 Claudia Ulbrich, *Leibherrschaft am Oberrhein im Spätmittelalter*, Veröffentlichungen des MPIG LVIII (Göttingen, 1979), p. 256.

94 'Articles of the Peasants of Memmingen, 24 February–3 March, and the Reply of the Memmingen Town Council', in Tom Scott and Bob Scribner, eds, *The German Peasants' War. A History in Documents* (Atlantic Highlands, NJ, 1991), p. 78, no. 3.

95 See Blickle, *Revolution of 1525*, pp. 171–80.

96 Wunder, *Die bäuerliche Gemeinde*, pp. 35–7; Du Boulay, *Germany in the Later Middle Ages*, pp. 176–8.

97 Wunder, *Die bäuerliche Gemeinde*, p. 58.

98 The chief force behind enserfment and the formation of the latifundia (*Gutsherrschaft*) east of the Elbe was the export boom in grain during the sixteenth century. Peter Kriedte, *Peasants, Landlords and Merchant Capitalists. Europe and the World Economy, 1500–1800*, trans. V. R. Berghahn (Cambridge, 1983), pp. 27–30.

99 A fact noted by Italian observers. See Antony Black, *Guilds and Civil Society in European Political Thought from the Twelfth Century to the Present* (Ithaca, NY, 1984), p. 74; the following quote on p. 71.

100 Ingrid Bátori, 'Das Patriziat der deutschen Stadt. Zu den Forschungsergebnissen über das Patriziat besonders der süddeutschen Städte', *Zeitschrift für Stadtgeschichte, Stadtsoziologie und Denkmalpflege* II (1975), p. 1–30.

101 Quoted by Brady, *Ruling Class*, p. 49.

102 Quoted by Isenmann, *Die deutsche Stadt*, p. 246.

103 Werner Danckert, *Unehrliche Leute. Die verfemten Berufe* (Berne, 1963), p. 23.

104 Sprandel, 'Gewerbe und Handel 1350–1500', p. 379.

105 Thomas Fischer, *Städtische Armut und Armenfürsorge im 15. und 16. Jahrhundert*, Göttinger Beiträge zur Wirtschafts- und Sozialgeschichte IV (Göttingen, 1979), pp. 128–9.

106 *Ibid.*, p. 115, n. 1.
107 Franz Irsigler and Arnold Lassotta, *Bettler, Gauker, Dirnen und Henker. Randgruppen und Aussenseiter in Köln 1300–1600* (Cologne, 1984), p. 47.
108 Alfred Haverkamp, 'The Jewish Quarters in German Towns during the Late Middle Ages' (unpublished paper). My thanks to Professor Haverkamp for allowing me to read this. See also Isenmann, *Die deutsche Stadt*, pp. 100–1.
109 Antony Black, 'The Individual and Society', in J. H. Burns, ed., *The Cambridge History of Medieval Political Thought, c.350–c.1450* (Cambridge, 1988), p. 596.
110 Quoted by Black, *Guilds and Civil Society*, p. 71.
111 See, in general, Léopold Genicot, *Rural Communities in the Medieval West* (Baltimore, MD, 1990), ch. 4; Isenmann, Die deutsche Stadt, ch. 5; Dietrich Kurze, *Pfarrerwahlen im Mittelalter. Ein Beitrag zur Geschichte der Gemeinde und des Niederkirchenwesens*, Forschungen zur Kirchengeschichte VI (Cologne/Graz, 1966).
112 See Wolfgang Reinhard, 'Die Verwaltung der Kirche', in Kurt G. A. Jeserich, Hans Pohl, and Georg-Christoph von Unruh, eds, *Deutsche Verwaltungsgeschichte I: Vom Spätmittelalter bis zum Ende des Reiches* (Stuttgart, 1983), pp. 156–7; Karl Siegfried Bader, 'Universitas subditorum parochie–des Pfarrers Untertanen. Zur Auffassung und Bezeichnung der spät-mittelalterlichen Pfarrgemeinde', in Klaus Obermayer, eds, *Festschrift Hans Liermann zum 70. Geburtstag* (Erlangen, 1964), pp. 11–25, reprinted in Karl Siegfried Bader, *Ausgewählte Schriften zur Rechts- und Landesgeschichte* (3 vols., Sigmaringen, 1984) II, pp. 240–54.
113 Kurze, *Pfarrerwahlen im Mittelalter*, p. 388.
114 Isenmann, *Die deutsche Stadt*, p. 211.
115 Luzian Pfleger, *Die elsässische Pfarrei. Ihre Entstehung und Entwicklung*, Forschungen zur Kirchengeschichte des Elsaß III (Strasbourg, 1936), pp. 113–46.
116 Kurze, *Pfarrwahlen*; Rosi Fuhrmann, 'Die Kirche im Dorf. Kommunale Initiativen zur Organisation von Seelsorge vor der Reformation', in Peter Blickle, ed., *Zugänge zur bäuerlichen Reformation*, Bauer und Reformation I (Zurich, 1987), pp. 147–86; idem, 'Dorfgemeinde und Pfründstiftung vor der Reformation. Kommunale Selbstbestimmungschancen zwischen Religion und Recht', in *Kommunalisierung und Christianisierung. Voraussetzungen und Folgen der Reformation 1400–1600*, eds, Peter Blickle and Johannes Kunisch, ZHF Supplement IX (Berlin, 1989), pp. 77112; Peter Blickle, 'Antiklerikalismus um den Vierwaldstättersee 1300–1500. Aufriß eines Modells, weshalb es nicht zur Reformation kommt', in Peter Dykema and Heiko A. Oberman, eds, *Anticlericalism in the Late Middle Ages and Reformation* (Leiden, 1992), pp. 115–32.
117 Blickle, *Communal Reformation*.
118 Isenmann, *Die deutsche Stadt*, pp. 183–90.
119 Bossy, *Christianity in the West*, p. 57.
120 This phrase from Gabriel Le Bras is quoted by Isenmann, *Die deutsche Stadt*, p. 223. See Robert W. Scribner, 'Elements of Popular Belief', in Brady *et al.*, *Handbook of European History, 1400–1600*, I, pp. 231–62, here pp. 241–2.
121 Irsigler and Lassotta, *Bettler, Gauker, Dirnen und Henker*, p. 47.
122 Reinhard, 'Die Verwaltung der Kirche', pp. 143–76.
123 See John Van Engen, 'The Church in the Fifteenth Century', in Brady *et al.*, *Handbook of European History, 1400–1600* I, 305–30.
124 I mean more the notion of property and its purpose than its precise legal status, for, as David Sabean points out, by the sixteenth century in regions of partible inheritance such as Württemberg, ownership was strictly individual; Sabean,

Property, Production and Family, p. 16.

125 Dietmar Willoweit, 'Die Entwicklung und Verwaltung der spätmittelalterlichen Landesherrschaft', Wolfgang Reinhard, 'Die Verwaltung der Kirche', and Dietmar Willoweit, 'Das landesherrliche Kirchenregiment', in Jeserich *et al.*, *Deutsche Verwaltungsgeschichte* I, pp. 77–8, 165–7, 361–2; Gerhard Kallen, *Die oberschwäbischen Pfründen des Bistums Konstanz und ihre Besetzung (1275–1508). Ein Beitrag zur Pfründgeschichte vor der Reformation*, Kirchenrechtliche Abhandlungen XLV–XLVI (Stuttgart, 1965), pp. 188–95; Jörn Sieglerschmidt, *Territorialstaat und Kirchenregiment. Studien zur Rechtsdogmatik des Kirchenpatronatsrechts im 15. und 16. Jahrhundert Forschungen zur kirchlichen Rechtsgeschichte und zum Kirchenrecht*, XV (Cologne/Vienna, 1987).

126 Wiesflecker, *Kaiser Maximilian I.* I, p. 79; V, pp. 156–7.

127 Francis Rapp, *Réformes et réformation à Strasbourg. Église et société dans le diocèse de Strasbourg (1450–1525)*, Collection de l'Institut des Hautes Études Alsaciennes XXIII (Paris, 1974), pp. 265–79, 284–7, 298–9, 306–18, 313, 430–4, 435–41, 451–2.

128 Among the common people, I think, this is nearer the mark than Bossy's thesis of a direct passage from spiritual kinship to individualism; Bossy, *Christianity in the West*. I owe much of this insight to David Sabean's writings.

129 Johann Geiler von Kaysersberg, *Die Emeis. Dis ist das buch von der Omeissen, und auch Herr der kónnig ich diente gern* (Strasburg, 1516), 28[b]. See Thomas A. Brady, Jr, 'You Hate us Priests': Anticlericalism, Communalism, and the Control of Women at Strasbourg in the Age of the Reformation', in Dykema and Oberman, eds., *Anticlericalism in the Late Middle Ages and Reformation*, pp. 167–207, on which this paragraph is based.

|11|

Communities and the Nature of Power

BOB SCRIBNER

Some historiography

There is a long tradition in German historiography which emphasizes the importance of 'community' in German political, social, and economic history. The interest arose from several directions, but mainly within the confines of nineteenth-century Prussia, in liberal-romantic desires to find specifically German origins of liberties and freedom. The mythic foundations were found in Tacitus' account of early Teutonic society as distinctively free and relatively democratic, and the theme was continued in interpretations of the German middle ages that stressed popular forms of democratic-egalitarian association as the foundation of both urban and rural society. Georg Ludwig von Maurer (1790–1872) set the tone with his theory, developed in the years 1854–66, that the Germanic form of free association for use of common lands (*Markgenossenschaft*) had formed the basis for the peasant commune of the high and late middle ages.[1] This theory, controversial in its own time, was taken over by Marx and Engels and passed into marxist historiography, as well as becoming conventional wisdom among many historians and jurists until after the First World War. Equally influential was the work of Otto von Gierke (1841–1921), partly influenced by Maurer, who published in 1868 the first of four massive volumes on the German law of association. Gierke argued for the continual importance in German history of voluntary forms of free association, imbued with a sense of individual liberty, a corporate ethos, and a sense of community, something he saw as a special contribution of the German people and which constituted for him a theory of corporatism or 'fellowship' (*Genossenschaft*).[2]

Gierke developed this viewpoint into a theory of history which distinguished five major epochs from the time of primitive Germanic society to his own day. In each he discerned a dialectic between fellowship and lordship (*Herrschaft*), from which either one or the other gained the upper hand. In early Germanic society (up to 800) fellowship was dominant, but was displaced by lordship with the emergence of feudal society (800–1200). In the high middle ages (1200–1525) the pendulum swung again in favour of fellowship, which experienced its fullest flowering in guilds, towns, confederations, and Estates, only to be subdued again by lordship in the period of absolutism (1525–1806). The fifth period (from 1806) was one in which the modern constitutional state brought about a synthesis of fellowship and lordship. Gierke's theory gave the concept of voluntary free association 'a star part in the history of liberty and of constitutional government' (Black). Although controversial and rebutted by other German historians with their own contemporary axes to grind, it was enormously influential, contributing to Tönnies' formulation of his distinction between affective community (*Gemeinschaft*) and rational instrumental association (*Gesellschaft*), and to Walter Ullmann's notion of the 'descending' and 'ascending' themes of the middle ages – the clash between vertical hierarchy and popular consensus. Indeed, it may even have decisively influenced Bernd Moeller's characterization of the religious ethos of late medieval imperial cities, which he saw as rendering them decisively receptive to the Reformation.[3]

The sharp distinction between lordship and an independent origin of communal association was blurred considerably by the research of agrarian and regional historians in the first three decades of the twentieth century, who mostly emphasized the role played by feudal lords in the creation of rural corporate and communal forms. This trend regarded lordship and rural community as complementary principles of local organization, but its reception was complicated by the rise of an often romanticized interest in folk community, which drew German *Volkskunde* (best understood as ethnology, rather than as 'folklore studies') into a long preoccupation with village and peasant communities which has endured to the present day. The beginnings in the early 1930s of a rural sociology, influenced by North American concepts of the subject, were snuffed out by the rise of the Nazi concern to identify peasant life and community as the quintessential expression of Germanic culture. Thus, from then until recently there has been a comparatively low level of general interest in village community, despite a growing body of specialist regional and local history, of which the most influential work was undoubtedly that of the legal historian K. S. Bader, who emphasized the legal self-determination of the village as a local immunity.[4] Much the same can be said for studies of urban community. The enormous body of work on urban history and on urban corporate life produced few works of synthesis directed at communal aspects or the experience of community. There was a trickle, rather than a steady flow, of work directed at particular aspects such as the idea of the 'common good', although notions of urban community were placed back on the agenda of Reformation studies nearly three decades ago now by Moeller's seminal work on the imperial cities. English scholarship of the 1970s began to interest itself in urban community and the theme was also taken up by North American scholarship on Renaissance Italy, but there was no echo in German urban history.[5]

When interest in 'community' as a theme in itself revived in Germany, it was as a consequence of citizens' initiative movements of the late 1960s, which emphasized the need for political engagement and autonomy at local government level. This merely continued an older interest from the 1930s in the origins of local self-government, born of an awareness of the importance of devolving administrative power from the modern central state.[6] However, a combination of increasing erosion of village life by relentless economic and cultural urbanization and a nostalgia for a rural world that was being lost (movingly chronicled in the film *Heimat*), focused attention on the 'crisis of village community' and so on rural life.[7] Around this time there appeared the first examples of a new historically-based 'empirical cultural research' (as *Volkskunde* was now called to free it from its Nazi past), with micro-historical studies of village community such as that by Utz Jeggle on Kiebingen.[8] The contemporary impulse inspiring this new wave of historical ethnography is also evident in the work of Peter Blickle, the historian most closely associated with recent German scholarship on community.

In a series of studies developed over almost thirty years, Blickle has identified the commune, rural and urban, as a fundamental building-block of pre-modern German society, and has offered an overarching interpretation, initially for his own specialist field, the Reformation, and then for German history as a whole (increasingly with reference to Switzerland as a prototypical model). According to Blickle, the demand for communal autonomy was a precondition for positive resistance by rural classes to attempts at domination by feudal-aristocratic classes, forming the basis for a German and Swiss tradition of populist, anti-feudal politics. The existence in some parts of Germany of forms of communal representation in territorial or regional assemblies (*Landschaften*) provided an alternative to princely rule supported by Estates comprised largely of social elites. Thus, Blickle argued, German history had not been a tale of continuous subjection of subordinate classes and could boast of an alternative parliamentarian tradition. This argument bears the stamp of the self-consciously 'emancipatory' history favoured by the post-1968 generation of historians, who looked for alternative paths to modernity not via the tradition of the absolutist states but in the corporatist, federalist modes of politics that characterized the early modern Holy Roman Empire (the so-called 'Old Empire', to distinguish it from the Bismarckian 'Second Empire'). Curiously enough, this model looked strangely like the Federal Republic of Germany, although in Blickle's later work, the model of the Swiss Confederation has also begun to influence the conceptualization, and his central concept, 'communalism', has been presented as a preliminary stage to 'democratization'. North American scholars working within the growing field of 'peasant studies' developed similar arguments in the 1970s: that the existence of strong communal forms was the precondition for active peasant resistance to the state.[9] However, the wider comparative and anthropological perspectives offered by 'peasant studies' were received only slowly in Germany, and in Blickle's version the communalism thesis has come to resemble a neo-Whig interpretation of German history, establishing an anti-authoritarian, popular representative tradition.[10] Blickle then widened the model to include the urban commune, thus binding together two traditions of scholarship in a way not seen since Gierke, while insisting that his notion of 'communalism' was not to be confused with Gierke's ideal of corporatism or 'fellowship'. The issue of 'communalism', an interpretation still under debate by historical specialists, has placed the study of community, and what should be understood by that term, squarely in the centre of historical discussion of late medieval and early modern Germany.

Concepts of community

The German usage of the notion of 'community' is fairly complex and is not wholly covered by either of the two corresponding English words 'community' or 'commune'. The word *Gemeinde*, which can be translated as either 'community' or 'commune', covers a range of concepts. It can refer to the common land held by a community, to a territorially limited set of social affiliations in the sense of 'neighbourhood', or to the 'commons' in the sense of the mass of ordinary people in a given community. It can designate a political-legal form of association, referring to the enfranchised inhabitants and area of a self-governing community or to a unit of local government within a state (here similar to the French *commune*). Associated terms which fall into the same semantic field are *Gemeinschaft*, denoting a closer, integrated, organic community; and *Genossenschaft*, designating forms of collective, sometimes corporate association or fellowship.[11]

We can see the complexity of the term *Gemeinde* in a set of village statutes issued in 1553 for Buxheim, a village subject to the Carthusian Priory of the same name not far from the imperial city of Memmingen. *Gemeinde* is used in this document to mean the collective property of the village commune, but also to designate such things as the village paths used by everyone, or to refer to the common land or *Allmende*. In referring to the legally constituted village commune, it designated only those farmers and cotters holding land in fee from the monastic lordship, thus encompassing only male heads of households and excluding all women, adult children living with the householder, servants, and employed workers; however, it could also include one married adult child living with the feeholder. It was also used to refer to an assembly of the legally constituted commune; and finally the word was used in a further, vaguer sense to mean all those subject to the commands and prohibitions (*Gebot und Verbot*) of the village officials, so, implicitly, everyone living in the village.[12]

This complexity of meaning arises from the multiplicity of usages attached in the later middle ages and early modern period to the term 'common' (*gemein*), from which the word *Gemeinde* was derived and which was very frequently used interchangeably with it. Jakob Grimm remarked that the word *gemein* was closely related to its Latin equivalent *communis*, derived from the notion of those who lived within the protection of an encircling wall, therefore enjoying common security and so common rights and obligations.[13] Thus, *gemein* denoted not only what was of general concern to all, but more specifically, what was a general concern to all who formed a commonality, signifying what was of public rather than private concern. Hence the most potent opposition found in our period was that between *gemeinnutz*, the 'common good', and *eigennutz*, private or self-interest, and which will be discussed below. Luther defined this usage in speaking of the community created by the eucharist: 'Community here means common possession, shared and enjoyed by the many ... for a common thing means that many persons enjoy it in common, such as the public fountain, the public street, public fields, meadows, woods'.[14] Here 'common' and 'public' are interchangeable notions, and are embodied in the word *gemein* as applied to public property, public wealth (in the sense of a public treasury), and the public good (in the fifteenth century, *res publica*, equivalent to the 'common weal'). It found particular embodiment in the *Allmende* (in Middle High German, *algemeine*) or common land, that is, public grazing land (along with its water and wood) open to all and regarded as no person's private property. The term extended to public streets, buildings, shelters for the sick and needy, the market where all could buy and sell without hindrance, public income and expenditure, public office and officeholders, and even a 'public opinion', information made available to all and sundry and common to all. According to Grimm, it is in this sense of 'available to all' and so private to no one that the notion of the *gemein weib* or 'common woman' is to be understood (alongside the *gemein frawenhaus*, or public brothel), rather than primarily signifying a woman of little personal value. The clear implication of this web of concepts is that there existed even in the middle ages a well-defined 'public sphere', carefully distinguished from a 'private sphere' (the Latin terms that correspond to *gemein* and *eigen* are *publicus* and *privatus*), and that these notions were not the creation of the early modern or modern periods or of any process of 'modernization'.

The designation 'commune' or 'commonality' (*gemeine*) was applied most specifically to an assembly or gathering of those with common concerns, imbued with the particular force of representing and expressing unity in their multiplicity. This applied whether the assembly was one of residents of a jurisdiction, tenants of a lordship, a guild, a group of merchants, or a parish community. It was further extended to cover formal assemblies meeting for the purpose of taking advice and making decisions, ranging from a parish community assembled to receive the parish accounts to gatherings of political bodies such as the Swabian League or the Reichstag. In these cases, the notion of unity in community was applied to the formal decisions made by majority agreement (whether by vote or not), enabling a single person to speak in the name of the whole. Hence we find the notion of the 'common council' (*gemein rat*) of a city, that is, one empowered to speak in the name of the entire citizenry. The idea was often reinforced by reference to 'the entire community' (*all gemein, die ganz gemein*), enabling it to speak with a 'common voice' (*gemeine stimme*) – a potent concept for the formation and expression of public opinion.

The notion was then extended more broadly to cover all those involved in any similar or collective forms of life, whether peasants (*gemeine bauerschafft*), citizens (*gemeine bürger*, used in both the singular and plural), or nobles (*gemeine edelleute*). It was applied to parishioners (*gemeine pfarrkinder*) and so to the parish itself (*gemeine pfarr*, thence to *Pfarrgemeinde*), even to a city as a form of collective living (*gemeine stadt*). Finally, it was applied to the highest political relationships, the assembly of Estates in the Imperial Diet, the assembled imperial cities, and anything concerning the Empire as issued from the Imperial Diet. Here we see an appropriation of the concept to cover more abstract notions of collectivity, revealing that it was not inimical to, indeed was rather useful for, hierarchy and lordship. In this sense it was also used to describe a lordship (*gemeine herrschaft*) or territory as a whole (*das gemein lant*) and its subjects (*gemeine unterthanen*), as well as government in general (*gemein regiment*).

This appropriation of a collective, horizontal concept for non-collective, hierarchical, vertical forms undoubtedly flowed from its considerable moral power (Grimm called it a 'wholly noble word' – *das ganze edle wort*), from which it derived a range of connotations of impartiality, embodied in the notion of a 'common man' or 'common people' (*gemein man, gemain leute*) called as adjudicators in disputes. Thus one designated someone standing above the self-interest of the disputing parties, and in the same way the concept was also applied to law and justice, which only retained their power in being *gemein* in this impartial sense. Thence was derived the potent idea that all should have the same rights under the law, the undoubted fount of the grievances of rebellious peasants, with whom the evident injustice of much law and its application rankled deeply. Also located in this part of the semantic field is the high value placed on those involved in communal service, as well as the idea of communal life in general, so embracing all forms of commmunity (*gemeinschaft*), including religious communities. The highest expression of this moral force in our period was undoubtedly the experience of the Eucharist, which we find strikingly expressed in Luther (and which rebuts the view that Luther fostered a wholly individual notion of religion): 'You have two fruits from the Holy Sacrament. One is that it makes us brothers and joint heirs of Christ the lord, also that from him and us we become one bread. The other is that we become one and common with all other people on earth, and also all one bread.'[15]

This seems to imply that the idea of communality could easily be taken as a universal concept; yet it was far from all-embracing and implicitly entailed a range of exclusions, of whose overtones we should be continually aware. First, the condition of commonality applied only to a body of persons insofar as they engaged in common concerns. Thus, the commonality of peasantry, citizens, or guildsmen excluded all those who did not belong to these categories, and was most strikingly evident where the notion of the commonality was set in opposition to nobles, lords, princes, or even to political authority. It also excluded those of lower social status, for example labourers in a town or village. These exclusions are seen most clearly in the antitheses to the term *gemein*, of which the oldest was perhaps that between 'commoner' and 'noble' (*gemeiner man* and *edel man*). They cover the antithesis 'common' versus 'eminent', 'high', or 'great' (*vornehm, hoch, grosz*), as well as that between 'common' and 'learned', similar to the Latin terms *illiteratus* and *literatus*, with overtones of simplicity and lesser understanding. Hence one derived the notion at the end of the fifteenth century that the 'common reader' was one who could read German but not Latin, embodied in Luther's sentiment that 'German books are made especially for the common man to read at home'.[16] Perhaps the most significant exclusion was contained in the antithesis between 'common folk' and the clergy, a contrast that was by no means the creation of either pre-Reformation or Reformation anti-clerical feeling. Rather, it was founded on a contrast with 'common' in the meaning of 'not holy', 'profane', 'impure', or 'unconsecrated'.

Some of these connotations were clearly intended as exclusions 'from above', attempts to retain notions of social hierarchy and differentiation possibly threatened by the way in which the notion of 'commonality' had spread throughout all areas of life. Thus, the *gemeine mann* was equated with the subject (*untertan*), analogous to the medieval usage of 'poor' (*arm*) to mean the powerless or servile. We can clearly discern here a hegemonic struggle over the moral weighting of the notion of commonality, which in many of the meanings discussed so far placed common folk (*gemeine leute, gemein man*), citizens, or guildsmen in a position of high honour and made the views of 'common people' morally authoritative. This was matched by an array of disparaging or belittling usages, equating the 'common man' or 'common folk' with the vulgar, the undiscriminating, and the ignorant, imbued with all the overtones attached to our modern use of the word 'mob' (in the period under discussion, *pöbel*). We can see the opposing tendencies in the differential weightings given to the notion of 'common understanding' (*des gemeinen mannes verstand*), on the one hand meaning accessible to everyone and according to general reason, but on the other contrasted with higher forms of understanding. This cultural separation of the 'common' from the 'elevated' was given impetus in the seventeenth century, as the norms of court life and of academic elites were gradually imposed as those of 'civilized' behaviour. Thus, the notion of 'common' was given stronger and more disparaging overtones of the everyday, the mediocre, belonging to the masses, and therefore undiscriminating and of poor quality.

The purpose of this brief exercise in sociolinguistics has been twofold. First, it reveals that concepts of community embodied universal, virtually hegemonic values, that led everyone to seek to appropriate them in social and political power plays in order to tilt the moral balance in their favour, or at least to disarm or discomfort opponents. It is therefore especially important to peer behind the façade of the term in every case to discern the content signified, since what was involved was strategies of representation in which meaning was continually constructed and reconstructed in different social contexts. Second, where the terms 'community' or 'commune' were used as formal social or political designations, we need to be conscious of the multi-vocality inherent in the words, something of which people of the time were only too aware as language-users. Indeed, they were clearly able to switch between one meaning and another as situation and occasion demanded, to exploit ambiguities or to insist on firm lines being maintained. That is, there was not one discourse on community but many, and we cannot discuss 'community' or 'commune' apart from speech strategies that were themselves part of wider power struggles. Bearing these principles in mind, we can now examine more closely how community was understood in both the rural and urban spheres.

Peasant communities

There exists a consensus in German scholarship about the origins of the peasant commune, which is seen to have emerged in the eleventh and twelfth centuries in consequence of the introduction of the three-field system, itself a response to pressure to increase production to meet the demands of a growing population. The need for more intensive cultivation led to the creation of nuclear villages with large areas of arable tilled according to the threefold rotation of winter crop, summer crop, and fallow. The necessity of regulating the use of the arable and enforcing conformity to the system on individual farmers created a structure of rules and regulations affecting such matters as what crops should be sown and when, the rights of equal access to the fields (now divided into strips farmed by different peasants), the fencing of the arable to protect it from animals, and the use of, and access to, grazing on the fallow. This practice emerged in most of Western Europe during the eleventh to fourteenth centuries, and in Eastern Europe, where land reserves were greater and population pressure less, only in the fifteenth and sixteenth centuries. The change from a manorial economy to one based on leasehold in payment for annual rents accentuated the trend towards collective endeavour, since the lords largely left the business of farming to the peasants. In a parallel development, there was an intensification of lordship and lordship rights over the countryside, expressed in the establishment of village courts with inferior jurisdiction. Indeed, in some areas the fragmentation of lordships led to lords controlling only a few villages, sometimes even a single village, so that the unit within which seigneurial commands and prohibitions were issued and implemented was the village. Village bodies such as the commune and village officials such as judges and jurors developed areas of legal competence and fields of action that contributed to the creation of a strong sense of village cohesion. The sense of peasant community, of belonging and working together, it is argued, was the result of the interaction of demographic, economic, sociopolitical, and legal developments.[17]

It is difficult to trace the origins of the formalized peasant commune (*Gemeinde*) as a corporate body with any certainty. The institution is not mentioned until the early thirteenth century, although it seems to have been in existence in the twelfth. The extant sources offer information only from the perspective of lordship until the beginning of the fifteenth century, when written documents from the communal perspective begin to flow in increasing volume. The latter certainly reveal a strong sense of the commune as a local locus of power, as a body willing to engage the lords in dispute, struggle, and even rebellion to uphold its viewpoint. However, it seems generally accepted that the peasant commune had a dualist origin, the legal conferral of communal institutions as a 'privilege' from the seigneurial side being matched by struggles from that of the peasants for recognition of existing communal forms. The peasants' awareness was strongly shaped by a sense that the rights of the lord were matched by those of the peasant commune, and that both sides could demand fulfilment of obligations. Thus, the peasant commune was built on a dynamic between lords and peasants that created a form of reciprocity: each side depended on the other for the fulfilment of certain duties and functions. It was this sense of reciprocity that was invoked by the rebels during the German Peasants' War of 1525. In some cases, the peasants demanded to know what the lords did for them in return for their allegiance and their dues, in others even arguing that the relationship had been broken by the lords' non-fulfilment, so that the peasants' allegiance was abrogated.[18]

It is worth at this point describing an ideal-typical form of the peasant commune, so that we can better appreciate the complex variations of the actual historical phenomenon. Every village constituted a commune, or rather, every village endowed with its own area of farmland, since it has been remarked that it was the farmland that provided the occasion for the commune, rather than merely the village itself.[19] A share of the farmland thus entailed a share in the commune, and hence it was only those in possession of farm holdings who were full members of the legally constituted commune. The commune was also often the seat of a court with inferior jurisdiction (with competence over minor disputes, drunkenness, petty theft, breach of the peace and affray – the boundary here was often that affray which involving wounding, that is, drawing blood, was reserved to the next higher court). Sometimes the lord who possessed the jurisdictional rights presided over this court, although often in silence; most commonly a judge or bailiff presided in his stead, sometimes assisted by a bench of jurors. The jurisdiction of the communal court was largely coextensive with the village, and constituted the village commune as a legal personality, entitled to issue commands and prohibitions (*Gebot und Verbot*) for the maintenance of peace and order, and to sue in a court of law. It was this legal-corporative character of the village commune that formed the bedrock of peasant political and social self-consciousness, since the peasant commune was thereby accorded a place in the structures of power and domination exercised through the law. It has indeed been called the basic unit of pre-modern society, a form of local power with whom lords had to negotiate if they were not to act extralegally. Much of the rich documentation from which we learn about peasant communes arose as a result of legal disputes between village communes and their lords, the so-called *Weistümer* or 'manifests', documents settling a dispute by calling attention to, and regulating, local affairs, and which therefore came to be equivalent to local law. Because they were legal personalities, village communes possessed seals and banners; the banner indicated the seat of the court, the seal attested the legal validity of documents it issued. Thus the commune had a legal authority comparable to that of other legal authorities above it in the power hierarchy, admittedly circumscribed within the area of the commune, but qualitatively no less important. The communal banner and seal were signs of peasant pride and social standing, along with the church bell, potent symbols of their communality.

The middle ages and early modern period were riddled with bodies which recognized the equality of their members and used principles of majority election to appoint their officers (hence that particular sense in which the word *gemein* was applied to them). They could thus be thought of as microscopic democracies, and the peasant commune was no exception. The commune elected its own officials annually, most importantly the headman (who bore different titles in different parts of Germany:

Bauermeister, Heimburg, Dorfmeister, Gemeinmeister, sometimes even *Bürgermeister*, as if the peasants were placing themselves on the same evaluative plane as the citizens of a town). Sometimes there was also a small council (*Bauernrat, Dorfrat*), comprising in larger villages as many as twelve members. Other officials were elected to oversee the important economic aspects of communal life: a constable to see that village statutes were observed, a field constable to check for breaches of statutes regulating use of the arable (observing boundaries between one strip of arable and another by keeping fences in good order was a major issue), a village herdsman, a forester (if the village controlled substantial amounts of forest). The constitutive organ of the commune was the communal assembly, a gathering summoned by the headman by ringing the church bell or by a drum-beat. All legal members of the commune were obliged to attend, with fines levied for unjustified absence. The communal assembly met on the village square, sometimes under the village oak or linden (in some places there were fixed seats arranged in a circle around the tree, although meeting must have been difficult in winter). Some communes seem to have met haphazardly in inns, although some villages possessed a 'communal hall' (*Gemeindehaus*) that also served as a refuge for the poor, the village herdsman, and sometimes the village school. Some villages (undoubtedly the wealthiest) possessed a council hall (*Rathaus*), which must have contributed considerably to communal pride.

It would be entirely misleading, however, to equate the village commune with any modern notion of democracy, since participation was tightly restricted to property-holders, essentially to male heads of farm households. Usually excluded from membership were all women, children, servants, day-labourers, artisans, cottagers, lodgers, tenants, foresters, servants or officials of the local lord, and any resident nobles. Even the pastor and schoolteacher were excluded insofar as they did not farm in the village lands. Some of these village residents could be incorporated in the legal association of the commune and placed under its protection by paying a fee (*Dorfgelt*), as could (in Bamberg territory) those born in the village but resident elsewhere. However this fee could be substantial, and where it was set as high as 10 fl. it clearly acted as a barrier against the undesirable. In some areas cottagers who also enjoyed a share of the common fields were admitted to membership, although the rule of thumb seems to have been the holding of sufficient land for a minimum subsistence. Smallholders such as cottagers were able to become members of the commune, but only after a long, hard struggle, a struggle which often began with disputes over access to communal grazing and woods, a central issue in intracommunal disputes in Upper Swabia during the Peasants' War of 1525. The two issues were often tied together, since smallholders or those without any land were unable to feed cattle over the winter (even the single cow essential for the survival of a small household), and there was a fear that they would do so by stealing fodder belonging to the commune. In some parts of Bavaria smallholders were excluded by the mechanism of tying membership of the commune to holding a full farmstead and prohibiting any subdivision of holdings. At the end of the early modern period there was even an attempt in Bavaria to prevent those without land, such as day labourers, from keeping even a single cow or goat.[20] We can see here a potent source of conflict, one that destroys any romanticized image of the commune as a haven of peace and harmony. Indeed, daily life in the village was often far from peaceful, with many ongoing petty disputes between families and individuals, the tinder from which the sparks of ill-will could ignite the flames of sorcery and witchcraft accusations via attacks on personal honour. Meetings of the village commune were often rowdy and disorganized affairs, so much so that some innkeepers refused to let the commune meet on their premises.[21]

For this reason, there were two ways of understanding the term *Gemeinde*. On the one hand it distinguished all those residents of a village who were feudal dependents, so excluding only those non-dependent persons such as pastor, churchwarden, schoolmaster or free wage-workers. This sense was often used by lords in their dealings with a village, to include all those subject to their authority. On the other hand, the villagers themselves perceived and applied a narrower sense of *Gemeinde*: the propertied and enfranchised commune, comprising only those agricultural producers with rights to common land, with their own farmstead and with sufficient agricultural land to nourish themselves, that is, farmers of complete or partial landholdings such as cotters (*Kossaten*). This peasant sense of the commune was in some east Elbian territories covered by the words 'peasantry' (*Bauernschaft*) and sometimes 'neighbourhood' (*Nachbarschaft*). The two terms were not synonymous, since *Nachbarschaft* excluded cotters, while *Bauernschaft* included them. Thus, one could distinguish virtually three layers within a peasant community: a narrower propertied group, an enfranchised commune, and a wider 'political' community. If there was any consistent principle of horizontal solidarity in all this, it was largely towards the outside world, and it may be as valid to speak of peasant factionalism as of peasant community.[22]

The communal principle of horizontal solidarity was weakened in another way by the intrusion of the vertical principle of lordship. Indeed, the presence of lordship within the commune was sufficiently strong for many historians to describe it as a dualist system. On the one hand, the commune fulfilled a function for seigneurial administration, for example, supplying rent in kind or other forms to the seigneurial bailiff as the lord's agent, so that lords did not have to deal directly with individual peasants. On the other hand, the commune was a means of regulating the internal and especially the economic affairs of community. Thus, it was at one and the same time a corporate association of agrarian producers and an instrument of feudal lordship to ensure the functioning of feudal exploitation and maintenance of feudal order. In older settlement areas of north

Germany, this distinction was signified by the presence of two different officials, a bailiff or judge (*Schultheiß, Richter, Amtmann*) as regulator of seigneurial affairs, and the headman (*Bauermeister, Heimburg*) as representative of corporate community. In colonized east Elbian territories, both functions were fulfilled by a single official, the judge or bailiff (*Schulze*). The judge or bailiff represented seigneurial interests within the village, but was also a member of the village community; indeed, often the most prominent member of the village. His role as a representative of lordship was so important that in some villages with several lords, there was also a corresponding number of bailiffs. If a particular lord's interests in a given village were relatively limited, his bailiff was a lesser light in the village community; but if they were considerable, the bailiff was one of the most powerful men of the commune, expected to induce obedience and compliance to the lord's wishes. Thus the bailiff was almost always chosen from farmers with full holdings, not from the ranks of cotters or the non-propertied. In rare cases where this did occur, either the cotters elected their own bailiff, or else the office alternated annually between full farmers and cotters.[23]

In any case, it was very rare for anyone other than the more well-to-do of a village to gain this office, and there is clearly a good reason why this was so, since the bailiff was expected to wield seigneurial authority within the village, if necessary to act sternly against peasant recalcitrance, even to the point of using violence and seizure of goods. The rewards were considerable, either in the form of conferral of lands free of feudal dues, exemption from the tithe, or privileges in the usufruct of seigneurial rights, such as the use of wood, water, meadows, or hay.[24] In some areas east of the Elbe, the office was hereditary by contrast with the elected position of headman, and the bailiff's holding was several times greater than that of ordinary peasants. Yet it would be incorrect to see the bailiff purely as a figure of seigneurial authority, acting repressively and against the will of the peasant community. Lords had a strong interest in maintaining good relations with peasant communities, and the bailiff fulfilled a function of harmonizing peasant and seigneurial interests. For this reason, bailiffs frequently appeared as spokesmen for the peasants in conflicts with their lord, and in numerous peasant rebellions the bailiffs took the role of peasant leaders.[25] They thus fulfilled a classic role as middlemen, mediating between two interests and seeking to reconcile them, with their own self-interest divided in two directions. They embodied the dualist character of the peasant community as incorporated into seigneurial structures while maintaining communal autonomy.

As well as the intrusion of lordship, the territorial state steadily began to permeate the peasant community, a process that has been traced in Thuringia from the 1570s as village statutes increasingly began to express the wishes of the ruling prince for that paternalist regulation of all aspects of daily life known as *Polizei*. Village statutes and regulations were trans-

mitted orally for most of the middle ages, although the interests of lords
and rulers gradually led to these being fixed in writing (in the so-called
Weistümer), often as a consequence of disputes between peasants and their
lords. Progressively the *Weistümer* were displaced by village statutes issued
in the name of the territorial ruler, and those promulgated during the late
sixteenth and throughout the seventeenth century increasingly embody the
dichotomy of sovereign prince and subjects, subsuming the older
dichotomy between lords and commune. A pattern of development has
been traced for Franconia, which begins after the German Peasants' War
and proceeds in waves until the end of the eighteenth century, with peaks
around 1600, at the end of the Thirty Years' War and in the middle of
the eighteenth century.[26] The impulse to state regulation after upheavals
such as the Peasants' War and the Thirty Years' War is evident, while the
earlier intervention was also given further impetus by the implementation
of the Reformation, which imposed new duties on village and parish communities, such as the maintenance of village schools or the administration
of poor chests. After the Thirty Years' War, governments anxious to reconstruct a devastated rural economy had no qualms about intervening in
property relationships and vesting in appointed bailiffs powers previously
left to the communal assembly. The state was also moved to intervention
at the end of the sixteenth century by its desire to deal with problems of
poverty and vagrancy, swelling numbers of rural artisans who operated
outside urban guild regulations and the control of day-labourers, all
matters once left to village communities but now grown into issues of territorial importance. The impulse to such measures was largely a desire to
increase state income, for example, by increasing the number of resident
households, even if this meant subdivision of protected peasant holdings,
or at least by diminishing poverty and so widening the tax-base. The
appetite of the state in the eighteenth century to regulate every aspect of
its subjects' lives led to an astonishing multiplication of regulations and
the penetration of state authority into the most minute areas of peasant
daily life. The village statutes issued in 1755 for Vorbachzimmern near
Mergentheim contained 328 articles, including 59 articles on what tasks
the villagers were to be commanded to perform on the Monday after
Whitsun each year, from sweeping the streets to removing overhanging
branches.[27]

State intervention of this kind clearly infringed communal autonomy,
and began after 1525 with strict controls in some territories over meetings
of the village commune and the removal of village courts. In the later
waves, this extended to princely appointment of village officials such as
the headman. Most notoriously, in Bayreuth the state expropriated all
village common land in the middle of the eighteenth century to counter-
balance the drain on public finances caused by the extravagant lifestyle of
Margrave Friedrich and his wife, Friedrike Sophie Wilhelmine. Although
an infringement of corporative rights, state intervention on the other hand

often served to widen communal participation, for example, by allowing all male inhabitants in a village to participate in the communal assembly (in the principality of Ansbach), or forcing the village commune to allow access to common land by non-members of the commune (Würzburg). These measures were bitterly resisted by the village communes, but represented a massive intervention of the state in the interests of the poor (albeit incidental to the pursuit of its own interests), and confound any romantic notions about the 'democratic' nature of peasant communities.[28]

The major difficulty in constructing any unified picture of peasant communities is the wide regional and territorial variation across all German-speaking lands. This was so even in Franconia, scene of the vigorous and successful actions during the German Peasants' War, with weakly developed peasant communes in the Upper Main region and principality of Bayreuth, while those in the area around Nuremberg and the principality of Ansbach profited from fragmented lordships. Competition and disputes between lords, as well as the absence of any single lordship over many villages (in which as many as seven seigneurs many have shared lordship rights), presented peasant communities with frequent opportunities to assert their independence. The varying strengths of peasant communities in Franconia reflected the mixture of elements that shaped the formation of communes. A mixed economic pattern of viticulture and arable farming determined the different kinds of co-operation required of peasant producers, as did the late medieval population decline and economic recession, which put a premium on direct producers and constituted the fifteenth century as a golden age of Franconian peasant community. In parts of Franconia, as in western and north-western Germany, peasant communes participated in supraregional legal jurisdictions, largely through their grasp of customary law. The last was displaced in the sixteenth century by the rise of Roman law, with courts staffed by territorial officials, reducing communal legal competence to the lowest level of village courts.[29]

In looking for patterns in German social and economic life, it is common to distinguish between the older, central settled areas of the medieval German Empire, and newly settled parts of the middle and east Elbian territories. Certainly the conditions of colonization imparted a distinctive character to many peasant communities that arose in these areas. Immigrant peasants from north, west, and south Germany, whose labour was needed to clear and settle these areas, had a strong bargaining hand which reflected itself in strong communal forms. This enabled peasant communities to lay claim to local autonomy and extract seigneurial recognition of their rights to manage their own affairs, legal, religious, economic, and personal. There were two main forms of communal institutions, one in which village headmen were prominent and one in which village judges (*Schulze*) appear as the main officials instead of headmen. Although it might be expected that the former was a more independent form than the latter, it has been argued that the reverse was the case: communities with headmen prominent in their affairs

represented a dualist form of peasant and seigneurial interest. While those
with judges prominent developed stronger independence of the lord (whereby
much turns on the role ascribed to the *Schulz*, and there is another tradition
of scholarship which tends to argue the reverse). Whatever the medieval
developments, the middle and east Elbian pattern in the early modern period
is indisputable. Local lords, backed by the power of the territorial state, progressively asserted control over peasant communities, especially by removing
hereditary village judges and replacing them with their own appointees. This
did not mean squeezing out village self-government so much as incorporating it into state structures.

Turning to the central areas, the situation in Hessen was complex, but
communal autonomy was more developed in the southern than in the
northern parts of the territory, where the territorial ruler began to intervene
in communal affairs in the later middle ages and increasingly in the
sixteenth century. Bavaria displays almost as much variation, from
scattered settlement patterns with individual homesteads forming a neigh-
bourhood-based community, as in Westphalia, to more dependent communities in which seigneurial officials took a role as strong as in middle
and east Elbian territories. In Swabia, peasants profited as in Franconia
from fragmented lordship and late medieval depopulation to create larger
villages and powerful communes, with village courts gaining competence
over both minor offences and major misdemeanours. In Rhineland territories, peasant communities had attained a high degree of independence,
taking over functions once exercised by seigneurial officials and sending
representatives to higher jurisdictional courts. In the Lower Rhine area,
with forms of secondary dispersed settlement, nucleated villages did not
play a role and the unit for the maintenance of peace and order was the
household. The basis of peasant collective organization was the neighbourhood, and the peasants formed themselves into *Bauerschaften* or
assemblies of neighbours. Several *Bauerschaften* could form into a corporation (*Markgenossenschaft*) to organize the exploitation of woods and
pastures. There was no village church at the centre of religious life: that
is, the religious unit of the parish (*Kirchspiel*) encompassed several
Bauerschaften. On the north German coast, peasant organization was
initially wholly detached from settlement patterns and constituted by associations of family clans, which only later became localized forms of organization. In Lauenburg, northern Lower Saxony, and Elbostfalen,
neighbourhood, economic association, and ecclesiastical unit all coincided
in the *Bauerschaft* form of organization. In thinly settled parts of lower
Saxony, there was no demand for any form of communal organization,
farming was extensive and used a single-field system, farmers settled dis-
agreements amongst themselves, and there was little need to unite against
outsiders, since there were few boundary disputes.

If any pattern is discernible in all this variation, it is that peasants in
areas with thin settlement and little incentive to group together into village

units tended to form communities on a wider geographical basis, as occurred in parts of the Black Forest and Switzerland. In the former region, the lordship of Hauenstein provides an interesting example in which peasants identified not with a local community but with a county community (*Landsgemeinde*). Settlement patterns were of small, loosely formed 'swarm villages' (*Schwarmsiedlung*), with weak village communal organization but with a developed cantonal organization, meeting regularly to discuss common affairs, administer justice, and maintain public peace. Perhaps because this wider community was detached from the connection between village landholding and communal regulation, participation was wider and encompassed both enfranchised and disenfranchised adult males, excluding only women, children, and the clergy. Yet for this very reason this kind of community presented a more vigorous form of peasant resistance, and Hauenstein was the scene of some bitter peasant uprisings, although it lacked the sense of local solidarity on which the notion of 'communalism' is predicated. Heide Wunder has argued that there is no uniform type of medieval peasant community with a universal parameter. Different geographical, demographic, and economic conditions, as well as different processes of interaction between lords and peasants, produced different outcomes, all of which can only be evaluated within their relevant regional context. Even the suggestion that one might distinguish peasant communities according to their position in the historical geography of the medieval German Empire and their temporal sequence – distinguishing between peasant communities in the central areas of the German Empire and those on the periphery – may be helpful for discerning origins, but not for studying long-term developments. Peasant communities were too multi-layered, we might even say multidimensional, to even create a meaningful spectrum. Even if we were to set up a spectrum of communal autonomy, which would undoubtedly place Switzerland and Ditmarschen at the most independent end, this would seriously mislead, because of the tendency towards rural oligarchy, found most notably in Ditmarschen and stretching back to the foundations of that famous peasant republic in an association of family clans. Indeed, it might be worth asking whether the iron law of oligarchy, present in all medieval and early modern cities, was not more characteristic of peasant communities than was 'communalism'. It may indeed have been more characteristic than 'communalism', since the mere form of a commune does not ensure against oligarchy, and may even encourage it: the wealthiest are always the leaders, and there is an inherent impossibility of the non-wealthy rising to communal prominence without a bitter struggle. Thus, as we have seen at several points, peasant communities are shot through with power struggles, which also form a unifying theme of communal life and which may even be more important to explore for communal life than the themes of reciprocity and communality emphasized in the literature. The discourse about communality discussed above was part of this power struggle and served to mask it.

A final important problem to mention in discussing the structure of the peasant commune is the relationship of the secular to the religious community. Since the same word (*Gemeinde*) is used for both, confusion can easily arise, not least if we too casually assume an identity of the two entities. The religious community was different from the secular community in at least two important respects. First, the religious community was far wider than the peasant commune, since it included all adults and children over the age when they were admitted to communion. Second, the village was often not coterminous with the parish, since many late medieval and early modern parishes could encompass several villages, sometimes only supplied with filial churches or chapels, if at all. This often entailed great inconvenience for parishioners in the outlying villages, who had to traverse poor paths in inclement weather to obtain basic religious services – not only for worship, but for baptisms, weddings, and burials. Hence the desire in any village which could scrape together the funds to establish first a chapel and then a parish church of its own, with all appropriate parish rights. This has been called a 'communalization' of the church, although the term leaves crucially ambiguous whether it was primarily a concern of the formal village commune or of the wider community, and so elides crucial differences in meaning.[30] In any case, such attempts to gain a degree of village religious autonomy often led to conflict between communities, since the creation of a new parish diminished the tithe and other incomes for the mother parish and so placed greater burdens on the remaining parishioners.

Here we see once again how the 'communal' impulse (however we define it) actually led to division among rural dwellers, rather than serving primarily to unify them. If we peer more closely into social relationships within the parish community, we see something similar occurring. In theory, the religious community was one in which all were equal before God, although there may have been various religious grounds for exclusion of certain persons, for example, notorious sinners excluded from communion and so from full realization of religious fellowship in the sense mentioned above by Luther. Indeed, in Ditmarschen, a quintessentially peasant communal polity, there existed a spiritual oligarchy, comprised of all men and women considered members of the 'sacramental community' (worthy of admission to the Lord's Supper), which constituted the parish assembly, met monthly in the churchyard, exercised discipline over morals and manners, and decided who should be counted as the 'deserving poor'. However, it was the social relationships within the parish community which most intruded into the Christian communal ideal. In many churches, seating was arranged according to social status, so that peasants with full holdings were ranked above those with half or partial holdings, and these again ahead of cotters and servants (the last usually had no seats in church, but had to stand at the back). It is unclear where parishioners from outlying villages were ranked in such classification systems, and the problem is largely unresearched. However, it is clear that the stratification implicit in the formal commune was imposed on the religious community, and this principle was extended to the church officers of elder and churchwarden, since these positions were also filled from the ranks of village notables (another under-researched field compared with the work on churchwardens now being undertaken for England). The sense of belonging to the religious community was therefore heavily qualified by the principles of exclusion inherent in the notion of the commune, especially since many persons – servants, day-labourers, the poor, those defined as dissolute or disreputable – were subjected to the surveillance of the parish authorities (and so of secular authority) in what was undoubtedly a relationship and exercise of power. We do not know how far the invocation of the community as a religious ideal by the evangelical movements of the sixteenth century transcended or merely conformed to this restricted sense of community, shot through with its inequalities of power and status, but it seriously misleads if we elide the distinction.

There is one last point to bear in mind when we reflect on the long-term fate of German peasant communities. Although peasants made up almost 90 per cent of the German population, village communities did not extend across the entire surface of the land (unlike today, where no area is excluded from local government boundaries and communal territory is continuous). Many areas were thus free of communal control, not least castles or monasteries, mills, and other enterprises.[31] In the middle ages, control over continuous tracts of land was ensured by legal jurisdictions, but the trend from the later middle ages was for territorial rulers to extend control over their lands, and here any form of polity built on peasant communities was intrinsically weak (Switzerland may be the exception that proves the rule, and in any case many Swiss cantons were in effect city-based states in which the rule of the town over the countryside was not dissimilar from that of any other territorial lord). It comes as no surprise from all that we have said here that the long-term development of peasant communities saw them progressively integrated into the growing princely territorial states. This was a relatively smooth process, in which the commune was accepted as the lowest unit of administration and allowed a considerable degree of control over its affairs, with the state enforcing its will for reasons of administrative efficiency, economic rationality, or simply to assert sovereign authority. Whether the waves of development Endres has discerned for Franconia, with peaks following the Peasants' War of 1525, around 1600, after the Thirty Years' War, and in the middle of the eighteenth century can be generalized for Germany as a whole must be explored further. However, the ease of the process, despite continuous peasant resistance, does seem to show, in contradistinction to the communalism thesis, that the status of subject and 'common man' (in the sense of the member of a commune) were not at all incompatible.

Urban communities

The urban community was entirely different in structure and character
from the peasant community. An older debate as to whether the peasant
community was prior and the urban community an imitation of it, or
whether the peasants were influenced by the example of the townsmen,
has been superseded by the view that development was simultaneous.[32]
However, the issue has little relevance to the understanding of urban
community in our period. It is more important to bear in mind that the
town of late medieval and early modern Germany was no less complex
and many-sided than the peasant community. It is even doubtful whether
we can speak of 'the' town, rather than of an agglomerate of many types
of urban settlement. There were towns smaller and less significant than
villages, towns which were scarcely economically viable, towns whose sole
existence depended on their attachment to a monastery or fortification,
and towns which never achieved any form of municipal government.[33] For
our purposes, it is only towns with a form of municipal self-government
that really figure as communities in a sense comparable to peasant communities. One similarity with the peasant community is that not all
residents of such towns were members of the commonality. The most usual
mark of inclusion was the category of citizenship (*Bürger*), which was
defined according to widely variable criteria. At one end of the spectrum,
citizenship could apply to all adult residents, but this was unusual. The
most common 'broad' definition admitted to citizenship all economically
independent persons, whether craftsmen, merchants, or landowners.
However, this usually meant male heads of households, since only those
with economic independence were allowed to marry and establish a
household. Thus the common body of citizens, which was usually thought
to constitute the urban 'commune', was typically very small. It excluded
women, children, unmarried adult males (these sometimes attained membership if they were sons of citizens), day-labourers, servants, lodgers and
guests, the clergy (before the Reformation), nobles, and their servants
resident in the town. Citizens could sometimes make up no more than a
fifth of a town's inhabitants.[34]

The urban 'commune' differed from the peasant community in another
crucial respect, in that its government, usually a town council (*Rat*), was
not always elected by the citizens. In some towns under the close control
of a city overlord (who could be a nobleman or a corporation such as a
cloister), the town council was appointed by the lord or his representative,
usually a bailiff or steward (*Vogt*). An intermediate position between
appointment and election occurred where a town had the right to present
a list of possible town councillors to the overlord, from whom the town
council was finally chosen or confirmed, thus allowing the appearance of

an election within a strictly hierarchical relationship. Even where they were not appointed from above, many town councils were co-optive bodies in which the councillors maintained their numbers by self-recruitment, often from the ranks of ruling families who constituted a governing elite. Indeed, even if the town council was elected by the body of citizens, in some cases councillors could only be elected from the ranks of those families eligible for council office (*ratsfähig*). In this and in many other respects, the urban commune is not at all comparable with the peasant commune, since the latter depended on a single principle of membership (holding of land) and the electoral principle for communal officials was wellnigh universal, something that cannot be said of the far more varied urban commune.[35]

We can see something of this variation in the different polities prevailing in German towns of the sixteenth century. There were towns ruled by oligarchies of elite families, from whose ranks alone town councillors were chosen. In the later middle ages, under the influence of humanism, such families attempted to present themselves in aristocratic guise, most notably by styling themselves 'patricians', in analogy with the senatorial patriciate of the Roman Republic – in Cologne such 'patrician' families even attempted to trace their descent from Roman senatorial families. These families were or had been powerful property-owners, mostly landowners, in the town for many generations – although this did not prevent downward mobility, and there were many poor 'patrician' families whose political privilege and status were resented by economically powerful families without the equivalent prestige conferred by public office. Ruling elites were not only constituted by property-holding, but could also be constituted by sheer wealth, as in the great mercantile towns of north Germany, where merchant families played the role of an urban patriciate. A merchant ruling elite was less closed to newcomers, but could preserve exclusivity by a number of mechanisms, either by guild membership (for example, a merchants' guild or a cloth-merchants' guild) or by forming a drinking-club, literally a society of those who met in a particular tavern or parlour. These were no less sites of power-broking than the London clubs of the modern period, but attained a greater significance where they formed the basis for election to municipal office. Because the term 'patrician' often has overtones of hereditary qualification for office and power, and the ruling elites of many towns were more complex and permeable than the notion allows, it is more common to use the word 'notables' (*Ehrbarkeit*) to describe such urban ruling elites, and they often referred to themselves in such a way.[36]

Some towns were governed by a guild constitution, that is, craft guilds formed the basis of representation on which the town council was elected, often the guild electing one or two representatives to the council. Guild constitutions were often achieved as a result of fierce struggles against rule by notables, especially in the fourteenth to sixteenth centuries. Historians of the nineteenth century tended to regard the struggles for guild repre-

sentation as akin to struggles for democracy, and the disputes of the fourteenth century were often misleadingly labelled 'guild revolutions'.[37] Yet
most guilds were far from democratic institutions, and towns with guild
constitutions were certainly not democracies even in any remote sense.
First, guilds were extremely hierarchical among themselves, with
merchants, cloth-merchants, and butchers often constituting extremely
powerful guilds which sought to arrogate control to themselves, either by
insisting on control of the office of mayor or by a differential weighting
in the number of councillors they could elect. Less influential guilds could
be excluded from representation on urban bodies altogether, or given
minimal representation, such as one councillor for several guilds. Struggles
for guild representation always had a twofold aspect: guilds against
notables, often older elites of non-craft background; and lesser guilds,
seeking to gain representation or to widen it, against more powerful guilds.
The issue of guild constitutions becomes even more complicated when we
realize that non-guild elites could also seek to preserve their influence and
grip on power, if acceptance of a guild constitution was unavoidable, by
forming themselves into a 'guild' or guild-like corporation and claiming
privileged rights over other guilds. Many 'societies' (*Gesellschaften*) or
drinking-clubs (*Trinkstuben*) arose in this way, and gave some towns a
curiously mixed (notable–guild) constitution.[38]

Guilds were also strongly hierarchical internally. Only guildmasters
counted as full members (that is, able to form their own household and
workshop), although journeymen and apprentices were encompassed by
the membership of the guild corporation and subject to its discipline. In
some trades, the journeymen sought to form their own associations,
although these were regarded with deep suspicion by guilds and city rulers
alike, and were only permitted after bitter struggles. In theory, most guilds
elected their own presiding officers, one or more guildmasters, although
this election could also be subject to political control from the town
council. Some councils, doubtless aware of how unruly an element guilds
could be, insisted on approving the election, or else choosing the guildmasters from a list presented by the guild, in some cases simply appointing
the guildmasters themselves. In any case, most town councils preferred to
keep guilds firmly under control by using the guildmaster as an instrument. A guildmaster had to take an oath of loyalty to the council (to coun-
terbalance his oath to serve the guild); he was responsible for ensuring that
all council statutes and ordinances were observed within the guild; and if
the guild was allowed a minimum of internal jurisdiction (for example,
over indiscipline among its members), he acted as an arm of the council.
Representatives on town councils were most commonly chosen from the
ranks of present and past guildmasters, if they were not the guildmasters
themselves virtually *ex officio*. Thus, guildmasters could wear two hats,
representing guild interests in city politics, but also representing the
interests of the city government within their own guild. This was especially

the case where a ruling elite formed across guild lines, often linked by ties of marriage and friendship to form ruling cliques, virtually pure power elites whose grip on power was difficult to challenge.[39]

Some towns developed a different principle of political organization, based on town quarters or parishes. This may possibly have arisen from the organization of citizen militias, and constituted a topographical basis for representation, cutting across elite or guild interests, although many town quarters were characterized by the concentration of a particular craft or trade within them. Representation by quarters was a means by which those citizens not organized in corporations such as guilds or societies could gain access to power. This could include poorer artisans, whose numbers were too few to constitute a guild or whose trades were so little regarded that they were excluded from guild representation. It could be a means by which disenfranchised residents could break into the process of representation. Thus, we find in some towns very complex patterns of representation: what may look like a guild constitution, but which also accords privileged representation to 'patrician' elites, a guild constitution which is heavily weighted towards certain privileged guilds, and a principle of representation by quarters alongside a structure of guild representation. Sometimes all these forms can be found in the same town constitution, the cumulative result of successive struggles to change the representation of various interest groups. One final aspect of urban constitutions is worthy of mention. In many towns, the gradual widening of representation often led to the creation of a large and unwieldy town council, and it was a common solution to draw more effective power, especially executive decision-making, into a smaller body, often designated as a Small Council by contrast to the Great Council formed by the wider body. Sometimes this body was known as a Privy Council, sometimes by the number of its members (the Thirteen or the Council of Ten). In towns with especially wide representation, the process of concentration of power could be taken a step further, with an Inner Council being formed from the Small Council, reserving to itself important financial, military, and foreign policy matters. We can see here one of the basic principles of oligarchy at work, whereby as the representation of any political body is widened, the site of effective power is withdrawn to a smaller, more intimate body.[40]

Early modern towns were, therefore, scarcely 'democratic' in any modern sense, despite the existence of principles of majority election at various levels. If any blanket term is applicable to the polity of German towns it is that they were inherently oligarchic. Indeed, we should not use modern categories of 'democracy' for early modern towns at any level, whether that of their internal constitution or their external status. An imperial city was virtually an independent republic, subject to no authority other than the Emperor, and for this reason imperial cities used to be held up as examples of the horizontal, communal principle. Yet a city such as Regensburg was willing at the end of the fifteenth century to cede its imperial status in the hope of gaining economic advantage, while Göttingen, technically an imperial city, steadfastly refused to heed repeated calls to the Imperial Diet, possibly because it did not wish to be subject to imperial taxation. It belonged to a group of north German towns, technically subject to local ruling princes, but which were virtually autonomous.[41] On the other hand, guild or communal representation was by no means inimical to lordship, and guilds could intrigue with a town's overlord or a local prince in the hope of gaining internal advantage, especially against a merchant or patrician government. Princes knew how to make mischief in times of internal dispute within towns by attempting to address letters to guilds or to the commune in opposition to the town council.[42] This brings us to the question of how the terms 'common' or 'commune' were applied in and to towns. It is important at this point to realize that towns, even more than villages, can be best understood as constituted by a complex pattern of interest groups, continually struggling to reconcile individual and sometimes multiple interests one with another, and achieving this through very diverse forms of balancing or reconciling of interests.[43] Because of the very nature of towns, their diversity both internally and from one to the other, the nature of what a 'commune' meant was highly varied, and in no way comparable to the relatively simple 'communal' principle in the peasant community.

In what sense, therefore, were the terms *gemein* or *Gemeinde* used in pre-modern German towns? Here the ranges of meaning are as complex as for peasant communities, in many ways perhaps more complex because of greater urban social differentiation. An entire city can be called a 'commune', and the term *gemein* used to mean the communality of all those living together within its walls. However, the term *Gemeinde* was also used in a series of progressively narrower meanings. It sometimes designated those residing within the urban community who did not hold citizenship, in the sense of an undifferentiated 'common folk'.[44] In the expression *Rat und Gemeinde*, it could express the idea that the council spoke in the name of the political community, often used to demonstrate that the council had consulted the 'commune', the body of enfranchised citizens. This does not necessarily mean that there had been a gathering of the commune which voted on the measure in question, although town councils did follow this procedure on especially weighty matters for which a show of unanimity or at least majority support was deemed essential. Thus, it could mean the assembled citizenry, voting by majority decision. However, it could also signify a contrast between office-holders and the commune, either a consequence of urban oppositional movements or the expression of a desire to impose the ruling council's authority on the commune as a distinct and subordinate entity.[45] It could also signify the narrower group of enfranchised citizens as opposed to mere inhabitants (in the phrase *gemeinde und inwoner*), the reverse of the meaning mentioned above. It could refer to those organized in guilds and conceived of as a communality, as in a document from Mainz in 1411, which speaks of 'the guildmasters, the guilds and the entire community belonging to the guilds'.[46] The term *Gemeinde* (along with all the associations of *gemein*) was therefore sufficiently elastic to be appropriated in urban politics to throw different kinds of cloaks over rather different groupings of interest. This will be especially clear if we examine communal movements.

Communal movements and 'communalism'

There is one important difference between peasant and urban communal movements that emphasizes their entirely distinct characters. Peasant movements were usually directed against a lord or some similar hierarchical person or body. Although there were deep internal divisions within peasant communities and these often surfaced on the occasion of anti-seigneurial resistance, in general the peasant community closed ranks against external threats, so that peasant movements can give a deceptive appearance of internal cohesion and communality. Yet even this was sometimes hard to achieve, and was the result of strenuous political action. Villages may have joined together in resistance to a common lord, but not all villages or villagers were willing to join in, and sometimes had to be moved to do so by threats or coercion. Creating an alliance of villages under different lords was an even more precarious enterprise. It could be achieved under certain circumstances, as the German Peasants' War showed to devastating effect, but such alliances were fragile and unstable, one of the reasons for the often rapid dissolution of large-scale peasant resistance.[47] Urban communal movements almost always occurred within a town: there was rarely any solidarity of the communal opposition from town to town. Even where towns had close relationships one with another, in the form of urban leagues or simply of agreements of mutual assistance, other towns were reluctant to become involved in the internal affairs of a town embroiled in political upheaval. The most that might be done was to offer refuge to fugitive town councillors, or to adopt a neutral, wait-and-see attitude. Thus, it can be very misleading to bundle together civic upheavals in many towns into any kind of 'burgher movement', since the internal issues may have varied from town to town, and there was certainly no wider sense of shared concern. Where towns made common cause, it was often against the nobility or the clergy, sometimes against a territorial prince, but never in terms of a shared 'communal movement'. This emphasizes the uniqueness of the evangelical movements of the early sixteenth century, which did supply a principle transcending the otherwise atomistic form of urban communal movements, an issue to which we shall return below.[48]

Urban communal movements may be seen as containing two different emphases, which sometimes overlapped or merged. On the one hand, there was the attempt of groups excluded from a share in political power or status to force their way into city government, and many urban communal movements had this character, aiming at widening representation or eligibility; at weakening oligarchic control; or even simply attacking mismanagement, corruption or political ineptitude, usually provoked by some spectacular disaster such as a lost military campaign or a public bankruptcy. A second occasion for urban communal movements involved the tendency of city governments to arrogate to themselves notions of hierarchical authority (*Obrigkeit*) modelled on those within the aristocratic world of lordship. On one view of it, this tendency had always been inherent in towns, since municipal governments had merely taken over offices and competences from the town's lord, especially marked in the case of legal jurisdiction. On the other hand, the most common legitimation of municipal government was horizontal and corporative, the authority of the town council being seen as derived from the oath of association taken by the body of the citizens that constituted them as a corporation, and in whose name the town council governed. It could even be said that the principles of lordship and of communality were not competing but complementary principles, to be found in every town.[49]

It was none the less a clear trend from the fifteenth century onwards in towns of all types that the council increasingly began to emphasize its power of authority 'from above', and to distinguish itself from its citizens as an agent of domination and hierarchical rule. Progressively, it began to regard and to speak of its citizens as subjects. Many communal movements were directed against this trend or its manifestations, which was not unconnected to the tendency towards oligarchy or plutocracy. Such communal movements developed as forms of opposition to council policy, often around well-defined issues, of which we can identify the most common and important.[50] *Financial mismanagement* often provoked the most frequent demand, that the town council present an annual, public accounting of the city's financial affairs to the commune. This was, of course, an impossible task and in effect a committee was often elected by the commune for the purpose, or sometimes just representatives of the commune, perhaps chosen from each quarter, to act as auditors. These representatives were often incorporated into the municipal government, sometimes even being drawn into the government of a clique, showing how easily the impulse towards communal control could be weakened or negated.

A second major issue was the *right of free assembly* of the commune. Town councils emphasizing a notion of magisterial authority (*Obrigkeit*) wished to control when, where, and how the commune might assemble, and regarded unauthorized assemblies of citizens as dangerous and akin to conspiracy. A town council wished to stage an assembly of the commune under its own control as infrequently as possible, minimally once a year, when a new council was inaugurated by taking oaths of office and when citizens renewed their oaths of allegiance to the city and obedience to its magistrates. Irregular assemblies of the commune could be called to decide especially weighty matters, but were regarded with caution, since there was always a danger when large numbers were assembled of dissent finding wider expression and turning into open opposition or even disturbance. Many councils thus preferred to consult communal representatives or guild-masters, or else to consult guilds individually, without allowing these bodies to meet collectively. The demand for free assembly was therefore a sensitive point on both sides of the opposition between council and commune.[51] It was linked to the third issue, *secrecy in government.*

Town councils insisted, for what we might today call 'reasons of state', that certain matters should be kept secret in order not to endanger civic policy or interests, especially in matters of foreign policy and military affairs. However, government by oligarchy or by clique often led to other matters being kept secret for reasons purely of political expediency. These could include the real condition of a city's finances (massive indebtedness, inability to meet interest repayments on loans), the alienation of civic property, suppression of communal or guild privileges, or merely wheeling and dealing in external affairs. Such issues were often revealed only when citizens assembled together in numbers or circumstances such that the council was forced to reveal what had been going on. Sometimes such secrets tumbled out as a result of another investigation. It was frequently the case when a communal movement formed in serious opposition to the town council that a communal committee was formed to deal with the council, sometimes to act almost as a counter-government.[52] It was the investigations of such committees that uncovered many such hidden trans-actions of great embarrassment to the council or its individual members. Occasions when such political secrets surfaced and led to communal dis-turbance were frequent enough for opposition movements to insist on more open government, or at least access to government business, and for town councils to wish to preserve secrecy at all costs.

These issues flowed into three other grievances: the demand for *frequent consultation* of the commune about important civic policy, the demand for *wider representation* in the organs of government, and the most paramount economic grievance, *communal approval of taxation*, which usually related less to direct taxation and more to the imposition of excises on foodstuffs, brewing, milling, and above all on the sale of beer and wine. A seventh major grievance touched the very nature of the city as a collective-corporate entity, that of *arbitrary arrest*. The sense of the town as a legal personality was every bit as strong among citizens as it was in peasant communities. It flowed from several aspects of the town's very origin and *raison d'être.* Towns were thought of as havens of peace and security against arbitrary force against the person or his property, including renunciation of revenge or blood-feud. To bid the keeping of the peace was the duty of every citizen, and an aspect of sharing in the benefits of collective urban life. Citizenship was also predicated on the freedom of the citizens and their equality before the law, a privilege which was also extended to every resident of a town. On this basis, the town council was also obliged to pursue and protect the legal interests of every citizen against the claims of outsiders and outside legal demands.[53] One of the major expressions of these legal principles was the right of the citizen not to be arrested arbitrarily, but to be summoned to explain himself before the town council in its judicial capacity, so that policing rested strongly on consent. This was a principle often breached in the interests of precluding flight of culprits or preventing disturbance, but one firmly upheld by oppositional movements against what were seen as arbitrary expressions of magisterial authority.

There were, therefore, potent issues to do with the nature of urban communality around which oppositional movements developed. For this reason, such movements often invoked the concept of the commune, and presented themselves as 'the commune' (*die Gemeinde*) in opposition to the council. The communal movement invoked the value of the 'common good' (*Gemeinnutz*), and invariably accused the council of pursuing self-interest (*Eigennutz*).[54] These terms often featured in the upheavals provoked by communal movements, and represented an attempt by both sides to appropriate communal discourse, with its high moral tone. In normal circumstances, town councils invoked the 'common good' in reconciling divergent interests and advancing particular policies. Opposition to policy was condemned as self-interest or sectional interest, most effective against one guild or alliance (in the sense of a clique of friends or relatives seeking advantage). However, the oppositional movements also appropriated the concept, not least by presenting themselves as the *Gemeinde*, a term which invoked both the formal commune and the communality of the town as a whole. We must recall here that a town council often called itself the *gemein Rat* when operating within collectivity, but it could also present itself as standing outside and above the commune, as in the expression 'mayor, council and commune' (*Bürgermeister, Rat und Gemeinde*), as an additive entity.[55] The opposition movements often invoked the polarity by electing *gemeine Männer* as communal representatives to negotiate with the council on grievances, a terminology which undoubtedly also carried with it the overtones of impartial mediation. This communal-oppositional ideology was sufficiently strong that in many towns the commune achieved what amounted to a 'right of rebellion', the recognition that in certain circumstances the commune could legitimately set itself against the town council.[56]

Urban communal movements thus justified themselves by excluding the town council from the notion of communality. But it would be naïve to see them as representing the collectivity of the town or its inhabitants against any principle of lordship or domination. The notion of communality they employed also involved downwards exclusion, against non-citizens, non-guildsmen, the *gemeine Leute* in the pejorative sense, a sense town councils exploited when they sought to discredit oppositional movements.[57] It is in some ways valid to use the term 'communalism' to describe this process of formation of urban opposition movements and their appropriation of hegemonic concepts of communality, although it is altogether rather more fluid and inward-looking than the 'communalism' that might be discerned among peasant movements. It was, however, a very restricted notion of community, shot through with inequalities of power and status, and in the last resort one which was easily reconcilable with notions of vertical hierarchy. Indeed, the progressive widening of urban government to include representatives of the 'commune', whether in the form of representatives elected from town quarters or simply a number of councillors elected by the citizenry at large, was in no way inimical to the processes either of urban oligarchy or of control by territorial rulers. Territorial rulers may even have welcomed this broadening of participation, since it ensured wider levels of compliance with the state's decrees, and the progressive widening of representation runs parallel to the strengthening of the territorial state in Germany over the entire early modern period. On the other hand, a prince could use the withdrawal of municipal autonomy as a mark of displeasure at the inability of the mayor or council to control its own citizens. This occurred in the small Thuringian town of Berga an der Elster in 1560 following disputes between council and citizens around the middle of the century. The citizens lost the right to elect their councillors (who had in any case been subject to confirmation), and instead had to endure the mayor and councillors being appointed by their lord.[58]

There is one final issue to discuss. The notion of communality has been placed for the last two decades firmly in the centre of discussion of Reformation history because of the way the religious reformers and the evangelical movements of the sixteenth century invoked community as a religious ideal.[59] We do not yet know how far this religious usage of the notion of community conformed to or transcended the sociopolitical meanings of *gemein* and *Gemeinde* in the sense we have been discussing them. Luther certainly believed that the notions could be hedged off into purely spiritual meanings, although we have seen some instances above where he was willing to mix spiritual and secular meanings. The issue is complicated by the fact that evangelical propaganda was willing to invoke all the positive moral weighting of the concept of community-commonality as a discursive strategy to disseminate its message. Thus, it summoned up all the allusions to the common good, the common man, community of interest, and communality as signifiers in evangelical discourse, most of all exploiting the ambiguity and overlap that often existed between the secular and the religious community, for example, by emphasizing the right of the community to elect its own pastors. Yet the resonances of the terms *gemein* and *Gemeinde* were so diverse, first between town and country, and then

within both the urban and the peasant community, that it is misleading to
represent them under a single notion of 'communalism'. Indeed, ignoring
these differences and distinctions can be seriously misleading because it
distracts from the fact that they were in themselves matters of contest, part
of power plays to impart particular forms of meaning in particular
contexts. The study of communities in the late medieval and early modern
period is of great importance because it opens up a sense of the dynamic
nature of social and political relationships within the urban and peasant
worlds. That dynamic, however, can be understood or recovered, not by
focusing on a single overarching concept, but rather by paying attention
to competing discourses and strategies of power.

Notes

1   His output on this theme was prodigious: see G. L. von Maurer, *Einleitung
    zur Geschichte der Mark-, Hof- und Stadtverfassung und der öffentlichen
    Gewalt* (Munich, 1854); *Geschichte der Markenverfassung in Deutschland*
    (Erlangen, 1856); *Geschichte der Fronhöfen, des Bauernhofs und der
    Hofverfassung in Deutschland* (4 vols., Erlangen, 1862–3); *Geschichte der
    Dorfverfassung in Deutschland* (2 vols., Erlangen, 1865–6).
2   O. von Gierke, *Das deutsche Genossenschaftsrecht* (4 vols., Berlin,
    1868–1913). On the continual preoccupation of German historiography with
    the theme of community, especially peasant community, see Werner Rösener,
    Die Bauern in der europäischen Geschichte (Munich, 1993), pp. 9–24; Heide
    Wunder, *Die bäuerliche Gemeinde in Deutschland* (Göttingen, 1986). On the
    importance of Maurer, see Wunder, *Bäuerliche Gemeinde*, p. 142; on Gierke,
    Otto von Gierke, *Community in Historical Perspective*, ed. Antony Black
    (Cambridge, 1990), pp. xiv–xxx. Especially illuminating on the origins of
    Gierke's views is Otto Gerhard Oexle, 'Die mittelalterliche Zunft als
    Forschungsproblem', *BdLG* CXVIII (1982), pp. 1–44, here pp. 14–28. I have
    followed Antony Black in translating *Genossenschaft* as 'fellowship', instead
    of the more usual 'corporatism', to capture the less impersonal notion in
    Gierke's viewpoint.
3   Oexle, 'Die mittelalterliche Zunft', pp. 33–5 shows, however, how Tönnies
    split Gierke's two dialectical concepts into a pair of polar opposites. The
    quotation from Black in Gierke, *Community*, p. xvii; the influences on
    Ullmann and Moeller on pp. xxv and 252, n. 28.
4   On agrarian and regional history I have followed the comments in Wunder,
    Bäuerliche Gemeinde, p. 145; for rural sociology, Leopold von Wiese, ed., *Das
    Dorf als soziales Gebilde* (Munich, 1928) and the references in his article
    'Ländliche Siedlungen', in A. Vierkandt, ed., *Handwörterbuch der Soziologie*
    (Stuttgart, 1931), p. 526; the Nazi tradition represented by H. F. K. Günther,
    *Bauernglaube. Zeugnisse über Glauben und Frömmigkeit der deutschen
    Bauern* (Berlin, 1942). For a slightly different view of 1920s German ethno-
    logical interest in community, G. Wiegelmann, 'Gemeindestudien in
    Deutschland. Trends – Probleme – Aufgaben', in Weigelmann, ed., *Gemeinde
    in Wandel. Volkskundliche Gemeindestudien in Europa* (Münster, 1979), pp.

67–86, esp. pp. 67–8. See also K. S. Bader, *Studien zur Rechtsgeschichte des mittelalterlichen Dorfes* (3 vols., Weimar, 1957; repr. Cologne, 1962; Vienna/Cologne/Graz, 1973).

5 Bernd Moeller, *Reichstadt und Reformation* (Gütersloh, 1962; 2nd edn Berlin, 1987). For an overview of work on the 'common good', Winfried Schulze, 'Vom Gemeinnutz zum Eigennutz. Über den Normenwandel in der ständischen Gesellschaft der frühen Neuzeit', *HZ* CCXLIII (1986), pp. 591–626. Representative of English interest in urban community, Charles Phythian-Adams, *Desolation of a City. Coventry and the Urban Crisis of the Later Middle Ages* (Cambridge, 1979); for North American studies, Mack Walker, *German Home Towns. Community, State and General Estate 1448–1871* (Ithaca, NY, 1971); R. F. E. Weissmann, *Ritual Brotherhood in Renaissance Florence* (New York, 1982). The trends in German urban history are reflected in Eberhard Isenmann, *Die deutsche Stadt im Spätmittelalter 1250–1500* (Stuttgart, 1988) and summarized by Heinz Schilling, *Die Stadt in der frühen Neuzeit* (Munich, 1993), pp. 51–6.

6 Wunder, *Bäuerliche Gemeinde*, pp. 7–8; for an example of the earlier interest, Franz Steinbach, 'Geschichtliche Grundlagen der kommunalen Selbstverwaltung in Deutschland', *Rheinisches Archiv* XX (1932), pp. 17–72.

7 Edgar Reitz and Peter Steinbach, *Heimat. Eine deutsche Chronik* (Nördlingen, 1988); see also the comments in Anton Kaes, *From Hitler to Heimat. The Return of History as Film* (Cambridge, Mass., 1989), pp. 161–92, esp. pp. 166–9.

8 Utz Jeggle, *Kiebingen. Eine Heimatgeschichte. Zum Prozeß der Zivilisation in einem schwäbischen Dorf* (Tübingen, 1977), the context of this work identified by Wunder, *Bäuerliche Gemeinde*, pp. 9–10. The strong focus on the crisis of the village community in U. Jeggle, 'Krise der Gemeinde. Krise der Gemeindeforschung', in G. Wiegelmann, ed., *Gemeinde im Wandel* (Münster, 1979), pp. 101–10; for sociological studies of community, R. König, *Grundformen der Gesellschaft: die Gemeinde* (Hamburg, 1958), English translation as *The Community* (London, 1968).

9 Jerome Blum, 'The Internal Structure and Politics of the European Village Community', *JMH* XLIII (1971), pp. 541–76; David Sabean, 'The Communal Basis of pre-1800 Risings in Western Europe', *Comparative Politics* VIII (1976), pp. 355–64.

10 This is most marked in his short *Deutsche Untertanen. Ein Widerspruch* (Munich, 1981). For a wider assessment of Blickle's work as a whole, R. W. Scribner, 'Communalism: Universal Category or Ideological Construct?', *Historical Journal* XXXVII (1994), pp. 199–207.

11 See Koenig, *The Community*, pp. 14–21; Black, in Gierke, *Community*, p. xxxi.

12 Peter Blickle, 'Die Dorfgerichtsordnung von Buxheim vom Jahre 1553', *Memminger Geschichtsblätter* (1965), pp. 15–89, esp. pp. 43–4.

13 Jakob Grimm, *Deutsches Wörterbuch* IV (Leipzig, 1897), col. 3170. Grimm's entries for the words *gemein* and *gemeinde*, cols. 3169–3242, constitute an extended essay in historical semantics, drawing on his extraordinary knowledge of a vast range of medieval and early modern sources. Despite its occasional romanticism, it is far superior in quality to many modern attempts at *Begriffsgeschichte*, especially because it is constructed not from philosophy, theology, or political theory but from the actual use of language in a wide variety of social settings. It provides the basis for the comments offered in the following paragraphs. I have also followed Grimm in using the pre-modern spellings of nouns throughout. For a more localized lexical overview, see Herbert Reyer, *Die Dorfgemeinde im nördlichen Hessen. Untersuchungen zur*

hessischen Dorfverfassung im Spätmittelalter und in der frühen Neuzeit (Marburg, 1983), pp. 12–16.

14   'Gemeinschaft heiszt hie das gemeine gut, des viel theilhaftig sind und geneiszen, als gemein born, gemeine gassen, gemeiner acker, wiesen, holz, feuer', *Vom Abendmahl Christi, Bekenntnis* (1528), M. Luther, *Werke. Kritische Gesamtausgabe* (58 vols., Weimar, 1883–1993), hereafter *WA* XXVI, p. 490.

15   'ir habt zwo frucht von dem heiligen sacrament. eine ist, das es uns machet brüder und miterben des herrn Christi, also, das aus im und uns werde ein kuche. die ander, das wir auch *gemein und eins* werden mit allen andern leuten auf erden, und auch all ein kuche', *Eyn Sermon am grunen donnerstag* (1523), *WA*, XII, p. 485.

16   'Deudsche bücher sind fürnemlich dem gemeinen man gemacht, im hause zu lesen', *Eine Predigt, daß man Kinder zur Schule halten soll* (1530), *WA* XXX(2), p. 519.

17   Rösener, *Bauern in der europäischen Geschichte*, pp. 80, 205–7.

18   Wunder, *Bäuerliche Gemeinde*, p. 13; on the 'contractual views' of the rebels of 1525, Tom Scott and Bob Scribner, eds, *The German Peasants' War. A History in Documents* (Atlantic Highlands, NJ, 1991), p. 68 (Article 23 of the Articles of the Peasants of Stühlingen).

19   M. Hofmann, 'Die Dorfverfassung im Obermaingebiet', *JbfränkLF* 6–7 (1941), pp. 140–96, here p. 149.

20   Hofmann, 'Dorfverfassung im Obermaingebiet', p. 152; Anton Schmid, Gemeinschafts- und Gemeinderechte im altbäyerisch-schwäbischen Gebiet', *ZBLG* IV (1931), pp. 377–98, here pp. 371–2, 378; David Sabean, *Landbesitz und Gesellschaft am Vorabend des Bauernkriegs* (Stuttgart, 1972), pp. 102–4. In East Swabia cottagers could be members of the commune – see Hermann Grees, *Ländliche Unterschichten und ländliche Siedlung in Ostschwaben* (Tübingen, 1975), p. 24 – but this seems to have been an exception.

21   On conflict in general, Rösener, *Bauern in der europäischen Geschichte* p. 211; for examples of internal disputes, revealing the tyranny of the collective will against the individual, Jochen Richter, 'Wesen und Funktion der spätfeudalen Landgemeinde. Erläutert an den Dörfern des Klosteramts Dobbertin', *JbG Feudalismus* XI (1987), pp. 223–69, here pp. 245–6, 249.

22   Richter, 'Wesen und Funktion der spätfeudalen Landgemeinde', pp. 228–9 draws the distinction between a 'real commune' and a 'political commune', following F. Keil, *Die Landgemeinde in den östlichen Provinzen Preußens und die Versuche eine Landgemeindeordnung zu Schaffen* (Leipzig, 1890), pp. 20–2. The terminology was taken up briefly by Bader, *Studien zur Rechtsgeschichte* III, p. 29, but rejected as a matter only of 'late forms', though he did recognize a distinction between corporate and communal-political character (p. 22). Von Maurer, *Geschichte der Dorfverfassung* I, pp. 162–71, recognized the distinction, and devoted a chapter to it. On peasant factionalism, D. M. Leubke, 'Factions and Communities in Early Modern Central Europe', *CEH* XXV (1992), pp. 281–301, and his forthcoming *Faction and Community in the 'Salpeter Wars'*. Ingomar Bog, *Dorfgemeinde, Freiheit und Unfreiheit in Franken* (Stuttgart, 1956), p. 69 suggested that the practice of majority voting in communal decision-making in the course of the fifteenth century was a result of factionalism (*Parteiungen*).

23   Hofmann, 'Dorfverfassung im Obermaingebiet', pp. 155–6; Richter, 'Wesen und Funktion der spätfeudalen Landgemeinde', p. 230 and n. 28; Hartmut Harnisch, 'Gemeindeeigentum und Gemeindefinanzen im Spätfeudalismus', *JbRegG* VIII (1981), pp. 126–74, here pp. 132–40. It was also possible for a

lord to influence elections through the presence of his representative and, in some parts of Brandenburg-Ansbach, to appoint a committee which made the election; Bog, *Dorfgemeinde, Freiheit und Unfreiheit*, p. 72.

24 Richter, 'Wesen und Funktion der spätfeudalen Landgemeinde', pp. 230–1, 243.

25 Wunder, *Bäuerliche Gemeinde*, pp. 48–9.

26 Karl Heinz Quirin, *Herrschaft und Gemeinde nach mitteldeutschen Quellen des 12. bis 18. Jarhunderts* (Göttingen, 1952), pp. 79–84; Rudolf Endres, 'Absolutistische Entwicklungen in fränkischen Territorien im Spiegel der Dorfordnungen', *JbRegG* XVI(2) (1989), pp. 81–93, here p. 93.

27 Endres, 'Absolutistische Entwicklungen', p. 83; see also Anton Schmid, Gemeinschafts- und Gemeinderechte im altbayerisch-schwäbischen Gebiet', *ZBLG* IV (1931), pp. 367–98, esp. pp. 371–5.

28 Hofmann, 'Dorfverfassung im Obermaingebiet', p. 161; Endres, 'Absolutistische Entwicklungen', pp. 86, 93.

29 This and the following paragraphs on regional variations are based on Wunder, *Bäuerliche Gemeinde*, 67–77; Heide Wunder, 'Peasant Communities in Early Modern Germany', in *Les Communautés rurales*, Receuils de la Société Jean Bodin XLIV (1987), pp. 9–52, esp. pp. 28–41; Endres, 'Absolutistische Entwicklung'; and various essays in P. Blickle, ed., *Landgemeinde und Stadtgemeinde in Mitteleuropa* (Munich, 1991).

30 See R. Fuhrmann, 'Dorfgemeinde und Pfründstiftung vor der Reformation. Kommunale Selbstbestimmungschancen zwischen Religion und Recht', in P. Blickle and J. Kunisch, eds, *Kommunalisierung und Christianisierung. Voraussetzungen und Folgen der Reformation 1400–1600* (Berlin, 1989), pp. 77–112.

31 Hofmann, 'Dorfverfassung im Obermaingebiet', p. 153, has usefully pointed this out.

32 Grimm, *Deutsches Wörterbuch* IV, col. 3232, held the former position; for a simultaneous development, Karlheinz Blaschke, 'Dorfgemeinde und Stadtgemeinde in Sachsen zwischen 1300 und 1800', in Blickle, *Landgemeinde und Stadtgemeinde*, pp. 119–43, here p. 120. The literature on German towns is vast and there is no recent comprehensive overview for the early modern period, although Schilling, *Stadt in der frühen Neuzeit* provides a good point of departure. For the medieval period, Isenmann, *Die deutsche Stadt im Spätmittelalter* is an excellent encyclopaedic survey, with enormously helpful bibliographies. The theme of urban communities is covered in Blickle, *Landgemeinde und Stadtgemeinde*, although under variable presuppositions by individual authors. The reflections that follow are based largely on my own work on German towns, accumulated in the course of exploring the nature of the urban Reformation.

33 On definition of what constitutes a 'town', see Ch. 5, pp. 114–15.

34 On citizens and citizenship, Isenmann, *Die deutsche Stadt*, pp. 93–7.

35 On town councils, *Ibid.*, pp. 131–43.

36 On notables, *Ibid.*, p. 249; on the trend to oligarchy, Eberhard Isenmann, 'Die stadtische Gemeinde im oberdeutsch-schweizerischen Raum (1300–1800)', in Blickle, *Landgemeinde und Stadtgemeinde*, pp. 189–261, here p. 203; also Heinz Schilling, 'Civic Republicanism in Late Medieval and Early Modern Cities', in idem, *Religion, Political Culture and the Emergence of Early Modern Society* (Leiden, 1992), p. 28, which emphasizes that communal and corporate ideas not only do not contradict oligarchy, they even presuppose it.

37 For a succinct summary of the discussion of 'guild revolutions', 'citizen struggles', and 'inner-urban conflict' up to the end of the 1980s, see Eva-Marie

Felschow, *Wetzlar in der Krise des Spätmittelalters* (Darmstadt/Marburg, 1985), pp. 177–9. On nineteenth-century views, Karl Schreiner, "Kommunebewegung" und "Zunftrevolution". Zur Gegenwart der mittelalterlichen Stadt im historisch-politischen Denken des 19. Jahrhunderts', in F. Quarthal and W. Setzler, eds, *Städteverfassung – Verfassungsstaat – Presseppolitik. Festschrift für E. Naujoks zum 65. Geburtstag* (Sigmaringen, 1980), pp. 139–68.

38 On guilds and similar organizations, Isenmann, *Die deutsche Stadt*, pp. 299–321; on Trinkstuben, p. 303.

39 On guild masters, Isenmann, *Die deutsche Stadt*, p. 316.

40 On parishes or quarters, Gierke, *Das deutsche Genossenschaftsrecht* II, p. 790, commented that some towns even resembled a federal polity (citing the example of Basel in the 1520s). On Small Councils and oligarchy, Isenmann, *Die deutsche Stadt*, pp. 131, 134, 195; Olaf Mörke. 'Die städtische Gemeinde in mittleren Deutschland', in Blickle, *Landgemeinde und Stadtgemeinde*, pp. 289–308, here p. 302.

41 On Regensburg, I. Striedinger, 'Der Kampf um Regensburg 1486–1492', *Verhandlungen des historischen Vereins für die Oberpfalz und Regensburg* XLIV (1890–1), pp. 1–88; Heft II, pp. 95–205; it is also clear from C. T. Gemeiner, *Die Regensburger Chronik* III (Regensburg, 1821), pp. 703–4, 715–17, that this was a decision of the commune, albeit of a group of notables. On Göttingen, A. Hasselblatt and G. Kaestner, eds, *Urkunden der Stadt Göttingen aus dem xvi. Jht, 1500–33* (Göttingen, 1881), nos. 29, 37–8, 41, 79, 88, 105, 131, 155, 241, 307, 314, 320, 346, 382, 537, 681 for the years 1506–33. On autonomous north German towns, Olaf Mörke, 'Integration und Desintegration. Kirche und Stadtentwicklung in Deutschland vom 14. bis ins 17. Jahrhundert', in N. Bulst and J.-P. Genet, eds, *La Ville, la bourgeoisie et la genèse de l'état moderne (xiie–xviiie siècles)* (Paris, 1988), p. 300 and n. 11 (with further literature).

42 For example, Duke Erich von Braunschweig to the Merchants' Guild in Göttingen, in Hasselblatt and Kaestner, *Urkunden der Stadt Göttingen*, nos. 30 (3 Nov. 1506), 31 (the Town Council's reply of 7 Nov. 1506).

43 On conflict as a continual aspect of urban life, Olaf Mörke, 'Der "Konflict" als Kategorie städtischer Sozialgeschichte der Reformationszeit', in B. Diestelkamp, ed., *Beiträge zum spätmittelalterlichen Städtewesen* (Cologne/Vienna, 1982), pp. 144–61.

44 On these meanings, Gierke, *Das deutsche Genossenschaftsrecht* II, pp. 596–8.

45 *Ibid.* II, pp. 616–17, 786.

46 *Die zunftmeister und die zünfte und die ganze gemeinde, die zu den zunften gehorit,* 'Die Einigung des Raths und der Gemeinde zu Mainz', 5 Feb. 1411, in *Die Chroniken der deutschen Städte* XVII (Leipzig, 1881), p. 368; cf. Grimm, *Deutsches Wörterbuch* IV, col. 3,237, who reads this rather differently as distinguishing guilds from the commune. On several of the terms mentioned here, see *ibid.* IV, cols. 3,202, 3,208, 3,237.

48 See Scott and Scribner, *The German Peasants' War*, pp. 18, 58, 135–8.

48 *Ibid.*, pp. 180–1, on urban tactics in dealing with rebellious peasants, the most common form of inter-urban co-operation.

49 For this view, Isenmann, *Die deutsche Stadt*, p. 131; cf. also Ludwig Remling. 'Formen und Ausmaß gewerblicher Autonomie in nordwestdeutschen Städten (14.–16. Jahrhundert)', in B. Kirchgässner and E. Naujoks, eds, *Stadt und wirtschaftliche Selbstverwaltung* (Sigmaringen, 1987), pp. 60–76, here p. 62, invoking Gierke.

50 The complete list of grievances was often voluminous, but for a succinct summary, Isenmann, *Die deutsche Stadt*, p. 197, with further bibliography.

51 All these issues appeared in exemplary fashion in the 1512 disturbance in Speyer, precipitated by the carpenters' guild meeting without command of the town council and in the absence of their guild masters to discuss a privilege that the council had kept secret from them; *Bericht Verhandlung der Gemeyn gegen Burgermeister und Rat der Stat Speyer*, Stadtarchiv Speyer 1 A 20/1, arts. 4–5; a new oath imposed after the disturbance explicitly obliged citizens to summon no assembly without the town council's knowledge and permission; Stadstarchiv Speyer 1 A 46. On the general opposition to free assembly, G. L. von Maurer, *Geschichte der Städteverfassung in Deutschland* III (Erlangen, 1870), p. 158, who cites the examples of Breslau, Esslingen, Munich, Mainz, Seligenstadt, and Speyer.

52 On these committees, Gudrun Glebe, *Die Gemeinde als alternatives Ordnungsmodell. Zur sozialen und politischen Differenzierung des Gemeindebegriffs in der innerstädtischen Auseinandersetzungen des 14. und 15. Jahrhunderts. Mainz, Magdeburg, München, Lübeck* (Cologne, 1989), pp. 251–2; W. Ehbrecht, 'Form und Bedeutung innerstädtischer Kämpfe am Übergang vom Mittelalter zur Neuzeit', in Ehbrecht, ed., *Städtische Führungsgruppen und Gemeinde in der werdenden Neuzeit* (Cologne/Vienna, 1980), pp. 115–52, here p. 116; R. Postel, 'Bürgerausschüsse und Reformation in Hamburg', in Ehbrecht, *Städtische Führungsgruppen*, pp. 369–83.

53 Isenmann, *Die deutsche Stadt*, pp. 74–5.

54 Schulze, 'Vom Gemeinnutz zum Eigennutz'; Winfried Eberhard, 'Der Legitimationsbegriff des "gemeinen Nutzens" im Streit zwischen Herrschaft und Genossenschaft im Spätmittelalter', in J. O. Fichte, ed., *Zusammenhänge, Einflüße, Wirkungen, Kongreßakten zum ersten Symposium des Mediävistenverbandes in Tübingen* (Berlin, 1986), pp. 241–54; and for a wider view, Hans-Christoph Rublack, 'Political and Social Norms in Urban Communities in the Holy Roman Empire', in P. Blickle, H.-C. Rublack and Winfried Schulze, *Religion, Politics and Social Protest. Three Studies on Early Modern Germany* (London, 1984), pp. 24–60.

55 See Gierke, *Das deutsche Genossenschaftsrecht* II, pp. 780–5.

56 See Grimm, *Deutsches Wörterbuch* IV, cols. 3,190, 3,202 for the two meanings of *gemeine männer*; on right of rebellion, Ehbrecht, 'Form und Bedeutung innerstädtischer Kämpfe', p. 131.

57 The double-exclusion principle has been established by Glebe, *Gemeinde als alternatives Ordnungsmodell*, p. 256.

58 Willy Flach, *Verfassungsgeschichte einer grundherrlichen Stadt Berga an der Elster* (Leipzig, 1934), p. 53.

59 Debate on this subject, provoked by the works of Moeller, *Reichstadt und Reformation*, and Blickle, *Gemeindereformation*, is still at an inconclusive stage. For recent critical assessments from different directions, see Euan Cameron, *The European Reformation* (Oxford, 1991), pp. 210–63; Mark U. Edwards, 'Gemeindereformation als Bindeglied der mittelalterlichen und der neuzeitlichen Welt', *HZ* CCXLIX (1989), pp. 95–105; Mörke, 'Integration und Desintegration'; B. Rüth, 'Reformation und Konfessionsbildung im städtischen Bereich. Perspektiven der Forschung', *ZRG KA* LXXVII (1991), pp. 197–282; Heinz Schilling, 'The Communal Reformation in Germany', in idem, *Religion, Political Culture and the Emergence of Early Modern Society* (Leiden, 1992), pp. 189–201; Tom Scott, 'The Common People in the German Reformation', *Historical Journal* XXXIV (1991), pp. 183–92; R. W. Scribner, 'Paradigms of Urban Reform: *Gemeindereformation* or Erastian Reformation' in Leif Grane and Kai Hørby, eds, *Die dänische Reformation vor ihrem internationalen Hintergrund* (Göttingen, 1990), pp. 111–28.

|12|

Daily Life in Late Medieval and Early Modern Germany

ROBERT JÜTTE

In search of material culture and daily life in Germany

Problems of conceptualization

German scholars have only recently discovered the history of daily life and material culture, and still have not yet fully emancipated themselves from a concept of *Kulturgeschichte* mainly based on literary sources.[1] Our information from literary evidence has in the meantime been supplemented by the study of physical artefacts, such as houses and furniture, or the description of such artefacts in probate inventories. German ethnologists have traditionally been closer to the people and their ways of life than the historians. It is only in the past ten years or so that German social historians and ethnologists have virtually converged on this broad approach to material culture, now understood in a wide sense, to include such cultural constructs as the categories of sickness or dirt and ritualized forms of behaviour such as feasting or violence. Like the notion of (material) 'culture', the term 'daily life' is equally problematic. The term *Alltagsgeschichte* became popular in Germany towards the late 1970s. However, it is a term with a long history in some Western European countries (e.g. France, England). The history of everyday life has often been reduced, explicitly or implicitly, to the study of the life of the popular classes, thus excluding by definition the 'elite'. Among the alternatives recently proposed is the view that everybody has 'his' (or 'her') daily life independent of social status.

Problems of periodization

Daily life, however stable it may appear in retrospect, is far from static.[2] In view of the relatively slow process of change in material culture in past centuries and the long periods required for innovations to be accepted and to be spread, the phases cannot be short. In terms of material culture as a whole, the phases in Germany should be defined as follows: (1) 1350–1600; (2) *c.*1600–*c.*1730; (3) *c.*1730–*c.*1840; (4) *c.*1840–1950. However, the amount of change is not the same in the various sectors of daily life and material culture. Günter Wiegelmann, for example, distinguishes the following periods in the consumption of food in Central Europe: 1300–1500, 1500–1680, 1680–1770, 1770–1850, and 1850 to the present.[3] In taking, as I suggest, the period 1350–1600 as a baseline, I am not suggesting that this period was static. The Black Death was certainly an important landmark, bringing about demographic and social turmoil as well as changes in people's attitudes and values. Other changes were more gradual, the most important being urbanization, innovations in agriculture, and the spread of literacy.

Settings and commodities

Housing

The range and variety of buildings to be found in late medieval and early modern Germany makes it difficult to describe their 'artefactual grammar'. None the less, two major urban types may be distinguished with respect to floor plan and means of construction.[4] The first type of housing, prevalent in north German towns since the later middle ages, is the *Dielenhaus*, a house with a large principal room or hall, used for working, cooking, and dining, with an adjacent, mostly stone-built chamber (functioning as bedroom and living-room) at its back. In southern Germany a vertical distribution of residential space became the common denominator of various architectural forms of urban housing. People lived and slept in rooms on the upper floor, while the ground floor was reserved for storage or business activities. In pre-industrial German towns, housing was strictly subjected to the parcelling out of units of land. The building was defined and shaped by the small plot of land, which therefore curbed individual planning considerably, making regrouping of building parts quite difficult. Since the late thirteenth century town councils had kept a watchful eye not only on the alignment but also on certain aesthetic and safety standards for houses.[5]

Projections of upper floors and the use of wood for some parts of the house were prohibited. On the other hand, financial incentives were given for buildings with stone structure, the use of bricks or natural stone varying from region to region. Even in places where timber-framed houses dominated the cityscape till the nineteenth and early twentieth centuries, the dividing walls were built out of stone and the highly decorated woodwork was restricted to the front of the building. Similar safety measures for framework and roofing were introduced in almost every German town from the later middle ages.

No account of urban architectural forms would be adequate without taking into account the substandard housing conditions of the lower classes, although it is quite difficult to reconstruct their humble houses. There is evidence from Nuremberg, Augsburg, Braunschweig, and Cologne that the houses of the lower middle class were relatively small (about 50 m² floor space).[6] The south German type consisted of a workshop in the basement and living-space (from the sixteenth century onward, divided in various mono-functional little rooms) on the upper floor. The north German type of lower class housing (*Bude, Gadem*) was initially built to simple storey-and-a-half, single-bay specifications.

The history of the German farmhouse is also one of steadily growing diversity.[7] However, two distinct features of architectural forms prevailed in north and south Germany. In the so-called *Einhaus* with its regional variants (Frisian, Lower Saxon, Lothringian, Upper German, etc.), animals and people lived under one roof, while in central Germany animals were kept in a separate part of the farmstead (*Gehöft*), which consisted of a farmhouse, barns, and stables built around a courtyard. Small farmers or farmworkers with a small plot of land lived in more humble houses which were small, crude buildings. The *Kossätenhaus* was the German equivalent of the English 'cottage'.[8] It normally consisted of a single room, though in some cases there may have been a tiny loft just under the roof.

Not everybody owned the house in which he lived. Available evidence from some German cities[9] shows that in the late middle ages renting was far more common than historians have assumed (see Table 12.1). As far as these two types of accommodation (renting and ownership) are concerned, it is clear that they confirm not only the contrast between artisans on the one hand and patricians, merchants, and town officials on the other, but also the unequal distribution of wealth among the artisans and occupational groups. In any case, a correlation exists between the habitat of tenants and the geography of poverty, as indicated by a recent case study (Augsburg). According to data from south-west German cities, the lower classes had to pay an annual rent of up to 1.5 fl., while the citizens who were better off could afford housing amenities which amounted to anything between 5 fl. and 20 fl. a year. The average annual rent in Cologne, for example, was over 23.6 marks (*c.*5.9 fl.), according to the tax-registers of the parish of St Columba (1487).

It is difficult to assess the degree of crowding in these lodgings (whether rented or owned by their occupants). In Nuremberg about 40 per cent of the houses had between three and four occupants. Only 25 per cent had an occupation rate between five and six persons. Crowding was the general rule for the popular classes in particular. More domestic space was available only for the 'happy few', such as families with fewer children, bachelors, widowers, and, always, those who were better off.

The domestic environment

Until the sixteenth century any specialized use of a room was, like the number of annexes, a luxury for German peasants and citizens alike.[10] At the beginning of the early modern period, only few people knew the luxury of a real bedroom. Kitchens devoted solely to the preparation of food were an exception, too. Most rooms were still multifunctional, judging by the furniture and household items mentioned in the probate inventories of late medieval German cities. Only from the sixteenth century onwards did the number of rooms increase everywhere, in towns at

Table 12.1 Categories of accommodation in selected German towns

Town	Year	Renting (%)	Ownership (%)
Rostock	1404	17	83
	1430	19	81
	1522	57	43
Görlitz	1426	39	61
	1472	47	53
Mühlhausen	1418	20	80
	1552	28	72
Leipzig (various quarters)	1554–6	23–65	77–35
Dresden	1488	44	56
	1502	52	48
Cologne (one parish)	1487	75	25
	1589	62	38
Frankfurt a.M.	1495	6	94
Esslingen	1384	23	77
Freiburg im Br.	1385	7	93
Schaffhausen	1402	4	96
	1502	29	71
Vienna	1563	63	37

least. At the same time the rooms changed their function. For the majority of the population, domestic life was rooted in a single living-space around the hearth. At first, annexes like the *Saal* or the heated parlour (*Stube, Dörnse*) were not really part of the lodging. They either represented an intermediate state between interior and exterior or served as a retreat during the cold season. It was only in the seventeenth century that such annexes became an integral part of the living-space in German town houses, when people learned to organize their immediate environment, assigning specific use to particular spaces and dividing the large hall into small, juxtaposed, partitioned units. The underlying trend throughout the early modern period was towards greater size and greater differentiation.

Any study of a domestic environment must be based on probate inventories.[11] Even cursory reading of these records, dating back in some cases to the thirteenth century, makes clear that households in late medieval and early modern Germany varied greatly with respect to the possession of material objects. This should be emphasized at the outset, since the delineation which follows refers largely to 'average' people and holdings. The German probate inventories show a clear trend toward ample and more diversified physical possessions. This was roughly true for all classes of people, although the lower classes moved much more slowly toward greater material prosperity, as evidence from some north and south-west German towns indicates (see Table 12.2).

In almost all German houses there was at least one fireplace. The hearth was a necessity, not a luxury. In sixteenth-century Cologne, 50 per cent of all households had only one chimney; the rest of the citizens who also paid chimney tax in 1582 had two or more fireplaces.[12] The traditional site of the hearth was the hall (*Diele*). The fireplace performed multiple functions – it served for cooking, heating, and lighting – and also stimulated people to come together and to communicate. The typical fireplace consisted of andirons or supports made out of stone for holding up the legs. Suspended from the 'lug-pole' at the chimney were a variety of hooks, bars, and chains. Along the sides of the fireplace were the tools used for the handling of fire and other equipment necessary for cooking (pots, pans, kettles, etc.).

In the late middle ages (*c.*1300–1350), when the stove made its debut in urban housing in most parts of Germany, people developed new styles of behaviour and a different psychological approach to the fire. The stove ensured better heating, providing more warmth and more calories for less fuel (wood, charcoal, or coal). At the same time the fire became almost invisible, and additional lighting facilities were called for. People gradually exchanged the symbolic values of an open fire (shining, leaping flames in the chimney) for a greater freedom of movement, as they no longer needed to sit close to the fireplace to feel warm and comfortable.

Linked to the hearth were those kitchen utensils which were necessary for the preparation of meals. For obvious reasons it is difficult to offer precise generalizations about this equipment. The lower classes owned fewer items than those who were better off. An average of 13.4 kitchen utensils was listed per household in early seventeenth-century Braunschweig. The richer families had an average of 19.5 items, while a lower-class household had to be content with fewer cooking and dining utensils (10.3 items). Most of the sixteenth-century rural households had at least a large cooking pot (74 per cent) and owned a kettle (85 per cent), as evidence from the north German region of Quernheim indicates.[13]

Table 12.2 Availability of kitchen utensils (percentage owning) in an early modern German city (Braunschweig, 1610–40)

| | Social rank | | | |
	I	II	III	IV
Silverware	90	83	79	37
Pewterware	100	100	100	95
Wooden utensils	70	67	74	53
Glassware	80	75	21	32
Pots and jugs	100	100	100	90
Cutlery	90	92	84	79
Bowls	100	100	100	84
Plates	100	100	90	84
Pewter plates	60	58	42	32

Source: Mohrmann, 'Wohnkultur', p. 132.

To judge by this scattered evidence from some German towns, it appears that in the period under discussion (1300–1600) permanency outweighed novelty as far as cooking utensils and crockery are concerned.

Our catalogue of furnishings likely to have been found in a late medieval German household is not necessarily a long one. There were, however, some class-related and regional varieties which make a delineation quite difficult. No estate was entirely without items of furniture (see Table 12.3). The key piece of furniture was the chest (*Kiste, Kastentruhe*), which was found in almost all German homes in pre-industrial times. By the end of the middle ages a new trend shows up quite clearly: wardrobe and chest dominate the probate inventories from the sixteenth century onwards. Thus the old system of storage, which continued well into the modern period, was slightly modified. Furniture for social gatherings among family and friends also did not change much, except for the introduction of more individual seating facilities (e.g. chairs). However, the most important item of furniture was the bed. Homes where each member of the household had a bed were rare exceptions until the eighteenth century, when the average was still 1.8 persons to a bed. A complete bed (including bedstead, palliasses, mattresses, and bed-linen) not only provided warmth and intimacy but was also associated with symbolic and social values.[14] Not everybody succeeded during

Table 12.3. Availability of furniture (%) in an early modern German city (Braunschweig, 1610–40)

	Social rank			
	I	II	III	IV
Storage				
Wardrobes	90	75	95	89
Chests	100	100	95	100
Party furnishings				
Tables	100	100	100	95
Chairs	90	83	95	89
Benches	70	67	74	58
Beds				
Bedsteads	100	100	100	95

Source: as Table 12.2.

his lifetime in acquiring such a prestigious and costly object. Up to the sixteenth century many people, at least in the rural parts of Germany, had to be content with bedding and fittings which were far from complete.

Food and eating

In 1563 the Flemish artist Pieter Bruegel the Elder (?1525–69) finished two copper engravings which he entitled *vette cuecken* ('fat cookery') and *arm ghasterije* ('poor cookery'). No other picture illustrates better the material basis of different lifestyles during our period than these two little master-pieces. The rich man considers what might please his palate; the popular classes are simply concerned to fill their stomach. The difference in social status generally correlates with the qualitative and quantitative feature of nutrition, but nourishment is only one aspect of food consumption. Taste and social prestige are other important determinants, and both are apt to change in the course of time and from one place to another.[15] Even chari-table institutions reflected this social hierarchy in consumption, as can be seen, for instance, in the regulations for the municipal hospital in Constance in 1470 (see Table 12.4).

In late medieval Germany the food of the well-to-do was both varied and plentiful, probably becoming somewhat richer and more elaborate towards the early modern period. The dinner accounts of noblemen and patricians show that emphasis was put on meat, fowl, and fish. Even the account-books of hospitals reveal that their inmates could often choose

Table 12.4 Class distinctions in the municipal hospital of Constance

Class	Pieces of meat per week	Index	Quantity of wine per day	Index
Priest	40	100.0	3.95 l	100
Rich prebendaries	17	42.5	2.96 l	75
Poor prebendaries	9	22.5	2.96 l	75
Poor inmates	6	15.0	1.96 l	50

Source: Dirlmeier, *Untersuchungen*, p. 378.

from an impressive variety of food. The Heilig-Geist-Hospital in Frankfurt am Main, for example, purchased between 1510 and 1515 the following types of foodstuff: milk, fried fish, pigeon, chives, onions, parsley, bread rolls, beef, mutton's pluck, mutton, veal, sugar, fresh herring, butter rolls, herbs, kale, flat(?)fish, deer, apples, turnips, dried fish, cheese, groundling, chicken, legs of veal, eggs, roast beef, lamb, lamb's head, strawberries, cherries, parsnips, horseradish, liver, birds, carp, flour, breast of veal, carrots, mulberries, almonds, wheaten flour, pike, sausages, pork, pears, calf's liver, peaches, juniper, geese, malmsey, and wine. This impressive list is, however, misleading: most of the foodstuffs were reserved for some feastdays, or for the opulent banquets given to the governors of the hospital in reward for their honorary service. The ordinary diet in most of these charitable institutions, reflecting the nutritional status of the lower middle class, was of meat, salt, fish, cheese, and beer.

Apart from travellers' tales and the occasional probate inventories, the most reliable source of information about the diet of the middle class consists of private account-books. Although this method of establishing a diet is not completely satisfactory, we gain at least an impression of how much food of a certain kind was consumed by the *petit bourgeois*. A typical representative of this middle group is Hermann Weinsberg (1518–97), alderman of the city of Cologne (see Table 12.5). Even if this diet was not very healthy by the standards of modern nutritionists, it provided at least the calories needed for people with modest or average physical activity.

As the leading German specialist in this field, Günter Wiegelmann, has pointed out, two major periods of food consumption can be distinguished. The first one runs from roughly 1300 up to 1500. The distinctive feature of this period is the large amount of meat consumed by people from all walks of life. Wilhelm Abel estimated that the average German ate 100 kg of meat per annum in the later middle ages, when the price of grain was relatively low and the wages unusually high because of the demographic and economic impact of the Black Death after 1350. The second period (1500–1680) saw a drastic decline in meat consumption and its substitution by grain dishes. In other words, the diet deteriorated, at least from the standpoint of preference. As people looked for cheaper grain alternatives, there was also a change from wheat to other bread grain (e.g. rye). The sixteenth and seventeenth centuries are also marked by a conspicuous consumption of imported sugar and exotic spices by those who could afford to buy such luxuries for their diet (*pauper non emit quia not potest*, 'a poor man does not buy what he cannot afford', Conrad Peutinger, 1522) and the introduction of new foodstuffs to the German consumer (e.g. potatoes, coffee). This period saw also the improvement of table manners and a rising concern for a healthy diet. It should be added that in both periods considerable regional variations existed. In the south, for example, people preferred farinaceous food (*Mehlspeisen*), while in the north the diet was mostly made up of meat and bread.

Table 12.5. Approximate daily intake of nutrients by members of the Weinsberg family in late sixteenth-century Cologne

Foodstuffs	Amount (g/ml)	Energy (kcal)	Protein (g)	Calcium (mg)	Iron (mg)
Meat days (206)					
Beef	50	97	10.0	6	1.3
Pork	76	204	13.7	6	1.5
Ham	184	543	40.5	17	4.6
Butter	26	196	0.3	5	0.1
Cheese	22	74	5.7	149	0.1
Bread	397	997	27.8	60	4.0
Beer	664	299	3.3	27	0.7
Wine	332	203	–	33	2.0
Total requirements		2,613	101.3	303	14.3
		2,400	56.0	800	10.0
Fish days (159)					
Stockfish	40	95	20.4	16	1.1
Plaice	216	189	34.5	24	0.9
Butter	26	196	0.3	5	0.1
Cheese	22	74	5.7	149	0.1
Bread	397	997	27.8	60	4.0
Beer	664	299	3.3	27	0.7
Wine	332	302	–	33	2.0
Total requirements		2,053	92.0	314	8.9
		2,400	56.0	800	10.0

Source: Jütte, 'Weinsberg', p. 280.

Clothing

In a society of orders and estates, clothing was an important measure of status. Clothes were a means of classification and distinction. In fact, German town magistrates and territorial rulers worked out a set of legal regulations concerning garments admissible for each class of men.[16] The first sumptuary laws referring to clothes were passed in the early thirteenth century. Legislation reached a first peak in the decade after the Black Death; another crucial period was the second half of the fifteenth century. (See Table 12.6.)

Table 12.6. German sumptuary laws concerning garments, 1200–1550

Period	Number of regulations		Regulations per decade
	No.	%	
1200–99	19	3.8	1.9
1300–48	36	7.2	6.2
1349–59	26	5.2	26.0
1360–99	63	12.6	15.8
1400–49	95	19.0	19.0
1450–99	140	28.1	28.0
1500–49	120	24.0	24.0
	499	100.0	

Source: Bulst, 'Luxusgesetzgebung', p. 35

From the beginning of our period until the middle of the sixteenth century, we can detect a fairly constant, rapid expansion in sumptuary laws, except for a very short period after the plague of 1348–50, when there appears to have been a sudden increase in legislation. It is easy to surmise that social change and economic developments in town and countryside threatened the old order, forcing the authorities to act. No one really questioned the existence of a hierarchy of distinct social orders. Faced with changes which threw the relatively clear stratification out of focus, first the magistrates and later some German territorial rulers considered it their Christian duty to define the orders of society in terms of clothing ordinances. However, specific regulations concerning the garments appropriate to each order (*Stand*) proved to be unenforceable; for the styles changed quickly, and social imitation combined with new wealth and social aspirations was a too powerful human factor.

Clothing not only confers a social identity, it also reveals the character and personality of the wearer. Nevertheless, one has to be careful in inter-

Table 12.7 The variation of clothing codes in late medieval Germany, according to different categories of source

Source	Person (rank)	Clothes	Quality of clothes
Testament	High rank (member of the town council; person filling an official position; merchant)	Cloak	Red (black); fur lining; foreign cloth
		Belt	Silver; gilt
	Low rank servant	Tunic	Not red; no quality mentioned
	Wealthy woman	Gown	Foreign cloth; fur lining
		Veil	Abundant use of linen or silk
Sumptuary law	Everybody	Any dress	Never yellow
	Everybody	Shoes	Not pointed
		Any dress	No new fashions
	Low rank (servant; peasant)	Any dress	No silk; no fur or cheap fur; low price; no jewellery
	Outcasts (Jews; prostitutes)	Part of dress	Yellow
Picture	High rank (official position), positive	Cloak	Red; fur lining; extravagant cloth (brocade, velvet, silk)
	High rank, negative (Oriental judge, etc.)	Cloak	Fur lining; extravagant cloth; orientalizing; 'fictional'
	High rank, young, positive (nobleman)	Doublet; hose	Red; tight; fashionable
	Low rank negative (torturer)	Doublet; hose	Multicoloured; yellow; tight; close-fitting; torn-up; extremely fashionable
	Low rank positive (peasant; the poor)	Tunic reaching to the knee	Grey; not coloured; cheap cloth

Source: Gerhard Jaritz, 'Daily Life in Medieval Literature', in *Medium Aevum Quotidianum Newsletter* II (1984), pp. 6–23, Table 2.

preting such clothing codes.[17] Different sources from late medieval Germany show some differences in characterization or in the use of terminology (see Table 12.7). Especially the matter of colour has been gravely misinterpreted in some traditional studies of medieval and early modern clothing.

In the medieval world of fashion, women undoubtedly took the lead. Their wardrobe showed enormous variety and underwent a few important changes. The *Tappert* or its shorter version, the *Schaube*, a tunic with a full knee-length or ankle-length skirt, became the most important element of women's fashions. The open-sided gown (*surcot*) was also very common among the well-to-do, and was soon imitated by others. Many different hoods, veils, and caps were worn by women during this period. The most spectacular head-dress was no doubt the *hennin*, a tall, cone-shaped structure which appeared at the beginning of the fifteenth century, and was worn with different types of veil until the 1480s.

Like women's clothes, but even more so, men's garments underwent many changes throughout the period. Skirtless doublets (*Wams*), with slashed sleeves and open, laced fronts showing the shirt, were worn from the 1480s. From the beginning of the eighteenth century a short-sleeved or sleeveless jerkin (*Koller*) was often worn over the doublet. Close-fitting breeches were worn over the hose and were sometimes attached to the inner edge of the doublet. Back caps (*Gugel*) were worn as head-dresses by men throughout the fourteenth and fifteenth centuries: a stiffened brimless cap (*Barett*), moulded to have four corners, became the most popular male head-dress in the sixteenth century. Long-pointed toes (*Schnabelschuhe*) were fashionable in the late fourteenth and then again in the late fifteenth century; after this date broad-toed mules (*Kuhmäuler*) were worn until the middle of the sixteenth century. Over their shoes men and women often wore clogs (*Trippen*) to protect against mud.

Women and men alike showed much more concern for effect, originality of styles, and colours than for the functionality of clothes. However, one should not forget that many could not afford to buy fashionable clothes. For these people, clothing was reduced to the bare essentials, not to speak of the rather ragged appearance of the poor. The *petit bourgeois* who did not fall below the poverty line spent between 3 and 10 fl. yearly on clothes. Among the German upper class conspicious consumption, spending dozens of florins on a single garment, was a way of emphasizing social rank and wealth.

Hygiene and sanitation

Most of the complaints that have come down to us from the middle ages as to filthy and evil-smelling streets suggest that this deplorable condition was the rule rather than the exception. However, one has to keep in mind that the crude sanitary arrangements of medieval towns were not necessarily as offensive as they have been pictured.[18] Various ordinances and, more especially, repeated legislation are indicative of public activity and widespread sentiment against such nuisances. As early as 1302 the Nuremberg magistrates issued an ordinance that forbade the throwing of filth and garbage into ditches, rivers, and waters; by the fifteenth century, such special provisions for sanitary control had become widespread. However, our evidence remains rather erratic, and therefore forbids any attempt at generalization. Not only are there marked differences between various towns: in many cases we can also detect a discrepancy in the policy of the same town at different periods. For instance, there are German towns in which at a very early stage a ban was imposed on keeping pigs in the street; according to later evidence from the same town, this ban was either lifted or disregarded (e.g. Cologne, Nuremberg, Hamburg).

One of the major problems with which every town had to cope was the disposal of faecal matter. Medieval ordinances decreed that sinks for the reception of urine and human excrement should be as far from the house as possible, and not too close to a neighbour's house (e.g. Nuremberg 1382, Munich 1484). Not every householder could afford to build his own privy and the necessary adjacent cesspool for the reception of faeces. In the late middle ages it gradually became the rule, at least for the well-do-do, to have private conveniences in their houses. By that time a considerable number of monasteries and feudal castles already had their latrines and in some cases even their own lavatories. Well known, amongst others, are the elaborate toilet facilities (*Danziger*) which were in use in fourteenth-century castles belonging to the Teutonic Order. The cleaning of the cesspits was not only disagreeable to smell and foul to the sight, it was also a rather costly matter. This despicable job was undertaken by the hangman or his assistants. Their official Latin name was *purgatores privete* (Vienna 1378/78), but usually they had derogatory popular names (e.g. *Kotkönige, Goldgräber*). These men usually worked during the night. There was no fixed payment for this unpleasant job; in the 1370s the city of Cologne paid its *cloacarii* between 2 and 9 marks silver for the clearance of a single cesspit. There is evidence that the first public conveniences did not make their debut in German towns before the fourteenth century (e.g. Frankfurt 1348). A more modern sewage system, by which the sewage was piped out to a disposal area, was in use in the city of Breslau in Silesia as early as 1543.

What applies to faecal matter applies also to garbage. Leftovers were usually disposed in the streets and were consumed by dogs, chickens, and pigs – those animals that acted as the town scavengers until the eighteenth century, despite many attempts by magistrates to ban them from the streets. Non-edible waste (tannery offal, ashes, broken glass, and earthenware) was harder to dispose of. It was either buried outside the city or thrown into the nearby cesspits, thus enabling the archaeologist to reconstruct the material culture of the medieval and early modern town.

The provision of drinkingwater very early became a collective function of the medieval town. German cities passed legislation in order to guard wells and springs, and also found it essential to find new water sources as well as to distribute the available water all over the town. A lead or wooden conduit was used to convey water from the area outside the walls to the inner city. As early as the thirteenth century the provision of water conduits became a public matter in some German towns (see Table 12.8).

Table 12.8 Water conduits in medieval German cities

1200	Breslau	1272
	Lübeck	1294
1300	Helmstedt	1329
	Braunschweig	1332
	Nuremberg	1361
	Zittau	1376
	Berne	1393
	Bremen	1394
1400	Augsburg	1412
	Hildesheim	1416
	Zurich	1421
	Ulm	1426
	Regensburg	1449
	Munich	1467
	Dresden	before 1478
1500	Hanover	1512
	Celle	1530

Source: Busch, 'Wasserversorgung', p. 302.

The piping of water to public fountains was indeed an important step forward in sanitation. However, the water still had to be distributed by hand. This was certainly an inconvenience, but it also had its advantages, as the public fountain remained a focus of sociability throughout the pre-industrial period.

Of great importance for the medieval attitude towards cleanliness was the existence of private baths and public bathhouses. The latter were widespread in late medieval German towns.[19] At the end of the middle ages there were 11 bathhouses in Ulm and Cologne, 12 in Nuremberg, 15 in Frankfurt am Main, 17 in Augsburg, and 29 in Vienna. These public baths were meant for sweating and steaming. Such a thorough cleaning of the body was customary at least once every month, sometimes once a week. The bathing establishments, which in some cases also served as semimedical resorts, declined in the sixteenth century mainly because people feared contagion (syphilis). The number of public baths was reduced also because of rising fuel prices, which lowered the profit of the bathhouse-keepers. The medieval practice of bathing began to disappear with the Reformation, but not because of it.

Travel and communication

Travel. Communication in medieval Germany consisted, in the first place, of shipping routes, either coastal or river routes.[20] There were also the many land routes, connecting the south with the north, the east with the west. No less important than the routes themselves were the various stopping places: a harbour, a town, an open roadstead, a fortified castle, a monastery, or a lonely inn in the countryside. Nodal points were the 3,000 urban settlements spread all over late medieval Germany. The towns of the Low Countries and southern Germany, as well as the towns which formed the Hanseatic League, made up a closely knit urban network.

At first sight there does not seem to have been any revolutionary change between 1300 and 1600 in either land or sea transport. The boats used were almost the same as before (only the loading capacity increased considerably from 50–80 tons to about 400) and so were the diverse imperfect vehicles (wheeled carts and pack animals). There was some improvement in roads and navigation. The speed and regularity of the postal service increased. The cost of transport fell. These changes, however, were never of revolutionary proportions. We have detailed records of hundreds of Hanseatic ships and we know their cargoes, their approximate cargoes, and their itineraries. This evidence indicates that small ships were still in a majority. River traffic all of which was paralleled by overland traffic was improved during the fourteenth century through the building of canals (the canal between the rivers Ilmenau and Elbe in Lüneburg, and the Stecknitz canal, which linked the important Hanseatic town of Lübeck with the river Elbe). Land transport was made easier through considerable progress in cartography (e.g. the famous compass map of central Europe by Erhard Etzlaub, 1501), and the pioneering atlas for Bavaria designed by Philipp Appian in 1568). We hear of new record speeds reached by sea and, for postal communication, by the overland route. On the whole, however, the average speed did not increase much. Typical of pre-industrial Europe in general and the Holy Roman Empire of the German Nation in particular is the wide range of times required to travel the same journey. According to the correspondence of a fifteenth-century German merchant (Hildebrand Veckinchusen), a letter from Danzig to Lübeck took between 10 and 37 days. Over the distance Bruges–Riga, recorded cases give a minimum length of 39 days, a maximum of 77. Higher speed had its special price. At the beginning of the sixteenth century the tariff between Venice and Nuremberg varied according to the time necessary to cover the distance: four days, 58 florins; six days, 25 florins. Such ultrafast and costly communication was, however, recorded only in exceptional cases. Everyday communications in late medieval Germany had a much slower rhythm (see Table 12.9).

Table 12.9 Average distance covered by various forms of transport on land routes in pre-modern Germany

Km/day (12 hrs)	Form of transport	Season	Period
23	wheeled vehicles	–	middle ages
46	messenger (mail)	winter	middle ages
53	messenger (mail)	summer	16th century
91	express messenger	winter	16th century
106	express messenger	summer	16th century

Source: Denecke, 'Straße', p. 217.

Travelling and transport became somewhat cheaper and more convenient by the end of the sixteenth century, yet constituted even then a major expense. Travelling, like everything else, could be a matter of luxury or a basic commodity, depending on the economic status of the people on the road (see Table 12.10)

Communication. Communication depended not only on how fast news travelled from one place to another but also on the channel by which news were transmitted, i.e. the language. Latin remained the lingua franca of the church, the institutions of higher learning and administration up to the sixteenth century. Nevertheless, late medieval Germany was already a multilingual society. The medieval German language consisted of a number of dialects which may be classified into broad categories such as Middle High German and Middle Low German. Linguistically speaking, the two are similar but not totally mutually comprehensible.[21] This linguistic dichotomy applies less to written texts than to the spoken language. Most people spoke rural or urban dialects, although some central German dialects tend to

Table 12.10 The variety and social range of travelling in sixteenth-century north-west Germany

Social rank of traveller	Expenses per day (Taler)	Purchase value in 1983 (DM)	Costs in no. of artisan work-days, 1600
Upper class	11.8	1,465	37.0
Middle class	1.3	158	3.9
Lower class	0.1	14	0.5

Source: Schwarzwälder, 'Reisemodalitäten', p. 203.

resemble standardized forms of the German language (*Kanzleisprachen*) more closely than others. The social and geographical pressures involved in the diffusion of linguistic standardization are, of course, a good deal more complex than those associated with fashions. It is possible, however, to demonstrate in a broad kind of way that some similar factors, such as the invention of printing, bureaucratization, the growth of commerce, and the spread of education, were at work in the moulding of a national language which gradually superseded Latin.

Life experiences

Birth and death

Despite the arguments of some influential non-German authors (Philippe Ariès and Edward Shorter) that the love of children is a comparatively new phenomenon, recent research[22] (including historical studies by German scholars) has stressed the fact that there are, of course, some differences between our modern attitude to children and the affection felt by our medieval ancestors towards their offspring. Yet there is no doubt that they loved their children just as intensely as we do, and perhaps even spoiled them too. Parental love was not the exception but rather the norm in medieval and early modern Germany. Otherwise it would be difficult to explain why the death or even illness of a young child, or a separation from it, could have been a source of great sorrow and real suffering for parents (such as the German town physician Johannes Tichtel, who spoke about *Dulcis mi puer* when mentioning the death of his two-year-old son in 1484). Emotions and interests were also displayed at the birth of a child. Emotionally, this biological event was usually perceived as a great happiness, except by the many unmarried mothers who had to fear the stigma of bearing an illegitimate child. Childbirth in late medieval Germany was undoubtedly a social occasion. It was common practice to have at least two or three 'honest women' present at the birth in order to help and to assist the midwife. The invitation of several 'gossips' to attend a birth was required by social convention; it was likewise encouraged by apprehensive secular and ecclesiastical authorities, trying to discipline and to control the private lives of their subjects. As early as the fourteenth century midwives had to take a special oath in order to receive a licence from the magistrates. However, we still have an abundance of cases in which women gave birth without the help of a midwife. Even when a midwife was there, her presence was not always regarded as an unmixed blessing, as we can learn from German witch-trials dating back to the fifteenth and sixteenth centuries. Once the birth was over, the mother's and the child's health was a subject of special concern for a few weeks at least. Medical vade-mecums written in the vernacular, such as the famous book by Eustachius Rösslin, *Der swangeren frauwen und hebamen rosegarten* (Strasbourg, 1513), listed the many grave and perilous diseases which commonly afflicted children in those days. Books of this kind were evidently a commercial success, as several editions were called for.

While confinement was always a kind of limbo for the woman giving birth to a child, baptism was a source of merriment and joy, not only for the immediate family but also for friends and neighbours.[23] Thus it comes as no surprise that German magistrates tried from the later middle ages onwards to limit spending on the christening feast, e.g. by prescribing the number of godparents and guests at the festive meal as well as the value of christening gifts (the upper limit in fourteenth-century Nuremberg was 32 pence). Because some members of the German upper and middle classes were so conscientious about recording details on their household expenses, it is possible for us to learn about the limited success of this kind of sumptuary legislation. The baptized child often received the christian name of one of his godparents, or the name of one of his brothers or sisters who had died during infancy. In some families it was customary to pass on a certain name from generation to generation.

Like birth, man's final stage on earth was attended by certain prescribed social activities. If possible, people preferred to die surrounded by members of their family, or at least by friends: the important thing was not to die alone. And yet not everybody showed the same attitude towards death.[24] Being put under collective pressure, people were forced to endure on the deathbed and to die an edifying death. Only a few held out heroically against pain and the dread of death. Before dying most people showed a considerable concern about their salvation, setting up special clauses in their wills which guaranteed enough money for commemorative as well as charitable acts (distributions of alms, donations for churches and hospitals, collective prayers, and the office for the dead). Indeed, people in pre-Reformation Germany were able to prepare themselves consciously for imminent death, on condition that illness did not deprive them of clear awareness. Catholics were not very different from Protestants when it came to the preoccupation with salvation. The main difference lay in the attitude towards the means (faith alone as opposed to good works, for example) rather than towards the ends (i.e. eternal life and salvation).

As elsewhere in medieval and early modern Europe, the clergy in Germany watched closely over the dying. People sent for a priest who could administer the Eucharist to the sick person on his deathbed. Mourning was also expressed in socialized forms (e.g. the custom of employing certain persons to invite mourners to a funeral). The funeral itself testified to the rank of the dead person, although the church and the secular authorities tried – often in vain – to forbid over-expensive funerals. The provincial synod of

Trier, for example, decreed in 1310: 'As dining seems nowadays more common than mourning at funerals, we forbid by law that such feasts and banquets commonly arranged by heirs at the funeral of the deceased person should proceed.' Similar and even more detailed ordinances by German magistrates can be found as early as the fourteenth century (e.g. in the by-laws of the city of Frankfurt am Main dating back to 1356). Although luxury at funerals was prohibited in most German towns from the fourteenth century onwards, and although the famous German examples of the 'dance of death' (e.g. Lübeck 1463, Basel *c.*1470) never stopped praising the Grim Reaper as the great leveller, the hour of death nevertheless provided a very good opportunity to remind people of rank. This is true for the period preceding the Reformation and even for the century which followed it. In the later middle ages and in the early modern period, the manner in which death was treated in the family differed significantly from that in the eighteenth century, when the cemeteries inside the city walls were closed down for hygienic reasons and elaborate public rituals related to the process of death and to the funeral had become the privilege of the most substantial pillars of society (such as statesmen and bishops). Before these changes took place, those who had enough means were buried in the church, close to the altar, while ordinary people were usually buried in the graveyard outside the church walls. Most unlucky were those who were excluded for some reason or another from a Christian burial. They received a stigmatizing form of a funeral, the 'ass's burial' (*sepultura asina*), which actually meant the disposal of the dead body somewhere outside the city walls in the so-called 'knacker's yard' – a practice which was gradually given up in the seventeenth and eighteenth centuries.

Childhood and old age

The first stage of childhood covered the period from birth to weaning. As far as late medieval Germany is concerned, we do not have sufficient statistical data to decide when exactly weaning took place.[25] The same problem arises when we attempt to answer the question whether wet-nursing was widespread or not. In any case, we do know whether children were usually breastfed, either by their mother or by a hired wet-nurse. Infants spent in general much more time in their mother's arms than they do nowadays. Whether it was the privilege of babies born to well-to-do parents to be swaddled is difficult to decide, although the cradle seems to have been a common motif in late medieval German painting. It is likely that infants under a year old did not sleep in their parents' bed for fear of being 'overlain', that is, suffocated when older persons lay on top of them.

Among the popular classes it was not unusual for several people, including young children, to share one bed, or what passed for a bed. The little ones therefore ran a permanent risk of being smothered by their elder bed-fellows.

In late medieval and early modern Germany, country children hardly had the opportunity to go to school. The few schools were located almost exclusively in the towns, where less than 20 per cent of the German people lived.[26] Until the high middle ages the educational system was almost entirely in the hands of the church. In the thirteenth century the first municipal schools were founded (Worms 1260, Lübeck 1262, Breslau 1266, Wismar 1269, Hamburg 1281). Other German towns quickly followed. These were Latin schools which gave instruction in the basic subjects of the Trivium. Young boys of 6 or 7 studied the alphabet and were drilled in simple Latin phrases. The older boys memorized their Donatus and Alexander of Villadei (authors of the most widely used Latin grammars in medieval Germany), and were taught to imitate the style and vocabulary of selected ancient writers like Cicero and Horace. However, in the long run magistrates all over Germany had to bow to parental pressure to stress practical skills over reading classical texts in the classroom. New primary schools under purely secular auspices were established (e.g. Lübeck 1418, Braunschweig 1420).

Even before the Reformation, German magistrates (such as the council of the city of Nuremberg in 1511) set up new school regulations, which contained some progressive ideas: separation of age groups with a more flexible programme for the youngest boys, special tutorials for gifted boys, bilingual teaching (German and Latin), and weekly inspections by town commissioners. By the end of the fifteenth century almost every town had its Latin school and a number of German schools officially sanctioned by the city government. The Latin schools catered for the social elite, while the official German schools provided a vernacular education for sons of less affluent parents. Finally there was a large number of unlicensed German schools (*Winkelschulen*) which offered instruction for poorer boys and girls. These schools were often located close to home, and their fees were certainly lower. They also concentrated on reading and writing rather than on the acquisition of classical languages and religious education. The content of the instruction varied from school to school, but the material culture of teaching was the same everywhere. Pupils sat on wooden benches and took notes on tablets made of wax or slate. More advanced pupils wrote with a quill-pen in notebooks made of cheap paper. In some schools pupils were obliged to supply firewood during winter in order to heat the classroom. Long working hours and attendance at mass were the rule in late medieval German schools. Holidays were short, but there were enough Christian feasts during which the pupils could stay at home. The size of grammar schools varied greatly. Some had fewer than 20 pupils; others had over 100.

Towards 12 or 14 years of age at the latest, the records switch to using the term *juvenis* (youth) instead of *puer* (boy). This change in terminology corresponded to yet another phase in the life-cycle. Those who had attended a Latin school continued their studies at university level, while those who had attended a German school, as well as those who had no access to such schools, began a new life as apprentices. While boys were able to embark on a profession at that age, girls of 12 or so did not usually leave the house, but instead took over various jobs in their parents' household. As in medieval and early modern France, where youth associations were known under the name of *abbayes de la jeunesse*, German teenagers formed youth groups (*Knabenschaften* or *Burschenschaften*) with their own rules and forms of entertainment.

Unlike today, life expectancy was very low in late medieval and early modern Germany. Barely half of those born reached adulthood, less than one-third lived through it, and only one-fifth reached old age. In their 30s, men were in their prime; but after about 50, a man was considered old, and his prestige did not increase with time.[27] The few men and women who reached old age did not enjoy the respect and affection lavished on elderly people in the ancient world, as we may learn from the German Renaissance author Pamphilus Gengenbach (*c.*1480–1525):

> For the first ten years a child./ At 20 years a youth./ At 30 years a man./ At 40 years stationary./ At 50 years well to do./ At 60 years on the decline./ At 70 years look after thy soul./ At 80 years the fool of the world./ At 90 years the laughing-stock of children./ At a hundred years, now God have mercy on thee.

Old parents no longer had authority over their sons and daughters. On the contrary, they depended on their children's mercy. There was no real provision for the aged in the middle ages, except for those few places available in multifunctional medieval hospitals. There was nothing like the modern old-age insurance or pension fund in late medieval and early modern Germany. In the countryside the *Altenteil* (old folks' portion), a share of property reserved by the farmer on his retirement, was the only provision for old age. Artisans had to find other solutions. One possibility was to buy life annuities issued by the city government and other institutions. People could buy (provided they had enough money: the price varied between 50 fl. and more than 200 fl. for a single person) a prebend in one of the municipal hospitals. Such opportunities were naturally restricted to a small minority of the urban population. The rest had to rely on a variety of urban social ties or support networks, of which the family-relative connection was the strongest; friend-neighbour was next in order of prevalence, coworker-employer followed. Despite some recent work on ageing in pre-industrial Germany we still know far too little about the impact of profession, income, assets, and education on chances of happiness or misery during old age.

Illness and health

Common beliefs about sickness and health, the behaviour of sick persons, and their expectations of treatment, as well as the attitude of family members and healers towards them, are all aspects of a social reality which is culturally defined or 'constructed' and thus varies as one moves from one locality to another, or from one historical period to another.[28]

People in late medieval and early modern Germany suffered from a multitude of discomforts and disorders. Medical treatises and diaries of middle- and upper-class people yield an impressive list of medical concerns (from apostema to wry neck). Luther, for example, identified nearly 300 symptoms or disorders which needed treatment by professional healers or folk practitioners. While parish registers are an unrivalled source of information about diseases from which people died, diaries are more concerned about the disorders people had to live with. Colds, for example, are frequently mentioned as minor ailments. They were treated, if at all, with casual remedies. More serious than colds were agues or intermittent fevers. As antibiotics were not yet known, people found ague worrying and debilitating, especially as the cold and hot fits of ague could be interpreted as the first symptoms of the most fatal contagious disease, the plague. Nowadays people are afraid of cancer although statistically more people die of heart diseases. Until the eighteenth century people were more terrified of the plague than of any other disease. The plague serves as a good example for the coexistence of secular and religious approaches to illness. It was generally agreed that the plague was the result of human sin. Consequently, people believed that the only medicine they could trust was prayer. Nevertheless they also took prophylactics (such as the popular mithridate known in Germany under the name of *Theriak*, and similar antidotes), or resorted to conventional remedies once they had contracted the disease.

In most other cases of illness the humoral/astrological approach provided a satisfactory basis for its explanation and treatment – a view which was not successfully challenged on the popular level until the nineteenth century! Medieval sufferers could thus be far more confident about explaining ailments than can their twentieth-century descendants. Discussions by medical experts and laymen reflect the theory of the humours and temperaments as well as the doctrine of the 'six non-naturals', one of the mainstays of ancient and medieval medical theory, which is connected with the name of Galen (d.199), the famous Roman-Greek physician. The medieval German reader was bound to encounter this doctrine in many popular manuals of health, for example, the numerous vernacular versions of the *Regimen Sanitatis Salernitatum*. Evidence from German diaries which have survived the last 400 or 500 years (such as the diary of Hermann Weinsberg) revealed how often people thought that illness was caused by vitiated air, intemperance in consuming food and drink, constipation, lack of physical exercise, insufficient sleep, or sexual debauchery.

Bleeding, purging and strong remedies – the stock-in-trade of most medieval physicians – were all too often disliked by the patients. People used the medical knowledge they gathered from former experiences of illness, from their scattered reading, and from oral tradition in order to treat themselves, their family members, and their friends and acquaintances. Self-treatment was surely the most common type of medical therapy in late medieval and early modern Germany, although there is sufficient statistical evidence from the sixteenth century onwards that more people than is generally believed obtained expert medical or surgical help. The majority of the middle and lower classes found the money to pay for the expensive services of physicians and barber-surgeons. In addition to taking self-made or prescribed internal medicine, people underwent minor surgical procedures for both prophylactic and curative purposes. Phlebotomy was common, although some patients and medical authors thought more highly of it than others. It seems that people only occasionally underwent this procedure, although medical treatises and popular calendars recommended a more frequent blood-letting. While evidence from a fifteenth-centry religious institution in Austria (Chorfrauenstift Klosterneuburg) suggests that the canonesses frequently let blood (two to three times a year), the Weinsberg family who lived in sixteenth-century Cologne was apparently less attracted to phlebotomy. Blood-letting could be dangerous, but the death rate (100 deaths per annum in an average-sized town) mentioned by contemporary authors like the Austrian physician Hippolytus Guarinonius (1571–1654) seems to be exaggerated.

People drank and bathed in the waters of the many natural springs around which fashionable spas had grown up since the middle ages. Sick and pleasure-loving men and women from all over Germany visited Aachen and Wiesbaden, or travelled as far as Lucca (such as the sixteenth-century Nuremberg merchant Balthasar Paumgartner), partly to take the waters and partly to amuse themselves.

Despite the considerable risks involved, medieval people were enthusiastic medicine-takers. Their attitude towards physic-taking was, however, different from ours. They expected a medicine to show its strength by producing an immediate result – usually in the form of multiple bowel movements or vomits. Medieval physicians usually complied with the wishes of their clients, as it was common for patients and medical practitioners to negotiate a mutually acceptable medicine. The real change in the doctor–patient relationship did not occur before the nineteenth century.

Notes

1   For methodological reflections and an updated bibliography see Uwe Meiners, 'Forschungen zur historischen Sachkultur', *Der Deutschunterricht* XXXIX (1987), pp. 173–6; Alf Lüdtke, ed., *Alltagsgeschichte* (Frankfurt a. M./New York, 1989); Gerhard Jaritz, *Zwischen Augenblick und Ewigkeit. Einführung in die Alltagsgeschichte des Mittelalters* (Vienna/Cologne, 1989); Konrad Köstlin and Hermann Bausinger, eds, *Umgang mit Sachen. Zur Kulturgeschichte des Dinggebrauchs* (Regensburg, 1983). For a general introduction, see Dietrich W. H. Schwarz, *Sachgüter und Lebensformen. Einführung in die materielle Kulturgeschichte des Mittelalters und der Neuzeit* (Berlin, 1970). The most complete bibliography is supplied by the Institut für mittelalterliche Realienkunde Österreichs: Gerhard Jaritz, ed., 'Alltag und materielle Kultur des Mittelalters. Eine Auswahlbibliographie' I: *Medium Aevum Quotidianum Newsletter* VII–VIII (1984), pp. 1–99.

2   The best introduction to the problems of periodization in German folk culture is Günter Wiegelmann, ed., *Wandel der Alltagskultur seit dem Mittelalter* (Münster, 1987). Cf. also Walter Hartinger, 'Epochen der deutschen Volkskultur', *Ethnologia Europaea* XV (1985), pp. 53–92.

3   Günter Wiegelmann, *Alltags- und Festspeisen. Wandel und gegenwärtige Stellung* (Marburg, 1967).

4   For urban housing in Germany, 1300–1800, Moriz Heyne, *Deutsche Hausaltertümer von den ältesten geschichtlichen Zeiten bis zum 16. Jahrhundert* I: *Wohnung* (Leipzig, 1899); Cord Meckseper, *Kleine Kunstgeschichte der deutschen Stadt im Mittelalter* (Darmstadt, 1982); Gertrud Benker, *Bürgerliches Wohnen und städtische Wohnkultur in Mitteleuropa von der Gotik bis zum Jugendstil* (Munich, 1984); Fred Kaspar, *Bauen und Wohnen in einer alten Hansestadt* (Bonn, 1985); as well as the articles by Wolfgang Erdmann and Sven Schütte in the collection of essays edited by Bernd Herrmann, *Mensch und Umwelt im Mittelalter* (Frankfurt a. M. 1989). See also the articles by Oskar Moser, Konrad Bedal, and Fred Kaspar in Günter Wiegelmann, ed., *Nord–Süd–Unterschiede in der städtischen und ländlichen Kultur Mitteleuropas* (Münster, 1985). For further research, J. Hähnel, ed., *Hauskundliche Bibliographie* (Münster, 1971–).

5   See the numerous examples given in Harry Kühnel, ed., *Alltag im Spätmittelalter*, 3rd edn (Graz/Vienna/Cologne, 1986), pp. 17 ff.

6   Helmuth Thomsen, *Der volkstümliche Wohnungsbau der Stadt Braunschweig im Mittelalter* (Borna-Leipzig, 1937); Peter Hans Ropertz, *Kleinbürgerlicher Wohnungsbau in Deutschland und im benachbarten Ausland* (Ph.D., Aachen, 1976); Ulf Dirlmeier, *Untersuchungen zu Einkommensverhältnissen und Lebenshaltungskosten in oberdeutschen Städten des Spätmittelalters* (Heidelberg, 1982), pp. 257 f.

7   Karl Baumgarten, *Das deutsche Bauernhaus. Eine Einführung in seine Geschichte vom 9. bis zum 19. Jahrhundert* (Berlin, 1980).

8   E.g. Karl Baumgarten, ' "Domus kotores". Ein mittelalterliches Kleinbauernhaus in Mecklenburg', *Rheinisch-Westfälische Zeitschrift für Volkskunde* XXVIII (1983), pp. 47–60.

9   Dirlmeier, *Untersuchungen*, p. 240; Joseph Greving, 'Wohnungs- und Besitzverhältnisse der einzelnen Bevölkerungsklassen im Kölner Kirchspiel St. Kolumba vom 13. bis 16. Jahrhundert', *Annalen des historischen Vereins für den Niederrhein* LXXVIII (1904), pp. 1–79, esp. p. 33; Erich Maschke, 'Die Unterschichten der mittelalterlichen Städte Deutschlands', in E. Maschke and

J. Sydow, eds, *Gesellschaftliche Unterschichten in den südwestdeutschen Städten* (Stuttgart, 1967), pp. 21 f.; Dietrich Denecke, 'Sozialtopographie und sozialräumliche Gliederung der spätmittelalterlichen Stadt', in J. Fleckenstein and K. Stackmann, eds, *Über Stadt, Bürger und städtische Literatur im Spätmittelalter* (Göttingen, 1980), pp. 161–202, esp. p. 186; Elisabeth Lichtenberger, *Die Wiener Altstadt. Von der mittelalterlichen Bürgerstadt zur City* (Vienna, 1977).

10 For the history of domestic environment in late medieval and early modern Germany, Walter Stengel, *Alte Wohnkultur in Berlin und in der Mark im Spiegel der Quellen des 16.–19. Jahrhunderts* (Berlin, 1958); Ruth-E Mohrmann, 'Städtische Wohnkultur in Nordwestdeutschland vom 17. bis zum 19. Jahrhundert (aufgrund von Inventaren)', in G. Wiegelmann, ed., *Nord-Süd-Unterschiede in der städtischen und ländlichen Kultur Mitteleuropas* (Münster, 1985), pp. 89–156; Ruth-E. Mohrmann, idem: *Alltagswelt im Land Braunschweig* (Münster, 1990); Max Hasse, 'Neues Hausgerät, neue Häuser, neue Kleider', *Zeitschrift für die Archäologie des Mittelalters* VII (1979), pp. 7–83. See also the articles by Horst Appuhn, Jürgen Wittstock, and others in two richly illustrated catalogues *Aus dem Alltag der mittelalterlichen Stadt* (Bremen, 1985) and C. Meckseper, ed., *Stadt im Wandel* (Stuttgart/Bad Cannstatt, 1985) III; Rainer Kahsnitz and Rainer Brandl, eds, *Aus dem Wirtshaus zum Wilden Mann. Funde aus dem mittelalterlichen Nürnberg* (Nuremberg, 1984); Valentin Groebner, *Ökonomie ohne Haus. Zum Wirtschaften armer Leute in Nürnberg am Ende des 15. Jahrhunderts* (Göttingen, 1993).

11 For a complete bibliography of published record material, Hildegard Mannheims and Klaus Roth, eds, *Nachlaßverzeichnisse. Probate Inventories* (Münster, 1984). For a methodologically interesting case study, see Uta Löwenstein, ' "Item ein Betth" ... Wohnungs- und Nachlaßinventare als Quellen zur Haushaltsführung im 16. Jahrhundert', in Trude Ehlert, ed., *Haushalt und Familie in Mittelalter und früher Neuzeit* (Sigmaringen, 1991) pp. 43–70.

12 See Robert Jütte, *Obrigkeitliche Armenfürsorge in deutschen Reichsstädten der frühen Neuzeit* (Cologne/Vienna, 1984), p. 230.

13 Christiane Homoet, Dietmar Sauermann and Joachim Schepes, *Sterbfallinventare des Stiftes Quernheim, 1525–1808* (Münster, 1982), pp. 70 ff.

14 Gottfried Korff, 'Einige Bemerkungen zum Wandel des Bettes', *Zeitschrift für Volkskunde* LXXVII (1981), pp. 1–16; Ruth-E. Mohrmann, ' "In der freywilligen Nachlassung der willkührlichen Bewegungen". Anmerkungen zur Geschichte des Schlafens', in B. Pötter, H. Eberhart, and E. Katschnig-Fasch, eds, *Innovation und Wandell. Festschrift für Oskar Moser zum 80. Geburtstag* (Graz, 1994), pp. 261–78.

15 For studies on food and nutrition in late medieval and early modern Germany, Wilhelm Abel, *Stufen der Ernährung* (Göttingen, 1981); Irmgard Bitsch, Trude Ehlert, Tenja V. Ertzdorff, *Essen und Trinken in Mittelalter und Neuzeit* (Sigmaringen, 1987); Dirlmeier, *Untersuchungen*, pp. 293 ff.; Hans J. Teuteberg and Günter Wiegelmann, *Unsere tägliche Kost. Geschichte und regionale Prägung*, 2nd edn (Münster, 1988); Robert Jütte, 'Diets in Welfare Institutions and in Outdoor Poor Relief in Early Modern Western Europe', *Ethnologia Europaea* XVII (1987), pp. 117–36; Wolfgang Sannwald, *Spitäler in Pest und Krieg. Untersuchungen zur Wirtschafts- und Sozialgeschichte südwestdeutscher Spitäler im 17. Jahrhundert* (Gomaringen, 1993); Barbara Krug-Richter, *Zwischen Fasten und Festmahl. Hospitalverpflegung in Münster 1540 bis 1650* (Stuttgart, 1994).

16 Liselotte Constanze Eisenbart, *Kleiderordnungen der deutschen Städte zwischen 1350 und 1700* (Göttingen, 1962); Veronika Baur, *Kleiderordnungen in Bayern vom 14. bis zum 19. Jahrhundert* (Munich, 1975); Neithard Bulst,

'Zum Problem städtischer und territorialer Kleider-, Aufwands- und Luxusgesetzgebung in Deutschland, 13.– Mitte 16. Jahrhundert', in A. Gouronu and A.
Rigaudiere, eds, *Renaissance du pouvoir législatif et genèse de l'état* (Perpig-
nan, 1988), pp. 29–57; Neithard Bulst and Robert Jütte, eds, *Kleidung und
Identität in der ständischen Gesellschaft*, Saeculum XLIV(1) (Freiburg im Br.,
1993).

17 For recent research on ethnological and psychological aspects of clothing in
pre-industrial Germany, see the bibliographical and methodological survey by
W. Hansen, 'Aufgaben der historischen Kleidungsforschung', in Günter
Wiegelmann, ed., *Geschichte der Alltagskultur* (Münster, 1980), pp. 149–174.
Important studies in these field include Helmut Ottenjahn, ed., *Mode-Tracht-
Regionale Identität. Historische Kleidungsforschung heute* (Cloppenburg,
1985); Harry Kühnel, ed., *Terminologie und Typologie mittelalterlicher
Sachgüter. Das Beispiel der Kleidung* (Vienna, 1988).

18 For new German research on sanitation and hygiene in historical times, Ulf
Dirlmeier, 'Die kommunalen Zuständigkeiten und Leistungen süddeutscher
Städte im Spätmittelalter (vor allem auf dem Gebiet der Ver- und Entsorgung)'
in J. Sydow, ed., *Städtische Versorgung und Entsorgung im Wandel der
Geschichte* (Sigmaringen, 1981), pp. 113–50; Gottfried Hösel, *Unser Abfall
aller Zeiten. Eine Geschichte der Städtereinigung* (Munich, 1987); Martin Illi,
Von der Schîssgrueb zur modernen Stadtentwässerung (Zurich, 1987). For one
particular aspect (water supply) see Rolf Busch, 'Die Wasserversorgung des
Mittelalters und der frühen Neuzeit in norddeutschen Städten', in C.
Meckseper, *Stadt im Wandel IV*, pp. 301–15.

19 Alfred Martin, *Deutsches Badewesen in vergangenen Tagen* (Jena, 1906), pp.
64 ff.

20 For the history of travel and transport in our period, see e.g. Norbert Ohler,
Reisen im Mittelalter (Munich, 1986); Herbert Schwarzwälder, 'Reisekosten
als Faktor der Reisemodalitäten in Nordwestdeutschland um 1600', in D.
Brosius and M. Last, eds, *Beiträge zur niedersächsischen Landesgeschichte*
(Hildesheim, 1984); Hans Conrad Peyer, ed., *Gastfreundschaft, Taverne und
Gasthaus im Mittelalter* (Munich, 1982); Dietrich Denecke, 'Straße und Weg
im Mittelalter als Lebensraum und Vermittler zwischen entfernten Orten', in
Herrmann, *Umwelt*, pp. 207–23; Helmut Hundsbichler, 'Selbstzeugnisse mit-
telalterlicher Reisetätigkeit und historische Migrationsforschung', in G. Jaritz
and A. Müller, eds, *Migration in der Feudalgesellschaft* (Frankfurt a. M./New
York, 1988), pp. 351–70.

21 E.g. Ludwig Erich Schmitt, *Untersuchungen zu Entstehung und Struktur der
neuhochdeutschen Schriftssprache* I (Cologne/Graz, 1966).

22 E.g. Klaus Arnold, *Kind und Gesellschaft in Mittelalter und Renaissance*
(Paderborn, 1980); August Nitschke, 'Die Stellung des Kindes in der Familie
im Spätmittelalter und in der Renaissance', in A. Haverkamp, ed., *Haus und
Familie in der spätmittelalterlichen Stadt* (Vienna/Cologne, 1984), pp. 215–43;
Jochen Martin and August Nitschke, eds, *Zur Sozialgeschichte der Kindheit*
(Freiburg im Br., 1986); Rudolf Lenz, 'Emotion und Affektion in der Familie
der frühen Neuzeit', in P. J. Schuler, ed., *Die Familie als sozialer und historischer
Verband. Untersuchungen zum Spätmittelalter und zur frühen Neuzeit*
(Sigmaringen, 1987), pp. 121–46; Steven Ozment, *Three Behaim Boys. Growing
Up in Early Modern Germany* (New Haven, Conn./London, 1990); Richard
van Dülmen, *Kultur und Alltag in der Frühen Neuzeit I: Das Haus und seine
Menschen 16.–18. Jahrhundert* (Munich, 1991). For German examples of the
history of childbirth, midwifery and weaning, Peter Ketsch, *Frauen im
Mittelalter* II (Düsseldorf, 1984), pp. 212 ff.; U. Ottmüller, 'Mutter und

Wickelkind in der vorindustriellen Gesellschaft des deutschsprachigen Raumes (ab ca. 1500)', in *Frauengeschichte* (Munich, 1981), pp. 101–6; Merry E. Wiesner, 'Early Modern Midwifery. A Case Study', in B. A. Hanawalt, ed., *Women and Work in Preindustrial Europe* (Bloomington, IN, 1986), pp. 94–113.

23   E.g., Alwin Schultz, *Deutsches Leben im XIV. und XV. Jahrhundert* (Prague/Vienna/Leipzig, 1892), pp. 120 ff.; Gottlieb Schnapper-Arndt, *Studien zur Geschichte der Lebenshaltung in Frankfurt a. M. während des 17. und 18. Jahrhunderts* (Frankfurt a. M., 1915) I, pp. 358 ff.

24   E.g. Paul Richard Blum, ed., *Studien zur Thematik des Todes im 16. Jahrhundert* (Wolfenbüttel, 1983); Werner Friedrich Kümmel, 'Der sanfte und der selige Tod', in R. Lenz, ed., *Leichenpredigten als Quellen historischer Wissenschaften* (Marburg, 1984), pp. 199–225; Arno Borst, 'Zwei mittelalterliche Sterbefälle', *Merkur* XXXIV (1980), pp. 1081–98; Bernhard Vogler, 'La Législation sur les sépultures dans l'Allemagne protestante au XVIᵉ siècle', *Revue d'histoire moderne et contemporaine* XXII (1975), pp. 191–232; Wolfgang Herborn, 'Alltagsleben in Siegburg und an der unteren Sieg im Mittelalter und in der frühen Neuzeit', *Jb des Geschichts- und Altertumsvereins für Siegburg und den Rhein-Sieg-Kreis* LIII (1985), pp. 84–108, esp. pp. 92 ff.; Christian Krötzl, 'Evidentissima signa mortis. Zu Tod und Todesfeststellung in mittelalterlichen Mirakelberichten', in Gertrud Blaschitz *et al.*, eds, *Symbole des Alltags – Alltag der Symbole. Festschrift für Harry Kühnel zum 65. Geburtstag* (Graz, 1992), pp. 765–76.

25   For the later period, Arthur E. Imhof, 'Säuglingssterblichkeit im europäischen Kontext, 17.–20. Jahrhundert', *Demographic Data Base Newsletter* II (1984), pp. 1–64.

26   For the history of German schools and education, see e.g. Edith Ennen 'Stadt und Schule in ihrem wechselseitigen Verhältnis vornehmlich im Mittelalter', *Rheinische Vierteljahresblätter* XXII (1957), pp. 56–72; Gerald Strauss, *Luther's House of Learning* (Baltimore, MD, 1978); Martin Kintzinger, *Das Bildungswesen in der Stadt Braunschweig im hohen und späten Mittelalter. Verfassungs- und institutionengeschichtliche Studien zur Schulpolitik und Bildungsförderung* (Cologne, 1990). See also the source-book by Johannes Müller, *Vor- und frühreformatorische Schulordnungen und Schulverträge in deutscher und niederländischer Sprache* I (Zschoppau, 1915).

27   E.g. Christoph Conrad and Hans-Joachim von Kondratowitz, eds., *Gerontologie und Sozialgeschichte. Wege zu einer historischen Betrachtung des Alters* (Berlin, 1983); Robert Jütte, 'Aging and Body Image in the Sixteenth Century. Hermann Weinsberg's (1518–97) Perception of the Aging Body', *European History Quarterly* XVIII (1987), pp. 259–90; Peter Borscheid, *Geschichte des Alters 16.–18. Jahrhundert* (Münster, 1987); Manfred Welte, 'Das Alter im Mittelalter und in der Frühen Neuzeit', *Schweizerische Zeitschrift für Geschichte* XXXVII (1987), pp. 1–32; Christoph Conrads and Hans-Joachim von Kondratowitz, eds, *Zur Kulturgeschichte des Alterns. Toward a Cultural History of Aging* (Berlin, 1993).

28   There are only a few studies on the experience of illness in late medieval and early modern Germany: Rudolf Schenda, 'Der "gemeine Mann" und sein medikales Verhalten im 16. und 17. in Jahrhundert', in Joachim Telle, ed., *Pharmazie und der gemeine Mann* (Wolfenbüttel, 1982), pp. 9–20; Peter Wunderli, ed., *Der kranke Mensch in Mittelalter und Renaissance* (Düsseldorf, 1986); Otto Döhner, *Krankheitsbegriff, Gesundheitsverhalten und Einstellung zum Tod im 16. bis 18. Jahrhundert* (Frankfurt a. M./Berne, 1986); Barbara Duden, *Geschichte unter der Haut* (Stuttgart, 1987); Heinrich Schipperges, *Die Kranken im Mittelalter* (Munich, 1990); Robert Jütte, *Ärzte, Heiler und Patienten. Medizinischer Alltag in der frühen Neuzeit* (Munich/Zurich, 1991).

|13|

The Structure of Belief: Confessionalism and Society, 1500–1600

R. PO-CHIA HSIA

To summarize adequately the multi-faceted research on sixteenth century German religious history is obviously a presumptuous aim. In posting a few signs of current research, this essay can only hope to serve as a mapping guide, directing further effort toward unknown territories in the landscape of historical knowledge. I shall begin with a brief introductory section on current concepts in Reformation research, a sort of *Begriffsgeschichte*, in order to examine both the achievements and the limitations of current historiography. The next section will offer an approximate chronology of the sixteenth century under the concept of 'generation'. Without any claim to the narrative comprehensiveness which the reader may find in standard texts of the Reformation, this section will suggest a way of understanding the development of confessionalism in sixteenth century Central Europe by focusing on central experiences of succeeding generations. The remaining three sections forsake narrative for structural analysis. They outline in turn the three central themes in the development of confessionalism by comparing the structural similarities of the three major Christian confessions: the social profile of the clergies and their relationship to ruling elites; the shaping of society through the institutionalization of confessional churches; and, finally, the relationship between official and unofficial religions, in other words, the social context and limitations of confessionalization.

The Reformation: contending concepts

To the extent that dominant historiographical concepts have shaped research and debate, a brief summary of their arguments may be in order.

Five contending concepts represent the religious transformation of the sixteenth century as variously the 'early bourgeois revolution' (*frühbürgerliche Revolution*), the 'urban Reformation' (*Stadtreformation*), 'the radical reformation' (*radikale Reformation*), the 'communal Reformation' (*Gemeindere-formation*), and 'confessionalization' (*Konfessionalisierung*). I shall briefly outline each historiographical tradition.

The concept of 'early bourgeois revolution', formally articulated in 1961 by the Leipzig historian Max Steinmetz, established the paradigm for sixteenth-century research in the former German Democratic Republic for more than two decades.[1] Itself derived from the concept of *Volksreformation* first proposed during the 1950s by the Soviet historian M. M. Smirin, this paradigm was closely identified with the political ideology of the GDR and the claims of official marxist historiography.[2] Its proponents argued that the popular reformation of the peasants, miners, and workers, the plebeian class of the sixteenth century, served as a forerunner to the English, Dutch, and French Revolutions, although that reformation was suppressed by the ruling classes. According to this school, the years 1525–35 witnessed the revolutionary climax, because the reform movement was directed at the Catholic church as the quintessential representative of the feudal regime. Betrayed by the bourgeois party – the followers of Luther and Zwingli – the people's Reformation was crushed by the Reformation of the princes. In addition to the Peasants' War of 1525, a great deal of attention was also lavished on the radical reformer Thomas Müntzer, who was elevated to a historical status equal to that of Martin Luther. Although limited by the arguments of class determinism and economic reductionism, the concept of the early bourgeois revolution represented an important challenge to traditional views of the Reformation. For more than two decades it served as a counterpoint to the dominant historicist discourse on the Reformation in West Germany, an interpretation shaped by Leopold von Ranke in the nineteenth century, with emphasis on the emperors, princes, the territorial state, and theology. The concept of early bourgeois revolution enjoyed only a limited reception outside the GDR.[3]

In 1962 Bernd Moeller argued in a seminal essay, *Imperial Cities and the Reformation*, that the political experience of the south German and Swiss urban communes shaped the theologies of the south German and Swiss reformers, men such as Huldrych Zwingli and Martin Bucer, whose views on the new reformed communities differed substantially from Luther's. Literate in religious matters, concerned for their salvation, experienced in parochial administration, hostile to clerical abuses and privileges within urban walls, citizens of these urban communes envisioned their cities as representations of the *corpus christianum*, the ideal communities of salvation.[4] The concept of city and Reformation, based in part on Moeller's own research on the Reformation in Constance, inspired many case studies of the urban reformation. It has also helped to direct research attention to the late sixteenth-century city, resulting in the related concepts of 'late city Reformation' and 'city and Counter-Reformation'.[5] The strength of Moeller's thesis is its emphasis on the polycentrism of reform and its critique of the narrow concentration of Reformation scholarship on Martin Luther. In turn, his critics argue that the ideology of urban corporate unity merely masked intense urban class struggles and neglected the connections between city and country.[6] Nevertheless, Moeller was an important advocate for combining the history of theology and society, and gave a strong impetus to the subsequent rise of social history of the Reformation.

In 1962 George H. Williams presented his concept of the 'radical Reformation' as an alternative to the 'magisterial Reformation' of the Lutheran and Calvinist reformers. Williams followed the tradition of Roland Bainton, who had stressed the contributions of the 'left wing of the Reformation,' a loose category including Anabaptists, spiritualists, and rational evangelists opposed to the theologies and the institutionalization of the official Protestant churches.[7] As a distant intellectual and spiritual heir to the hitherto marginal Anabaptist and Schwenckfeldian scholarship, the paradigm of the radical Reformation also echoes the analysis of German Lutheranism in the work of Ernst Troeltsch, although it does not follow his distinction between the ideal types of 'church' and 'sect'.[8] The concept of radical Reformation has opened research into areas ignored by traditional Lutheran scholarship, especially in casting light on neglected intellectual figures of the sixteenth century.[9] Except for limited quantitative research, studies in the radical Reformation have focused on theology and biography, often to the neglect of the larger social-political context.[10]

Proposed in the work of Peter Blickle, the concept of 'communal Reformation' argues for the central significance of self-governing village and urban communes in early modern Central European history, not the least in serving as the driving force behind the popular reform movement. Based on his previous work on political representation in the German south-west and on the revolution of 1525, Blickle developed his model to bridge the gap between city and country and to find an alternative populist perspective in understanding early modern German history.[11]

Chronologically, Blickle's ideas evolved from a focus on political-institutional history to religious history; and the concept of 'communal Reformation' is predicated upon the centrality of 'commune' and the 'common man' in his earlier research. Critics of Blickle's thesis point to the inapplicability of the model in north Germany, to the neglected role of the territorial state, and to the contrary examples of Swiss communes that remained Catholic.[12]

While the preceding four concepts are derived primarily from the analysis of the early sixteenth century, especially from the intense study of the early reform movement between 1520 and 1535, the concept of confessionalization (*Konfessionalisierung*) describes the development of the later sixteenth and seventeenth centuries. It goes beyond the idea of confessional formation (*Konfessionsbildung*), first developed by Ernst W. Zeeden, whose work focuses on the parallel consolidation of competing confessional systems of doctrines, institutions, and rituals.[13] In the research of Heinz Schilling, Wolfgang Reinhard, and R. Po-chia Hsia, the study of the confessional churches is closely tied to the analysis of the social and cultural impact of the religious divisions of Central Europe after 1555.[14]

The generations of reform

Using the concept of 'generations', we can identify four distinct periods which shaped the experiences of contemporaries in sixteenth century Germany. The four generation-periods were themselves characterized by a cluster of crucial events: the revolutionary years of the early Reformation, 1520-1535; the confirmation of Protestant identity, 1535–55; the achievement of religious peace, 1555–80; and the rise of confessional parties, 1580-1600.

Within a few years of the publication of Luther's reformation pamphlets, the simmering resentment of the church boiled over in a flood of revolts and rebellions: in town after town, artisans disrupted the Catholic mass, threatened the clergy, and removed idols; in the countryside, peasants refused to pay the tithe and flocked to hear wandering preachers; ultimately, in the spring of 1525, unrest in town and country flared up in a full-scale revolution that challenged not only the church but also traditional social order.

By first questioning and then condemning the theology and practice of salvation of the Roman church, Luther and his followers made the evangelical movement a lightning-rod for the discharge of deep and widespread anger against the established order. Before the Reformation, anger at the abuses and privileges of the clergy was balanced by devotion to the system of salvation provided by the church. The vehement criticism of the clergy's conduct reflected rather the laity's devotion to the sacramental system over which the clergy supervised. The laity wanted a better educated clergy, who would say mass, hear confession, and tend to the parishioners' spiritual needs. Except for a small minority of dissidents, the efficacy of Catholic sacraments was not questioned by the laity. Luther shattered this delicate balance. In arguing for a salvation by faith, in attacking the theology of 'good works', Luther in fact condemned the sacramental system as the fraudulent concoction of the Roman clergy. In one stroke, therefore, reform theology annulled the efficacy of the Catholic sacramental system and the authority of its practitioners, the Roman clergy. Once delegitimized, the Roman church became in the eyes of its critics merely a fraudulent and exploitative institution.

During the massive uprisings of 1525, which historians have variously called the 'revolution of the common man' or the 'Peasants' War',[15] monasteries became favourite targets for plunder, while noble estates were usually spared. Refusal to pay the tithe, as in the countryside around Nuremberg, was justified by peasants with appeal to Luther's slogan of 'priesthood of all believers'.[16] While economic grievances predominated in the articles of the peasant armies, there was evidence of a high degree of religious mobilization among the Alsatian and Thuringian rebels.[17]

Although the peasant armies were defeated in 1525, the vision of a religious transformation of society did not fade away. Millenarian voices calling for perfect justice and saintly rule on earth, echoes of the radical heretical movements of the later middle ages, were heard among the Anabaptist sects that grew rapidly after 1525. This sectarian movement reached its height in 1534, when the Anabaptist followers of Jan Matthys, a follower of the self-proclaimed prophet Melchior Hoffmann, took control of the city of Münster. The brief social and religious experiment of the Anabaptist Kingdom of Münster (March 1534 to June 1535) was a deep shock to the Catholic and Lutheran rulers of the Empire. Catholic and Lutheran churchmen were vociferous in condemning the community of property and the polygyny of the Münsteraners; and the combined forces of Catholic and Lutheran princes crushed this most dangerous challenge to the ordained order of church and government.

Between 1533 and 1535, under the leadership of the reformer Martin Bucer and the patrician councillor Jakob Sturm, the evangelical preachers in Strasbourg drafted ordinances of worship and church organization that were endorsed by the magistrates. The Evangelical Church Ordinance of Strasbourg defined the character of the new emerging Reformed church. It specified the nature of the Lord's Supper, the organization of the pastorate, the constitution of the community of worship, and the articles of faith. It also condemned the teachings of Melchior Hoffmann, the spiritual father of the Münster Anabaptists, who was languishing in a Strasbourg gaol.

As an explicit response to the sectarian challenge of the Anabaptists, the Strasbourg Evangelical Ordinance, one of the many evangelical ordinances promulgated during the 1520s and 1530s, represented an important development in the Reformation.[18] Having challenged the authority of the Roman church, the reformers found their own teachings attacked by lay prophets and turned to secular magistrates in order to prevent a complete collapse of clerical authority. The promulgation of evangelical church ordinances, the first step in the institutionalization of the reform movement, was in part a direct reaction to the instability of the revolutionary years 1525–35. In addition to firming up reformed identity against sectarian agitation, the new church ordinances also gave the Protestant church a legal basis to contest the orthodoxy of the Catholic church.

To be sure, the institutionalization of reform was an uneven process.

While many territories and cities such as Ernestine Saxony, Hesse, Württemberg, Memmingen, Strasbourg, and Nuremberg confidently adopted reformed worship, other areas such as Albertine Saxony and Regensburg did not declare for the Confessio Augustana until the 1540s.[19] Nevertheless, by the early 1540s Protestant Germany was a political reality in the existence of the Schmalkaldic League, a military alliance based on the central axis Saxony–Hesse and directed against the Catholic Habsburg emperor.

Military defeat at Mühlberg (1547) was another significant experience for the formation of German Protestant identity. Defeat brought a sense of martyrdom: the leading Protestant princes were captured and humiliated; imperial cities were occupied and their privileges rescinded; reform worship was forbidden; and the abhorred Catholic mass was restored. To Protestant Germany the catastrophe, following so soon after Luther's death in 1546, seemed to signify the imminent Second Coming of Christ and the Last Judgment, before which the Antichrist would reign and the faithful persecuted. Leading reformers who refused to accept the Interim lost their positions: Martin Bucer of Strasbourg, Andreas Osiander of Nuremberg, and many others. A torrent of sermons and pamphlets poured forth from the pulpit and printing presses condemning the Interim, the religious settlement that was meant to be a bridge before a final resolution of the religious schism by a general church council. The reintroduction of Catholicism was effectively sabotaged. In Strasbourg, for example, apprentices and youths harassed the Roman clergy, who were allowed to celebrate mass under the terms of the Interim, while the magistrates turned a blind eye.[20] If military defeat in 1547 tested the faith of the Lutherans, it also strengthened their sense of identity by giving them an experience of persecution, martyrdom, and resistance. The figure of the Antichrist and the expectation of the apocalypse, so central in mid-century, would become ideological structures in the identity and discourse of German Lutheranism.

The years 1555–80 seemed on the surface a period of relative stability and religious peace. After the turmoil of the previous generations, the religious settlement of Augsburg gave the Empire a constitutional framework for confessional toleration. In many cities, Lutheran and Catholic communities coexisted peacefully, in spite of the polemics of their clergies: the south German Imperial cities of Augsburg, Ulm, Ravensburg, Biberach, and Dinkelsbühl evolved into biconfessional urban communities, where the confessions even shared the use of church space.[21] The spirit of the times was reflected in Münster, where the civic community still had living memory of the Anabaptist débâcle but grew to tolerate a small Lutheran and Anabaptist minority.[22] For the generations who had experienced the religious strife of mid-century, the relative quiet of the 1560s and 1570s seemed to reflect the wisdom of the religious peace, which shielded Germans from the savage religious warfare that tore apart the body politic in France and the Netherlands.

Yet the toleration of the elders struck a younger generation as compromise. Brought up in the confessional schools established in these decades of peace – the universities, academies, gymnasia, and schools of the Lutherans and Calvinists, and the Jesuit colleges of the Catholics – a new generation of political and ecclesiastical leaders challenged the religious compromise struck by their elders. Even in this period of stability, the constitutional framework of Augsburg proved inadequate to prevent the confessionalization of German society. In Lutheran Germany, the ascendancy of conservative theologians, the so-called Gnesio-Lutherans, helped to consolidate Lutheran identity against both Tridentine Catholicism and Calvinism. In Catholic Germany, signs of the Counter-Reformation were apparent in Bavaria and in the ecclesiastical principalities, particularly in Würzburg, where Protestantism was combated by political repression. A more ominous sign of future conflicts was the rise of Calvinism in the Holy Roman Empire. Calvinism made its initial political inroad in 1563, with the conversion of Frederick III (1559–1576), Elector Palatine, who remained isolated until the conversions of the counts of Sayn-Wittgenstein and Nassau-Dillenburg in 1578. Others followed. Soon Calvinism in the Empire became a political force to be reckoned with. Events would soon prove the impossibility of shielding the Empire from the larger clash of arms that pitched Protestant against Catholic Europe.

The 1580s were a crucial decade. In historical hindsight, it may be said that events pointed clearly to the eventual shattering of the system of religious peace in the Thirty Years' War. Many signs pointed to the hardening of confessional fronts.

In 1580 the Book of Concord, a confession of doctrines formulated by orthodox Lutheran theologians, was formally adopted by most of the subscribers to the *Confessio Augustana*. The Formula of Concord provided Lutheran Germany with a theological and political clarity amidst confessional competition from Catholicism and Calvinism; it was the final step in the definition of Lutheran confessional identity and unity.

In the meantime, Calvinism continued to make headway among the estates of the Empire: Bremen and Neuenahr in 1581, Solms-Braunfels in 1582, East Friesland in 1583, Isenburg-Ronneburg, Palatinate-Zweibrücken, and Bentheim-Tecklenburg in 1588, Hanau-Münzenberg in 1595, Isenburg-Büdingen, and Anhalt in 1596, Baden-Durlach in 1599, and other territories into the early seventeenth century. Most of the conversions were at the expense of the Lutheran church, although the conversion of Archbishop Gebhard Truchsess of Cologne in 1583 was an exception that threatened to upset completely the balance of power in imperial politics.

A powerful political bloc, Calvinism was by and large an elite phenomenon in the Holy Roman Empire and enjoyed limited success among the populace at large. Princes, magistrates, and officials who converted to Calvinism encountered strong opposition from their Lutheran subjects when they attempted to impose the new official religion. Intra-Protestant polemics certainly rivalled, if not exceeded, the vituperation of Protestant Catholic diatribes.

The Calvinist challenge was met head-on by a more self-confident and militant Catholicism in the Empire, a force embodied by the Wittelsbach dynasty of Bavaria and by the ecclesiastical principalities. Determined to prevent any further erosion of the Catholic position, and indeed poised to reconquer Protestant souls, a younger generation of Catholic princes and officials, many educated by the Jesuits, were bitterly opposed to the 'political' compromise of their predecessors. Having suppressed Protestants at home, the Wittelsbachs undertook a strategy to safeguard the ecclesiastical principalities in north-west Germany for the dynasty and for Catholicism. The victory of Archbishop Ernst of Bavaria over his rival, Gebhard Truchsess, in the War of Cologne (1583) opened the way for the accumulation of north-west German bishoprics and for the importation of the methods of the Counter-Reformation Bavarian state into north Germany.

The clergy and the regimes

Since the reform movement was initiated by clerics, one may speak of the Reformation as a massive internal revolt within the official church. Two themes are central to this discussion: the pervasive anti-clericalism leading up to the Reformation and its persistence into the confessional age; and the transformation of the clergy after the Reformation and their relationship to secular authorities. The prominence given to the Lutheran clergy in the following discussion is a reflection of the uneven scholarship on the subject rather than of the historical significance of the Lutheran clergy.

Anti-clericalism can be massively documented in the decades leading up to the Reformation.[23] The clergy was hated for its privileges and abuses; Robert Scribner has characterized the clerics as holding political, economic, legal, social, sexual, and sacral powers over the laity.[24] Pamphlets, songs, chronicles, and popular actions represented a broad sentiment of anti-clericalism. Most of the research, however, has not clearly differentiated between different kinds of anti-clericalism. Although the clergy as a privileged estate was under general attack, it seemed that the religious orders suffered especially harsh criticism.

A more important point was the phenomenon of clerical anti-clericalism, which went beyond the traditional self-criticism of the clergy and provided the first impetus of the anti-Roman, anti-papal evangelical movement. The 176 evangelical preachers active in Germany during the years between 1520 and 1550 included 74 priests and 54 monks, about three-quarters of the total.[25] Again, about three-quarters of the total group had attended university. Two conclusions can be drawn. First, there was a remarkable continuity between the old Catholic priesthood and the new evangelical reformers, a thesis fully documented by regional studies of the Lutheran clergy.[26] Second, the first clerical supporters of reform seemed to have been proportionally better educated than the clergy as a whole. As Scribner has shown, 105 of the 176 preachers were initially appointed to preach (as opposed to parish priests, canons, etc.). One of the expressions of lay piety before the Reformation was precisely the endowment of preacherships, undertaken either by the city council or by wealthy lay patrons. These benefices remained in lay magisterial control, and called for educated clerics to serve the needs of the urban communities. To provide suitable candidates, city councils often established scholarships for native sons; and the general growth of German university enrolments between 1385 and 1517 helped to raise the educational level of the urban parish clergy.[27] And it was this stratum of the clergy, the urban preachers – Bernhard Rothmann in Münster, Balthasar Hubmaier in Regensburg, Matthis Zell in Strasbourg, Andreas Osiander in Nuremberg, Huldrych Zwingli in Zurich, and Johannes Brenz in Schwäbisch Hall, to name only some of the most prominent – who first sounded the evangelical challenge to Rome.[28]

The success of the new evangelical church, however, failed to diminish traditional anti-clericalism. The gap between the Protestant pastorate and the laity continued, despite the integration of the reformed clergy in the body politic, because the new clerical estate distanced itself both socially and intellectually from the laity, a result of its own self-perception, social recruitment, and official church policy.

Among the Lutheran pastorate, the overwhelming majority came from the lower and middle strata of urban society. To take Nuremberg as an example, in the sixteenth century 80 per cent of the pastors came from artisanal-burgher families; 6.6 per cent came from merchant families; 5.3 were of peasant stock; and 4 per cent were recruited from elite jurist families.[29] The strongly urban character of the Lutheran pastorate not only reflected the importance of cities in the reform movement, but also structured the interaction between urban and rural cultures as the official Protestant churches extended their influence into the countryside.

By the second half of the sixteenth century the Lutheran pastorate had established an enduring pattern of recruitment and a distinct social profile. As the older generation of ex-Catholic pastors passed away – a Lutheran pastorate created as much by fiat as by voluntary conversion, when cities and territories professed the evangelical faith – a new generation of pastors, schooled in the confessional polemics of territorial universities, took their place. Overwhelmingly urban in background, these pastors embodied both the authority of the territorial or urban evangelical churches and secular officialdom to their peasant parishioners. The distance between pastor and rural parishioner was further increased by the tendency of the Lutheran clergy to recruit from its own ranks. In sixteenth century Württemberg, of the 511 pastors whose social background can be ascertained (out of a total of 2,716 pastors), 323 were sons of pastors and only four came from peasant families.[30] These percentages corresponded almost exactly to the breakdown for figures of the Palatinate pastorate in Bernard Vogler's detailed study.[31] This urban preponderance became even more pronounced in the following centuries: for eighteenth-century Württemberg, we know the social background for 3,067 out of the total of 3,208 pastors; only six came from peasant families and 1,352 were sons of clerics.[32]

Peasant alienation can be seen in the sermon collection of the Rostock professor Simon Pauli, who recorded one parishioner saying to him: 'Let our clerk pray, he is paid for it. I don't pray, since I get no money doing it' (*Vnser Pfaff mag beten, der hat Gelt dafuer. Ich bete nicht, denn ich habe kein Gelt dafuer*). Or, when a peasant was asked what he was receiving in Easter communion, replied in his Saxon dialect: 'Maybe our pope knows what it is, why should I care?' (*Wat dat ys, mag vnse Pape weten, wat kuemmert my dat?*).[33]

Anti-clericalism persisted in Catholic territories as well. During the sixteenth century, the Council of Trent had a limited impact on the German Catholic church. True, several reform bishops published the decrees of the Council, and a handful of conscientious bishops actually carried out diocesan visitations – Bishop Hoya of Münster in 1573, for example. But these early efforts encountered numerous entrenched privileges in the various collegiate and corporate bodies of the regular and secular clergy. To renew Catholicism, disciplining the clergy and replenishing its depleted ranks became the most important goals of the territories that remained steadfast to Rome. The initiative came from a group of reformist prince-bishops and the newly constituted Society of Jesus.

As a rule, reform in Catholic Germany during the sixteenth century was imposed from above, and measures taken to discipline the clergy and laity were closely linked to efforts to consolidate secular authority.[34] Unlike the Lutheran pastorate, who became *de facto* civil servants of princes and magistrates, the Catholic clergy represented a heterogeneous group. In ecclesiastical territories, the leading church officials (the archbishops, bishops, abbots, officials, and vicars) combined secular and spiritual jurisdictions. To implement reform, the bishops relied more heavily on their secular authority, since the exercise of their spiritual authority was impeded by the privileges of clerical corporations. For the sixteenth century, Catholic reform meant in the first place a reform of the clergy, undertaken by the clerical elite (reform bishops, their officials, and Jesuits), often against the fierce resistance of the secular clergy and the established religious orders. In this light, it is important to note the internal divisions of the Catholic clergy, who were everywhere split between support for reform and tradition. Battles were fought over episcopal election, jurisdiction of visitations, reform of cloisters, control of benefices, and the administration of sacraments. On one side were the partisans of Tridentine discipline: reforming bishops, canons, and episcopal officials educated in the German College in Rome, the Jesuits, and a handful of zealous clerics; on the other side stood the defenders of tradition and corporate privileges: the masses of secular and regular clergy who more often than not resisted rather than supported the centralization of episcopal authority and the imposition of tighter clerical discipline.

Unlike its counterpart in Western Europe, Calvinism in the Empire, with the exception of Emden and some urban communities on the Lower Rhine, resembled by and large the structure of the Lutheran territorial church. The prince, not the congregation, officials, rather than presbyters, played the dominant role in shaping religion. In contrast to their Scottish, English, Dutch, Swiss, and French colleagues, German Calvinist ministers seldom contradicted the policy of their princes and magistrates. Some of them had been former Lutheran pastors, like those in the Palatinate, who switched confession by decree of their prince. A politically precarious religion dependent on the princes, Calvinism in the Empire developed the strongest arguments in support of the absolutist godly prince: the doctrine of erastianism (the supremacy of secular authority over the clerical) which came out of Heidelberg was a case in point. *Struggle for Stability*

Reshaping society

By abolishing the rites and institutions of the Catholic church, the Reformation accelerated changes which were reshaping Central European society since the fifteenth century. For all its imprecision and generality, the idea of increased patriarchal secular authority summarizes the complexity of many of these social, cultural, and political transformations. The three estates of medieval society (clergy, nobility, and people) were replaced by the three estates of *politia*, *ecclesia*, and *oeconomia*, now unified in the authority of the male ruler/minister/householder. This section will discuss the consolidation of this secular, patriarchal authority by examining the impact of the Reformation on marriage, sexuality, poor relief, and schooling.

During the first years of the evangelical movement, reformers often wed publicly as a sign of their allegiance to the new cause. More than a simple repudiation of their former Catholic clerical status, the celebration of civic marriage also proclaimed the desirability of sexual union in the scheme of reformed theology and social ethics. Praised in the writings of Luther and other reformers, marriage became the cornerstone of a reformed Christian society and the family the institution of religious instruction. Opposed to the Catholic ideal of clerical celibacy, the holy household, in Protestant theology, was both an institution and metaphor in the proper structuring of society. In the words of Bernhard Rothmann, the Münster reformer before he joined the cause of the Anabaptists, the wife stood in relation to the husband exactly as the husband stood to Christ, to be instructed in the proper doctrines and the worship of God. Not surprisingly, civic magistrates (with territorial princes following their example) quickly established their authority over marriage in cities where the authority of church courts had been swept away by the reform movement. One of the earliest civic marriage courts was set up in May 1525 in Zurich. Comprising lay councillors and ministers, the court adjudicated adultery and divorce cases which were then enforced by the city council. In other Protestant territories, consistories of churchmen took up the task of policing adultery, incest, 'whoredom', marital discord, and divorce.

Although the introduction of divorce in theory gave women a greater right of control, in practice it was seldom granted, even in cases of physical abuse. The preservation of patriarchal household was the most important aim of Protestant marital reforms. To that effect, magistrates and pastors collaborated to exercise a more repressive sexual regime than the medieval church had achieved. They closed brothels, cited adulterers, enforced child support, and attempted to control youthful sexuality by prohibiting dances, spinning bees, and marriages between young unpropertied couples who had not obtained parental consent. As recent studies have shown, Protestant sexual reform reinforced the authority of the patriarchal householders, especially for the urban artisans and the propertied families in rural areas.[35]

If property and morality were central to the Christian family, the idea of unregulated poverty threatened the sense of well-being in the Christian polity. In attacking clerical indolence in general and the mendicant friars in particular, the Reformation affirmed the value of productive labour in the scheme of salvation. The poor, who played a significant role in the economy of Catholic salvation, were deprived of their privileged position in the new moral economy. The liquidation of church properties gave civic officials the means to establish new institutions of poor relief and bring under uniform control the myriad private charities in existence. These 'common chests' were created as early as 1522 in Nuremberg, before the official adoption of the Reformation. Drawing on humanist and reform writings, Protestant church ordinances universally included programmes for poor relief: compulsory work for the able-bodied, centralized charity for the disabled, public alms for women and children, and the strict prohibition of vagrancy and public begging. For the authorities of Protestant territories, policing the poor and policing sexuality were intricately related: unwanted pregnancies, illegitimate children, abandoned wives, and destitute households made poor subjects and bad Christians; they drained public resources and undermined the divinely ordained estates of polity, church, and household.

As family fathers themselves, Protestant ruling elites arrogated to their governance the image of paternal authority, at once benign and strict. The patriarchal figure became a commonplace in theological and political discourse.[36] It was invoked in the language of numerous civic legislations in Regensburg after the adoption of Lutheran reform.[37] It was implicit in the Foreword to the 1563 Heidelberg Catechism, wherein Elector Frederick III explained:

> in Our remembrance of God's Word, and due to Our natural duty and inclination, we have finally recognized and undertaken to fulfil Our divinely ordained office, vocation, and governance, not only keep peace and order, but also to maintain a disciplined, upright, and virtuous life and behaviour among Our subjects, furthermore, and especially, to instruct them and bring them step by step to the righteous knowledge and fear of the Almighty and His sanctifying Word as the only basis of all virtues and obedience .... to help them gain eternal and transient well-being.[38]

Convinced of the inherent sinfulness of human nature, Protestant authorities sought to restrain this nature not only by legislation but also by instruction.[39] The sixteenth century saw the introduction of a comprehensive system of public schools for boys and girls in Protestant Germany which, however underfunded and inadequate, was superior to the educational system in Catholic Germany. Protestant schools consisted of two categories: elite Latin gymnasia that trained students for the universities; and German schools that trained the sons of craftsmen and peasants, and separate girls' schools that imparted literacy as well as 'feminine virtues'. Confessional indoctrination was of course inevitable in Protestant schools, as was true in their Catholic counterparts, but with rudimentary religious instruction for a broader segment of the population possible, literacy and book-ownership gradually increased in Protestant Germany.[40] Naturally, the central significance of 'the Word' in reformed theology provided the motive for educational reform. However, reading and literacy did not enhance individual spirituality, at least not in the sixteenth century. The experience of 'the Word' was mediated in the church and the household: song-books, prayer-books, and catechisms were far more common than the Bible; and the picture of the father reading from an edifying text to his household was a more accurate picture than the individual deep in solitary reading.

The religions of the people

Despite the numerous church ordinances, catechisms, sermons, and visitations, the religion of the clergies was far from the religion of the laity.

Already during the early years of the Reformation, there were cries against
'a new clerical tyranny' when reformers tried to impose church discipline.
Later in the sixteenth century, there was little evidence that the intra- and
inter-confessional polemics between the Lutheran, Calvinist, and Catholic
clergies attracted much lay attention. In fact, quite the opposite was true.
In 1598 David Altenstetter, a goldsmith in Augsburg, was arrested by the
magistrates on suspicion of being a follower of the spiritualist Caspar von
Schwenckfeld. When asked whether he was a Catholic, Lutheran, or
Schwenckfeldian, Altenstetter replied, in the words of the records:

> since up to now the theologians of the Catholic religion and the
> Augsburg confession have been opposing one another most vehe-
> mently, he does not like either one but is free from both and had
> read all sorts of Christian books at home, namely: Tauler, the *Imitatio
> Christi*, Erasmus' exegesis of the New Testament, and an old Bible
> which was printed in Nuremberg one hundred years ago. In the
> meantime, he had gone to the Lutheran church ... and although from
> time to time he had heard things in this place or that he did not
> like, he had often heard many good things preached in both
> churches ... He did not have any particular belief, but adheres to
> some articles of the Catholic church and other articles of the
> Augsburg Confession.[41]

Such a detailed testimony such as Altenstetter's was uncommon; but his
example reflected the attitude of many laypeople who were either indifferent
or hostile to any official religion, be it Protestant or Catholic. Aside from
the numerically insignificant Anabaptist sects and spiritualist coteries, it is
simply impossible to obtain any accurate picture of the proportion of the
religiously indifferent in the population at large. Nevertheless, from current
research we can draw some tentative conclusions on this elusive subject.

The laity and the clergy did not necessarily share the same ideas of confessional allegiance. In other words, laypeople who considered themselves
good Lutherans or Catholics in the sixteenth century often disagreed with
their respective clergies in religious matters. A few examples should suffice:
in Strasbourg, pious Lutheran burghers bound and read biblical books
regardless of the confessional origins of the commentators; in Lutheran
Strasbourg and Catholic Münster, citizens often sympathized with the
pacifist Anabaptists who were sought out and exiled by the magistrates
and the clergy; in Cologne, the city councillor Hermann von Weinsberg
(1518–98), who thought of himself as a good Catholic, excoriated the
clergy in his journal; and many Protestant parents, lured by the quality of
Jesuit colleges, had no qualms in sending their sons to the Catholic
fathers.[42]

The above discussion clearly implies that a specifically confessional
culture, entirely exclusive of other cultural elements, did not exist for the
laity of the sixteenth century, nor, for that matter, for the early modern

period. Confessions were porous cultural systems that grew over a sub-stratum of existing cultural beliefs and practices. This idea of cultural strat-ification was more than simply a matter of 'Catholic vestiges' in Protestantism. Instead, the phenomenon reflected the survival of many late medieval, unofficial, popular religious beliefs and practices into the con-fessional age. And because these practices corresponded with the more permanent structures of material life, they could not be readily reshaped by the religious cultures created in the sixteenth century. Condemned by the clergy as magical and superstitious, the practice of popular religion transcended both confessional and social boundaries, at least for the sixteenth century. At the heart of this popular attitude was a pervasive and pragmatic materialism.

Late medieval Catholicism, through its rituals and symbols, represented a cultural system that linked theories of the cosmos to the practices of daily existence. In abolishing Catholic rites, Protestant reformers could only partially fill in the void: the exhortation to heed the Word of God through sermons, readings, prayers, and hymns found greater reception among the urban populace than among the rural folk, who made up about nine-tenths of the Empire's population. Overwhelmingly successful in the imperial and free cities of the Holy Roman Empire, the Reformation was much slower in penetrating the rural hinterlands. Protestant reform followed the main roads out from the urban centres, affecting first the villages in the environs of the major reformed cities such as Strasbourg and Nuremberg; it pene-trated the major routes of communication, establishing a stronger presence in market towns and compact village settlements of the plains than in the scattered hamlets of the forests and mountains. In Württemberg, for example, the Protestant church was more strongly established in the rural parishes closer to Stuttgart (the ducal capital) and Tübingen (the univer-sity town); in the Palatinate, villages along the Rhine were open to the suc-cessive waves of Lutheran and Calvinist confessionalization, whereas the relatively inaccessible Hunsrück remained, from the perspective of official religion, a backwater of folk magic and superstitions throughout the sixteenth century.

Above all, Protestantism (more true of Calvinism than Lutheranism) failed to develop a fully viable system of symbols and practices quickly to win over the rural population. The gap between official and popular religions was more than an urban/rural split: the dynamics of demographic exchange between the countryside and the city clearly favoured the latter; and rural immigrants to the cities brought with them their own beliefs and practices.

During the last decades of the sixteenth century, the Counter-Reformation church was able to exploit this gap for recapturing lost souls. By offering a reinvigorated system of rites and symbols, the Catholic clergy enjoyed some successes in converting Protestants and, above all, in pre-venting further defections to the reformed cause. Protestant pastors, on the other hand, had to contend with the challenge of the Catholic clergy, who offered a paraphernalia of 'magical' services and objects seemingly desired by the people: exorcism, consecrations with holy water, blessed amulets, and pilgrimages, among others. Partly to combat this Catholic threat, the Lutheran church sanctioned and even encouraged popular forms of devotion that verged on the magical, most notably in the promotion of a cult of Luther that resembled the Catholic cult of the saints.[43]

Hard put to explain away Catholic claims to miracles, the Protestant clergy concentrated their effort on condemning popular superstitions which were often no more than popular healing practices. A whole array of popular prophylactics came under clerical attack. Two examples will illustrate the scope of this problem for the Protestant clergy; they spanned the spectrum of the 'Protestant sixteenth century' and included both Lutheran and Calvinist condemnations of popular healing practices. In 1528 Luther lashed out at the superstitions of the people because the Saxon visitation turned up numerous amulets, many with Hebrew incantations, which the people wore to ward off diseases and ill fortune; he was particularly incensed that some of these were found in the possession of the clergy. Towards the end of the century the Calvinist pastor Samuel Hochholtzer published a book, *On Disciplining Children. How the Disobedient, Evil, and Corrupted Youth of These Anxious Last Days Can Be Bettered* (1591). He singled out mothers as responsible for the corruption of youth:

> how they [the women] love to accept strange, false beliefs, and go about with benedictions and witches' handwork. When they are not firm in faith and the Devil comes to tempt them, they follow him and go about with supernatural fantasies. Daily experience also teaches us that many of them hide in the serious error that they could cure their children and others with blessings and devilish things, such as the many stories about herbs, which they first empowered with supernatural blessings.[44]

In this passage, the practice of herbal medicine and benedictions, condemned as superstitions, was linked to the much more dangerous charge of demonic delusion. Witchcraft and popular healing both sprouted from the same soil that was barren for the seeds of official religion.

The above citation also underscores another significant theme: the complex relationship between gender, religion, magic, confessionalization, urban and rural cultures in the witch-hunts. As recent research has shown, the first great wave of witch-hunts in the Empire during the 1580s corresponded both with a subsistence crisis and with heightened confessional confrontations.[45] While the stereotypes of witchcraft were developed by the elites, and the confessional states provided the institutional mechanism for the widespread prosecution of magic, the actual denunciations usually came from below: villagers and artisans were overwhelmingly the instigators of witch trials by denouncing suspected neighbours to the authorities. In both city and countryside, in Protestant and Catholic areas, the great majority of victims were women. This particular fact seemed to have been the result of a conjunction of factors: the identification of black magic as practised by wise women as essentially a feminine trait, the patriarchal nature of confessionalism, and the dynamics of social conflict within rural communities that pitted households against marginal social elements. It was certainly no accident that the most intense witch-hunts and confessional confrontation fell between the 1580s and the middle of the seventeenth century.

Simply put, the official churches and the confessional states simply lacked the resources to impose confessional identities on populations that they could scarcely police.[46] In addition to the clergy and the officials, the confessional state depended on the co-operation – or at least the acquiescence – of urban magistrates, guild artisans, civic militia, village bailiffs, and the burghers and peasants of the various communities. In other words, the confessionalization of the late sixteenth century was as much a political process imposed from above as it was a social process from below, whether expressed in terms of support or opposition to religious changes. The urban unrests and confessional confrontations near the end of the century clearly formed part of a pattern of urban protests and revolts that lasted into the early years of the Thirty Years' War. Aachen (1580), Augsburg (1584), Emden (1595), Lübeck (1598), Worms (1612), and Frankfurt (1612) experienced open conflicts, while tensions were almost as high in many other civic communities.

The confessional character of many of these urban conflicts was itself both an expression and a cause. An equally important element was the larger structural change in the socioeconomic matrix of urban communities: the steady erosion of real income for artisans after mid-century and a redistribution of wealth and status between urban groups. The losers were the craftsmen of the guilds. Caught between capitalistic entrepreneurs and more cost-efficient competitors (rural artisans and Jews), urban guildsmen defended their corporate privileges by restricting guild entry and appealing for protective legislations against economic competition. Political decline often accompanied economic decline. Some guilds lost their political representation during the tumultuous years of the Reformation. In Münster, for example, the *Gesamtgilde*, the corporation of the seventeen enfranchised guilds, was suppressed in 1535 after the Anabaptist revolt and, although restored in 1555, was in a politically weaker position versus the city council and the patrician-burgher elite. In Augsburg, an imperial city where artisans played an important role during the Reformation, guilds were suppressed after 1548 by Emperor Charles V and a Catholic patrician oligarchy (with minority Lutheran representation) ruled over a Lutheran majority in the city.

The confessional conflicts of the 1580s and 1590s were predicated upon these structures of political and economic conflicts. When the Catholic magistrates of Augsburg (with the support of several Lutheran colleagues) voted to adopt the Catholic Gregorian calender in 1584, they precipitated a political crisis. They arrested Georg Müller, a Lutheran pastor who challenged the authority of the council, and stirred up an armed uprising that nearly toppled the regime. As Bernd Roeck has shown, the Lutheran crowd that assembled before the city hall consisted largely of weavers and butchers, artisans who had been most adversely affected by the economic restructuring of the late sixteenth century.[47] One can discern a similar pattern in the confrontations in late sixteenth-century Münster between the guildsmen who argued for toleration and the magistrates who tried to impose Catholic conformity. The Protestants and their sympathizers were concentrated in the traditional trades of the *Gesamtgilde*, especially in the clothing trades, whereas the Catholic clerical party drew its strength from the administrative professions that had gained status and prominence at the expense of the crafts.[48]

As more regional studies are undertaken, especially for the countryside, we shall gain a better understanding of the social processes behind confessionalization. The development of confessionalism was by no means an even process; and any generalization must be considered against the particularities of local and regional developments. On the basis of current research some tentative hypotheses can be advanced which may prove useful as guidelines to test future investigation:

1. The driving force behind confessionalization consisted of a coalition of official and clerical elites in the service of princes, who constituted a cohesive social network connected by school, connubial, and economic ties.
2. As a cultural system, confessionalism served more than the interests of the governing elites; it also appealed to the religious sensibilities and world-view of crucial mediating social groups – merchants, artisans, and peasant householders. The imposition of religious conformity and social discipline must thus be understood as an acculturation process by which members of certain social groups internalized greater self-control and also acquired external control over others, whether in the context of the household, the craft guild, the village community, or the city.
3. The conceptual polarity of elite versus popular culture is inadequate for understanding the process of confessionalization. Neither does a simple contrast between urban and rural culture give us a complete picture. Although both models may describe certain historical phenomena, such as the character of the witch-hunts, they fail to take account of the unstable and changing historical contexts in which confessional conflicts could be expressed in different patterns of religious and socioeconomic alignments.

4. And finally, confessionalization represented parallel though not similar processes of the formation of social identity and of individual identity. The contrast between external conformity and individual conscience, visible rituals and invisible spirituality became a significant motif during the last quarter of the sixteenth century. In contrast to the conversion experiences of the early Reformation, conversions between the Christian confessions in the late sixteenth century were thus simultaneously a social convention as well as a matter of the self.

In conclusion, some remarks are in order on the relationship between the Christian confessions and the minority Jewish population in the Holy Roman Empire. The enthusiasm for massive Jewish conversion in the early evangelical movement quickly turned to disappointment and, in the well-known case of Luther, personal bitterness. Nevertheless, the Protestant tradition did represent a break in the anti-Judaic stance of the Catholic church. Several reformers were known for their avid support of Hebrew studies, among them Wolfgang Capito in Strasbourg and Andreas Osiander in Nuremberg. The latter also composed an anonymous treatise defending Jews against the blood libel. During the first years of the evangelical movement, many reformers, willing or not, were identified as sympathetic to Judaism. In part this was due to the initial contact between reformers and rabbis, who quickly discovered the chasm between them. Moreover, Catholic polemicists tried to blacken the evangelical cause by associating reformers with Jews: Johannes Eck, for example, cursed Osiander as a 'Jew-lover' (*Judenfreund*); and Johannes Staffelstein, a minor reformer who took his name from a community with an established Jewish presence, was forced to publish a pamphlet disavowing any Jewish ancestry.

By the second half of the sixteenth century, both Protestants and Catholics settled down to a comfortable hostility toward Jews and their religion. While the Catholic church retained its traditional anti-Judaic stance, the Lutheran church, by claiming an identity as the 'New Israel', gradually developed an identity parallel to the image of the Old Testament Israelites but in sharp contradistinction to the Jews of the sixteenth century. As confessional tempers heated up during the last decades of the century, the early philo-Semitism of the Protestants vanished in the face of a new anti-Jewish polemic. Embedded in the larger controversy directed against Catholics and Calvinists, anti-Semitism in the Lutheran church drew upon Luther's vitriolic writings of the 1540s and ignored the earlier writings that advocated toleration. Such was the case, for example, in 1595 in Dortmund, a Lutheran city where a small Catholic patrician minority tried to sponsor the Jesuits with the support of Emperor Rudolf II. The handful of Jewish families who lived in Dortmund under imperial protection became casualties of the confessional struggle and were expelled by the Lutheran community in retaliation for the emperor's support of the Counter-Reformation.[49]

Anti-Jewish prejudices transcended confessional divides and class barriers. While the accusation of Jewish host-desecration vanished in Protestant Germany together with Catholic eucharistic theology, the belief in the kidnapping and ritual murder of Christian children by Jews never went away.[50] In spite of imperial prohibitions of ritual murder trials in any territorial or urban courts, Jews were imprisoned and interrogated on the charge of child-kidnapping and murder in Catholic Würzburg and Lutheran Worms during the sixteenth century. And among the rural populace this long-standing suspicion persisted well into the modern period and demonstrated, at least in this example, the durability and strength of magical beliefs over confessional acculturation.

Notes

1   Max Steinmetz, 'Thesen zur frühbürgerlichen Revolution' in Gerhard Brendler, ed., *Die frühbürgerliche Revolution in Deutschland. Referat und Diskussion zum Thema Probleme der frühbürgerlichen Revolution in Deutschland 1476 bis 1535* (Berlin, 1961).

2   M. M. Smirin, *Die Volksreformation des Thomas Müntzer* (Berlin, 1952); for two prominent examples of the formulation of the official marxist paradigm, see Max Steinmetz, *Deutschland von 1476 bis 1648. Von der frühbürgerlichen Revolution bis zum Westfälischen Frieden* (Berlin, 1965); and Adolf Laube, Max Steinmetz, and Günther Vogler, *Illustrierte Geschichte der deutschen frühbürgerlichen Revolution* (Berlin, 1974).

3   For sympathetic reception of marxian class analysis, see Thomas A. Brady, *Ruling Class, Regime and Reformation at Strasbourg, 1420–1555* (Leiden, 1978), pp. 1–47; Robert Scribner, 'Is There a Social History of the Reformation?', *Social History* IV (1977), pp. 483–505.

4   Bernd Moeller, *Reichsstadt und Reformation* (Gütersloh, 1962).

5   Kaspar von Greyerz, *The Late City Reformation in Germany, The Case of Colmar, 1522–1628* (Wiesbaden, 1980); R. Po-chia Hsia, *Society and Religion in Münster, 1535–1618* (New Haven, CT, 1984).

6   For a review of the 'Moeller thesis', see R. Po-chia Hsia, 'The Myth of the Commune. Recent Historiography on City and Reformation in Germany', *CEH* XX (3–4) (1987), pp. 203–15. For the most recent literature review, see Kaspar von Greyerz, 'Stadt und Reformation. Stand und Aufgaben der Forschung, *ARG* LXXVI (1985), pp. 6–63.

7   George H. Williams, *The Radical Reformation* (Philadelphia, 1962).

8   Ernst Troelsch, *Die soziallehren Lehren der christlichen Kirchen und Gruppen* (Tübingen, 1912).

9   See Hans-Jürgen Goertz, *Umstrittenes Täufertum, 1525–1975* (Hamburg, 1975); and the collection of biographies under his editorship, *Radikale Reformatoren* (1978).

10   For the only quantitative study of the radical reformation, see Claus-Peter Clasen, *Anabaptism. A Social History, 1525–1618* (Ithaca, NY, 1972).

11   The central arguments are presented in Peter Blickle, *Landschaften im Alten Reich. Die staatliche Funktion des gemeinen Mannes in Oberdeutschland*

(Munich, 1973); *Deutsche Untertanen, Ein Widerspruch?* (Munich, 1981); 'Kommunalismus, Parlamentarismus, Republikanismus', *HZ* CCXLII (1986), pp. 529–56; and *Gemeindereformation. Die Menschen des 16. Jahrhunderts auf dem Weg zum Heil* (Munich, 1985).

12 See Volker Press, 'Kommunalismus oder Territorialismus? Bemerkungen zur Ausbildung des frühmodernen Staates in Mitteleuropa', in Heiner Timmermann, ed., *Die Bildung des frühmodernen Staates. Stände und Konfessionen* (Saarbrücken, 1989), pp. 109–35; Hsia, 'The Myth of the Commune'; Tom Scott, 'The Communal Reformation between City and Land', in *Die Reformation in Deutschland und Europa. Interpretationen und Debatten*, special issue of *ARG* (1993), pp. 175–92.

13 Ernst Walter Zeeden, *Die Entstehung der Konfessionen. Grundlagen und Formen der Konfessionsbildung* (Munich, 1965).

14 See Heinz Schilling, 'Die Konfessionalisierung im Reich. Religiöser und gesellschaftlicher Wandel in Deutschland zwischen 1555 und 1620', *HZ* CCXLVI (1988), pp. 1–45; Wolfgang Reinhard, 'Zwang zur Konfessionalisierung? Prologemena zu einer Theorie des konfessionellen Zeitalters', *ZhF* X (1983), pp. 257–77; 'Konfession und Konfessionalisierung in Deutschland', in W. Reinhard, ed., *Bekenntnis und Geschichte* (Augsburg, 1981), pp. 165–89; R. Po-chia Hsia, *Social Discipline in the Reformation. Central Europe, 1550–1750* (London, 1989).

15 Peter Blickle, *The Revolution of 1525. The German Peasants' War from a New Perspective*, trans. Thomas A. Brady and H. C. Erik Midelfort (Baltimore, MD, 1981); on the traditional concept of the Peasants' War, see Günther Franz, *Der deutsche Bauernkrieg* (Darmstadt, 1977).

16 Günther Vogler, *Nürnberg 1524/25. Studien zur Geschichte der reformatorischen und sozialen Bewegung in der Reichsstadt* (Berlin, 1982).

17 See Franziska Conrad, *Reformation in der bäuerlichen Gesellschaft. Zur Rezeption reformatorischer Theologie im Elsass* (Stuttgart, 1984); Tom Scott, *Freiburg and the Breisgau. Town–Country Relations in the Age of Reformation and Peasants' War* (Oxford, 1986).

18 On the development of evangelical church ordinances, see Emil Sehling, ed., *Die evangelischen Kirchenordnungen des 16. Jahrhunderts* (Leipzig, 1901–13), continued by the Institut für Evangelisches Kirchenrecht der Evangelischen Kirche in Deutschland (Tübingen, 1955–   ).

19 See Günther Wartenberg, *Landesherrschaft und Reformation. Moritz von Sachsen und die albertinischen Kirchenpolitik bis 1546* (Gütersloh, 1988); Kristin E. S. Zapalac, *In His Image and Likeness. Political Iconography and Religious Change in Regensburg, 1500–1600* (Ithaca, NY, 1990).

20 Erdmann Weyrauch, *Konfessionelle Krise und soziale Stabilität. Das Interim in Strassburg (1548–1562)* (Stuttgart, 1978).

21 See Paul Warmbrunn, *Zwei Konfessionen in einer Stadt. Das Zusammenleben von Katholiken und Protestanten in den paritätischen Reichsstädten Augsburg, Biberach, Ravensburg, und Dinkelsbühl von 1548 bis 1648* (Wiesbaden, 1983).

22 R. Po-chia Hsia, *Society and Religion in Münster, 1535–1618* (New Haven, CT, 1984).

23 For the most important literature on anti-clericalism, see Henry J. Cohn, 'Anticlericalism in the German Peasants' War 1525', *P & P* LXXXIII (1979), pp. 3–31; Hans-Jürgen Goertz, *Pfaffenhass und gross Geschrei. Die reformatorischen Bewegungen in Deutschland 1517–1529* (Munich, 1987); Robert Scribner, 'Antiklerikalismus in Deutschland um 1500', in Ferdinand Seibt and Winfried Eberhardt, eds, *Europa 1500. Integrationsprozesse im Widerstreit* (Stuttgart, 1986), pp. 368–82; Peter A. Dykema and Heiko A. Oberman, eds,

Anticlericalism in Late Medieval and Early Modern Europe (Leiden, 1993), pp. 147–66.

24 See the contribution by Robert Scribner in Heiko A. Oberman, ed., *Anticlericalism in Late Medievalism and Early Modern Europe* (Leiden, 1992).

25 Robert Scribner, 'Practice and Principle in the German Towns. Preachers and People', in Peter N. Brooks, ed., *Reformation Principle and Practice. Essays in Honour of Arthur Geoffrey Dickens* (London, 1980), pp. 97–117.

26 Susan Karant-Nunn, *Luther's Pastors. The Reformation in the Ernestine Countryside* (Philadelphia, 1979).

27 Rainer Christoph Schwinges identified two periods of rapid growth in university enrolment (1385–1434, 1450–80), followed by two periods of relative stagnation (1428/34–1450, 1480–1500); 'Universitätsbesuch im Reich von 14. zum 16. Jahrhundert. Wachstum und Konjunkturen', *GG* X (1984), pp. 5–30.

28 On the relationship between preacherships and the reform movement, see Steven E. Ozment, *The Reformation in the Cities. The Appeal of Protestantism to Sixteenth-Century Germany and Switzerland* (New Haven, CT, 1975), pp. 38–41.

29 Bernhard Klaus, 'Soziale Herkunft und theologische Ausbildung lutherischer Pfarrer der reformatorischen Frühzeit', *ZKG* LXXX (1969), pp. 22–49.

30 Martin Brecht, 'Herkunft und Ausbildung der protestantischen Geistlichen des Herzogtum Württembergs im 16. Jahrhunderts', *ZKG* LXXX (1969), pp. 163–75.

31 In the Palatinate, Vogler has reconstructed the social origins of 250 out of a total of 1,544 pastors for the period 1555–1619: 155 were sons of pastors and only 4 came from peasant families. See his *Le Clergé protestant rhénan au siècle de la réforme (1555–1619)* (Paris, 1976), p. 18.

32 Martin Hasselhorn, *Der altwürttembergische Pfarrstand im 18. Jahrhundert* (Stuttgart, 1958).

33 Quoted in Hans-Christoph Rublack, ' "Der wohlgeplagte Priester". Vom Selbstverständnis lutherischer Geistlichkeit im Zeitlater der Orthodoxie', *ZhF* XVI (1989), pp. 1–30; here pp. 1–2.

34 There is as yet no single study of Catholic reform in sixteenth-century Central Europe. Some useful monographs are: Franz Ortner, *Reform, katholische Reform und Gegenreformation in Erzstift Salzburg* (Salzburg, 1981); Hansgeorg Molitor, *Kirchliche Reformversuche der Kurfürsten und Erzbischöfe von Trier* (Wiesbaden, 1967); Marc Forster, *The Counter-Reformation in the Villages. Popular Catholicism and the Catholic Reform in the Bishopric of Speyer 1560–1720* (Ithaca, NY, 1992).

35 See Thomas Robisheaux, 'Peasants and Pastors. Rural Youth Control and the Reformation in Hohenlohe, 1540–1680', *Social History* VI (1981), pp. 281–300; Lyndal Roper, *The Holy Household. Religion, Morals, and Order in Reformation Augsburg* (Oxford, 1989).

36 Paul Münch, 'Die "Obrigkeit im Vaterstand". Zur Definition und Kritik des "Landesvaters" während der frühen Neuzeit', in Elger Blühm, Jörn Garber, and Klaus Garber, eds, *Hof, Staat und Gesellschaft der Literatur des 17. Jahrhunderts*, special issue of *Daphnis*, XI(1–2) (1982), pp. 15–40.

37 Zapalac, *In His Image and Likeness*.

38 Cited in R. Po-chia Hsia, *Social Discipline in the Reformation. Central Europe 1550–1750* (London, 1989), pp. 34–5.

39 On Lutheran schooling, see Gerald Strauss, *Luther's House of Learning. Indoctrination of the Young in the German Reformation* (Baltimore, MD, 1978).

40 Rolf Engelsing, *Analphabetentum und Lektüre. Zur Sozialgeschichte des Lesens in Deutschland zwischen feudaler und industrieller Gesellschaft*

(Stuttgart, 1973).

41 Cited in Bernd Roeck, *Eine Stadt in Krieg und Frieden. Studien zur Geschichte der Reichsstadt Augsburg zwischen Kalenderstreit und Parität* (2 vols., Göttingen, 1989), I, pp. 118–19.

42 For references, see L. Jane Abray, *The People's Reformation. Magistrates, Clergy, and Commons in Strasbourg 1500–1598* (Ithaca, NY, 1985); Hsia, *Society and Religion in Münster*; Warmbrunn, *Zwei Konfessionen in einer Stadt*; Wolfgang Herborn, 'Die Protestanten in Schilderung und Urteil des Kölner Chronisten Hermann von Weinsberg (1518–1598)', in W. Ehbrecht and H. Schilling, eds, *Niederlande und Nordwestdeutschland. Studien zur Regional- und Stadtgeschichte Nordwestkontinentaleuropas im Mittelalter und in der Neuzeit* (Cologne, 1983).

43 Robert Scribner, *Popular Culture and Popular Movements in Reformation Germany* (London, 1987), pp. 323–53.

44 Cited in Hsia, *Social Discipline*, pp. 147–8.

45 Wolfgang Behringer, *Hexenverfolgung in Bayern. Volksmagie, Glaubenseifer und Staatsräson in der Frühen Neuzeit* (Munich, 1987).

46 Robert Scribner, 'Police and the Territorial State in Sixteenth Century Württemberg', in E. I. Kouri and Tom Scott, eds, *Politics and Society in Reformation Europe* (London, 1987).

47 Roeck, *Eine Stadt in Krieg und Frieden* I, pp. 140–69.

48 Hsia, *Society and Religion in Münster*.

49 See R. Po-chia Hsia, 'Printing, Censorship, and Antisemitism in Reformation Germany', in Sherrin Marshall and Philip Bebb, eds, *The Process of Change in Early Modern Europe. Festschrift for Miriam Usher Chrisman* (Athens, OH, 1988).

50 See R. Po-chia Hsia, *The Myth of Ritual Murder. Jews and Magic in Reformation Germany* (New Haven, CT, 1988).

General Index

Wissemburg 5
witchcraft (witch trials) 49, 343, 370-71
Wittelsbach dynasty 362
wives, idealized roles 214
woad 15, 17, 20, 67, 138, 139, 159, 161-2, 200
Wörnitz 135
Wolfach 134
Wolff, Hans of Gemünd 195
women
  age of first marriage 45
  and childbirth 53, 343-4
  and citizenship 216
  and domestic work 215, 218
  and guilds 221-22, 269-70
  and popular magic 370
  and sexual liaisons 47
  guild masters 239, 269
  labourers 219
  taxpayers 246
  clothing 338
  excluded from commune 301, 307, 310
  legal rights 216-7
  life expectancy 54
  literacy rates 212
  occupations 16, 17, 213
  patrician 242
  restrictions on work 224, 268
  rural occupations 217-18
  skilled work 215, 269-70
  social status 210
  unmarried 45, 217
  unskilled work 215
  women's labour as productive force 221-2
wool (wool-weaving) 1, 4, 5, 13-17 *passim*, 20, 159-64 *passim*, 182, 184, 198-200
wool-dealers 163
  investing in mining 195
work and gender 213
Worms 124-33 *passim*, 169, 200, 245, 346, 371, 374

Wrocław
  see Breslau
Wunsiedel 22
Württemberg 7, 15, 17, 57, 67, 92, 158, 263, 360, 364
  dukes of 127
population density 42
  Protestantism in 369
  towns in 127-9, 135
  viticulture 12, 13, 157
  wine exports 157
  wool production 16, 163, 198
Würzburg 148, 163, 167, 265, 305, 374
Wurm, river 137
Wurmser family (Strasbourg merchants) 279

Xanten, 12

yarn 159, 160, 161
  dealers 59
  markets 159-60
youth 48, 49, 346-7, 370
  and Reformation 360, 366
  and sexuality 366
  in population 53
  mortality 53

Zangmeister, merchants in Memmingen 16
Zell 134
Zell, Matthias (Strasbourg Reformer) 363
Zerbst 114
Zimmern, counts of 41
Zimmern, Werner von, knight 265
zinc 192
Zink, Burkard 90
Zittau 125, 138, 340
Zurich 18, 41, 51, 267, 276, 340
  marriage court in 366
Zurich, canton 36
Zurzach 148, 170
Zwickau 125, 139, 157, 247
Zwingli, Huldrych 356, 363

Index of Modern Authors

Printed in the United States
38714LVS00003B/13